21st-CENTURY OXFORD AUTHORS

GENERAL EDITOR

SEAMUS PERRY

21st-CENTURY OXFORD AUTHORS

Emily Brontë

EDITED BY
FRANCIS O'GORMAN

OXFORD
UNIVERSITY PRESS

Great Clarendon Street, Oxford, OX2 6DP,
United Kingdom

Oxford University Press is a department of the University of Oxford.
It furthers the University's objective of excellence in research, scholarship,
and education by publishing worldwide. Oxford is a registered trade mark of
Oxford University Press in the UK and in certain other countries

Introduction and Editorial Material © Francis O'Gorman 2023

The moral rights of the author have been asserted

All rights reserved. No part of this publication may be reproduced, stored in
a retrieval system, or transmitted, in any form or by any means, without the
prior permission in writing of Oxford University Press, or as expressly permitted
by law, by licence or under terms agreed with the appropriate reprographics
rights organization. Enquiries concerning reproduction outside the scope of the
above should be sent to the Rights Department, Oxford University Press, at the
address above

You must not circulate this work in any other form
and you must impose this same condition on any acquirer

Published in the United States of America by Oxford University Press
198 Madison Avenue, New York, NY 10016, United States of America

British Library Cataloguing in Publication Data
Data available

Library of Congress Control Number: 2022944401

ISBN 978–0–19–886816–3

Printed and bound by
CPI Group (UK) Ltd, Croydon, CR0 4YY

Links to third party websites are provided by Oxford in good faith and
for information only. Oxford disclaims any responsibility for the materials
contained in any third party website referenced in this work.

ACKNOWLEDGEMENTS

My first thanks are to the large number of people with whom I have discussed the Brontë family and their work, not least after I arrived in Yorkshire in the summer of 1999, and where I lived for nearly a quarter of a century. This includes the many master's degree students I had the pleasure of teaching on my Brontë course at the University of Leeds until 2016, and most especially Heidi Freer-Hay. I am grateful to my former graduate student at Leeds and then Edinburgh, Dr Tricia Ayrton, for her exceptional care for Emily Brontë and her works. Tricia has generously shared information with me as well as a complete scan of the Gondal notebook in the British Library, St Pancras.

I am likewise grateful to my mother, Joyce O'Gorman, and my friends, especially Professor Dinah Birch CBE; Professor Ian Campbell; Professor Matthew Campbell; Valerie Cotter; Professor Robert Douglas-Fairhurst; Sally Gray; all at number 14 and number 20; Professor Graham Huggan; Celia Ienco; the late Dr Kevin Jackson; Professor Elisabeth Jay; Professor Juliet John; Aaron, Felix, Freddie, Isobel, Milo, and Maya Killingworth; Professor Brent Kinser; the late Christopher Kwiatowski; Dr Nigel Mortimer; Jacqueline Norton; David Pipe; Rosslie Platten; the Right Revd Dr Stephen Platten; Professor Fiona Robertson; Dr Iain Quinn; Dr Nicholas Shrimpton; Professor Helen Small FBA; Professor David Sorensen; the late Professor E.G. Stanley FBA; Bethany Thomas; Professor Alex Thomson; Alice and Sam Williams; and Professor Greg Walker FRSE.

It is a true sadness to record that my first tutor at Oxford, Miss Elizabeth Mackenzie—for whom I wrote my first undergraduate essay, which was, as it happens, on Emily Brontë—died the very day before I completed this edition. She was 100 years of age. I thank her heartily for everything she taught me.

As my Introduction describes, editors and critics have tended to regard Emily Brontë as either extremely well-read or hardly at all. In the absence of much definite evidence one way or the other, I have simply remained cautious. I am particularly grateful to editions of the poetry by Janet Gezari (Harmondsworth: Penguin, 1992) and Derek Roper and Edward Chitham (Oxford: Clarendon, 1995), and to Hilda Marsden and Ian Jack's edition of the novel in the Clarendon Edition of the Novels of the Brontës, 1976, even where I have taken a different view. It is not possible to proceed very far into Brontë scholarship, which I have been thinking about for nearly thirty years, without recognizing, and admiring, the contribution in the first half of the twentieth century of, among others, Clement K. Shorter (1857–1926), C.W. Hatfield (1877?–1942), and (with the obvious substantial reservation) Thomas James Wise (1859–1937), as well as the many scholars and readers connected with the Brontë Society and the Brontë Parsonage Museum, and

vi ACKNOWLEDGEMENTS

their related publications. The late Margaret Smith's more recent work on Charlotte's letters is unrivalled; Juliet Barker's biographical accounts are essential.

Images of Emily Brontë's drawings and watercolours, together with the MSS, are easily available for free online. Much of the final preparation for this edition was undertaken during the strange conditions of the Covid-19 pandemic. I did once make it out to the Parsonage during a brief lull in a lockdown and stood in the graveyard looking at the silent and closed building. The family could easily have been behind those shutters in this now immaculately kept house. I took some local comfort in the flourishing in my garden of Ausearnshaw, Rose Emily Brontë, which David Austin Roses of Albrighton, Shropshire, created for the Brontë Society to mark her bicentenary in 2018. As it did for many other scholars, the disease significantly curtailed my opportunities to work in research libraries: the book has, in turn, been slower in the making than planned. This also explains my greater reliance on digital copies of texts than normal.

When not confined to home, I continued to profit, as I have done for nearly a quarter of a century, from the kindness, friendliness, and reliability of the British Library Reading Room at Boston Spa. I thank warmly also the staff of the British Library at St Pancras, particularly those in the Rare Books and Music Reading Room; the National Library of Scotland; the Athenæum Club, 107 Pall Mall; the New Club, 86 Princes Street, Edinburgh; the Library of the University of Edinburgh; the Brotherton Library, University of Leeds; the Bodleian Library, University of Oxford; and the Leeds Library. I am very grateful to the Department of English Literature at the University of Edinburgh for a semester's research leave in 2021. My thanks to the General Editor of this series, Professor Seamus Perry, and to the production team at Oxford University Press. At proof stage, serious illness intervened, and I wish warmly to thank Ela Kotkowska and Seamus Perry for managing the consequence of this. I also dearly thank Professor John Bowen for travelling to the British Library to check some important references for me.

The editorial part of this book is for my wife, Kate Williams, who shows me what love is.

Francis O'Gorman
The Feastday of St Margaret of Antioch
Cambridge, 2022

CONTENTS

Illustrations	xi
Abbreviations	xiii
Introduction	xv
Note on the Text	xlix

TEXTS	1
Diary Paper, 24 November 1834	3
Diary Paper, 26 June 1837	4
Poems in MSS from 1838 to 1846 later included in 'Poems by Ellis Bell', in *Poems by Currer, Ellis, and Acton Bell*, ed. Currer Bell, 2nd edn (London: Smith & Elder, 1850), with other personal documents inserted as chronologically appropriate	5
30 August 1838 ('For him who struck thy foreign string')	5
17 October 1838, 'Song by J. Brenzaida to G.S.'	5
11 November 1838 ('Loud without the wind was roaring')	6
4 December 1838 ('A little while, a little while')	8
18 December 1838 ('The blue bell is the sweetest flower')	10
11 September 1840 ('In summer's mellow midnight')	11
16 May 1841 ('Shall earth no more inspire thee')	12
6 July 1841 ('Aye there it is! It wakes tonight')	13
Diary Paper, 30 July 1841	14
19 December 1841, 'A.S. to G.S.'	15
Letter to Ellen Nussey, 22? May 1843	16
6 September 1843 ('In the earth, the earth thou shalt be laid')	17
11 March 1844, 'E.W. to A.G.A.'	17
11 November 1844, 'From a Dungeon Wall in the Southern College'	19
28 May 1845, 'A.E. and R.C.'	20

viii CONTENTS

Letter to Ellen Nussey, 16? July 1845 23

Diary Paper, 30 July 1845 24

2 January 1846 ('No coward soul is mine') 26

Undated ('Love is like the wild rose briar') 27

Ellis Bell [Emily Brontë]'s contribution to *Poems by Currer, Ellis, and Acton Bell* (London: Aylott and Jones, 1846) 29

Faith and Despondency 29

Stars 31

The Philosopher 32

Remembrance 33

A Death-Scene 34

Song 36

Anticipation 37

The Prisoner (A Fragment) 38

Julian M. and A.G. Rochelle 40

18 December 1843 ('Hope was but a timid friend') 44

A Day Dream 45

To Imagination 47

How clear she shines 48

Sympathy 49

Plead for me 49

Self-interrogation 50

Death 52

Stanzas to— 53

Honour's Martyr 53

Stanzas 55

My Comforter 56

The Old Stoic 57

Ellis Bell [Emily Brontë], *Wuthering Heights: A Novel* (London: Newby, 1847) 59

CONTENTS ix

APPENDICES 309

i. Currer Bell [Charlotte Brontë]'s accounts in *'Wuthering Heights' and 'Agnes Grey'. By Ellis and Acton Bell. A New Edition Revised, with a Biographical Notice of the Authors, a Selection from their Literary Remains, and a Preface, by Currer Bell* (1850) 311

Currer Bell [Charlotte Brontë], 'Biographical Notice of Ellis and Acton Bell' (1850) 311

Currer Bell [Charlotte Brontë], 'Selections from the Literary Remains of Ellis and Acton Bell' (1850) 316

Currer Bell [Charlotte Brontë], 'Editor's Preface to the new edition of *Wuthering Heights*' (1850) 317

ii. Early Poems about Emily Brontë 322

[Charlotte Brontë], 'On the Death of Emily Jane Brontë' (1848) 322

'A' [Matthew Arnold], 'Haworth Churchyard, April 1855' (1855) 322

Francis William Lauderdale Adams, 'To Emily Brontë' (1887) 327

Lionel Johnson, 'Brontë' (1890) 328

Stephen Phillips, 'Emily Brontë' (1913) 329

Robert Bridges, 'Emily Brontë' (1923) 330

iii. The First Criticism 332

George Barnett Smith, from 'The Brontës' (1873/5) 332

A. Mary F. Robinson, ' "Wuthering Heights": Its Origins' (1883) 335

Algernon Charles Swinburne, 'Emily Brontë' (1883) 342

Explanatory Notes 349

Index of First Lines 433

Index of Titles (where given) 434

ILLUSTRATIONS

1. Ponden Hall (photograph by the editor, 7 July 2021). EJB might have read in the library here.   381

2. The inscription at Ponden Hall (photograph by the editor, 7 July 2021), possibly a model—possibly not—for properties in *WH*. Like the inscription in *Wuthering Heights*, the instruction above the door at Ponden Hall is dated 1801.   382

ABBREVIATIONS

1846	*Poems by Currer, Ellis, and Acton Bell* (London: Aylott and Jones, 1846)
1847	Ellis Bell [Emily Brontë], *Wuthering Heights: A Novel* and Acton Bell [Anne Brontë], *Agnes Grey*, 3 vols (London: Newby, 1847)
1850	*'Wuthering Heights' and 'Agnes Grey'. By Ellis and Acton Bell. A New Edition Revised, with a Biographical Notice of the Authors, a Selection from their Literary Remains, and a Preface, by Currer Bell* (London: Smith, Elder, 1850)
1850*	*Poems by Currer, Ellis, and Acton Bell*, ed. Currer Bell [Charlotte Brontë], 2nd edn (London: Smith & Elder, 1850)
1998	Emily Brontë, *Wuthering Heights*, ed. Ian Jack and Patsy Stoneman, Oxford World's Classics (Oxford: Oxford University Press, 1998 [first published as a World's Classics paperback in 1995])
2009	Emily Brontë, *Wuthering Heights*, ed. Ian Jack and Helen Small, Oxford World's Classics (Oxford: Oxford University Press, 2009)
AB	Anne Brontë (1820–49)
Barker	Juliet Barker, *The Brontës*, 2nd revised edn (Hachette Digital/ Little, Brown, 2010), ebook
Books	'Books belonging to or inscribed by Members of the Brontë Family & held in The Brontë Parsonage Museum', accessible from the Parsonage website
BPM	Brontë Parsonage Museum, Church Street, Haworth, BD22 8DR
Brontësaurus	John Sutherland, *The Brontësaurus: An A to Z of Charlotte, Emily, and Anne Brontë (and Branwell)* (London: Icon, 2016)
CB	Charlotte Brontë (1816–55)
CH	Miriam Allott, ed., *The Brontës: The Critical Heritage* (London: Routledge & Kegan Paul, 1974)
Chitham	Edward Chitham, *A Life of Emily Brontë*, revised edn (Stroud: Amberley, 2010)
Companion	Christine Alexander and Margaret Smith, *The Oxford Companion to the Brontës* (Oxford: Oxford University Press, 2006)
The Complete Poems of Charlotte Brontë	*The Complete Poems of Charlotte Brontë*, ed. Clement Shorter (London: Hodder and Stoughton, n.d. [1923])
EJB	Emily Jane Brontë (1818–48)
Gezari	Emily Brontë, *The Complete Poems*, ed. Janet Gezari (Harmondsworth: Penguin, 1992)

GP	Emily Brontë, *Gondal Poems* notebook (sometimes called 'B'), begun February 1844 and continued till May 1848. Now in the British Library, Add MS 43483, and partially available as https://www.bl.uk/collection-items/manuscript-of-emily-bronts-gondal-poetry
Hewish	John Hewish, *Emily Brontë: A Critical and Biographical Study* (London: Macmillan, 1969)
HM	Honresfield Manuscript (sometimes called 'A'), once in the possession of Sir Alfred Law MP (1860–1939) of Honresfield House, Littleborough. There is a facsimile (omitting some fine detail and often quite difficult to read) in the Shakespeare Head Brontë, *Poems of Emily and Anne Brontë*, ed. Thomas James Wise and J. Alexander Symington (Oxford: Blackwell for Shakespeare Head, 1934), pp. 310–29. The original photographs, made either in 1926 or 1934 (where some of that detail is recoverable), are in BPM.

As this edition went to print, HM, included within what is now to be called the Blavatnik Honresfield Library, was purchased by a consortium of libraries and private donors for the United Kingdom. In due course, HM should be accessible to scholars.

As with *GP*, EJB commenced her transcriptions in this book in February 1844 (the MS's first line is 'EJB. Transcribed Febuary [*sic*] 1844.')

JE	*Jane Eyre: An Autobiography*, ed. Currer Bell, 3 vols (London: Smith, Elder, 1847)
LCB	E.C. [Elizabeth] Gaskell, *The Life of Charlotte Brontë, Author of 'Jane Eyre', 'Shirley', 'Villette' &c*, 2 vols (London: Smith, Elder, 1857)
Letters	Margaret Smith, ed., *The Letters of Charlotte Brontë with a Selection of Letters by Family and Friends*, 3 vols (Oxford: Clarendon, 1995–2004)
ODNB	*Oxford Dictionary of National Biography*, online
OED	*Oxford English Dictionary*, online
Shirley	Currer Bell [Charlotte Brontë], *Shirley: A Tale*, 3 vols (London: Smith, Elder, 1849)
ST	[Juliet Barker], *Sixty Treasures: The Brontë Parsonage Museum* (Haworth: Brontë Parsonage Museum, 1988)
Villette	Currer Bell [Charlotte Brontë], *Villette*, 3 vols (London: Smith, Elder, 1853)
WH	Ellis Bell [Emily Brontë], *Wuthering Heights*, this edition
Wright	Joseph Wright, *The English Dialect Dictionary*, 6 vols (London: English Dialect Society, 1898–1905), available from http://eddonline-proj.uibk.ac.at/edd/

INTRODUCTION

Quickly, as if she were recalled by something over there, she turned to her canvas. There it was—her picture. Yes, with all its greens and blues, its lines running up and across, its attempt at something. It would be hung in the attics, she thought; it would be destroyed. But what did that matter? she asked herself, taking up her brush again. She looked at the steps; they were empty; she looked at her canvas; it was blurred. With a sudden intensity, as if she saw it clear for a second, she drew a line there, in the centre. It was done; it was finished. Yes, she thought, laying down her brush in extreme fatigue, I have had my vision.

Virginia Woolf, *To the Lighthouse* (1927)

Literary scholars who are, for instance, Classicists, Anglo-Saxonists, or Medievalists in European literature are obliged to accept the fact that they rarely can know much about *whom* they are talking. I mean, simply, that the authors from these periods, often enough, are completely unrecoverable. No-one, for instance, can identify Homer. And we know, now, that there was no such man—he is best thought, in Nigel Nicolson's great formulation, a combination of memory and power.[1] Who was the author, assuming there was a single one, of the Old English rumination on redemption, 'The Dream of the Rood'? And who was the 'Gawain poet'? There have been some tentative suggestions. But nothing like certainty. He wrote the late fourteenth-century Middle English masterpiece, the alliterative romance *Sir Gawayn and þe Grene Knyȝt*. And possibly 'Pearl', 'Patience', and 'Cleanness'. But, of his identity, what he did, what he thought, and how he lived—nothing is known for sure. William Shakespeare, customarily assumed to be an elusive figure in terms of biography, looks as if he has a well-documented life in comparison with these absences.

By the time of the nineteenth century, literary scholars are, differently, habituated to a wealth of resource. For some writers—Charles Dickens, for example, John Ruskin, George Eliot, Henry James, Michael Field (Katharine Bradley and Edith Cooper)—it is at times possible to reconstruct an hour-by-hour account of a particular day in their lives. A single example would be John Ruskin's Christmas Day walk in Venice in 1876.[2] What would it be like if we could do that for *Chaucer*? Dickens has his secrets, for sure, and we would, apart from anything else, like to know more about Ellen (Nelly) Ternan, the

---

[1] Adam Nicolson, *The Mighty Dead: Why Homer Matters* (London: Collins, 2014), p. 25.
[2] See Van Akin Burd, ed., *Christmas Story: John Ruskin's Venetian Letters of 1876–1877* (Newark: University of Delaware Press, 1990).

xvi INTRODUCTION

young woman with whom he had a long affair *sub rosa*.[3] There are plenty of letters, nevertheless, and the memories of other people. This is a different world from *Gawain*, let alone the *Odyssey*.

So it is a curious problem that usually belongs with those at work on much earlier periods of literature that the reader of Emily Brontë knows almost nothing about her. We understand more about the famously reclusive Emily Dickinson (who admired Emily Brontë and, memorably, Charlotte[4]) or, in the following century, the oddly unreachable Flann O'Brien (Brian Ó Nualláin). But Emily Jane Brontë—the only one of the Brontë writers to have a middle name, of which she was proud—is a mystery. As she possibly was to herself.

Part of the trouble with this—if trouble it quite is—is that readers of Emily Brontë, faced with the near blank sheet of her life have become inventive, sometimes wildly so, in an effort to fill in the gaps. Those readers have, understandably, made an attempt to address the difficult question: how can one of the most admired, as well as original, of nineteenth-century novelists and one of the most moving of nineteenth-century poets not have had a life—a mind and a heart—that can be known, or at least thought to be known? How and why has she slipped away—assuming that there was a lyrical centre, a full personality, *to* slip away? (I will return to this point.) Hidden selves preoccupied Charlotte Brontë, for sure. The aristocratic Lord Byron would no doubt have dismissed this as mere bourgeois fussing about the supposedly organic wholeness, the integrity, of the 'self'. But it is, all the same, with such wholenesses, and whether we can know them or not, that the Brontë sisters were often concerned. There was something of a family fascination with the difference between the outer person and the inner, a private life shown to very few. In terms of the sisters' imaginative literature, the summary of this fascination is *Villette* (1853). One remembers Miss Fanshawe's astonished question to Charlotte's heroine: ' "Who *are* you, Miss Snowe?" '[5]

Akin to the oddity of the difference between Robert Browning's public persona—bluff, hearty, loud—and his psychologically/emotionally penetrating poetry,[6] the question of who Emily Brontë was has felt to many readers,

---

[3] On this, see most recently, Claire Tomalin, *The Invisible Woman: The Story of Nelly Ternan and Charles Dickens*, new edition (London: Penguin, 2014); Michael Slater, *The Great Charles Dickens Scandal* (New Haven: Yale University Press, 2012); Brian Ruck, 'Ellen Ternan and Charles Dickens: A Re-evaluation of the "Evidence" ', *The Dickensian*, 110 (2014), pp. 118–30; and Francis O'Gorman, 'Trollope, *Orley Farm*, and Dickens's Marriage Break-down', *English Studies*, 99 (2018), pp. 624–41.

[4] 'Oh what an afternoon for Heaven | When Brontë entered there!', ['Charlotte Brontë's Grave'], *c*.1859: Thomas H. Johnson, ed., *The Complete Poems of Emily Dickinson* (Boston: Little, Brown, 1951 [1960 edn]), p. 70. There is some brief discussion of the relation between the two poets in Wendy Anne Powers, 'Emily Brontë and Emily Dickinson: Parallel Lives on Opposing Shores', *Brontë Studies*, 32.2 (2007), pp. 145–50.

[5] Currer Bell, *Villette*, 3 vols (London: Smith, Elder, 1853), i.289.

[6] Cf. Henry James's short story, 'The Private Life', published in *The Atlantic Monthly*, 69 (April 1892), pp. 463–83, and Sidney E. Lind, 'James's "The Private Life" and Browning', *American Literature*, 23 (1951), pp. 315–22.

INTRODUCTION   xvii

from the first, in need of an answer. And perhaps to be *the* question about her. The historian of science, Herbert Dingle, incidentally, was a lone voice in 1974 when he turned his attention to 'the mind of Emily Brontë' and concluded, with a view as surprising as it is hard to comprehend, that 'so far from being a sphinx of literature as she has been called, [she] is more open to our understanding than almost any other writer'.[7]

The concern, though, with what could not be known about the author of *Wuthering Heights* started—if not among the Brontë family members themselves—early in the history of Emily's reception. That properly began in the second and third last decades of the nineteenth century: prior to that, Emily Brontë rarely figured. The British novelist Romer Wilson (1891–1930) was, for example, unabashed in her speculative—sometimes extremely speculative—account, with its finely ambiguous title, *All Alone: The Life and Private History of Emily Jane Brontë* (1928). 'This life of Emily Jane Brontë', Wilson said at the beginning, 'is based chiefly upon the internal evidence of her poems.'[8] Yet, as I go on to discuss, the internal evidence, such that it is, reveals more about Emily's imaginative world of Gondal than her own life (though it becomes important, as I will indicate, to recognize how difficult it is to make a separation between these two). Even in her opening remarks, Romer Wilson found herself on the back foot, with the paucity of information about Emily: a few scraps of diary pages, a tiny number of uninformative letters, some reminiscences, not all of them revealing or even appealing. 'I do not care', Wilson found herself obliged to report, 'how erroneous my statements of fact are, provided these statements draw forth clear and correct evidence from secret hiding-places.'[9] It is hard not to be sympathetic to, although slightly appalled by, this sentence. Wilson wanted to achieve the impossible: to 'explain' as well as to document Emily Brontë.

Dame Millicent Garrett Fawcett (1847–1929), the high-profile suffragist, author, and champion of women's higher education, had ventured into the enigma of Emily Brontë earlier. In *Some Eminent Women of Our Times* (1889), Fawcett had tried to match at least something of Emily's life with the nature of her imagination. This was more promising, though the vital element of Gondal was unknown to Fawcett and she was following the public lead of Charlotte Brontë in pointing, innocently, to the landscape around Haworth as a major, explanatory force. 'The development of Emily's genius was different [from Charlotte's]', Fawcett said:

Her love of the moors around Haworth was so intense that it was impossible for her to thrive when she was away from them. It became a fact recognized by all the family that Emily must not be taken away from home. The solitude of the wild, dark moors, and

---

[7] Herbert Dingle, *The Mind of Emily Brontë* (London: Brian & O'Keefe, 1974), p. 101.
[8] Romer Wilson, *All Alone: The Life and Private History of Emily Jane Brontë* (London: Chatto & Windus, 1928), p. xi.
[9] Ibid.

xviii INTRODUCTION

the communing with her own heart, together with the dark tragedy of Branwell's wasted life, were the sole sources of Emily's inspiration.[10]

Again, Fawcett, who is dependent, as we still are, on Elizabeth Gaskell's splendid but contested *Life of Charlotte Brontë* (1857), knows nothing of Gondal. And what exactly, one wonders, is actually revealed by asserting that the moors were a source of 'inspiration'? This view was apparent, too, even earlier among the critics and biographers, in A. Mary F. Robinson's chapter of 1883, reproduced here on pp. 335–42. What *kind* of knowledge is this? Certainly, it is knowledge that Winifred Gérin (1901–81), one of Emily Brontë's most influential later biographers, thought worth pursuing extensively; and, indeed, Gérin spent ten years living at Haworth and walking on 'Emily's moors'[11] to try to understand what they had meant to her. In a plain sense, it is true that Emily writes *about* the moors—though not so much in *Wuthering Heights* as is often assumed[12]—but what substantively that reveals about Emily's mind, or individuality, is not easy to be sure of. Perhaps that is exactly what Charlotte intended: in this interpretative move, the presence of the moors stands in for a mind and heart that cannot, in other terms, be apprehended or comprehended. Charlotte, indeed, might have emphasized Emily's attachment to the outdoors (see, for instance, pp. 316–18 and notes) because it was a safe, uncontroversial thing she *could* say about her sister, whose peculiar ways she did not, it might be, otherwise grasp.

A specific and more abstractly historical issue—still unresolved—in the 'problem' of Emily Brontë concerns what she had read. Fawcett might be taken to imply that the answer was: nothing. At any rate, whatever she read, according to Fawcett, made no impression on her writing, which was spurred solely by the moors and Branwell's decline. Alice Meynell (1847–1922), suffragist, writer, and poet, was, in the same spirit, more explicit in her *Hearts of Controversy* (1917). 'Emily Brontë', Meynell said, 'was no student of books. It was not from among the fruits of any other author's labour that she gathered [her] eminent words.'[13] Much depends, there, on what Meynell means by 'student'. It certainly appears that Emily knew something of Byron and something of Moore's account of Byron's life (originally 1830: see note to p. 117, '*He had listened. . .*'); some of the poetry appears to echo Shelley and Wordsworth, though the Blake-like language of the poem called in 1850 'The Two Children' can only be coincidental (see note to p. 20). Emily Brontë quotes from a book by Sir Walter Scott in *Wuthering Heights* (see p. 114 and

---

[10] Millicent Garrett Fawcett, *Some Eminent Women of Our Times: Short Biographical Sketches* (London: Macmillan, 1889), p. 105.

[11] Winifred Gérin, *Emily Brontë: A Biography* (Oxford: Oxford University Press, 1978 [1971]), p. viii.

[12] The word 'moors' appears twenty-two times in a novel of 108,000 words.

[13] Alice Meynell, *Hearts of Controversy* (London: Burns & Oates, 1917), p. 96.

INTRODUCTION   xix

the note), and his Border dialect terms might, perhaps, be heard in some of hers. It is hard not to think of *King Lear* (1606) in parts of the novel. But it cannot be certain that she had *studied* these texts. We simply do not know. Emily herself noted in 1841: 'I have a good many books on hands but I am sorry to say that as usual I make small progress with any' (p. 14). Culturally approved female modesty? That seems unlikely, for this is not a letter to an outsider but a diary paper for Anne. It is part of Lucasta Miller's contention in *The Brontë Myth* (2001) that Emily's wide reading was down-played by many early critics, who preferred to see her as a solitary genius, creating *Wuthering Heights* out of her own imagination—I will return to this point— yet hard evidence either to back up or interrogate Miller's argument remains out of our reach. And, besides, it is never quite clear why this dispute matters so much to Dr Miller in the first place, not least because the Romantic-derived conception of solitary genius has been so vigorously challenged from various other perspectives, and in ways relevant to Emily Brontë.[14]

Many have thought, to pursue this same idea about Emily the reader, that E.T.A. Hoffmann's *Das Majorat* (*The Entail*) (1817) could have a little to do with the opening of *Wuthering Heights* (in *Das Majorat* the narrator visits a castle in a 'wild and desolate place', and his first night is plagued by strange sounds, scratchings, and disturbance[15]). Yet the imaginative ingredients—a haunted castle, a disturbed night—seem hardly to need a specific 'source'. Charlotte, as observed in the note to p. 76 ('*Catherine Linton*'), had her own youthful version of this kind of scene: elements of shared imaginings are far from uncommon between the sisters (I suggest other examples in the notes). Emily could read German, though we do not know how well (her French was good[16]). But

---

[14] For a reconsideration of the book, see Lucasta Miller, 'Lives and Afterlives: The Brontë Myth Revisited', *Brontë Studies*, 39.4 (2014), pp. 254–66. On the Romantic notion (or apparent Romantic notion) of genius, see, for instance, Jack Stillinger, *Multiple Authorship and the Myth of Solitary Genius* (Oxford: Clarendon, 1991).

[15] '[...] Just as I was reading of the entrance of Jeronimo's bloody figure, the door leading from the gallery into the antechamber flew open with a tremendous bang. I started to my feet in terror; the book fell from my hands. In the very same moment, however, all was still again, and I began to be ashamed of my childish fears. The door must have been burst open by a strong gust of wind or in some other natural manner. It is nothing; my over-strained fancy converts every ordinary occurrence into the supernatural. Having thus calmed my fears, I picked up my book from the ground, and again threw myself in the arm-chair; but there came a sound of soft, slow, measured footsteps moving diagonally across the hall, whilst there was a sighing and moaning at intervals, and in this sighing and moaning there was expressed the deepest trouble, the most hopeless grief, that a human being can know. "Ha! it must be some sick animal locked up somewhere in the basement storey. Such acoustic deceptions at night time, making distant sounds appear close at hand, are well known to everybody. Who will suffer himself to be terrified at such a thing as that?" Thus I calmed my fears again. But now there was a scratching at the new portion of the wall, whilst louder and deeper sighs were audible, as if gasped out by some one in the last throes of mortal anguish [...]', *Weird Tales*, vol. 1, trans. J.T. Bealby, Project Gutenberg.

[16] For her French writing, see *The Belgian Essays: Charlotte Brontë and Emily Brontë: A Critical Edition*, ed. and trans. Sue Lonoff (New Haven: Yale University Press, 1996).

INTRODUCTION

whether, as Helen Small suggests, following the Clarendon Edition,[17] Emily Brontë knew of Hoffmann not directly in the German but through Scott we do not have any proof (and Scott, anyway, was no uncritical admirer of Hoffmann).

Arguing that Emily Brontë was bookish and that her work alludes to that wide reading remains part, for many scholars, of the critical assumptions necessary for assessing this remarkable writer. Certainly, she seems to be imbued with some of the Romantic poets' most celebrated topics: the supremacy of the imagination, the affective connection with the natural world, the private mind, how one might imaginatively inhabit a land, a Wollstonecraft-like surety of female self-possession. She might be consciously writing in the light of having read, say, in addition, Shelley, Coleridge, Wordsworth, and Byron (the 'real father' of Heathcliff, Hilda Marsden and Ian Jack observe pithily[18]). My notes do not avoid hesitant suggestions of what could be parallels, but my emphasis is on *could*. The argument that Emily Brontë's work is richly intertextual has a long heritage, almost as long as that which declares her writing has no such thing. A noticeable early example of the literary origin argument was Florence Swinton Dry's *The Sources of 'Wuthering Heights'* (1937), which was particularly keen to identify Sir Walter Scott's *Black Dwarf* (1816) as a creative starting point. The approach essentially remains the same for some critics. Both Patsy Stoneman's 1998 annotations to Ian Jack's text of *Wuthering Heights*, for example, and Helen Small's updating of that same edition in 2009 dwell, as already noted, on possible verbal parallels.[19] Dinah Birch, more generally, wrote in 2011 that '[o]ne of the few certain facts about Emily Brontë's retired life is that she was an eager reader'.[20] Yet we can neither be certain *how* nor, for the most part, *what* she read. Or, indeed, *if* she read very much at all. This last point seems an outside possibility. But it would be good to know definitely. There are precious few records of her reading, no detailed annotations—so far as is known—to a book or essay; little hard evidence. A comparison with Charlotte's often-quoted response to the first and second volumes of Ruskin's *Modern Painters* (1843, 1846) points up a notable contrast.[21]

---

[17] 'Introduction', Emily Brontë, *Wuthering Heights*, ed. Ian Jack and Helen Small, Oxford World's Classics (Oxford: Oxford University Press, 2009), p. 324; Emily Brontë, *Wuthering Heights*, ed. Hilda Marsden and Ian Jack (Oxford: Clarendon, 1976), p. 418.

[18] *Wuthering Heights*, ed. Marsden and Jack, p. 419n.

[19] A good example, and summary, of some possible 'source' discussion where the novel is concerned is A.J. Hoenselaars, 'Emily Brontë, Hamlet, and Wilhelm Meister', *Notes & Queries*, 39 (1992), pp. 177–8.

[20] Dinah Birch, 'Emily Brontë', in Claude Rawson, ed., *The Cambridge Companion to English Poets* (Cambridge: Cambridge University Press, 2011), pp. 408–21 (p. 415).

[21] 'I have lately been reading "Modern Painters," and I have derived from the work much genuine pleasure and, I hope, some edification; at any rate it made me feel how ignorant I had previously been on the subject which it treats. Hitherto I have only had instinct to guide me in judging of art; I feel now as if I had been walking blindfold—this book seems to give me eyes—

INTRODUCTION · xxi

And this matters. It matters because to concentrate on seeking out 'sources' (as distinct from direct allusion/quotation, as from a ballad noted by Walter Scott) is, in the case of Emily Jane Brontë, to imply that she wrote like many other major writers. That is, that she wrote out of both imagination and extensive studies. That she was inspired by—whatever that might quite mean—her close attention to the achievements of predecessors and peers. This is now a familiar way, especially for editors, of understanding, and presenting, what good literary writing is. It is the staple of modern literary editions, and source-searching might indeed be regarded as partly a by-product of the invention of the 'scholarly editor'. Yet we cannot be *certain* that this is a secure approach to, or for, Emily Brontë. After all, in many kinds of ways, both as a person and a writer, Emily Brontë did not do what others did.

One thing we can be sure that she wrote out of was—Gondal. And we can also, alas, be sure that we know very little about it. Gondal was Emily and Anne's invented land; the previous Glass Town, created by all four surviving children, was no doubt its origin and it, Gondal, diverged from Charlotte and Branwell's subsequent Angria. The British Library, which holds the tiny and fragmentary *The History of 'Angria'* (1836–7?) written by Branwell, tells the same story of the beginning of Gondal as follows: Glass Town was the 'original fictional land', the British Library remarks, but Emily and Anne subsequently invented their 'own private world'.[22] What is interesting is the slip between 'fictional land' and 'private world'. Perhaps, unintentionally or otherwise, the British Library delineates something that seems, on the slender evidence we have, to be a real possibility: that Gondal is not best understood simply as a child's game, as an imaginative project, but as a secret shared between two sisters and, especially necessary to, and pursued by, Emily. Anne took part. But she increasingly did without Gondal. Her published fiction shows no sign, so far as can be detected, of the clandestine island world(s) of the imagination. Emily's, it might be, is profoundly shaped by Gondal—written for and from it. Charlotte said, in what is known as the fragment, 'Farewell to Angria' (*c.*1839?), that it was 'no easy thing to dismiss from my imagination

---

I *do* wish I had pictures within reach by which to test this new sense. Who can read these glowing descriptions of Turner's works without longing to see them? [...]', letter to W.S. Williams, 31 July 1848, in Margaret Smith, ed., *The Letters of Charlotte Brontë with a Selection of Letters by Family and Friends*, 3 vols (Oxford: Clarendon, 1995–2004), ii.94.

[22] See Brontë Juvenilia: *The History of Angria*, British Library, https://www.bl.uk/collection-items/bront-juvenilia-the-history-of-angria. Consequential and/or interesting work on Gondal includes Fannie Ratchford, *The Brontës' Web of Childhood* (London: Oxford University Press, 1941) and her *Gondal's Queen, A Novel in Verse* (Austin: University of Texas Press, 1955). W.D. Paden's *An Investigation of Gondal* (New York: Bookman, 1958) took issue with both of these in a detailed bibliographical study.

xxii INTRODUCTION

the images which have filled it so long'.[23] Emily, I think, never did that. And if one takes the implications of that remark seriously, then one begins to realize just how unique, and misunderstood, Emily Brontë's imagination is. It is not, it seems, possible to draw a distinction between what was a Gondal poem and what was not. Gondal contexts allow for the expression of what might be private emotion, after all; apparently non-Gondal poems might have taken their starting point from a Gondal event and then been changed. No-one knows. Certainly, Emily Brontë in 1844 decided to transcribe some of her poems into a 'Gondal Poems' notebook, which is now in the British Library (Add MS 43483). She obviously thought she *could* make a distinction— or wanted to persuade herself she could. Something of the strange world of gusting passions, regret and remembrance, rebellion and imprisonment, infidelity and loyalty—a world of characters written on a huge scale, the Brocken Spectres of Emily Brontë's inner life—are glimpsed, though not more than that, in these poems. What was published as 'Remembrance', for instance (see pp. 33–4), is explicitly a Gondal poem, titled in the manuscript 'R. Alcona to J. Brenzaida'. Alcona, who might (at least sometimes) be the same person as 'A.G.A.', to whom I will return, had caused Brenzaida's imprisonment and then, apparently, married him or at least became his lover before his death. (See also the cognate story sketched in 'Julian M. and A.G. Rochelle' (pp. 40–4).) The reader catches for a moment a ray of reflected light, as from a dark ocean, of a whole invented world in this exceptional elegiac piece, which once read is hard ever to get out of one's mind (that is partly to do with the extraordinarily slow rhythm).

Emily was often at work on her invented Pacific islands. Gaaldine, a tropical island, is discovered by the Gondals in the south Pacific; Gondal itself, with a Scottish-Yorkshire landscape, is in the north Pacific. We can reconstruct a small number of facts about them both. In 1837, for example, Emily, then aged 18, wrote in one of the few surviving diary-like pages that she was composing 'Augusta Almeda's life 1st V. 1—4th page from the last—' (see p. 4). Augusta Almeida is that already-mentioned 'A.G.A.', the leading heroine of the whole saga, so far as is known, and clearly a passionate, cruel, sexually exciting figure who re-emerges, it might be, as Catherine Earnshaw.[24]

---

[23] The Brontës, *Tales of Glass Town, Angria, and Gondal*, ed. Christine Alexander (Oxford: Oxford University Press, 2010), p. 314.

[24] 'A.G.A.' is appropriately summed up by Christine Alexander and Margaret Smith as follows: 'Born in Gondal, to whose natural landscape of snowy mountains, heather, and bluebells she is deeply attached. She is a passionate dark beauty, ruthless in both political and personal relationships; a female alternative to the Byronic heroes of the Glass Town and Angrian saga. When she tires of Amedeus, the lover of her childhood friend Angelica, she sends both into exile. After an affair and marriage with Alfred Sidonia of Aspin Castle, she abandons him to die of a broken heart. Her relationship with Alexander, Lord of Elbë, also ends in his violent death by Lake Elmor. Fernando de Samara too she loves, imprisons, then drives into exile and suicide. And when her "passionate youth was nearly past", she is murdered by the outlaw Douglas at the instigation of Angelica, while alone on Elmor Hill. The faithful Lord Eldred contemplates her

INTRODUCTION   xxiii

In the diary-like page, Emily continued in her characteristic way of oscillating without comment between the imagined world and the real, an oscillation that might have been the condition of her whole life. '[F]ine', she went on, turning abruptly to the weather,

rather coolish thin grey cloudy but sunny day Aunt working in the little room the old nursery Papa gone out Tabby in the kitchen—the Emperors and Empresses of Gondal and Gaaldine preparing to depart from Gaaldine to Gondal to prepare for the coronation which will be on the 12th July Queen Vittoria ascended the throne this month. Northangerland in Monkey's Isle—Zamora at Eversham.

p. 4.

The punctuation drought, except for a dash or two, offers a kind of textual confirmation, as differently for Emily Dickinson or John Clare, of the uncertain but fructive relationships between thoughts, events, and images as they are written out on paper on the run; possibilities of connections within the disruptions are suggested, allowed, but not confirmed.[25] It was Emily Brontë's way of seeing the world. The imagined infused it all the time.

The poems, as I will conclude, give more evidence of the emotions in Gondal. As searing as 'Remembrance', there is the already-mentioned 'Julian M. and A.G. Rochelle'. Imprisonment, political conflict, a woman's strength, the force of the imagination: these magnificent Emily Brontë themes are brought into a taut relationship here in a poem that dwells on the opposite of the fissile. Then there is the grief over the death of 'Edward' articulated in what was first published as 'A Death-Scene' (see pp. 34–6):

> [...] Then his eyes began to weary,
> Weighed beneath a mortal sleep;
> And their orbs grew strangely dreary,
> Clouded, even as they would weep.
>
> But they wept not, but they changed not,
> Never moved, and never closed;
> Troubled still, and still they ranged not—
> Wandered not, nor yet reposed!
>
> So I knew that he was dying—
> Stooped, and raised his languid head;
> Felt no breath, and heard no sighing,
> So I knew that he was dead.

---

tempestuous life that inspired both hate and devotion but never fulfilled its promise', Christine Alexander and Margaret Smith, *The Oxford Companion to the Brontës* (Oxford: Oxford University Press, 2006), p. 11.

[25] I do not mean to imply that the dash was peculiar to any particular writer in the age of ink-dip pens (where a dash was safer than a full stop because there was less of a chance of blotting). Dashes were a norm. But all the same they create some interesting ambiguities in Emily Brontë's writing, worthy of comment.

xxiv INTRODUCTION

This poem was entitled in the manuscript: 'From A D— W— in the N.C.';
that is, 'From a Dungeon Wall in the Northern College' (though it is not
obviously a dungeon poem). But 'A Death-Scene's' first readers, and those
for many decades afterwards, did not know anything about Gondal. The
imaginative world from which this poem, as others, came was long severed
from its context (to be clear, Emily Brontë stripped out most references to
Gondal in the poems published in 1846 and Charlotte removed them, largely,
from the 1850 additions) so that the words appeared simply to arise from the
imagination or perhaps from some private experience. In fact, they arose
from fantasy. 'Edward' in the manuscript, for instance, was 'Elbë', that is,
Alexander, Lord of Elbë (Emily had, understandably, an attraction to another
name ending with an ë). He was a lover of A.G.A.; Elbë's lonely grave is at
Lake Elnor. This is Gondal territory. Lonely tombs; a strong-minded woman
loved by several men; a tormented death scene; a perpetual remembrance.[26]
The connections with *Wuthering Heights* are obvious.

Emily Brontë enveloped Gondal—or the other way around. Aged nearly
twenty-seven, on a train to York with Anne, Emily was, extraordinarily, still
absorbed with, or by, playing made-up people from her childhood world. She
wrote unselfconsciously in her diary paper (see p. 24):

Anne and I went our first long journey by ourselves together—leaving Home on the
30th of June—monday sleeping at York—returning to Keighley Tuesday evening
sleeping there and walking home on Wednesday morning—though the weather was
broken, we enjoyed ourselves very much except during a few hours at Bradford and
during our excursion we were Ronald Macelgin, Henry Angora, Juliet Augusteena,
Rosobelle Esualdar, Ella and Julian Egramont Catherine Navarre and Cordelia
Fitzaphnold escaping from the palaces of Instruction to join the Royalists who are
hard driven at present by the victorious Republicans—The Gondals still flourish
bright as ever I am at present writing a work on the First Wars—Anne has been writing some articles on this and a book by Henry Sophona—We intend sticking firm by
the rascals as long as they delight us which I am glad to say they do at present[.]

More than old enough to be married and with small children herself, Emily
Brontë presents a strange impression here. It is almost like finding
J.R.R. Tolkien pretending in all seriousness to be a character from *The Lord
of the Rings* (1954–5). The imagined fantasy overtakes the real. In turn, the
wonders of the ancient city of York, for instance, receive no mention: her
memory of the role-playing is everything. In this glimpse of what Emily
needed to feel safe, we perceive perhaps—truly one has to speculate where
Emily Brontë is concerned—a woman deeply anxious about how to navigate
the outside world. She does so, it appears, by retaining the certainties of

---

[26] On this broad subject, there is a survey of possibilities in Teddi Lynn Chichester, 'Evading
"Earth's Dungeon Tomb": Emily Brontë, A.G.A., and the Fatally Feminine', *Victorian Poetry*, 29
(1991), pp. 1–15.

INTRODUCTION   XXV

familiar things as a compensation for, or a barrier against, interaction with the unfamiliar. Her well-documented inability to make contact with strangers; her intensely withdrawn nature so resistant to the new, even when that newness is her own terminal illness (the story of her trying to live her usual life despite the last stages of consumption is as upsetting as it is peculiar[27]); her repetitive returns to the same narratives set out first in childhood even in her mid-twenties; the apparent near-impossibility of living away from the routines of home; the acute self-consciousness that led her both into privacy and fiercely to insist on anonymity in print, a privacy that included her horror that her poems had been discovered in the first place: the modern reader cannot but wonder whether this anxious, protective, and routine-needful Emily Brontë had some form of autism. She would hardly be the first major writer of whom this is true.

It is not possible, as I have said, to be sure whether a poem is a Gondal one or separate from Emily's secret imagined world, if such separation can be countenanced. And it is also hard to extract *Wuthering Heights* from Gondal. The novel looks different from its popular image as a great romance—even the astute and original writer Lydia Davis still calls the novel one of the 'more classical romances',[28] though it is hard to know what this means—if this context is understood. (And the cinema, as I will continue to note, has played a part here, doing much to transform the perception of the novel away from the text itself: the 1939 Hollywood version, directed by Samuel Goldwyn, for example, starring Laurence Olivier and Merle Oberon, famously missed out the whole second half of the novel, so it is easier to think, watching the film, of Heathcliff as an angry but passionate lover instead of a man who is also bent on fearful, cruel, and unnatural revenge.[29])

Sometimes the novel's connections with what we know of Gondal are unmissable. The British poet, novelist, and biographer Philip Henderson (1906–77), in the still valuable 'Introduction' to his selection of Emily Brontë's poems (1947), made a strong early case, for example, for the Gondal context of the fiction. These stanzas from 1838 were, as Henderson aptly put it, '*Wuthering Heights* in essence':

---

[27] Cf. Charlotte's account: 'When illness came her indomitable will still enabled her to present an unflinching front to sympathising friends. She refused to see the doctor, and would not have it that she was ill. To the last she retained an independent spirit, and on the day of her death she arose and dressed herself as usual. Her end reminds us of that of her brother Branwell whose will was so strong that he insisted on standing up to die and did actually so die. Emily did everything for herself on that last day, but as the hours drew on got manifestly worse, and could only whisper in gasps. The end came when it was too late to profit by human skill', see p. 333.

[28] 'A Beloved Duck Gets Cooked: Forms and Influences (I)', in Lydia Davis, *Essays* (London: Penguin, 2019), pp. 3–27 (p. 5).

[29] Goldwyn's dislike of the novel and preference for his film version are discussed in A. Scott Berg's *Goldwyn: A Biography* (New York: Knopf, 1989), pp. 319–34.

INTRODUCTION

> Do I not see thee now? Thy black resplendant [*sic*] hair;
> The glory-beaming brow, and smile how heavenly fair!
> Thine eyes are turned away—those eyes I would not see;
> Their dark, their deadly ray would more than madden me [...]
> And yet for all Her hate, each parting glance would tell
> A stronger passion breathed, burned in this last farewell—
> Unconquered in my soul the Tyrant rules me still—
> *Life* bows to my control, but, *Love* I cannot kill![30]

Henderson is not wrong. And feelings, in such writing, because they are Gondal feelings, are of a magnitude that can only belong to, or with, imagined worlds.

There is something further in the texture of Emily Brontë's novel that bonds it with Gondal: fantasy itself. *Wuthering Heights* has been thought a fiery fiction about what true love could be (not least thanks to that 1939 Hollywood version). Yet it is really a Gondal story, reconceived (no surprise, then, that another writer of wonders and the fabulous, Lewis Carroll, reading the novel as early as 1856, called it 'extraordinary'[31]). There is the dreadful dream at the beginning of *Wuthering Heights*, for sure, and the ghostly figures of the end. But there is also, more importantly, fantasy in the narrative as a whole. This distance from the fabric of lived experience is most visible in the figuring of violence, but that is only a pointer to a greater, more general, detachment from the actual throughout the text. I do not mean that the kinds of violence depicted in the novel cannot occur, alas, in the world beyond the page. Yet what is revealing about the novel's aesthetic is the lack of comment, or self-consciousness, about that violence. Many readers and critics have drawn attention to the absence of a moral compass in *Wuthering Heights*. It is important, nevertheless, to think through what this means for comprehending the roots of the novel's imagination and not simply for projecting a view of Emily as some kind of defiant radical, scornful of ethical 'convention'. The lack of a moral compass suggests something of how deeply *Wuthering Heights* is lodged in the realm, not of the other-worldly, but the non-world.[32]

---

[30] Emily Brontë, *Poems*, ed. Peter Henderson (London: Lawson and Dunn, 1947), p. xx, though following the text in *The Poems of Emily Brontë*, ed. Derek Roper and Edward Chitham (Oxford: Clarendon, 1995), pp. 65–6. Curiously, Henderson does not observe that the original title of this poem, which is dated 1 November 1838, is not, as he says, 'Light Up Thy Halls!' but 'F. De Samara to A.G.A.', *The Poems of Emily Brontë*, p. 64.

[31] Quoted in Robert Douglas-Fairhurst, *The Story of Alice: Lewis Carroll and the Secret History of Wonderland* (Harvard: Harvard University Press, 2016), p. 163.

[32] One reviewer of the 1850 edition of *Wuthering Heights* put the non-worldly element of Heathcliff in these thought-provoking terms: 'It might have been added, that to those whose experience of men and manners is neither extensive nor various, the construction of a self-consistent monster is easier than the delineation of an imperfect or inconsistent reality', '*Wuthering Heights* and *Agnes Grey*', *The Athenæum* (28 December 1850), pp. 1368–9 (p. 1369).

INTRODUCTION   xxvii

The poems hint at the violence and emotional extremes of Gondal—the unnamed prisoner shackled in the depths of an *oubliette* awaiting the visit of imaginative insight; the recoverable history of 'A Death-Scene'. The reader is in the territory of Beethoven's *An die ferne Geliebte* (April 1816), the first ever song cycle, only multiplied in intensity.[33] And the violence, and more particularly the response to violence, of *Wuthering Heights* is as startling as it is suggestive.

There are many examples. They include such passages as these.

Lockwood repulsed:

With these words she suddenly splashed a pint of icy water down my neck, and pulled me into the kitchen.

p. 71.

The near murder of Heathcliff with a measuring weight:

'Off dog!' cried Hindley, threatening him with an iron weight, used for weighing potatoes, and hay.

'Throw it,' he replied, standing still, 'and then I'll tell how you boasted that you would turn me out of doors as soon as he died, and see whether he will not turn you out directly.'

Hindley threw it, hitting him on the breast and down he fell but staggered up, immediately, breathless and white, and had not I prevented it he would have gone just so to the master, and got full revenge by letting his condition plead for him, intimating who had caused it.

p. 86.

Heathcliff attacks Master Linton:

He seized a tureen of hot apple-sauce, the first thing that came under his gripe, and dashed it full against the speaker's face and neck—who instantly commenced a lament that brought Isabella and Catherine hurrying to the place.

Mr. Earnshaw snatched up the culprit directly and conveyed him to his chamber, where, doubtless, he administered a rough remedy to cool the fit of passion, for he reappeared red and breathless.

p. 101.

Earnshaw's decline:

The master's bad ways and bad companions formed a pretty example for Catherine and Heathcliff. His treatment of the latter was enough to make a fiend of a saint. And, truly, it appeared as if the lad *were* possessed of something diabolical at that period. He delighted to witness Hindley degrading himself past redemption; and became daily more notable for savage sullenness and ferocity.

p. 106.

---

[33] I am not implying that Emily Brontë knew this work. There is a highly speculative set of claims about Emily and Beethoven (including that the composer served as a model for Heathcliff) in John Hennessy's *Emily Jane Brontë and Her Music* (York: W.K. Publishing, 2018).

xxviii INTRODUCTION

Heathcliff accidentally saves Hareton from Earnshaw:

It expressed, plainer than words could do, the intensest anguish at having made himself the instrument of thwarting his own revenge. Had it been dark, I dare say, he
would have tried to remedy the mistake by smashing Hareton's skull on the steps; but,
we witnessed his salvation; and I was presently below with my precious charge pressed
to my heart.

p. 113.

There are a plurality of similar scenes, their extremity largely unregistered in
the text. A thrown heavy weight, a bowl of hot apple sauce tipped onto flesh,
a thought of smashing a skull: these are instances of almost unthinkable damage. Charlotte and Anne come nowhere near this kind of writing (though
Huntingdon in *The Tenant of Wildfell Hall* (1848) is a chilling figure).
'I knocked over Hareton,' we read in *Wuthering Heights* (on p. 194), 'who was
hanging a litter of puppies from a chair back in the doorway; and, blest as a
soul escaped from purgatory, I bounded, leaped, and flew down the steep
road.' Emily Brontë's habit in her diary pages of moving from one subject to
another without reflecting on the alterations in direction is unambiguously
evident here too. Symptomatically, suffering is narrated but not, as it were,
noted. (And Emily cared about dogs.)

Around *Wuthering Heights*, evident even in these accounts of rage, cruelty,
intemperance, and, to use a word from the original reviews, savagery, there is
a curious kind of authorial separateness. About that separateness there is an
unanswerable question concerning both the poetry and the novel: we will
never know whether Emily Brontë was feeling or describing feeling. Certainly,
we, as readers, become oddly acculturated, even immune, to the extremities
of *Wuthering Heights*. It is a daring comparison, but something of a similar
effect is experienced in the writing of the Marquis de Sade (1740–1814). Eye-
watering violence is depicted in his work, an astonishing account of what a
human being can imagine doing to another, in a way that is also unself-aware,
innocent of perspective. As Edmund Wilson aptly put it in 'The Vogue of the
Marquis de Sade' (1952):

The horrors that are perpetrated by his characters are made to take place in a kind of
void: they rarely have any of the consequences that they would have in actual life, and
that they did, to his sorrow, for Sade himself.[34]

There is a connection with *Wuthering Heights*, though I am not for one
moment suggesting Emily Brontë read de Sade. And the unselfconscious-
ness, the fantastic, relates, too, as I have implied, to the huge and sometimes
inexplicable emotions the novel so captivatingly narrates. Emily Brontë
does not always, in an important sense, *do* narrative—at least explanatory

[34] Edmund Wilson, 'The Vogue of the Marquis de Sade', in *The Bit Between My Teeth: A Literary Chronicle of 1950–1965* (New York: Farrar, Straus and Giroux, 1965), pp. 158–73 (p. 167).

INTRODUCTION   xxix

narrative. Revenge, on the one hand, *is* the motif for Heathcliff's stratagems in the second half of the novel, certainly; class affiliation for the first Catherine's marriage to Linton. The novel allows us to 'explain' these characters' actions by giving us bold, even stark, psychological motives—however little real people might be so single-minded in their ways of managing life. Yet Isabella's infatuation for Heathcliff, so necessary to the latter's devilish schemes, is, on the other hand, as sudden as it is 'unnarrated', created rather than accounted for.

The overall coherence of Emily Brontë's scheme—the satisfaction of Heathcliff's anger at his treatment as a child and his reunion with Catherine—absorbs, or rather dilutes, this psychological oddity that, in another novel, would feel a fault. Here, instead, we sense what kind of narrative art can be the result of, looked at unsympathetically, incoherence or the inexplicable. This is far from the creative, constructive features of what John Bayley would call 'the uses of division'.[35] Charlotte and Emily's interest in intense privacy becomes in this case about narrative silences, absent explanations, or psychological motives, which, importantly, we do not fully notice because there are larger things to hold our attention. *Wuthering Heights*, refusing to tell us where Heathcliff came from, who he is, where he goes, and how he obtains his money, makes of absences and puzzles, like that of Isabella's desire, a staple of its aesthetic.[36] The novel's aim, at this level, is not at making narrative sense but in conveying what being *in* the narrative feels like (whether Emily herself felt it or not). Emily Brontë has sometimes been said to have a Shakespearian element to her imagination. She is Shakespearian in this sense: that the work of art must lead to climatic moments and that those are more important than carefully contriving the way that leads to them. Walt Whitman does something of the same. Shakespeare permits us to know nothing substantial about Iago's motives, for example: Iago needs to act in the way he does for Shakespeare to stage his climactic disaster. We can no more account for Angelo in *Measure for Measure* than for Heathcliff or Isabella. They are caused by the dramas that need them.

Gondal is the key to Emily Brontë's imagination. And a key we will never properly find. In turn, it is hard to avoid noticing the remarkable consistency of her themes, approaches, characters, and moods. Even when not writing—at least, so it seems—about Gondal, she is still within the theatre of its desires, plots, and personalities. Tellingly, it is possible to see Gondal even in the *devoirs* that she wrote in Brussels for her tutor, Constantin Héger (1809–96), in 1842. Asked to compose a practice letter, Emily Brontë on 5 August 1842

---

[35] See John Bayley, *The Uses of Division: Unity and Disharmony in Literature* (London: Chatto & Windus, 1976).

[36] Among the most bracing and suggestive accounts of this matter of Heathcliff and his origins is Terry Eagleton's daring study *Heathcliff and the Great Hunger: Studies in Irish Culture* (London: Verso, 1995).

XXX INTRODUCTION

wrote (in Sue Lonoff's English translation) the following. It is the letter from one brother to another:

My brother,
A letter received from me will be for you as a letter received from the tomb. Ten long years, ten years of suffering, of work and change have gone by since we departed from our father's house, angry with each other and vowing an eternal separation. Those years have dissipated many hopes, in my case they have brought many griefs, but admidst it all, I kept hidden in my heart that vow, born of anger and fed by pride [...]
Forgive, this last act of the tyrant who had so long usurped the place of nature in my breast; an instant later I was on my knees praying and crying and abjuring my enmity forever; I went to bed happy, I awake ~~happy~~ sad; perhaps my repentance comes too late, perhaps that your heart is hardened more than mine. But in the past my brother was always the last to become angry and the first to forget an injury. Edward, come assure me that your nature has not changed—do not write but come.[37]

This could be an early draft of a Gondal poem in prose (if Emily Brontë, like Thomas Hardy, had begun her poems in such a way). But *Wuthering Heights* seems present, in a pre-echo, already. The emotions are extreme and the language terse. An 'eternal separation', long-held vows, long-standing enmity, a desire for reunion. They come back in 1847. And that desire for a loved one to return—'do not write but come'—reminds one not only of the poems in which the dead are mourned as lost forever, but of the aftermath of Lockwood's dream where Heathcliff calls on Cathy to come back, of the disinterment of her body, and of Heathcliff's yearning, and Linton's, to be reunited with her after death ('I am going to her', Linton says on his deathbed, not, conspicuously, 'I am going to God': p. 267.)

One other Brussels example, and this, again, about siblings, is in the *devoir* called, in English, 'Filial Love'. Part of this reads, again in translation, as follows:

The hour will come when conscience will awake; then there will be a terrible retribution. What mediator will plead then for the criminal? It is God who accuses him. What power will save the wretch? It is God who condemns him. He has rejected happiness in mortal life to assure himself of torment in eternal life.
Let angels and men weep for his fate—he was their brother.[38]

'Terrible retribution', pleading for a criminal, condemned by the highest power, tormented for ever, a domestic relationship destroyed: *Wuthering Heights* reverberates here too—a novel F.R. Leavis was obliged to miss out of *The Great Tradition* (1948) as he rightly observed that there was no tradition

---

[37] *The Belgian Essays: Charlotte Brontë and Emily Brontë*, pp. 164–6.
[38] Ibid., p. 158.

INTRODUCTION   xxxi

in which to place it.[39] But Emily Brontë was, as it were, in her own tradition, writing persistently from the same perspectives: the Gondal saga is detectable even in her French homework.

Charlotte Brontë was keen to shape the public views of her sister both before and after her death. There was something about Emily Brontë that had to be amended not commended or, even, in the case of the mystery of what happened at Law Hill, missed out of the records.[40] This had some rather extreme consequences, however much the excisions led from Charlotte's genuine bafflement about how to understand her sister. The 1846 *Poems of Currer, Ellis, and Acton Bell*—the sisters' first foray into print—had, according to her own testimony, been Charlotte's idea. After Emily's death, she, Charlotte, managed the reception of *Wuthering Heights* in part with her new 1850 edition and its Preface (see pp. 317–21), in part by re-organizing the text. It is worth reflecting on that opening line to the Preface: Charlotte Brontë says that she has just reread the text, and has 'obtained a clear glimpse of what are termed (and, perhaps, really are) its faults; [I] have gained a definite notion of how it appears to other people' (p. 317). Charlotte tells her reader, first, that *Wuthering Heights* is flawed. *Wuthering Heights* is something to apologize for. And yet, in some way, perhaps that reveals just how difficult even Emily Brontë's sister found it to 'account' for this text and for the author behind it. Charlotte could not comprehend Emily. It is worth remembering, to Charlotte's credit, that no-one has been able securely to do so since.

---

[39] Leavis memorably says, in comments still worth thinking about:

> It is tempting to retort that there is only one Brontë. Actually, Charlotte, though claiming no part in the great line of English fiction (it is significant that she couldn't see why any value should be attached to Jane Austen), has a permanent interest of a minor kind. She had a remarkable talent that enabled her to do some-thing first-hand and new in the rendering of personal experience, above all in *Villette*.
>
> The genius, or course, was Emily. I have said nothing about *Wuthering Heights* because that astonishing work seems to me a kind of sport. It may, all the same, very well have had some influence of an essentially undetectable kind: she broke completely, and in the most challenging way, both with the Scott tradition that imposed on the novelist a romantic resolution of his themes, and with the tradition coming down from the eighteenth century that demanded a plane-mirror reflection of the surface of 'real' life. Out of her a minor tradition comes, to which belongs, most notably, [George Douglas Brown's] *The House with the Green Shutters* [1901]).
>
> > *The Great Tradition: George Eliot, Henry James, Joseph Conrad*
> > (New York: Stewart, second impression, 1950), p. 27.

The view of the work of Charlotte Brontë is a curious example of Leavis's blindspots (it is worth remembering he gave no time to Dickens in *The Great Tradition* except for *Hard Times* (1854) and then changed his mind—without commenting on that change—in his and Q.D. Leavis's study, *Dickens the Novelist* (London: Chatto & Windus, 1970)). Given the moral strenuousness of Charlotte's fiction, its grasp of 'life', that important Leavis criterion for fiction, one wonders whether he might eventually have changed his mind on her work too. Leavis is, of course, right about the new 'rendering of personal experience'.

[40] See notes to pp. 8, 61–2, ' "*Wuthering*". . .', and 316, '*At that period . . .*'.

xxxii INTRODUCTION

Charlotte Brontë's 'Biographical Notice' (see pp. 311–16), also in the 1850 edition, gave a picture of Emily that has endured, despite its considerable limitations and the extent of its assertions (as distinct from evidenced arguments). These again are signs of Charlotte's bemusement over Emily, and her desire to protect her memory from strangers' inquiries into what she herself did not quite understand. In terms of texts, there were some reasonable interventions and some that were not. Certainly, as the reader knows from my edition, the original text of the novel was a mess. Charlotte sorted out many of the typos. That was obviously the right thing to do. She also rewrote Joseph the servant's speech to make it more accessible (many readers might have sympathy with that[41]). She built up much longer paragraphs from the original's often short ones. There is nothing especially wrong with that—and who knows if Newby followed Emily Brontë's paragraphing anyway, since we have no manuscript, regrettably. Charlotte's textual interventions here are more or less justifiable, or, at any rate, not wildly significant. But with the posthumous poetry, from the 1850 edition, that is not the case.

Charlotte is, alas, both unprincipled and over-principled with these poems. She added, on first glance, seventeen more pieces to the corpus, which was a gain for readers (though one was almost certainly not by Emily Brontë and another was a fragment from a larger piece: see Note on the Text, pp. l–li). But, making these additions involved, as my explanations indicate, changing things. Punctuation, for a start, was significantly altered (as it was in the novel: Charlotte's ear for subtle rhythms was not as fine as Emily's in either prose or poetry: cf. note to p. 308). It might be possible to argue that Emily Brontë, like John Clare, expected a sympathetic or friendly editor to 'sort out' the punctuation of the manuscript texts, assuming—and it is a large assumption—that Emily considered publishing any more of her poetry. Yet again, this is not known. But there are other problems too.

Gondal, for a start, is, at least from the surface, banished. And that is not the only issue. Further confusing the biographical record (see, for instance, pp. 6–8 and notes); mistakenly claiming—or at least apparently claiming—what was the last poem (see p. 26 and note); and, most astonishing of all, writing poetry *for* Emily: these were serious matters in 1850. As my notes indicate, Charlotte Brontë's more minor changes—of a word here or there, a collocation or even a line—can often seem inexplicable. One looks at some of the revisions and wonders simply, *why?* And then Charlotte adds more of her own poetry. She might well—no-one knows for sure—have written 'Stanzas' herself (see note to p. 27); she certainly did write, among other additions to poems, the last lines of 'The Elder's Rebuke' (see pp. 19–20 and notes).

---

[41] There is a challenge for an editor in the original form of Joseph's speech in that it is partly or largely incomprehensible now. I have provided standard English-language versions in the notes for clarity while accepting that this changes how the reader perceives what Joseph says.

INTRODUCTION   xxxiii

Many of the poems' titles are hers. Her interventions in 'A little while, a little while, | The weary task is put away' significantly change the meaning of the poem (see pp. 8–9 and the note). Perhaps Charlotte thought that she could fill in what Emily had meant to say, or would have said if she had thought, or felt, more carefully. And Charlotte Brontë, of course, could have had no idea of how famous her sister would become (happily, Charlotte was able to glimpse something of her own fame before her equally untimely death) and, as a result, how much readers would want of the real Emily Brontë. In turn, it might be, that Charlotte did not consider her editor's pencil mattered greatly. It was more about family privacy, protecting a curious sister, protecting a sister from curiosity.

The 21st-Century Oxford Authors series is distinctive in that it offers the contemporary reader the works of authors as they were first known (in print, usually but not always[42]) in the chronological order in which they were first available. There are occasionally some modifications to this in other volumes where MS material is included among printed texts,[43] but the overall principle remains to reproduce the first published version of a text with any significant subsequent alterations, as well as any significant deviations from surviving MS versions, recorded in footnotes or appendices. But Emily Brontë needs some disclaimers and some explanation of both compromises, and riskily strict adherence, to the series' principles. First, one must note that the earliest published texts are ones, to an extent, which scholars and critics have been trying to move away from for more than a century. This is partly to do with completion and partly to do with getting around Charlotte. In terms of completion, there is a major matter. Emily's poetic output, as published in 1846 and then supplemented in 1850, was, or at least appeared to be, thirty-eight poems. In Janet Gezari's Penguin edition of *The Complete Poems* (1992), there are 182 poems and two of doubtful authorship.[44] Merely on a matter of scale, Emily Brontë the poet reproduced as she was first read provides a very limited sense of what she did. Second, there is the matter, already mentioned, of Charlotte's interventions. My 'solutions', where the poems are concerned, and amid many competing issues, are described in the 'Note on the Text', pp. xlix–li.

Then, third, there is the challenge of the novel, aside from Charlotte's interventions in 1850. The trouble, as noted, is that the first edition, from

---

[42] John Donne is an obvious exception as his poems circulated in MS before his death and publication of the 1633 edition.

[43] For instance, in my Swinburne edition for the same series (2016), the first poem given, the 'Ode to Mazzini' (1857), was not published in Swinburne's lifetime. But given its significance as a starting point, and as evidence of some ideas that Swinburne never abandoned, the poem seemed necessary to include and was reproduced from the MS. Seamus Perry's edition of Arnold (2020) includes poems in their MS form that were not published till later.

[44] Cf. Susan R. Bauman, 'In the Market for Fame: The Victorian Publication History of the Brontë Poems', *Victorian Review*, 30 (2004), pp. 44–71.

xxxiv INTRODUCTION

the shifty London publisher Thomas Cautley Newby (1797–1882) of 72 Mortimer Street, Cavendish Square, was badly produced. Its badness is here faithfully rendered. What is in my edition is, nevertheless, a version of Emily Brontë worth remembering. Not least because it is this version that has been debated, challenged, and revised ever since. It is a revealing experience to see *Wuthering Heights* with its typographical blemishes, usually tidied up in modern editions. The original state of the text leaves the reader with a visible sense of Emily Brontë's early obscurity—in every mistake there is a sign of the fact that Ellis Bell was an unknown writer making it into print under fairly amateurish circumstances. (This, incidentally, had nothing to do with sex: Newby did not know with whom he was dealing.) And, as for the poetry, we understand now that Emily Brontë wrote a lot more. But the most important thing to say is that the 1846 volume represents, once Emily was reconciled to publishing at all, what she herself—with collective agreement[45]—was prepared to be known by. She is hardly the first or last poet to think the most important thing after writing is tact. Yeats and Auden spring to mind as poets who edited, even censored, themselves. Peter McDonald's volumes of Yeats from the Longman Annotated English Poets series (2020–) is beginning to reveal, for instance, something of the difference between the poet known through the official complete poems and the working poet, publishing what and when he could, and then refining what he wished to be known by in selective, selected, volume form.[46] More thinking, though, could be profitably done on *why* Emily Brontë chose the poems, or perhaps allowed the choice of the poems, that she did for 1846.[47]

Charlotte tried, perhaps because she was confused, to shape posthumous knowledge of Emily Brontë. But Anne had something firmer to say about her sister in public too, or at least, so it seems. *The Tenant of Wildfell Hall* (1848) can easily be perceived as Anne's response to the non-realism, the un-realism, of *Wuthering Heights*. (J. Hillis Miller makes, incidentally, the peculiar assertion in an otherwise illuminating essay in *Fiction and Repetition: Seven English Novels* (1982), that *Wuthering Heights* 'obeys most of the conventions of Victorian realism'.[48] This is a mis-hit, not only because *Wuthering Heights* is far from realism, but also because, apart from anything else, such 'conventions'

---

[45] I am grateful to Tricia Ayrton for pointing out to me the various pencil marks in the MSS which appear to indicate how the sisters, including Emily herself, chose which of Emily's poems should be included in the collection of 1846. Cf. Stillinger, *Multiple Authorship and the Myth of Solitary Genius*.

[46] There are 184 pieces in McDonald's first two volumes (2020) but Yeats preserved only seventy-nine of them in subsequent collections. In due course, this will be the standard text.

[47] See the forthcoming study by Tricia Ayrton.

[48] J. Hillis Miller, *Fiction and Repetition: Seven English Novels* (Cambridge, MA: Harvard University Press, 1982), p. 42.

INTRODUCTION

had hardly had time to become established.) The link between Anne's novel and her views on her sister's is possible to discern even in the title: the plot of both novels concerns, and this is not a minor point, tenancy (the centre of Heathcliff's ruthless ambition is, of course, to make himself landlord to his enemies) and the central dwelling of each is a remote, weather-swept house with the initials W.H. Here is Wildfell Hall:

> Near the top of this hill, about two miles from Linden-Car, stood Wildfell Hall, a superannuated mansion of the Elizabethan era, built of dark grey stone,—venerable and picturesque to look at, but, doubtless, cold and gloomy enough to inhabit, with its thick stone mullions and little latticed panes, its time-eaten airholes, and its too lonely, too unsheltered situation,—only shielded from the war of wind and weather by a group of Scotch firs, themselves half blighted with storms, and looking as stern and gloomy as the Hall itself.[49]

And here Wuthering Heights:

> Wuthering Heights is the name of Mr Heathcliff's dwelling. 'Wuthering' being a significant provincial adjective, descriptive of the atmospheric tumult to which its station is exposed, in stormy weather. Pure, bracing ventilation they must have up there, at all times, indeed: one may guess the power of the north wind, blowing over the edge, by the excessive slant of a few, stunted firs at the end of the house; and by a range of gaunt thorns all stretching their limbs one way, as if craving alms of the sun. Happily, the architect had foresight to build it strong: the narrow windows are deeply set in the wall; and the corners defended with large jutting stones.

pp. 61–2.

They are more or less the same place.

Yet the connections implicit in the title and in the houses are only the first clues to a more substantial link—a link and an objection. Anne's objection is to essential things. First, it is to Emily's portrait of what living with violent, dissolute, and chaotic men is really like. The non-reality of Emily Brontë's Gondalian violence and emotional extremes are countered in Anne's level-headed, realist, and profoundly uncomfortable novel. In Lord Lowborough before his reformation, Ralph Hattersley, and Mr Grimsby, Anne dramatizes the awfulness of alcoholism, drug addiction, and infidelity. And her central male character in this debauched set, Arthur Huntingdon, shocks: his open affair, drinking, and his capacity, as Anne depicts it, to damage other lives, not least his son's, is unstintingly lain out. *The Tenant of Wildfell Hall*, it is not difficult to assume, took as its starting point not only Anne's doubts about *Wuthering Heights'* preference for fantasy over the reality in depicting life with debased men. She might well also have been musing on Emily's apparent blindness to what real life in Haworth Parsonage was actually like as she wrote.

---

[49] Acton Bell, *The Tenant of Wildfell Hall*, 3 vols (London: Newby, 1848), i.31.

xxxvi INTRODUCTION

Branwell Brontë, drunkard, drug taker, and possible adulterer, died on 24 September 1848. *The Tenant of Wildfell Hall* was published in June as the end approached. Anne Brontë, countering Emily's absorption in a made-up world with a portrait of what, as she saw it, was the authentic experience of dwelling among such moral, physical, and emotional disarray, had created for herself both a powerful novel and a problem. Anne, simply put, could only think she had succeeded if her novel was not liked. Repulsive behaviour is hardly the easiest subject for an appealing book. Each 'revolting detail', said, not unreasonably, *Sharpe's London Magazine* in July, 'is dwelt on with painful minuteness, each brutal or profane expression chronicled with hateful accuracy.'[50] But, for Anne, in *Wildfell Hall*, that was what she thought truthfulness: a reviewer's objection (to her objection to *Wuthering Heights*) was a version of literary, moral, and personal bravery. 'My object', Anne Brontë said frankly in the Preface to the second edition,

in writing the following pages was not simply to amuse the Reader; neit'her was it to gratify my own taste, nor yet to ingratiate myself with the Press and the Public: I wished to tell the truth, for truth always conveys its own moral to those who are able to receive it.[51]

She was, perhaps, primarily talking to Emily, beyond the grave. *Wuthering Heights*, Anne Brontë is implying, is all very well. Yet, in an important sense, it is false because it represents, but does not comment on, what is in truth, outside the pages of a fantasy novel, intolerable.

Anne Brontë's second novel pitched an alternative, felt world at Emily's. And a kinder one. Helen Huntingdon endeavours to reform, and for a long time to think the best of, her wayward husband. His attempts to corrupt their son drive her away but Helen is still willing, in a turn of the plot many modern readers find hard to take, to return to nurse him. There is nothing of Heathcliff's implacable revenge here. Forgiveness, universal redemption, recovery in a second marriage: these are the benign presences of Anne Brontë's world (she is the only one of the sisters who, in *Agnes Grey* (1847), published in the same volumes as *Wuthering Heights*, imagines the pleasures of falling in love with a man who is kind and decent) in defiance of her curious sister's curious book, a novel which *Douglas Jerrold's Weekly Magazine* described as having episodes that made a reader, 'shocked, disgusted, almost sickened by details of cruelty, inhumanity'.[52] Anne seems to have felt something of the same.

---

[50] 'The Tenant of Wildfell Hall', *Sharpe's London Magazine*, 7 (July 1848), pp. 181–4 (p. 182).
[51] Anne Brontë, *The Tenant of Wildfell Hall*, ed. Herbert Rosengarten (Oxford: Clarendon, 1992), p. 3.
[52] *Douglas Jerrold's Weekly Magazine*, 15 January 1848, in Miriam Allott, ed., *The Brontës: The Critical Heritage* (London: Routledge & Kegan Paul, 1974), pp. 227–8 (p. 228).

INTRODUCTION   xxxvii

The Tenant of Wildfell Hall, furthermore, reminds the reader, as I have already implied, of another (a)moral aspect of *Wuthering Heights*. *Wuthering Heights* is an adultery novel. And, as with the physical violence, it does not mind. It is even more indifferent to the implications of this topic than, say, Evelyn Waugh's *Brideshead Revisited* (1945), where the readiness of Waugh's magnificently dismaying plot to envisage infidelity as a norm is not, differently from *Wuthering Heights*, without some furtive recognition of moral and emotional consequence. Just before Catherine explains, in the most famous speech in the text, that she *is* Heathcliff though she intends to marry Linton nevertheless, Nelly Dean remarks how lonely and deserted Heathcliff will be after this separation. ' "He quite deserted! we separated!" ' Catherine exclaims 'with an accent of indignation':

'Who is to separate us, pray? They'll meet the fate of Milo! Not as long as I live, Ellen—for no mortal creature. Every Linton on the face of the earth might melt into nothing, before I could consent to forsake Heathcliff. Oh, that's not what I intend— that's not what I mean! I shouldn't be Mrs. Linton were such a price demanded! He'll be as much to me as he has been all his lifetime.[']

p. 118.

A Gondal proposition, it seems, from the same imagination that envisaged the turbulent sexual life of A.G.A. Adultery, or at least adulterous feelings, intrigued the sisters. And Branwell, perhaps, had practical knowledge of it, or them.[53] But only Emily Brontë seemed to remain on the outside, as it were, of her own narrative proposal, indifferent to the ethical and personal turmoil that is lightly dispensed with in this speech. Charlotte has Jane Eyre nearly, unknowingly, enter not only an adulterous but a bigamous relationship; Huntingdon is unfaithful to Helen and disaster follows; Catherine, however, proposes to marry one man while continuing intently to love another. There is a difference. The two other sisters step back from the brink, avoiding narrating the reality of such possibilities. Charlotte Brontë does not permit Jane to marry bigamously any more than she permits her to consent to Rochester's invitation to become his mistress. And Helen remains firmly faithful, despite Gilbert Markham's efforts. Only Emily Brontë, with characteristic distance from ethical comment/conduct, allows Catherine's proposition to commit adultery of the heart (or does the novel suggest more than this?) without reflecting on the emotional disaster that would be involved in real life. (It is, speculatively, interesting to wonder what Emily knew of Charlotte's actual adulterous feelings for Constantin Héger—she had been in Belgium with her sister on the first visit, after all—and whether somehow she has come to think from this that such feelings were common.) Whatever the case, these desires are magnified in *Wuthering Heights* into a passion, the strength and single-mindedness of which negate self-consciousness.

[53] See note to p. 18, ll. 21–4.

xxxviii INTRODUCTION

Where the commentary comes from—when it does come—in *Wuthering Heights* is, principally, from Nelly Dean. She might be thought an intellectualish version of Tabby Ackroyd, the much-cherished servant in Haworth Parsonage. But she, Nelly, is also a kind of anchor; a crossing point between the Gondal world and a version of the solid realities of the terrestrial. Both Anne and Emily Brontë were interested in embedded narratives—perhaps the starting point for this was Sir Walter Scott in the Waverley novels or William Wordsworth in *The Excursion* (1814)? Whatever the case, the Brontës explore, and exploit, the fine, sometimes exceptionally subtle, distances, and differences in meaning, which arise from a narrator relating someone else's story. Anne has the letters and journal in *Wildfell Hall*; Emily has Lockwood narrating Mrs Dean narrating Cathy...The 'steady, reasonable kind of body' (p. 104) of Wuthering Heights' housekeeper, though she is made to cause various crises in the plot, not least because she is late to realize Cathy's dire illness, deepens the complexity of voice in the novel, the layers of irony and artfully muted commentary. Mrs Dean also, more importantly, grounds *Wuthering Heights* in the earth (or perhaps, like Emily Brontë often was said to be, in the kitchen), disguising its Gondal nature. *The Examiner* said on 8 January 1848, in a review that Emily kept in her writing desk:

> This is a strange book. It is not without evidences of considerable power: but, as a whole, it is wild, confused, disjointed, and improbable; and the people who make up the drama, which is tragic enough in its consequences, are savages ruder than those who lived before the days of Homer.[54]

Although it is fashionable to dismiss negative comments from the first reviewers of *Wuthering Heights*—and it is hard to forget George Saintsbury's later general assertion that the 'English literary criticism of 1830–1860, speaking in round numbers, is curiously and to this day rather unintelligibly

---

[54] 'Wuthering Heights', *The Examiner*, 2084 (8 January 1848), pp. 21–2 (p. 21). *Douglas Jerrold's Weekly Newspaper* on 15 January 1848 began in the same way (cf. p. xxxvi above). The review is a further example of both the sympathy and the bafflement the novel created among the first readers who knew nothing of Gondal. Again, Emily Brontë kept a copy of this in her writing desk:

> Wuthering Heights is a strange sort of book,—baffling all regular criticism; yet, it is impossible to begin and not finish it; and quite as impossible to lay it aside afterwards and say nothing about it. In the midst of the reader's perplexity the ideas predominant in his mind concerning this book are likely to be—brutal cruelty, and semi-savage love. What may be the moral which the author wishes the reader to deduce from his work, it is difficult to say; and we refrain from assigning any, because to speak honestly, we have discovered none but mere glimpses of hidden morals or secondary meanings. [...] We strongly recommend all our readers who love novelty to get this story, for we can promise them that they never have read anything like it before. It is very puzzling and very interesting, and if we had space we would willingly devote a little more time to the analysis of this remarkable story, but we must leave it to our readers to decide what sort of book it is.
>
> *CH*, p. 228.

INTRODUCTION xxxix

bad'[55]—*The Examiner*'s piece is not unperceptive, not least given the fact that the writer could know nothing of Emily Brontë's invented imagined islands. But the invention of Mrs Dean, with her homely ways, knitting, and competence in domestic management under absurd circumstances, pulls the novel as best Emily Brontë can from the days of Homer, from the ways of Gondal. The tangibility of the moors and the changing moods of the weather and seasons secure the novel in the terrene too, endeavouring to provide a counterbalance to the—using *The Examiner*'s word—'improbable' Gondal-derived plot of characters who could not all coherently be explained, whose emotions were far beyond a natural scale, and whose motives were either unknowable or shockingly plain. Miriam Allott, in a penetrating essay from 1958, describes an element of this with appealing mildness when she says that 'for the purposes of ordinary life [Heathcliff] will not do'.[56] Such matters—the 'steady' housekeeper and the natural world—are the equivalent of Emily Brontë's editing-out Gondal references for the 1846 *Poems*. They are a way of introducing an illusion of, or an allusion to, realism. And, for sure, it is worth underlining that the illusion of the real is compelling and and makes us, despite our literary alertness, forget how illusory it is. As Virginia Woolf adroitly put it in an essay on ' "Jane Eyre" and "Wuthering Heights" ' (1916) in *The Common Reader: First Series* (1925), '[Emily Brontë] could free life from its dependence on facts; with a few touches indicate the spirit of a face so that it needs no body; by speaking of the moor make the wind blow and the thunder roar.'[57]

The Tenant of Wildfell Hall is the first creative response to *Wuthering Heights*. And *Shirley* (1849), which involved Charlotte working on Emily Brontë's image before the 1850 edition of *Wuthering Heights*, is the second. This time, in *Shirley*, by figuring Emily—in Shirley herself—as the personality Emily Brontë might have been in happier circumstances.[58] Setting aside for a moment, though, the memories that Anne and Charlotte wanted to leave of their sister, there is a broader question of what other writers had made of Emily Brontë as both novelist and poet. Leavis was not wrong—to start with

[55] George Saintsbury, *Matthew Arnold* (Edinburgh: Blackwood, 1902), p. 56. For an example of wholesale disapproval of initial critics, see Keith Sagar, 'The Originality of *Wuthering Heights*', in Anne Smith, ed., *The Art of Emily Brontë* (London: Vision, 1976), pp. 121–59 (pp. 128–32).

[56] Miriam Allott, '*Wuthering Heights*: The Rejection of Heathcliff?', *Essays in Criticism*, 8 (1958), pp. 27–47 (p. 47).

[57] Virginia Woolf, ' "Jane Eyre" and "Wuthering Heights" ' [1916], in *The Common Reader: First Series* (London: Hogarth Press, 1925), ebook.

[58] The idea that *Wuthering Heights* was a comment on *Jane Eyre*—as I am suggesting *The Tenant* was of *Wuthering Heights*—appeared in early reviews. 'The two novels appeared to be written by one hand', said *Tait's Edinburgh Magazine* in December 1848, for instance: ' "Wuthering Heights" as an exaggeration of "Jane Eyre," with its blemishes raised, and its virtues depressed', 'Poems by Currer, Ellis, and Acton Bell', *Tait's Edinburgh Magazine*, 15 (December 1848), pp. 860–1 (p. 860).

xl INTRODUCTION

the novel—to think, as I have said, that little that could be called a tradition followed from *Wuthering Heights*—and certainly not a tradition of moral earnestness like that from Jane Austen to George Eliot to Henry James to D.H. Lawrence. But, as Leavis acknowledged, this did not diminish the stature of *Wuthering Heights*. Algernon Charles Swinburne thought he could compare Emily Brontë's novel only to a now forgotten one by the Anglican priest and folklorist Sabine Baring-Gould (1834–1924: see p. 343 and note). Mary Webb's *Precious Bane* (1924), with its Heathcliff-like Gideon Sarn, nods back just after the First World War to Emily Brontë. And the multiple film versions, some now lost, of *Wuthering Heights* have added in another way to the *Rezeptionsgeschichte*, each director re-working the narrative to leave new generations of audiences with different memories of what they believe the novel is (the 1992 version with Ralph Fiennes as a ferocious Heathcliff and Juliette Binoche as both Catherines must rank as one of the most startling modern visual up-turnings of the experience of reading the text, with as much of a transformative effect as the 1939 version). Popular fictions derived from the plot—for example, recently, Clare B. Dunkle's *The House of Dead Maids: A Chilling Prequel to 'Wuthering Heights'* (2010) and Michael Stewart's *Ill Will: The Untold Story of Heathcliff* (2018)—confirm the novel's enduring imaginative presence, and also other writers' sense that things are missing in *Wuthering Heights*, that explanatory narratives are absent but can be imagined (Jean Rhys did something not unrelated for Charlotte Brontë in *Wide Sargasso Sea* (1966), though with rather more serious consequences; Daphne du Maurier's *Rebecca* (1938) is a (Gothic) gloss on *Jane Eyre* of a different kind). But such supplementary fictions do not comprise a tradition.[59]

It is different with the poetry, its *Nachleben*. To return to the difficult question of what Emily Brontë had read (and how she had read): her verse follows, it seems, some of the ideas and principles of William Wordsworth in *Lyrical Ballads* (1798) with its decisive metricality, plainness of diction, interest in strong human emotion, attention to the extraordinariness of the ordinary, and, often, its focus on the rural world charged with higher forces.[60] We cannot

---

[59] On the broad topic, see Patsy Stoneman, 'Adaptations, Prequels, Sequels, Translations', in Marianne Thormählen, ed., *The Brontës in Context* (Cambridge: Cambridge University Press, 2012), pp. 207–14. See also, more specifically, and at greater length, Valérie V. Hazette, *'Wuthering Heights' on Film and Television: A Journey across Time and Cultures* (Bristol: Intellect, 2015). See also the special edition of *Brontë Studies*, 39.4 (2014), *Afterlives of the Brontës: Biography, Fiction and Literary Criticism*.

[60] It is important to acknowledge the revisionist point that Wordsworth's 'Preface' to *Lyrical Ballads* (1800, 1802) was belated and was arguing for principles already substantially in practice. See, for example, the case made in David Fairer, *English Poetry of the Eighteenth Century, 1700–1789* (Harlow: Longman, 2003).

INTRODUCTION   xli

know, of course, if this is coincidence; we cannot know if Emily Brontë read Wordsworth's ambition of 'fitting to metrical arrangement a selection of the real language of men in a state of vivid sensation'[61] and found it akin to, or helpful for, her own poetics. After Emily Brontë there is, nevertheless, in the same post-Wordsworthian spirit, a significant succession of poets writing in English, and often enough in *England*, who replay and reposition something of the emotional clarity, rhythmic control, and direct gaze of Brontë's best poems, written, it may be, in the long shadow of the author of *Lyrical Ballads*. Here is Thomas Hardy in 'Your Last Journey', the second of *Poems of 1912–1913*:

> Here by the moorway you returned,
> And saw the borough lights ahead
> That lit your face—all undiscerned
> To be in a week the face of the dead,
> And you told of the charm of that haloed view
> That never again would beam on you.
>
> And on your left you passed the spot
> Where eight days later you were to lie,
> And be spoken of as one who was not;
> Beholding it with a heedless eye
> As alien from you, though under its tree
> You soon would halt everlastingly.
>
> I drove not with you.... Yet had I sat
> At your side that eve I should not have seen
> That the countenance I was glancing at
> Had a last-time look in the flickering sheen,
> Nor have read the writing upon your face,
> 'I go hence soon to my resting-place;
>
> 'You may miss me then. But I shall not know
> How many times you visit me there,
> Or what your thoughts are, or if you go
> There never at all. And I shall not care.
> Should you censure me I shall take no heed
> And even your praises no more shall need.'
>
> True: never you'll know. And you will not mind.
> But shall I then slight you because of such?
> Dear ghost, in the past did you ever find

---

[61] William Wordsworth, 'Preface' (1800/1802) to *Lyrical Ballads*, ed. Celia de Piro (Oxford: Oxford University Press, 2006), p. 227.

xlii INTRODUCTION

> The thought 'What profit', move me much?
> Yet abides the fact, indeed, the same,—
> You are past love, praise, indifference, blame.[62]

The rhythm is not Emily Brontë's, though Hardy does not wholly spurn the trochee, which Emily's ear so valued.[63] But, in Hardy's poem, the reader finds the spareness and focus of emotion—Hardy the husband mourning the death

---

[62] *Collected Poems of Thomas Hardy* (London: Macmillan, 1923), pp. 319–20. Cf. my longer effort to place the 'Emma' poems in the context of Hardy's writing: Francis O'Gorman, 'Hardy getting out of...', *Thomas Hardy Society Journal*, 34 (2018), pp. 35–51.

[63] For a poem that does catch something of Emily Brontë's metrical preferences, pace, and diction, and is alert to her landscapes and feelings, see C. Day Lewis's 'Emily Brontë', in *The Complete Poems of C. Day Lewis* (Vintage Digital, 2012):

> All is the same still. Earth and heaven locked in
> A wrestling dream the seasons cannot break:
> Shrill the wind tormenting my obdurate thorn trees,
> Moss-rose and stone-chat silent in its wake.
> Time has not altered here the rhythms I was rocked in,
> Creation's throb and ache.
>
> All is yet the same, for mine was a country
> Stoic, unregenerate, beyond the power
> Of man to mollify or God to disburden—
> An ingrown landscape none might long endure
> But one who could meet with a passion wilder-wintry
> The scalding breath of the moor.
>
> All is yet the same as when I roved the heather
> Chained to a demon through the shrieking night,
> Took him by the throat while he flailed my sibylline
> Assenting breast, and won him to delight.
> O truth and pain immortally bound together!
> O lamp the storm made bright!
>
> Still on those heights prophetic winds are raving,
> Heath and harebell intone a plainsong grief:
> 'Shrink, soul of man, shrink into your valleys—
> Too sharp that agony, that spring too brief!
> Love, though your love is but the forged engraving
> Of hope on a stricken leaf!'
>
> Is there one whom blizzards warm and rains enkindle
> And the bitterest furnace could no more refine?
> Anywhere one too proud for consolation,
> Burning for pure freedom so that he will pine,
> Yes, to the grave without her? Let him mingle
> His barren dust with mine.
>
> But is there one who faithfully has planted
> His seed of light in the heart's deepest scar?
> When the night is darkest, when the wind is keenest,
> He, he shall find upclimbing from afar
> Over his pain my chaste, my disenchanted
> And death-rebuking star.

For more on Lewis and Emily Brontë, see note to p. 33.

INTRODUCTION
xliii

of his first wife, Emma, from whom he had become estranged—together with the telling concision of diction, unLatinate, but elevated, almost solemn; the sudden detail (the 'flickering sheen') and the poised use of the monosyllabic ('You may miss me then') together with the weight of regret: this is not a poem 'in the manner of Emily Brontë' in any merely imitative way. But the two poets are in a conversation: he, as T.S. Eliot would have it in the proposal of 'Tradition and the Individual Talent' (1919), modifying what we know of her as much as she enabling—directly or indirectly—Hardy to write as he did.

This is about the indefinite matter, as Eliot would have recognized, of one writer creating the conditions, aesthetically, for the possibility of another. And it is also about how the later writer subtly alters how we read the earlier (as Milton shifts the way we read Shakespeare; Vikram Seth how we read George Eliot or Thomas Mann; Anthony Powell how we read Proust). Edward Thomas, Edmund Blunden, Lascelles Abercrombie, Siegfried Sassoon, Robert Frost, W.B. Yeats, Vita Sackville-West in *The Land* (1926), D.H. Lawrence—none is without their own version of the Emily Brontë mode at times, a freshness, an investment in the revelations that occur in ordinary experience, sadness, lucidity, and, sometimes, quiet grandness. (And it is worth noting that Thomas Hardy and D.H. Lawrence compare with Emily Brontë as writers of both lyrical fiction *and* lyrical poetry, an uncommon achievement.) If Wordsworth is the primary source of all this in terms of poetics, then Emily Brontë is a kind of confirmation or reiteration of that source. Modernism would largely dispel these things from poetry in English and take readers elsewhere, even as the number of Brontë-related books, plays, and films began significantly to increase at the same time, perhaps in some kind of oblique defiance of the fractures and ambitions of, say, Eliot, Pound, H.D., David Jones, and Marianne Moore. But the return of emotional directness, of plainer diction and metre, of a sense of the poem as an expression of feeling that was not impersonal (though that does not mean it was necessarily authorial) emerges again in Movement poetry and most notably in Philip Larkin. It emerges elsewhere in, for example, Edwin Muir,[64] Seamus Heaney, and Elizabeth Jennings (who edited a selection of Emily Brontë's

---

[64] Muir's manner can be close to Emily Brontë's. His observation in 'For Ann Scott-Moncrieff (1914–1943)' (1946) is more directly thought-provoking:

> [...] Under the years' assaults,
> In the storm of good and bad,
> You too had the faults
> That Emily Brontë had,
> Ills of body and soul,
> Of sinner and saint and all
> Who strive to make themselves whole,
> Smashed to bits by the Fall. [...]
>
> Edwin Muir, *Collected Poems*
> (London: Faber, 1960), p. 157.

xliv INTRODUCTION

poems and *Wuthering Heights* in 1967 as she also wrote on Emily Dickinson and, separately, Robert Frost). Emily Brontë belongs, and is one of the jewels, in a deep seam of Romantic and post-Romantic poetry in English that makes out of familiar language a point of entry into moving and sometimes revelatory experience.

Emily Brontë is, once, invoked by a poet in the twentieth century remarkably, though not absolutely, different from her. Ted Hughes, born in Mytholmroyd, eleven miles north of Haworth, shared, for sure, a cognate alertness to the wild world and a sense of quasi-spiritual experience of the secular revelation that is Wordsworthian in origin.[65] His landscapes are, at least empirically, hers too. Hughes, nevertheless, is not in her tradition, as I have been describing it: Hughes' 'Emily Brontë' in *Remains of Elmet: A Pennine Sequence* (1979), for example, neither is in her manner nor does it conjure her likeness. 'The wind on Crow Hill was her darling', Hughes begins his four unrhymed tercets, a kind of relic of a *terza rima* as much as an abandoned mill is an engram of old Elmet:

> His fierce, high tale in her ear was her secret.
> But his kiss was fatal.[66]

The poem, as a whole, is a return, almost a parodic one, to the biographer's fascination with Emily Brontë's projected romantic life, ending with a final strange, and provocative, image: 'Her death is a baby-cry on the moor.'[67] The sense that Emily must have had an erotic relationship with a man, or how could she have written *Wuthering Heights*, is implicitly, it might be, revived, despite decades of scholarship, in the tough, torn landscapes of Hughes' image of Emily Brontë in West Yorkshire. Hughes, more generally, invokes that long-standing idea of an 'elemental' Emily Brontë—he is an 'elemental' poet if ever there were one—which had its starting point in criticism with Charlotte's claim that *Wuthering Heights* was 'hewn in a wild workshop' (see p. 320), and was still being affirmed, in a completely different idiom, in the memorable song by Kate Bush (who, as it happens, shares Emily's birthday), 'Wuthering Heights' (1978). Hughes prompts a re-animation of the old argument: raw talent rather than worked-at? the untaught *savant* or the reflective, well-read artist? The questions about Emily Brontë remain unyieldingly the same. And it is not certain that answers would tell us much anyway.

Sir Frank Kermode observes in *Forms of Attention: Botticelli and 'Hamlet'* (1985) that the endurance of great works of art is dependent on an interpretative community, and that that interpretative community will oscillate between opinion and argument. 'The success', he continues, thinking of how works of

---

[65] The poet and critic Edward Larrissy objects to this form of poetry in 'Edward Larrissy Interview', *The Argotist Online*, https://www.argotistonline.co.uk/Larrissy%20interview.htm.
[66] Ted Hughes, *Remains of Elmet: A Pennine Sequence* (London: Faber, 1979), ebook.
[67] Ibid.

INTRODUCTION   xlv

art do or do not survive, 'of interpretative argument as a means of conferring or endorsing value is [...] not to be measured by the survival of the comment but by the survival of its object.'[68] Yet the case of Emily Brontë provokes a different line of thought. Kermode is interested in *Forms of Attention* in the ways interpretation—Sandro Botticelli and *Hamlet* are offered as examples, not unique cases—has changed through centuries: the former only discovered in the later nineteenth century to be of value; the second regarded as a masterpiece from the beginning and, in turn, posing a challenge to generations of readers to reinterpret, to see it afresh. Yet the interpretative community around *Wuthering Heights* and the relatively small corpus of Emily's poetry has been more notable for its consistent, one might even say, limited, approaches, questions, and accounts. Ted Hughes reminds us of that. *Wuthering Heights* is a peculiar example of a novel that determines its own readings to a remarkable degree. Ezra Pound memorably observed that literature 'is news that *stays* news'.[69] But it is wondrously hard to say much new about *Wuthering Heights*, though its vitality as a reading experience remains undiminished. Its survival and endorsement then, different from Kermode's analysis, is not dependent on the refreshing of critical interpretation. *Wuthering Heights* has made of interpretive consistency its own form of perpetuation.

But what of Kermode's important distinction between argument and opinion in the critical afterlife of a work of art, or of an artist as a whole?

In Kermode's *The Uses of Error* (1991), the proposition, in the final essay, originally a sermon in King's College Chapel, Cambridge, is that the history of interpretation is 'to an incalculable extent a history of error'.[70] I end, then, with my assertion—opinion not argument—that this is true of the reception of *Wuthering Heights*, which has been repeatedly and bafflingly read, as Helen Small correctly describes, as 'one of the greatest love stories in the English language'.[71] The novel has, at the most extreme, been bizarrely elevated into a kind of *Ur*-text of human life. Taking up the text, Stevie Davies, the Welsh novelist and writer, said in *Emily Brontë: Heretic* (1994), makes us feel 'as if we had always been living somewhere near or somehow within the book'.[72] But *Wuthering Heights*' profound *strangeness*, its unreality, have been my topics here. We need a better vocabulary for talking about a text that has been, in the popular conception, transformed by film and television, and in intellectual circles by criticism with, often enough, a distinctive *parti pris*, into something easier, plainer, and more easily loveable, or championable, than

---

[68] Frank Kermode, *Forms of Attention: Botticelli and 'Hamlet'* (Chicago: University of Chicago Press, 1985), p. 67.

[69] Ezra Pound, *ABC of Reading* (New York: New Directions, 1960 [1934]), p. 29.

[70] Frank Kermode, *The Uses of Error* (London: Fontana, 1991), p. 431.

[71] *Wuthering Heights*, ed. Jack and Small, p. vii.

[72] Stevie Davies, *Emily Brontë: Heretic* (London: Women's Press, 1994), p. 60.

xlvi INTRODUCTION

itself. Northrop Frye, in his prickly *Anatomy of Criticism: Four Essays* (1957), declared:

It is generally accepted that a critic is a better judge of the *value* of a poem than its creator, but there is still a lingering notion that it is somehow ridiculous to regard the critic as the final judge of its meaning, even though in practice it is clear that he must be.[73]

Frye might, presumably, have said novel as much as poem. But what to do with assessing the 'meaning' of Emily Brontë's work? *Wuthering Heights* is no realist text, and the magnitude and nature of the represented feelings, despite the creation of Nelly to anchor it in the quotidian, are, as I have said, those that can only belong to ingenuity. Its meaning, in the most general sense, is something unobtainable, however much Frye thinks that critics can obtain such things. *Wuthering Heights'* real nature lies in the fact that it is a Gondal narrative. If it were Charlotte Brontë who destroyed her sister's Gondal prose, then that was an act of distortion that makes Charlotte's editing of the 1850 poems look like minor interference. *Wuthering Heights* comes from an imaginary, secret domain, in which its author seemed to live throughout her life, and which Anne grew out of as much as Charlotte left Angria behind. Whether Emily *could* have grown out of her imaginary world, with all its security, is an intriguing question about her cognitive state and what matters allayed the anxiety of, it seems, the demands of her being alive. We will never know. But the uses of error are, and remain, at the heart of the interpretative history, if history it quite is, of this uniquely curious fantasy that is both impossible—and impossible to put down.

Accordingly, to return, it is the poetry, Gondal or apparently otherwise, which invites the reader first, and consequentially, into the unique mental landscape of this short-lived author whose legacy is nothing of the kind. The poems of 1846 give us, however faintly, the mental parameters in which to try to read the novel of the following year. This is the last of Emily Brontë's contributions to the 1846 collection, one of her most celebrated lyrics:

> Riches I hold in light esteem;
>   And Love I laugh to scorn;
> And lust of fame was but a dream
>   That vanished with the morn:
>
> And if I pray, the only prayer
>   That moves my lips for me
> Is, 'Leave the heart that now I bear,
>   And give me liberty!'

[73] Northrop Frye, *An Anatomy of Criticism: Four Essays* (Princeton: Princeton University Press, 1957), p. 5.

INTRODUCTION   xlvii

> Yes, as my swift days near their goal,
> 'Tis all that I implore;
> In life and death, a chainless soul,
> With courage to endure.

(pp. 57).

Here is highly crafted poetry masked as simplicity. Its sound patterns, for instance, provide filigree coherence, not merely through end rhyme but inner chimes: 'Leave the heart that now I bear, | And give me liberty!', for example, a sentiment book-ended by two <l>s. Making the most of that letter <l>, more generally, and especially in the first stanza, the poem also wields the polysyllable amid a preponderance of monosyllables, to effect: they are most numerous in the final stanza, matching the growing word lengths with the increasing elevation of the sentiment. Yet who speaks the poem? And what is it about (Frye again)?

As usual, we do not know for certain. The poet, characteristically, leaves only a trace of her private world and allows the reader no real clue—Margaret Maison tried, alas, to my mind, unpersuasively, to argue for the presence of Epictetus in the poem[74]—as to what part of an ongoing saga, an ongoing set of human relationships in a rebellious, erotically charged, and death-absorbed world, this poem belongs. The yearning for liberty and the figure of the 'chainless soul', the assumption of death at hand, and the determination like that of 'Julian M. and A.G. Rochelle' to 'endure', are familiar terms of Emily Brontë's imaginary *desmaine*; interchangeable counters, as it were, of the human scenes of her art with its emphasis on a woman's strength and emotion's depth. The poems, exquisitely valuable in themselves, are also the only hints we have to what might be the real context, or source, or meaning, of *Wuthering Heights*. What might *Wuthering Heights* have been rewriting, and what fixed terms of the poet's creative existence might be being repositioned and wrought afresh there? An edition that puts Emily Brontë's poetry and fiction side-by-side produces something as close as we can get, I think, to the real mysteries and irreducible pleasures of this writer whose only novel did not come from nowhere.

---

[74] See Margaret Maison, 'Emily Brontë and Epictetus', *Notes & Queries*, 25 (1978), pp. 230–31. The case made in this note is speculative and based on what might be coincidences. The book at the heart of the argument, Hester Chapone's, *Letters on the Improvement of the Mind: Letters to a Lady*, 2 vols (London: Walter, 1773), was, Maison contends, a staple of Roe Head school where Emily was a pupil. The book was, as Maison admits, hostile to Stoicism (and it never uses the word: the ground of Chapone's book is Christianity, not Hellenistic ethics from the third century BC). See note to p. 26 for a different possibility.

NOTE ON THE TEXT

The texts reproduced here, as I have said, take (mostly) literally the 21st-Century Oxford Authors principle of presenting authors as readers first found them. There is one *major* exception to the whole version/vision of the author in this edition and one, so far as can be known, of which Emily Brontë would have vehemently disapproved. That is: she never wished to be read under her own name. Properly speaking, this should be a book of the first writing and publications of Ellis Bell, whose brothers (?) had also published verse and fiction, but about whom nothing else was known. It was not even certain to first readers—see, for instance, note to p. 62, '*pointer*'—that there were three writers anyway: perhaps only one writing under different names? Authors might use a pseudonym for many reasons, as they still do. But the reason for Emily Brontë's determination on Ellis Bell was to do with what seems to have been intense self-consciousness. It appears from Charlotte's bitterly regretful comment—see note to p. 311, '*It has been thought. . .*'—on having broken the anonymity with the publisher that it was privacy that mattered. Emily Brontë did not want to be known to a public at all—she did not want, in fact, to be known personally to anyone, apparently, except a handful of family and family servants, and a tiny number of friends. Self-exposure more than troubled her and, in the world of print, she guarded herself behind her *nom-de-plume*. It would be impossible now to publish this present volume as by Ellis Bell though the name is retained within the edition in the titles of her volumes to respect Emily Brontë's preference to be in public simply enigmatic, even as to sex.

The Emily Brontë represented here takes the series' principles plainly in terms of what actual texts are reproduced but, as I have said, with qualifications. The plainness of application includes, as discussed in the Introduction, pp. xxxiii–xxxiv, reproducing (almost all of) the errors in the text of *Wuthering Heights*. This is a very different practice from other editions, including the Clarendon edition of the novel, edited by Hilda Marsden and Ian Jack for Oxford University Press in 1976, which has been the basis for subsequent (Oxford) World's Classics editions. Marsden and Jack retained Newby's paragraphing but corrected spelling, removed stray commas, otherwise re-punctuated, and made many other alterations to accidentals 'where we believe them to be wrong, misleading, irritating, or disconcerting to the reader'.[1] I have taken a different view, though recognize it can easily be challenged, in an effort to capture something of what reading this new novelist, Ellis Bell,

---

[1] 'Introduction' to Emily Brontë, *Wuthering Heights*, ed. Hilda Marsden and Ian Jack (Oxford: Clarendon, 1976), p. xxxii.

NOTE ON THE TEXT

actually felt like in 1847—which might indeed have been at points irritating or disconcerting. Note that I have retained the typography of the original texts so, for instance, initial words of chapters (and poems) are usually given in capitals; these have been reproduced along with the periodic moments when the typesetter forgot to do this (recorded in the notes).

Some of the errors in the printed text of the novel are, it should be added, clearly mistakes by the compositor. But others prompt thought about what the MS that Emily Brontë submitted was like. Some persistent misspellings, as documented in my notes, might be explicable by Emily's erratic orthography (of which the diary-like pieces provide more evidence). The trouble, then, would be a different kind of inattention in the printer's workshop: an over-scrupulousness in reproducing the presented text. One particular issue is worth underlining as it does affect reading in both an interesting and, perhaps, distinctively frustrating way, which must have puzzled new readers of the novel to a special degree. That is the omission of speech marks, faithfully reproduced here. Rather than burdening the text with notes indicating 'sic', the large majority of these omissions are, following my practice elsewhere, reproduced without comment. (I have added just a few notes about these omissions simply to retain the reader's awareness of this ongoing problem.) The omission of speech marks in the original text must have further confused the embedded narratives in *Wuthering Heights*, which can be challenging enough to disentangle even with the full complement of punctuation. In Newby's edition, one voice accidentally merges with another as if there is some kind of dream-like state inhabiting the whole novel, fusing one character with another, as elsewhere characters double each other like the two Catherines.

For the 1846 volume of poems by the three sisters, I reproduce exactly what Emily Brontë allowed into print, with one exception. The exception is 'Julian M. and A.G. Rochelle', pp. 40–4, which I give in the main text as a complete poem from the MS. It follows after the adapted extract that Emily did agree to print, named 'The Prisoner (A Fragment)' (pp. 38–40). This inconsistency I allow—though I can see, again, a good reason to object—because the (narrative) poem in full is so substantial that it seems worth giving the reader the whole piece in the main text so as to leave him or her better able to judge the scale of the poet's achievements at this point in her writing life rather than banishing the text in its complete version to the notes. It is also worth seeing this poem before reading *Wuthering Heights* because it is, unusually, a romance in poetic form where love between man and woman proves to be, or reaches, a moving resolution. 'Julian M. and A.G. Rochelle' appeared, as I have said, in a modified extract in 1846 and then another short extract was selected for the 1850 volume as 'The Visionary', which I give in the notes: see note to p. 27. Both miss out the ending. For the 1850 volume, I reproduce in the main text, in chronological order, the poems as originally

NOTE ON THE TEXT   li

written—I will shortly slightly qualify this statement—and provide Charlotte's versions in the notes. There might be a good argument to justify the opposite approach, including the Oxford series' commitment to placing in the foreground the versions of texts as first read. That opposite approach has historical value, of course, but the reader of this volume still has both the MS versions and the edited/written-over versions from Charlotte. I have simply chosen to give Emily Brontë's voice more prominence in the texts for the 1850 collection than her sister's adaptation of it.

The slight qualification. Emily Brontë's poems have been checked against the photographic and digital surrogates of the two MS sources (detailed in the Abbreviations, pp. xiii–xiv). I have not attempted a comprehensive account of corrections in the MSS, not least because there are difficulties in legibility and, anyway, this is not the principle of the series. Where there is alainly visible change, I have nevertheless included the first version, as far as I can discern it, in ~~strike-through~~. Most, if not all, of the changes look to me like errors in copying (both MSS that survive are of poems copied from pre-existing and now lost drafts). On quite a few occasions, there has to be some judgement. This most frequently concerns Emily Brontë's punctuation: colons might be semi-colons in places, dashes could be commas in others. I have had to use my judgement in deciding what to reproduce, and other editors have sometimes taken other views. This is also true of the diary papers (where deciding between hypens and n-/m-dashes is often impossible except for context, for instance). I have faithfully reproduced, I hope, even the oddities and errors of the MSS (as the quirks of the published novel are reproduced), in the hope that something of the living, at-work poet and writer is not lost as she might have been in a completely tidied-up text. Many of the MS poems have hand-written titles, and the assumption is that these are Charlotte's. If not used in the published version, the added titles are given in the notes. Very occasionally, I am uncertain that the usually given word in published versions is actually what is in the relevant MS (Emily Brontë copied her poems in a noticeably small hand), and in turn I indicate this hesitation in square brackets. As with so much for this great writer, one can never be wholly sure.

TEXTS

DIARY PAPER, 24 NOVEMBER 1834

Emily and Anne Brontë's Diary Paper, 24 November 1834

November the 24 1834 Monday

Emily Jane Brontë

Anne Brontë

I fed Rainbow, Diamond Snowflake Jasper pheasant (alias this morning Branwell went down to Mr. Driver's and brought news that Sir Robert Peel was going to be invited to stand for Leeds Anne and I have been peeling apples for Charlotte to make us an apple pudding and for Aunt nuts and apples Charlotte said she made puddings perfectly and she was of a quick but limited intellect. Taby said just now Come Anne pilloputate (i.e. pill a potato Aunt has come into the kitchen just now and said where are your feet Anne Anne answered On the floor Aunt papa opened the parlour door and gave Branwell a letter saying here Branwell read this and show it to your Aunt and Charlotte—The Gondals are discovering the interior of Gaaldine Sally Mosley is washing in the back kitchen

It is past Twelve o'clock Anne and I have not tidied ourselves, done our bedwork or done our lessons and we want to go out to play we are going to have for Dinner Boiled Beef, Turnips, potatoes and applepudding. The Kitchin is in a very untidy state Anne and I have not done our music exercise which consists of b major Taby said on my putting a pen in her face Ya pitter pottering there instead of pilling a potate I answered O Dear, O Dear, O dear I will directly with that I get up, take a knife and begin pilling (finished) pilling the potatoes papa going to walk Mr. Sunderland expected.

Anne and I say I wonder what we shall be like and what we shall be and where we shall be if all goes on well in the year 1874—in which year I shall be in my 54th year Anne will be going in her 55th year Branwell will be going in his 58th year And Charlotte in her 59th year hoping we shall all be well at that time we close our paper

Emily and Anne

Emily and Anne Brontë's Diary Paper, 26 June 1837

Monday evening June 26th 1837 A bit past 4 o'clock Charlotte working in Aunt's room, Branwell reading Eugene Aram to her—Anne and I writing in the drawing-room—Anne a poem beginning "Fair was the evening and brightly the sun"—I Augusta Almeda's life 1st V. 1–4th page from the last—fine rather coolish thin grey cloudy but sunny day Aunt working in the little room the old nursery Papa gone out Tabby in the kitchen—the Emperors and Empresses of Gondal and Gaaldine preparing to depart from Gaaldine to Gondal to prepare for the coronation which will be on the 12th July Queen Vittoria ascended the throne this month. Northangerland in Monkey's Isle—Zamora at Eversham. All tight and right in which condition it is hoped we shall all be this day 4 years at which time Charlotte will be 25 and 2 months Branwell just 24 it being his birthday—myself 22 and 10 months and a piece Anne 21 and nearly a half I wonder where we shall be and how we shall be and what kind of a day it will be then—let us hope for the best

Emily Jane Brontë—Anne Brontë

I guess that this day 4 years we shall all be in this drawing-room comfortable I hope it may be so. Anne guesses we shall all be gone somewhere comfortable We hope it may be so indeed. Aunt: Come Emily it's past 4 o'clock

Emily: Yes, Aunt Exit Aunt

Ann: Well, do you intend to write in the evening Emily: Well, what think you (We agreed to go out 1st to make sure if we got into the humour. We may stay in—)

POEMS IN MSS FROM 1838 TO 1846 LATER INCLUDED IN 'POEMS BY ELLIS BELL', IN *POEMS BY CURRER, ELLIS, AND ACTON BELL*, ED. CURRER BELL, 2ND EDN (LONDON: SMITH & ELDER, 1850), WITH OTHER PERSONAL DOCUMENTS INSERTED AS CHRONOLOGICALLY APPROPRIATE

---

30 August 1838

For him who struck thy foreign string
I ween this heart has ceased to care
Then why dost thou such feelings bring
To my sad spirit, old guitar?

It is as if the warm sunlight   5
In some deep glen should lingering stay
When clouds of tempest and of night
Have wrapped the parent orb away—

It is as if the glassy brook
Should image still its willows fair   10
Though years ago the woodman's stroke
Laid low in dust their gleaming hair:

Even so, guitar, thy magic tone
Hath moved the tear and waked the sigh
Hath bid the ancient torrent flow   15
Although its very source is dry!

17 October 1838, 'Song by J. Brenzaida to G.S.'

I knew not 'twas so dire a crime
To say the word, Adieu:
But this shall be the only time
My slighted heart shall sue.

The wild moorside, the winter morn,   5
The gnarled and ancient tree—
If in your breast they waken scorn
Shall wake the same in me.

I can forget black eyes and brows
And lips of rosy charm   10
If you forget the sacred vows
Those faithless lips could form—

If hard commands can tame your love,
Or prison walls can hold
I would not wish to grieve above   15
A thing so false and cold—

And there are bosoms bound to mine
With links both tried and strong;
And there are eyes whose lightning shine
Has warmed and blessed me long: 20

Those eyes shall make my only day,
Shall set my spirit free
And chase the foolish thoughts away
That mourn your memory!

11 November 1838

Loud without the wind was roaring
    Through the waned autumnal sky,
Drenching wet, the cold rain pouring
    Spoke of stormy winters nigh.

All too like that dreary eve   5
Sighed within repining grief—
Sighed at first—but sighed not long
Sweet—How softly sweet it came!
Wild words of an ancient song—
Undefined, without a name—   10

"It was spring, and the skylark was singing."
Those words they awakened a spell—
They unlocked a deep fountain whose springing,
Nor Absence nor Distance can quell.

In the gloom of a cloudy November   15
They uttered the music of May—

POEMS IN MSS FROM 1838 TO 1846

They kindled the perishing ember
Into fervour that could not decay

Awaken on all my dear moorland,
The wind in its glory and pride!
O call me from valley and lowland,
To walk by the hill-river's side!

It is swelled with the first snowy weather;
The rocks they are icy and hoar
And darker waves round the long heather,
And the fern-leaves are sunny no more.

There are no yellow-stars on the mountain,
The blue-bells have long died away
From the brink of the moss-bedded fountain,
From the side of the wintry brae—

But lovelier than corn-fields all waving
In emerald and scarlet and gold
Are the slopes where the north-wind is raving
And the crags where I wandered of old—

"It was morning: the bright sun was beaming."
How sweetly it brought back to me
The time when nor labour nor dreaming
Broke the sleep of the happy and free

But blithely we rose as the dusk heaven
Was melting to amber and blue—
And swift were the wings to our feet given,
As we traversed the meadows of dew.

For the moors, for the moors where the short grass
Like velvet beneath us should lie!
For the moors, for the moors where each high pass
Rose sunny against the clear sky!

For the moors, where the linnet was trilling
Its song on the old granite stone—
Where the lark—the wild sky-lark was filling
Every breast with delight like its own.

What language can utter the feeling
Which rose when, in exile afar,
On the brow of a lonely hill kneeling
I saw the brown heath growing there?

EMILY BRONTË

It was scattered and stunted, and told me   55
That soon even that would be gone
It whispered; "The grim walls enfold me
I have bloomed in my last summer's sun"

But not the loved music, whose waking
Makes the soul of the Swiss die away,   60
Has a spell more adored and heart-breaking
Than in its half-blighted bells lay—

The spirit which bent 'neath its power
How it longed, how it burned to be free!
If I could have wept in that hour   65
Those tears had been heaven to me—

Well, well the sad minutes are moving
Though loaded with trouble and pain—
And sometime the loved and the loving
Shall meet on the mountains again—   70

4 December 1838

A little while, a little while,
The noisy crowd are barred away;
And I can sing and I can smile
A little while I've holyday!

Where wilt thou go my harassed heart?   5
Full many a land invites thee now;
And places near, and far apart
Have rest for thee, my weary brow—

There is a spot mid barren hills
Where winter howls and driving rain   10
But if the dreary tempest chills
There is a light that warms again

The house is old, the trees are bare
And moonless bends the misty dome
But what on earth is half so dear—   15
So longed for as the hearth of home ?

The mute bird sitting on the stone,
The dank moss dripping from the wall,

POEMS IN MSS FROM 1838 TO 1846

The garden-walk with weeds o'ergrown
I love them—how I love them all!   20

Shall I go there? or shall I seek
Another clime, another sky—
Where tongues familiar music speak
In accents dear to memory?

Yes, as I mused, the naked room,   25
The flickering firelight died away
And from the midst of cheerless gloom
I passed to bright unclouded day—

A little and a lone green lane
That opened on a common wide   30
A distant, dreamy, dim blue chain
Of mountains circling every side—

A heaven so clear, an earth so calm,
So sweet, so soft, so hushed an air
And, deepening still the dreamlike charm,   35
Wild moor-sheep feeding everywhere—

That was the scene—I knew it well
I knew the pathways far and near
That winding o'er each billowy swell
Marked out the tracks of wandering deer   40

Could I have lingered but an hour
It well had paid a week of toil
But truth has banished fancy's power
I hear my dungeon bars recoil—

Even as I stood with raptured eye   45
Absorbed in bliss so deep and dear
My hour of rest had fleeted by
And given me back to weary care—

18 December 1838

The blue bell is the sweetest flower
That waves in summer air
Its blossoms have the mightiest power
To soothe my spirit's care

There is a spell in purple heath   5
Too wildly, sadly drear
The violet has a fragrant breath
But fragrance will not cheer

The trees are bare, the sun is cold
And seldom, seldom seen—   10
The heavens have lost their zone of gold
The earth its robe of green

And ice upon the glancing stream
Has cast its sombre shade
And distant hills and valleys seem   15
In frozen mist arrayed—

The blue bell cannot charm me now
The heath has lost its bloom
The violets in the glen below
They yield no sweet perfume   20

But though I mourn the heather-bell
'Tis better far, away
I know how fast my tears would swell
To see it smile today

And that wood flower that hides so shy   25
Beneath the mossy stone
Its balmy scent and dewy eye
'Tis not for them I moan

It is the slight and stately stem
The blossom's silvery blue   30
The buds hid like a sapphire gem
In sheaths of emerald hue

'Tis these that breathe upon my heart
A calm and softening spell
That if it makes the tear-drop start   35
Has power to soothe as well

POEMS IN MSS FROM 1838 TO 1846   11

For these I weep, so long divided
Through winter's dreary day
In longing weep—but most when guided
On withered banks to stray   40

If chilly then the light should fall
Adown the dreary sky
And gild the dank and darkened wall
With transient brilliancy

How do I yearn, how do I pine   45
For the time of flowers to come
And turn me from that fading shine
To mourn the fields of home—

11 September 1840

In summer's mellow midnight
    A cloudless moon shone through
Our open parlour window
And rosetrees wet with dew—

I sat in silent musing—   5
    The soft wind waved my hair
It told me Heaven was glorious
And sleeping Earth was fair—

I needed not its breathing
To bring such thoughts to me   10
But still it whispered lowly
"How dark the woods will be!—

"The thick leaves in my murmur
"Are rustling like a dream,
"And all their myriad voices   15
"Instinct with spirit seem"

I said, "Go gentle singer,
"Thy wooing voice is kind
"But do not think its music
"Has power to reach my mind—   20

"Play with the scented flower,
"The young tree's supple bough—
"And leave my human feelings
"In their own course to flow"

EMILY BRONTË

The Wanderer would not heed me;   25
Its kiss grew warmer still—
"O come," it sighed so sweetly
"I'll win thee 'gainst thy will—

"Have we not been from childhood friends?
"Have I not loved thee long?   30
"As long as thou hast loved the night
"Whose silence wakes my song?

"And when thy heart is laid at rest
"Beneath the church-yard stone,
"I shall have time enough to mourn,   35
"And thou for being alone"—

16 May 1841

Shall earth no more inspire thee,
Thou lonely dreamer now?
Since passion may not fire thee
Shall Nature cease to bow?

Thy mind is ever moving   5
In regions dark to thee;
Recall its useless roving—
Come back and dwell with me—

I know my mountain breezes
Enchant and soothe thee still—   10
I know my sunshine pleases
Despite thy wayward will—

When day with evening blending
Sinks from the summer sky,
I've seen thy spirit bending   15
In fond idolatry—

I've watched thee every hour—
I know my mighty sway—
I know my magic power
To drive thy griefs away—   20

Few hearts to mortals given
On earth so wildly pine

POEMS IN MSS FROM 1838 TO 1846   13

Yet few would ask a Heaven
More like this Earth than thine—

Then let my winds caress thee—   25
Thy comrade let me be—
Since nought beside can bless thee
Return and dwell with me—

6 July 1841

Aye there it is! It wakes tonight
Sweet thoughts that will not die
And feeling's fires flash all as bright
As in the years gone by!—

And I can tell by thine altered cheek   5
And by thy kindled gaze
And by the words thou scarce dost speak,
How wildly fancy plays—

Yes I could swear that glorious wind
Has swept the world aside   10
Has dashed its memory from thy mind
Like foam-bells from the tide—

And thou art now a spirit pouring
Thy presence into all—
The essence of the Tempest's roaring   15
And of the Tempest's fall—

A universal influence
From Thine own influence free—
A principle of life intense
Lost to mortality—   20

Thus truly when that breast is cold
Thy prisoned soul shall rise
The dungeon mingle with the mould—
The captive with the skies—

Diary Paper, 30 July 1841

A Paper to be opened
when Anne is
25 years old
or my next birthday after—
if
—all be well—

It is Friday evening—near 9 o'clock—wild rainy weather I am seated in the dining room alone—having just concluded tidying our desk-boxes—writing this document—Papa is in the parlour. Aunt up stairs in her room—she has been reading Blackwood's Magazine to papa—Victoria and Adelaide are ensconced in the peat-house—Keeper is in the kitchen—Hero in his cage—We are all stout and hearty as I hope is the case with Charlotte, Branwell, and Anne, of whom the first is at John White Esq., Upperwood. House, Rawden; the second is at Luddenden foot and the third is I beleive at Scarborough—enditing [inditing] perhaps a paper corresponding to this— A scheme is at present in agitation for setting us up in a school of our own as yet nothing is determined but I hope and trust it may go on and prosper and answer our highest expectations. This day 4 years I wonder whether we shall still be dragging on in our present condition or established to our heart's content Time will show—

I guess that at the time appointed for the opening of this paper—we (i.e.) Charlotte, Anne and I—shall be all merrily seated in our own sitting-room in some pleasant and flourishing seminary having just gathered in for the midsummer holydays our debts will be paid off and we shall have cash in hand to a considerable amount. papa Aunt and Branwell will either have been—or be coming—to visit us—it will be a fine warm summery evening. very different from this bleak look-out Anne and I will perchance slip out into the garden a minutes to peruse our papers. I hope either this or something better will be the case—

The Gondalians are at present in a threatening state but there is no open rupture as yet—all the princes and princesses of the royal royaltys are at the palace of Instruction—I have a good many books on hands but I am sorry to say that as usual I make small progress with any—however I have just made a new regularity paper! and I mean verb sap—to do great things—and now I close sending from far an exhortation of course courage! to exiled and harassed Anne wishing she was here

POEMS IN MSS FROM 1838 TO 1846   15

19 December 1841, 'A.S. to G.S.'

I do not weep, I would not weep;
Our Mother needs no tears:
Dry thine eyes, too, 'tis vain to keep
This causeless grief for years

What though her brow be changed and cold,   5
Her sweet eyes closed for ever?
What though the stone—the darksome mould
Our mortal bodies sever?

What though her hand smooth ne'er again
Those silken locks of thine?   10
Nor through long hours of future pain
Her kind face o'er thee shine?

Remember still, she is not dead;
She sees us Gerald now;
Laid where her angel spirit fled   15
Mid heath and frozen snow

And from the world of heavenly light
Will she not always bend
To guide us in our lifetime's night
And guard us to the end?   20

Thou knowst she will, and well mayst mourn
That we are left below
But not that she can ne'er return
To share our earthly woe—

Letter to Ellen Nussey, [Monday] 22? May 1843

Dear Miss Ellen,

I should be wanting in common civility if I did not thank you for your kindness in letting me know of an opportunity to send "postage-free."

I have written as you directed though if "next Tuesday" means tomorrow, I fear it will be too late to go with Mr. Taylor.

Charlotte has never mentioned a word about coming home. if you would go over for half a year perhaps you might be able to bring her back with you otherwise she might vegetate "there" till the age of Methusaleh for mere lack of courage to face the voyage.

All here are in good health so was Anne according to the last accounts—the holydays will be here in a week or two and then if "she" be willing I will get her to write you a proper letter—a feat that I have never performed.

With love and good wishes,
E J Brontë

POEMS IN MSS FROM 1838 TO 1846

6 September 1843

In the earth, the earth thou shalt be laid
A grey stone standing over thee;
Black mould beneath thee spread
And black mould to cover thee—

"Well, there is rest there   5
"So fast come thy prophecy—
"The time when my sunny hair
"Shall with grass roots twined be."

    But cold, cold is that resting place
    Shut out from Joy and Liberty   10
    And all who loved thy living face
    Will shrink from its gloom and thee

    "Not so, *here* the world is chill,
    "And sworn friends fall from me
    "But *there*, they'll own me still   15
    "And prize my memory"

    Farewell, then, all that love
    All that deep sympathy;
    Sleep on, heaven laughs above—
    Earth never misses thee   20

    Turf-sod and tombstone drear
    Part human company
    One heart broke, only, there
    That heart was worthy thee!—

11 March 1844, 'E.W. to A.G.A.'

How few, of all the hearts that loved,
are grieving for thee now!
And why should mine, tonight, be moved
With such a sense of woe?

Too often, thus, when left alone   5
Where none my thoughts can see,
Comes back a word, a passing tone
From thy strange history.

Sometimes I seem to see thee rise
A glorious child again—
All virtues beaming from thine eyes
That ever honoured men—

Courage and Truth, a generous breast
Where Love and Gladness lay;
A being whose very Memory blest
And made the mourner gay—

O, fairly spread thy early sail
And fresh and pure and free
Was the first impulse of the gale
That urged life's wave for thee!

Why did the pilot, too confiding
Dream o'er that Ocean's foam?
And trust in Pleasure's careless guiding
To bring his vessel home?

For, well he knew what dangers frowned,
What mists would gather dim,
What rocks and shelves and sands lay round
Between his port and him—

The very brightness of the sun,
The splendour of the main,
The wind which bore him wildly on
Should not have warned in vain

An anxious gazer from the shore,
I marked the whitening wave
And wept above thy fate the more
Because I could not save—

It recks not now, when all is over,
But, yet my heart will be
A mourner still, though friend and lover
Have both forgotten thee!

POEMS IN MSS FROM 1838 TO 1846

11 November 1844, 'From a Dungeon Wall in the Southern College'—JB Sept. 1825

"Listen! when your hair, like mine
"Takes a tint of silver grey,
"When your eyes, with dimmer shine,
"Watch life's bubbles float away,

W'hen you, young man, have borne like me 5
"The weary weight of sixty-three
"Then shall penance sore be paid
"For those hours so wildly squandered;
"And the words that now fall dead
"On your ears be deeply pondered 10
"Pondered and approved at last
"But their virtue will be past!

"Glorious is the prize of Duty,
"Though she be a serious power
"Treacherous all the lures of Beauty 15
"Thorny bud and poisonous flower!

"Mirth is but a mad beguiling
"Of the golden-gifted Time—
"Love—a demon-meteor wiling
"Heedless feet to gulfs of crime. 20

"Those who follow earthly pleasure,
"Heavenly Knowledge will not lead
"Wisdom hides from them her treasure,
"Virtue bids them evil speed!

"Vainly may their hearts, repenting, 25
"Seek for aid in future years—
"Wisdom, scorned, knows no relenting—
"Virtue is not won by tears

"Fain would we your steps reclaim
"Waken fear and holy shame 30
"And to this end, our council well
"And kindly doomed you to a cell
"Whose darkness, may perchance, disclose
"A beacon-guide from sterner woes"—

 So spake my judge—then seized his lamp 35
 And left me in the dungeon damp,

A vault-like place whose stagnant air
Suggests and nourishes despair!

Rosina, this had never been
Except for you, my despot queen!   40
Except for you the billowy sea
Would now be tossing under me
The wind's wild voice my bosom thrill
And my glad heart bound wilder still

Flying before the rapid gale   45
Those wondrous southern isles to hail
Which wait for my companions free
But thank your passion—not for me!

You know too well—and so do I
Your haughty beauty's sovereignty   50
Yet have I read those falcon eyes—
Have dived into their mysteries—
Have studied long their glance and feel
It is not love those eyes reveal—

They Flash—they burn with lightning shine   55
But not with such fond fire as mine;
The tender star fades faint and wan
Before Ambition's scorching sun—
So deem I now—and Time will prove
If I have wronged Rosina's love—   60

28 May 1845, 'A.E. and R.C.'

Heavy hangs the raindrop ~~from~~
From the burdened spray;
Heavy broods the damp mist
On Uplands far away;

Heavy looms the dull sky,   5
Heavy rolls the sea—
And heavy beats the young heart
Beneath that lonely tree—

Never has a blue streak
Cleft the clouds since morn—   10
Never has his grim Fate
Smiled since he was born—

POEMS IN MSS FROM 1838 TO 1846

Frowning on the infant,
Shadowing childhood's joy,
Guardian angel knows not   15
That melancholy boy—

Day is passing swiftly
Its sad and sombre prime;
Youth is fast invading
Sterner manhood's time—   20

All the flowers are praying
For sun before they close
And he prays too, unknowing,
That sunless human rose!

Blossom, that the westwind   25
Has never wooed to blow
Scentless are thy petals,
Thy dew is cold as snow.

Soul, where kindred kindness
No early promise woke   30
Barren is your beauty
As weed upon a rock—

Wither, Brothers, wither,
You were vainly given—
Earth reserves no blessing   35
For the unblest of Heaven!

Child of Delight! with ~~golden~~ sunbright hair,
And seablue seadeep eyes
Spirit of Bliss, what brings thee here
Beneath these sullen skies?   40

Thou shouldst live in eternal spring
Where endless day is never dim
Why, seraph, has thy erring wing
Borne thee down to weep with him?

"Ah, not from heaven am I descended   45
"And I do not come to mingle tears
"But sweet is day, though with shadows blended
"And though clouded, sweet are youthful years—

"I, the image of light and gladness
"Saw and pitied that mournful boy   50
"And I swore to take his gloomy sadness
"And give to him my beamy joy—.

"Heavy and dark the night is closing
"Heavy and dark may its biding be
"Better for all from grief reposing   55
"And better for all who watch like me—

"Guardian angel, he lacks no longer;
"Evil fortune he need not fear;
"Fate is strong but love is stronger
"And more unsleeping than angel's care—" 60

Letter to Ellen Nussey, 16? July 1845

Dear Miss Ellen,

If you have set your heart on Charlotte saying [staying] another week she has our united consent: I for one will take everything easy on Sunday—I'm glad she is enjoying herself: let her make the most of the next seven days & return stout and hearty—

Love to her and you from Anne & myself and tell her all are well at home—Your affect—

E J Brontë

Diary Paper, Thursday, 30 July 1845

My birthday—showery—breezy—cool—I am twenty seven years old today—this morning Anne and I opened the papers we wrote 4 years since on my twenty third birthday—this paper we intend, if all be well, to open on my 30th three years hence in 1848—since the 1841 paper, the following events have taken place

Our school-scheme has been abandoned and instead Charlotte and I went to Brussels on the 8th of Febrary 1842 Branwell left his place at Luddenden Foot C and I returned from Brussels November 8th 1842 in consequence of Aunt's death—Branwell went to Thorp Green as a tutor where Anne still continued—January 1843 Charlotte returned to Brussels the same month and after staying a year came back again on new years day 1844 Anne left her situation at Thorp Green of her own accord—June 1845 Branwell left—July 1845

Anne and I went our first long journey by ourselves together—leaving Home on the 30th of June—monday sleeping at York—returning to Keighley Tuesday evening sleeping there and walking home on Wednesday morning—though the weather was broken, we enjoyed ourselves very much except during a few hours at Bradford and during our excursion we were Ronald Macelgin, Henry Angora, Juliet Augusteena, Rosobelle Esualdar, Ella and Julian Egramont Catherine Navarre and Cordelia Fitzaphnold escaping from the palaces of Instruction to join the Royalists who are hard driven at present by the victorious Republicans—The Gondals still flourish bright as ever I am at present writing a work on the First Wars—Anne has been writing some articles on this and a book by Henry Sophona—We intend sticking firm by the rascals as long as they delight us which I am glad to say they do at present—I should have mentioned that last summer the school scheme was revived in full vigor—We had prospectuses printed, despatched letters to all aquaintances imparting our plans and did our little all—but it was found no go—now I dont desire a school at all and none of us have any great longing for it. We have cash enough for our present wants with a prospect of accumulation—we are all in decent health—only that papa has a complaint in his eyes and with the exception of B who I hope will be better and do better, hereafter. I am quite contented for myself—not as idle as formerly, altogether as hearty and having learnt to make the most of the present and hope for the future with less fidgetiness that I cannot do all I wish—seldom or ever troubled with nothing to do, and merely desiring that every body could be as comfortable as myself and as undesponding and then we should have a very tolerable world of it

By mistake I find we have opened the paper on the 31st instead of the 30th Yesterday was much such a day as this but the morning was devine—

DIARY PAPER, 30 JULY 1845

Tabby who was gone in our last paper is come back and has lived with us—two years and a half and is in good health—Martha who also departed is here too. We have got Flossey, got and lost Tiger—lost the Hawk. Hero which with the geese was given away and is doubtless dead for when I came back from Brussels I enquired on all hands and could hear nothing of him—Tiger died early last year—Keeper and Flossey are well also the canary acquired 4 years since

We are now all at home and likely to be there some time—Branwell went to Liverpool on Tuesday to stay a week. Tabby has just been teasing me to turn as formerly to—"pilloputate". Anne and I should have picked the black currants if it had been fine and sunshiny. I must hurry off now to my [darning?] and ironing I have plenty of work on hands and writing and am altogether full of buisness with best wishes for the whole House till 1848 July 30th and as much longer as may be I conclude

E J Brontë

2 January 1846

No coward soul is mine
No trembler in the world's storm-troubled sphere
I see Heaven's glories shine
And Faith shines equal arming me from fear.

O God within my breast   5
Almighty ever-present Deity
Life, that in me has rest
As I Undying Life, have power in thee

Vain are the thousand creeds
That move men's hearts, unutterably vain,   10
Worthless as withered weeds
Or idle froth amid the boundless main

To waken doubt in one
Holding so fast by thy infinity
So surely anchored on   15
The steadfast rock of Immortality

With wide-embracing love
Thy spirit animates eternal years
Pervades and broods above
Changes, sustains, dissolves, creates and rears   20

Though Earth and moon were gone
And suns and universes ceased to ~~shine~~ be
And thou were left alone
Every Existence would exist in ~~thine~~ thee

There is not room for Death   25
Nor atom that his might could render void
Since thou art Being and Breath
And what thou art may never be destroyed

POEMS IN MSS FROM 1838 TO 1846

Undated

Love is like the wild rose briar,
Friendship, like the holly tree.
The holly is dark when the rose briar blooms,
But which will bloom most constantly?

The wild rose briar is sweet in spring,   5
Its summer blossoms scent the air
Yet wait till winter comes again
And who will call the wild-briar fair

Then scorn the silly rose-wreath now
And deck thee with the holly's sheen   10
That when December blights thy brow
He still may leave thy garland green—

ELLIS BELL [EMILY BRONTË]'S CONTRIBUTION TO *POEMS BY CURRER, ELLIS, AND ACTON BELL* (LONDON: AYLOTT AND JONES, 1846)

Faith and Despondency

"The winter wind is loud and wild,
Come close to me, my darling child;
Forsake thy books, and mateless play;
And, while the night is gathering gray,
We'll talk its pensive hours away;—   5

"Iernë, round our sheltered hall
November's gusts unheeded call;
Not one faint breath can enter here
Enough to wave my daughter's hair,
And I am glad to watch the blaze   10
Glance from her eyes, with mimic rays;
To feel her cheek, so softly pressed,
In happy quiet on my breast.

"But, yet, even this tranquillity
Brings bitter, restless thoughts to me;   15
And, in the red fire's cheerful glow,
I think of deep glens, blocked with snow;
I dream of moor, and misty hill,
Where evening closes dark and chill;
For, lone, among the mountains cold,   20
Lie those that I have loved of old.
And my heart aches, in hopeless pain
Exhausted with repinings vain,
That I shall greet them ne'er again!"

"Father, in early infancy,   25
When you were far beyond the sea,
Such thoughts were tyrants over me!
I often sat, for hours together,
Through the long nights of angry weather,

Raised on my pillow, to descry 30
The dim moon struggling in the sky;
Or, with strained ear, to catch the shock,
Of rock with wave, and wave with rock;
So would I fearful vigil keep,
And, all for listening, never sleep. 35
But this world's life has much to dread,
Not so, my Father, with the dead.

"Oh! not for them, should we despair,
The grave is drear, but they are not there;
Their dust is mingled with the sod, 40
Their happy souls are gone to God!
You told me this, and yet you sigh,
And murmur that your friends must die.
Ah! my dear father, tell me why?
For, if your former words were true, 45
How useless would such sorrow be;
As wise, to mourn the seed which grew
Unnoticed on its parent tree,
Because it fell in fertile earth,
And sprang up to a glorious birth— 50
Struck deep its root, and lifted high
Its green boughs in the breezy sky.

"But, I'll not fear, I will not weep
For those whose bodies rest in sleep,—
I know there is a blessed shore, 55
    Opening its ports for me and mine;
And, gazing Time's wide waters o'er,
    I weary for that land divine,
Where we were born, where you and I
Shall meet our Dearest, when we die; 60
From suffering and corruption free,
Restored into the Deity."

"Well hast thou spoken, sweet, trustful child!
    And wiser than thy sire;
And worldly tempests, raging wild, 65
    Shall strengthen thy desire—
Thy fervent hope, through storm and foam,
    Through wind and ocean's roar,
To reach, at last, the eternal home,
    The steadfast, changeless shore!" 70

Stars

Ah! why, because the dazzling sun
    Restored our Earth to joy,
Have you departed, every one,
    And left a desert sky?

All through the night, your glorious eyes
    Were gazing down in mine,
And, with a full heart's thankful sighs,
    I blessed that watch divine.

I was at peace, and drank your beams
    As they were life to me;
And revelled in my changeful dreams,
    Like petrel on the sea.

Thought followed thought, star followed star,
    Through boundless regions, on;
While one sweet influence, near and far,
    Thrilled through, and proved us one!

Why did the morning dawn to break
    So great, so pure, a spell;
And scorch with fire, the tranquil cheek,
    Where your cool radiance fell?

Blood-red, he rose, and, arrow-straight,
    His fierce beams struck my brow;
The soul of nature, sprang, elate,
    But mine sank sad and low!

My lids closed down, yet through their veil,
    I saw him, blazing, still,
And steep in gold the misty dale,
    And flash upon the hill.

I turned me to the pillow, then,
    To call back night, and see
Your worlds of solemn light, again,
    Throb with my heart, and me!

It would not do—the pillow glowed,
    And glowed both roof and floor;
And birds sang loudly in the wood,
    And fresh winds shook the door;

EMILY BRONTË

The curtains waved, the wakened flies
   Were murmuring round my room,
Imprisoned there, till I should rise,
   And give them leave to roam.   40

Oh, stars, and dreams, and gentle night;
   Oh, night and stars return!
And hide me from the hostile light,
   That does not warm, but burn;

That drains the blood of suffering men;   45
   Drinks tears, instead of dew;
Let me sleep through his blinding reign,
   And only wake with you!

The Philosopher

"ENOUGH of thought, philosopher!
   Too long hast thou been dreaming
Unlightened, in this chamber drear,
   While summer's sun is beaming!
Space-sweeping soul, what sad refrain   5
Concludes thy musings once again?

  "Oh, for the time when I shall sleep
   Without identity,
  And never care how rain may steep,
   Or snow may cover me!   10
  No promised heaven, these wild desires,
   Could all, or half fulfil;
  No threatened hell, with quenchless fires,
   Subdue this quenchless will!"

"So said I, and still say the same;   15
   Still, to my death, will say–
Three gods, within this little frame,
   Are warring night and day;
Heaven could not hold them all, and yet
   They all are held in me;   20
And must be mine till I forget
   My present entity!
Oh, for the time, when in my breast
   Their struggles will be o'er!

POEMS BY CURRER, ELLIS, AND ACTON BELL 33

Oh, for the day, when I shall rest,   25
   And never suffer more!"

"I saw a spirit, standing, man,
   Where thou dost stand—an hour ago,
And round his feet three rivers ran,
   Of equal depth, and equal flow—   30
A golden stream—and one like blood;
   And one like sapphire, seemed to be;
But, where they joined their triple flood
   It tumbled in an inky sea.
The spirit sent his dazzling gaze   35
   Down through that ocean's gloomy night
Then, kindling all, with sudden blaze,
   The glad deep sparkled wide and bright—
White as the sun, far, far more fair
   Than its divided sources were!"   40

"And even for that spirit, seer,
   I've watched and sought my life-time long;
Sought him in heaven, hell, earth and air—
   An endless search, and always wrong!
Had I but seen his glorious eye   45
   Once light the clouds that wilder me,
I ne'er had raised this coward cry
   To cease to think and cease to be;
I ne'er had called oblivion blest,
   Nor, stretching eager hands to death,   50
Implored to change for senseless rest
   This sentient soul, this living breath—
Oh, let me die—that power and will
   Their cruel strife may close;
And conquered good, and conquering ill   55
   Be lost in one repose!"

Remembrance

COLD in the earth—and the deep snow piled above thee,
Far, far, removed, cold in the dreary grave!
Have I forgot, my only Love, to love thee,
Severed at last by Time's all-severing wave?

Now, when alone, do my thoughts no longer hover   5
Over the mountains, on that northern shore,
Resting their wings where heath and fern-leaves cover
Thy noble heart for ever, ever more?

Cold in the earth—and fifteen wild Decembers,
From those brown hills, have melted into spring: 10
Faithful, indeed, is the spirit that remembers
After such years of change and suffering!

Sweet Love of youth, forgive, if I forget thee,
While the world's tide is bearing me along;
Other desires and other hopes beset me,   15
Hopes which obscure, but cannot do thee wrong!

No later light has lightened up my heaven,
No second morn has ever shone for me;
All my life's bliss from thy dear life was given,
All my life's bliss is in the grave with thee.   20

But, when the days of golden dreams had perished,
And even Despair was powerless to destroy;
Then did I learn how existence could be cherished,
Strengthened, and fed without the aid of joy.

Then did I check the tears of useless passion—   25
Weaned my young soul from yearning after thine;
Sternly denied its burning wish to hasten
Down to that tomb already more than mine.

And, even yet, I dare not let it languish,
Dare not indulge in memory's rapturous pain;   30
Once drinking deep of that divinest anguish,
How could I seek the empty world again?

A Death-Scene

"O DAY! he cannot die
When thou so fair art shining!
O Sun, in such a glorious sky,
So tranquilly declining;

He cannot leave thee now,   5
While fresh west winds are blowing,

And all around his youthful brow
Thy cheerful light is glowing!

Edward, awake, awake—
The golden evening gleams 10
Warm and bright on Arden's lake—
Arouse thee from thy dreams!

Beside thee, on my knee,
My dearest friend! I pray
That thou, to cross the eternal sea, 15
Wouldst yet one hour delay:

I hear its billows roar—
I see them foaming high;
But no glimpse of a further shore
Has blest my straining eye. 20

Believe not what they urge
Of Eden isles beyond;
Turn back, from that tempestuous surge,
To thy own native land.

It is not death, but pain 25
That struggles in thy breast—
Nay, rally, Edward, rouse again;
I cannot let thee rest!"

One long look, that sore reproved me
For the woe I could not bear— 30
One mute look of suffering moved me
To repent my useless prayer:

And, with sudden check, the heaving
Of distraction passed away;
Not a sign of further grieving 35
Stirred my soul that awful day.

Paled, at length, the sweet sun setting;
Sunk to peace the twilight breeze:
Summer dews fell softly, wetting
Glen, and glade, and silent trees. 40

Then his eyes began to weary,
Weighed beneath a mortal sleep;
And their orbs grew strangely dreary,
Clouded, even as they would weep.

EMILY BRONTË

But they wept not, but they changed not,   45
Never moved, and never closed;
Troubled still, and still they ranged not—
Wandered not, nor yet reposed!

So I knew that he was dying—
Stooped, and raised his languid head;   50
Felt no breath, and heard no sighing,
So I knew that he was dead.

Song

THE linnet in the rocky dells,
    The moor-lark in the air,
The bee among the heather bells,
    That hide my lady fair:

The wild deer browse above her breast;   5
    The wild birds raise their brood;
And they, her smiles of love caressed,
    Have left her solitude!

I ween, that when the grave's dark wall
    Did first her form retain;   10
They thought their hearts could ne'er recall
    The light of joy again.

They thought the tide of grief would flow
    Unchecked through future years;
But where is all their anguish now,   15
    And where are all their tears?

Well, let them fight for honour's breath,
    Or pleasure's shade pursue—
The dweller in the land of death
    Is changed and careless too.   20

And, if their eyes should watch and weep
    Till sorrow's source were dry,
She would not, in her tranquil sleep,
    Return a single sigh!

Blow, west-wind, by the lonely mound,   25
    And murmur, summer-streams—
There is no need of other sound
    To sooth my lady's dreams.

Anticipation

How beautiful the earth is still,
To thee—how full of happiness!
How little fraught with real ill,
Or unreal phantoms of distress!
How spring can bring thee glory, yet,   5
And summer win thee to forget
December's sullen time!
Why dost thou hold the treasure fast,
Of youth's delight, when youth is past,
   And thou art near thy prime?   10

When those who were thy own compeers,
Equals in fortune and in years,
Have seen their morning melt in tears,
   To clouded, smileless day;
Blest, had they died untried and young,   15
Before their hearts went wandering wrong,
Poor slaves, subdued by passions strong,
   A weak and helpless prey!

"Because, I hoped while they enjoyed,
And, by fulfilment, hope destroyed;   20
As children hope, with trustful breast,
I waited bliss—and cherished rest.
A thoughtful spirit taught me, soon,
That we must long till life be done;
That every phase of earthly joy   25
Must always fade, and always cloy:

This I foresaw—and would not chase
   The fleeting treacheries;
But, with firm foot and tranquil face,
Held backward from that tempting race,   30
Gazed o'er the sands the waves efface,
   To the enduring seas—
There cast my anchor of desire
Deep in unknown eternity;
Nor ever let my spirit tire,   35
With looking for *what is to be*!

It is hope's spell that glorifies,
Like youth, to my maturer eyes,

All Nature's million mysteries,
   The fearful and the fair—   40
Hope soothes me in the griefs I know;
She lulls my pain for others' woe,
And makes me strong to undergo
   What I am born to bear.

Glad comforter! will I not brave,   45
Unawed, the darkness of the grave?
Nay, smile to hear Death's billows rave—
   Sustained, my guide, by thee?
The more unjust seems present fate,
The more my spirit swells elate,   50
Strong, in thy strength, to anticipate
   Rewarding destiny!"

The Prisoner

A Fragment

In the dungeon-crypts, idly did I stray,
Reckless of the lives wasting there away;
"Draw the ponderous bars! open, Warder stern!"
He dared not say me nay—the hinges harshly turn.

"Our guests are darkly lodged," I whisper'd, gazing through   5
The vault, whose grated eye showed heaven more grey than blue;
(This was when glad spring laughed in awaking pride;)
"Aye, darkly lodged enough!" returned my sullen guide.

Then, God forgive my youth; forgive my careless tongue;
I scoffed, as the chill chains on the damp flag-stones rung: 10
"Confined in triple walls, art thou so much to fear,
That we must bind thee down and clench thy fetters here?"

The captive raised her face, it was as soft and mild
As sculpted marble saint, or slumbering unwean'd child;
It was so soft and mild, it was so sweet and fair,   15
Pain could not trace a line, nor grief a shadow there!

The captive raised her hand and pressed it to her brow;
"I have been struck," she said, "and I am suffering now;
Yet these are little worth, your bolts and irons strong,
And, were they forged in steel, they could not hold me long." 20

Hoarse laughed the jailor grim: "Shall I be won to hear;
Dost think, fond, dreaming wretch, that *I* shall grant thy prayer?

POEMS BY CURRER, ELLIS, AND ACTON BELL   39

Or, better still, wilt melt my master's heart with groans?
Ah! sooner might the sun thaw down these granite stones.

"My master's voice is low, his aspect bland and kind,   25
But hard as hardest flint, the soul that lurks behind;
And I am rough and rude, yet not more rough to see
Than is the hidden ghost that has its home in me."

About her lips there played a smile of almost scorn,
"My friend," she gently said, "you have not heard me mourn;   30
When you my kindred's lives, my lost life, can restore,
Then I may weep and sue,—but never, friend, before!

Still, let my tyrants know, I am not doom'd to wear
Year after year in gloom, and desolate despair;
A messenger of Hope, comes every night to me,   35
And offers for short life, eternal liberty.

He comes with western winds, with evening's wandering airs,
With that clear dusk of heaven that brings the thickest stars.
Winds take a pensive tone, and stars a tender fire,
And visions rise, and change, that kill me with desire.   40

Desire for nothing known in my maturer years,
When Joy grew mad with awe, at counting future tears.
When, if my spirit's sky was full of flashes warm,
I knew not whence they came, from sun, or thunder storm.

But, first, a hush of peace—a soundless calm descends;   45
The struggle of distress, and fierce impatience ends.
Mute music soothes my breast, unuttered harmony,
That I could never dream, till Earth was lost to me.

Then dawns the Invisible; the Unseen its truth reveals;
My outward sense is gone, my inward essence feels: 50
Its wings are almost free—its home, its harbour found,
Measuring the gulph, it stoops, and dares the final bound.

Oh, dreadful is the check—intense the agony—
When the ear begins to hear, and the eye begins to see;
When the pulse begins to throb, the brain to think again,   55
The soul to feel the flesh, and the flesh to feel the chain.

Yet I would lose no sting, would wish no torture less;
The more that anguish racks, the earlier it will bless;
And robed in fires of hell, or bright with heavenly shine,
If it but herald death, the vision is divine!"   60

EMILY BRONTË

She ceased to speak, and we, unanswering, turned to go—
We had no further power to work the captive woe:
Her cheek, her gleaming eye, declared that man had given
A sentence, unapproved, and overruled by Heaven.

'Julian M. and A.G. Rochelle'

Silent is the House—all are laid asleep;
One, alone, looks out o'er the snow-wreaths deep;
Watching every cloud, dreading every breeze
That whirls the wildering drifts and bends the groaning trees—

Cheerful is the hearth, soft the matted floor   5
Not one shivering gust creeps through pane or door
The little lamp burns straight; its rays shoot strong and far
I trim it well to be the Wanderer's guiding-star—

Frown, my haughty sire, chide my angry Dame;
Set your slaves to spy, threaten me with shame;   10
But neither sire nor dame, nor prying serf shall know
What angel nightly tracks that waste of winter snow—

In the dungeon crypts idly did I stray
Reckless of the lives wasting there away;
"Draw the ponderous bars, open Warder stern!"   15
He dare not say me nay—the hinges harshly turn—

"Our guests are darkly lodged" I whispered gazing through
The vault whose grated eye showed heaven more grey than blue;
(This was when glad spring laughed in awaking pride.)
"Aye, darkly lodged enough!" returned my sullen guide—   20

Then, God forgive my youth, forgive my careless tongue!
I scoffed as the chill chains on the damp flagstones rung;
"Confined in triple walls, art thou so much to fear,
"That we must bind thee down and clench thy fetters here?"

The captive raised her face; it was as soft and mild   25
As sculptured marble saint or slumbering, unweaned child
It was so soft and mild, it was so sweet and fair
Pain could not trace a line nor grief a shadow there!

The captive raised her hand and pressed it to her brow
"I have been struck, she said, and I am suffering now   30

POEMS BY CURRER, ELLIS, AND ACTON BELL　　41

"Yet these are little worth, your bolts and irons strong
"And were they forged in steel they could not hold me long!"

Hoarse laughed the jailer grim, "Shall I be won to hear
"Dost think fond, dreaming wretch, that *I* shall grant thy prayer?
"Or better still, wilt melt my master's heart with groans?　　35
"Ah sooner might the sun thaw down these granite stones!—

"My master's voice is low, his aspect bland and kind
"But hard as hardest flint the soul that lurks behind:
"And I am rough and rude, yet, not more rough to see
"Than is the hidden ghost which has its home in me!"　　40

About her lips there played a smile of almost scorn
"My friend, she gently said, you have not heard me mourn
"When you, my parent's lives—*my* lost life can restore
"Then may I weep and sue, but, never, Friend, before!"

Her head sank on her hands its fair curls swept the ground　　45
The Dungeon seemed to swim in strange confusion round—
"Is she so near to death?" I murmured half aloud
And kneeling, parted back the floating golden cloud

Alas, how former days upon my heart were borne
How memory mirrored then the prisoner's joyous morn　　50
Too blithe, too loving Child, too warmly, ~~too~~ wildly gay!
Was that the wintry close of thy celestial May?

She knew me and she sighed "Lord Julian, can it be,
"Of all my playmates, you, alone, remember me?
"Nay start not at my words, unless you deem it shame　　55
"To own from conquered foe, a once familiar name—

"I cannot wonder now at aught the world will do
"And insult and contempt I lightly brook from you,
"Since those who vowed away their souls to win my love
"Around this living grave like utter strangers move:　　60

"Nor has one voice been raised to plead that I might die
"Not buried under earth but in the open sky;
"By ball or speedy knife or headsman's [hodsman's? herdsman's?]
　skilful blow—
"A quick and welcome pang instead of lingering woe!

"Yet, tell them, Julian, all, I am not doomed to wear　　65
"Year after year in gloom and desolate despair;

"A messenger of Hope comes every night to me
"And offers, for short life, eternal liberty.

"He comes with western winds, with evening's wandering airs,
"With that clear dusk of heaven that brings the thickest stars;   70
"Winds take a pensive tone and stars a tender fire
"And visions rise and change which kill me with desire—

"Desire for nothing known in my maturer years
"When joy grew mad with awe at counting future tears;
"When, if my spirit's sky was full of flashes warm,   75
"I knew not whence they came from sun or thunderstorm:

"But first a hush of peace, a soundless calm descends;
"The struggle of distress and fierce impatience ends;
"Mute music soothes my breast—unuttered harmony
"That I could never dream till earth was lost to me.   80

"Then dawns the Invisible, the Unseen its truth reveals;
"My outward sense is gone, my inward essence feels—
"Its wings are almost free, its home, its harbour found;
"Measuring the gulf it stoops and dares the final bound!—

["]Oh, dreadful is the check—intense the agony   85
["]When the ear begins to hear and the eye begins to see;
["]When the pulse begins to throb, the brain to think again,
["]The soul to feel the flesh and the flesh to feel the chain!

"Yet I would lose no sting, would wish no torture less;
"The more that anguish racks the earlier it will bless: 90
"And robed in fires of Hell, or bright with heavenly shine
"If it but herald Death, the vision is divine—"

She ceased to speak and I, unanswering watched her there
Not daring now to touch one lock of silken hair—
As I had knelt in scorn, on the dank floor I knelt still,   95
My fingers in the links of that iron hard and chill,

I heard and yet heard not the surly keeper growl;
I saw, yet did not see, the flagstone damp and foul;
The keeper, to and fro, paced by the bolted door
And shivered as he walked and as he shivered, swore—   100

While my cheek glowed in flame, I marked that he did rave
Of air that froze his blood and moisture like the grave—
"We have been two hours good!" he muttered peevishly,
Then, loosing off his belt the rusty dungeon key,

POEMS BY CURRER, ELLIS, AND ACTON BELL 43

He said, "You may be pleased, Lord Julian, still to stay 105
"But duty will not let me linger here all day;
"If I might go, I'd leave this badge of mine with you
"Not doubting that you'd prove a jailer stern and true"

I took the proffered charge; the captive's drooping lid
Beneath its shady lash a sudden lightning hid 110
Earth's hope was not so dead heaven's home was not so dear
I read it in that flash of longing quelled by fear

Then like a tender child whose hand did just enfold
Safe in its eager grasp a bird it wept to hold
When pierced with one wild glance from the troubled hazel eye 115
It gushes into tears and lets its treasure fly

Thus ruth and selfish love together striving tore
The heart all newly taught to pity and adore;
If I should break the chain, I felt my bird would go
Yet I must break the chain or seal the prisoner's woe— 120

Short strife what rest could soothe—what peace could visit me
While she lay pining there for Death to set her free?
"Rochelle, the dungeons teem with foes to gorge our hate—
Thou art too young to die by such a bitter fate!"

With hurried blow on blow I struck the fetters through 125
Regardless how that deed my after hours might rue
Oh, I was over-blest by the warm unasked embrace
By the smile of grateful joy that lit her angel face!

And I was over-blest—aye, more than I could dream
When, faint, she turned aside from noon's unwonted beam; 130
When though the cage was wide—the heaven around it lay—
Its pinion would not waft my wounded dove away—

Through thirteen anxious weeks of terror-blent delight
I guarded her by day and guarded her by night
While foes were prowling near and Death gazed greedily 135
And only Hope remained a faithful friend to me—

Then oft with taunting smile, I heard my kindred tell
"How Julian loved his hearth and sheltering rooftree well,—
How the trumpet's voice might call the battle-standard wave
But Julian had no heart to fill a patriot's grave." 140

And I, who am so quick to answer sneer with sneer;
So ready to condemn to scorn a coward's fear,

EMILY BRONTË

I held my peace like one whose conscience keeps him dumb
And saw my kinsmen go—and lingered still at home.

Another hand than mine, my rightful banner held   145
And gathered my renown on Freedom's crimson field
Yet I had no desire the glorious prize to gain—
It needed braver nerve to face the world's disdain—

And by the patient strength that could that world defy;
By suffering with calm mind, contempt and calumny;   150
By never-doubting love, unswerving constancy,
Rochelle, I earned at last an equal love from thee!

18 December 1843

HOPE was but a timid friend;
    She sat without the grated den,
Watching how my fate would tend,
    Even as selfish-hearted men.

She was cruel in her fear;   5
    Through the bars, one dreary day,
I looked out to see her there,
    And she turned her face away!

Like a false guard, false watch keeping,
    Still, in strife, she whispered peace;   10
She would sing while I was weeping;
    If I listened, she would cease.

False she was, and unrelenting;
    When my last joys strewed the ground,
Even Sorrow saw, repenting,   15
    Those sad relics scattered round;

Hope, whose whisper would have given
    Balm to all my frenzied pain,
Stretched her wings, and soared to heaven,
    Went, and ne'er returned again!   20

A Day Dream

On a sunny brae alone I lay
    One summer afternoon;
It was the marriage-time of May
    With her young lover, June.

From her mother's heart, seemed loath to part   5
    That queen of bridal charms,
But her father smiled on the fairest child
    He ever held in his arms.

The trees did wave their plumy crests,
    The glad birds caroled clear;   10
And I, of all the wedding guests,
    Was only sullen there!

There was not one, but wished to shun
    My aspect void of cheer;
The very grey rocks, looking on,   15
    Asked, "What do you do here?"

And I could utter no reply;
    In sooth, I did not know
Why I had brought a clouded eye
    To greet the general glow.   20

So, resting on a heathy bank,
    I took my heart to me;
And we together sadly sank
    Into a reverie.

We thought, "When winter comes again,   25
    Where will these bright things be?
All vanished, like a vision vain,
    An unreal mockery!

The birds that now so blithely sing,
    Through deserts, frozen dry,   30
Poor spectres of the perished spring,
    In famished troops, will fly.

And why should we be glad at all?
    The leaf is hardly green,
Before a token of its fall   35
    Is on the surface seen!"

Now, whether it were really so,
  I never could be sure;
But as in fit of peevish woe,
  I stretched me on the moor. 40

A thousand thousand gleaming fires
  Seemed kindling in the air;
A thousand thousand silvery lyres
  Resounded far and near:

Methought, the very breath I breathed 45
  Was full of sparks divine,
And all my heather-couch was wreathed
  By that celestial shine!

And, while the wide earth echoing rung
  To their strange minstrelsy, 50
The little glittering spirits sung,
  O seemed to sing, to me.

"O mortal! mortal! let them die;
  Let time and tears destroy,
That we may overflow the sky 55
  With universal joy!

Let grief distract the sufferer's breast,
  And night obscure his way;
They hasten him to endless rest,
  And everlasting day. 60

To thee the world is like a tomb,
  A desert's naked shore;
To us, in unimagined bloom,
  It brightens more and more!

And, could we lift the veil, and give 65
  One brief glimpse to thine eye,
Thou wouldst rejoice for those that live,
  Because they live to die."

The music ceased; the noonday dream,
  Like dream of night, withdrew; 70
But Fancy, still, will sometimes deem
  Her fond creation true.

To Imagination

WHEN weary with the long day's care,
　And earthly change from pain to pain,
And lost and ready to despair,
　Thy kind voice calls me back again:
Oh, my true friend! I am not lone,　　　　5
While thou canst speak with such a tone!

So hopeless is the world without;
　The world within I doubly prize;
Thy world, where guile, and hate, and doubt,
　And cold suspicion never rise;　　　　10
Where thou, and I, and Liberty,
Have undisputed sovereignty.

What matters it, that, all around,
　Danger, and guilt, and darkness lie,
If but within our bosom's bound　　　　15
　We hold a bright, untroubled sky,
Warm with ten thousand mingled rays
Of suns that know no winter days?

Reason, indeed, may oft complain
　For Nature's sad reality,　　　　20
And tell the suffering heart, how vain
　Its cherished dreams must always be;
And Truth may rudely trample down
The flowers of Fancy, newly-blown:

But, thou art ever there, to bring　　　　25
　The hovering vision back, and breathe
New glories o'er the blighted spring,
　And call a lovelier Life from Death,
And whisper, with a voice divine,
Of real worlds, as bright as thine.　　　　30

I trust not to thy phantom bliss,
　Yet, still, in evening's quiet hour,
With never-failing thankfulness,
　I welcome thee, Benignant Power;
Sure solacer of human cares,　　　　35
And sweeter hope, when hope despairs!

EMILY BRONTË

How clear she shines.

How clear she shines! How quietly
   I lie beneath her guardian light;
While heaven and earth are whispering me,
   "To morrow, wake, but, dream to-night."
Yes, Fancy, come, my Fairy love!   5
   These throbbing temples softly kiss;
And bend my lonely couch above
   And bring me rest, and bring me bliss.

The world is going; dark world, adieu!
   Grim world, conceal thee till the day;   10
The heart, thou canst not all subdue,
   Must still resist, if thou delay!

Thy love I will not, will not share;
   Thy hatred only wakes a smile;
Thy griefs may wound—thy wrongs may tear,   15
   But, oh, thy lies shall ne'er beguile!
While gazing on the stars that glow
   Above me, in that stormless sea,
I long to hope that all the woe
   Creation knows, is held in thee!   20

And, this shall be my dream to-night;
   I'll think the heaven of glorious spheres
Is rolling on its course of light
   In endless bliss, through endless years;
I'll think, there's not one world above,   25
   Far as these straining eyes can see,
Where Wisdom ever laughed at Love,
   Or Virtue crouched to Infamy;

Where, writhing 'neath the strokes of Fate,
   The mangled wretch was forced to smile;   30
To match his patience 'gainst her hate,
   His heart rebellious all the while.
Where Pleasure still will lead to wrong,
   And helpless Reason warn in vain;
And Truth is weak, and Treachery strong;   35
   And Joy the surest path to Pain;
And Peace, the lethargy of Grief;

And Hope, a phantom of the soul;
And Life, a labour, void and brief;
   And Death, the despot of the whole!   40

Sympathy

THERE should be no despair for you
   While nightly stars are burning;
While evening pours its silent dew
   And sunshine gilds the morning.
There should be no despair—though tears   5
   May flow down like a river:
Are not the best beloved of years
   Around your heart for ever?

They weep, you weep, it must be so;
   Winds sigh as you are sighing,   10
And Winter sheds his grief in snow
   Where Autumn's leaves are lying:
Yet, these revive, and from their fate
   Your fate cannot be parted:
Then, journey on, if not elate,   15
   Still, *never* broken-hearted!

Plead for me

OH, thy bright eyes must answer now,
When Reason, with a scornful brow,
Is mocking at my overthrow!
Oh, thy sweet tongue must plead for me
And tell, why I have chosen thee!   5

Stern Reason is to judgment come,
Arrayed in all her forms of gloom:
Wilt thou, my advocate, be dumb?
No, radiant angel, speak and say,
Why I did cast the world away.   10

Why I have persevered to shun
The common paths that others run,

And on a strange road journeyed on,
Heedless, alike, of wealth and power—
Of glory's wreath and pleasure's flower. 15

These, once, indeed, seemed Beings Divine;
And they, perchance, heard vows of mine,
And saw my offerings on their shrine;
But, careless gifts are seldom prized,
And *mine* were worthily despised. 20

So, with a ready heart I swore
To seek their altar-stone no more;
And gave my spirit to adore
Thee, ever-present, phantom thing;
My slave, my comrade, and my king, 25

A slave, because I rule thee still;
Incline thee to my changeful will,
And make thy influence good or ill:
A comrade, for by day and night
Thou art my intimate delight,— 30

My darling pain that wounds and sears
And wrings a blessing out from tears
By deadening me to earthly cares;
And yet, a king, though Prudence well
Have taught thy subject to rebel. 35

And am I wrong to worship, where
Faith cannot doubt, nor hope despair,
Since my own soul can grant my prayer?
Speak, God of visions, plead for me,
And tell why I have chosen thee! 40

Self-interrogation

"THE evening passes fast away,
   'Tis almost time to rest;
What thoughts has left the vanished day,
   What feelings, in thy breast?

"The vanished day? It leaves a sense 5
   Of labour hardly done;
Of little, gained with vast expense,—
   A sense of grief alone!

"Time stands before the door of Death,
    Upbraiding bitterly;
And Conscience, with exhaustless breath,
    Pours black reproach on me:

"And though I've said that Conscience lies,
    And Time should Fate condemn;
Still, sad Repentance clouds my eyes,
    And makes me yield to them!["]

"Then art thou glad to seek repose?
    Art glad to leave the sea,
And anchor all thy weary woes
    In calm Eternity?

"Nothing regrets to see thee go—
    Not one voice sobs 'farewell,'
And where thy heart has suffered so,
    Canst thou desire to dwell?"

"Alas! The countless links are strong
    That bind us to our clay;
The loving spirit lingers long,
    And would not pass away!

"And rest is sweet, when laurelled fame
    Will crown the soldier's crest;
But, a brave heart, with a tarnished name,
    Would rather fight than rest."

"Well, thou hast fought for many a year,
    Hast fought thy whole life through,
Hast humbled Falsehood, trampled Fear;
    What is there left to do?"

"'Tis true, this arm has hotly striven,
    Has dared what few would dare;
Much have I done, and freely given,
    But little learnt to bear!"

"Look on the grave, where thou must sleep,
    Thy last, and strongest foe;
It is endurance not to weep,
    If that repose seem woe.

"The long war closing in defeat,
    Defeat serenely borne,
Thy midnight rest may still be sweet,
    And break in glorious morn!"

Death

DEATH! that struck when I was most confiding
In my certain faith of joy to be—
Strike again, Time's withered branch dividing
From the fresh root of Eternity!

Leaves, upon Time's branch, were growing brightly,   5
Full of sap, and full of silver dew;
Birds beneath its shelter gathered nightly;
Daily round its flowers the wild bees flew.

Sorrow passed, and plucked the golden blossom;
Guilt stripped off the foliage in its pride;   10
But, within its parent's kindly bosom,
Flowed for ever Life's restoring tide.

Little mourned I for the parted gladness,
For the vacant nest and silent song—
Hope was there, and laughed me out of sadness;   15
Whispering, "Winter will not linger long!"

And, behold! with tenfold increase blessing,
Spring adorned the beauty-burdened spray;
Wind and rain and fervent heat, caressing,
Lavished glory on that second May!   20

High it rose—no winged grief could sweep it;
Sin was scared to distance with its shine;
Love, and its own life, had power to keep it
From all wrong—from every blight but thine!

Cruel Death! The young leaves droop and languish;   25
Evening's gentle air may still restore—
No! the morning sunshine mocks my anguish—
Time, for me, must never blossom more!

Strike it down, that other boughs may flourish
Where that perished sapling used to be;   30
Thus, at least, its mouldering corpse will nourish
That from which it sprung—Eternity.

Stanzas to—

WELL, some may hate, and some may scorn,
And some may quite forget thy name;
But my sad heart must ever mourn
Thy ruined hopes, thy blighted fame!
'Twas thus I thought, an hour ago,   5
Even weeping o'er that wretch's woe;
One word turned back my gushing tears,
And lit my altered eye with sneers.
Then "Bless the friendly dust," I said,
"That hides thy unlamented head!   10
Vain as thou wert, and weak as vain,
The slave of Falsehood, Pride, and Pain,—
My heart has nought akin to thine;
Thy soul is powerless over mine."

But these were thoughts that vanished too; 15
Unwise, unholy, and untrue:
Do I despise the timid deer,
Because his limbs are fleet with fear?
Or, would I mock the wolf's death-howl,
Because his form is gaunt and foul?   20
Or, hear with joy the leveret's cry,
Because it cannot bravely die?
No! Then above his memory
Let Pity's heart as tender be;
Say, "Earth, lie lightly on that breast, 25
And, kind Heaven, grant that spirit rest!"

Honour's Martyr

THE moon is full this winter night;
 The stars are clear, though few;
And every window glistens bright,
 With leaves of frozen dew.

The sweet moon through your lattice gleams 5
 And lights your room like day;
And there you pass, in happy dreams,
 The peaceful hours away!

While I, with effort hardly quelling
    The anguish in my breast,
Wander about the silent dwelling,
    And cannot think of rest.

The old clock in the gloomy hall
    Ticks on, from hour to hour;
And every time its measured call
    Seems lingering slow and slower:

And oh, how slow that keen-eyed star
    Has tracked the chilly grey!
What, watching yet! how very far
    The morning lies away!

Without your chamber door I stand;
    Love, are you slumbering still?
My cold heart, underneath my hand,
    Has almost ceased to thrill.

Bleak, bleak the east wind sobs and sighs,
    And drowns the turret bell,
Whose sad note, undistinguished, dies
    Unheard, like my farewell!

To-morrow, Scorn will blight my name,
    And Hate will trample me,
Will load me with a coward's shame—
    A traitor's perjury.

False friends will launch their covert sneers;
    True friends will wish me dead;
And I shall cause the bitterest tears
    That you have ever shed.

The dark deeds of my outlawed race
    Will then like virtues shine;
And men will pardon their disgrace,
    Beside the guilt of mine.

For, who forgives the accursed crime
    Of dastard treachery?
Rebellion, in its chosen time,
    May Freedom's champion be;

Revenge may stain a righteous sword,
    It may be just to slay;

But, traitor, traitor,—from *that* word
  All true breasts shrink away!

Oh, I would give my heart to death,
  To keep my honour fair;   50
Yet, I'll not give my inward faith
  My honour's *name* to spare!

Not even to keep your priceless love,
  Dare I, Beloved, deceive;
This treason should the future prove,   55
  Then, only then, believe!

I know the path I ought to go;
  I follow fearlessly,
Inquiring not what deeper woe
  Stern duty stores for me.   60

So foes pursue, and cold allies
  Mistrust me, every one:
Let me be false in others' eyes,
  If faithful in my own.

Stanzas

I'LL not weep that thou art going to leave me,
  There's nothing lovely here;
And doubly will the dark world grieve me,
  While thy heart suffers there.

I'll not weep, because the summer's glory   5
  Must always end in gloom;
And, follow out the happiest story—
  It closes with a tomb!

And I am weary of the anguish
  Increasing winters bear;   10
Weary to watch the spirit languish
  Through years of dead despair.

So, if a tear, when thou art dying,
  Should haply fall from me,
It is but that my soul is sighing,   15
  To go and rest with thee.

My Comforter

WELL hast thou spoken, and yet, not taught
　A feeling strange or new;
Thou hast but roused a latent thought,
A cloud-closed beam of sunshine, brought
　To gleam in open view.　　　　　　　　　　5

Deep down, concealed within my soul,
　That light lies hid from men;
Yet, glows unquenched—though shadows roll,
Its gentle ray cannot control,
　About the sullen den.　　　　　　　　　　10

Was I not vexed, in these gloomy ways
　To walk alone so long?
Around me, wretches uttering praise,
Or howling o'er their hopeless days,
　And each with Frenzy's tongue;—　　　　15

A brotherhood of misery,
　Their smiles as sad as sighs;
Whose madness daily maddened me,
Distorting into agony
　The bliss before my eyes!　　　　　　　　20

So stood I, in Heaven's glorious sun,
　And in the glare of Hell;
My spirit drank a mingled tone,
Of seraph's song, and demon's moan;
What my soul bore, my soul alone　　　　25
　Within itself may tell!

Like a soft air, above a sea,
　Tossed by the tempest's stir;
A thaw-wind, melting quietly
The snow-drift, on some wintry lea;　　　30
No: what sweet thing resembles thee,
　My thoughtful Comforter?

And yet a little longer speak,
　Calm this resentful mood;
And while the savage heart grows meek,　35
For other token do not seek,
But let the tear upon my cheek
　Evince my gratitude!

The Old Stoic

RICHES I hold in light esteem;
 And Love I laugh to scorn;
And lust of fame was but a dream
 That vanished with the morn:

And if I pray, the only prayer
 That moves my lips for me
Is, "Leave the heart that now I bear,
 And give me liberty!"

Yes, as my swift days near their goal,
 'Tis all that I implore;
In life and death, a chainless soul,
 With courage to endure.

Ellis Bell [Emily Brontë],
Wuthering Heights: A Novel
(London: Newby, 1847)

Chapter I.

1801—I have just returned from a visit to my landlord—the solitary neighbour that I shall be troubled with. This is certainly, a beautiful country! In all England, I do not believe that I could have fixed on a situation so completely removed from the stir of society. A perfect misanthropist's Heaven—and Mr. Heathcliff and I are such a suitable pair to divide the desolation between us. A capital fellow! He little imagined how my heart warmed towards him when I beheld his black eyes withdraw so suspiciously under their brows, as I rode up, and when his fingers sheltered themselves, with a jealous resolution, still further in his waistcoat, as I announced my name.

"Mr. Heathcliff?" I said.

A nod was the answer.

"Mr. Lockwood your new tenant, sir—I do myself the honour of calling as soon as possible, after my arrival, to express the hope that I have not inconvenienced you by my perseverance in soliciting the occupation of Thrushcross Grange: I heard, yesterday, you had had some thoughts—"

"Thrushcross Grange is my own, sir," he interrupted wincing, "I should not allow any one to inconvenience me, if I could hinder it—walk in!"

The "walk in," was uttered with closed teeth and expressed the sentiment, "Go to the Deuce!" even the gate over which he leant manifested no sympathizing movement to the words; and I think that circumstance determined me to accept the invitation: I felt interested in a man who seemed more exaggeratedly reserved than myself.

When he saw my horse's breast fairly pushing the barrier, he did pull out his hand to unchain it, and then sullenly preceded me up the causeway, calling, as we entered the court:

"Joseph, take Mr. Lockwood's horse; and bring up some wine."

"Here we have the whole establishment of domestics, I suppose," was the reflection, suggested by this compound order, "No wonder the grass grows up between the flags, and cattle are the only hedge-cutters."

Joseph was an elderly, nay, an old man, very old, perhaps, though hale and sinewy.

"The Lord help us!" he soliloquised in an undertone of peevish displeasure, while relieving me of my horse: looking, meantime, in my face so sourly that I charitably conjectured he must have need of divine aid to digest his dinner, and his pious ejaculation had no reference to my unexpected advent.

Wuthering Heights is the name of Mr. Heathcliff's dwelling. "Wuthering" being a significant provincial adjective, descriptive of the atmospheric tumult

62   EMILY BRONTË

to which its station is exposed, in stormy weather. Pure, bracing ventilation
they must have up there, at all times, indeed: one may guess the power of the
north wind, blowing over the edge, by the excessive slant of a few, stunted firs
at the end of the house; and by a range of gaunt thorns all stretching their
limbs one way, as if craving alms of the sun. Happily, the architect had foresight to build it strong: the narrow windows are deeply set in the wall; and the
corners defended with large jutting stones.

Before passing the threshold, I paused to admire a quantity of grotesque
carving lavished over the front, and especially about the principal door, above
which, among a wilderness of crumbling griffins, and shameless little boys,
I detected the date "1500," and the name "Hareton Earnshaw," I would have
made a few comments, and requested a short history of the place, from the
surly owner, but his attitude at the door appeared to demand my speedy
entrance, or complete departure, and I had no desire to aggravate his impatience, previous to inspecting the penetralium.

One step brought us into the family sitting-room, without any introduc-
tory lobby, or passage: they call it here "the house" preeminently. It includes
kitchen, and parlor, generally, but I believe at Wuthering Heights, the kitchen
is forced to retreat altogether, into another quarter, at least I distinguished a
chatter of tongues, and a clatter of culinary utensils, deep within; and
I observed no signs of roasting, boiling, or baking, about the huge fire-place;
nor any glitter of copper saucepans and tin cullenders on the walls. One end,
indeed, reflected splendidly both light and heat, from ranks of immense pewter dishes; interspersed with silver jugs, and tankards, towering row after row,
in a vast oak dresser, to the very roof. The latter had never been under-drawn,
its entire anatomy lay bare to an inquiring eye, except where a frame of wood
laden with oatcakes, and clusters of legs of beef, mutton and ham, concealed
it. Above the chimney were sundry villanous old guns, and a couple of horse-
pistols, and, by way of ornament, three gaudily painted canisters disposed
along its ledge. The floor was of smooth, white stone: the chairs, high-backed,
primitive structures, painted green: one or two heavy black ones lurking in
the shade. In an arch, under the dresser, reposed a huge, liver-coloured bitch
pointer surrounded by a swarm of squealing puppies, and other dogs, haunted
other recesses.

The apartment, and furniture would have been nothing extraordinary as
belonging to a homely, northern farmer with a stubborn countenance, and
stalwart limbs, set out to advantage in knee-breeches, and gaiters. Such an
individual, seated in his arm-chair, his mug of ale frothing on the round table
before him, is to be seen in any circuit of five or six miles among these hills, if
you go at the right time, after dinner. But, Mr. Heathcliff forms a singular
contrast to his abode and style of living. He is a dark skinned gypsy, in aspect,
in dress, and manners, a gentleman, that is, as much a gentleman as many a
country squire: rather slovenly, perhaps, yet not looking amiss, with his

WUTHERING HEIGHTS

negligence, because he has an erect and handsome figure—and rather morose—possibly, some people might suspect him of a degree of under-bred pride—I have a sympathetic chord within that tells me it is nothing of the sort; I know, by instinct, his reserve springs from an aversion to showy displays of feeling—to manifestations of mutual kindliness. He'll love and hate, equally under cover, and esteem it a species of impertinence, to be loved or hated again—No, I'm running on too fast—I bestow my own attributes over liberally on him. Mr. Heathcliff may have entirely dissimilar reasons for keeping his hand out of the way, when he meets a would be acquaintance, to those which actuate me. Let me hope my constitution is almost peeuliar: my dear mother used to say I should never have a comfortable home, and only last summer, I proved myself perfectly unworthy of one.

While enjoying a month of fine weather at the sea-coast, I was thrown into the company of a most fascinating creature, a real goddess, in my eyes, as long as she took no notice of me. I "never told my love" vocally; still, if looks have language, the merest idiot might have guessed I was over head and ears: she understood me, at last, and looked a return—the sweetest of all imaginable looks—and what did I do? I confess it with shame—shrunk icily into myself, like a snail, at every glance retired colder and farther; till, finally, the poor innocent was led to doubt her own senses, and, overwhelmed with confusion at her supposed mistake, persuaded her mamma to decamp.

By this curious turn of disposition I have gained the reputation of deliberate heartlessness, how undeserved, I alone can appreciate.

I took a seat at the end of the hearthstone opposite that towards which my landlord advanced, and filled up an interval of silence by attempting to caress the canine mother, who had left her nursery, and was sneaking wolfishly to the back of my legs, her lip curled up, and her white teeth watering for a snatch.

My caress provoked a long, guttural gnarl.

"You'd better let the dog alone," growled Mr. Heathcliff, in unison, checking fiercer demonstrations with a punch of his foot. "She's not accustomed to be spoiled—not kept for a pet."

Then, striding to a side-door, he shouted again.

"Joseph!"

Joseph mumbled indistinctly in the depths of the cellar; but, gave no intimation of ascending; so, his master dived down to him, leaving me *vis-à-vis* the ruffianly bitch, and a pair of grim, shaggy sheep dogs, who shared with her a jealous guardianship over all my movements.

Not anxious to come in contact with their fangs, I sat still—but, imagining they would scarcely understand tacit insults, I unfortunately indulged in winking and making faces at the trio, and some turn of my physiognomy so irritated madam, that she suddenly broke into a fury, and leapt on my knees. I flung her back, and hastened to interpose the table between us. This proceeding roused the whole hive. Half-a-dozen four-footed fiends, of various sizes, and ages, issued from hidden dens to the common centre. I felt my heels, and coat-laps peculiar subjects of assault; and, parrying off the larger combatants, as effectually as I could, with the poker, I was constrained to demand, aloud, assistance from some of the household, in re-establishing peace.

Mr. Heathcliff and his man climbed the cellar steps with vexatious phlegm. I don't think they moved one second faster than usual, though the hearth was an absolute tempest of worrying and yelping.

Happily, an inhabitant of the kitchen made more dispatch; a lusty dame, with tucked up gown, bare arms, and fire-flushed cheeks, rushed into the midst of us flourishing a fryingpan; and used that weapon, and her tongue to such purpose, that the storm subsided magically, and she only remained, heaving like a sea after a high wind, when her master entered on the scene.

"What the devil is the matter?" he asked, eyeing me in a manner that I could ill endure after this inhospitable treatment.

"What the devil, indeed!" I muttered. "The herd of possessed swine could have had no worse spirits in them than those animals of yours, sir. You might as well leave a stranger with a brood of tigers!"

"They wont meddle with persons who touch nothing," he remarked, putting the bottle before me, and restoring the displaced table. "The dogs do right to be vigilant. Take a glass of wine?"

"No, thank you."

"Not bitten, are you?"

"If I had been, I would have set my signet on the biter."

Heathcliff's countenance relaxed into a grin.

"Come, come," he said, "you are flurried, Mr. Lockwood. Here, take a little wine. Guests are so exceedingly rare in this house that I and my dogs, I am willing to own, hardly know how to receive them. Your health, sir!"

I bowed and returned the pledge; beginning to perceive that it would be foolish to sit sulking for the misbehaviour of a pack of curs: besides, I felt loath to yield the fellow further amusement, at my expense; since his humour took that turn.

He—probably swayed by prudential considerations of the folly of offending a good tenant—relaxed, a little, in the laconic style of chipping of his pronouns, and auxiliary verbs; and introduced, what he supposed would be a subject of interest to me, a discourse on the advantages and disadvantages of my present place of retirement.

I found him very intelligent on the topics we touched; and, before I went home, I was encouraged so far as to volunteer another visit, to-morrow.

He evidently wished no repetition of my intrusion. I shall go, notwithstanding. It is astonishing how sociable I feel myself compared with him.

CHAPTER II.

YESTERDAY afternoon set in misty and cold. I had half a mind to spend it by my study fire, instead of wading through heath and mud to Wuthering Heights.

On coming up from dinner, however, (N.B. I dine between twelve and one o'clock; the housekeeper, a matronly lady taken as a fixture along with the house, could not, or would not comprehend my request that I might be served at five.) On mounting the stairs with this lazy intention, and stepping into the room, I saw a servant-girl on her knees, surrounded by brushes, and coal-scuttles; and raising an infernal dust as she extinguished the flames with heaps of cinders. This spectacle drove me back immediately; I took my hat, and, after a four miles walk, arrived at Heathcliff's garden gate just in time to escape the first feathery flakes of a snow shower.

On that bleak hill top the earth was hard with a black frost, and the air made me shiver through every limb. Being unable to remove the chain, I jumped over, and, running up the flagged causeway bordered with straggling gooseberry bushes, knocked vainly for admittance, till my knuckles tingled, and the dogs howled.

"Wretched inmates!" I ejaculated, mentally, "you deserve perpetual isolation from your species for your churlish inhospitality. At least, I would not keep my doors barred in the day time—I don't care—I will get in!"

So resolved, I grasped the latch, and shook it vehemently. Vinegar-faced Joseph projected his head from a round window of the barn.

"Whet are ye for?" he shouted. "T'maisters dahn i' t'fowld. Goa rahnd by th' end ut' laith, if yah went tuh spake tull him."

"Is there nobody inside to open the door?" I hallooed, responsively.

"They's nobbut t' missis; and shoo'll nut oppen't an ye mak yer flaysome dins till neeght."

"Why? cannot you tell her who I am, eh, Joseph?"

"Nor-ne me! Aw'll hae noa hend wi't," muttered the head vanishing.

The snow began to drive thickly. I seized the handle to essay another trial; when a young man, without coat, and shouldering a pitchfork, appeared in the yard behind. He hailed me to follow him, and, after marching through a washhouse, and a paved area containing a coal-shed, pump, and pigeon cote, we at length arrived in the large, warm, cheerful apartment, where I was formerly received.

It glowed delightfully in the radiance of an immense fire, compounded of coal, peat, and wood: and near the table, laid for a plentiful evening meal, I was pleased to observe the "missis," an individual whose existence I had never previously suspected.

66 EMILY BRONTË

I bowed and waited, thinking she would bid me take a seat. She looked at me, leaning back in her chair, and remained motionless and mute.

"Rough weather!" I remarked. "I'm afraid, Mrs. Heathcliff, the floor must bear the consequence of your servant's leisure attendance: I had hard work to make them hear me!"

She never opened her mouth. I stared—she stared also. At any rate, she kept her eyes on me, in a cool, regardless manner, exceedingly embarrassing and disagreeable.

"Sit down," said the young man, gruffly. "He'll be in soon."

I obeyed; and hemmed, and called the villain Juno, who deigned, at this second interview, to move the extreme tip of her tail, in token of owning my acquaintance.

"A beautiful animal!" I commenced again. "Do you intend parting with the little ones, madam?"

"They are not mine," said the amiable hostess more repellingly than Heathcliff himself could have replied.

"Ah, your favourites are among these!" I continued, turning to an obscure cushion full of something like cats.

"A strange choice of favourites," she observed scornfully.

Unluckily, it was a heap of dead rabbits—I hemmed once more, and drew closer to the hearth, repeating my comment on the wildness of the evening.

"You should not have come out," she said, rising and reaching from the chimney piece two of the painted canisters.

Her position before was sheltered from the light: now, I had a distinct view of her whole figure and countenance. She was slender, and apparently scarcely past girlhood: an admirable form, and the most exquisite little face that I have ever had the pleasure of beholding: small features, very fair; flaxen ringlets, or rather golden, hanging loose on her delicate neck; and eyes—had they been agreeable in expression, they would have been irresistible—fortunately for my susceptible heart, the only sentiment they evinced hovered between scorn and a kind of desperation, singularly unnatural to be detected there.

The canisters were almost out of her reach; I made a motion to aid her; she turned upon me as a miser might turn, if any one attempted to assist him in counting his gold.

"I don't want your help," she snapped, "I can get them for myself."

"I beg your pardon," I hastened to reply.

"Were you asked to tea?" she demanded, tying an apron over her neat black frock, and standing with a spoonful of the leaf poised over the pot.

"I shall be glad to have a cup," I answered.

"Were you asked?" she repeated.

"No;" I said, half smiling. "You are the proper person to ask me."

She flung the tea back, spoon and all; and resumed her chair in a pet, her forehead corrugated, and her red under-lip pushed out, like a child's, ready to cry.

Meanwhile, the young man had slung onto his person a decidedly shabby upper garment, and, erecting himself before the blaze, looked down on me, from the corner of his eyes, for all the world as if there were some mortal feud unavenged between us. I began to doubt whether he were a servant or not; his dress and speech were both rude, entirely devoid of the superiority observable in Mr. and Mrs. Heathcliff; his thick, brown curls were rough and uncultivated, his whiskers encroached bearishly over his cheeks, and his hands were embrowned like those of a common labourer, still his bearing was free, almost haughty; and he showed none of a domestic's assiduity in attending on the lady of the house.

In the absence of clear proofs of his condition, I deemed it best to abstain from noticing his curious conduct, and, five minutes afterwards, the entrance of Heathcliff relieved me, in some measure, from my uncomfortable state.

"You see, sir, I am come according to promise!" I exclaimed, assuming the cheerful "and I fear I shall be weather-bound for half an hour, if you can afford me shelter during that space."

"Half an hour?" he said, shaking the white flakes from his clothes; "I wonder you should select the thick of a snow-storm to ramble about in. Do you know that you run a risk of being lost in the marshes? People familiar with these moors often miss their road on such evenings, and, I can tell you, there is no chance of a change at present."

"Perhaps I can get a guide among your lads, and he might stay at the Grange till morning—could you spare me one?"

"No, I could not."

"Oh, indeed! Well then, I must trust to my own sagacity."

"Umph!"

"Are you going to mak th 'tea?" demanded he of the shabby coat, shifting his ferocious gaze from me to the young lady.

"Is *he* to have any?" she asked, appealing to Heathcliff.

"Get it ready, will you?" was the answer, uttered so savagely that I started. The tone in which the words were said, revealed a genuine bad nature. I no longer felt inclined to call Heathcliff a capital fellow.

When the preparations were finished, he invited me with—

"Now, sir, bring forward your chair." And we all, including the rustic youth, drew round the table, an austere silence prevailing while we discussed our meal.

I thought, if I had caused the cloud, it was my duty to make an effort to dispel it. They could not every day sit so grim and taciturn, and it was impossible, however ill-tempered they might be, that the universal scowl they wore was their every day countenance.

"It is strange," I began in the interval of swallowing one cup of tea, and receiving another, "it is strange how custom can mould our tastes and ideas; many could not imagine the existence of happiness in a life of such complete

68 EMILY BRONTË

exile from the world as you spend, Mr. Heathcliff; yet, I'll venture to say, that, surrounded by your family, and with your amiable lady as the presiding genius over your home and heart—"

"My amiable lady!" he interrupted, with an almost diabolical sneer on his face. "Where is she—my amiable lady?"

"Mrs. Heathcliff, your wife, I mean."

"Well, yes—Oh! you would intimate that her spirit has taken the post of ministering angel, and guards the fortunes of Wuthering Heights, even when her body is gone. Is that it?"

Perceiving myself in a blunder, I attempted to correct it. I might have seen there was too great a disparity between the ages of the parties to make it likely that they were man and wife. One was about forty; a period of mental vigour at which men seldom cherish the delusion of being married for love, by girls: that dream is reserved for the solace of our declining years. The other did not look seventeen.

Then it flashed upon me; "the clown at my elbow, who is drinking his tea out of a basin, and eating his bread with unwashed hands, may be her husband. Heathcliff, junior, of course. Here is the consequence of being buried alive: she has thrown herself away upon that boor, from sheer ignorance that better individuals existed! A sad pity—I must beware how I cause her to regret her choice."

The last reflection may seem conceited; it was not. My neighbour struck me as bordering on repulsive. I knew, through experience, that I was tolerably attractive.

"Mrs. Heathcliff is my daughter-in-law," said Heathcliff, corroborating my surmise. He turned, as he spoke, a peculiar look in her direction, a look of hatred unless he has a most perverse set of facial muscles that will not, like those of other people, interpret the language of his soul.

"Ah, certainly—I see now; you are the favoured possessor of the beneficent fairy," I remarked, turning to my neighbour.

This was worse than before: the youth grew crimson, and clenched his fist with every appearance of a meditated assault. But he seemed to recollect himself, presently; and smothered the storm in a brutal curse, muttered on my behalf, which, however, I took care not to notice."

"Unhappy in your conjectures, sir!" observed my host; "we neither of us have the privilege of owning your good fairy; her mate is dead. I said she was my daughter-in-law, therefore, she must have married my son."

"And this young man is—"

"Not my son, assuredly!"

Heathcliff smiled again, as if it were rather too bold a jest to attribute the paternity of that bear to him.

"My name is Hareton Earnshaw," growled the other; "and I'd counsel you to respect it!"

WUTHERING HEIGHTS 69

"I've shown no disrespect," was my reply, laughing internally at the dignity with which he announced himself.

He fixed his eye on me longer than I cared to return the stare, for fear I might be tempted either to box his ears, or render my hilarity audible. I began to feel unmistakably out of place in that pleasant family circle. The dismal spiritual atmosphere overcame, and more than neutralized the glowing physical comforts round me; and I resolved to be cautious how I ventured under those rafters a third time.

The business of eating being concluded, and no one uttering a word of sociable conversation, I approached a window to examine the weather. A sorrowful sight I saw; dark night coming down prematurely, and sky and hills mingled in one bitter whirl of wind and suffocating snow.

"I don't think it possible for me to get home now, without a guide," I could not help exclaiming. "The roads will be buried already; and, if they were bare, I could scarcely distinguish a foot in advance."

"Hareton, drive those dozen sheep into the barn porch. They'll be covered if left in the fold all night; and put a plank before them," said Heathcliff.

"How must I do?" I continued, with rising irritation.

There was no reply to my question; and, on looking round, I saw only Joseph bringing in a pail of porridge for the dogs; and Mrs. Heathcliff, leaning over the fire, diverting herself with burning a bundle of matches which had fallen from the chimney-piece as she restored the tea-canister to its place.

The former, when he had deposited his burden, took a critical survey of the room; and, in cracked tones, grated out:

"Aw woonder hagh yah can faishion tuh stand thear i' idleness un war, when all on 'em's goan aght! Bud yah're a nowt, and it's noa use talking— yah'll niver mend uh yer ill ways; bud, goa raight tuh t' divil, like yer mother afore ye!"

I imagined, for a moment, that this piece of eloquence was addressed to me; and, sufficiently enraged, stepped towards the aged rascal with an intention of kicking him out of the door.

Mrs. Heathcliff, however, checked me by her answer.

"You scandalous old hypocrite!" she replied. "Are you not afraid of being carried away bodily, whenever you mention the devil's name? I warn you to refrain from provoking me, or I'll ask your abduction as a special favour. Stop, look here, Joseph," she continued, taking a long, dark book from a shelf. "I'll show you how far I've progressed in the Black Art—I shall soon be competent to make a clear house of it. The red cow didn't die by chance; and your rheumatism can hardly be reckoned among providential visitations!"

"Oh, wicked, wicked!" gasped the elder, "may the Lord deliver us from evil!"

"No, reprobate! you are a castaway—be off, or I'll hurt you seriously! I'll have you all modlled in wax and clay; and the first who passes the limits, I fix,

70   EMILY BRONTË

shall—I'll not say what he shall be done to—but, you'll see! Go, I'm looking at you!"

The little witch put a mock malignity into her beautiful eyes, and Joseph, trembling with sincere horror, hurried out praying and ejaculating "wicked" as he went.

I thought her conduct must be prompted by a species of dreary fun; and, now that we were alone, I endeavoured to interest her in my distress.

"Mrs. Heathcliff," I said, earnestly, "you must excuse me for troubling you—I presume, because, with that face, I'm sure you cannot help being good-hearted. Do point out some landmarks by which I may know my way home—I have no more idea how to get there than you would have how to get to London!"

"Take the road you came," she answered, ensconcing herself in a chair, with a candle, and the long book open before her. "It is brief advice; but, as sound as I can give."

"Then, if you hear of me being discovered dead in a bog, or a pit full of snow, your conscience wont whisper that it is partly your fault?"

"How so? I cannot escort you. They wouldn't let me go to the end of the garden-wall."

"*You*! I should be sorry to ask you to cross the threshold, for my convenience, on such a night," I cried. "I want you to *tell* me my way, not to *show* it; or else to persuade Mr. Heathcliff to give me a guide."

"Who? There is himself, Earnshaw, Zillah, Joseph, and I. Which would you have?"

"Are there no boys at the farm?"

"No, those are all."

"Then, it follows that I am compelled to stay."

"That you may settle with your host. I have nothing to do with it."

"I hope it will be a lesson to you, to make no more rash journeys on these hills," cried Heathcliff's stern voice from the kitchen entrance. "As to staying here, I don't keep accommodations for visiters; you must share a bed with Hareton, or Joseph, if you do."

"I can sleep on a chair in this room," I replied.

"No, no! A stranger is a stranger, be he rich or poor—it will not suit me to permit any one the range of the place while I am off guard!" said the unmannerly wretch.

With this insult my patience was at an end. I uttered an expression of disgust, and pushed past him into the yard, running against Earnshaw in my haste. It was so dark that I could not see the means of exit, and, as I wandered round, I heard another specimen of their civil behaviour amongst each other.

At first, the young man appeared about to befriend me.

"I'll go with him as far as the park," he said.

"You'll go with him to hell!" exclaimed his master, or whatever relation he bore. "And who is to look after the horses, eh?"

WUTHERING HEIGHTS

"A man's life is of more consequence than one evening's neglect of the horses; somebody must go," murmured Mrs. Heathcliff, more kindly than I expected.

"Not at your command!" retorted Hareton.

"If you set store on him, you'd better be quiet."

"Then I hope his ghost will haunt you; and I hope Mr. Heathcliff will never get another tenant, till the Grange is a ruin!" she answered sharply.

"Hearken, hearken, shoo's cursing on em!" muttered Joseph, towards whom I had been steering.

He sat within earshot, milking the cows, by the aid of a lantern which I seized unceremoniously, and calling out that I would send it back on the morrow, rushed to the nearest postern.

"Maister, maister, he's staling t' lantern!" shouted the ancient, pursuing my retreat. "Hey, Gnasher! Hey, dog! Hey, wolf, holld him, holld him!"

On opening the little door, two hairy monsters flew at my throat, bearing me down, and extinguishing the light, while a mingled guffaw, from Heathcliff and Hareton, put the copestone on my rage and humiliation.

Fortunately, the beasts seemed more bent on stretching their paws, and yawning, and flourishing their tails, than devouring me alive; but, they would suffer no resurrection, and I was forced to lie till their malignant masters pleased to deliver me: then hatless, and trembling with wrath, I ordered the miscreants to let me out—on their peril to keep me one minute longer—with several incoherent threats of retaliation, that in their indefinite depth of virulency, smacked of King Lear.

The vehemence of my agitation brought on a copious bleeding at the nose, and still Heathcliff laughed, and still I scolded. I don't know what would have concluded the scene had there not been one person at hand rather more rational than myself, and more benevolent than my entertainer. This was Zillah, the stout housewife; who at length issued forth to inquire into the nature of the uproar. She thought that some of them had been laying violent hands on me; and, not daring to attack her master, she turned her vocal artillery against the younger scoundrel.

"Well, Mr. Earnshaw," she cried, "I wonder what you'll have agait next! Are we going to murder folk on our very door-stones? I see this house will never do for me—look at t' poor lad, he's fair choking! Wisht, wisht! you mun'n't go on so—come in, and I'll cure that. There now, hold ye still."

With these words she suddenly splashed a pint of icy water down my neck, and pulled me into the kitchen. Mr. Heathcliff followed, his accidental merriment expiring quickly in his habitual moroseness.

I was sick exceedingly, and dizzy and faint; and thus compelled, perforce, to accept lodgings under his roof. He told Zillah to give me a glass of brandy, and then passed on to the inner room, while she condoled with me on my sorry predicament, and having obeyed his orders, whereby I was somewhat revived, ushered me to bed.

Chapter III.

While leading the way up-stairs, she recommended that I should hide the candle, and not make a noise, for her master had an odd notion about the chamber she would put me in; and never let anybody lodge there willingly.

I asked the reason.

She did not know, she answered; she had only lived there a year or two; and they had so many queer goings on, she could not begin to be curious.

Too stupified to be curious myself, I fastened my door and glanced round for the bed. The whole furniture consisted of a chair, a clothes-press, and a large oak case, with squares cut out near the top, resembling coach windows.

Having approached this structure, I looked inside, and perceived it to be a singular sort of old-fashioned couch, very conveniently designed to obviate the necessity for every member of the family having a room to himself. In fact, it formed a little closet, and the ledge of a window, which it enclosed, served as a table.

I slid back the panelled sides, got in with my light, pulled them together again, and felt secure against the vigilance of Heathcliff, and every one else.

The ledge, where I placed my candle, had a few mildewed books piled up in one corner; and it was covered with writing scratched on the paint. This writing, however, was nothing but a name repeated in all kinds of characters, large and small—*Catherine Earnshaw*; here and there varied to *Catherine Heathcliff*, and then again to *Catherine Linton*."

In vapid listlessness I leant my head against the window, and continued spelling over Catherine Earnshaw—Heathcliff—Linton, till my eyes closed; but they had not rested five minutes when a glare of white letters started from the dark, as vivid as spectres—the air swarmed with Catherines; and rousing myself to dispel the obtrusive name, I discovered my candle wick reclining on one of the antique volumes, and perfuming the place with an odour of roasted calf-skin.

I snuffed it off, and, very ill at ease, under the influence of cold and lingering nausea, sat up, and spread open the injured tome on my knee. It was a Testament, in lean type, and smelling dreadfully musty: a fly-leaf bore the inscription—"Catherine Earnshaw, her book," and a date some quarter of a century back.

I shut it, and took up another, and another, till I had examined all. Catherine's library was select; and its state of dilapidation proved it to have been well used, though not altogether for a legitimate purpose; scarcely one chapter had escaped a pen and ink commentary, at least, the appearance of one, covering every morsel of blank that the printer had left.

WUTHERING HEIGHTS

Some were detached sentences; other parts took the form of a regular diary, scrawled in an unformed, childish hand. At the top of an extra page, quite a treasure probably when first lighted on, I was greatly amused to behold an excellent caricature of my friend Joseph, rudely yet powerfully sketched.

An immediate interest kindled within me for the unknown Catherine, and I began, forthwith, to decypher her faded hieroglyphics.

"An awful Sunday!" commenced the paragraph beneath. "I wish my father were back again. Hindley is a detestable substitute—his conduct to Heathcliff is atrocious—H. and I are going to rebel—we took our initiatory step this evening.

"All day had been flooding with rain; we could not go to church, so Joseph must needs get up a congregation in the garret; and, while Hindley and his wife basked down stairs before a comfortable fire, doing anything but reading their bibles, I'll answer for it; Heathcliff, myself, and the unhappy plough-boy, were commanded to take our Prayer-books, and mount—we were ranged in a row, on a sack of corn, groaning and shivering, and hoping that Joseph would shiver too, so that he might give us a short homily for his own sake. A vain idea! The service lasted precisely three hours; and yet my brother had the face to exclaim, when he saw us descending,

"'What, done already?'

"On Sunday evenings we used to be permitted to play, if we did not make much noise; now a mere titter is sufficient to send us into corners!

"'You forget you have a master here,' says the tyrant. 'I'll demolish the first who puts me out of temper! I insist on perfect sobriety and silence. Oh, boy! was that you? Frances, darling, pull his hair as you go by; I heard him snap his fingers.

"Frances pulled his hair heartily; and then went and seated herself on her husband's knee, and there they were, like two babies, kissing and talking non-sense by the hour—foolish palaver that we should be ashamed of.

"We made ourselves as snug as our means allowed in the arch of the dresser. I had just fastened our pinafores together, and hung them up for a curtain; when in comes Joseph, on an errand from the stables. He tears down my handywork, boxes my ears, and croaks:

"'T' maister nobbut just buried, and Sabbath nut oe'red, und t' sabnd, uh't gospel still i' yer lugs, and yah darr be laiking! shame on ye! sit ye dahn, ill chllder! they's good books eneugh if ye'll read 'em; sit ye dahn, and think uh yer sowls!'"

Saying this, he compelled us so to square our positions that we might receive, from the far-off fire, a dull ray to show us the text of the lumber he thrust upon us.

"I could not bear the employment. I took my dingy volume by the scroop, and hurled it into the dog-kennel, vowing I hated a good book.

"Heathcliff kicked his to the same place.

74 EMILY BRONTË

"Then there was a hubbub!

"'Maister Hindley!' shouted our chaplain. 'Maister, coom hither! Miss Cathy's riven th' back off 'Th' Helmet uh Salvation,' un' Heathcliff's pawsed his fit intuh t' first part uh 'T' Brooad Way to Destruction!' It's fair flaysome ut yah let 'em goa on this gait. Ech! th' owd man ud uh laced 'em properly—bud he's goan!'

"Hindley hurried up from his paradise on the hearth, and seizing one of us by the collar, and the other by the arm, hurled both into the back-kitchen; where, Joseph asseverated, "owd Nick" would fetch us as sure as we were living; and, so comforted, we each sought a separate nook to await his advent.

"I reached this book, and a pot of ink from a shelf, and pushed the house-door ajar to give me light, and I have got the time on with writing for twenty minutes; but my companion is impatient and proposes that we should appropriate the dairy woman's cloak, and have a scamper on the moors, under its shelter. A pleasant suggestion—and then, if the surly old man come in, he may believe his prophesy verified—we cannot be damper, or colder, in the rain than we are here."

* * * * *

I suppose Catherine fulfilled her project, for the next sentence took up another subject; she waxed lachrymose.

"How little did I dream that Hindley would ever make me cry so!" she wrote. "My head aches, till I cannot keep it on the pillow; and still I can't give over. Poor Heathcliff! Hindley calls him a vagabond, and wont let him sit with us, nor eat with us any more; and, he says, he and I must not play together, and threatens to turn him out of the house if we break his orders.

"He has been blaming our father (how dared he?) for treating H. too liberally; and swears he will reduce him to his right place—"

* * * * *

I began to nod drowsily over the dim page; my eye wandered from manuscript to print. I saw a red ornamented title . . . "Seventy Times Seven, and the First of the Seventy First. A Pious Discourse delivered by the Reverend Jabes Branderham, in the Chapel of Gimmerden Sough."

And while I was, half consciously, worrying my brain to guess what Jabes Branderham would make of his subject, I sank back in bed, and fell asleep.

Alas, for the effects of bad tea and bad temper! what else could it be that made me pass such a terrible night? I don't remember another that I can at all compare with it since I was capable of suffering.

I began to dream, almost before I ceased to be sensible of my locality. I thought it was morning; and I had set out on my way home, with Joseph for a guide. The snow lay yards deep in our road; and, as we floundered on, my companion wearied me with constant reproaches that I had not brought a pilgrim's staff: telling me I could never get into the house without one, and

WUTHERING HEIGHTS

75

boastfully flourishing a heavy-headed cudgel, which I understood to be so denominated.

For a moment I considered it absurd that I should need such a weapon to gain admittance into my own residence. Then, a new idea flashed across me. I was not going there; we were journeying to hear the famous Jabes Branderham preach from the text—"Seventy Times Seven;" and either Joseph, the preacher, or I had committed the "First of the Seventy First," and were to be publicly exposed and excommunicated.

We came to the chapel—I have passed it really in my walks, twice or thrice: it lies in a hollow, between two hills—an elevated hollow—near a swamp, whose peaty moisture is said to answer all the purposes of embalming on the few corpses deposited there. The roof has been kept whole hitherto, but, as the clergyman's stipend is only twenty pounds per annum, and a house with two rooms, threatening speedily to determine into one, no clergyman will undertake the duties of pastor, especially, as it is currently reported that his flock would rather let him starve than increase the living by one penny from their own pockets. However, in my dream, Jabes had a full and attentive con- gregation: and he preached—good God—what a sermon! Divided into *four hundred and ninety* parts—each fully equal to an ordinary address from the pulpit—and each discussing a separate sin! Where he searched for them, I cannot tell; he had his private manner of interpreting the phrase, and it seemed necessary the brother should sin different sins on every occasion.

They were of the most curious character—odd trangressions that I never imagined previously.

Oh, how weary I grew. How I writhed, and yawned, and nodded, and revived! How I pinched and pricked myself, and rubbed my eyes, and stood up, and sat down again, and nudged Joseph to inform me if he would *ever* have done!"

I was condemned to hear all out—finally, he reached the "*First of the Seventy-First*." At that crisis, a sudden inspiration descended on me; I was moved to rise and denounce Jabes Branderham as the sinner of the sin that no christian need pardon.

"Sir," I exclaimed, "sitting here, within these four walls, at one stretch, I have endured and forgiven the four hundred and ninety heads of your dis- course. Seventy times seven times have I plucked up my hat, and been about to depart—Seventy times seven times have you preposterously forced me to resume my seat. The four hundred and ninety-first is too much. Fellow mar- tyrs, have at him! Drag him down, and crush him to atoms, that the place which knows him may know him no more!"

"*Thou art the Man!*" cried Jabes, after a solemn pause, leaning over his cushion. "Seventy times seven times didst thou gapingly contort thy visage— seventy times seven did I take counsel with my soul—Lo, this is human weak- ness; this also may be absolved! The First of the Seventy-First is come.

76   EMILY BRONTË

Brethren, execute upon him the judgment written! such honour have all His saints!"

With that concluding word, the whole assembly, exalting their pilgrim's staves, rushed round me in a body, and I, having no weapon to raise in self-defence, commenced grappling with Joseph, my nearest and most ferocious assailant, for his. In the confluence of the multitude, several clubs crossed; blows, aimed at me, fell on other sconces. Presently the whole chapel resounded with rappings and counter-rappings. Every man's hand was against his neighbour; and Branderham, unwilling to remain idle, poured forth his zeal in a shower of loud taps on the boards of the pulpit which responded so smartly, that, at last, to my unspeakable relief, they woke me.

And what was it that had suggested the tremendous tumult, what had played Jabes' part in the row? Merely, the branch of a fir-tree that touched my lattice, as the blast wailed by, and rattled its dry cones against the panes!

I listened doubtingly an instant; detected the disturber, then turned and dosed, and dreamt again; if possible, still more disagreebly than before.

This time, I remembered I was lying in the oak closet, and I heard distinctly the gusty wind, and the driving of the snow; I heard also, the firbough repeat its teasing sound, and ascribed it to the right cause: but, it annoyed me so much, that I resolved to silence it, if possible; and, I thought, I rose and endeavoured to unhasp the casement. The hook was soldered into the staple, a circumstance observed by me, when awake, but forgotten.

"I must stop it, nevertheless!" I muttered, knocking my knuckles through the glass, and stretching an arm out to seize the importunate branch: instead of which, my fingers closed on the fingers of a little, ice-cold hand!

The intense horror of nightmare came over me; I tried to draw back my arm, but, the hand clung to it, and a most melancholy voice, sobbed, "Let me in—let me in!"

"Who are you?" I asked struggling, meanwhile, to disengage myself.

"Catherine Linton," it replied, shiveringly, (why did I think of *Linton*? I had read *Earnshaw*, twenty times for Linton) "I'm come home, I'd lost my way on the moor!"

As it spoke, I discerned, obscurely, a child's face looking through the window—Terror made me cruel; and, finding it useless to attempt shaking the creature off, I pulled its wrist on to the broken pane, and rubbed it to and fro till the blood ran down and soaked the bed-clothes: still it wailed, "Let me in!" and maintained its tenacious gripe, almost maddening me with fear.

"How can I?" I said at length. "Let *me* go, if you want me to let you in!"

The fingers relaxed, I snatched mine through the hole, hurriedly piled the books up in a pyramid against it, and stopped my ears to exclude the lamentable prayer.

I seemed to keep them closed above a quarter of an hour, yet, the instant I listened, again, there was the doleful cry moaning on!

WUTHERING HEIGHTS

"Begone!" I shouted, "I'll never let you in, not if you beg for twenty years!"

"It's twenty years," mourned the voice, "twenty years, I've been a waif for twenty years!"

Thereat began a feeble scratching outside, and the pile of books moved as if thrust forward.

I tried to jump up; but, could not stir a limb; and so, yelled aloud, in a frenzy of fright.

To my confusion, I discovered the yell was not ideal. Hasty footsteps approached my chamber door: somebody pushed it open, with a vigorous hand, and a light glimmered through the squares at the top of the bed. I sat shuddering, yet, and wiping the perspiration from my forehead: the intruder appeared to hesitate and muttered to himself.

At last, he said in a half-whisper, plainly not expecting an answer,

"Is any one here?"

I considered it best to confess my presence, for I knew Heathcliff's accents, and feared he might search further, if I kept quiet.

With this intention, I turned and opened the panels—I shall not soon forget the effect my action produced.

Heathcliff stood near the entrance, in his shirt and trousers; with a candle dripping over his fingers, and his face as white as the wall behind him. The first creak of the oak startled him like an electric shock: the light leaped from his hold to a distance of some feet, and his agitation was so extreme, that he could hardly pick it up.

"It is only your guest, sir," I called out, desirous to spare him the humiliation of exposing his cowardice further. "I had the misfortune to scream in my sleep, owing to a frightful nightmare. I'm sorry I disturbed you."

"Oh, God confound you, Mr. Lockwood! I wish you were at the—" commenced my host setting the candle on a chair, because he found it impossible to hold it steady.

"And who showed you up to this room?" he continued, crushing his nails into his palms, and grinding his teeth to subdue the maxillary convulsions. "Who was it? I've a good mind to turn them out of the house, this moment!"

"It was your servant, Zillah," I replied flinging myself, on to the floor, and rapidly resuming my garments. "I should not care if you did, Mr. Heathcliff; she richly deserves it. I suppose that she wanted to get another proof that the place was haunted, at my expense—Well, it is—swarming with ghosts and goblins! You have reason in shutting it up, I assure you. No one will thank you for a dose in such a den!"

"What do you mean?" asked Heathcliff, "and what are you doing? Lie down and finish out the night, since you *are* here; but, for Heaven's sake! don't repeat that horrid noise—Nothing could excuse it, unless you were having your throat cut!"

EMILY BRONTË

"If the little fiend had got in at the window, she probably would have strangled me!" I returned. "I'm not going to endure the persecutions of your hospitable ancestors, again—Was not the Reverend Jabes Branderham akin to you on the mother's side? And that minx, Catherine Linton, or Earnshaw, or however she was called—she must have been a changling—wicked little soul! She told me she had been walking the earth these twenty years: a just punishment for her mortal transgressions, I've no doubt!"

Scarcely were these words uttered, when I recollected the association of Heathcliff's with Catherine's name in the book, which had completely slipped from my memory till thus awakened. I blushed at my inconsideration; but without showing further consciousness of the offence, I hastened to add,

"The truth is, sir, I passed the first part of the night in—" Here, I stopped afresh—I was about to say "perusing those old volumes," then it would have revealed my knowledge of their written, as well as their printed contents; so correcting myself, I went on,

"In spelling over the name scratched on that window-ledge. A monotonous occupation, calculated to set me asleep, like counting, or—"

"What *can* you mean, by talking in this way to *me*!" thundered Heathcliff with savage vehemence. "How—how *dare* you, under my roof—God! he's mad to speak so!" And he struck his forehead with rage.

I did not know whether to resent this language, or pursue my explanation; but he seemed so powerfully affected that I took pity and proceeded with my dreams; affirming I had never heard the appellation of "Catherine Linton," before, but, reading it often over produced an impression which personified itself when I had no longer my imagination under control.

Heathcliff gradually fell back into the shelter of the bed, as I spoke, finally, sitting down almost concealed behind it. I guessed, however, by his irregular and intercepted breathing, that he struggled to vanquish an access of violent emotion.

Not liking to show him that I heard the conflict, I continued my toilette rather noisily, looked at my watch, and soliloquised on the length of the night:

"Not three o'clock, yet! I could have taken oath it had been six—time stagnates here—we must surely have retired to rest at eight!"

"Always at nine in winter, and always rise at four," said my host, suppressing a groan; and, as I fancied, by the motion of his shadow's arm, dashing a tear from his eyes.

"Mr Lockwood," he added, "you may go into my room; you'll only be in the way, coming down stairs so early: and your childish outcry has sent sleep to the devil for me."

"And for me too," I replied. "I'll walk in the yard till daylight, and then I'll be off; and you need not dread a repetition of my intrusion. I am now quite cured of seeking pleasure in society, be it country or town. A sensible man ought to find sufficient company in himself."

"Delightful company!" muttered Heathcliff. "Take the candle, and go where you please. I shall join you directly. Keep out of the yard though the dogs are unchained; and the house—Juno mounts sentinel there—and—nay, you can only ramble about the steps and passages—but, away with you! I'll come in two minutes."

I obeyed, so far as to quit the chamber; when, ignorant where the narrow lobbies led, I stood still, and was witness, involuntarily, to a piece of superstition on the part of my landlord, which belied, oddly, his apparent sense.

He got on to the bed, and wrenched open the lattice, bursting, as he pulled at it, into an uncontrollable passion of tears.

"Come in! come in!" he sobbed. "Cathy, do come. Oh do—*once* more! Oh! my heart's darling, hear me *this* time—Catherine, at last!"

The spectre showed a spectre's ordinary caprice; it gave no sign of being; but the snow and wind whirled wildly through, even reaching my station, and blowing out the light.

There was such anguish in the gush of grief that accompanied this raving, that my compassion made me overlook its folly, and I drew off, half angry to have listened at all, and vexed at having related my ridiculous nightmare, since it produced that agony; though *why*, was beyond my comprehension.

I descended cautiously to the lower regions and landed in the back-kitchen, where a gleam of fire, raked compactly together, enabled me to rekindle my candle.

Nothing was stirring except a brindled, grey cat, which crept from the ashes, and saluted me with a querulous mew.

Two benches, shaped in sections of a circle, nearly enclosed the hearth; on one of these I stretched myself, and Grimalkin mounted the other. We were both of us nodding, ere any one invaded our retreat; and then it was Joseph shuffling down a wooden ladder that vanished in the roof, through a trap, the assent to his garret, I suppose.

He cast a sinister look at the little flame which I had enticed to play between the ribs, swept the cat from its elevation, and bestowing himself In the vacancy, commenced the operation of stuffing a three-inch pipe with tobacco; my presence in his sanctum was evidently esteemed a piece of impudence too shameful for remark. He silently applied the tube to his lips, folded his arms, and puffed away.

I let him enjoy the luxury, unannoyed; and after sucking out the last wreath, and heaving a profound sigh, he got up, and departed as solemnly as he came.

A more elastic footstep entered next, and now I opened my mouth for a "good morning," but closed it again, the salutation unachieved; for Hareton Earnshaw was performing his orisons, *sotto voce*, in a series of curses directed against every object he touched, while he rummaged a corner, for a spade or shovel to dig through the drifts. He glanced over the back of the bench

EMILY BRONTË

dilating his nostrils, and thought as little of exchanging civilities with me, as with my companion, the cat.

I guessed by his preparations that egress was allowed, and leaving my hard couch, made a movement to follow him. He noticed this, and thrust at an inner door with the end of his spade, intimating by an inarticulate sound, that there was the place where I must go, if I changed my locality.

It opened into the house, where the females were already astir. Zillah urging flakes of flame up the chimney with a colossal bellows; and Mrs. Heathcliff, kneeling on the hearth, reading a book by the aid of the blaze.

She held her hand interposed between the furnace-heat and her eyes; and seemed absorbed in her occupation: desisting from it only to chide the servant for covering her with sparks, or to push away a dog, now and then, that snoozled its nose over forwardly into her face.

I was surprised to see Heathcliff there also. He stood by the fire, his back towards me, just finishing a stormy scene to poor Zillah, who ever and anon interrupted her labour to pluck up the corner of her apron, and heave an indignant groan.

"And you, you worthless—" he broke out as I entered, turning to his daughter-in-law, and employing an epithet as harmless as duck, or sheep, but generally represented by a dash.

"There you are at your idle tricks again! The rest of them do earn their bread—you live on my charity! Put your trash away, and find something to do. You shall pay me for the plague of having you eternally in my sight—do you hear, damnable jade?"

"I'll put my trash away, because you can make me, if I refuse," answered the young lady, closing her book, and throwing it on a chair. "But I'll not do anything, though you should swear your tongue out, except what I please!"

Heathcliff lifted his hand, and the speaker sprang to a safer distance, obviously acquainted with its weight.

Having no desire to be entertained by a cat and dog combat, I stepped forward briskly, as if eager to partake the warmth of the hearth, and innocent of any knowledge of the interrupted dispute. Each had enough decorum to suspend further hostilities; Heathcliff placed his fists, out of temptation, in his pockets: Mrs. Heathcliff curled her lip, and walked to a seat far off; where she kept her word by playing the part of a statue during the remainder of my stay.

That was not long. I declined joining their breakfast, and, at the first gleam of dawn, took an opportunity of escaping into the free air, now clear, and still, and cold as impalpable ice.

My landlord hallooed for me to stop ere I reached the bottom of the garden, and offered to accompany me across the moor. It was well he did, for the whole hill-back was one billowy, white ocean; the swells and falls not indicating corresponding rises and depressions in the ground—many pits, at least,

WUTHERING HEIGHTS

were filled to a level; and entire ranges of mounds, the refuse of the quarries, blotted from the chart which my yesterday's walk left pictured in my mind.

I had remarked on one side of the road, at intervals of six or seven yards, a line of upright stones, continued through the whole length of the barren: these were erected, and daubed with lime, on purpose to serve as guides in the dark, and also, when a fall, like the present, confounded the deep swamps on either hand with the firmer path: but, excepting a dirty dot pointing up, here and there, all traces of their existence had vanished; and my companion found it necessary to warn me frequently to steer to the right, or left, when I imagined I was following, correctly, the windings of the road.

We exchanged little conversation, and he halted at the entrance of Thrushcross park, saying, I could make no error there. Our adieux were limited to a hasty bow, and then I pushed forward, trusting to my own resources, for the porter's lodge is untenanted as yet.

The distance from the gate to the Grange is to miles: I believe I managed to make it four; what with losing myself among the trees, and sinking up to the neck in snow, a predicament which only those who have experienced it can appreciate. At any rate, whatever were my wanderings, the clock chimed twelve as I entered the house; and that gave exactly an hour for every mile of the usual way from Wuthering Heights.

My human fixture, and her satellites rushed to welcome me; exclaiming, tumultuously, they had completely given me up; everybody conjectured that I perished last night; and they were wondering how they must set about the search for my remains.

I bid them be quiet, now that they saw me returned, and, benumbed to my very heart, I dragged up-stairs, whence, after putting on dry clothes, and pacing to and fro, thirty or forty minutes, to restore the animal heat, I am adjourned to my study, feeble as a kitten, almost too much so to enjoy the cheerful fire, and smoking coffee which the servant has prepared for my refreshment.

Chapter IV.

What vain weather-cocks we are! I, who had determined to held myself independent of all social intercourse, and thanked my stars that, at length, I had lighted on a spot where it was next to impracticable. I, weak wretch, after maintaining till dusk a struggle with low spirits, and solitude, was finally compelled to strike my colours; and, under pretence of gaining information concerning the necessities of my establishment, I desired Mrs. Dean, when she brought in supper, to sit down while I ate it, hoping sincerely she would prove a regular gossip, and either rouse me to animation, or lull me to sleep by her talk.

"You have lived here a considerable time," I commenced; "did you not say sixteen years?"

"Eighteen, sir; I came, when the mistress was married, to wait on her; after she died, the master retained me for his house-keeper."

"Indeed."

There ensued a pause. She was not a gossip, I feared, unless about her own affairs, and those could hardly interest me.

However, having studied for an interval, with a fist on either knee, and a cloud of meditation over her ruddy countenance, she ejaculated—

"Ah, times are greatly changed since then!"

"Yes," I remarked, "you've seen a good many alterations, I suppose?"

"I have: and troubles too," she said.

"Oh, I'll turn the talk on my landlord's family!" I thought to myself. "A good subject to start—and that pretty girl—widow, I should like to know her history; whether she be a native of the country, or, as is more probable, an exotic that the surly indigenae will not recognise for kin."

With this intention I asked Mrs. Dean why Heathcliff let Thrushcross Grange, and preferred living in a situation and residence so much inferior.

"Is he not rich enough to keep the estate in good order?" I enquired.

"Rich sir!" she returned. "He has, nobody knows what money, and every year it increases. Yes, yes, he's rich enough to live in a finer house than this; but he's very near—close-handed; and, if he had meant to flit to Thrushcross Grange, as soon as he heard of a good tenant, he could not have borne to miss the chance of getting a few hundreds more. It is strange people should be so greedy, when they are alone in the world!"

"He had a son, it seems?"

"Yes, he had one—he is dead."

"And that young lady, Mrs. Heathcliff, is his widow?"

"Yes."

"Where did she come from originally?"

"Why, sir, she is my late master's daughter; Catherine Linton was her maiden name. I nursed her, poor thing! I did wish Mr. Heathcliff would remove here, and then we might have been together again."

"What, Catherine Linton!" I exclaimed, astonished. But a minute's reflection convinced me it was not my ghostly Catherine. "Then," I continued, "my predecessor's name was Linton?"

"It was."

"And who is that Earnshaw, Hareton Earnshaw, who lives with Mr. Heathcliff? are they relations?"

"No; he is the late Mrs. Linton's nephew."

"The young lady's cousin then?"

"Yes; and her husband was her cousin also—one, on the mother's—the other, on the father's side—Heathcliff married Mr. Linton's sister."

"I see the house at Wuthering Heights has 'Earnshaw' carved over the front door. Are they an old family?"

"Very old, sir; and Hareton is the last of them, as our Miss Cathy is of us—I mean, of the Lintons. Have you been to Wuthering Heights? I beg pardon for asking; but I should like to hear how she is!"

"Mrs. Heathcliff? she looked very well, and very handsome; yet, I think, not very happy."

"Oh dear, I don't wonder!" And how did you like the master?"

"A rough fellow, rather, Mrs. Dean. Is not that his character?"

"Rough as a saw-edge, and hard as whinstone! The less you meddle with him the better."

"He must have had some ups and downs in life to make him such a churl. Do you know anything of his history?"

"It's a cuckoo's; sir—I know all about it; except where he was born, and who were his parents, and how he got his money, at first—And Hareton has been cast out like an unfledged dunnock—The unfortunate lad is the only one, in all this parish, that does not guess how he has been cheated!"

"Well, Mrs. Dean, it will be a charitable deed to tell me something of my neighbours—I feel I shall not rest, if I go to bed; so, be good enough to sit, and chat an hour."

"Oh, certainly, sir! I'll just fetch a little sewing, and then I'll sit as long as you please but you've caught cold, I saw you shivering, and you must have some gruel to drive it out."

The worthy woman bustled off; and I crouched nearer the fire: my head felt hot, and the rest of me chill: moreover I was excited, almost to a pitch of foolishness through my nerves and brain. This caused me to feel, not uncomfortable, but rather fearful, as I am still, of serious effects from the incidents of today and yesterday.

84   EMILY BRONTË

She returned presently, bringing a smoking basin, and a basket of work; and, having placed the former on the hob, drew in her seat, evidently pleased to find me so companionable.

"Before I came to live here," she commenced, waiting no further invitation to her story; "I was almost always at Wuthering Heights; because, my mother had nursed Mr. Hindley Earnshaw, that was Hareton's father, and I got used to playing with the children—I ran errands too, and helped to make hay, and hung about the farm ready for anything that anybody would set me to.

"One fine summer morning—it was the beginning of harvest, I remember—Mr. Earnshaw, the old master, came down stairs, dressed for a journey; and, after he had told Joseph what was to be done during the day, he turned to Hindley, and Cathy, and me—for I sat eating my porridge, with them, and he said, speaking to his son,

"Now my bonny man, I'm going to Liverpool, to-day . . . What shall I bring you? You may choose what you like; only let it be little, for I shall walk there and back; sixty miles each way, that is a long spell!"

Hindley named a fiddle, and then he asked Miss Cathy; she was hardly six years old, but she could ride any horse in the stable, and she chose a whip.

He did not forget me, for, he had a kind heart, though he was rather severe, sometimes. He promised to bring me a pocketful of apples, and pears, and then he kissed his children, good bye, and set off.

It seemed a long while to us all—the three days of his absence—and often did little Cathy ask when he would be home: Mrs. Earnshaw, expected him by supper-time, on the third evening; and she put the meal off hour after hour; there were no signs of his coming, however, and at last the children got tired of running down to the gate to look—Then it grew dark, she would have had them to bed, but they begged sadly to be allowed to stay up: and, just about eleven o'clock, the door-latch was raised quietly and in stept the master. He threw himself into a chair, laughing and groaning, and bid them all stand off, for he was nearly killed—he would not have such another walk for the three kingdoms.

"And at the end of it, to be flighted to death!" he said opening his great coat, which he held bundled up in his arms, "See here, wife; I was never so beaten with anything in my life; but you must e'en take it as a gift of God; though it's as dark almost as if it came from the devil."

We crowded round, and, over Miss Cathy's head, I had a peep at a dirty, ragged, black-haired child; big enough both to walk and talk—indeed, its face looked older than Catherine's—yet, when it was set on its feet, it only stared round, and repeated over and over again, some gibberish that nobody could understand. I was frightened, and Mrs. Earnshaw was ready to fling it out of doors: she did fly up—asking how he could fashion to bring that gipsy brat into the house, when they had their own bairns to feed, and fend for? What he meant to do with it, and whether he were mad?

WUTHERING HEIGHTS 85

The master tried to explain the matter; but, he was really half dead with fatigue, and all that I could make out, amongst her scolding, was a tale of his seeing it starving, and houseless, and as good as dumb in the streets of Liverpool where he picked it up and inquired for its owner—Not a soul knew to whom it belonged, he said, and his money and time, being both limited, he thought it better, to take it home with him, at once, than run, into vain expences there; because he was determined he would not leave as he found it.

Well, the conclusion was that my mistress grumbled herself calm; and Mr Earnshaw told me to wash it, and give it clean things, and let it sleep with the children.

Hindley and Cathy contented themselves with looking and listening till peace was restored: then, both began searching their father's pockets for the presents he had promised them. The former was a boy of fourteen, but when he drew out, what had been a fiddle crushed to morsels in the great coat, he blubbered aloud, and Cathy, when she learnt the master had lost her whip in attending on the stranger, showed her humour by grinning and spitting at the stupid little thing, earning for her pains, a sound blow from her father to teach her cleaner manners.

They entirely refused to have it in bed with them, or even in their room, and I had no more sense, so, I put it on the landing of the stairs, hoping it might be gone on the morrow. By chance, or else attracted by hearing his voice, it crept to Mr. Earnshaw's door and there he found it on quitting his chamber. Inquiries were made as to how it got there; I was obliged to confess, and in recompense for my cowardice and inhumanity was sent out of the house.

This was Heathcliff's first introduction to the family: on coming back a few days afterwards, for I did not consider my banishment perpetual, I found they had christened him "Heathcliff," it was the name of a son who died in childhood, and it has served him ever since, both for christian and surname.

Miss Cathy and he were now very thick; but Hindley hated him, and to say the truth I did the same; and we plagued and went on with him shamefully, for I was'nt reasonable enough to feel my injustice, and the mistress never put in a word on his behalf, when she saw him wronged.

He seemed a sullen, patient child; hardened, perhaps, to ill-treatment: he would stand Hindley's blows without winking or shedding a tear, and my pinches moved him only to draw in a breath, and open his eyes as if he had hurt himself by accident, and nobody was to blame.

This endurance made old Earnshaw furious when he discovered his son persecuting the poor, fatherless child, as he called him. He took to Heathcliff strangely, believing, all he said, (for that matter, he said precious little, and generally the truth,) and petting him up far above Cathy, who was too mischievous and wayward for a favourite.

So, from the very beginning, he bred bad feeling in the house; and at Mrs Earnshaw's death, which happened in less than two years after, the young

86 EMILY BRONTË

master had learnt to regard his father as an oppressor rather than a friend, and Heathcliff as a usurper of his parent's affections, and his privileges, and he grew bitter with brooding over these injuries.

I sympathised awhile, but, when the children fell ill of the measles and I had to tend them, and take on me the cares of a woman, at once, I changed my ideas. Heathcliff was dangerously sick, and while he lay at the worst he would have me constantly by his pillow; I suppose he felt I did a good deal for him, and he had'nt wit to guess that I was compelled to do it. However, I will say this, he was the quietest child that ever nurse watched over. The difference between him and the others forced me to be less partial: Cathy and her brother harassed me terribly: *he* was as uncomplaining as a lamb; though hardness, not gentleness, made him give little trouble.

He got through, and the doctor affirmed it was in a great measure owing to me, and praised me for my care. I was vain of his commendations, and softened towards the being by whose means, I earned them, and thus Hindley lost his last ally; still I couldn't dote on Heathcliff, and I wondered often what my master saw to admire so much in the sullen boy who never, to my recollection, repaid his indulgence by any sign of gratitude. He was not insolent to his benefactor; he was simply insensible, though knowing perfectly the hold he had on his heart, and conscious he had only to speak and all the house would be obliged to bend to his wishes.

As an instance, I remember Mr. Earnshaw once bought a couple of colts at the parish fair, and gave the lads each one. Heathcliff took the handsomest, but it soon fell lame, and when he discovered it, he said to Hindley,

"You must exchange horses with me; I don't like mine, and, if you won't I shall tell your father of the three thrashings you've given me this week, and show him my arm which is black to the shoulder."

Hindley put out his tongue, and cuffed him over the ears.

"You'd better do it, at once," he persisted escaping to the porch, (they were in the stable) "you will have to, and, if I speak, of these blows, you'll get them again with interest."

"Off dog!" cried Hindley, threatening him with an iron weight, used for weighing potatoes, and hay.

"Throw it," he replied, standing still, "and then I'll tell how you boasted that you would turn me out of doors as soon as he died, and see whether he will not turn you out directly."

Hindley threw it, hitting him on the breast and down he fell but staggered up, immediately, breathless and white, and had not I prevented it he would have gone just so to the master, and got full revenge by letting his condition plead for him, intimating who had caused it."

"Take my colt, gipsy, then!" said young Earnshaw, "And I pray that he may break your neck, take him, and be damned, you beggarly interloper! and

WUTHERING HEIGHTS 87

wheedle my father out of all he has, only, afterwards, show him what you are, imp of Satan—And take that, I hope he'll kick out your brains!"

Heathcliff had gone to loose the beast, and shift it to his own stall—He was passing behind it, when Hindley finished his speech by knocking him under its feet, and without stopping to examine whether his hopes were fulfilled, ran away as fast as he could.

I was surprised to witness how coolly the child gathered himself up, and went on with his intention, exchanging saddles and all; and then sitting down on a bundle of hay to overcome the qualm which the violent blow occasioned, before he entered the house.

I persuaded him easily to let me lay the blame of his bruises on the horse; he minded little what tale was told since he had what he wanted. He complained so seldom, indeed, of such stirs as these, that I really thought him not vindictive—I was deceived, completely, as you will hear.

Chapter V.

In the course of time, Mr. Earnshaw began to fail. He had been active and healthy, yet his strength left him suddenly; and when he was confined to the chimney-corner he grew grievously irritable. A nothing vexed him, and suspected slights of his authority nearly threw him into fits.

This was especially to be remarked if any one attempted to impose upon, or domineer over his favourite; he was painfully jealous lest a word should be spoken amiss to him, seeming to have got into his head the notion that, because he liked Heathcliff, all hated, and longed to do him an ill-turn.

It was a disadvantage to the lad, for the kinder among us did not wish to fret the master, so we humoured his partiality; and that humouring was rich nourishment to the child's pride and black tempers. Still it became in a manner necessary; twice, or thrice, Hindley's manifestations of scorn, while his father was near, roused the old man to a fury. He seized his stick to strike him, and shook with rage that he could not do it.

At last, our curate, (we had a curate then who made the living answer by teaching the little Lintons and Earnshaws, and farming his bit of land himself,) he advised that the young man should be sent to college, and Mr, Earnshaw agreed, though with a heavy spirit, for he said—

"Hindley was naught, and would never thrive as where he wandered."

I hoped heartily we should have peace now. It hurt me to think the master should be made uncomfortable by his own good deed. I fancied the discontent of age and disease arose from his family disagreements, as he would have it that it did—really, you know, sir, it was in his sinking frame.

We might have got on tolerably, notwithstanding; but, for two people. Miss Cathy, and Joseph, the servant; you saw him, I dare say, up yonder. He was, and is yet, most likely, the wearisomest, self-righteous pharisee that ever ransacked a bible to rake the promises to himself, and fling the curses on his neighbours. By his knack of sermonizing and pious discoursing, he contrived to make a great impression on Mr. Earnshaw, and, the more feeble the master became, the more influence he gained.

He was relentless in worrying him about his soul's concerns, and about ruling his children rigidly. He encouraged him to regard Hindley as a reprobate; and, night after night, he regularly grumbled out a long string of tales against Heathcliff and Catherine; always minding to flatter Earnshaw's weakness by heaping the heaviest blame on the last.

Certainly, she had ways with her such as I never saw a child take up before; and she put all of us past our patience fifty times and oftener in a day: from

WUTHERING HEIGHTS 89

the hour she came down stairs, till the hour she went to bed, we had not a minute's security that she wouldn't be in mischief. Her spirits were always at high-water mark, her tongue always going—singing, laughing, and plaguing everybody who would not do the same. A wild, wick slip she was—but, she had the bonniest eye, and sweetest smile, and lightest foot in the parish; and, after all, I believe she meant no harm; for when once she made you cry in good earnest, it seldom happened that she would not keep you company; and oblige you to be quiet that you might comfort her.

She was much too fond of Heathcliff. The greatest punishment we could invent for her was to keep her separate from him: yet, she got chided more than any of us on his account.

In play, she liked, exceedingly, to act the little mistress; using her hands freely, and commanding her companions: she did so to me, but I would not bear slapping, and ordering; and so I let her know.

Now, Mr. Earnshaw did not understand jokes from his children: he had always been strict and grave with them; and Catherine, on her part, had no idea why her father should be crosser and less patient in his ailing condition, than he was in his prime.

His peevish reproofs wakened in her a naughty delight to provoke him; she was never so happy as when we were all scolding her at once, and she defying us with her bold, saucy look, and her ready words; turning Joseph's religious curses into ridicule, baiting me, and doing just what her father hated most, showing how her pretended insolence, which he thought real, had more power over Heathcliff than his kindness. How the boy would do *her* bidding in anything, and *his* only when it suited his own inclination.

After behaving as badly as possible all day, she sometimes came fondling to make it up at night.

"Nay, Cathy," the old man would say, "I cannot love thee; thou'rt worse than thy brother. Go, say thy prayers, child, and ask God's pardon. I doubt thy mother and I must rue that we ever reared thee!"

That made her cry, at first; and then, being repulsed continually hardened her, and she laughed if I told her to say she was sorry for her faults, and beg to be forgiven.

But the hour came, at last, that ended Mr. Earnshaw's troubles on earth. He died quietly in his chair one October evening, seated by the fire-side.

A high wind blustered round the house, and roared in the chimney: it sounded wild and stormy, yet it was not cold, and we were all together—I, a little removed from the hearth, busy at my knitting, and Joseph reading his Bible near the table, (for the servants generally sat in the house then, after their work was done.) Miss Cathy had been sick, and that made her still; she leant against her father's knee, and Heathcliff was lying on the floor with his head in her lap.

I remember the master, before he fell into a doze, stroking her bonny hair—it pleased him rarely to see her gentle—and saying—

EMILY BRONTË

"Why canst thou not always be a good lass, Cathy?"

And she turned her face up to his, and laughed, and answered,

"Why cannot you always be a good man, father?"

But as soon as she saw him vexed again, she kissed his hand, and said she would sing him to sleep. She began singing very low, till his fingers dropped from hers, and his head sank on his breast. Then I told her to hush, and not stir, for fear she should wake him. We all kept as mute as mice a full half-hour, and should have done longer, only Joseph, having finished his chapter, got up and said that he must rouse the master for prayers and bed. He stepped forward, and called him by name, and touched his shoulder, but he would not move—so he took the candle and looked at him.

I thought there was something wrong as he set down the light; and seizing the children each by an arm, whispered them to "frame up-stairs, and make little din—they might pray alone that evening—he had summut to do."

"I shall bid father good-night first," said Catherine, putting her arms round his neck, before we could hinder her.

The poor thing discovered her loss directly—she screamed out—

"Oh, he's dead, Heathcliff! he's dead!"

And they both set up a heart-breaking cry.

I joined my wail to theirs, loud and bitter; but Joseph asked what we could be thinking of to roar in that way over a saint in Heaven.

He told me to put on my cloak and run to Gimmerton for the doctor and the parson. I could not guess the use that either would be of, then. However, I went, through wind and rain, and brought one, the doctor, back with me; the other said he would come in the morning.

Leaving Joseph to explain matters, I ran to the children's room; their door was ajar, I saw they had never laid down, though it was past midnight; but they were calmer, and did not need me to console them. The little souls were comforting each other with better thoughts than I could have hit on; no parson in the world ever pictured Heaven so beautifully as they did, in their innocent talk; and, while I sobbed, and listened, I could not help wishing we were all there safe together.

Chapter VI.

Mr. Hindley came home to the funeral; and—a thing that amazed us, and set the neighbours gossiping right and left—he brought a wife with him.

What she was, and where she was born he never informed us; probably, she had neither money nor name to recommend her, or he would scarcely have kept the union from his father.

She was not one that would have disturbed the house much on her own account. Every object she saw, the moment she crossed the threshold, appeared to delight her; and every circumstance that took place about her, except the preparing for the burial, and the presence of the mourners.

I thought she was half silly from her behaviour while that went on; she ran into her chamber, and made me come with her, though I should have been dressing the children; and there she sat shivering and clasping her hands, and asking repeatedly—

"Are they gone yet?"

Then she began describing with hysterical emotion the effect it produced on her to see black; and started, and trembled, and, at last, fell a weeping—and when I asked what was the matter? answered, she didn't know; but she felt so afraid of dying!

I imagined her as little likely to die as myself. She was rather thin, but young, and fresh complexioned, and her eyes sparkled as bright as diamonds. I did remark, to be sure, that mounting the stairs made her breathe very quick, that the least sudden noise set her all in a quiver, and that she coughed troublesomely sometimes: but, I knew nothing of what these symptoms portended, and had no impulse to sympathize with her. We don't in general take to foreigners here, Mr. Lockwood, unless they take to us first.

Young Earnshaw was altered considerably in the three years of his absence. He had grown sparer, and lost his colour, and spoke and dressed quite differently: and, on the very day of his return, he told Joseph and me we must thenceforth quarter ourselves in the back-kitchen, and leave the house for him. Indeed he would have carpeted and papered a small spare room for a parlour; but his wife expressed such pleasure at the white floor, and huge glowing fire-place, at the pewter dishes, and delf-case, and dog-kennel, and the wide space there was to move about in, where they usually sat, that he thought it unnecessary to her comfort, and so dropped the intention.

She expressed pleasure, too, at finding a sister among her new acquaintance, and she prattled to Catherine, and kissed her, and ran about with her, and gave her quantities of presents, at the beginning. Her affection tired very

EMILY BRONTË

soon, however, and when she grew peevish, Hindley became tyrannical. A few words from her, evincing a dislike to Heathcliff, were enough to rouse in him all his old hatred of the boy. He drove him from their company to the servants, deprived him of the instructions of the curate, and insisted that he should labour out of doors instead, compelling him to do so, as hard as any other lad on the farm.

He bore his degradation pretty well at first, because Cathy taught him what she learnt, and worked or played with him in the fields. They both promised fair to grow up as rude as savages, the young master being entirely negligent how they behaved, and what they did, so they kept clear of him. He would not even have seen after their going to church on Sundays, only Joseph and the curate reprimanded his carelessness when they absented themselves, and that reminded him to order Heathcliff a flogging, and Catherine a fast from dinner or supper.

But it was one of their chief amusements to run away to the moors in the morning and remain there all day, and the after punishment grew a mere thing to laugh at. The curate might set as many chapters as he pleased for Catherine to get by heart, and Joseph might thrash Heathcliff till his arm ached; they forgot everything the minute they were together again, at least the minute they had contrived some naughty plan of revenge, and many a time I've cried to myself to watch them growing more reckless daily, and I not daring to speak a syllable for fear of losing the small power I still retained over the unfriended creatures.

One Sunday evening, it chanced that they were banished from the sitting-room, for making a noise, or a light offence of the kind, and when I went to call them to supper, I could discover them nowhere.

We searched the house, above and below, and the yard, and stables, they were invisible; and, at last, Hindley in a passion told us to bolt the doors, and swore nobody should let them in that night.

The household went to bed; and I, too anxious to lie down, opened my lattice and put my head out to hearken, though it rained, determined to admit them in spite of the prohibition, should they return.

In a while, I distinguished steps coming up the road, and the light of a lantern glimmered through the gate.

I threw a shawl over my head and ran to prevent them from waking Mr. Earnshaw by knocking. There was Heathcliff, by himself; it gave me a start to see him alone.

"Where is Miss Catherine?" I cried hurriedly. "No accident, I hope?"

"At Thrushcross Grange," he answered, "and I would have been there too, but they had not the manners to ask me to stay."

"Well, you will catch it!" I said, "you'll never be content till you're sent about your business. What in the world led you wandering to Thrushcross Grange?"

WUTHERING HEIGHTS 93

"Let me get off my wet clothes, and I'll tell you all about it, Nelly," he replied.

I bid him beware of rousing the master, and while he undressed, and I waited to put out the candle, he continued—

"Cathy and I escaped from the wash house to have a ramble at liberty, and getting a glimpse of the Grange lights, we thought we would just go and see whether the Lintons passed their Sunday evenings standing shivering in corners, while their father and mother sat eating and drinking and singing and laughing, and burning their eyes out before the fire. Do you think they do? Or reading sermons, and being catechised by their manservant, and set to learn a column of Scripture names, if they don't answer properly?"

"Probably not," I responded. "They are good children, no doubt, and don't deserve the treatment you receive, for your bad conduct."

"Don't you cant, Nelly," he said "nonsense! We ran from the top of the Heights to the park, without stopping—Catherine completely beaten in the race, because she was barefoot. You'll have to seek for her shoes in the bog to-morrow. We crept through a broken hedge, groped our way up the path, and planted ourselves on a flower-plot under the drawing room window. The light came from thence; they had not put up the shutters, and the curtains were only half closed. Both of us were able to look in by standing on the basement, and clinging to the ledge, and we saw—ah! it was beautiful—a splendid place carpeted with crimson, and crimson-covered chairs and tables, and a pure white ceiling bordered by gold, a shower of glass-drops hanging in silver chains from the centre, and shimmering with little soft tapers. Old Mr. and Mrs. Linton were not there. Edgar and his sister had it entirely to themselves; shouldn't they have been happy? We should have thought ourselves in heaven! And now, guess what your good children were doing? Isabella, I believe she is eleven, a year younger than Cathy, lay screaming at the farther end of the room, shrieking as if witches were running red hot needles into her. Edgar stood on the hearth weeping silently, and in the middle of the table sat a little dog shaking its paw and yelping, which, from their mutual accusations, we understood they had nearly pulled in two between them. The idiots! That was their pleasure! to quarrel who should hold a heap of warm hair, and each begin to cry because both, after struggling to get it, refused to take it. We laughed outright at the petted things, we did despise them! When would you catch me wishing to have what Catherine wanted? or find us by ourselves, seeking entertainment in yelling, and sobbing, and rolling on the ground, divided by the whole room? I'd not exchange, for a thousand lives, my condition here, for Edgar Linton's at Thrushcross Grange—not if I might have the privilege of flinging Joseph off the highest gable, and painting the house-front with Hindley's blood!"

"Hush, hush!" I interrupted. "Still you have not told me, Heathcliff, how Catherine is left behind?"

"I told you we laughed," he answered. The Linton's heard us, and with one accord, they shot like arrows to the door; there was silence, and then a cry, 'Oh, mamma, mamma! Oh, papa! Oh, mamma, come here. Oh papa, oh!' They really did howl out, something in that way. We made frightful noises to terrify them still more, and then we dropped off the ledge, because somebody was drawing the bars, and we felt we had better flee. I had Cathy by the hand, and was urging her on, when all at once she fell down.

"Run, Heathcliff, run!" she whispered. "They have let the bull-dog loose, and he holds me!"

"The devil had seized her ankle, Nelly; I heard his abominable snorting. She did not yell out—no! She would have scorned to do it, if she had been spitted on the horns of a mad cow. I did, though, I vociferated curses enough to annihilate any fiend in Christendom, and I got a stone and thrust it between his jaws, and tried with all my might to cram it down his throat. A beast of a servant came up with a lantern, at last, shouting—

"Keep fast, Skulker, keep fast!"

"He changed his note, however, when he saw Skulker's game. The dog was throttled off, his huge, purple tongue hanging half a foot out of his mouth, and his pendant lips streaming with bloody slaver.

"The man took Cathy up; she was sick; not from fear, I'm certain, but from pain. He carried her in; I followed grumbling execrations and vengeance."

"What prey, Robert?" hallooed Linton from the entrance."

"Skulker has caught a little girl, sir," he replied, and there's a lad here," he added, making a clutch at me, "who looks an out-and-outer! Very like, the robbers were for putting them through the window, to open the doors to the gang, after all were asleep, that they might murder us at their ease. Hold your tongue, you foul-mouthed thief, you! you shall go to the gallows for this. Mr. Linton, sir, don't lay by your gun!"

"No, no, Robert!" said the old fool. "The rascals knew that yesterday was my rent day; they thought to have me cleverly. Come in; I'll furnish them a reception. There, John, fasten the chain. Give Skulker some water, Jenny. To beard a magistrate in his strong-hold, and on the Sabbath, too! where will their insolence stop? Oh, my dear Mary, look here! Don't be afraid, it is but a boy—yet, the villain scowls so plainly in his face, would it not be a kindness to the country to hang him at once, before he shows his nature in acts, as well as features?"

He pulled me under the chandelier, and Mrs. Linton placed her spectacles on her nose and raised her hands in horror. The cowardly children crept nearer also, Isabella lisping—

"Frightful thing! Put him in the cellar, papa. He's exactly like the son of the fortune-teller, that stole my tame pheasant. Isn't he, Edgar?"

"While they examined me, Cathy came round; she heard the last speech, and laughed. Edgar Linton, after an inquisitive stare, collected sufficient wit

WUTHERING HEIGHTS

to recognise her. They see us at church, you know, though we seldom meet them elsewhere."

"That's Miss Earnshaw!" he whispered to his mother, "and look how Skulker has bitten her—how her foot bleeds!"

"Miss Earnshaw? Nonsense!" cried the dame, "Miss Earnshaw scouring the country with a gipsy! And yet, my dear, the child is in mourning—surely it is—and she may be lamed for life!"

"What culpable carelessness in her brother!" exclaimed Mr. Linton, turning from me to Catherine. "I've understood from Shielders (that was the curate sir) that he lets her grow up in absolute heathenism. But who is this? Where did she pick up this companion? Oho! I declare he is that strange acquisition my late neighbour made in his journey to Liverpool—a little Lascar, or an American or Spanish castaway."

"A wicked boy, at all events," remarked the old lady, "and quite unfit for a decent house! Did you notice his language, Linton? I'm shocked that my children should have heard it."

"I recommenced cursing—don't be angry Nelly—and so Robert was ordered to take me off—I refused to go without Cathy—he dragged me into the garden, pushed the lantern into my hand, assured me that Mr. Earnshaw, should be informed of my behaviour, and bidding me march, directly, secured the door again.

"The curtains were still looped up at one corner; and I resumed my station as spy, because, if Catherine had wished to return, I intended shattering their great glass panes to a million fragments, unless they let her out.

"She sat on the sofa quietly, Mrs. Linton took off the grey cloak of the dairy maid which we had borrowed for our excursion; shaking her head, and expostulating with her, I suppose; she was a young lady and they made a distinction between her treatment, and mine. Then the woman servant brought a basin of warm water, and washed her feet; and Mr. Linton mixed a tumbler of negus, and Isabella emptied a plateful of cakes into her lap, and Edgar, stood gaping at a distance. Afterwards, they dried and combed her beautiful hair, and gave her a pair of enormous slippers, and wheeled her to the fire, and I left her, as merry as she could be, dividing her food, between the little dog and Skulker whose nose she pinched as he ate; and kindling a spark of spirit in the vacant blue eyes of the Lintons—a dim reflection from her own enchanting face—I saw they were full of stupid admiration; she is so immeasurably superior to them—to everybody on earth; is she not, Nelly?"

"There will more come of this business than you reckon on." I answered covering him up and extinguishing the light, "You are incurable Heathcliff, and Mr. Hindley will have to proceed to extremities, see if he wont."

My words came truer than I desired. The luckless adventure made Earnshaw furious—And then, Mr. Linton, to mend matters, paid us a visit himself, on the morrow; and read the young master such a lecture on the road he guided his family, that he was stirred to look about him, in earnest.

Heathcliff received no flogging, but he was told that the first word he spoke to Miss Catherine should ensure a dismissal; and Mrs. Earnshaw undertook to keep her sister-in-law in due restraint, when she returned home employing art, not force—with force she would have found it impossible.

Chapter VII.

Cathy stayed at Thrushcross Grange five weeks, till Christmas. By that time her ankle was thoroughly cured, and her manners much improved. The mistress visited her often, in the interval, and commenced her plan of reform, by trying to raise her self-respect with fine clothes, and flattery, which she took readily: so that, instead of a wild, hatless little savage jumping into the house, and rushing to squeeze us all breathless, there lighted from a handsome black pony a very dignified person with brown ringlets falling from the cover of a feathered beaver, and a long cloth habit which she was obliged to hold up with both hands that she might sail in.

Hindley lifted her from her horse exclaiming delightedly,

"Why Cathy, you are quite a beauty! I should scarcely have known you—you look like a lady now—Isabella Linton is not to be be compared with her, is she Frances?"

"Isabella has not her natural advantages," replied his wife, "but she must mind and not grow wild again here. Ellen, help Miss Catherine off with her things—Stay, dear, you will disarrange your curls—let me untie your hat."

I removed the habit, and there shone forth, beneath a grand plaid silk frock, white trousers, and burnished shoes; and, while her eyes sparkled joyfully when the dogs came bounding up to welcome her, she dare hardly touch them lest they should fawn upon her splendid garments.

She kissed me gently, I was all flour making the Christmas cake, and it would not have done to give me a hug; and, then, she looked round for Heathcliff. Mr. and Mrs. Earnshaw watched anxiously their meeting, thinking it would enable them to judge, in some measure, what grounds they had for hoping to succeed in separating the two friends.

Heathcliff was hard to discover, at first—If he were careless, and uncared for, before Catherine's absence, he had been ten times more so, since.

Nobody, but I even did him the kindness to call him a dirty boy, and bid him wash himself, once a week; and children of his age, seldom have a natural pleasure in soap and water. Therefore, not to mention his clothes, which had seen three month's service, in mire and dust, and his thick uncombed hair; the surface of his face and hands was dismally beclouded. He might well skulk behind the settle, on beholding such a bright, graceful damsel enter the house, instead of a rough-headed counterpart to himself, as he expected.

"Is Heathcliff not here?" she demanded pulling off her gloves, and displaying fingers wonderfully whitened with doing nothing, and staying in doors.

EMILY BRONTË

"Heathcliff you may come forward," cried Mr. Hindley enjoying his discomfiture and gratified to see what a forbidding young blackguard he would be compelled to present himself. "You may come and wish Miss Catherine welcome, like the other servants."

Cathy, catching a glimpse of her friend in his concealment, flew to embrace him, she bestowed seven or eight kisses on his cheek within the second, and, then, stopped, and drawing back, burst into a laugh, exclaiming,

"Why, how very black and cross you look! and how—how funny and grim! But that's because I'm used to Edgar, and Isabella Linton. Well, Heathcliff, have you forgotten me?"

She had some reason to put the question, for shame, and pride threw double gloom over his countenance, and kept him immoveable.

"Shake hands, Heathcliff," said Mr. Earnshaw, condescendingly; "once in a way, that is permitted."

"I shall not!" replied the boy finding his tongue at last, "I shall not stand to be laughed at, I shall not bear it!"

And he would have broken from the circle, but Miss Cathy seized him again.

"I did not mean to laugh at you," she said, "I could not hinder myself, Heathcliff, shake hands, at least! What are you sulky for? It was only that you looked odd—If you wash your face, and brush your hair it will be all right. But you are so dirty!"

She gazed concernedly at the dusky fingers she held in her own, and also at her dress which she feared had gained no embellishment from its contact with his.

"You needn't have touched me!" He answered, following her eye and snatching away his hand. I shall be as dirty as I please, and I like to be dirty, and I will be dirty."

With that he dashed head foremost out of the room, amid the merriment of the master and mistress, and to the serious disturbance of Catherine who could not comprehend how her remarks should have produced such an exhibition of bad temper.

After playing lady's maid to the new comer, and putting my cakes in the oven, and making the house and kitchen cheerful with great fires befitting Christmas eve, I prepared to sit down and amuse myself by singing carols, all alone; regardless of Joseph's affirmations that he considered the merry tunes I chose as next door to songs.

He had retired to private prayer in his chamber, and Mr. and Mrs. Earnshaw were engaging Missy's attention by sundry gay trifles bought for her to present to the little Lintons, as an acknowledgment of their kindness[.]

They had invited them to spend the morrow at Wuthering Heights, and the invitation had been accepted, on one condition, Mrs. Linton begged that her darlings might be kept carefully apart from that "naughty, swearing boy."

WUTHERING HEIGHTS

Under these circumstances I remained solitary. I smelt the rich scent of the heating spices; and admired the shining kitchen utensils, the polished clock, decked in holly, the silver mugs ranged on a tray ready to be filled with mulled ale for supper; and, above all, the speckless purity of my particular care—the scoured and well-swept floor.

I gave due inward applause to every object and, then, I remembered how old Earnshaw used to come in when all was tidied, and call me a cant lass, and slip a shilling into my hand, as a christmas box: and, from that, I went on to think of his fondness for Heathcliff, and his dread lest he should suffer neglect after death had removed him; and that naturally led me to consider the poor lad's situation now, and from singing I changed my mind to crying. It struck me soon, however, there would be more sense in endeavouring to repair some of his wrongs than shedding tears over them—I got up and walked into the court to seek him.

He was not far, I found him smoothing the glossy coat of the new pony in the stable, and feeding the other beasts, according to custom.

"Make haste, Heathcliff!" I said "the kitchen is so comfortable—and Joseph is upstairs; make haste, and let me dress you smart before Miss Cathy comes out—and then you can sit together, with the whole hearth to yourselves, and have a long chatter till bedtime."

He proceeded with his task and never turned his head towards me.

"Come—are you coming?" I continued, "There's a little cake for each of you, nearly enough; and you'll need half an hour's donning."

I waited five minutes, but getting no answer left him . . . Catherine supped with her brother and sister-in law: Joseph and I joined at an unsociable meal seasoned with reproofs on one side, and sauciness on the other. His cake and cheese remained on the table all night, for the fairies. He managed to continue work till nine o'clock, and, then, marched dumb and dour, to his chamber.

Cathy sat up late; having a world of things to order for the reception of her new friends: she came into the kitchen, once, to speak to her old one, but he was gone, and she only staid [*sic*] to ask what was the matter with him, and then went back.

"In the morning, he rose early; and, as it was a holiday, carried his ill-humour onto the moors; not re-appearing till the family were departed for church. Fasting, and reflection seemed to have brought him to a better spirit. He hung about me, for a while, and having screwed up his courage, exclaimed abruptly,

"Nelly, make me decent, I'm going to be good."

"High time, Heathcliff," I said, "you *have* grieved Catherine; she's sorry she ever came home, I dare say! It looks as if you envied her, because she is more thought of than you."

The notion of *envying* Catherine was incomprehensible to him, but the notion of grieving her, be understood clearly enough.

100 EMILY BRONTË

"Did she say she was grieved?" he inquired looking very serious.

"She cried when I told her you were off again this morning."

"Well, *I* cried last night" he returned, "and I had more reason to cry than she."

"Yes, you had the reason of going to bed, with a proud heart, and an empty stomach," said I, "Proud people breed sad sorrows for themselves—But, if you be ashamed of your touchiness, you must ask pardon, mind, when she comes in. You must go up, and offer to kiss her, and say—you know best what to say, only, do it heartily, and not as if you thought her converted into a stranger by her grand dress. And now, though I have dinner to get ready, I'll steal time to arrange you so that Edgar Linton shall look quite a doll beside you: and that he does—You are younger, and yet, I'll be bound, you are taller and twice as broad across the shoulders—you could knock him down in a twinkling; don't you feel that you could?"

Heathcliff's face brightened a moment; then, it was overcast afresh, and he sighed.

"But, Nelly, if I knocked him down twenty times, that wouldn't make him less handsome, or me more so. I wish I had light hair and a fair skin, and was dressed, and behaved as well, and had a chance of being as rich as he will be!"

"And cried for mamma, at every turn—" I added, "and trembled if a country lad heaved his fist against you, and sat at home all day for a shower of rain.—O, Heathcliff, you are showing a poor spirit! Come to the glass, and I'll let you see what you should wish. Do you mark those two lines between your eyes, and those thick brow, that instead of rising arched, sink in the middle, and that couple of black fiends, so deeply buried, who never open their windows boldly, but lurk glinting under them, like devil's spies? Wish and learn to smooth away the surly wrinkles, to raise your lids frankly, and change the fiends to confidant, innocent angels, suspecting and doubting nothing, and always seeing friends where they are not sure of foes—Don't get the expression of a vicious cur that appears to know the kicks it gets are its desert, and yet, hates all the world, as well as the kicker, for what it suffers."

"In other words, I must wish for Edgar Linton's great blue eyes, and even forehead," he replied. "I do—and that wont help me to them."

"A good heart will help you to a bonny face my lad," I continued, "if you were a regular black; and a bad one will turn the bonniest into something worse than ugly. And now that we've done washing, and combing, and sulking—tell me whether you don't think yourself rather handsome? I'll tell you, I do. You're fit for a prince in disguise. Who knows, but your father was Emperor of China, and your mother an Indian queen, each of them able to buy up, with one week's income, Wuthering Heights and Thrushcross Grange together? And you were kidnapped by wicked sailors, and brought to England. Were I in your place, I would frame high notions of my birth; and the thoughts of what I was should give me courage and dignity to support the oppressions of a little farmer!"

WUTHERING HEIGHTS
101

So I chattered on; and Heathcliff gradually lost his frown, and began to look quite pleasant; when, all at once, our conversation was interrupted by a rumbling sound moving up the road and entering the court. He ran to the window, and I to the door, just in time to behold the two Lintons descend from the family carriage, smothered in cloaks and furs, and the Earnshaws dismount from their horses—they often rode to church in winter. Catherine took a hand of each of the children, and brought them into the house, and set them before the fire which quickly put colour into their white faces.

I urged my companion to hasten now, and show his amiable humour; and he willingly obeyed: but ill luck would have it, that as he opened the door leading from the kitchen on one side, Hindley opened it on the other; they met, and the master irritated at seeing him clean and cheerful, or, perhaps, eager to keep his promise to Mrs. Linton shoved him back with a sudden thrust, and angrily bade Joseph "keep the fellow out of the room—send him into the garret till dinner is over. He'll be cramming his fingers in the tarts, and stealing the fruit, if left alone with them a minute."

"Nay, sir," I could not avoid answering, "he'll touch nothing, not he—and, I suppose, he must have his share of the dainties as well as we."

"He shall have his share of my hand, if I catch him down stairs again till dark," cried Hindley. "Begone, you vagabond! What, you are attempting the coxcomb, are you? Wait till I get hold of those elegant locks—see if I won't pull them a bit longer!"

"They are long enough already," observed Master Linton, peeping from the door-way, "I wonder they don't make his head ache. It's like a colt's mane over his eyes!"

He ventured this remark without any intention to insult; but, Heathcliff's violent nature was not prepared to endure the appearance of impertinence from one whom he seemed to hate, even then, as a rival. He seized a tureen of hot apple-sauce, the first thing that came under his gripe, and dashed it full against the speaker's face and neck—who instantly commenced a lament that brought Isabella and Catherine hurrying to the place.

Mr. Earnshaw snatched up the culprit directly and conveyed him to his chamber, where, doubtless, he administered a rough remedy to cool the fit of passion, for he reappeared red and breathless. I got the dishcloth, and, rather spitefully, scrubbed Edgar's nose and mouth, affirming, it served him right for meddling. His sister began weeping to go home, and Cathy stood by confounded, blushing for all.

"You should not have spoken to him!" she expostulated with Master Linton. "He was in a bad temper, and now you've spoilt your visit, and he'll be flogged—I hate him to be flogged! I can't eat my dinner. Why did you speak to him, Edgar?"

EMILY BRONTË

"I didn't," sobbed the youth, escaping from my hands, and finishing the remainder of the purification with his cambric pocket-handkerchief. "I promised mamma that I wouldn't say one word to him, and I didn't!"

"Well, don't cry!" replied Catherine, contemptuously. "You're not killed— don't make more mischief—my brother is coming—be quiet! Give over, Isabella! Has any body hurt *you*?"

"There, there, children—to your seats!" cried Hindley, bustling in. "That brute of a lad has warmed me nicely. Next time, Master Edgar, take the law into your own fists—it will give you an appetite!'

The little party recovered its equanimity at sight of the fragrant feast. They were hungry, after their ride, and easily consoled, since no real harm had befallen them.

Mr. Earnshaw carved bountiful platefuls; and the mistress made them merry with lively talk. I waited behind her chair, and was pained to behold Catherine, with dry eyes and an indifferent air, commence cutting up the wing of a goose before her.

"An unfeeling child," I thought to myself, "how lightly she dismisses her old playmate's troubles. I could not have imagined her to be so selfish."

She lifted a mouthful to her lips; then, she set it down again: her cheeks flushed, and the tears gushed over them. She slipped her fork to the floor, and hastily dived under the cloth to conceal her emotion. I did not call her unfeeling long, for, I perceived she was in purgatory throughout the day, and wearying to find an opportunity of getting by herself, or paying a visit to Heathcliff, who had been locked up by the master, as I discovered, on endeavouring to introduce to him a private mess of victuals.

In the evening we had a dance, Cathy begged that he might be liberated then, as Isabella Linton had no partner; her entreaties were vain, and I was appointed to supply the deficiency.

We got rid of all gloom in the excitement of the exercise, and our pleasure was increased by the arrival of the Gimmerton band, mustering fifteen strong; a trumpet, a trombone, clarionets, bassoons, French horns, and a bass viol, besides singers. They go the rounds of all the respectable houses, and receive contributions every Christmas, and we esteemed it a first-rate treat to hear them.

After the usual carols had been sung, we set them to songs and glees. Mrs. Earnshaw loved the music, and, so, they gave us plenty.

Catherine loved it too; but she said it sounded sweetest at the top of the steps, and she went up in the dark: I followed. They shut the house door below, never noting our absence, it was so full of people. She made no stay at the stairs' head, but mounted farther, to the garret where Heathcliff was confined; and called him. He stubbornly declined answering for a while—she persevered, and finally persuaded him to hold communion with her through the boards.

WUTHERING HEIGHTS

I let the poor things converse unmolested, till I supposed the songs were going to cease, and the singers to get some refreshment: then, I clambered up the ladder to warn her.

Instead of finding her outside, I heard her voice within. The little monkey had crept by the skylight of one garret, along the roof, into the skylight of the other, and it was with the utmost difficultly I could coax her out again.

When she did come, Heathcliff came with her; and she insisted that I should take him into the kitchen, as my fellow-servant had gone to a neighbour's to be removed from the sound of our "devil's psalmody," as it pleased him to call it.

I told them I intended, by no means, to encourage their tricks; but as the prisoner had never broken his fast since yesterday's dinner, I would wink at his cheating Mr. Hindley that once.

He went down; I set him a stool by the fire, and offered him a quantity of good things; but, he was sick and could eat little: and my attempts to entertain him were thrown away. He leant his two elbows on his knees, and his chin on his hands, and remained wrapt in dumb meditation. On my inquiring the subject of his thoughts, he answered gravely—

"I'm trying to settle how I shall pay Hindley back. I don't care how long I wait, if I can only do it, at last. I hope he will not die before I do!"

"For shame, Heathcliff!" said I. "It is for God to punish wicked people; we should learn to forgive."

"No, God wont have the satisfaction that I shall," he returned. "I only wish I knew the best way! Let me alone, and I'll plan it out: while I'm thinking of that, I don't feel pain."

"But, Mr. Lockwood, I forget these tales cannot divert you. I'm annoyed how I should dream of chattering on at such a rate; and your gruel cold, and you nodding for bed! I could have told Heathcliff's history, all that you need hear, in half-a-dozen words."

Thus interrupting herself, the housekeeper rose, and proceeded to lay aside her sewing; but I felt incapable of moving from the hearth, and I was very far from nodding.

"Sit still, Mrs. Dean," I cried, "do sit still, another half hour! You've done just right to tell the story leisurely. That is the method I like; and you must finish in the same style. I am interested in every character you have mentioned, more or less."

"The clock is on the stroke of eleven, sir."

"No matter—I'm not accustomed to go to bed in the long hours. One or two is early enough for a person who lies till ten."

"You shouldn't lie till ten. There's the very prime of the morning gone long before that time. A person who has not done one half his day's work by ten o'clock, runs a chance of leaving the other half undone."

104   EMILY BRONTË

"Nevertheless, Mrs. Dean, resume your chair; because to-morrow I intend lengthening the night till afternoon. I prognosticate for myself an obstinate cold, at least."

"I hope not, sir. Well, you must allow me to leap over some three years, during that space, Mrs. Earnshaw—"

"No, no, I'll allow nothing of the sort! Are you acquainted with the mood of mind in which, if you were seated alone, and the cat licking its kitten on the rug before you, you would watch the operation so intently that puss's neglect of one ear would put you seriously out of temper?"

"A terribly lazy mood, I should say."

"On the contrary, a tiresomely active one. It is mine, at present, and, therefore, continue minutely. I perceive that people in these regions acquire over people in towns the value that a spider in a dungeon does over a spider in a cottage, to their various occupants; and yet the deepened attraction is not entirely owing to the situation of the looker-on. They *do* live more in earnest, more in themselves, and less in surface change, and frivolous external things. I could fancy a love for life here almost possible; and I was a fixed unbeliever in any love of a year's standing—one state resembles setting a hungry man down to a single dish on which he may concentrate his entire appetite, and do it justice—the other, introducing him to a table laid out by French cooks; he can perhaps extract as much enjoyment from the whole; but each part is a mere atom in his regard and remembrance."

"Oh! here we are the same as anywhere else, when you get to know us," observed Mrs. Dean, somewhat puzzled at my speech.

"Excuse me," I responded; "you, my good friend, are a striking evidence against that assertion. Excepting a few provincialisms of slight consequence; you have no marks of the manners that I am habituated to consider as peculiar to your class. I am sure you have thought a great deal more than the generality of servants think. You have been compelled to cultivate your reflective faculties, for want of occasions for frittering your life away in silly trifles."

Mrs. Dean laughed.

"I certainly esteem myself a steady, reasonable kind of body," she said, "not exactly from living among the hills, and seeing one set of faces, and one series of actions, from year's end to year's end: but I have undergone sharp discipline which has taught me wisdom; and then, I have read more than you would fancy, Mr. Lockwood. You could not open a book in this library that I have not looked into, and got something out of also; unless it be that range of Greek and Latin, and that of French—and those I know one from another, it is as much as you can expect of a poor man's daughter."

However, if I am to follow my story in true gossip's fashion, I had better go on; and instead of leaping three years, I will be content to pass to the next summer—the summer of 1778, that is nearly twenty-three years ago.

CHAPTER VIII.

On the morning of a fine June day, my first bonny little nursling, and the last of the ancient Earnshaw stock was born.

We were busy with the hay in a far away field, when the girl that usually brought our breakfasts came running, an hour too soon, across the meadow and up the lane, calling me as she ran.

"Oh, such a grand bairn!" she panted out. "The finest lad that ever breathed! but the doctor says missis must go; he says she's been in a consumption these many months. I heard him tell Mr. Hindley—and now she has nothing to keep her, and she'll be dead before winter. You must come home directly. You're to nurse it, Nelly—to feed it with sugar and milk, and take care of it, day and night—I wish I were you, because it will be all yours when there is no missis!"

"But is she very ill?" I asked, flinging down my rake, and tying my bonnet.

"I guess she is; yet she looks bravely," replied the girl, "and she talks as if she thought of living to see it grow a man. She's out of her head for joy, it's such a beauty! If I were her I'm certain I should not die. I should get better at the bare sight of it, in spite of Kenneth. I was fairly mad at him. Dame Archer brought the cherub down to master, in the house, and his face just began to light up, then the old croaker steps forward, and, says he:—'Earnshaw, it's a blessing your wife has been spared to leave you this son. When she came, I felt convinced we shouldn't keep her long; and now, I must tell you, the winter will probably finish her. Don't take on, and fret about it too much, it can't be helped. And besides, you should have known better than to choose such a rush of a lass!"

"And what did the master answer?" I enquired.

"I think he swore—but, I didn't mind him, I was straining to see the bairn," and she began again to describe it rapturously. I, as zealous as herself, hurried eagerly home to admire, on my part, though I was very sad for Hindley's sake; he had room in his heart only for two idols—his wife and himself—he doted on both, and adored one, and I couldn't conceive how he would bear the loss.

When we got to Wuthering Heights, there he stood at the front door; and, as I passed in, I asked, how was the baby?"

"Nearly ready to run about, Nell!" he replied, putting on a cheerful smile.

"And the mistress?" I ventured to inquire, "the doctor says she's—"

"Damn the doctor!" he interrupted, reddening. "Frances is quite right— she'll be perfectly well by this time next week. Are you going up-stairs? will

106 EMILY BRONTË

you tell her that I'll come, if she'll promise not to talk. I left her because she would not hold her tongue; and she must—tell her Mr. Kenneth says she must be quiet."

I delivered this message to Mrs. Earnshaw; she seemed in flighty spirits, and replied merrily—

"I hardly spoke a word, Ellen, and there he has gone out twice, crying. Well, say I promise I wont speak; but that does not bind me not to laugh at him!"

Poor soul! Till within a week of her death that gay heart never failed her; and her husband persisted doggedly, nay, furiously, in affirming her health improved every day. When Kenneth warned him that his medicines were useless at that stage of the malady, and he needn't put him to further expense by attending her, he retorted—

"I know you need not—she's well—she does not want any more attendance from you! She never was in a consumption. It was a fever; and it is gone—her pulse is as slow as mine now, and her cheek as cool."

He told his wife the same story, and she seemed to believe him; but one night, while leaning on his shoulder, in the act of saying she thought she should be able to get up to-morrow, a fit of coughing took her—a very slight one—he raised her in his arms; she put her two hands about his neck, her face changed, and she was dead.

As the girl had anticipated; the child Hareton, fell wholly into my hands. Mr. Earnshaw, provided he saw him healthy, and never heard him cry, was contented, as far as regarded him. For himself, he grew desperate; his sorrow was of that kind that will not lament, he neither wept nor prayed—he cursed and defied—execrated God and man, and gave himself up to reckless dissipation.

The servants could not bear his tyrannical and evil conduct long: Joseph and I were the only two that would stay. I had not the heart to leave my charge; and besides, you know, I had been his foster sister, and excused his behaviour more readily than a stranger would.

Joseph remained to hector over tenants and labourers; and because it was his vocation to be where he had plenty of wickedness to reprove.

The master's bad ways and bad companions formed a pretty example for Catherine and Heathcliff. His treatment of the latter was enough to make a fiend of a saint. And, truly, it appeared as if the lad *were* possessed of something diabolical at that period. He delighted to witness Hindley degrading himself past redemption; and became daily more notable for savage sullenness and ferocity.

I could not half tell what an infernal house we had. The curate dropped calling, and nobody decent came near us, at last; unless, Edgar Linton's visits to Miss Cathy might be an exception. At fifteen she was the queen of the country-side; she had no peer: and she did turn out a haughty, headstrong

WUTHERING HEIGHTS 107

creature! I own I did not like her, after her infancy was past; and I vexed her frequently by trying to bring down her arrogance; she never took an aversion to me though. She had a wondrous constancy to old attachments; even Heathcliff kept his hold on her affections unalterably, and young Linton, with all his superiority, found it difficult to make an equally deep impression.

He was my late master; that is his portrait over the fireplace. It used to hang on one side, and his wife's on the other; but her's has been removed, or else you might see something of what she was. Can you make that out?

Mrs. Dean raised the candle, and I discerned a soft-featured face, exceedingly resembling the young lady at the Heights, but more pensive and amiable in expression. It formed a sweet picture. The long light hair curled slightly on the temples; the eyes were large and serious; the figure almost too graceful. I did not marvel how Catherine Earnshaw could forget her first friend for such an individual. I marvelled much how he, with a mind to correspond with his person, could fancy my idea of Catherine Earnshaw.

"A very agreeable portrait," I observed to the housekeeper. "Is it like?"

"Yes," she answered; "but he looked better when he was animated, that is his every day countenance; he wanted spirit in general."

Catherine had kept up her acquaintance with the Lintons since her five weeks' residence among them; and as she had no temptation to show her rough side in their company, and had the sense to be ashamed of being rude where she experienced such invariable courtesy, she imposed unwittingly on the old lady and gentleman, by her ingenious cordiality; gained the admiration of Isabella, and the heart and soul of her brother—acquisitions that flattered her from the first, for she was full of ambition—and led her to adopt a double character without exactly intending to deceive anyone.

In the place where she heard Heathcliff termed a "vulgar young ruffian," and "worse than a brute," she took care not to act like him; but at home she had small inclination to practise politeness that would only be laughed at, and restrain an unruly nature when it would bring her neither credit, nor praise.

Mr. Edgar seldom mustered courage to visit Wuthering Heights openly. He had a terror of Earnshaw's reputation, and shrunk from encountering him, and yet, he was always received with our best attempts at civility: the master himself, avoided offending him—knowing why he came, and if he could not be gracious, kept out of the way. I rather think his appearance there was distasteful to Catherine; she was not artful, never played the coquette, and had evidently an objection to her two friends meeting at all: for when Heathcliff expressed contempt of Linton, in his presence, she could not half coincide, as she did in his absence; and when Linton evinced disgust, and antipathy to Heathcliff, she dare not treat his sentiments with indifference, as if depreciation of her playmate were of scarcely any consequence to her.

I've had many a laugh at her perplexities, and untold troubles, which she vainly strove to hide from my mockery. That sounds ill-natured—but she was

108   EMILY BRONTË

so proud, it became really impossible to pity her distresses, till she should be chastened into more humility.

She did bring herself, finally, to confess, and confide in me. There was not a soul else that she might fashion into an adviser.

Mr. Hindley had gone from home, one afternoon; and Heathcliff presumed to give himself a holiday, on the strength of it. He had reached the age of sixteen then, I think, and without having bad features or being deficient in intellect, he contrived to convey an impression of inward and outward repulsiveness that his present aspect retains no traces of.

In the first place, he had, by that time, lost the benefit of his early education: continual hard work, begun soon and concluded late, had extinguished any curiosity he once possessed in pursuit of knowledge, and any love for books, or learning. His childhood's sense of superiority, instilled into him by the favours of old Mr. Earnshaw, was faded away. He struggled long to keep up an equality with Catherine in her studies and yielded with poignant though silent regret: but, he yielded completely; and there was no prevailing on him to take a step in the way of moving upward, when he found he must, necessarily, sink beneath his former level. Then personal appearance sympathised with mental deterioration; he acquired a slouching gait, and ignoble look; his naturally reserved disposition was exaggerated into an almost idiotic excess of unsociable moroseness; and he took a grim pleasure, apparently, in exciting the aversion rather than the esteem of his few acquaintance.

Catherine and he were constant companions still, at his seasons of respite from labour; but, he had ceased to express his fondness for her in words, and recoiled with angry suspicion from her girlish caresses, as if conscious there could be no gratification in lavishing such marks of affection on him. On the before-named occasion he came into the house to announce his intention of doing nothing, while I was assisting Miss Cathy to arrange her dress—she had not reckoned on his taking it into his head to be idle, and imagining she would have the whole place to herself, she managed, by some means, to inform Mr. Edgar of her brother's absence, and was then preparing to receive him.

"Cathy, are you busy, this afternoon?" asked Heathcliff, "Are you going anywhere?"

"No, it is raining," she answered.

"Why have you that silk frock on, then?" he said, "Nobody coming here I hope?"

"Not that I know of;" stammered Miss, "but you should be in the field now, Heathcliff. It is an hour past dinner time; I thought you were gone."

"Hindley does not often free us from his accursed presence;" observed the boy, "I'll not work any more to-day, I'll stay with you."

"O, but Joseph will tell;" she suggested, "you'd better go!"

"Joseph is loading lime on the farther side of Pennistow Crag, it will take him till dark, and he'll never know."

WUTHERING HEIGHTS 109

So saying he lounged to the fire, and sat down, Catherine reflected an instant, with knitted brows—she found it needful to smooth the way for an intrusion.

"Isabella, and Edgar Linton talked of calling this afternoon;" she said at the conclusion of a minute's silence. "As it rains, I hardly expect them; but, they may come, and if they do, you run the risk of being scolded for no good."

"Order Ellen to say you are engaged, Cathy," he persisted, "Don't turn me out for those pitiful, silly friends of yours! I'm on the point, sometimes, of complaining that they—but I'll not—"

"That they what?" cried Catherine, gazing at him with a troubled countenance. "Oh Nelly!" she added petulantly jerking her head away from my hands, "you've combed my hair quite out of curl! That's enough, let me alone. What are you on the point of complaining about, Heathcliff?"

"Nothing—only look at the almanack, on that wall," he pointed to a framed sheet hanging near the window, and continued;

"The crosses are for the evenings you have spent with the Lintons, the dots for those spent with me—Do you see, I've marked every day?"

"Yes—very foolish; as if I took notice!" replied Catherine in a peevish tone. "And where is the sense of that?"

"To show that I *do* take notice." said Heathcliff.

"And should I always be sitting with you," she demanded, growing more irritated. "What good do I get—What do you talk about? you might be dumb or a baby for anything you say to amuse me, or for anything you do, either!"

"You never told me, before, that I talked too little, or that you disliked my company, Cathy!" exclaimed Heathcliff in much agitation.

"It is no company at all, when people know nothing and say nothing," she muttered.

Her companion rose up, but he hadn't time to express his feelings further, for a horse's feet were heard on the flags, and, having knocked gently, young Linton entered, his face brilliant with delight at the unexpected summons he had received.

Doubtless Catherine marked the difference between her friends as one came in, and the other went out. The contrast resembled what you see in exchanging a bleak, hilly, coal country, for a beautiful fertile valley; and his voice, and greeting were as opposite as his aspect—He had a sweet, low manner of speaking, and pronounced his words as you do, that's less gruff than we talk here and softer.

"I'm not come too soon, am I?" he said, casting a look at me, I had begun to wipe the plate, and tidy some drawers at the far end in the dresser.

"No," answered Catherine. "What are you doing there, Nelly?"

"My work, Miss," I replied. (Mr. Hindley had given me directions to make a third party in any private visits Linton chose to pay.)

110   EMILY BRONTË

She stepped behind me and whispered crossly, "Take yourself and your dusters off! when company are in the house, servants don't commence scouring and cleaning in the room where they are!"

"It's a good opportunity, now that master is away," I answered aloud, "he hates me to be fidgetting over these things in his presence—I'm sure Mr. Edgar will excuse me."

"I hate you to be fidgetting in *my* presence," exclaimed the young lady imperiously, not allowing her guest time to speak—she had failed to recover her equanimity since the little dispute with Heathcliff.

"I'm sorry for it, Miss Catherine!" was my response; and I proceeded assiduously with my occupation.

She, supposing Edgar could not see her, snatched the cloth from my hand, and pinched me, with a prolonged wrench, very spitefully on the arm.

I've said I did not love her; and rather relished mortifying her vanity, now and then; besides, she hurt me extremely, so I started up from my knees, and screamed out.

"O, Miss, that's a nasty trick! you have no right to nip me, and I'm not going to bear it!"

"I didn't touch you, you lying creature!" cried she, her fingers tingling to repeat the act, and her ears red with rage. She never had power to conceal her passion, it always set her whole complexion in a blaze.

"What's that then?" I retorted showing a decided purple witness to refute her.

She stamped her foot, wavered a moment, and then, irresistibly impelled by the naughty spirit within her, slapped me on the cheek a stinging blow that filled both eyes with water.

"Catherine, love! Catherine!" interposed Linton, greatly shocked at the double fault of falsehood, and violence which his idol had committed.

"Leave the room, Ellen!" she repeated, trembling all over.

Little Hareton, who followed me everywhere, and was sitting near me on the floor, at seeing my tears commenced crying himself, and sobbed out complaints against "wicked aunt Cathy," which drew her fury on to his unlucky head: she seized his shoulders, and shook him till the poor child waxed livid, and Edgar thoughtlessly laid hold of her hands to deliver him. In an instant one was wrung free, and the astonished young man felt it applied over his own ear in a way that could not be mistaken for jest.

He drew back in consternation—I lifted Hareton in my arms, and walked off to the kitchen with him; leaving the door of communication open, for I was curious to watch how they would settle their disagreement.

The insulted visiter moved to the spot where he had laid his hat, pale and with a quivering lip.

"That's right!" I said to myself, "Take warning and begone! It's a kindness to let you have a glimpse of her genuine disposition."

"Where are you going?" demanded Catherine, advancing to the door.

WUTHERING HEIGHTS

He swerved aside and attempted to pass.

"You must not go!" she exclaimed energetically.

"I must and shall!" he replied in a subdued voice.

"No," she persisted, grasping the handle; "not yet, Edgar Linton—sit down, you shall not leave me in that temper. I should be miserable, all night, and I won't be miserable for you!"

"Can I stay after you have struck me?" asked Linton.

Catherine was mute.

"You've made me afraid, and ashamed of you;" he continued; "I'll not come here again!"

Her eyes began to glisten and her lids to twinkle.

"And you told a deliberate untruth!" he said.

"I didn't!" she cried, recovering her speech "I did nothing deliberately— Well, go, if you please—get away! And now I'll cry—I'll cry myself sick!"

She dropped down on her knees by a chair and set to weeping in serious earnest.

Edgar persevered in his resolution as far as the court; there, he lingered. I resolved to encourage him.

"Miss is dreadfully wayward, sir!" I called out. "As bad as any marred child—you'd better be riding home, or else she will be sick, only to grieve us."

The soft thing looked askance through the window—he possessed the power to depart, as much as a cat possesses the power to leave a mouse half killed, or a bird half eaten—

Ah, I thought; there will be no saving him—He's doomed, and flies to his fate!

And, so it was; he turned abruptly, hastened into the house again, shut the door behind him; and, when I went in a while after to inform them that Earnshaw had come home rabid drunk, ready to pull the old place about our ears, (his ordinary frame of mind in that condition) I saw the quarrel had merely affected a closer intimacy—had broken the outworks of youthful timidity, and enabled them to forsake the disguise of friendship, and confess themselves lovers.

Intelligence of Mr. Hindley's arrival drove Linton speedily to his horse, and Catherine to her chamber. I went to hide little Hareton, and to take the shot out of the master's fowling piece which he was fond of playing with in his insane excitement, to the hazard of the lives of any who provoked, or even, attracted his notice too much; and I had hit upon the plan of removing it, that he might do less mischief, if he did go the length of firing the gun.

Chapter IX.

He entered, vociferating oaths dreadful to hear; and caught me in the act of stowing his son away in the kitchen cupboard. Hareton was impressed with a wholesome terror of encountering either his wild-beast's fondness, or his madman's rage—for in one he ran a chance of being squeezed and kissed to death, and in the other of being flung into the fire, or dashed against the wall—and the poor thing remained perfectly quiet wherever I chose to put him.

"There I've found it out at last!" cried Hindley, pulling me back by the skin of the neck, like a dog, "By Heaven and Hell, you've sworn between you to murder that child! I know how it is, now, that he is always out of my way. But, with the help of Satan, I shall make you swallow the carving knife, Nelly! you needn't laugh; for I've just crammed Kenneth head-downmost, in the Blackhorse marsh; and two is the same as one—and I want to kill some of you, I shall have no rest till I do!"

"But I don't like the carving knife, Mr. Hindley;" I answered, it has been cutting red herrings—I'd rather be shot if you please."

"You'd rather be damned!" he said, "and so you shall—No law in England can hinder a man from keeping his house decent, and mine's abominable! open your mouth."

He held the knife in his hand, and pushed its point between my teeth: but, for my part I was never much afraid of his vagaries. I spat out, and affirmed it tasted detestably—I would not take it on any account."

"Oh!" said he releasing me, I see that hideous little villain is not Hareton—I beg your pardon, Nell—if it be he deserves flaying alive for not running to welcome me, and for screaming as if I were a goblin. Unnatural cub, come hither! I'll teach thee to impose on a good-hearted, deluded father—Now, don't you think the lad would be handsomer cropped? It makes a dog fiercer, and I love something fierce—Get me a scissors—something fierce and trim! Besides, it's infernal affectation—devilish conceit, it is to cherish our ears—we're asses enough without them. Hush, child, hush! well then, it is my darling I wisht, dry thy eyes—there's a joy; kiss me; what it won't? kiss me, Hareton! Dam'n thee, kiss me! By God, as if I would rear such a monster! As sure as I'm living, I'll break the brat's neck."

Poor Hareton was squalling and kicking in his father's arms with all his might, and re-doubled his yells when he carried him up-stairs and lifted him over the bannister. I cried out that he would frighten the child into fits, and ran to rescue him.

As I reached them, Hindley leant forward on the rails to listen to a noise below; almost forgetting what he had in his hands.

"Who is that?" he asked, hearing some one approaching the stair's-foot.

I leant forward, also, for the purpose of signing to Heathcliff, whose step I recognized, not to come further; and, at the instant when my eye quitted Hareton, he gave a sudden spring, delivered himself from the careless grasp that held him, and fell.

There was scarcely time to experience a thrill of horror before we saw that the little wretch was safe. Heathcliff arrived underneath just at the critical moment; by a natural impulse, he arrested his descent, and setting him on his feet, looked up to discover the author of the accident.

A miser who has parted with a lucky lottery ticket for five shillings and finds next day he has lost in the bargain five thousand pounds, could not show a blanker countenance than he did on beholding the figure of Mr. Earnshaw above—It expressed, plainer than words could do, the intensest anguish at having made himself the instrument of thwarting his own revenge. Had it been dark, I dare say, he would have tried to remedy the mistake by smashing Hareton's skull on the steps; but, we witnessed his salvation; and I was presently below with my precious charge pressed to my heart.

Hindley descended more leisurely, sobered and abashed.

"It is your fault, Ellen," he said, "you should have kept him out of sight; you should have taken him from me! Is he injured anywhere?"

"Injured!" I cried angrily, "If he's not killed, he'll be an idiot! Oh! I wonder his mother does not rise from her grave to see how you use him. You're worse than a heathen—treating your own flesh and blood in that manner!"

He attempted to touch the child, who on finding himself with me sobbed off his terror directly. At the first finger his father laid on him, however, he shrieked again louder than before, and struggled as if he would go into convulsions.

"You shall not meddle with him!" I continued, "He hates you—they all hate you—that's the truth! A happy family you have; and a pretty state you're come to!"

"I shall come to a prettier, yet! Nelly," laughed the misguided man, recovering his hardness.

"At present, convey yourself and him away—And, hark you, Heathcliff! clear you too, quite from my reach and hearing . . . I wouldn't murder you to-night, unless, perhaps I set the house on fire; but that's as my fancy goes—"

While saying this he took a pint bottle of brandy from the dresser, and poured some into a tumbler.

"Nay don't!" I entreated, "Mr. Hindley do take warning. Have mercy on this unfortunate boy, if you care nothing for yourself!"

"Any one will do better for him, than I shall," he answered.

EMILY BRONTË

"Have mercy on your own soul!" I said, endeavouring to snatch the glass from his hand.

"Not I! on the contrary, I shall have great pleasure in sending it to perdition, to punish its maker," exclaimed the blasphemer, "Here's to its hearty damnation!"

He drank the spirits, and impatiently bade us go; terminating his command with a sequel of horrid imprecations, too bad to repeat, or remember.

"It's a pity he cannot kill himself with drink," observed Heathcliff, muttering an echo of curses back when the door was shut. "He's doing his very utmost; but his constitution defies him—Mr. Kenneth says he would wager his mare, that he'll outlive any man on this side Gimmerton, and go to the grave a hoary sinner; unless, some happy chance out of the common course befall him."

I went into the kitchen and sat down to lull my little lamb to sleep. Heathcliff, as I thought, walked through to the barn. It turned out, afterwards, that he only got as far as the other side the settle, when he flung himself on a bench by the wall, removed from the fire, and remained silent.

I was rocking Hareton on my knee, and humming a song that began;

> "It was far in the night, and the bairnies grat,
> The mither beneath the mools heard that."

when Miss Cathy, who had listened to the hubbub from her room, put her head in, and whispered,

"Are you alone, Nelly?"

"Yes, Miss," I replied.

She entered and approached the hearth. I, supposing she was going to say something, looked up. The expression of her face seemed disturbed and anxious. Her lips were half asunder as if she meant to speak; and she drew a breath, but it escaped in a sigh, instead of a sentence.

I resumed my song: not having forgotten her recent behaviour.

"Where's Heathcliff?" she said, interrupting me.

"About his work in the stable," was my answer.

He did not contradict me; perhaps, he had fallen into a dose.

There followed another long pause, during which I perceived a drop or two trickle from Catherine's cheek to the flags.

Is she sorry for her shameful conduct? I asked myself. That will be a novelty, but, she may come to the point as she will—I shan't help her!

No, she felt small trouble regarding any subject, save her own concerns.

"Oh, dear!" she cried at last. "I'm very unhappy!"

"A pity," observed I, "you're hard to please—so many friends and so few cares, and can't make yourself, content!"

"Nelly, will you keep a secret for me?" she pursued, kneeling down by me, and lifting her winsome eyes to my face with that sort of look which turns off bad temper, even, when one has all the right in the world to indulge it.

"Is it worth keeping?" I inquired less sulkily.

"Yes, and it worries me, and I must let it out! I want to know what I should do—Today, Edgar Linton has asked me to marry him, and I've given him an answer—Now, before I tell you whether it was a consent, or denial—you tell me which it ought to have been."

"Really, Miss Catherine, how can I know?" I replied. "To be sure, considering the exhibition you performed in his presence, this afternoon, I might say it would be wise to refuse him—since he asked you after that, he must either be hopelessly stupid, or a venturesome fool."

"If you talk so, I wont tell you any more," she returned, peevishly, rising to her feet, "I accepted him, Nelly; be quick, and say whether I was wrong!"

"You accepted him? then, what good is it discussing the matter? You have pledged your word, and cannot retract."

"But, say whether I should have done so—do!" she exclaimed in an irritated tone; chafing her hands together, and frowning.

"There are many things to be considered, before that question can be answered properly." I said sententiously, "First and foremost, do you love Mr. Edgar?"

"Who can help it? of course I do," she answered.

Then I put her through the following catechism—for a girl of twenty-two it was not injudicious.

"Why do you love him, Miss Cathy?"

"Nonsense, I do—that's sufficient."

"By no means; you must say why?"

"Well, because he is handsome, and pleasant to be with."

"Bad," was my commentary.

"And because he is young and cheerful."

"Bad, still."

"And, because he loves me."

"Indifferent, coming there."

"And he will be rich, and I shall like to be the greatest woman of the neighbourhood, and I shall be proud of having such a husband."

"Worst of all! And, now, say how you love him?"

"As every body loves—You're silly, Nelly."

"Not at all—Answer."

"I love the ground under his feet, and the air over his head, and everything he touches, and every word he says—I love all his looks, and all his actions, and him entirely, and altogether. There now!"

"And why?"

"Nay—you are making a jest of it; it is exceedingly ill-natured! It's no jest to me!" said the young lady scowling, and turning her face to the fire.

"I'm very far from jesting, Miss Catherine," I replied, "you love Mr. Edgar, because he is handsome, and young, and cheerful, and rich, and loves you. The last, however, goes for nothing—You would love him without that, probably, and with it, you wouldn't unless he possessed the four former attractions."

"No, to be sure not—I should only pity him—hate him, perhaps, if he were ugly, and a clown."

"But, there are several other handsome, rich young men in the world; handsomer, possibly, and richer than he is—What should hinder you from loving them?"

"If there be any, they are out of my way—I've seen none like Edgar."

"You may see some; and he won't always be handsome, and young, and may not always be rich."

"He is now; and I have only to do with the present—I wish you would speak rationally."

"Well, that settles it—if you have only to do with the present, marry Mr. Linton."

"I don't want your permission for that—I *shall* marry him; and yet, you have not told me whether I'm right."

"Perfectly right; if people be right to marry only for the present. And now, let us hear what you are unhappy about. Your brother will be pleased . . . The old lady and gentleman will not object, I think—you will escape from a disorderly, comfortless home into a wealthy respectable one; and you love Edgar, and Edgar loves you. All seems smooth and easy—where is the obstacle?"

"*Here!* and *here!*" replied Catherine, striking one hand on her forehead, and the other on her breast. "In whichever place the soul lives—in my soul, and in my heart, I'm convinced I'm wrong!"

"That's very strange! I cannot make it out."

"It's my secret; but if you will not mock at me, I'll explain it; I can't do it distinctly—but I'll give you a feeling of how I feel."

She seated herself by me again: her countenance grew sadder and graver, and her clasped hands trembled.

"Nelly, do you never dream queer dreams?" she said, suddenly, after some minutes' reflection."

"Yes, now and then," I answered.

"And so do I. I've dreamt in my life dreams that have stayed with me ever after, and changed my ideas; they've gone through and through me, like wine through water, and altered the colour of my mind. And this is one—I'm going to tell it—but take care not to smile at any part of it."

"Oh! don't. Miss Catherine!" I cried. "We're dismal enough without conjuring up ghosts, and visions to perplex us. Come, come, be merry, and like yourself! Look at little Hareton—*he's* dreaming nothing dreary. How sweetly he smiles in his sleep!"

"Yes; and how sweetly his father curses in his solitude! You remember him, I dare say, when he was just such another as that chubby thing—nearly as

WUTHERING HEIGHTS

young and innocent. However, Nelly, I shall oblige you to listen—it's not long; and I've no power to be merry to-night."

"I wont hear it, I wont hear it!" I repeated, hastily.

I was superstitious about dreams then, and am still; and Catherine had an unusual gloom in her aspect, that made me dread something from which I might shape a prophecy, and foresee a fearful catastrophe.

She was vexed, but she did not proceed. Apparently taking up another subject, she re-commenced in a short time.

"If I were in heaven, Nelly, I should be extremely miserable."

"Because you are not fit to go there," I answered. "All sinners would be miserable in heaven."

"But it is not for that. I dreamt, once, that I was there."

"I tell you I wont harken to your dreams, Miss Catherine! I'll go to bed," I interrupted again.

She laughed, and held me down, for I made a motion to leave my chair.

"This is nothing," cried she; "I was only going to say that heaven did not seem to be my home; and I broke my heart with weeping to come back to earth; and the angels were so angry that they flung me out, into the middle of the heath on the top of Wuthering Heights: where I woke sobbing for joy. That will do to explain my secret, as well as the other. I've no more business to marry Edgar Linton than I have to be in heaven; and if the wicked man in there, had not brought Heathcliff so low I shouldn't have thought of it. It would degrade me to marry Heathcliff, now; so he shall never know how I love him; and that, not because he's handsome, Nelly, but because he's more myself than I am. Whatever our souls are made of, his and mine are the same, and Linton's is as different as a moonbeam from lightning, or frost from fire."

Ere this speech ended I became sensible of Heathcliff's presence. Having noticed a slight movement, I turned my head, and saw him rise from the bench, and steal out, noiselessly. He had listened till he heard Catherine say it would degrade her to marry him, and then he staid to hear no farther.

My companion, sitting on the ground, was prevented by the back of the settle from remarking his presence or departure; but I started, and bade her hush!

"Why?" she asked, gazing nervously round.

"Joseph is here," I answered, catching, opportunely, the roll of his cart-wheels up the road; "and Heathcliff will come in with him. I'm not sure whether he were not at the door this moment."

"Oh, he couldn't overhear me at the door!" said she. "Give me Hareton, while you get the supper, and when it is ready ask me to sup with you. I want to cheat my uncomfortable conscience, and be convinced that Heathcliff has no notion of these things—he has not, has be? He does not know what being in love is?"

"I see no reason that he should not know, as well as you," I returned; "and if *you* are his choice, he'll be the most unfortunate creature that ever was born! As soon as you become Mrs. Linton, he loses friend, and love, and all!

EMILY BRONTË

Have you considered how you'll bear the separation, and how he'll bear to be quite deserted in the world? Because, Miss Catherine—"

"He quite deserted! we separated!" she exclaimed, with an accent of indignation. "Who is to separate us, pray? They'll meet the fate of Milo! Not as long as I live, Ellen—for no mortal creature. Every Linton on the face of the earth might melt into nothing, before I could consent to forsake Heathcliff. Oh, that's not what I intend—that's not what I mean! I shouldn't be Mrs. Linton were such a price demanded! He'll be as much to me as he has been all his lifetime. Edgar must shake off his antipathy, and tolerate him, at least. He will when he learns my true feelings towards him. Nelly, I see now, you think me a selfish wretch, but, did it never strike you that, if Heathcliff and I married, we should be beggars? whereas, if I marry Linton, I can aid Heathcliff to rise, and place him out of my brother's power."

"With your husband's money, Miss Catherine?" I asked. "You'll find him not so pliable as you calculate upon: and, though I'm hardly a judge, I think that's the worst motive you've given yet for being the wife of young Linton."

"It is not," retorted she, "it is the best! The others were the satisfaction of my whims; and for Edgar's sake, too, to satisfy him. This is for the sake of one who comprehends in his person my feelings to Edgar and myself. I cannot express it; but surely you and every body have a notion that there is, or should be an existence of yours beyond you. What were the use of my creation if I were entirely contained here? My great miseries in this world have been Heathcliff's miseries, and I watched and felt each from the beginning; my great thought in living is himself. If all else perished, and *he* remained, I should still continue to be; and, if all else remained, and he were annihilated, the Universe would turn to a mighty stranger. I should not seem a part of it. My love for Linton is like the foliage in the woods. Time will change it, I'm well aware, as winter changes the trees—my love for Heathcliff resembles the eternal rocks beneath—a source of little visible delight, but necessary. Nelly, I *am* Heathcliff—he's always, always in my mind—not as a pleasure, any more than I am always a pleasure to myself—but, as my own being—so, don't talk of our separation again—it is impracticable; and—"

She paused, and hid her face in the folds of my gown; but I jerked it forcibly away. I was out of patience with her folly!

"If I can make any sense of your nonsense, Miss," I said, "it only goes to convince me that you are ignorant of the duties you undertake in marrying; or else, that you are a wicked, unprincipled girl. But, trouble me with no more secrets. I'll not promise to keep them."

"You'll keep that?" she asked, eagerly.

"No, I'll not promise," I repeated.

She was about to insist, when the entrance of Joseph finished our conversation; and Catherine removed her seat to a corner, and nursed Hareton, while I made the supper.

WUTHERING HEIGHTS 119

After it was cooked, my fellow servant and I began to quarrel who should carry some to Mr. Hindley; and we didn't settle it till all was nearly cold. Then we came to the agreement that we would let him ask, if he wanted any, for we feared particularly to go into his presence when he had been sometime alone.

"Und hah isn't that nowt comed in frough th' field, be this time? What is he abaht? girt eedle seeght!" demanded the old man, looking round for Heathcliff.

"I'll call him," I replied. "He's in the barn, I've no doubt."

I went and called, but got no answer. On returning, I whispered to Catherine that he had heard a good part of what she said, I was sure; and told how I saw him quit the kitchen just as she complained of her brother's conduct regarding him.

She jumped up in a fine fright—flung Hareton onto the settle, and ran to seek for her friend herself, not taking leisure to consider why she was so flurried, or how her talk would have affected him.

She was absent such a while that Joseph proposed we should wait no longer. He cunningly conjectured they were staying away in order to avoid hearing his protracted blessing. They were "ill eneugh for ony fahl manners," he affirmed. And, on their behalf, he added, that night a special prayer to the usual quarter of an hour's supplication before meat, and would have tacked another to the end of the grace, had not his young mistress broken in upon him with a hurried command, that he must run down the road, and, wherever Heathcliff had rambled, find and make him re-enter directly!"

"I want to speak to him, and I *must*, before I go up-stairs, she said. "And the gate is open, he is somewhere out of hearing; for he would not reply, though I shouted at the top of the fold as loud as I could."

Joseph objected at first; she was too much in earnest, however, to suffer contradiction; and, at last, he placed his hat on his head, and walked grumbling forth.

Meantime, Catherine paced up and down the floor, exclaiming—

"I wonder where he is—I wonder where he *can* be!" What did I say, Nelly? I've forgotten. Was he vexed at my bad humour this afternoon? Dear! tell me what I've said to grieve him? I do wish he'd come. I do wish he would!"

"What a noise for nothing!" I cried, though rather uneasy myself. "What a trifle scares you! It's surely no great cause of alarm that Heathcliff should take a moonlight saunter on the moors, or, even lie too sulky to speak to us, in the hay-loft. I'll engage he's lurking there. See, if I don't ferret him out!"

I departed to renew my search; its result was disappointment, and Joseph's quest ended in the same.

"Yon lad gets war un war!" observed he on re-entering. "He's left th' yate ut t' full swing, and miss's pony has trodden dahn two rigs uh corn, un plottered through, raight o'er intuh t' meadow! Hahsomdiver, t' maister 'ull play t'

EMILY BRONTË

divil to-morn, and he'll do weel. He's patience itsseln wi' sich careless, offald craters—patience itsseln he is! Bud he'll nut be soa allus—yah's see, all on ye! Yah mumn't drive him aht uf his heead fur nowt!"

"Have you found Heathcliff, you ass?" interrupted Catherine. "Have you been looking for him, as I ordered?"

"Aw sud more likker look for th' horse," he replied. "It 'ud be tuh more sense. Bud, aw can look for norther horse, nur man uf a neeght loike this—as black as t' chimbley! und Hathecliff's noan t' chap tuh coom ut *maw* whistle—happen he'll be less hard uh hearing wi' *ye*!"

It *was* a very dark evening for summer: the clouds appeared inclined to thunder, and I said we had better all sit down; the approaching rain would be certain to bring him home without further trouble.

However, Catherine would not be persuaded into tranquillity. She kept wandering to and fro, from the gate to the door, in a state of agitation, which permitted no repose: and, at length, took up a permanent situation on one side of the wall, near the road; where, heedless of my expostulations, and the growling thunder, and the great drops that began to plash around her, she remained calling, at intervals, and then listening, and then crying outright. She beat Hareton, or any child, at a good, passionate fit of crying.

About midnight, while we still sat up, the storm came rattling over the Heights in full fury. There was a violent wind, as well as thunder, and either one or the other split a tree off at the corner of the building; a huge bough fell across the roof, and knocked down a portion of the east chimney-stack, sending a clatter of stones and soot into the kitchen fire.

We thought a bolt had fallen in the middle of us, and Joseph swung onto his knees, beseeching the Lord to remember the Patriarchs Noah and Lot; and, as in former times, spare the righteous, though he smote the ungodly. I felt some sentiment that it must be a judgment on us also. The Jonah, in my mind, was Mr. Earnshaw, and I shook the handle of his den that I might ascertain if he were yet living. He replied audibly enough, in a fashion which made my companion vociferate more clamorously than before that a wide distinction might be drawn between saints like himself, and sinners like his master. But, the uproar passed away in twenty minutes, leaving us all unharmed, excepting Cathy, who got thoroughly drenched for her obstinacy in refusing to take shelter, and standing bonnetless and shawlless to catch as much water as she could with her hair and clothes.

She came in, and lay down on the settle, all soaked as she was, turning her face to the back, and putting her hands before it.

"Well Miss!" I exclaimed, touching her shoulder. "You are not bent on getting your death, are you? Do you know what o'clock it is? Half-past twelve. Come! come to bed; there's no use waiting longer on that foolish boy—he'll be gone to Gimmerton, and he'll stay there now. He guesses we should n't wake for him till this late hour; at least, he guesses that only

WUTHERING HEIGHTS   121

Mr. Hindley would be up; and he'd rather avoid having the door opened by the master."

"Nay, nay, he's noan at Gimmerton!" said Joseph. "Aw's niver wonder, bud he's at t' bothoin uf a bog-hoile. This visitation worn't for nowt, und aw wod hev ye tub look aht. Miss,—yah muh be t' next. Thank Hivin for all! tuh them as is chozzen, and piked aht froo' th' rubbidge! Yah knaw whet t' Scripture ses—"

And he began quoting several texts; refering us to the chapters and verses, where we might find them.

I having vainly begged the wilful girl to rise and remove her wet things, left him preaching, and her shivering, and betook myself to bed with little Hareton; who slept as fast as if every one had been sleeping round him.

I heard Joseph read on a while afterwards; then, I distinguished his slow step on the ladder, and then I dropt asleep.

Coming down somewhat later than usual, I saw, by the sunbeams piercing the chinks of the shutters, Miss Catherine still seated near the fire-place. The house door was ajar, too light entered from its unclosed windows, Hindley had come out, and stood on the kitchen hearth, haggard and drowsy.

"What ails you, Cathy?" he was saying when I entered; "You look as dismal as a drowned whelp—Why are you so damp and pale child?"

"I've been wet;" she answered reluctantly "and I'm cold, that's all."

"Oh, she is naughty!" I cried, perceiving the master to be tolerably sober; "She got steeped in the shower of yesterday evening, and there she has sat, the night through, and I couldn't prevail on her to stir."

Mr. Earnshaw stared at us in surprise. "The night through," he repeated. "What kept her up, not fear of the thunder, surely? That was over, hours since."

Neither of us wished to mention Heathcliff's absence, as long as we could conceal it; so, I replied, I didn't know how she took it into her head to sit up; and she said nothing.

The morning was fresh and cool; I threw back the lattice, and presently the room filled with sweet scents from the garden: but Catherine called peevishly to me.

"Ellen, shut the window. I'm starving!" And her teeth chattered as she shrunk closer to the almost extinguished embers.

"She's ill—" said Hindley, taking her wrist, "I suppose that's the reason she would not go to bed—Damn it! I don't want to be troubled with more sickness, here—What took you into the rain?"

"Running after t'lads, as usuald!" croaked Joseph, catching an opportunity, from our hesitation, to thrust in his evil tongue.

"If Aw wur yah, maister, Aw'd just slam t'boards i' their faces all on 'em, gentle and simple! Never a day ut yah're off, but yon cat uh Linton comes sneaking hither—and Miss Nelly shoo's a fine lass! shoo sits watching for ye i' t'kitchen; and as yah're in at one door, he's aht at t'other—Und, then, wer grand lady goes a coorting uf hor side! It's bonny behaviour, lurking amang t'flields, after twelve ut' night, wi that fahl, flaysome divil uf a gipsy, Heathcliff,! They think *Aw'm* blind; but Aw'm noan, now't ut t'soart! Aw seed young Linton, boath coming and going, and Aw seed *yah* (directing his discourse to me.) Yah gooid fur nowt, slattenly witch! nip up nud bolt intuh th' haks, t' minute yah heard t'maister's horse fit clatter up t' road.

"Silence, eavesdropper!" cried Catherine, "None of your insolence, before me!" Edgar Linton, came yesterday, by chance, Hindley: and it was *I* who told him to be off: because, I knew you would not like to have met him as you were."

"You lie, Cathy, no doubt," answered her brother, "and you are a confounded simpleton! But, never mind Linton, at present—Tell me, were you not with Heathcliff, last night? Speak the truth, now. You need not be afraid of harming him—Though I hate him as much as ever, he did me a good turn, a short time since, that will make my conscience tender of breaking his neck. To prevent it, I shall send him about his business, this very morning; and after he's gone, I'd advise you all to look sharp, I shall only have the more humour for you!"

"I never saw Heathcliff last night," answered Catherine, beginning to sob bitterly: "and if yon do turn him out of doors, I'll go with him. But, perhaps, you'll never have an opportunity—perhaps, he's gone." Here she burst into uncontrollable grief, and the remainder of her words were inarticulate.

Hindley lavished on her a torrent of scornful abuse, and bid her get to her room immediately, or she shouldn't cry for nothing! I obliged her to obey; and I shall never forget what a scene she acted, when we reached her chamber. It terrified me—I thought she was going mad, and I begged Joseph to run for the doctor.

It proved the commencement of delirium: Mr. Kenneth, as soon as he saw her, pronounced her dangerously ill; she had a fever.

He bled her, and he told me to let her live on whey, and water gruel; and take care she did not throw herself down stairs, or out of the window; and then he left; for, he had enough to do in the parish where two or three miles was the ordinary distance between cottage and cottage.

Though I cannot say I made a gentle nurse, and Joseph and the master were no better; and, though our patient was as wearisome and headstrong as a patient could be, she weathered it through.

Old Mrs. Linton paid us several visits, to be sure; and set things to rights, and scolded and ordered us all; and when Catherine was convalescent, she insisted on conveying her to Thrushcross Grange; for which deliverance we were very grateful. But, the poor dame had reason to repent of her kindness; she, and her husband, both took the fever, and died within a few days of each other.

WUTHERING HEIGHTS 123

Our young lady returned to us, saucier, and more passionate, and haughtier than ever. Heathcliff had never been heard of since the evening of the thunderstorm, and, one day, I had the misfortune, when she had provoked me exceedingly, to lay the blame of his disappearance on her (where indeed it belonged, as she well knew.) From that period for several months, she ceased to hold any communication with me save in the relation of a mere servant. Joseph fell under a ban also; he *would* speak his mind, and lecture her all the same as if she were a little girl; and she esteemed herself a woman, and our mistress; and thought that her recent illness gave her a claim to be treated with consideration. Then the doctor had said that she would not bear crossing much, she ought to have her own way; and it was nothing less than murder, in her eyes, for any one, to presume to stand up and contradict her.

From Mr. Earnshaw, and his companions she kept aloof, and tutored by Kenneth, and serious threats of a fit that often attended her rages, her brother allowed her whatever she pleased to demand, and generally avoided aggravating her fiery temper. He was rather too indulgent in humouring her caprices; not from affection, but from pride; he wished earnestly to see her bring honour to the family by an alliance with the Lintons, and, as long as she let him alone, she might trample us like slaves for ought he cared!

Edgar Linton, as multitudes have been before, and will be after him, was infatuated; and believed himself the happiest man alive on the day he led her to Gimmerton chapel, three years subsequent to his father's death.

Much against my inclination, I was persuaded to leave Wuthering Heights and accompany her here. Little Hareton was nearly five years old, and I had just began to teach him his letters: We made a sad parting, but Catherine's tears were more powerful than ours—When I refused to go, and when she found her entreaties did not move me, she went lamenting to her husband, and brother. The former offered me munificent wages; the latter ordered me to pack up—he wanted no women in the house, he said, now that there was no mistress; and as to Hareton, the curate should take him in hand, by and bye. And so, I had but one choice left, to do as I was ordered—I told the master he got rid of all decent people only to run to ruin a little faster; I kissed Hareton good bye; and, since then, he has been a stranger, and it's very queer to think it, but I've no doubt, he has completely forgotten all about Ellen Dean and that he was ever more than all the world to her, and she to him!

At this point of the housekeeper's story she chanced to glance towards the time-piece over the chimney; and was in amazement, on seeing the minute-hand measure half past one. She would not hear of staying a second longer—In truth, I felt rather disposed to defer the sequel of her narrative, myself: and now, that she is vanished to her rest, and I have meditated for another hour or two, I shall summon courage to go, also, in spite of aching laziness of head and limbs.

Chapter X.

A CHARMING introduction to a hermit's life! Four weeks' torture, tossing and sickness! Oh, these bleak winds, and bitter, northern skies, and impassable roads, and dilatory country surgeons! And, oh, this dearth of the human physiognomy, and, worse than all, the terrible intimation of Kenneth that I need not expect to be out of doors till spring!

Mr. Heathcliff has just honoured me with a call. About seven days ago he sent me a brace of grouse—the last of the season. Scoundrel! He is not altogether guiltless in this illness of mine; and that I had a great mind to tell him. But, alas! how could I offend a man who was charitable enough to sit at my bedside a good hour, and talk on some other subject than pills, and draughts, blisters, and leeches?

This is quite an easy interval. I am too weak to read, yet I feel as if I could enjoy something interesting. Why not have up Mrs. Dean to finish her tale? I can recollect its chief incidents, as far as she had gone. Yes, I remember her hero had run off, and never been heard of for three years; and the heroine was married. I'll ring; she'll be delighted to find me capable of talking cheerfully.

Mrs. Dean came.

"It wants twenty minutes, sir, to taking the medicine," she commenced.

"Away, away with it!" I replied; "I desire to have—"

"The doctor says you must drop the powders."

"With all my heart! Don't interrupt me. Come and take your seat here. Keep your fingers from that bitter phalanx of vials. Draw your knitting out of your pocket—that will do—now continue the history of Mr. Heathcliff, from where you left off, to the present day. Did he finish his education on the Continent, and come back a gentleman? or did he get a sizer's place at college? or escape to America, and earn honours by drawing blood from his foster country? or make a fortune more promptly, on the English highways?"

"He may have done a little in all these vocations, Mr. Lockwood; but I couldn't give my word for any. I stated before that I didn't know how he gained his money; neither am I aware of the means he took to raise his mind from the savage ignorance into which it was sunk; but, with your leave, I'll proceed in my own fashion, if you think it will amuse, and not weary you. Are you feeling better this morning?"

"Much."

"That's good news. I got Miss Catherine and myself to Thrushcross Grange: and to my agreeable disappointment, she behaved infinitely better than I dared to expect. She seemed almost over fond of Mr. Linton; and even to his sister, she showed plenty of affection. They were both very attentive to her comfort, certainly. It was not the thorn bending to the honeysuckles, but the honeysuckles embracing the thorn. There were no mutual concessions; one stood erect, and the others yielded; and who *can* be ill-natured, and bad-tempered, when they encounter neither opposition, nor indifference?

"I observed that Mr. Edgar had a deep-rooted fear of ruffling her humour. He concealed it from her; but if ever he heard me answer sharply, or saw any other servant grow cloudy at some imperious order of hers, he would show his trouble by a frown of displeasure that never darkened on his own account. He, many a time, spoke sternly to me about my pertness; and averred that the stab of a knife could not inflict a worse pang than he suffered at seeing his lady vexed.

"Not to grieve a kind master I learnt to be less touchy; and, for the space of half a year, the gunpowder lay as harmless as sand, because no fire came near to explode it. Catherine had seasons of gloom and silence, now and then, they were respected with sympathizing silence by her husband, who ascribed them to an alteration in her constitution, produced by her perilous illness, as she was never subject to depression of spirits before. The return of sunshine was welcomed by answering sunshine from him. I believe I may assert that they were really in possession of deep and growing happiness.

"It ended. Well, we *must* be for ourselves in the long run; the mild and generous are only more justly selfish than the domineering—and it ended when circumstances caused each to feel that the one's interest was not the chief consideration in the other's thoughts.

"On a mellow evening in September, I was coming from the garden with a heavy basket of apples which I had been gathering. It had got dusk, and the moon looked over the high wall of the court, causing undefined shadows to lurk in the corners of the numerous projecting portions of the building. I set my burden on the house steps by the kitchen door, and lingered to rest, and draw in a few more breaths of the soft, sweet air; my eyes were on the moon, and my back to the entrance, when I heard a voice behind me say—

"'Nelly, is that you?'

"It was a deep voice, and foreign in tone: yet, there was something in the manner of pronouncing my name which made it sound familiar. I turned about to discover who spoke, fearfully, for the doors were shut, and I had seen nobody on approaching the steps.

"Something stirred in the porch; and moving nearer, I distinguished a tall man dressed in dark clothes, with dark face and hair. He leant against the side, and held his fingers on the latch, as if intending to open for himself.

"'Who can it be?' I thought. 'Mr. Earnshaw? Oh, no! The voice has no resemblance to his.'

"'I have waited here an hour,' he resumed, while I continued staring; 'and the whole of that time all round has been as still as death I dared not enter. You do not know me? Look, I'm not a stranger!'

EMILY BRONTË

126

A ray fell on his features; the cheeks were sallow, and half covered with black whiskers; the brows lowering, the eyes deep set and singular. I remembered the eyes."

"What!" I cried, uncertain whether to regard him as a worldly visiter, and I raised my hands in amazement. "What! you come back? Is it really you? Is it?"

"Yes, Heathcliff," he replied, glancing from me up to the windows which reflected a score of glittering moons, but showed no lights from within. "Are they at home—where is she? Nelly, you are not glad—you needn't be so disturbed. Is she here? Speak! I want to have one word with her—your mistress. Go, and say some person from Gimmerton desires to see her."

"How will she take it?" I exclaimed, "what will she do? The surprise bewilders me—it will put her out of her head! And you *are* Heathcliff? But altered! Nay, there's no comprehending it. Have you been for a soldier?"

"Go, and carry my message," he interrupted impatiently; "I'm in hell till you do!"

He lifted the latch, and I entered; but when I got to the parlour where Mr. and Mrs. Linton were, I could not persuade myself to proceed.

At length, I resolved on making an excuse to ask if they would have the candles lighted, and I opened the door.

They sat together in a window whose lattice lay back against the wall, and displayed beyond the garden trees, and the wild green park, the valley of Gimmerton, with a long line of mist winding nearly to its top, (for very soon after you pass the chapel, as you may have noticed, the sough that runs from the marshes joins a beck which follows the bend of the glen), Wuthering Heights rose above this silvery vapour,; [*sic*] but our old house was invisible— it rather dips down on the other side.

Both the room, and its occupants, and the scene they gazed on, looked wondrously peaceful. I shrank reluctantly from performing my errand: and was actually going away, leaving it unsaid, after having put my question about the candles, when a sense of my folly compelled me to return, and mutter:

"A person from Gimmerton wishes to see you, ma'am."

"What does he want?" asked Mrs. Linton.

"I did not question him," I answered.

"Well, close the curtains, Nelly," she said; "and bring up tea. I'll be back again directly."

She quitted the apartment; Mr. Edgar inquired carelessly, who it was?

"Some one the mistress does not expect," I replied. "That Heathcliff, you recollect him, sir, who used to live at Mr. Earnshaw's."

"What, the gipsy—the plough-boy?" he cried. "Why did you not say so to Catherine?"

"Hush! you must not call him by those names, master," I said. "She'd be sadly grieved to hear you. She was nearly heartbroken when he ran off; I guess his return will make a jubilee to her."

Mr. Linton walked to a window on the other side of the room that overlooked the court. He unfastened it, and leant out. I suppose they were below, for he exclaimed, quickly:—

"Don't stand there love! Bring the person in, if it be any one particular."

Ere long, I heard the click of the latch, and Catherine flew up-stairs, breathless and wild, too excited to show gladness; indeed, by her face, you would rather have surmised an awful calamity.

"Oh, Edgar, Edgar!" she panted, flinging her arms round his neck. "Oh, Edgar, darling! Heathcliff's come back—he is!" And she tightened her embrace to a squeeze.

"Well, well," cried her husband, crossly, "don't strangle me for that! He never struck me as such a marvellous treasure. There is no need to be frantic!"

"I know you didn't like him," she answered, repressing a little the intensity of her delight. "Yet for my sake, you must be friends now. Shall I tell him to come up?"

"Here," he said, "into the parlour?"

"Where else?" she asked.

He looked vexed, and suggested the kitchen as a more suitable place for him.

Mrs. Linton eyed him with a droll expression—half angry, half laughing at his fastidiousness.

"No," she added, after a while; "I cannot sit in the kitchen. Set two tables here, Ellen; one for your master and Miss Isabella, being gentry; the other for Heathcliff and myself, being of the lower orders. Will that please you, dear? Or must I have a fire lighted elsewhere? If so, give directions. I'll run down and secure my guest. I'm afraid the joy is too great to be real!"

She was about to dart off again; but Edgar arrested her.

"*You* bid him step up," he said, addressing me; "and, Catherine, try to be glad, without being absurd! The whole household need not witness the sight of your welcoming a runaway servant as a brother."

I descended and found Heathcliff waiting under the porch, evidently anticipating an invitation to enter. He followed my guidance without waste of words, and I ushered him into the presence of the master and mistress, whose flushed cheeks betrayed signs of warm talking. But the lady's glowed with another feeling when her friend appeared at the door; she sprang forward, took both his hands, and led him to Linton; and then she seized Linton's reluctant fingers and crushed them into his.

Now fully revealed by the fire and candlelight, I was amazed, more than ever, to behold the transformation of Heathcliff. He had grown a tall, athletic, well-formed man; beside whom, my master seemed quite slender and youthlike. His upright carriage suggested the idea of his having been in the army. His countenance was much older in expression, and decision of feature than

128 EMILY BRONTË

Mr. Linton's; it looked intelligent, and retained no marks of former degradation. A half-civilized ferocity lurked yet in the depressed brows, and eyes full of black fire, but it was subdued; and his manner was even dignified, quite divested of roughness though too stern for grace.

My master's surprise equalled or exceeded mine: he remained for a minute at a loss how to address the ploughboy, as he had called him; Heathcliff dropped his slight hand, and stood looking at him coolly till he chose to speak.

"Sit down, sir," he said, at length. "Mrs. Linton, recalling old times, would have me give you a cordial reception, and, of course, I am gratified when anything occurs to please her."

"And I also," answered Heathcliff, "especially if it be anything in which I have a part. I shall stay an hour or two willingly."

He took a seat opposite Catherine, who kept her gaze fixed on him as if she feared he would vanish were she to remove it. He did not raise his to her, often; a quick glance now and then sufficed; but it flashed back, each time, more confidently, the undisguised delight he drank from hers.

They were too much absorbed in their mutual joy to suffer embarrassment; not so Mr. Edgar, he grew pale with pure annoyance, a feeling that reached its climax when his lady rose—and stepping across the rug, seized Heathcliff's hands again, and laughed like one beside herself.

"I shall think it a dream to-morrow!" she cried. "I shall not be able to believe that I have seen, and touched, and spoken to you once more—and yet, cruel Heathcliff! you don't deserve this welcome. To be absent and silent for three years, and never to think of me!"

"A little more than you have thought of me!" he murmured. "I heard of your marriage, Cathy, not long since; and, while waiting in the yard below, I meditated this plan—just to have one glimpse of your face—a stare of surprise, perhaps, and pretended pleasure; afterwards settle my score with Hindley; and then prevent the law by doing execution on myself. Your welcome has put these ideas out of my mind; but beware of meeting me with another aspect next time! Nay, you'll not drive me off again—you were really sorry for me, were you? Well, there was cause. I've fought through a bitter life since I last heard your voice, and you must forgive me, for I struggled only for you!"

"Catherine, unless we are to have cold tea, please to come to the table," interrupted Linton, striving to preserve his ordinary tone, and a due measure of politeness. "Mr. Heathcliff will have a long walk, wherever he may lodge to-night; and I'm thirsty."

She took her post before the urn; and Miss Isabella came, summoned by the bell; then, having handed their chairs forward, I left the room.

The meal hardly endured ten minutes—Catherine's cup was never filled, she could neither eat, nor drink. Edgar had made a slop in his saucer, and scarcely swallowed a mouthful.

WUTHERING HEIGHTS 129

Their guest did not protract his stay, that evening, above an hour longer. I asked, as he departed, if he went to Gimmerton?

"No, to Wuthering Heights," he answered, "Mr. Earnshaw invited me when I called this morning."

Mr. Earnshaw invited *him*! and *he* called on Mr. Earnshaw! I pondered this sentence painfully, after he was gone. Is he turning out a bit of a hypocrite, and coming into the country to work mischief under a cloak? I mused—I had a presentiment, in the bottom of my heart, that he had better have remained away.

About the middle of the night, I was wakened from my first nap by Mrs. Linton gliding into my chamber, taking a seat on my bed-side, and pulling me by the hair to rouse me.

"I cannot rest, Ellen;" she said by way of apology. "And I want some living creature to keep me company in my happiness! Edgar is sulky, because I'm glad of a thing that does not interest him—He refuses to open his mouth, except to utter pettish, silly speeches; and he affirmed I was cruel and selfish for wishing to talk when he was so sick and sleepy. He always contrives to be sick at the least cross! I gave a few sentences of commendation to Heathcliff, and he, either for a headache or a pang of envy, began to cry: so I got up and left him."

"What use is it praising Heathcliff to him?" I answered, "As lads they had an aversion to each other, and Heathcliff would hate just as much to hear him praised—it's human nature. Let Mr. Linton alone about him, unless you would like an open quarrel between them."

"But does it not show great weakness?" pursued she. "I'm not envious—I never feel hurt at the brightness of Isabella's yellow hair, and the whiteness of her skin; at her dainty elegance, and the fondness all the family exhibit for her. Even you Nelly, if we have a dispute sometimes, you back Isabella, at once; and I yield like a foolish mother—I call her a darling, and flatter her into a good temper. It pleases her brother to see us cordial, and that pleases me. But, they are very much alike they are spoiled children, and fancy the world was made for their accommodation; and, though I humour both, I think a smart chastisement might improve them, all the same."

"You're mistaken, Mrs. Linton," said I, "They humour you—I know what there would be to do if they did not! You can well afford to indulge their passing whims, as long as their business is to anticipate all your desires—You may, however, fall out, at last, over something of equal consequence to both sides; and, then those you term weak are very capable of being as obstinate as you!"

"And then we shall fight to the death, shan't we, Nelly?" she returned laughing, "No! I tell you, I have such faith in Linton's love that I believe I might kill him, and he wouldn't wish to retaliate."

I advised her to value him the more for his affection.

"I do," she answered, "but, he needn't resort to whining for trifles. It is childish; and, instead of melting into tears, because I said that Heathcliff was now worthy of any one's regard, and it would honour the first gentleman in the country to be his friend; he ought to have said it for me, and been delighted from sympathy—He must get accustomed to him, and he may as well like him—considering how Heathcliff has reason to object to him, I'm sure he behaved excellently!"

"What do you think of his going to Wuthering Heights?" I inquired, "He is reformed in every respect, apparently—quite a christian—offering the right hand of fellowship to his enemies all round!"

"He explained it," she replied. "I wondered as much as you—He said he called to gather information concerning me, from you, supposing you resided there still; and Joseph told Hindley who came out, and fell to questioning him of what he had been doing, and how he had been living: and finally, desired him to walk in—There were some persons sitting at cards—Heathcliff joined them; my brother lost some money to him; and, finding him plentifully supplied, he requested that he would come again in the evening, to which he consented. Hindley is too reckless to select his acquaintance prudently; he doesn't trouble himself to reflect on the causes he might have for mistrusting one whom he has basely injured—But, Heathcliff affirms his principal reason for resuming a connection with his ancient persecutor is a wish to install himself in quarters at walking distance from the Grange, and an attachment to the house where we lived together, and, likewise a hope that I shall have more opportunities of seeing him there than I could have if he settled in Gimmerton. He means to offer liberal payment for permission to lodge at the Heights; and doubtless my brother's covetousness will prompt him to accept the terms; he was always greedy, though what he grasps with one hand, he flings away with the other."

"It's a nice place for a young man to fix his dwelling in!" said I, "Have you no fear of the consequences, Mrs. Linton?"

"None for my friend," she replied, "his strong head will keep him from danger—a little for Hindley; but, he can't be made morally worse than he is; and I stand between him and bodily harm—The event of this evening has reconciled me to God, and humanity! I had risen in angry rebellion against providence—Oh, I've endured very, very bitter misery. Nelly! If that creature knew how bitter, he'd be ashamed to cloud its removal with idle petulance—It was kindness for him which induced me to bear it alone: had I expressed the agony I frequently felt, he would have been taught to long for its alleviation as ardently as I—However, it's over, and I'll take no revenge on his folly—I can afford to suffer anything, hereafter! should the meanest thing alive slap me on the cheek, I'd not only turn the other, but, I'd ask pardon for provoking it— and, as a proof, I'll, go make my peace with Edgar instantly—Good night— I'm an angel!"

In this self-complacent conviction she departed; and the success of her fulfilled resolution was obvious on the morrow—Mr. Linton had not only abjured his peevishness (though his spirits seemed still subdued by Catherine's

WUTHERING HEIGHTS 131

exuberance of vivacity) but he ventured no objection to her taking Isabella with her to Wuthering Heights, in the afternoon; and she rewarded him with such a summer of sweetness and affection, in return, as made the house a paradise for several days; both master, and servants profiting from the perpetual sunshine.

Heathcliff—Mr. Heathcliff I should say in future, used the liberty of visiting at Thrushcross Grange cautiously, at first: he seemed estimating how far its owner would bear his intrusion. Catherine also, deemed it judicious to moderate her expressions of pleasure in receiving him; and he gradually established his right to be expected.

He retained a great deal of the reserve for which his boyhood was remarkable, and that served to repress all startling demonstrations of feeling. My master's uneasiness experienced a lull, and further circumstances diverted it into another channel for a space.

His new source of trouble sprang from the not anticipated misfortune of Isabella Linton evincing a sudden and irresistible attraction towards the tolerated guest—She was at that time a charming young lady of eighteen; infantile in manners, though possessed of keen wit, keen feelings, and a keen temper, too, if irritated. Her brother, who loved her tenderly, was appalled at this fantastic preference. Leaving aside the degradation of an alliance with a nameless man, and the possible fact that his property, in default of heirs male, might pass into such a one's power, he had sense to comprehend Heathcliff's disposition—to know that, though his exterior was altered, his mind was unchangeable, and unchanged. And he dreaded that mind; it revolted him; he shrank forebodingly from the idea of committing Isabella to its keeping.

He would have recoiled still more had he been aware that her attachment rose unsolicited, and was bestowed where it awakened no reciprocation of sentiment; for the minute he discovered its existence, he laid the blame on Heathcliff's deliberate designing.

We had all remarked, during some time, that Miss Linton fretted and pined over something. She grew cross and wearisome, snapping at and teazing Catherine, continually, at the imminent risk of exhausting her limited patience. We excused her to a certain extent, on the plea of ill health—she was dwindling and fading before our eyes—But, one day "when she had been peculiarly wayward, rejecting her breakfast, complaining that the servants did not do what she told them; that the mistress would allow her to be nothing in the house, and Edgar neglected her; that she had caught a cold with the doors being left open, and we let the parlour fire go out on purpose to vex her; with a hundred yet more frivolous accusations; Mrs. Linton peremptorily insisted that she should get to-bed; and, having scolded her heartily, threatened to send for the doctor.

Mention of Kenneth, caused her to exclaim, instantly, that her health was perfect, and it was only Catherine's harshness which made her unhappy.

EMILY BRONTË

"How can you say I am harsh, you naughty fondling?" cried the mistress, amazed at the unreasonable assertion. "You are surely losing your reason. When have I been harsh, tell me?"

"Yesterday," sobbed Isabella, "and now!"

"Yesterday!" said her sister-in-law. "On what occasion?"

"In our walk along the moor; you told me to ramble where I pleased, while you sauntered on with Mr. Heathcliff!"

"And that's your notion of harshness?" said Catherine, laughing. "It was no hint that your company was superfluous; we didn't care whether you kept with us or not; I merely thought Heathcliff's talk would have nothing entertaining for your ears."

"Oh, no," wept the young lady, "you wished me away, because you knew I liked to be there!"

"Is she sane?" asked Mrs. Linton, appealing to me. "I'll repeat our conversation, word for word, Isabella; and you point out any charm it could have had for you."

"I don't mind the conversation," she answered: "I wanted to be with—"

"Well!" said Catherine, perceiving her hesitate to complete the sentence.

"With him; and I wont be always sent off!" she continued, kindling up. "You are a dog in the manger, Cathy, and desire no one to be loved but yourself!"

"You are an impertinent little monkey!" exclaimed Mrs. Linton, in surprise. "But I'll not believe this idiocy! It is impossible that you can covet the admiration of Heathcliff —that you can consider him an agreeable person! I hope I have misunderstood you, Isabella?

"No, you have not," said the infatuated girl. "I love him more than ever you loved Edgar; and he might love me if you would let him!"

"I wouldn't be you for a kingdom, then!" Catherine declared, emphatically— and she seemed to speak sincerely. "Nelly, help me to convince her of her madness. Tell her what Heathcliff is—an unreclaimed creature, without refinement—without cultivation; an arid wilderness of furze and whinstone. I'd as soon put that little canary into the park on a winter's day as recommend you to bestow your heart on him! It is deplorable ignorance of his character, child, and nothing else, which makes that dream enter your head, pray don't imagine that he conceals depths of benevolence and affection beneath a stern exterior! He's not a rough diamond—a pearl-containing oyster of a rustic; he's a fierce, pitiless, wolfish man. I never say to him let this or that enemy alone, because it would be ungenerous or cruel to harm them—I say let them alone, because *I* should hate them to be wronged: and he'd crush you, like a sparrow's egg, Isabella, if he found you a troublesome charge. I know he couldn't love a Linton; and yet, he'd be quite capable of marrying your fortune, and expectations. Avarice is growing with him a besetting sin. There's my picture; and I'm his friend—so much so, that had he thought seriously

WUTHERING HEIGHTS 133

to catch you, I should, perhaps, have held my tongue, and let you fall into his trap."

Miss Linton regarded her sister-in-law with indignation.

"For shame! for shame!" she repeated, angrily. "You are worse than twenty foes, you poisonous friend!"

"Ah! you wont believe me, then?" said Catherine. "You think I speak from wicked selfishness?"

"I'm certain you do," retorted Isabella; "and I shudder at you!"

"Good!" cried the other. "Try for yourself, if that be your spirit; I have done, and yield the argument to your saucy insolence."

"And I must suffer for her egotism!" she sobbed, as Mrs. Linton left the room. "All, all is against me; she has blighted my single consolation. But she uttered falsehoods, didn't she? Mr. Heathcliff is not a fiend; he has an honourable soul, and a true one, or how could he remember her?"

"Banish him from your thoughts, miss," I said. "He's a bird of bad omen; no mate for you. Mrs. Linton spoke strongly, and yet, I can't contradict her. She is better acquainted with his heart than I, or any one besides; and she never would represent him as worse than he is. Honest people don't hide their deeds. How has he been living? how has he got rich? why is he staying at Wuthering Heights, the house of a man whom he abhors? They say Mr. Earnshaw is worse and worse since he came. They sit up all night together continually; and Hindley has been borrowing money on his land; and does nothing but play and drink, I heard only a week ago; it was Joseph who told me—I met him at Gimmerton."

"Nelly," he said, "we's hae a Crahnr's 'quest enah, at ahr folks. One on 'em's a' most getten his finger cut off wi' hauding t'other froo' sticking hisseln loike a cawlf. That's maister, yah knaw, ut's soa up uh going tuh t'grand 'sizes. He's noan feard uh t' Bench uh judges, norther Paul, nur Peter, nur John, nor Mathew, nor noan on 'em, nut he! He fair like's he langs tuh set his brazened face agean 'em! And yon bonny lad Heathcliff, yah mind, he's a rare un! He can girn a laugh, as weel's onybody at a raight divil's jest. Does he niver say nowt of his fine living amang us, when he goas tuh t' Grange? This is t' way on't—up at sun-dahn; dice, brandy, cloised shutters, und can'le lught till next day, at nooin—then, t' fooil gangs banning un raving tuh his cham'er, makking dacent fowks dig thur fingers i' thur higs fur varry shaume; un' the' knave, wah he carn cahnt his brass, un ate, un' sleep, un' off tuh his neighbour's tuh gossip wi' t' wife. I' course, be tells Dame Catherine hah hor father's goold runs intuh his pocket, and her fathur's son gallops dahn t' Broad road, while he flees afore tuh oppen t' pikes?" Now, Miss Linton, Joseph is an old rascal, but no liar; and, if his account of Heathcliff's conduct be true, you would never think of desiring such a husband, would you?"

"You are leagued with the rest, Ellen!" she replied. "I'll not listen to your slanders. What malevolence you must have to wish to convince me that there is no happiness in the world!"

134   EMILY BRONTË

Whether she would have got over this fancy if left to herself, or persevered in nursing it perpetually, I cannot say; she had little time to reflect. The day after, there was a justice-meeting at the next town; my master was obliged to attend; and Mr. Heathcliff, aware of his absence, called rather earlier than usual.

Catherine and Isabella were sitting in the library, on hostile terms, but silent. The latter alarmed at her recent indiscretion, and the disclosure she had made of her secret feelings in a transcient fit of passion; the former, on mature consideration, really offended with her companion; and, if she laughed again at her pertness, inclined to make it no laughing matter to *her*.

She did laugh as she saw Heathcliff pass the window. I was sweeping the hearth, and I noticed a mischievous smile on her lips. Isabella, absorbed in her meditations, or a book, remained till the door opened, and it was too late to attempt an escape, which she would gladly have done had it been practicable.

"Come in, that's right!" exclaimed the mistress, gaily, pulling a chair to the fire. "Here are two people sadly in need of a third to thaw the ice between them; and you are the very one we should both of us choose. Heathcliff, I'm proud to show you, at last, somebody that dotes on you more than myself. I expect you to feel flattered—nay, it's not Nelly; don't look at her! My poor little sister-in-law is breaking her heart by mere contemplation of your phys- ical and moral beauty. It lies in your own power to be Edgar's brother! No, no, Isabella, you sha'n't run off," she continued, arresting, with feigned playful- ness, the confounded girl who had risen indignantly.

"We were quarrelling like cats about you, Heathcliff; and I was fairly beaten in protestations of devotion, and admiration; and, moreover, I was informed that if I would but have the manners to stand aside, my rival, as she will have herself to be, would shoot a shaft into your soul that would fix you for ever, and send my image into eternal oblivion!"

"Catherine," said Isabella, calling up her dignity, and disdaining to strug- gle from the tight grasp that held her. "I'd thank you to adhere to the truth and not slander me, even in joke! Mr. Heathcliff, be kind enough to bid this friend of yours release me—she forgets that you and I are not intimate acquaintances, and what amuses her is painful to me beyond expression."

As the guest answered nothing, but took his seat, and looked thoroughly indifferent what sentiments she cherished concerning him, she turned, and whispered an earnest appeal for liberty to her tormentor.

"By no means!" cried Mrs. Linton in answer. "I wont be named a dog in the manger again. You *shall* stay, now then! Heathcliff, why don't you evince satisfaction at my pleasant news? Isabella swears that the love Edgar has for me, is nothing to that she entertains for you. I'm sure she made some speech of the kind, did she not, Ellen? And she has fasted ever since the day before

WUTHERING HEIGHTS 135

yesterday's walk, from sorrow and rage that I despatched her out of your society, under the idea of its being unacceptable."

"I think you belie her," said Heathcliff, twisting his chair to face them. "She wishes to be out of my society now, at any rate!"

And he stared hard at the object of discourse, as one might do at a strange repulsive animal, a centipede from the Indies, for instance, which curiosity leads one to examine in spite of the aversion it raises.

The poor thing couldn't bear that; she grew white and red in rapid succession, and, while tears beaded her lashes, bent the strength of her small fingers to loosen the firm clutch of Catherine, and perceiving that, as fast as she raised one finger off her arm, another closed down, and she could not remove the whole together, she began to make use of her nails, and their sharpness presently ornamented the detainer's with crescents of red.

"There's a tigress!" exclaimed Mrs. Linton, setting her free, and shaking her hand with pain. "Begone, for God's sake, and hide your vixen face! How foolish to reveal those talons to *him*. Can't you fancy the conclusions he'll draw? Look, Heathcliff! they are instruments that will do execution—you must beware of your eyes."

"I'd wrench them off her fingers, if they ever menaced me," he answered, brutally, when the door had closed after her. "But, what did you mean by teasing the creature in that manner, Cathy? You were not speaking the truth, were you?"

"I assure you I was," she returned. "She has been pining for your sake several weeks; and raving about you this morning, and pouring forth a deluge of abuse, because I represented your failings in a plain light for the purpose of mitigating her adoration. But don't notice it further. I wished to punish her sauciness, that's all—I like her too well, my dear Heathcliff, to let you absolutely seize and devour her up."

"And I like her too ill to attempt it," said he, "except in a very ghoulish fashion. You'd hear of odd things, if I lived alone with that mawkish, waxen face; the most ordinary would be painting on its white the colours of the rainbow, and turning the blue eyes, black, every day or two; they detestably resemble Linton's."

"Delectably," observed Catherine. "They are dove's eyes—angel's!"

"She's her brother's heir, is she not?" he asked, after a brief silence.

"I should be sorry to think so," returned his companion. "Half-a-dozen nephews shall erase her title, please Heaven! Abstract your mind from the subject, at present—you are too prone to covet your neighbour's goods: remember *this* neighbour's goods are mine."

"If they were *mine*, they would be none the less that," said Heathcliff, "but though Isabella Linton may be silly, she is scarcely mad; and—in short we'll dismiss the matter as you advise."

EMILY BRONTË

From their tongues, they did dismiss it; and Catherine, probably, from her thoughts. The other, I felt certain, recalled it often in the course of the evening; I saw him smile to himself—grin rather—and lapse into ominous musing whenever Mrs. Linton had occasion to be absent from the apartment.

I determined to watch his movements. My heart invariably cleaved to the master's, in preference to Catherine's side; with reason, I imagined, for he was kind, and trustful, and honourable: and she—she could not be called the *opposite*, yet, she seemed to allow herself such wide latitude, that I had little faith in her principles, and still less sympathy for her feelings. I wanted something to happen which might have the effect of freeing both Wuthering Heights and the Grange of Mr. Heathcliff, quietly, leaving us as we had been prior to his advent. His visits were a continual nightmare to me; and, I suspected, to my master also. His abode at the Heights was an oppression past explaining. I felt that God had forsaken the stray sheep there to its own wicked wanderings, and an evil beast prowled between it and the fold, waiting his time to spring and destroy.

Chapter XI.

Sometimes, while meditating on these things in solitude, I've got up in a sudden terror, and put on my bonnet to go see how all was at the farm; I've persuaded my conscience that it was a duty to warn him how people talked regarding his ways; and then I've recollected his confirmed bad habits, and, hopeless of benefiting him, have flinched from re-entering the dismal house, doubting if I could bear to be taken at my word.

One time, I passed the old gate, going out of my way, on a journey to Gimmerton. It was about the period that my narrative has reached—a bright, frosty afternoon; the ground bare, and the road hard and dry.

I came to a stone where the highway branches off on to the moor at your left hand; a rough sand-pillar, with the letters W. H. cut on its north side, on the east, G., and on the south-west, T. G. It serves as guide-post to the Grange, and Heights, and village.

The sun shone yellow on its grey head, reminding me of summer; and I cannot say why, but all at once, a gush of child's sensations flowed into my heart. Hindley and I held it a favourite spot twenty years before.

I gazed long at the weather-worn block; and, stooping down, perceived a hole near the bottom still full of snail-shells and pebbles which we were fond of storing there with more perishable things—and, as fresh as reality, it appeared that I beheld my early play-mate seated on the withered turf; his dark, square head bent forward, and his little hand scooping out the earth with a piece of slate.

"Poor Hindley!" I exclaimed, involuntarily.

I started—my bodily eye was cheated into a momentary belief that the child lifted its face and stared straight into mine! It vanished in a twinkling; but, immediately, I felt an irresistible yearning to be at the Heights. Superstition urged me to comply with this impulse—supposing he should be dead! I thought—or should die soon!—supposing it were a sign of death!

The nearer I got to the house the more agitated I grew: and on catching sight of it, I trembled every limb. The apparition had outstripped me; it stood looking through the gate. That was my first idea on observing an elf-locked, brown-eyed boy setting his ruddy countenance against the bars. Further reflection suggested this must be Hareton, *my* Hareton, not altered greatly since I left him, ten months since.

"God bless thee, darling!" I cried, forgetting instantaneously my foolish fears. "Hareton, it's Nelly—Nelly, thy nurse."

He retreated out of arm's length, and picked up a large flint.

138 EMILY BRONTË

"I am come to see thy father, Hareton," I added, guessing from the action that Nelly, if she lived in his memory at all, was not recognised as one with me.

He raised his missile to hurl it; I commenced a soothing speech, but could not stay his hand. The stone struck my bonnet, and then ensued, from the stammering lips of the little fellow, a string of curses which, whether he comprehended them or not, were delivered with practised emphasis, and distorted his baby features into a shocking expression of malignity.

You may be certain this grieved, more than angered me. Fit to cry, I took an orange from my pocket, and offered it to propitiate him.

He hesitated, and then snatched it from my hold, as if he fancied I only intended to tempt, and disappoint him.

I showed another keeping it out of his reach.

"Who has taught you those fine words, my barn," I inquired. "The curate?"

"Damn the curate, and thee! Gie me that," he replied.

"Tell us where you got your lessons, and you shall have it," said I. "Whose your master?"

"Devil daddy," was his answer.

"And what do you learn from Daddy?" I continued.

He jumped at the fruit; I raised it higher. "What does he teach you?" I asked.

"Naught," said he, "but to keep out of his gait—Daddy cannot bide me, because I swear at him."

"Ah! and the devil teaches you to swear at Daddy?" I observed.

"Aye—nay," he drawled.

"Who then?"

"Heathcliff."

"I asked if he liked Mr. Heathcliff?

"Aye!" he answered again.

Desiring to have his reasons for liking him, I could only gather the sentences. I known't—he pays Dad back what he gies to me—he curses Daddy for cursing me—He says I mun do as I will."

"And the curate does not teach you to read and write, then?" I pursued.

"No, I was told the curate should have his—teeth dashed down his—throat, if he stepped over the threshold—Heathcliff, had promised that!"

I put the orange in his hand; and bade him tell his father that a woman called Nelly Dean, was waiting to speak with him, by the garden gate.

He went up the walk, and entered the house; but, instead of Hindley, Heathcliff appeared on the door stones, and I turned directly and ran down the road as hard as ever I could race, making no halt till I gained the guide post, and feeling as scared as if I had raised a goblin.

This is not much connected with Miss Isabella's affair; except, that it urged me to resolve further, on mounting vigilant guard, and doing my utmost to

WUTHERING HEIGHTS 139

check the spread of such bad influence at the Grange, even though I should wake a domestic storm, by thwarting Mrs. Linton's pleasure.

The next time Heathcliff came, my young lady chanced to be feeding some pigeons in the court. She had never spoken a word to her sister-in-law, for three days; but, she had likewise dropped her fretful complaining, and we found it a great comfort.

Heathcliff had not the habit of bestowing a single unnecessary civility on Miss Linton, I knew. Now, as soon as he beheld her, his first precaution was to take a sweeping survey of the house-front. I was standing by the kitchen window, but I drew out of sight. He then stept across the pavement to her, and said something: she seemed embarrassed, and desirous of getting away; to prevent it, he laid his hand on her arm: she averted her face; he apparently put some question which she had no mind to answer. There was another rapid glance at the house, and supposing himself unseen, the scoundrel had the impudence to embrace her.

"Judas! Traitor!" I ejaculated "you are a hypocrite too, are you? A deliberate deceiver."

"Who is Nelly?" said Catherine's voice at my elbow—I had been over-intent on watching the pair outside to mark her entrance.

"Your worthless friend!" I answered warmly, "the sneaking rascal yonder— Ah, he has caught a glimpse of us—he is coming in! I wonder will he have the art to find a plausible excuse, for making love to Miss, when he told you he hated her?"

Mrs. Linton saw Isabella tear herself free, and run into the garden; and a minute after, Heathcliff opened the door.

I couldn't withhold giving some loose to my indignation; but Catherine angrily insisted on silence, and threatened to order me out of the kitchen, if I dared be so presumptuous as to put in my insolent tongue.

"To hear you, people might think *you* were the mistress!" She cried. "You want setting down in your right place! Heathcliff, what are you about, raising this stir? I said you must let Isabella alone!—I beg you will unless you are tired of being received here, and wish Linton to draw the bolts against you!"

"God forbid that he should try!" answered the black villain—I detested him just then. "God keep him meek and patient! Every day I grow madder after sending him to heaven!"

"Hush!" said Catherine shutting the inner door! "Don't vex me. Why have you disregarded my request? Did she come across you on purpose?"

"What is it to you?" he growled, "I have a right to kiss her, if she chooses, and you have no right to object—I'm not *your* husband *you* needn't be jealous of me!"

"I'm not jealous of you;" replied the mistress, I'm jealous for you. Clear your face, you shan't scowl at me! If you like Isabella, you shall marry her. But, do you like her, tell the truth, Heathcliff? There, you wont answer. I'm certain you don't!"

140 EMILY BRONTË

"And would Mr. Linton approve of his sister marrying that man?" I inquired.

"Mr. Linton should approve," returned my lady decisively.

"He might spare himself the trouble," said Heathcliff, "I could do as well without his approbation—And, as to you, Catherine, I have a mind to speak a few words, now, while we are at it—I want you to be aware that I *know* you have treated me infernally—infernally! Do you hear? And, if you flatter yourself that I don't perceive it you are a fool—and if you think I can be consoled by sweet words you are an idiot—and if you fancy I'll suffer unrevenged, I'll convince you of the contrary, in a very little while! Meantime, thank you for telling me your sister-in-law's secret—I swear I'll make the most of it, and stand you aside!"

"What new phase of his character is this?" exclaimed Mrs. Linton, in amazement. "I've treated you infernally—and you'll take revenge! How will you take it, ungrateful brute? How have I treated you infernally?"

"I seek no revenge on you," replied Heathcliff less vehemently. "That's not the plan—The tyrant grinds down his slaves and they don't turn against him, they crush those beneath them—You are welcome to torture me to death for your amusement, only, allow me me [*sic*] to amuse myself a little in the same style—And refrain from insult, as much as you are able. Having levelled my palace, don't erect a hovel and complacently admire your own charity in giving me that for a home. If I imagined you really wished me to marry Isabella, I'd cut my throat!"

"Oh the evil is that I am *not* jealous, is it?" cried Catherine. "Well, I won't repeat my offer of a wife—It is as bad as offering Satan a lost soul—Your bliss lies, like his, in inflicting misery—You prove it—Edgar is restored from the ill-temper he gave way to at your coming; I begin to be secure and tranquil; and, you, restless to know us at peace, appear resolved on exciting a quarrel— quarrel with Edgar if you please, Heathcliff, and deceive his sister; you'll hit on exactly the most efficient method of revenging yourself on me."

The conversation ceased—Mrs. Linton sat down by the fire, flushed and gloomy. The spirit which served her was growing intractable: she could neither lay nor control it. He stood on the hearth, with folded arms brooding on his evil thoughts; and in this position I left them, to seek the master who was wondering what kept Catherine below so long.

"Ellen," said he, when I entered, "have you seen your mistress?"

"Yes, she's in the kitchen, sir," I answered. "She's sadly put out by Mr. Heathcliff's behaviour: and, indeed, I do think it's time to arrange his visits on another footing. There's harm in being too soft, and now it's come to this—." And I related the scene in the court, and, as near as I dared, the whole subsequent dispute. I fancied it could not be very prejuicial to Mrs. Linton, unless she made it so, afterwards, by assuming the defensive for her guest.

Edgar Linton had difficulty in hearing me to the close—His first words revealed that he did not clear his wife of blame.

"This is insufferable!" he exclaimed. "It is disgraceful that she should own him for a friend, and force his company on me! Call me two men out of the hall, Ellen—Catherine shall linger no longer to argue with the low ruffian—I have humoured her enough."

He descended, and, bidding the servants wait in the passage, went, followed by me, to the kitchen. Its occupants had recommenced their angry discussion; Mrs. Linton, at least, was scolding with renewed vigour; Heathcliff had moved to the window, and hung his head somewhat cowed by her violent rating apparently.

He saw the master first, and made a hasty motion that she should be silent; which she obeyed, abruptly, on discovering the reason of his intimation.

"How is this?" said Linton, addressing her; "what notion of propriety must you have to remain here, after the language which has been held to you by that blackguard? I suppose, because it is his ordinary talk, you think nothing of it—you are habituated to his baseness, and, perhaps, imagine I can get used to it too!"

"Have you been listening at the door, Edgar?" asked the mistress, in a tone particularly calculated to provoke her husband, implying both carelessness and contempt of his irritation.

Heathcliff, who had raised his eyes at the former speech, gave a sneering laugh at the latter, on purpose, it seemed, to draw Mr. Linton's attention to him.

He succeeded; but Edgar did not mean to entertain him with any high flights of passion.

"I have been so far forbearing with you, sir," he said, quietly; "not that I was ignorant of your miserable, degraded character, but, I felt you were only partly responsible for that; and Catherine, wishing to keep up your acquaintance, I acquiesced—foolishly. Your presence is a moral poison that would contaminate the most virtuous—for that cause, and to prevent worse consequences, I shall deny you, hereafter, admission into this house, and give notice, now, that I require your instant departure. Three minutes' delay will render it involuntary and ignominious."

Heathcliff measured the height and breadth of the speaker with an eye full of derision.

"Cathy, this lamb of yours threatens like a bull!" he said. "It is in danger of splitting its skull against my knuckles. By God, Mr. Linton, I'm mortally sorry that you are not worth knocking down!"

My master glanced towards the passage, and signed me to fetch the men—he had no intention of hazarding a personal encounter.

I obeyed the hint; but Mrs. Linton suspecting something, followed, and when I attempted to call them, she pulled me back, slammed the door to, and locked it.

"Fair means!" she said, in answer to her husband's look of angry surprise. "If you have not the courage to attack him, make an apology, or allow yourself to be beaten. It will correct you of feigning more valour than you possess. No, I'll swallow the key before you shall get it! I'm delightfully rewarded for my kindness to each! After constant indulgence of one's weak nature, and the other's bad one, I earn, for thanks, two samples of blind ingratitude, stupid to absurdity! Edgar, I was defending you, and yours; and I wish Heathcliff may flog you sick, for daring to think an evil thought of me!"

It did not need the medium of a flogging to produce that effect on the master. He tried to wrest the key from Catherine's grasp; and for safety she flung it into the hottest part of the fire; whereupon Mr. Edgar was taken with a nervous trembling, and his countenance grew deadly pale. For his life he could not avert that access of emotion—mingled anguish and humiliation overcame him completely. He leant on the back of a chair, and covered his face.

"Oh! Heavens! In old days this would win you knighthood!" exclaimed Mrs. Linton. "We are vanquished, we are vanquished! Heathcliff would as soon lift a finger at you as the king would march his army against a colony of mice. Cheer up, you sha'n't be hurt! Your type is not a lamb, it's a sucking leveret."

"I wish you joy of the milk-blooded coward, Cathy!" said her friend. "I compliment you on your taste: and that is the slavering, shivering thing you preferred to me! I would not strike him with my fist, but I'd kick him with my foot, and experience considerable satisfaction. Is he weeping, or is he going to faint for fear?"

The fellow approached and gave the chair on which Linton rested a push. He'd better have kept his distance: my master quickly sprang erect, and struck him full on the throat a blow that would have levelled a slighter man.

It took his breath for a minute; and, while he choked, Mr. Linton walked out by the back door into the yard, and from thence, to the front entrance.

"There! you've done with coming here," cried Catherine. "Get away, now—he'll return with a brace of pistols, and half-a-dozen assistants. If he did overhear us, of course, he'd never forgive you. You've played me an ill turn, Heathcliff! But, go—make haste! I'd rather see Edgar at bay than you."

"Do you suppose I'm going with that blow burning in my gullet?" he thundered. "By Hell, no! I'll crush his ribs in like a rotten hazel-nut, before I cross the threshold! If I don't floor him now, I shall murder him sometime, so, as you value his existence, let me get at him!"

"He is not coming." I interposed, framing a bit of a lie. "There's the coachman, and the two gardeners; you'll surely not wait to be thrust into the road by them! Each has a bludgeon, and master will, very likely, be watching from the parlour windows to see that they fulfil his orders."

The gardeners, and coachman *were* there; but Linton was with them. They had already entered the court—Heathcliff, on second thoughts resolved to avoid a struggle against three underlings; he seized the poker, smashed the lock from the inner door, and made his escape as they tramped in.

Mrs. Linton who was very much excited, bid me accompany her up stairs. She did not know my share in contributing to the disturbance, and I was anxious to keep her in ignorance.

"I'm nearly distracted, Nelly!" she exclaimed, throwing herself on the sofa. "A thousand smiths' hammers are beating in my head! Tell Isabella to shun me—this uproar is owing to her; and should she or any one else aggravate my anger at present, I shall get wild. And, Nelly, say to Edgar, if you see him again to-night, that I'm in danger of being seriously ill—I wish it may prove true. He has startled and distressed me shockingly! I want to frighten him. Besides, he might come and begin a string of abuse, or complainings; I'm certain I should recriminate, and God knows where we should end! Will you do so, my good Nelly? You are aware that I am no way blameable in this matter. What possessed him to turn listener? Heathcliff's talk was outrageous, after you left us; but I could soon have diverted him from Isabella, and the rest meant nothing. Now, all is dashed wrong by the fool's craving to hear evil of self that haunts some people like a demon! Had Edgar never gathered our conversation, he would never have been the worse for it. Really, when he opened on me in that unreasonable tone of displeasure, after I had scolded Heathcliff till I was hoarse for *him*; I did not care, hardly, what they did to each other, especially as I felt that, however the scene closed, we should all be driven asunder for nobody knows how long! Well, if I cannot keep Heathcliff for my friend—if Edgar will be mean and jealous, I'll try to break their hearts by breaking my own. That will be a prompt way of finishing all, when I am pushed to extremity! But it's a deed to be reserved for a forlorn hope—I'd not take Linton by surprise with it. To this this point he has been discreet in dreading to provoke me; you must represent the peril of quitting that policy; and remind him of my passionate temper, verging, when kindled, on frenzy—I wish you could dismiss that apathy out of your countenance, and look rather more anxious about me!"

The stolidity with which I received these instructions was, no doubt, rather exasperating; for they were delivered in perfect sincerity, but I believed a person who could plan the turning of her fits of passion to account, beforehand, might, by exerting her will, manage to control herself tolerably even while under their influence; and I did not wish to "frighten" her husband, as she said, and multiply his annoyances for the purpose of serving her selfishness.

Therefore I said nothing when I met the master coming towards the parlour; but I took the liberty of turning back to listen whether they would resume their quarrel together.

He began to speak first.

144 EMILY BRONTË

"Remain where you are, Catherine," he said, without any anger in his voice, but with much sorrowful despondency. "I shall not stay. I am neither come to wrangle, nor be reconciled: but I wish just to learn whether, after this evening's events, you intend to continue your intimacy with—"

"Oh, for mercy's sake," interrupted the mistress, stamping her foot, "for mercy's sake, let us hear no more of it now! Your cold blood cannot be worked into a fever—your veins are full of ice-water—but mine are boiling, and the sight of such chillness makes them dance."

"To get rid of me—answer my question," persevered Mr. Linton. "You *must* answer it; and that violence does not alarm me. I have found that you can be as stoical as any one, when you please. Will you give up Heathcliff hereafter, or will you give up me? It is impossible for you to be *my* friend, and *his* at the same time; and I absolutely *require* to know which you choose."

"I require to be let alone!" exclaimed Catherine, furiously. "I demand it! Don't you see I can scarcely stand? Edgar, you—you leave me!"

She rung the bell till it broke with a twang: I entered leisurely. It was enough to try the temper of a saint, such senseless, wicked rages! There she lay dashing her head against the arm of the sofa, and grinding her teeth, so that you might fancy she would crash them to splinters!

Mr. Linton stood looking at her in sudden compunction and fear. He told me to fetch some water. She had no breath for speaking.

I brought a glass full; and, as she would not drink, I sprinkled it on her face. In a few seconds she stretched herself out stiff, and turned up her eyes, while her cheeks, at once blanched and livid, assumed the aspect of death.

Linton looked terrified.

"There is nothing in the world the matter," I whispered. I did not want him to yield, though I could not help being afraid in my heart.

"She has blood on her lips!" he said, shuddering.

"Never mind!" I answered, tartly. And I told him how she had resolved, previous to his coming, on exhibiting a fit of frenzy.

I incautiously gave the account aloud, and she heard me, for she started up—her hair flying over her shoulders, her eyes flashing, the muscles of her neck and arms standing out preternaturally. I made up my mind for broken bones, at least; but she only glared about her, for an instant, and then rushed from the room.

The master directed me to follow; I did, to her chamber door; she hindered me from going farther by securing it against me.

As she never offered to descend to breakfast next morning, I went to ask whether she would have some carried up.

"No!" she replied, peremptorily.

The same question was repeated at dinner, and tea; and again on the morrow after, and received the same answer.

Mr. Linton, on his part, spent his time in the library, and did not inquire concerning his wife's occupations. Isabella and he had had an hour's interview, during which he tried to elicit from her some sentiment of proper horror for Heathcliff's advances; but he could make nothing of her evasive replies, and was obliged to close the examination, unsatisfactorily; adding, however, a solemn warning, that if she were so insane as to encourage that worthless suitor, it would dissolve all bonds of relationship between herself and him.

Chapter XII.

While Miss Linton moped about the park and garden, always silent, and almost always in tears; and her brother shut himself up among books that he never opened; wearying, I guessed, with a continual vague expectation that Catherine, repenting her conduct, would come of her own accord to ask pardon, and seek a reconciliation; and *she* fasted pertinaciously, under the idea, probably, that at every meal, Edgar was ready to choke for her absence, and pride alone held him from running to cast himself at her feet; I went about my household duties, convinced that the Grange had but one sensible soul in its walls, and that lodged in my body.

I wasted no condolences on miss, nor any expostulations on my mistress, nor did I pay attention to the sighs of my master who yearned to hear his lady's name, since he might not hear her voice.

I determined they should come about as they pleased for me; and though it was a tiresomely slow process, I began to rejoice at length in a faint dawn of its progress, as I thought at first.

Mrs. Linton, on the third day, unbarred her door; and having finished the water in her pitcher and decanter, desired a renewed supply, and a basin of gruel, for she believed she was dying. That I set down as a speech meant for Edgar's ears, I believed no such thing, so I kept it to myself, and brought her some tea and dry toast.

She eat and drank eagerly; and sank back on her pillow again clenching her hands and groaning.

"Oh, I will die," she exclaimed, "since no one cares anything about me. I wish I had not taken that."

Then a good while after I heard her murmur,

"No, I'll not die—he'd be glad—he does not love me at all—he would never miss me!"

"Did you want anything, ma'am?" I enquired, still preserving my external composure, in spite of her ghastly countenance, and strange exaggerated manner.

"What is that apathetic being doing?" she demanded, pushing the thick entangled locks from her wasted face. "Has he fallen into a lethargy, or is he dead?"

"Neither," replied I; "if you mean Mr. Linton. He's tolerably well, I think, though his studies occupy him rather more than they ought; he is continually among his books, since he has no other society."

I should not have spoken so, if I had known her true condition, but I could not get rid of the notion that she acted a part of her disorder.

WUTHERING HEIGHTS 147

"Among his books!" she cried, confounded. "And I dying! I on the brink of the grave! My God! does he know how I'm altered?" continued she, staring at her reflection in a mirror, hanging against the opposite wall. "Is that Catherine Linton? He imagines me in a pet—in play, perhaps. Cannot you inform him that it is frightful earnest? Nelly, if it be not too late, as soon as I learn how he feels, I'll choose between these two—either to starve, at once, that would be no punishment unless he had a heart—or to recover and leave the country. Are you speaking the truth about him now? Take care. Is he actually so utterly indifferent for my life?"

"Why, ma'am," I answered, "the master has no idea of your being deranged; and, of course, he does not fear that you will let yourself die of hunger."

"You think not? Cannot you tell him I will?" she returned; "persuade him—speak of your own mind—say you are certain I will!"

"No, you forget, Mrs. Linton," I suggested, "that you have eaten some food with a relish this evening, and to-morrow you will perceive its good effects."

"If I were only sure it would kill him," she interrupted, "I'd kill myself directly! These three awful nights, I've never closed my lids—and oh, I've been tormented! I've been haunted, Nelly! But I begin to fancy you don't like me. How strange! I thought, though everybody hated and despised each other, they could not avoid loving me—and they have all turned to enemies in a few hour?. *They* have, I'm positive; the people *here*. How dreary to meet death, surrounded by their cold faces! Isabella, terrified and repelled, afraid to enter the room, it would be so dreadful to watch Catherine go. And Edgar standing solemnly by to see it over; then offering prayers of thanks to God for restoring peace to his house, and going back to his *books*! What in the name of all that feels, has he to do with *books*, when I am dying?"

She could not bear the notion which I had put into her head of Mr. Linton's philosophical resignation. Tossing about, she increased her feverish bewilderment to madness, and tore the pillow with her teeth, then raising herself up all burning, desired that I would open the window. We were in the middle of winter, the wind blew strong from the north-east, and I objected.

Both the expressions flitting over her face, and the changes of her moods, began to alarm me terribly; and brought to my recollection her former illness, and the doctor's injunction that she should not be crossed.

A minute previously she was violent; now, supported on one arm, and not noticing my refusal to obey her, she seemed to find childish diversion in pulling the feathers from the rents she had just made, and ranging them on the sheet according to their different species: her mind had strayed to other associations.

"That's a turkey's," she murmured to herself; "and this is a wild-duck's; and this is a pigeon's. Ah, they put pigeons' feathers in the pillows—no wonder I couldn't die! Let me take care to throw it on the floor when I lie down.

148 EMILY BRONTË

And here is a moor-cock's; and this—I should know it among a thousand—it's a lapwing's. Bonny bird; wheeling over our heads in the middle of the moor. It wanted to get to its nest, for the clouds touched the swells, and it felt rain coming. This feather was picked up from the heath, the bird was not shot—we saw its nest in the winter, full of little skeletons. Heathcliff set a trap over it, and the old ones dare not come. I made him promise he'd never shoot a lapwing, after that, and he didn't. Yes, here are more! Did he shoot my lapwings, Nelly? Are they red, any of them? Let me look."

"Give over with that baby-work!" I interrupted, dragging the pillow away, and turning the holes towards the mattress, for she was removing its contents by handfuls. "Lie down and shut your eyes, you're wandering. There's a mess! The down is flying about like snow!"

I went here and there collecting it.

"I see in you, Nelly," she continued, dreamily, "an aged woman—you have grey hair, and bent shoulders. This bed is the fairy cave under Peniston Crag, and you are gathering elf-bolts to hurt our heifers; pretending, while I am near, that they are only locks of wool. That's what you'll come to fifty years hence; I know you are not so now. I'm not wandering, you're mistaken, or else I should believe you really *were* that withered hag, and I should think I *was* under Penistone Crag, and I'm conscious it's night, and there are two candles on the table making the black press shine like jet."

"The black press? where is that?" I asked. "You are talking in your sleep!"

"It's against the wall, as it always is," she replied. "It *does* appear odd—I see a face in it!"

"There is no press in the room, and never was," said I, resuming my seat, and looping up the curtain that I might watch her.

"Don't *you* see that face?" she enquired, gazing earnestly at the mirror.

And say what I could, I was incapable of making her comprehend it to be her own; so I rose and covered it with a shawl.

"It's behind there still!" she pursued, anxiously. "And it stirred. Who is it?" I hope it will not come out when you are gone! Oh! Nelly, the room is haunted! I'm afraid of being alone!"

I took her hand in mine, and bid her be composed, for a succession of shudders convulsed her frame, and she *would* keep straining her gaze towards the glass.

"There's nobody here!" I insisted. "It was *yourself*, Mrs. Linton; you knew it a while since."

"Myself," she gasped, "and the clock is striking twelve! It's true then; that's dreadful!"

Her fingers clutched the clothes, and gathered them over her eyes. I attempted to steal to the door with an intention of calling her husband; but I was summoned back by a piercing shriek. The shawl had dropped from the frame.

WUTHERING HEIGHTS 149

"Why what *is* the matter?" cried I. "Who is coward now? Wake up! That is the glass—the mirror, Mrs. Linton; and you see yourself in it, and there am I too by your side."

Trembling and bewildered, she held me fast, but the horror gradually passed from her countenance; its paleness gave place to a glow of shame.

"Oh, dear! I thought I was at home," she sighed. "I thought I was lying in my chamber at Wuthering Heights. Because I'm weak, my brain got confused, and I screamed unconsciously. Don't say anything; but stay with me. I dread sleeping, my dreams appal me."

"A sound sleep would do you good, ma'am," I answered; "and I hope this suffering will prevent your trying starving again."

"Oh, if I were but in my own bed in the old house!" she went on bitterly, wringing her hands. "And that wind sounding in the firs by the lattice. Do let me feel it—it comes straight down the moor—do let me have one breath!"

To pacify her, I held the casement ajar, a few seconds. A cold blast rushed through, I closed it, and returned to my post.

She lay still, now: her face bathed in tears—Exhaustion of body had entirely subdued her spirit; our fiery Catherine was no better than a wailing child!

"How long is it since I shut myself in here?" she asked suddenly reviving.

"It was Monday evening," I replied, "and this is Thursday night, or rather Friday morning, at present."

"What! of the same week?" she exclaimed. "Only that brief time?"

"Long enough to live on nothing but cold water, and ill-temper," observed I.

"Well, it seems a weary number of hours," she muttered doubtfully, "it must be more—I remember being in the parlour, after they had quarrelled; and Edgar being cruelly provoking, and me running into this room desperate—As soon as ever I had barred the door, utter blackness overwhelmed me, and I fell on the floor—I couldn't explain to Edgar how certain I felt of having a fit, or going raging mad, if he persisted in teasing me! I had no command of tongue, or brain, and he did not guess my agony, perhaps; it barely left me sense to try to escape from him and his voice—Before I recovered, sufficiently to see, and hear, it began to be dawn; and Nelly, I'll tell you what I thought, and what has kept recurring and recurring till I feared for my reason—I thought as I lay there with my head against that table leg, and my eyes dimly discerning the grey square of the window, that I was enclosed in the oak-panelled bed at home; and my heart ached with some great grief which, just waking, I could not recollect—I pondered, and worried myself to discover what it could be; and most strangely, the whole last seven years of my life grew a blank! I did not recall that they had been at all. I was a child; my father was just buried, and my misery arose from the separation that Hindley had ordered between me, and Heathcliff—I was laid alone, for the first time, and rousing from a dismal dose after a night of weeping—I lifted my hand to push the panels aside, it struck the table-top! I swept it along the carpet, and

EMILY BRONTË

then, memory burst in—my late anguish was swallowed in a paroxysm of despair—I cannot say why I felt so wildly wretched—it must have been temporary derangement for there is scarcely cause—But, supposing at twelve years old, I had been wrenched from the Heights, and every early association, and my all in all, as Heathcliff was at that time, and been converted, at a stroke into Mrs. Linton, the lady of Thrushcross Grange, and the wife of a stranger; an exile, and outcast, thenceforth, from what had been my world—You may fancy a glimpse of the abyss where I grovelled! Shake your head, as you will, Nelly, *you* have helped to unsettle me! You should have spoken to Edgar, indeed you should, and compelled him to leave me quiet! Oh, I'm burning! I wish I were out of doors—I wish I were a girl again, half savage and hardy, and free . . . and laughing at injuries, not maddening under them! Why am I so changed? why does my blood rush into a hell of tumult at a few words? I'm sure I should be myself were I once among the heather on those hills . . . Open the window again wide, fasten it open! Quick, why don't you move?"

"Because, I won't give you your death of cold," I answered.

"You won't give me a chance of life, you mean," she said sullenly. "However, I'm not helpless yet, I'll open it myself."

And sliding from the bed before I could hinder her, she crossed the room, walking very uncertainly, threw it back, and bent out, careless of the frosty air that cut about her shoulders as keen as a knife.

I entreated, and finally attempted to force her to retire. But I soon found her delirious strengh much surpassed mine; (she *was* delirious I became convinced by her subsequent actions, and ravings.)

There was no moon, and every thing beneath lay in misty darkness; not a light gleamed from any house, far or near; all had been extinguished long ago; and those at Wuthering Heights were never visible . . . still she asserted she caught their shining.

"Look!" she cried eagerly, "that's my room, with the candle in it, and the trees swaying before it . . . and the other candle is in Joseph's garret . . . Joseph sits up late, doesn't he? He's waiting till I come home that he may lock the gate . . . Well, he'll wait a while yet. It's a rough journey, and a sad heart to travel it; and we must pass by Gimmerton Kirk, to go that journey! We've braved it's ghosts often together, and dared each other to stand among the graves and ask them to come . . . But Heathcliff, if I dare you now, will you venture? If you do, I'll keep you. I'll not lie there by myself; they may bury me twelve feet deep, and throw the church down over me; but I won't rest till you are with me . . . I never will!"

She paused, and resumed with a strange smile, "He's considering . . . he'd rather I'd come to him! Find a way, then! not through that Kirkyard . . . You are slow! Be content, you always followed me!"

Perceiving it vain to argue against her insanity, I was planning how I could reach something to wrap about her, without quitting my hold of herself, for

WUTHERING HEIGHTS

I could not trust her alone by the gaping lattice; when to my consternation, I heard the rattle of the door-handle, and Mr. Linton entered. He had only then come from the library; and, in passing through the lobby, had noticed our talking and been attracted by curiosity, or fear to examine what it signified, at that late hour.

"Oh, sir!" I cried, checking the exclamation risen to his lips at the sight which met him, and the bleak atmosphere of the chamber.

"My poor Mistress is ill, and she quite masters me; I cannot manage her at all, pray, come and persuade her to go to bed. Forget your anger, for she's hard to guide any way but her own."

"Catherine ill?" he said hastening to us. "Shut the window, Ellen! Catherine! why . . ."

He was silent; the haggardness of Mrs. Linton's appearance smote him speechless, and he could only glance from her to me in horrified astonishment.

"She's been fretting here," I continued, "and eating scarcely anything, and never complaining, she would admit none of us till this evening, and so we couldn't inform you of her state, as we were not aware of it ourselves," but it is nothing."

I felt I uttered my explanations awkwardly; the master frowned. "It is nothing is it, Ellen Dean?" he said sternly. "You shall account more clearly for keeping me ignorant of this!" And he took his wife in his arms, and looked at her with anguish.

At first she gave him no glance of recognition . . . he was invisible to her abstracted gaze. The delirium was not fixed, however; having weaned her eyes from contemplating the outer darkness; by degrees, she centred her attention on him, and discovered who it was that held her.

"Ah! you are come, are you, Edgar Linton?" she said with angry animation . . . "You are one of those things that are ever found when least wanted, and when you are wanted never! I suppose we shall have plenty of lamentations, now . . . I see we shall . . . but they can't keep me from my narrow home out yonder—My resting place where I'm bound before Spring is over! There it is, not among the Lintons, mind, under the chapel-roof; but in the open air with a head-stone, and you may please yourself, whether you go to them, or come to me!"

"Catherine, what have you done?" commenced the master. "Am I nothing to you, any more? Do you love that wretch, Heath—"

"Hush!" cried Mrs. Linton. "Hush, this moment! You mention that name and I end the matter, instantly, by a spring from the window! What you touch at present, you may have; but my soul will be on that hill-top before you lay hands on me again. I don't want you, Edgar; I'm past wanting you . . . Return to your books . . . I'm glad you possess a consolation, for all you had in me is gone."

EMILY BRONTË

"Her mind wanders, sir," I interposed. "She has been talking nonsense the whole evening; but, let her have quiet and proper attendance, and she'll rally . . . Hereafter, we must be cautious how we vex her."

"I desire no further advice from you," answered Mr. Linton. "You knew your mistress's nature, and you encouraged me to harass her. And not to give me one hint of how she has been these three days! It was heartless! months of sickness could not cause such a change!"

I began to defend myself, thinking it too bad to be blamed for another's wicked waywardness!

"I knew Mrs. Linton's nature to be headstrong and domineering," cried I; "but I didn't know that you wished to foster her fierce temper! I didn't know that, to humour her, I should wink at Mr. Heathcliff. I performed the duty of a faithful servant in telling you, and I have got a faithful servant's wages! Well, it will teach me to be careful next time. Next time you may gather intelligence for yourself!"

"The next time you bring a tale to me, you shall quit my service, Ellen Dean," he replied.

"You'd rather hear nothing about it, I suppose, then, Mr. Linton?" said I. "Heathcliff has your permission to come a courting to Miss and to drop in at every opportunity your absence offers, on purpose to poison the mistress against you?"

Confused as Catherine was, her wits were alert at applying our conversation.

"Ah! Nelly has played traitor," she exclaimed, passionately. "Nelly is my hidden enemy—you witch! So you do seek elf-bolts to hurt us! Let me go, and I'll make her rue! I'll make her howl a recantation!"

A maniac's fury kindled under her brows; she struggled desperately to disengage herself from Linton's arms. I felt no inclination to tarry the event; and resolving to seek medical aid on my own responsibility, I quitted the chamber.

In passing the garden to reach the road, at a place where a bridle hook is driven into the wall, I saw something white moved irregularly evidently by another agent than the wind. Notwithstanding my hurry, I staid to examine it, lest ever after I should have the conviction impressed on my imagination that it was a creature of the other world.

My surprise and perplexity were great to discover, by touch more than vision, Miss Isabella's springer Fanny, suspended to a handkerchief, and nearly at its last gasp.

I quickly released the animal, and lifted it into the garden. I had seen it follow its mistress up-stairs, when she went to bed, and wondered much how it could have got out there, and what mischievous person had treated it so.

While untying the knot round the hook, it seemed to me that I repeatedly caught the beat of horses' feet galloping at some distance; but there were such a number of things to occupy my reflections that I hardly gave the

WUTHERING HEIGHTS 153

circumstance a thought, though it was a strange sound, in that place, at two o'clock in the morning.

Mr. Kenneth was fortunately just issuing from his house to see a patient in the village as I came up the street; and my account of Catherine Linton's malady induced him to accompany me back immediately.

He was a plain, rough man; and he made no scruple to speak his doubts of her surviving this second attack; unless she were more submissive to his directions than she had shown herself before.

"Nelly Dean," said he, "I can't help fancying there's an extra cause for this. What has there been to do at the Grange? We've odd reports up here. A stout, hearty lass like Catherine does not fall ill for a trifle; and that sort of people should not either. It's hard work bringing them through fevers, and such things. How did it begin?"

"The master will inform you," I answered; "but you are acquainted with the Earnshaw's violent dispositions, and Mrs. Linton caps them all. I may say this; it commenced in a quarrel. She was struck during a tempest of passion with a kind of fit. That's her account, at least; for she flew off in the height of it, and locked herself up. Afterwards, she refused to eat, and now she alternately raves, and remains in a half dream, knowing those about her, but having her mind filled with all sorts of strange ideas and illusions."

"Mr. Linton will be sorry?" observed Kenneth, interrogatively.

"Sorry? he'll break his heart should anything happen!" I replied. "Don't alarm him more than necessary."

"Well, I told him to beware," said my companion, "and he must bide the consequences of neglecting my warning! Hasn't he been thick with Mr. Heathcliff lately?"

"Heathcliff frequently visits at the Grange," answered I, "though more on the strength of the mistress having known him when a boy, than because the master likes his company. At present, he's discharged from the trouble of calling; owing to some presumptuous aspirations after Miss Linton which he manifested. I hardly think he'll be taken in again."

"And does Miss Linton turn a cold shoulder on him?" was the doctor's next question.

"I'm not in her confidence," returned I, reluctant to continue the subject.

"No, she's a sly one," he remarked, shaking his head. "She keeps her own counsel! But she's a real little fool. I have it from good authority, that, last night, and a pretty night it was! she and Heathcliff were walking in the plantation at the back of your house, above two hours; and he pressed her not to go in again, but just mount his horse and away with him! My informant said she could only put him off by pledging her word of honour to be prepared on their first meeting after that, when it was to be, he didn't hear, but you urge Mr. Linton to look sharp!"

This news filled me with fresh fears; I outstripped Kenneth, and ran most of the way back. The little dog was yelping in the garden yet. I spared a minute to open the gate for it, but instead of going to the house door, it coursed up and down snuffing the grass, and would have escaped to the road, had I not seized and conveyed it in with me.

On ascending to Isabella's room, my suspicions were confirmed; it was empty. Had I been a few hours sooner, Mrs. Linton's illness might have arrested her rash step. But what could be done now? There was a bare possibility of overtaking them if pursued instantly. *I* could not pursue them, however; and I dare not rouse the family, and fill the place with confusion; still less unfold the business to my master, absorbed as he was in his present calamity, and having no heart to spare for a second grief!

I saw nothing for it, but to hold my tongue, and suffer matters to take their course: and Kenneth being arrived, I went with a badly composed countenance to announce him.

Catherine lay in a troubled sleep; her husband had succeeded in soothing the access of frenzy; he now hung over her pillow, watching every shade, and every change of her painfully expressive features.

The doctor, on examining the case for himself, spoke hopefully to him of its having a favourable termination, if we could only preserve around her perfect and constant tranquillity. To me, he signified the threatening danger was, not so much death, as permanent alienation of intellect.

I did not close my eyes that night, nor did Mr. Linton; indeed, we never went to bed: and the servants were all up long before the usual hour, moving through the house with stealthy tread, and exchanging whispers as they encountered each other in their vocations. Every one was active, but Miss Isabella; and they began to remark how sound she slept—her brother too asked if she had risen, and seemed impatient for her presence, and hurt that she showed so little anxiety for her sister-in-law.

I trembled lest he should send me to call her; but I was spared the pain of being the first proclaimant of her flight. One of the maids, a thoughtless girl, who had been on an early errand to Gimmerton, came panting up stairs, open-mouthed, and dashed into the chamber, crying.

"Oh, dear, dear! What mun we have next? Master, master, our young lady—"

"Hold your noise!" cried I hastily, enraged at her clamorous manner.

"Speak lower, Mary—What is the matter?" said Mr. Linton. "What ails your young lady?"

"She's gone, she's gone! Yon' Heathcliff's run off wi' her!" gasped the girl.

"That is not true!" exclaimed Linton, rising in agitation. "It cannot be— how has the idea entered your head? Ellen Dean, go and seek her—it is incredible—it cannot be."

As he spoke he took the servant to the door, and, then, repeated his demand to know her reasons for such an assertion.

WUTHERING HEIGHTS

"Why, I met on the road a lad that fetches milk here," she stammered, "and he asked whether we wern't in trouble at the Grange—I thought he meant for Missis's sickness, so I answered, yes. Then says he, they's somebody gone after 'em, I guess?" I stared. He saw I knew naught about it, and he told how a gentleman and lady had stopped to have a horse's shoe fastened at a black-smith's shop, two miles out of Gimmerton, not very long after midnight! and how the blacksmith's lass had got up to spy who they were: she knew them both directly—And she noticed the man, Heathcliff it was, she felt certain, nob'dy could mistake him, besides—put a sovereign in her father's hand for payment. The lady had a cloak about her face; but having desired a sup of water, while she drank, it fell back, and she saw her very plain—Heathcliff held both bridles as they rode on, and they set their faces from the village, and went as fast as the rough roads would let them. The lass said nothing to her father, but she told it al over Gimmerton this morning."

I ran and peeped, for form's sake into Isabella's room: confirming, when I returned, the servant's statement—Mr. Linton had resumed his seat by the bed; on my re-entrance, he raised his eyes, read the meaning of my blank aspect, and dropped them without giving an order, or uttering a word.

"Are we to try any measures for overtaking and bringing her back," I inquired. "How should we do?"

"She went of her own accord," answered the master; "she had a right to go if she pleased—Trouble me no more about her—Hereafter she is only my sister in name; not because I disown her, but because she has disowned me."

And that was all he said on the subject; he did not make a single inquiry further, or mention her in any way, except directing me to send what property she had in the house to her fresh home, wherever it was, when I knew it.

Chapter XIII.

For two months the fugitives remained absent, in those two months, Mrs. Linton encountered and conquered the worst shock of what was denominated a brain fever. No mother could have nursed an only child more devotedly than Edgar tended her. Day and night, he was watching, and patiently enduring all the annoyances that irritable nerves and a shaken reason could inflict: and, though Kenneth remarked that what he saved from the grave would only recompense his care by forming the source of constant future anxiety, in fact, that his health and strength were being sacrificed to preserve a mere ruin of humanity, he knew no limits in gratitude and joy, when Catherine's life was declared out of danger; and hour after hour, he would sit beside her, tracing the gradual return to bodily health, and flattering his too sanguine hopes with the illusion that her mind would settle back to its right balance also, and she would soon be entirely her former self.

The first time she left her chamber, was at the commencement of the following March. Mr. Linton had put on her pillow, in the morning, a handful of golden crocuses; her eye, long stranger to any gleam of pleasure, caught them in waking, and shone delighted as she gathered them eagerly together.

"These are the earliest flowers at the Heights!" she exclaimed. "They remind me of soft thaw winds, and warm sunshine, and nearly melted snow— Edgar, is there not a south wind, and is not the snow almost gone?"

"The snow is quite gone; down here, darling!" replied her husband, "and I only see two white spots on the whole range of moors—The sky is blue, and the larks are singing, and the becks and brooks are all brim full. Catherine; last spring at this time, I was longing to have you under this roof—now, I wish you were a mile or two up those hills, the air blows so sweetly, I feel that it would cure you."

"I shall never be there, but once more!" said the invalid; "and then you'll leave me, and I shall remain, for ever. Next spring you'll long again to have me under this roof, and you'll look back and think you were happy to-day."

Linton lavished on her the kindest caresses, and tried to cheer her by the fondest words; but vaguely regarding the flowers, she let the tears collect on her lashes, and stream down her cheeks unheeding.

We knew she was really better, and therefore, decided that long confinement to a single place produced much of this despondency, and it might be partially removed by a change of scene.

The master told me to light a fire in the many-week's deserted parlour, and to set an easy-chair in the sunshine by the window; and then he brought her

WUTHERING HEIGHTS 157

down, and she sat a long while enjoying the genial heat, and, as we expected, revived by the objects round her, which, though familiar, were free from the dreary associations investing her hated sick-chamber. By evening, she seemed greatly exhausted; yet no arguments could persuade her to return to that apartment, and I had to arrange the parlour sofa for her bed, till another room could be prepared.

To obviate the fatigue of mounting and descending the stairs, we fitted up this, where you lie at present; on the same floor with the parlour: and she was soon strong enough to move from one to the other, leaning on Edgar's arm.

Ah, I thought myself, she might recover, so waited on as she was. And there was double cause to desire it, for on her existence depended that of another; we cherished the hope that in a little while, Mr. Linton's heart would be gladdened, and his lands secured from a stranger's gripe, by the birth of an heir.

I should mention that Isabella sent to her brother, some six weeks from her departure a short note, announcing her marriage with Heathcliff. It appeared dry and cold; but at the bottom, was dotted in with pencil, an obscure apology, and an entreaty for kind remembrance, and reconciliation, if her proceeding had offended him; asserting that she could not help it then, and being done, she had now no power to repeal it.

Linton did not reply to this, I believe; and, in a fortnight more, I got a long letter which I considered odd coming from the pen of a bride just out of the honeymoon. I'll read it, for I keep it yet. Any relic of the dead is precious, if they were valued living.

"DEAR ELLEN," it begins.

"I came, last night, to Wuthering Heights, and heard, for the first time, that Catherine has been, and is yet, very ill. I must not write to her I suppose, and my brother is either too angry, or too distressed to answer what I send him. Still, I must write to somebody, and the only choice left me is you.

Inform Edgar that I'd give the world to see his face again—that my heart returned to Thrushcross Grange in twenty-four hours after I left it, and is there at this moment, full of warm feelings for him, and Catherine! *I can't follow it though*—(those words are underlined) they need not expect me, and they may draw what conclusions they please; taking care however, to lay nothing at the door of my weak will, or deficient affection.

The remainder of the letter is for yourself, alone. I want to ask you two questions: the first is,

How did you contrive to preserve the common sympathies of human nature when you resided here? I cannot recognise any sentiment which those around, share with me.

The second question, I have great interest in; it is this—

Is Mr. Heathcliff a man? If so, is he mad? And if not, is he a devil? I shan't tell my reasons for making this inquiry; but, I beseech you to explain, if you

158 EMILY BRONTË

can, what I have married—that is, when you call to see me; and you must call Ellen, very soon. Don't write, but come, and bring me something from Edgar.

Now, you shall hear how I have been received in my new home, as I am led to imagine the Heights will be. It is to amuse myself that I dwell on such subjects as the lack of external comforts; they never occupy my thoughts, except at the moment when I miss them—I should laugh and dance for joy, if I found their absence was the total of my miseries, and the rest was an unnatural dream!

The sun set behind the Grange, as we turned on to the moors; by that, I judged it to be six o'clock; and my companion halted half-an-hour, to inspect the park, and the gardens, and, probably, the place itself, as well as he could; so it was dark when we dismounted in the paved yard of the farmhouse, and your old fellow-servant, Joseph, issued out to receive us by the light of a dip candle. He did it with a courtesy that redounded to his credit. His first act was to elevate his torch to a level with my face, squint malignantly, project his under lip, and turn away.

Then he took the two horses, and led them into the stables; reappearing for the purpose of locking the outer gate, as if we lived in an ancient castle.

Heathcliff stayed to speak to him, and I entered the kitchen—a dingy, untidy hole; I dare say you would not know it, it is so changed since it was in your charge.

By the fire stood a ruffianly child, strong in limb, and dirty in garb, with a look of Catherine in his eyes, and about his mouth.

"This is Edgar's legal nephew," I reflected—"mine in a manner; I must shake hands, and—yes—I must kiss him. It is right to establish a good understanding at the beginning."

I approached, and, attempting to take his chubby fist, said—

"How do you do, my dear?"

He replied in a jargon I did not comprehend.

"Shall you and I be friends, Hareton?" was my next essay at conversation.

An oath, and a threat to set Throttler on me if I did not "frame off" rewarded my perseverance.

"Hey, Throttler, lad!" whispered the little wretch, rousing a half-bred bull-dog from its lair in a corner. "Now, wilt tuh be ganging?" he asked authoritatively.

Love for my life urged a compliance; I stepped over the threshold to wait till the others should enter. Mr. Heathcliff was nowhere visible; and Joseph, whom I followed to the stables, and requested to accompany me in, after staring and muttering to himself, screwed up his nose and replied—

"Mim! mim! mim! Did iver Christian body hear owt like it? Minching un' munching! Hah can Aw tell whet ye say?"

"I say, I wish you to come with me into the house!" I cried, thinking him deaf, yet highly disgusted at his rudeness.

WUTHERING HEIGHTS 159

"Nor nuh me! Aw getten summut else to do," he answered, and continued his work, moving his lantern jaws meanwhile, and surveying my dress and countenance (the former a great deal too fine, but the latter, I'm sure, as sad as he could desire) with sovereign contempt.

I walked round the yard, and through a wicket, to another door, at which I took the liberty of knocking, in hopes some more civil servant might shew himself.

After a short suspense it was opened by a tall, gaunt man, without neckerchief, and otherwise extremely slovenly; his features were lost in masses of shaggy hair that hung on his shoulders; and *his* eyes, too, were like a ghostly Catherine's, with all their beauty annihilated.

"What's your business here?" he demanded, grimly. "Who are you?"

"My name *was* Isabella Linton," I replied. "You've seen me before, sir. I'm lately married to Mr. Heathcliff; and he has brought me here—I suppose by your permission."

"Is he come back, then?" asked the hermit, glaring like a hungry wolf.

"Yes—we came just now," I said; "but he left me by the kitchen door; and when I would have gone in, your little boy played sentinel over the place, and frightened me off by the help of a bull-dog."

"It's well the hellish villain has kept his word!" growled my future host, searching the darkness beyond me in expectation of discovering Heathcliff, and then he indulged in a soliloquy of execrations, and threats of what he would have done had the "fiend" deceived him.

I repented having tried this second entrance; and was almost inclined to slip way before he finished cursing, but ere I could execute that intention, he ordered me in, and shut and re-fastened the door.

There was a great fire, and that was all the light in the huge apartment, whose floor had grown a uniform grey; and the once brilliant pewter dishes which used to attract my gaze when I was a girl partook of a similar obscurity, created by tarnish and dust.

I inquired whether I might call the maid, and be conducted to a bed-room? Mr. Earnshaw vouchsafed no answer. He walked up and down, with his hands in his pockets, apparently quite forgetting my presence; and his abstraction was evidently so deep, and his whole aspect so misanthropical, that I shrank from disturbing him again.

"You'll not be surprised, Ellen, at my feeling particularly cheerless, seated in worse than solitude, on that inhospitable hearth, and remembering that four miles distant lay my delightful home, containing the only people I loved on earth: and there might as well be the Atlantic to part us, instead of those four miles, I could not overpass them!

I questioned with myself—where must I turn for comfort? and—mind you don't tell Edgar, or Catherine—above every sorrow beside, this rose pre-eminent—despair at finding nobody who could or would be my ally against Heathcliff!

I had sought shelter at Wuthering Heights, almost gladly, because I was secured by that arrangement from living alone with him; but he knew the people we were coming amongst, and he did not fear their intermeddling.

I sat and thought a doleful time; the clock struck eight, and nine, and still my companion paced to and fro, his head bent on his breast, and perfectly silent, unless a groan, or a bitter ejaculation forced itself out at intervals.

I listened to detect a woman's voice in the house, and filled the interim with wild regrets, and dismal anticipations, which, at last, spoke audibly in irrepressible sighing, and weeping.

I was not aware how openly I grieved, till Earnshaw halted opposite, in his measured walk, and gave me a stare of newly awakened surprise. Taking advantage of his recovered attention, I exclaimed—

"I'm tired with my journey, and I want to go to bed! Where is the maid-servant? Direct me to her, as she wont come to to me!"

"We have none," he answered; "you must wait on yourself!"

"Where must I sleep, then?" I sobbed—I was beyond regarding self-respect, weighed down by fatigue and wretchedness.

Joseph will show you Heathcliff's chamber," said he; "open that door—he's in there."

"I was going to obey, but he suddenly arrested me, and added in the strangest tone—

"Be so good as to turn your lock, and draw your bolt—don't omit it!"

"Well!" I said. "But why, Mr. Earnshaw?" I did not relish the notion of deliberately fastening myself in with Heathcliff.

"Look here!" he replied, pulling from his waistcoat a curiously constructed pistol, having a double edged spring knife attached to the barrel. "That's a great tempter to a desperate man, is it not? I cannot resist going up with this, every night, and trying his door, if once I find it open he's done for! I do it invariably, even though the minute before I have been recalling a hundred reasons that should make me refrain—it is some devil that urges me to thwart my own schemes by killing him—you fight against that devil, for love, as as long as you may; when the time comes, not all the angels in heaven shall save him!

I surveyed the weapon inquisitively; a hideous notion struck me. How powerful I should be possessing such an instrument! I took it from his hand, and touched the blade. He looked astonished at the expression my face assumed during a brief second. It was not horror, it was covetousness. He snatched the pistol back, jealously; shut the knife, and returned it to its concealment.

"I don't care if you tell him," said he. Put him on his guard, and watch for him. You know the terms we are on, I see; his danger does not shock you."

"What has Heathcliff done to you?" I asked. "In what has he wronged you to warrant this appalling hatred? Wouldn't it be wiser to bid him quit the house?"

WUTHERING HEIGHTS   161

"No," thundered Earnshaw, "should he offer to leave me, he's a dead man, persuade him to attempt it, and you are a murderess! Am I to lose *all* without a chance of retrieval? Is Hareton to be a beggar? Oh, damnation! I *will* have it back; and I'll have *his* gold too; and then his blood; and hell shall have his soul! It will be ten times blacker with that guest than ever it was before!"

"You've acquainted me, Ellen, with your old master's habits. He is clearly on the verge of madness—he was so last night, at least. I shuddered to be near him, and thought on the servant's ill-bred moroseness as comparatively agreeable.

He now recommenced his moody walk, and I raised the latch, and escaped into the kitchen.

Joseph was bending over the fire, peering into a large pan that swung above it; and a wooden bowl of oatmeal stood on the settle close by. The contents of the pan began to boil, and he turned to plunge his hand into the bowl; I conjectured that this preparation was probably for our supper, and, being hungry, I resolved it should be eatable—so crying out, sharply—"*I'll* make the porridge!" I removed the vessel out of his reach, and proceeded to take off my hat and riding habit. "Mr. Earnshaw," I continued, "directs me to wait on myself—I will—I'm not going to act the lady among you, for fear I should starve."

"Gooid Lord!" he muttered, sitting down, and stroking his ribbed stockings from the knee to the ankle. "If they's tuh be fresh ortherings—just when Aw getten used tuh two maisters, if aw mun hev a *mistress* set o'er my heead, it's loike time tuh be flitting. Aw niver *did* think tuh say t' day ut aw mud lave th' owld place—but aw daht it's nigh at hend!"

This lamentation drew no notice from me; I went briskly to work; sighing to remember a period when it would have been all merry fun; but compelled speedily to drive off the remembrance. It racked me to recall past happiness, and the greater peril there was of conjuring up its apparition, the quicker the thible ran round, and the faster the handfuls of meal fell into the water.

Joseph beheld my style of cookery with growing indignation.

"Thear!" he ejaculated. "Hareton, thah willut sup thy porridge tuh neeght; they'll be nowt bud lumps as big as maw nave. Thear, agean! Aw'd fling in bowl un all, if aw wer yah! Thear, pale t' guilp off, un' then yah'll hae done wi't. Bang, bang. It's a marcy t' bothom isn't deaved aht!"

It *was* rather a rough mess, I own, when poured into the basins; four had been provided, and a gallon pitcher of new milk was brought from the dairy, which Hareton seized and commenced drinking and spilling from the expansive lip.

I expostulated, and desired that he should have his in a mug; affirming that I could not taste the liquid treated so dirtily. The old cynic chose to be vastly offended at this nicety; assuring me, repeatedly, that "the barn was every bit as gooid" as I, "and every bit as wollsome," and wondering how I could fashion to be so conceited; meanwhile, the infant ruffian continued sucking; and glowered up at me defyingly, as he slavered into the jug.

162   EMILY BRONTË

"I shall have my supper in another room," I said. "Have you no place you call a parlour?"

"*Parlour!*" he echoed, sneeringly, "*parlour!* Nay, we've noa *parlours*. If yah dunnut loike wer company, they's maister's; un' if yah dunnut loike maister, they's us."

"Then I shall go up-stairs," I answered; "shew me a chamber!"

I put my basin on a tray, and went myself to fetch some more milk.

With great grumblings, the fellow rose, and preceded me in my ascent: we mounted to the garrets; he opening a door, now and then, to look into the apartments we passed.

"Here's a rahm," he said, at last, flinging back a cranky board on hinges. "It's weel eneugh tuh ate a few porridge in. They's a pack uh corn i' t' corner, thear, meeterly clane; if yah're feared uh muckying yer grand silk cloes, spread yer hankerchir ut t' top on't."

The "rahm" was a kind of lumber-hole smelling strong of malt and grain; various sacks of which articles were piled around, leaving a wide, bare space in the middle.

"Why, man!" I exclaimed, facing him angrily, "this is not a place to sleep in. I wish to see my bed-room."

"*Bed-rume!*" he repeated, in a tone of mockery. "Yah's see all t' *bed-rumes* thear is—yon's mine."

He pointed into the second garret, only differing from the first in being more naked about the walls, and having a large, low, curtainless bed, with an indigo-coloured quilt, at one end.

"What do I want with yours?" I retorted. "I suppose Mr. Heathcliff does not lodge at the top of the house, does he?"

"Oh! it's Maister *Hathecliff's* yah're wenting?" cried he, as if making a new discovery. "Couldn't ye uh said soa, at onst? un then, aw mud uh telled ye, baht all this wark, ut that's just one yah cannut sea—he allas keeps it locked, un' nob'dy iver mells on't but hisseln."

"You've a nice house, Joseph," I could not refrain from observing, "and pleasant inmates; and I think the concentrated essence of all the madness in the world took up its abode in my brain the day I linked my fate with theirs! However that is not to the present purpose—there are other rooms. For heaven's sake, be quick, and let me settle somewhere!"

He made no reply to this adjuration; only plodding doggedly down the wooden steps, and halting before an apartment which, from that halt, and the superior quality of its furniture, I conjectured to be the best one.

There was a carpet, a good one; but the pattern was obliterated by dust; a fire-place hung with cut paper dropping to pieces; a handsome oak-bedstead with ample crimson curtains of rather expensive material, and modern make. But they had evidently experienced rough usage, the valances hung in festoons, wrenched from their rings; and the iron rod supporting them was bent

WUTHERING HEIGHTS   163

in an arc, on one side, causing the drapery to trail upon the floor. The chairs were also damaged, many of them severely; and deep indentations deformed the panels of the walls.

I was endeavouring to gather resolution for entering, and taking possession, when my fool of a guide announced—

"This here is t' maister's."

My supper by this time was cold, my appetite gone, and my patience exhausted. I insisted on being provided instantly with a place of refuge, and means of repose.

"Whear the divil," began the religious elder. "The Lord bless us! The Lord forgie us! Whear the *hell*, wold ye gang? ye marred, wearisome nowt! Yah seen all bud Hareton's bit uf a cham'er. They's nut another hoile tuh lig dahn in i' th' hahse!"

I was so vexed, I flung my tray, and its contents on the ground; and then seated myself at the stairs-head, hid my face in my hands, and cried.

"Ech! ech!" exclaimed Joseph. "Weel done, Miss Cathy! weel done, Miss Cathy! Hahsiver, t' maister sall just tum'le o'er them brocken pots; un' then we's hear summut; we's hear hah it's tuh be. Gooid-fur-nowt madling! yah desarve pining froo this tuh Churstmas, flinging t' precious gifts uh God under fooit i' yer flaysome rages! Bud, aw'm mista'en if yah shew yer sperrit lang. Will Hathecliff bide sich bonny ways, think ye? Aw nobbut wish he muh cotch ye i' that plisky. Aw nobbut wish he may."

And so he went scolding to his den beneath, taking the candle with him, and I remained in the dark.

The period of reflection succeeding this silly action, compelled me to admit the necessity of smothering my pride, and choking my wrath, and bestirring myself to remove its effects.

An unexpected aid presently appeared in the shape of Throttler, whom I now recognised as a son of our old Skulker; it had spent its whelphood at the Grange, and was given by my father to Mr. Hindley. I fancy it knew me—it pushed its nose against mine by way of salute, and then hastened to devour the porridge, while I groped from step to step, collecting the shattered earthenware, and drying the spatters of milk from the bannister with my pocket-handherchief.

Our labours were scarcely over when I heard Earnshaw's tread in the passage; my assistant tucked in his tail, and pressed to the wall; I stole into the nearest doorway. The dog's endeavour to avoid him was unsuccessful; as I guessed by a scutter down stairs, and a prolonged, piteous yelping. I had better luck. He passed on, entered his chamber, and shut the door.

Directly after Joseph came up with Hareton, to put him to bed. I had found shelter in Hareton's room, and the old man on seeing me, said—

"They's rahm fur boath yah, un yer pride, nah, aw sud think i' th hahse. It's empty; yah muh hev it all tuh yerseln, un Him as allas maks a third, i' sich ill company!"

164 EMILY BRONTË

Gladly did I take advantage of this intimation; and the minute I flung myself into a chair, by the fire, I nodded, and slept.

My slumber was deep, and sweet; though over far too soon. Mr. Heathcliff awoke me; he had just come in, and demanded, in his loving manner, what I was doing there?

I told him the cause of my staying up so late—that he had the key of our room in his pocket.

The adjective *our* gave mortal offence. He swore it was not, nor ever should be mine; and he'd—but I'll not repeat his language, nor describe his habitual conduct; he is ingenious and unresting in seeking to gain my abhorrence! I sometimes wonder at him with an intensity that deadens my fear: yet, I assure you, a tiger, or a venomous serpent could not rouse terror in me equal to that which he wakens. He told me of Catherine's illness, and accused my brother of causing it; promising that I should be Edgar's proxy in suffering, till he could get a hold of him.

"I do hate him—I am wretched—I have been a fool! Beware of uttering one breath of this to any one at the Grange. I shall expect you every day—don't disappoint me!

"ISABELLA."

CHAPTER XIV.

As soon as I had perused this epistle, I went to the master, and informed him that his sister had arrived at the Heights, and sent me a a letter expressing her sorrow for Mrs. Linton's situation, and her ardent desire to see him; with a wish that he would transmit to her, as early as possible, some token of forgiveness by me.

"Forgiveness?" said Linton. "I have nothing to forgive her, Ellen—you may call at Wuthering Heights this afternoon, if you like, and say that I am not *angry*, but I'm *sorry* to have lost her: especially as I can never think she'll be happy. It is out of the question my going to see her, however; we are eternally divided; and should she really wish to oblige me, let her persuade the villain she has married to leave the country."

"And you wont write her a little note, sir?" I asked, imploringly.

"No," he answered. "It is needless. My communication with Heathcliff's family shall be as sparing as his with mine. It shall not exist!"

Mr. Edgar's coldness depressed me exceedingly; and all the way from the Grange, I puzzled my brains how to put more heart into what he said, when I repeated it; and how to soften his refusal of even a few lines to console Isabella.

I dare say she had been on the watch for me since morning: I saw her looking through the lattice, as I came up the garden causeway and I nodded to her; but she drew back, as if afraid of being observed.

I entered without knocking. There never was such a dreary, dismal scene as the formerly cheerful house presented! I must confess that, if I had been in the young lady's place, I would, at least, have swept the hearth, and wiped the tables with a duster. But she already partook of the pervading spirit of neglect which encompassed her. Her pretty face was wan and listless; her hair uncurled; some locks hanging lankly down, and some carelessly twisted round her head. Probably she had not touched her dress since yester evening.

Hindley was not there. Mr. Heathcliff sat at a table, turning over some papers in his pocket-book; but he rose when I appeared, asked me how I did, quite friendly, and offered me a chair.

He was the only thing there that seemed decent, and I thought he never looked better. So much had circumstances altered their positions, that he would certainly have struck a stranger as a born and bred gentleman, and his wife as a thorough little slattern!

She came forward eagerly to greet me; and held out one hand to take the expected letter.

EMILY BRONTË

I shook my head. She wouldn't understand the hint, but followed me to a sideboard, where I went to lay my bonnet, and importuned me in a whisper to give her directly what I had brought.

Heathcliff guessed the meaning of her manœuvres, and said—

"If you have got anything for Isabella, as no doubt you have, Nelly, give it to her. You needn't make a secret of it; we have no secrets between us."

"Oh, I have nothing," I replied, thinking it best to speak the truth at once. "My master bid me tell his sister that she must not expect either a letter or a visit from him at present. He sends his love, ma'am, and his wishes for your happiness, and his pardon for the grief you have occasioned; but he thinks that after this time, his household, and the household here, should drop intercommunication; as nothing good could come of keeping it up.

Mrs. Heathcliff's lip quivered slightly, and she returned to her seat in the window. Her husband took his stand on the hearthstone, near me, and began to put questions concerning Catherine.

I told him as much as I thought proper of her illness, and he extorted from me, by cross-examination, most of the facts connected with its origin.

I blamed her, as she deserved, for bringing it all on herself; and ended by hoping that he would follow Mr. Linton's example, and avoid future interference with his family, for good or evil.

"Mrs Linton is now just recovering," I said, "she'll never be like she was, but her life is spared, and if you really have a regard for her, you'll shun crossing her way again. Nay you'll move out of this country entirely; and that you may not regret it, I'll inform you Catherine Linton is as different now, from your old friend Catherine Earnshaw, as that young lady is different from me! Her appearance is changed greatly, her character much more so; and the person, who is compelled, of necessity, to be her companion, will only sustain his affection hereafter, by the remembrance of what she once was, by common humanity, and a sense of duty!"

"That is quite possible," remarked Heathcliff forcing himself to seem calm, "quite possible that your master should have nothing but common humanity, and a sense of duty to fall back upon. But do you imagine that I shall leave Catherine to his *duty* and *humanity?* and can you compare my feelings respecting Catherine, to his? Before you leave this house, I must exact a promise from you, that you'll get me an interview with her—consent, or refuse, I *will* see her! What do you say?"

"I say Mr. Heathcliff," I replied, "you must not—you never shall through my means. Another encounter between you and the master, would kill her altogether!"

"With your aid that may be avoided;" he continued, "and should there be danger of such an event—should he be the cause of adding a single trouble more to her existence—Why, I think, I shall be justified in going to extremes! I wish you had sincerity enough to tell me whether Catherine would suffer

WUTHERING HEIGHTS 167

greatly from his loss. The fear that she would restrains me: and there you see the distinction between our feelings—Had he been in my place, and I in his, though I hated him with a hatred that turned my life to gall, I never would have raised a hand against him. You may look incredulous, if you please! I never would have banished him from her society, as long as she desired his. The moment her regard ceased, I would have torn his heart out, and drank his blood! But, till then, if you don't believe me, you don't know me—till then, I would have died by inches before I touched a single hair of his head!"

"And yet, I interrupted, you have no scruples in completely ruining all hopes of her perfect restoration, by thrusting yourself in to her remembrance, now, when she has nearly forgotten you, and involving her in a new tumult of discord, and distress."

"You suppose she has nearly forgotten me?" he said. "Oh Nelly! you know she has not! You know as well as I do, that for every thought she spends on Linton, she spends a thousand on me! At a most miserable period of my life, I had a notion of the kind, it haunted me on my return to the neighbourhood, last summer, but only her own assurance, could make me admit the horrible idea again. And then, Linton would be nothing, nor Hindley, nor all the dreams that ever I dreamt. Two words would comprehend my future *death* and *hell*—existence, after losing her would be hell.

"Yet I was a fool to fancy for a moment that she valued Edgar Linton's attachment more than mine—If he loved with all the powers of his puny being, he couldn't love as much in eighty years, as I could in a day. And Catherine has a heart as deep as I have; the sea could be as readily contained in that horse-trough, as her whole affection be monopolized by him—Tush! He is scarcely a degree dearer to her than her dog, or her horse—It is not in him to be loved like me, how can she love in him what he has not?

"Catherine and Edgar are as fond of each other, as any two people can be!" cried Isabella with sudden vivacity. "No one has a right to talk in that manner, and I won't hear my brother depreciated in silence!"

"Your brother is wondrous fond of you too, isn't he?" observed Heathcliff scornfully. "He turns you adrift on the world with surprising alacrity."

"He is not aware of what I suffer," she replied. "I didn't tell him that."

"You have been telling him something, then—you have written, have you?"

"To say that I was married, I did write—you saw the note."

"And nothing since?"

"No."

"My young lady is looking sadly the worse, for her change of condition," I remarked. "Somebody's love comes short in her case, obviously—whose I may guess; but, perhaps, I shouldn't say."

"I should guess it was her own," said Heathcliff. "She degenerates into a mere slut! She is tired of trying to please me, uncommonly early—You'd

168 EMILY BRONTË

hardly credit it, but the very morrow of our wedding, she was weeping to go home. However, she'll suit this house so much the better for not being over nice, and I'll take care she does not disgrace me by rambling abroad."

"Well, sir;" returned I, "I hope you'll consider that Mrs. Heathcliff is accustomed to be looked after, and waited on; and that she has been brought up like an only daughter whom every one was ready to serve—You must let her have a maid to keep things tidy about her, and you must treat her kindly—Whatever be your notion of Mr. Edgar, you cannot doubt that she has a capacity for strong attachments or she wouldn't have abandoned the elegancies, and comforts, and friends of her former home, to fix contentedly, in such a wilderness as this, with you."

"She abandoned them under a delusion;" he answered, "picturing in me a hero of romance, and expecting unlimited indulgences from my chivalrous devotion. I can hardly regard her in the light of a rational creature, so obstinately has she persisted in forming a fabulous notion of my character, and acting on the false impressions she cherished. But at last, I think she begins to know me—I don't perceive the silly smiles and grimaces that provoked me, at first; and the senseless incapability of discerning that I was in earnest when I gave her my opinion of her infatuation, and herself—It was a marvellous effort of perspicacity to discover that I did not love her. I believed at one time, no lessons could teach her that! aud yet it is poorly learnt; for this morning she announced, as a piece of appalling intelligence, that I had actually succeeded in making her hate me! A positive labour of Hercules, I assure you! If it be achieved, I have cause to return thanks—Can I trust your assertion, Isabella, are you sure you hate me? If I let you alone for half-a-day, won't you come sighing and wheedling to me again? I dare say she would rather I had seemed all tenderness before you; it wounds her vanity to have the truth exposed. But, I don't care who knows that the passion was wholly on one side, and I never told her a lie about it. She cannot accuse me of showing a bit of deceitful softness. The first thing she saw me do, on coming out of the Grange, was to hang up her little dog, and when she pleaded for it the first words I uttered, were a wish that I had the hanging of every being belonging to her, except one: possibly, she took that exception for herself—But no brutality disgusted her—I suppose, she has an innate admiration of it, if only her precious person were secure from injury! Now, was it not the depth of absurdity—of genuine idiocy, for that pitiful slavish, mean-minded brach to dream that I could love her? Tell your master, Nelly, that I never, in all my life, met with such an abject thing as she is—She even disgraces the name of Linton; and I've sometimes relented, from pure lack of invention, in my experiments on what she could endure, and still creep shamefully cringing back! But tell him also, to set his fraternal and magisterial heart at ease, that I keep strictly within the limits of the law—I have avoided, up to this period, giving her the slightest right to claim a separation; and what's more, she'd thank nobody for dividing us—if

WUTHERING HEIGHTS 169

she desired to go she might—the nuisance of her presence outweighs the gratification to be derived from tormenting her!"

"Mr. Heathcliff," said I, "this is the talk of a madman, and your wife, most likely is convinced you are mad; and, for that reason, she has borne with you hitherto: but now that you say she may go, she'll doubtless avail herself of the permission—You are not so bewitched ma'am, are you, as to remain with him, of your own accord?"

"Take care, Ellen!" answered Isabella, her eyes sparkling irefully—there was no misdoubting by their expression, the full success of her partner's endeavours to make himself detested, "Don't put faith in a single word he speaks. He's a lying fiend, a monster, and not a human being! I've been told I might leave him before; and I've made the attempt, but I dare not repeat it! Only Ellen, promise you'll not mention a syllable of his infamous conversation to my brother or Catherine—whatever he may pretend, he wishes to provoke Edgar to desperation—he says he has married me on purpose to obtain power over him; and he shan't obtain it—I'll die first! I just hope, I pray that he may forget his diabolical prudence, and kill me! The single pleasure I can imagine is, is to die, or to see him dead!"

"There—that will do for the present!" said Heathcliff. "If you are called upon in a court of law, you'll remember her language, Nelly! And take a good look at that countenance—she's near the point which would suit me. No, you're not fit to be your own guardian, Isabella now; and I, being your legal protector, must retain you in my custody, however distasteful the obligation may be—Go up stairs; I have something to say to Ellen Dean, in private. That's not the way—up-stairs, I tell you! Why this is the road up-stairs, child!"

He seized, and thrust her from the room; and returned muttering,

"I have no pity! I have no pity! The worms writhe, the more I yearn to crush out their entrails! It is a moral teething, and I grind with greater energy, in proportion to the increase of pain."

"Do you understand what the word pity means?" I said hastening to resume my bonnet. "Did you ever feel a touch of it in your life?"

"Put that down!" he interrupted, perceiving my intention to depart. "You are not going yet—Come here now, Nelly—I must either persuade, or compel you to aid me in fulfilling my determination to see Catherine, and that without delay—I swear that I meditate no harm; I don't desire to cause any disturbance, or to exasperate, or insult Mr. Linton; I only wish to hear from herself how she is, and why she has been ill; and to ask, if anything that I could do would be of use to her. Last night, I was in the Grange garden six hours, and I'll return there to-night; and every night I'll haunt the place, and every day, till I find an opportunity of entering. If Edgar Linton meets me, I shall not hesitate to knock him down, and give him enough to ensure his quiescence while I stay—If his servants oppose me, I shall threaten them off with these pistols—But wouldn't it be better to prevent my coming in contact with

170 EMILY BRONTË

them, or their master. And you could do it so easily! I'd warn you when I came, and then you might let me in unobserved, as soon as she was alone, and watch till I departed—your conscience quite calm, you would be hindering mischief."

I protested against playing that treacherous part in my employer's house; and besides, I urged the cruelty, and selfishness of his destroying Mrs. Linton's tranquillity, for his satisfaction.

"The commonest occurrence startles her painfully," I said. "She's all nerves, and she couldn't bear the surprise, I'm positive—Don't persist, sir! or else, I shall be obliged to inform my master of your designs, and he'll take measures to secure his house and its inmates from any such unwarrantable intrusions!

In that case, I'll take measures to secure you, woman!" exclaimed Heathcliff, "you shall not leave Wuthering Heights till to-morrow morning. It is a foolish story to assert that Catherine could not bear to see me; and as to surprising her, I don't desire it, you must prepare her—ask her if I may come. You say she never mentions my name, and that I am never mentioned to her. To whom should she mention me if I am a forbidden topic in the house? She thinks you are all spies for her husband—Oh, I've no doubt she's in hell among you! I guess, by her silence as much as any thing, what she feels. You say she is often restless, and anxious looking—is that a proof of tranquillity? You talk of her mind, being unsettled—How the devil could it be otherwise, in her frightful isolation. And that insipid, paltry creature attending her from *duty* and *humanity*! From *pity* and *charity*. He might as well plant an oak in a flower-pot, and expect it to thrive, as imagine he can restore her to vigour in the soil of his shallow cares! Let us settle it at once; will you stay here, and am I to fight my way to Catherine over Linton, and his footmen? Or will you be my friend, as you have been hitherto, and do what I request? Decide! because there is no reason for my lingering another minute, if you persist in your stubborn ill-nature!"

Well, Mr. Lockwood, I argued, and complained, and flatly refused him fifty times; but in the long run he forced me to an agreement—I engaged to carry a letter from him to my mistress; and should she consent, I promised to let him have intelligence of Linton's next absence from home, when he might come, and get in as he was able—I wouldn't be there, and my fellow servants should be equally out of the way.

Was it right, or wrong? I fear it was wrong, though expedient. I thought I prevented another explosion by my compliance; and I thought too, it might create a favourable crisis in Catherine's mental illness: and then I remembered Mr. Edgar's stern rebuke of my carrying tales; and I tried to smooth away all disquietude on the subject, by affirming, with frequent iteration, that, that betrayal of trust, if it merited so harsh an appellation, should be the last.

Notwithstanding my journey homeward was sadder than my journey thither; and many misgivings I had, ere I could prevail on myself to put the missive into Mrs. Linton's hand.

But here is Kenneth—I'll go down, and tell him how much better you are. My history is *dree'* as we say, and will serve to wile away another morning.

Dree, and dreary! I reflected as the good woman descended to receive the doctor; and not exactly of the kind which I should have chosen to amuse me; but never mind! I'll extract wholesome medicines from Mrs. Dean's bitter herbs; and firstly, let me beware of the fascination that lurks in Catherine Heathcliff's brilliant eyes. I should be in a curious taking if I surrendered my heart to that young person, and the daughter turned out a second edition of the mother!

The End of Vol. I.

Volume II

Chapter I.

Another week over—and I am so many days nearer health, and spring! I have now heard all my neighbour's history, at different sittings, as the housekeeper could spare time from more important occupations. I'll continue it in her own words, only a little condensed. She is, on the whole, a very fair narrator and I don't think I could improve her style.

"In the evening," she said, "the evening of my visit to the Heights, I knew as well as if I saw him, that Mr. Heathcliff was about the place; and I shunned going out, because I still carried his letter in my pocket, and didn't want to be threatened, or teased any more.

I had made up my mind not to give it till my master went somewhere; as I could not guess how its receipt would affect Catherine. The consequence was, that it did not reach her before the lapse of three days. The fourth was Sunday, and I brought it into her room, after the family were gone to church.

There was a man servant left to keep the house with me, and we generally made a practice of locking the doors during the hours of service; but on that occasion, the weather was so warm and pleasant that I set them wide open; and to fulfil my engagement, as I knew who would be coming, I told my companion that the mistress wished very much for some oranges, and he must run over to the village, and get a few, to be paid for on the morrow. He departed, and I went up-stairs.

Mrs. Linton sat in a loose, white dress, with a light shawl over her shoulders, in the recess of the open window, as usual. Her thick, long hair had been partly removed at the beginning of her illness; and now, she wore it simply combed in its natural tresses over her temples and neck. Her appearance was altered, as I had told Heathcliff, but when she was calm, there seemed unearthly beauty in the change.

The flash of her eyes had been succeeded by a dreamy and melancholy softness; they no longer gave the impression of looking at the objects around her; they appeared always to gaze beyond, and far beyond—you would have said out of this world—Then, the paleness of her face, its haggard aspect having vanished as she recovered flesh, and the peculiar expression arising from her mental state, though painfully suggestive of their causes, added to the touching interest, which she wakened, and invariably to me, I know, and to any person who saw her, I should think, refuted more tangible proofs of convalescence and stamped her as one doomed to decay.

A book lay spread on the sill before her, and the scarcely perceptible wind fluttered its leaves at intervals. I believe Linton had laid it there, for she never

176 EMILY BRONTË

endeavoured to divert herself with reading, or occupation of any kind; and he would spend many an hour in trying to entice her attention to some subject which had formerly been her amusement.

She was conscious of his aim, and in her better moods, endured his efforts placidly; only showing their uselessness by now and then suppressing a wearied sigh, and cheeking him at last, with the saddest of smiles and kisses. At other times, she would turn petulantly away, and hide her face in her hands, or even push him off angrily; and then he took care to let her alone, for he was certain of doing no good.

Gimmerton chapel bells were still ringing: and the full, mellow flow, of the beck in the valley, came soothingly on the ear. It was a sweet substitute for the yet absent murmur of the summer foliage which drowned that music about the Grange, when the trees were in leaf. At Wuthering Heights it always sounded on quiet days, following a great thaw, or a season of steady rain— and, of Wuthering Heights, Catherine was thinking as she listened; that is, if she thought, or listened, at all; but she had the vague, distant look, I mentioned before, which expressed no recognition of material things either by ear or eye.

"There's a letter for you, Mrs. Linton," I said, gently inserting it in one hand that rested on her knee. "You must read it immediately, because it wants an answer. Shall I break the seal?"

"Yes," she answered, without altering the direction of her eyes.

I opened it—it was very short.

"Now," I continued, "read it."

She drew away her hand, and let it fall. I replaced it in her lap, and stood waiting till it should please her to glance down; but that movement was so long delayed that at last I resumed—

"Must I read it, ma'am? It is from Mr. Heathcliff."

There was a start, and a troubled gleam of recollection, and a struggle to arrange her ideas. She lifted the letter, and seemed to peruse it; and when she came to the signature she sighed; yet still I found she had not gathered its import; for upon my desiring to hear her reply she merely pointed to the name, and gazed at me with mournful and questioning eagerness.

"Well, he wishes to see you," said I, guessing her need of an interpreter. "He's in the garden by this time, and impatient to know what answer I shall bring."

As I spoke, I observed a large dog lying on the sunny grass beneath, raise its ears, as if about to bark; and then smoothing them back, announce by a wag of the tail that some one approached whom it did not consider a stranger.

Mrs. Linton bent forward, and listened breathlessly. The minute after a step traversed the hall; the open house was too tempting for Heathcliff to resist walking in: most likely he supposed that I was inclined to shirk my promise, and so resolved to trust to his own audacity.

WUTHERING HEIGHTS 177

With straining eagerness Catherine gazed towards the entrance of her chamber. He did not hit the right room directly; she motioned me to admit him; but he found it out, ere I could reach the door, and in a stride or two was at her side, and had her grasped in his arms.

He neither spoke, nor loosed his hold, for some five minutes, during which period he bestowed more kisses than ever he gave in his life before, I dare say; but then my mistress had kissed him first, and I plainly saw that he could hardly bear, for downright agony, to look into her face! The same conviction had stricken him as me, from the instant he beheld her, that there was no prospect of ultimate recovery there—she was fated, sure to die.

"Oh, Cathy! Oh my life! how can I bear it?" was the first sentence he uttered, in a tone that did not seek to disguise his despair.

And now he stared at her so earnestly that I thought the very intensity of his gaze would bring tears into his eyes; but they burned with anguish, they did not melt.

"What now?" said Catherine, leaning back, and returning his look with a suddenly clouded brow—her humour was a mere vane for constantly varying caprices. "You and Edgar have broken my heart, Heathcliff! And you both come to bewail the deed to me, as if you were the people to be pitied! I shall not pity you, not I. You have killed me—and thriven on it, I think. How strong you are! How many years do you mean to live after I am gone?"

Heathcliff had knelt on one knee to embrace her; he attempted to rise, but she seized his hair, and kept him down.

"I wish I could hold you," she continued, bitterly, "till we were both dead! I shouldn't care what you suffered. I care nothing for your sufferings. Why shouldn't you suffer? I do! Will you forget me—will you be happy when I am in the earth? Will you say twenty years hence, 'That's the grave of Catherine Earnshaw. I loved her long ago, and was wretched to lose her; but it is past. I've loved many others since—my children are dearer to me that she was, and, at death, I shall not rejoice that I am going to her, I shall be sorry that I must leave them!' Will you say so, Heathcliff?"

"Don't torture me till I'm as mad as yourself," cried he, wrenching his head free, and grinding his teeth.

The two, to a cool spectator, made a strange and fearful picture. Well might Catherine deem that Heaven would be a land of exile to her, unless, with her mortal body, she cast away her mortal character also. Her present countenance had a wild vindictiveness in its white cheek, and a bloodless lip, and scintillating eye; and she retained, in her closed fingers, a portion of the locks she had been grasping. As to her companion, while raising himself with one hand, he had taken her arm with the other; and so inadequate was his stock of gentleness to the requirements of her condition, that on his letting go, I saw four distinct impressions left blue in the colourless skin.

178   EMILY BRONTË

"Are you possessed with a devil," he pursued, savagely, "to talk in that manner to me, when you are dying? Do you reflect that all those words will be branded in my memory, and eating deeper eternally, after you have left me? You know you lie to say I have killed you; and, Catherine, you know that I could as soon forget you, as my existence! Is it not sufficient for your infernal selfishness, that while you are at peace I shall writhe in the torments of hell?"

"I shall not be at peace," moaned Catherine, recalled to a sense of physical weakness by the violent, unequal throbbing of her heart, which beat visibly, and audibly under this excess of agitation.

She said nothing further till the paroxysm was over; then she continued, more kindly—

"I'm not wishing you greater torment than I have, Heathcliff! I only wish us never to be parted—and should a word of mine distress you hereafter, think I feel the same distress underground, and for my own sake, forgive me! Come here and kneel down again! You never harmed me in your life. Nay, if you nurse anger, that will be worse to remember than my harsh words! Wont you come here again? Do!"

Heathcliff went to the back of her chair, and leant over, but not so far as to let her see his face, which was livid with emotion. She bent round to look at him; he would not permit it; turning abruptly, he walked to the fire-place, where he stood, silent, with his back towards us.

Mrs. Linton's glance followed him suspiciously: every movement woke a new sentiment in her. After a pause, and a prolonged gaze, she resumed, addressing me in accents of indignant disappointment.

"Oh, you see, Nelly! he would not relent a moment, to keep me out of the grave! *That* is how I'm loved! Well, never mind! That is not *my* Heathcliff. I shall love mine yet; and take him with me—he's in my soul. And," added she, musingly, "the thing that irks me most is this shattered prison, after all. I'm tired, tired of being enclosed here. I'm wearying to escape into that glorious world, and to be always there; not seeing it dimly through tears, and yearning for it through the walls of an aching heart; but really with it, and in it. Nelly, you think you are better and more fortunate than I; in full health and strength—you are sorry for me—very soon that will be altered. I shall be sorry for *you*. I shall be incomparably beyond and above you all. I *wonder* he wont be near me!" She went on to herself. "I thought he wished it. Heathcliff dear! you should not be sullen now. Do come to me, Heathcliff."

In her eagerness she rose, and supported herself on the arm of the chair. At that earnest appeal, he turned to her, looking absolutely desperate. His eyes wide, and wet, at last, flashed fiercely on her; his breast heaved convulsively. An instant they held asunder; and then how they met I hardly saw, but Catherine made a spring, and he caught her, and they were locked in an embrace from which I thought my mistress would never be released alive. In fact, to my eyes, she seemed directly insensible. He flung himself into the

WUTHERING HEIGHTS

nearest seat, and on my approaching hurriedly to ascertain if she had fainted, he gnashed at me, and foamed like a mad dog, and gathered her to him with greedy jealousy. I did not feel as if I were in the company of a creature of my own species; it appeared that he would not understand, though I spoke to him; so, I stood off, and held my tongue, in great perplexity.

A movement of Catherine's relieved me a little presently: she put up her hand to clasp his neck, and bring her cheek to his, as he held her: while he, in return, covering her with frantic caresses, said wildly—

"You teach me now how cruel you've been—cruel and false. *Why* did you despise me? *Why* did you betray your own heart, Cathy? I have not one word of comfort—you deserve this. You have killed yourself. Yes, you may kiss me, and cry; and wring out my kisses and tears. They'll blight you—they'll damn you, You loved me—then what *right* had you to leave me? What right—answer me—for the poor fancy you felt for Linton? Because misery, and degradation, and death, and nothing that God or satan could inflict would have parted us, *you*, of your own will, did it. I have not broken your heart—*you* have broken it—and in breaking it, you have broken mine. So much the worse for me, that I am strong. Do I want to live? What kind of living will it be when you—oh God! would *you* like to live with your soul in the grave?"

"Let me alone. Let me alone," sobbed Catherine. "If I've done wrong, I'm dying for it. It is enough! You left me too; but I wont upbraid you! I forgive you. Forgive me!"

"It is hard to forgive, and to look at those eyes, and feel those wasted hands," he answered. "Kiss me again; and don't let me see your eyes! I forgive what you have done to me. I love *my* murderer—but *yours*! How can I?"

They were silent—their faces hid against each other, and washed by each other's tears. At least, I suppose the weeping was on both sides; as it seemed Heathcliff *could* weep on a great occasion like this.

I grew very uncomfortable, meanwhile; for the afternoon wore fast away, the man whom I had sent off returned from his errand, and I could distinguish, by the shine of the westering sun up the valley, a concourse thickening outside Gimmerton chapel porch.

"Service is over," I announced. "My master will be here in half-an-hour."

Heathcliff groaned a curse, and strained Catherine closer—she never moved.

Ere long I perceived a group of the servants passing up the road towards the kitchen wing. Mr. Linton was not far behind; he opened the gate himself, and sauntered slowly up, probably enjoying the lovely afternoon that breathed as soft as summer.

"Now he is here," I exclaimed. "For Heaven's sake, hurry down! You'll not meet any one on the front stairs. Do be quick; and stay among the trees till he is fairly in."

180   EMILY BRONTË

"I must go, Cathy," said Heathcliff, seeking to extricate himself from his companion's arms. "But, if I live, I'll see you again before you are asleep. I wont stray five yards from your window."

"You must not go!" she answered, holding him as firmly as her strength allowed. "You shall not, I tell you."

"For one hour," he pleaded, earnestly.

"Not for one minute," she replied.

"I *must*—Linton will be up immediately," persisted the alarmed intruder.

He would have risen, and unfixed her fingers by the act—she clung fast gasping; there was mad resolution in her face.

"No!" she shrieked. "Oh, don't, don't go. It is the last time! Edgar will not hurt us. Heathcliff, I shall die! I shall die!"

"Damn the fool. There he is," cried Heathcliff, sinking back into his seat. "Hush, my darling! Hush, hush, Catherine! I'll stay. If he shot me so, I'd expire with a blessing on my lips."

And there they were fast again. I heard my master mounting the stairs— the cold sweat ran from my forehead; I was horrified.

"Are you going to listen to her ravings?" I said, passionately. "She does not know what she says. Will you ruin her, because she has not wit to help herself? Get up! you could be free instantly. That is the most diabolical deed that ever you did. We are all done for—master, mistress, and servant."

I wrung my hands, and cried out; and Mr. Linton hastened his step at the noise. In the midst of my agitation, I was sincerely glad to observe that Catherine's arms had fallen relaxed, and her head hung down.

"She's fainted or dead," I thought, "so much the better. Far better that she should be dead, than lingering a burden, and a misery-maker to all about her."

Edgar sprang to his unbidden guest, blanched with astonishment and rage. What he meant to do, I cannot tell; however, the other stopped all demonstrations, at once, by placing the lifeless-looking form in his arms.

"Look there," he said, "unless you be a fiend, help her first—then you shall speak to me!"

He walked into the parlour, and sat down. Mr. Linton summoned me, and, with great difficulty, and after resorting to many means, we managed to restore her to sensation; but she was all bewildered; she sighed, and moaned, and knew nobody. Edgar, in his anxiety for her, forgot her hated friend. I did not. I went, at the earliest opportunity, and besought him to depart, affirming that Catherine was better, and he should hear from me in the morning, how she passed the night.

"I shall not refuse to go out of doors," he answered; "but I shall stay in the garden; and, Nelly, mind you keep your word to-morrow. I shall be under those larch trees, mind! or I pay another visit, whether Linton be in or not."

He sent a rapid glance through the half-open door of the chamber, and ascertaining that what I stated was apparently true, delivered the house of his luckless presence.

Chapter II.

About twelve o'clock, that night, was born the Catherine you saw at Wuthering Heights, a puny, seven months' child; and two hours after the mother died, having never recovered sufficient consciousness to miss Heathcliff, or know Edgar.

The latter's distraction at his bereavement is a subject too painful to be dwelt on; its after effects showed how deep the sorrow sunk.

A great addition, in my eyes, was his being left without an heir. I bemoaned that, as I gazed on the feeble orphan; and I mentally abused old Linton for, what was only natural partiality, the securing his estate to his own daughter, instead of his son's.

An unwelcomed infant it was, poor thing! It might have wailed out of life, and nobody cared a morsel, during those first hours of existence. We redeemed the neglect afterwards; but it's beginning was as friendless as its end is likely to be.

Next morning—bright and cheerful out of doors—stole softened in through the blinds of the silent room, and suffused the couch and its occupant with a mellow, tender glow.

Edgar Linton had his head laid on the pillow, and his eyes shut. His young and fair features were almost as death-like as those of the form beside him, and almost as fixed; but *his* was the hush of exhausted anguish, and *her's* of perfect peace. Her brow smooth, her lids closed, her lips wearing the expression of a smile. No angel in heaven could be more beautiful than she appeared; and I partook of the infinite calm in which she lay. My mind was never in a holier frame, than while I gazed on that untroubled image of Divine rest. I instinctively echoed the words she had uttered, a few hours before. "Incomparably beyond, and above us all! Whether still on earth or now in Heaven her spirit is at home with God!"

I don't know if it be a peculiarity in me, but I am seldom otherwise than happy while watching in the chamber of death, should no frenzied or despairing mourner share the duty with me. I see a repose that neither earth nor hell can break; and I feel an assurance of the endless and shadowless hereafter— the Eternity they have entered—where life is boundless in its duration, and love in its sympathy, and joy in its fulness. I noticed on that occasion how much selfishness there is even in a love like Mr. Linton's, when he so regretted Catherine's blessed release!

To be sure one might have doubted, after the wayward and impatient existence she had led, whether she merited a haven of peace at last. One might doubt in seasons of cold reflection, but not then, in the presence of her corpse.

EMILY BRONTË

It asserted its own tranquillity, which seemed a pledge of equal quiet to its former inhabitants.

"Do you believe such people *are* happy in the other world, sir? I'd give a great deal to know."

I declined answering Mrs. Dean's question, which struck me as something heterodox. She proceeded:

"Retracing the course of Catherine Linton I fear we have no right to think she is: but we'll leave her with her Maker."

The master looked asleep, and I ventured soon after sunrise to quit the room and steal out to the pure, refreshing air. The servants thought me gone to shake off the drowsiness of my protracted watch; in reality my chief motive motive was seeing Mr. Heathcliff. If he had remained among the larches all night he would have heard nothing of the stir at the Grange, unless, perhaps, he might catch the gallop of the messenger going to Gimmerton. If he had come nearer he would probably be aware, from the lights flitting to and fro, and the opening and shutting of the outer doors, that all was not right within.

I wished yet feared to find him. I felt the terrible news must be told, and I longed to get it over, but *how* to do it I did not know.

He was there—at least a few yards further in the park; leant against an old ash tree, his hat off, and his hair soaked with the dew that had gathered on the budded branches, and fell pattering round him. He had been standing a long time in that position, for I saw a pair of ousels passing and repassing, scarcely three feet from him, busy in building their nest, and regarding his proximity no more than that of a piece of timber. They flew off at my approach, and he raised his eyes and spoke:

"She's dead!" he said; "I've not waited for you to learn that. Put your handkerchief away—don't snivel before me. Damn you all! she wants none of *your* tears!"

I was weeping as much for him as her: we do sometimes pity creatures that have none of the feeling either for themselves or others; and when I first looked into his face I perceived that he had got intelligence of the catastrophe; and a foolish notion struck me that his heart was quelled, and he prayed, because his lips moved, and his gaze was bent on the ground.

"Yes, she's dead!" I answered, checking my sobs, and drying my cheeks. "Gone to to heaven, I hope, where we may, everyone, join her, if we take due warning, and leave our evil ways to follow good!"

"Did *she* take due warning, then?" asked Heathcliff, attempting a sneer. "Did she die like a saint? Come, give me a true history of the event. How did—"

He endeavoured to pronounce the name, but could not manage it; and compressing his mouth, he held a silent combat with his inward agony, defying, meanwhile, my sympathy with an unflinching, ferocious stare.

WUTHERING HEIGHTS 183

"How did she die?" he resumed, at last—fain, notwithstanding his hardihood, to have a support behind him, for, after the struggle, he trembled, in spite of himself, to his very finger-ends.

"Poor wretch!" I thought; "you have a heart and nerves the same as your brother men! Why should you be so anxious to conceal them? Your pride cannot blind God! You tempt him to wring them, till he forces a cry of humiliation!"

"Quietly as a lamb!" I answered, aloud. "She drew a sigh, and stretched herself, like a child reviving, and sinking again to sleep; and five minutes after I felt one little pulse at her heart, and nothing more!"

"And—and did she ever mention me?" he asked, hesitating, as if he dreaded the answer to his question would introduce details that he could not bear to hear.

"Her senses never returned—she recognised nobody from the time you left her," I said. "She lies with a sweet smile on her face; and her latest ideas wandered back to pleasant early days. Her life closed in a gentle dream—may she wake as kindly in the other world!"

"May she wake in torment?" he cried, with frightful vehemence, stamping his foot, and groaning in a sudden paroxysm of ungovernable passion. "Why, she's a liar to the end! Where is she? Not *there*—not in heaven—not perished—where? Oh! you said you cared nothing for my sufferings! And I pray one prayer—I repeat it till my tongue stiffens—Catherine Earnshaw, may you not rest, as long as I am living! You said I killed you—haunt me then! The murdered *do* haunt their murderers. I believe—I know that ghosts *have* wandered on earth. Be with me always—take any form—drive me mad! only *do* not leave me in this abyss, where I cannot find you! Oh, God! it is unutterable! I *cannot* live without my life! I *cannot* live without my soul!"

He dashed his head against the knotted trunk; and, lifting up his eyes, howled, not like a man, but like a savage beast getting goaded to death with knives and spears.

I observed several splashes of blood about the bark of the tree, and his band and forehead were both stained; probably the scene I witnessed was a repetition of others acted during the night. It hardly moved my compassion—it appalled me; still I felt reluctant to quit him so. But the moment he recollected himself enough to notice me watching, he thundered a command for me to go, and I obeyed. He was beyond my skill to quiet or console!

Mrs. Linton's funeral was appointed to take place on the Friday following her decease; and till then her coffin remained uncovered, and strewn with flowers and scented leaves, in the great drawing-room. Linton spent his days and nights there, a sleepless guardian; and—a circumstance concealed from all but me—Heathcliff spent his nights, at least, outside, equally a stranger to repose.

I held no communication with him; still I was conscious of his design to enter, if he could; and on the Tuesday, a little after dark, when my master

184 EMILY BRONTË

from sheer fatigue, had been compelled to retire a couple of hours, I went and opened one of the windows, moved by his perseverance to give him a chance of bestowing on the fading image of his idol one final adieu.

He did not omit to avail himself of the opportunity, cautiously and briefly; too cautiously to betray his presence by the slightest noise; indeed, I shouldn't have discovered that he had been there, except for the disarrangement of the drapery about the corpse's face, and for observing on the floor a curl of light hair, fastened with a silver thread, which, on examination, I ascertained to have been taken from a locket hung round Catherine's neck. Heathcliff had opened the trinket, and cast out its contents, replacing them by a black lock of his own. I twisted the two, and enclosed them together.

Mr. Earnshaw was, of course, invited to attend the remains of his sister to the grave; and he sent no excuse, but he never came; so that besides her husband, the mourners were wholly composed of tenants and servants. Isabella was not asked.

The place of Catherine's interment, to the surprise of the villagers, was neither in the chapel, under the carved monument of the Lintons', nor yet by the tombs of her own relations, outside. It was dug on a green slope, in a corner of the kirkyard, where the wall is so low that heath and bilberry plants have climbed over it from the moor; and peat mould almost buries it. Her husband lies in the same spot, now; and they have each a simple headstone, above, and a plain grey block at their feet, to mark the graves.

Chapter III.

That Friday made the last of our fine days, for a month. In the evening, the weather broke; the wind shifted from south to north-east, and brought rain, first, and then sleet, and snow.

On the morrow one could hardly imagine that there had been three weeks of summer: the primroses and crocuses were hidden under wintry drifts: the larks were silent, the young leaves of the early trees smitten and blackened— And dreary, and chill, and dismal that morrow did creep over! My master kept his room—I took possession of the lonely parlour, converting it into a nursery; and there I was sitting, with the moaning doll of a child laid on my knee; rocking it to and fro, and watching, meanwhile the still driving flakes build up the uncurtained window, when the door opened, and some person entered out of breath, and laughing!"

My anger was greater than my astonishment for a minute; I supposed it one of the maids, and I cried,

"Have done! How dare you show your giddiness, here? What would Mr. Linton say if he heard you?"

"Excuse me!" answered a familiar voice, "but I know Edgar is in bed, and I cannot stop myself."

With that, the speaker came forward to the fire, panting and holding her hand, to her side.

"I have run the whole way from Wuthering Heights!" she continued, after a pause. "Except where I've flown—I couldn't count the number of falls I've had—Oh, I'm aching all over! Don't be alarmed—There shall be an explanation as soon as I can give it—only just have the goodness to step out, and order the carriage to take me on to Gimmerton, and tell a servant to seek up a few clothes in my wardrobe."

The intruder was Mrs. Heathcliff—she certainly seemed in no laughing predicament: her hair streamed on her shoulders dripping with snow and water; she was dressed in the girlish dress she commonly wore, befitting her age more than her position; a low frock, with short sleeves, and nothing on either head, or neck. The frock was of light silk, and clung to her with wet; and her feet were protected merely by thin slippers; add to this a deep cut under one ear, which only the cold prevented from bleeding profusely, a white face scratched and bruised, and a frame hardly able to support itself through fatigue, and you may fancy my first fright was not much allayed when I had leisure to examine her.

"My dear young lady," I exclaimed "I'll stir no-where, and hear nothing, till you have removed every article of your clothes, and put on dry things; and

186   EMILY BRONTË

certainly you shall not go to Gimmerton to-night; so it is needless to order the carriage."

"Certainly, I shall;" she said; "walking or riding—yet I've no objection to dress myself decently; and—ah, see how it flows down my neck now! the fire does make it smart."

She insisted on my fulfilling her directions, before she would let me touch her; and not till after the coachman had been instructed to get ready, and a maid set to pack up some necessary attire, did I obtain her consent for binding the wound, and helping to change her garments.

"Now Ellen," she said when my task was finished, and she was seated in an easy chair on the hearth, with a cup of tea before her, "You sit down opposite me, and put poor Catherine's baby away—I don't like to see it! You mustn't think I care little for Catherine, because I behaved so foolishly on entering—I've cried too, bitterly—yes, more than any one else has reason to cry—we parted unreconciled, you remember, and I shan't forgive myself. But for all that, I was not going to sympathise with him—the brute beast! O give me the poker! This is the last thing of his I have about me," she slipped the gold ring from her third finger, and threw it on the floor. "I'll smash it!" she continued striking with childish spite. "And then I'll burn it!" and she took and dropped the misused article among the coals. "There! he shall buy another, if he gets me back again. He'd be capable of coming to seek me, to tease Edgar—I dare not stay, lest that notion should possess his wicked head! And besides, Edgar has not been kind, has he? And I won't come suing for his assistance; nor will I bring him into more trouble—Necessity compelled me to seek shelter here; though if I had not learnt he was out of the way, I'd have halted at the kitchen, washed my face, warmed myself, got you to bring what I wanted, and departed again to anywhere out of the reach of my accursed—of that incarnate goblin! Ah, he was in such a fury—if he had caught me! It's a pity, Earnshaw is not his match in strength—I wouldn't have run, till I'd seen him all but demolished, had Hindley been able to do it!"

"Well, don't talk so fast, Miss!" I interrupted, "you'll disorder the handkerchief I have tied round your face, and make the cut bleed again—Drink your tea, and take breath and give over laughing—Laughter is sadly out of place under this roof, and in your condition!"

"An undeniable truth," she replied, "Listen to that child! It maintains a constant wail—send it out of my hearing, for an hour; I shan't stay any longer."

I rang the bell, and committed it to a servant's care; and then I inquired what had urged her to escape from Wuthering Heights in such an unlikely plight—and where she meant to go, as she refused remaining with us?"

"I ought, and I wish to remain;" answered she; "to cheer Edgar, and take care of the baby, for two things, and because the Grange is my right home—but I tell you, he wouldn't let me! Do you think he could bear to see me grow fat, and merry; and could bear to think that we were tranquil, and not resolve on poisoning our comfort? Now, I have the satisfaction of being sure that he detests me to the point of its annoying him seriously to have me within ear shot, or eye-sight—I notice, when I enter his presence, the muscles of his countenance are involuntarily distorted into an expression of hatred; partly arising from his knowledge of the good causes I have to feel that sentiment for him, and partly from original aversion—It is strong enough to make me feel pretty certain that he would not chase me over England, supposing I contrived a clear escape; and therefore I must get quite away. I've recovered from my first desire to be killed by him. I'd rather he'd kill himself! He has extinguished my love effectually, and so I'm at my ease. I can recollect yet how I loved him; and can dimly imagine that I could still be loving him, if—No, no! Even, if he had doted on me, the devilish nature would have revealed its existence, somehow. Catherine had an awfully perverted taste to esteem him so dearly, knowing him so well—Monster! would that he could be blotted out of creation, and out of my memory!"

"Hush, hush! He's a human being," I said. "Be more charitable; there are worse men than he is yet!"

"He's not a human being:" she retorted; "and he has no claim on my charity—I gave him my heart, and he took and pinched it to death; and flung it back to me—people feel with their hearts, Ellen, and since he has destroyed mine, I have not power to feel for him, and I would not, though he groaned from this, to his dying day; and wept tears of blood for Catherine! No, indeed, indeed, I wouldn't!" And here Isabella began to cry; but, immediately dashing the water from her lashes, she recommenced.

"You asked, what has driven me to flight at last? I was compelled to attempt it, because, I had succeeded in rousing his rage a pitch above his malignity. Pulling out the nerves with red hot pincers, requires more coolness than knocking on the head. He was worked up to forget the fiendish prudence he boasted of, and proceeding to murderous violence: I experienced pleasure in being able to exasperate him: the sense of pleasure woke my instinct of self-preservation; so, I fairly broke free, and if ever I come into his hands again he is welcome to a signal revenge.

"Yesterday, you know, Mr. Earnshaw should have been at the funeral. He kept himself sober, for the purpose—tolerably sober; not going to-bed mad, at six o'clock and getting up drunk, at twelve. Consequently, he rose, in suicidal low spirits; as fit for the church, as for a dance; and instead, he sat down by the fire, and swallowed gin or brandy by tumblerfuls.

"Heathcliff—I shudder to name him! has been a stranger in the house from last Sunday till to-day—Whether the angels have fed him, or his kin beneath, I cannot tell; but, he has not eaten a meal with us for nearly a week—He has just come home at dawn, and gone up-stairs to his chamber; locking himself in—as if anybody dreamt of coveting his company! There he has continued,

188 EMILY BRONTË

praying like a methodist; only the deity he implored is senseless dust and ashes; and God, when addressed, was curiously confounded with his own black father! After concluding these precious orisons and they lasted generally till he grew hoarse, and his voice was strangled in his throat, he would be off again; always straight down to the Grange! I wonder Edgar did not send for a constable, and give him into custody! For me, grieved as I was about Catherine, it was impossible to avoid regarding this season of deliverance from degrading oppression as a holiday.

"I recovered spirits sufficient to hear Joseph's eternal lectures without weeping; and to move up and down the house, less with the foot of a frightened thief, than formerly. You wouldn't think that I should cry at anything Joseph could say, but he and Hareton are detestable companions. I'd rather sit with Hindley, and hear his awful talk, than with 't' little maister,' and his staunch supporter, that odious old man!

"When Heathcliff is in, I'm often obliged to seek the kitchen, and their society, or starve among the damp, uninhabited chambers; when he is not, as was the case this week, I establish a table, and chair, at one corner of the house fire, and never mind how Mr. Earnshaw may occupy himself; and he does not interfere with my arrangements: he is quieter, now, than he used to be, if no one provokes him; more sullen and depressed, and less furious. Joseph affirms he's sure he's an altered man; that the Lord has touched his heart, and he is saved "so as by fire." I'm puzzled to detect signs of the favourable change, but it is not my business.

"Yester-evening, I sat in my nook reading some old books, till late on towards twelve. It seemed so dismal to go up-stairs, with the wild snow blowing outside, and my thoughts continually reverting to the kirkyard, and the new made grave! I dared hardly lift my eyes from the page before me, that melancholy scene so instantly usurped its place.

"Hindley sat opposite; his head leant on his hand, perhaps meditating on the same subject. He had ceased drinking at a point below irrationality, and had neither stirred, nor spoken during two or three hours. There was no sound through the house, but the moaning wind which shook the windows every now and then: the faint crackling of the coals; and the click of my snuffers as I removed at intervals the long wick of the candle. Hareton and Joseph were probably fast asleep in bed. It was very, very sad, and while I read, I sighed, for it seemed as if all joy had vanished from the world, never to be restored.

The doleful silence was broken, at length, by the sound of the kitchen latch—Heathcliff had returned from his watch earlier than usual, owing, I suppose, to the sudden storm.

"That entrance was fastened; and we heard him coming round to get in by the other. I rose with an irrepressible expression of what I felt on my lips, which induced my companion, who had been staring towards the door, to turn and look at me.

WUTHERING HEIGHTS 189

"I'll keep him out five minutes." He exclaimed. "You won't object?"

"No, you may keep him out the whole night, for me," I answered. "Do! put the key in the lock, and draw the bolts."

Earnshaw accomplished this, ere his guest reached the front; he then came, and brought his chair to the other side of my table; leaning over it, and searching in my eyes, a sympathy with the burning hate that gleamed from his: as he both looked, and felt like an assassin, he couldn't exactly find that; but he discovered enough to encourage him to speak.

"You, and I," he said, "have each a great debt to settle with the man out yonder! If we were neither of us cowards, we might combine to discharge it. Are you as soft as your brother? Are you willing to endure to the last, and not once attempt a repayment?"

"I'm weary of enduring now;" I replied, "and I'd be glad of a retaliation that wouldn't recoil on myself; but treachery, and violence, are spears pointed at both ends—they wound those who resort to them, worse than their enemies."

"Treachery and violence are a just return for treachery and violence!" cried Hindley. "Mrs. Heathcliff, I'll ask you to do nothing, but sit still, and be dumb—Tell me now, can you? I'm sure you would have as much pleasure as I, in witnessing the conclusion of the fiend's existence, he'll be *your* death unless you overreach him—and he'll be *my* ruin—Damn the hellish villain! He knocks at the door, as if he were master here, already! Promise to hold your tongue, and before that clock strikes—it wants three minutes of one— you're a free woman!"

He took the implements which I described to you in my letter from his breast, and would have turned down the candle—I snatched it away, however, and seized his arm.

"I'll not hold my tongue!" I said, "You mustn't touch him . . . Let the door remain shut and be quiet!"

"No! I've formed my resolution, and by God, I'll execute it!" cried the desperate being, "I'll do you a kindness, in spite of yourself, and Hareton justice! And you needn't trouble your head to screen me, Catherine is gone— Nobody alive would regret me, or be ashamed though I cut my throat, this minute—and it's time to make an end!"

I might as well have struggled with a bear; or reasoned with a lunatic. The only resource left me was to run to a lattice, and warn his intended victim of the fate which awaited him.

"You'd better seek shelter somewhere else to-night!" I exclaimed in a rather triumphant tone. "Mr. Earnshaw has a mind to shoot you, if you persist in endeavouring to enter."

"You'd better open the door, you—" he answered, addressing me by some elegant term that I don't care to repeat.

"I shall not meddle in the matter," I retorted again, "Come in, and get shot, if you please! I've done my duty."

190 EMILY BRONTË

With that I shut the window, and returned to my place by the fire; having too small a stock of hypocrisy at my command to pretend any anxiety for the danger that menaced him.

Earnshaw swore passionately at me; affirming that I loved the villain yet: and calling me all sorts of names for the base spirit I evinced. And I, in my secret heart, (and conscience never reproached me) thought what a blessing it would be for *him*, should Heathcliff put him out of misery: and what a blessing for *me*, should he send Heathcliff to his right abode! As I sat nursing these reflections, the casement behind me, was banged on to the floor by a blow from the latter individual; and his black countenance looked blightingly through. The stanchions stood too close to suffer his shoulders to follow; and I smiled, exulting in my fancied security. His hair and clothes were whitened with snow, and his sharp cannibal teeth, revealed by cold and wrath, gleamed through the dark.

"Isabella let me in, or I'll make you repent!" he 'girned', as Joseph calls it.

"I cannot commit murder;" I replied "Mr. Hindley stands sentinel with a knife, and loaded pistol."

"Let me in by the kitchen door!" he said.

"Hindley will be there before me," I answered. And that's a poor love of yours, that cannot bear a shower of snow! We were left at peace in our beds, as long as the summer moon shone, but the moment a blast of winter returns, you must run for shelter! Heathcliff, if I were you, I'd go stretch myself over her grave, and die like a faithful dog . . . The world is surely not worth living in now, is it? You had distinctly impressed on me, the idea that Catherine was the whole joy of your life—I can't imagine how you think of surviving her loss."

"He's there . . . is he?" exclaimed my companion, rushing to the gap. "If I can get my arm out I can hit him!"

"I'm afraid Ellen, you'll set me down, as really wicked—but you don't know all, so don't judge! I wouldn't have aided or abetted an attempt on even *his* life, for anything—Wish that he were dead, I must; and therefore, I was fearfully disappointed, and unnerved by terror for the consequences of my taunting speech when he flung himself on Earnshaw's weapon and wrenched it from his grasp.

The charge exploded, and the knife, in springing back, closed into its owner's wrist. Heathcliff pulled it away by main force, slitting up the flesh as it passed on, and thrust it dripping into his pocket. He then took a stone, struck down the division between two windows and sprung in. His adversary had fallen senseless with excessive pain, and the flow of blood that gushed from an artery, or a large vein.

The ruffian kicked and trampled on him, and dashed his head repeatedly against the flags; holding me with one hand, meantime, to prevent me summoning Joseph.

He exerted preter-human self denial in abstaining from finishing him, completely; but getting out of breath, he finally desisted, and dragged the apparently inanimate body onto the settle.

There he tore off the sleeve of Earnshaw's coat, and bound up the wound with brutal roughness, spitting and cursing, during the operation, as energetically as he had kicked before.

Being at liberty, I lost no time in seeking the old servant; who, having gathered by degrees the purport of my hasty tale, hurried below, gasping, as he descended the steps two at once.

"Whet is thur tuh do, nah? whet is thur tuh do, nah?"

"There's this to do," thundered Heathcliff, "that your master's mad; and should he last another month, I'll have him to an asylum. And how the devil did you come to fasten me out, you toothless hound? Don't stand muttering and mumbling there. Come, I'm not going to nurse him. Wash that stuff away: and mind the sparks of your candle—it is more than half brandy!"

"Und soa, yah been murthering on him?" exclaimed Joseph, lifting his hands and eyes in horror. "If iver Aw seed a seeght loike this! May the Lord—"

Heathcliff gave him a push onto his knees, in the middle of the blood; and flung a towel to him; but instead of proceeding to dry it up, he joined his hands, and began a prayer which excited my laughter from its odd phraseology. I was in the condition of mind to be shocked at nothing; in fact, I was as reckless as some malefactors show themselves at the foot of the gallows.

"Oh, I forgot you," said the tyrant, "you shall do that. Down with you. And you conspire with him against me, do you, viper? There, that is work fit for you!"

He shook me till my teeth rattled, and pitched me beside Joseph, who steadily concluded his supplications, and then rose, vowing he would set off for the Grange directly. Mr. Linton was a magistrate, and though he had fifty wives dead, he should inquire into this.

He was so obstinate in his resolution that Heathcliff deemed it expedient to compel, from my lips, a recapitulation of what had taken place; standing over me, heaving with malevolence, as I reluctantly delivered the account in answer to his questions.

It required a great deal of labour to satisfy the old man that he was not the aggressor; especially with my hardly wrung replies. However, Mr. Earnshaw soon convinced him that he was alive still; he hastened to administer a dose of spirits, and by their succour his master presently regained motion and consciousness.

Heathcliff, aware that he was ignorant of the treatment received while insensible, called him deliriously intoxicated; and said he should not notice his atrocious conduct further; but advised him to get to bed. To my joy, he left us after giving this judicious counsel, and Hindley stretched himself on the hearth-stone. I departed to my own room, marvelling that I had escaped so easily.

This morning, when I came down, about half-an-hour before noon, Mr. Earnshaw was sitting by the fire, deadly sick; his evil genius almost as guant and ghastly, leant against the chimney. Neither appeared inclined to dine; and having waited till all was cold on the table, I commenced alone.

Nothing hindered me from eating heartily; and I experienced a certain sense of satisfaction and superiority, as, at intervals, I cast a look towards my silent companions, and felt the comfort of a quiet conscience within me.

After I had done, I ventured on the unusual liberty of drawing near the fire; going round Earnshaw's seat, and kneeling in the corner beside him.

Heathcliff did not glance my way, and I gazed up, and contemplated his features, almost as confidently as if they had been turned to stone. His forehead, that I once thought so manly, and that I now think so diabolical, was shaded with a heavy cloud; his basilisk eyes were nearly quenched by sleeplessness—and weeping, perhaps, for the lashes were wet then: his lips devoid of their ferocious sneer, and sealed in an expression of unspeakable sadness. Had it been another,, I would have covered my face, in the presence of such grief. In *his* case, I was gratified: and ignoble as it seems to insult a fallen enemy, I couldn't miss this chance of sticking in a dart; his weakness was the only time when I could taste the delight of paying wrong for wrong.

"Fie, fie, Miss!" I interrupted. "One might suppose you had never opened a Bible in your life. If God afflict your enemies, surely that ought to suffice you. It is both mean and presumptuous to add your torture to his!"

"In general, I'll allow that it would be, Ellen," she continued. "But what misery laid on Heathcliff could content me, unless I have a hand in it? I'd rather he suffered *less*, if I might cause his sufferings, and he might *know* that I was the cause. Oh, I owe him so much. On only one condition can I hope to forgive him. It is, if I may take an eye for an eye, a tooth for a tooth, for every wrench of agony, return a wrench, reduce him to my level. As he was the first to injure, make him the first to implore pardon; and then—why then, Ellen, I might show you some generosity. But it is utterly impossible I can ever be revenged, and therefore I cannot forgive him. Hindley wanted some water, and I handed him a glass, and asked him how he was."

"Not as ill as I wish," he replied. "But leaving out my arm, every inch of me is as sore as if I had been fighting with a legion of imps!"

"Yes, no wonder," was my next remark. "Catherine used to boast that she stood between you and bodily harm—she meant that certain persons would not hurt you, for fear of offending her. It's well people don't *really* rise from their grave, or, last night, she might have witnessed a repulsive scene! Are not you bruised, and cut over your chest and shoulders?"

"I can't say," he answered; "but what do you mean? Did he dare to strike me when I was down?"

WUTHERING HEIGHTS 193

"He trampled on, and kicked you, and dashed you on the ground," I whispered. "And his mouth watered to tear you with his teeth; because, he's only half a man—not so much."

Mr. Earnshaw looked up, like me, to the countenance of our mutual foe; who, absorbed in his anguish, seemed insensible to anything around him; the longer he stood, the plainer his reflections revealed their blackness through his features.

"Oh, if God would but give me strength to strangle him in my last agony, I'd go to hell with joy," groaned the impatient man writhing to rise, and sinking back in despair, convinced of his inadequacy for the struggle.

"Nay, it's enough that he has murdered one of you," I observed aloud. "At the Grange, every one knows your sister would have been living now, had it not been for Mr. Heathcliff. After all, it is preferable to be hated, than loved by him. When I recollect how happy we were—how happy Catherine was before he came—I'm fit to curse the day."

Most likely, Heathcliff noticed more the truth of what was said, than the spirit of the person who said it. His attention was roused, I saw, for his eyes rained down tears among the ashes, and he drew his breath in suffocating sighs.

I stared full at him, and laughed scornfully. The clouded windows of hell flashed, a moment towards me; the fiend which usually looked out, however, was so dimmed and drowned that I did not fear to hazard another sound of derision.

"Get up, and begone out of my sight," said the mourner.

I guessed he uttered those words, at least, though his voice was hardly intelligible.

"I beg your pardon," I replied. "But I loved Catherine too; and her brother requires attendance which, for her sake, I shall supply. Now that she's dead, I see her in Hindley; Hindley has exactly her eyes, if you had not tried to gouge them out, and made them black and red, and her—"

"Get up, wretched idiot, before I stamp you to death!" he cried, making a movement that caused me to make one also."

"But then," I continued, holding myself ready to flee; "if poor Catherine had trusted you, and assumed the ridiculous, contemptible, degrading title of Mrs. Heathcliff, she would soon have presented a similar picture! *She* wouldn't have borne your abominable behaviour quietly; her detestation and disgust must have found voice."

The back of the settle, and Earnshaw's person interposed between me and him; so instead of endeavouring to reach me, he snatched a dinner knife from the table, and flung it at my head. It struck beneath my ear, and stopped the sentence I was uttering; but pulling it out, I sprang to the door, and delivered another which I hope went a little deeper than his missile.

The last glimpse I caught of him was a furious rush, on his part, checked by the embrace of his host; and both fell locked together on the hearth.

EMILY BRONTË

In my flight through the kitchen I bid Joseph speed to his master; I knocked over Hareton, who was hanging a litter of puppies from a chair back in the doorway; and, blest as a soul escaped from purgatory, I bounded, leaped, and flew down the steep road: then, quitting its windings, shot direct across the moor, rolling over banks, and wading through marshes; precipitating myself, in fact, towards the beacon light of the Grange. And far rather would I be condemned to a perpetual dwelling in the infernal regions, than even for one night abide beneath the roof of Wuthering Heights again."

Isabella ceased speaking, and took a drink of tea; then she rose, and bidding me put on her bonnet, and a great shawl I had brought, and turning a deaf ear to my entreaties for her to remain another hour, she stepped onto a chair, kissed Edgar's and Catherine's portraits, bestowed a similar salute on me, and descended to the carriage accompanied by Fanny, who yelped wild with joy at recovering her mistress, She was driven away, never to revisit this neighbourhood; but a regular correspondence was established between her and my master when things were more settled.

I believe her new abode was in the south, near London; there she had a son born, a few months subsequent to her escape. He was christened Linton, and, from the first, she reported him to be an ailing, peevish creature.

Mr. Heathcliff, meeting me one day in the village, inquired where she lived. I refused to tell. He remarked that it was not of any moment, only she must beware of coming to her brother; she should not be with him, if he had to keep her himself.

Though I would give no information, he discovered, through some of the other servants, both her place of residence, and the existence of the child. Still he didn't molest her; for which forbearance she might thank his aversion, I suppose.

He often asked about the infant, when he saw me; and on hearing its name, smiled grimly, and observed:

"They wish me to hate it too, do they?"

"I don't think they wish you to know any thing about it," I answered.

"But I'll have it," he said, "when I want it. They may reckon on that!"

Fortunately, its mother died before the time arrived, some thirteen years after the decease of Catherine, when Linton was twelve, or a little more.

On the day succeeding Isabella's unexpected visit, I had no opportunity of speaking to my master: he shunned conversation, and was fit for discussing nothing. When I could get him to listen, I saw it pleased him that his sister had left her husband, whom he abhorred with an intensity which the mildness of his nature would scarcely seem to allow. So deep and sensitive was his aversion, that he refrained from going anywhere where he was likely to see or hear of Heathcliff. Grief, and that together, transformed him into a complete hermit: he threw up his office of magistrate, ceased even to attend church, avoided the village on all occasions, and spent a life of entire seclusion within

WUTHERING HEIGHTS 195

the limits of his park and grounds: only varied by solitary rambles on the moors, and visits to the grave of his wife, mostly at evening, or early morning, before other wanderers were abroad.

But he was too good to be thoroughly unhappy long. *He* didn't pray for Catherine's soul to haunt him: Time brought resignation, and a melancholy sweeter than common joy. He recalled her memory with ardent, tender love, and hopeful aspiring to the better world, where, he doubted not she was gone.

And he had earthly consolation and affections, also. For a few days, I said, he seemed regardless of the puny successor to the departed: that coldness melted as fast as snow in April, and ere the tiny thing could stammer a word or totter a step, it wielded a despot's sceptre in his heart.

It was named Catherine, but he never called it the name in full, as he had never called the first Catherine short, probably because Heathcliff, had a habit of doing so. The little one was always Cathy, it formed to him a distinction from the mother, and yet, a connection with her; and his attachment sprang from its relation to her, far more than from its being his own.

I used to draw a comparison between him, and Hindley Earnshaw and perplex myself to explain satisfactorily, why their conduct was so opposite in similar circumstances. They had both been fond husbands, and were both attached to their children; and I could not see how they shouldn't both have taken the same road, for good or evil. But, I thought in my mind, Hindley with apparently the stronger head, has shown himself sadly the worse and the weaker man. When his ship struck, the captain abandoned his post; and the crew, instead of trying to save her, rushed into riot, and confusion, leaving no hope for their luckless vessel. Linton, on the contrary, displayed the true courage of a loyal and faithful soul: he trusted God; and God comforted him. One hoped, and the other despaired: they chose their own lots, and were righteously doomed to endure them.

But you'll not want to hear my moralizing, Mr. Lockwood: you'll judge as well as I can, all these things; at least, you'll think you will and that's the same.

The end of Earnshaw was what might have been expected: it followed fast on his sister's, there was scarcely six months between them. We, at the Grange, never got a very succinct account of his state preceding it; all that I did learn, was on occasion of going to aid in the preparations for the funeral. Mr. Kenneth came to announce the event to my master.

"Well, Nelly;" said he, riding into the yard, one morning, too early not to alarm me with an instant presentiment of bad news.

"It's yours, and my turn to go into mourning at present. Who's given us the slip, now do you think?"

"Who?" I asked in a flurry.

"Why, guess!" he returned, dismounting, and slinging his bridle on a hook by the door. "And nip up the corner of your apron; I'm certain you'll need it."

"Not Mr. Heathcliff, surely? I exclaimed."

"What! would you have tears for him?" said the doctor. No, Heathcliff's a tough young fellow; he looks blooming to-day—I've just seen him. He's rapidly regaining flesh since he lost his better half.

"Who is it, then Mr. Kenneth?" I repeated impatiently.

"Hindley Earnshaw! Your old friend Hindley—" he replied. "And my wicked gossip; though he's been too wild for me this long while. There! I said we should draw water—But cheer up! He died true to his character drunk as a lord—Poor lad; I'm sorry too. One can't help missing an old companion; though he had the worst tricks with him that ever man imagined; and has done me many a rascally turn—He's barely twenty-seven, it seems; that's your own age; who would have thought you were born in one year!"

I confess this blow was greater to me than the shock of Mrs. Linton's death: ancient associations lingered round my heart; I sat down in the porch, and wept as for a blood relation, desiring Kenneth to get another servant to introduce him to the master.

I could not hinder myself from pondering on the question—"Had he had fair play?" Whatever I did that idea would bother me: it was so tiresomely pertinacious that I resolved on requesting leave to go to Wuthering Heights, and assist in the last duties to the dead. Mr. Linton was extremely reluctant to consent, but I pleaded eloquently for the friendless condition in which he lay; and I said my old master, and foster brother had a claim on my services as strong as his own. Besides, I reminded him that the child, Hareton, was his wife's nephew; and, in the absence of nearer kin, he ought to act as its guardian; and he ought to and must inquire how the property was left, and look over the concerns of his brother-in-law.

He was unfit for attending to such matters then, but he bid me speak to his lawyer; and at length, permitted me to go. His lawyer had been Earnshaw's also: I called at the village, and asked him to accompany me. He shook his head, and advised that Heathcliff should be let alone; affirming, if the truth were known, Hareton would be found little else than a beggar.

"His father died in debt;" he said, "the whole property is mortgaged, and the sole chance for the natural heir is to allow him an opportunity of creating some interest in the creditor's heart, that he may be inclined to deal leniently towards him."

When I reached the Heights, I explained that I had come to see everything carried on decently, and Joseph, who appeared in sufficient distress, expressed satisfaction at my presence. Mr. Heathcliff said he did not perceive that I was wanted, but I might stay and order the arrangements for the funeral, if I chose.

"Correctly," he remarked, "that fool's body should be buried at the crossroads, without ceremony of any kind—I happened to leave him ten minutes, yesterday afternoon; and, in that interval, he fastened the two doors of the house against me, and he has spent the night in drinking himself to death deliberately! We broke in this morning, for we heard him snorting like a horse;

WUTHERING HEIGHTS 197

and there he was, laid over the settle—flaying and scalping would not have wakened him—I sent for Kenneth, and he came; but not till the beast had changed into carrion—he was both dead and cold, and stark; and so you'll allow, it was useless making more stir about him!"

The old servant confirmed this statement, but muttered,

"Aw'd rayther he'd goan hisseln fur t'doctor! Aw sud uh taen tent uh t'maister better nur him—un he warn't deead when Aw left, nowt uh t'soart!"

I insisted on the funeral being respectable—Mr. Heathcliff said I might have my own way there too; only, he desired me to remember, that the money for the whole affair came out of his pocket.

He maintained a hard, careless deportment, indicative of neither joy nor sorrow; if anything, it expressed a flinty gratification at a piece of difficult work, successfully executed, I observed once, indeed, something like exultation in his aspect. It was just when the people were bearing the coffin from the house; he had the hypocrisy to represent a mourner; and previous to following with Hareton he lifted the unfortunate child on to the table, and muttered with peculiar gusto,

"Now my bonny lad you are *mine*! And we'll see if one tree won't grow as crooked as another, with the same wind to twist it!"

The unsuspecting thing was pleased at this speech; he played with Heathcliff's whiskers, and stroked his cheek, but I divined its meaning and observed tartly,

"That boy must go back with me to Thrushcross Grange, Sir—There is nothing in the world less yours than he is!"

"Does Linton say so?" he demanded.

"Of course—he has ordered me to take him." I replied.

"Well," said the scoundrel, "We'll not argue the subject now; but I have a fancy to try my hand at rearing a young one, so intimate to your master, that I must supply the place of this with my own, if he attempt to remove it; I don't engage to let Hareton go, undisputed: but, I'll be pretty sure to make the other come! remember to tell him."

This hint was enough to bind our hands. I repeated its substance, on my return, and Edgar Linton, little interested at the commencement, spoke no more of interfering. I'm not aware that he could have done it to any purpose, had he been ever so willing.

The guest was now the master of Wuthering Heights: he held firm possession, and proved to the attorney, who, in his turn, proved it to Mr. Linton, that Earnshaw had mortgaged every yard of land he owned for cash to supply his mania for gaming: and he, Heathcliff, was the mortgagee.

In that manner, Hareton, who should now be the first gentleman in the neighbourhood, was reduced to a state of complete dependence on his father's inveterate enemy; and lives in his own house as a servant deprived of the advantage of wages, and quite unable to right himself, because of his friendlessness, and his ignorance that he has been wronged.

CHAPTER IV.

"THE twelve years," continued Mrs. Dean, "following that dismal period, were the happiest of my life: my greatest troubles, in their passage, rose from our little lady's trifling illnesses which she had to experience in common with all children, rich and poor.'

For the rest, after the first six months, she grew like a larch; and could walk and talk too, in her own way, before the heath blossomed a second time over Mrs. Linton's dust.

She was the most winning thing that ever brought sunshine into a desolate house—a real beauty in face—with the Earnshaws' handsome dark eyes, but the Lintons' fair skin, and small features, and yellow curling hair. Her spirit was high, though not rough, and qualified by a heart, sensitive and lively to excess in its affections. That capacity for intense attachments reminded me of her mother; still she did not resemble her; for she could be soft and mild as a dove, and she had a gentle voice, and pensive expression: her anger was never furious; her love never fierce; it was deep and tender.

However, it must be acknowledged, she had faults to foil her gifts. A propensity to be saucy was one; and a perverse will that indulged children invariably acquire, whether they be good tempered or cross. If a servant chanced to vex her, it was always: "I shall tell papa!" And if he reproved her, even by a look, you would have thought it a heartbreaking business: I don't believe he ever did speak a harsh word to her.

He took her education entirely on himself, and made it an amusement: fortunately, curiosity, and a quick intellect urged her into an apt scholar; she learnt rapidly and eagerly, and did honour to his teaching.

Till she reached the age of thirteen, she had not once been beyond the range of the park by herself. Mr. Linton would take her with him, a mile or so outside, on rare occasions; but he trusted her to no one else. Gimmerton was an unsubstantial name in her ears; the chapel, the only building she had approached, or entered, except her own home; Wuthering Heights and Mr. Heathcliff did not exist for her; she was a perfect recluse; and, apparently, perfectly contented. Sometimes, indeed, while surveying the country from her nursery window, she would observe—

"Ellen, how long will it be before I can walk to the top of those hills? I wonder what lies on the other side—is it the sea?"

"No, Miss Cathy," I would answer, "it is hills again just like these."

"And what are those golden rocks like, when you stand under them?" she once asked.

WUTHERING HEIGHTS 199

The abrupt descent of Penistone Craggs particularly attracted her notice, especially when the setting sun shone on it, and the top-most Heights; and the whole extent of landscape besides lay in shadow.

I explained that they were bare masses of stone, with hardly enough earth in their clefts to nourish a stunted tree.

"And why are they bright so long after it is evening here?" she pursued.

"Because they are a great deal higher up than we are," replied I; "you could not climb them, they are too high and steep. In winter the frost is always there before it comes to us; and, deep into summer, I have found snow under that black hollow on the north-east side!"

"Oh, you have been on them!" she cried, gleefully. "Then I can go, too, when I am a woman. Has papa been, Ellen?"

"Papa would tell you, Miss," I answered, hastily, "that they are not worth the trouble of visiting. The moors, where you ramble with him, are much nicer; and Thrushcross park is the finest place in the world."

"But I know the park, and I don't know those," she murmured to herself. "And I should delight to look round me, from the brow of that tallest point—my little pony, Minny, shall take me sometime."

One of the maids mentioning the Fairy cave, quite turned her head with a desire to fulfil this project; she teased Mr. Linton about it; and he promised she should have the journey when she got older: but Miss Catherine measured her age by months, and—

"Now, am I old enough to go to Penistone Craggs?" was the constant question in her mouth.

The road thither wound close by Wuthering Heights. Edgar had not the heart to pass it; so she received as constantly the answer.

"Not yet, love, not yet."

I said Mrs. Heathcliff lived above a dozen years after quitting her husband. Her family were of a delicate constitution: she and Edgar both lacked the ruddy health that you will generally meet in these parts. What her last illness was, I am not certain; I conjecture, they died of the same thing, a kind of fever, slow at its commencement, but incurable, and rapidly consuming life towards the close.

She wrote to inform her brother of the probable conclusion of a four months' indisposition, under which she had suffered; and entreated him to come to her, if possible, for she had much to settle, and she wished to bid him adieu, and deliver Linton safely into his hands. Her hope was, that Linton might be left with him, as he had been with her; his father, she would fain convince herself, had no desire to assume the burden of his maintenance or education.

My master hesitated not a moment in complying with her request; reluctant as he was to leave home at ordinary calls, he flew to answer this; commending Catherine to my peculiar vigilance, in his absence; with reiterated

200 EMILY BRONTË

orders that she must not wander out of the park, even under my escort; he did not calculate on her going unaccompanied.

He was away three weeks: the first day or two, my charge sat in a corner of the library, too sad for either reading or playing: in that quiet state she caused me little trouble; but it was succeeded by an interval of impatient, fretful weariness; and being too busy, and too old then, to run up and down amusing her, I hit on a method by which she might entertain herself.

I used to send her on her travels round the grounds—now on foot, and now on a pony; indulging her with a patient audience of all her real and imaginary adventures, when she returned.

The summer shone in full prime; and she took such a taste for this solitary rambling that she often contrived to remain out from breakfast till tea; and then the evenings were spent in recounting her fanciful tales. I did not fear her breaking bounds, because the gates were generally locked, and I thought she would scarcely venture forth alone, if they had stood wide open.

Unluckily, my confidence proved misplaced. Catherine came to me, one morning, at eight o'clock, and said she was that day an Arabian merchant, going to cross the Desert with his caravan; and I must give her plenty of provision for herself, and beasts, a horse, and three camels, personated by a large hound, and a couple of pointers.

I got together good store of dainties, and slung them in a basket on one side of the saddle; and she sprang up as gay as a fairy, sheltered by her wide-brimmed hat and gauze veil from the July sun, and trotted off with a merry laugh, mocking my cautious counsel to avoid galloping, and come back early.

The naughty thing never made her appearance at tea. One traveller, the hound, being an old dog, and fond of its ease, returned; but neither Cathy, nor the pony, nor the two pointers were visible in any direction; and I despatched emissaries down this path, and that path, and, at last, went wandering in search of her myself.

There was a labourer working at a fence round a plantation, on the borders of the grounds. I enquired of him if he had seen our young lady?

"I saw her at morn," he replied, "she would have me to cut her a hazel switch; and then she leapt her galloway over the hedge yonder, where it is lowest, and gallopped out of sight."

You may guess how I felt at hearing this news. It struck me directly she must have started for Penistone Craggs.

"What will become of her?" I ejaculated, pushing through a gap which the man was repairing, and making straight to the high road.

I walked as if for a wager, mile after mile, till a turn brought me in view of the Heights, but no Catherine could I detect, far or near.

The Craggs lie about a mile and a half beyond Mr. Heathcliff's place, and that is four from the Grange, so I began to fear night would fall ere I could reach them.

WUTHERING HEIGHTS 201

"And what if she should have slipped in clambering among them," I reflected, "and been killed, or broken some of her bones?"

My suspense was truly painful; and, at first, it gave me delightful relief to observe, in hurrying by the farm-house, Charlie, the fiercest of the pointers, lying under a window, with swelled head, and bleeding ear.

I open the wicket, and ran to the door, knocking vehemently for admittance. A woman whom I knew, and who formerly lived at Gimmerton, answered—she had been servant there since the death of Mr Earnshaw.

"Ah," said she, "you are come a seeking your little mistress! don't be frightened. She's here safe—but I'm glad it isn't the master."

"He is not at home then, is he?" I panted, quite breathless with quick walking and alarm.

"No, no," she replied, "both he and Joseph are off, and I think they wont return this hour or more. Step in and rest you a bit."

I entered, and beheld my stray lamb, seated on the hearth, rocking herself in a little chair that had been her mother's, when a child. Her hat was hung against the wall, and she seemed perfectly at home, laughing and chattering, in the best spirits imaginable, to Hareton, now a great, strong lad of eighteen, who stared at her with considerable curiosity and astonishment; comprehending precious little of the fluent succession of remarks and questions which her tongue never ceased pouring forth.

"Very well, Miss," I exclaimed, concealing my joy under an angry countenance. "This is your last ride, till papa comes back. I'll not trust you over the threshold again, you naughty, naughty girl."

"Aha, Ellen!" she cried, gaily, jumping up, and running to my side. "I shall have a pretty story to tell to-night—and so you've found me out. Have you ever been here in your life before?"

"Put that hat on, and home at once," said I. "I'm dreadfully grieved at you, Miss Cathy, you've done extremely wrong! It's no use pouting and crying; that wont repay the trouble I've had, scouring the country after you. To think how Mr. Linton charged me to keep you in; and you stealing off so; it shows you are a cunning little fox, and nobody will put faith in you any more."

"What have I done?" sobbed she, instantly checked, "Papa charged me nothing—he'll not scold me, Ellen—he's never cross, like you!"

"Come, come!" I repeated. "I'll tie the riband. Now, let us have no petulance. Oh, for shame. You thirteen years old, and such a baby!"

This exclamation was caused by her pushing the hat from her head, and retreating to the chimney out of my reach.

"Nay," said the servant, "don't be hard on the bonny lass, Mrs. Dean. We made her stop—she'd fain have ridden forwards, afeard you should be uneasy. But Hareton offered to go with her, and I thought he should. It's a wild road over the hills."

202 EMILY BRONTË

Hareton, during the discussion, stood with his hands in his pockets, too awkward to speak, though he looked as if he did not relish my intrusion.

"How long am I to wait?" I continued, disregarding the woman's interference. "It will be dark in ten minutes. Where is the pony, Miss Cathy? And where is Phenix? I shall leave you, unless you be quick, so please yourself."

"The pony is in the yard," she replied, "and Phenix is shut in there. He's bitten—and so is Charlie. I was going to tell you all about it; but you are in a bad temper, and don't deserve to hear."

I picked up her hat, and approached to reinstate it; but perceiving that the people of the house took her part, she commenced capering round the room; and, on my giving chase, ran like a mouse, over and under, and behind the furniture, rendering it ridiculous for me to pursue.

Hareton and the woman laughed; and she joined them, and waxed more impertinent still; till I cried, in great irritation.

"Well, Miss Cathy, if you were aware whose house this is, you'd be glad enough to get out."

"It's *your* father's, isn't it?" said she, turning to Hareton.

"Nay," he replied, looking down, and blushing bashfully.

He could not stand a steady gaze from her eyes, though they were just his own.

"Whose then—your master's?" she asked.

He coloured deeper, with a different feeling, muttered an oath, and turned away.

"Who is his master?" continued the tiresome girl, appealing to me. "He talked about 'our house,' and 'our folk.' I thought he had been the owner's son. And he never said, Miss; he should have done, shouldn't he, if he's a servant?"

Hareton grew black as a thunder-cloud, at this childish speech. I silently shook my questioner, and, at last, succeeded in equipping her for departure.

"Now, get my horse," she said, addressing her unknown kinsman as she would one of the stable-boys at the Grange. "And you may come with me. I want to see where the goblin hunter rises in the marsh, and to hear about the *fairishes*, as you call them—but, make haste! What's the matter? Get my horse, I say."

"I'll see thee damned, before I be *thy* servant!" growled the lad.

"You'll see me me *what?*" asked Catherine in surprise.

"Damned—thou saucy witch!" he replied.

"There, Miss Cathy! you see you have got into pretty company," I interposed. "Nice words to be used to a young lady! Pray don't begin to dispute with him—Come, let us seek for Minny ourselves, and begone."

"But Ellen," cried she, staring, fixed in astonishment. "How dare he speak so to me? Mustn't he be made to do as I ask him? You wicked creature, I shall tell papa what you said—Now then!"

WUTHERING HEIGHTS 203

Hareton did not appear to feel this threat; so the tears sprung into her eyes with indignation. "You bring the pony," she exclaimed, turning to the woman, "and let my dog free this moment!"

"Softly, Miss," answered the addressed. "You'll lose nothing, by being civil. Though Mr. Hareton, there, be not the master's son, he's your cousin; and I was never hired to serve you."

"*He* my cousin!" cried Cathy with a scornful laugh.

"Yes, indeed," responded her reprover.

"Oh, Ellen! don't let them say such things," she pursued in great trouble. Papa is gone to fetch my cousin from London—my cousin is a gentleman's son—That my—" she stopped, and wept outright; upset at the bare notion of relationship with such a clown.

"Hush, hush!" I whispered, "people can have many cousins and of all sorts, Miss Cathy, without being any the worse for it; only they needn't keep their company, if they be disagreeable, and bad."

"He's not, he's not my cousin, Ellen!" she went on, gathering fresh grief from reflection, and flinging herself into my arms for refuge from the idea.

I was much vexed at her and the servant for their mutual revelations; having no doubt of Linton's approaching arrival, communicated by the former, being reported to Mr. Heathcliff; and feeling as confident that Catherine's first thought on her father's return, would be to seek an explanation of the latter's assertion, concerning her rude-bred kindred.

Hareton, recovering from his disgust at being taken for a servant, seemed moved by her distress; and, having fetched the pony round to the door, he took, to propitiate her, a fine crooked-legged terrier whelp from the kennel; and putting it into her hand, bid her wisht for he meant naught.

Pausing in her lamentations, she surveyed him with a glance of awe, and horror, then burst forth anew.

I could scarcely refrain from smiling at this antipathy to the poor fellow; who was a well-made, athletic youth, good looking in features, and stout and healthy, but attired in garments befitting his daily occupations of working on the farm, and lounging among the moors after rabbits and game. Still, I thought I could detect in his physiognomy a mind owning better qualities than his father ever possessed. Good things lost amid a wilderness of weeds, to be sure, whose rankness far over-topped their neglected growth; yet notwithstanding, evidence of a wealthy soil that might yield luxuriant crops, under other and favourable circumstances. Mr. Heathcliff, I believe, had not treated him physically ill; thanks to his fearless nature which offered no temptation to that course of oppression; it had none of the timid susceptibility that would have given zest to ill-treatment, in Heathcliff's judgment. He appeared to have bent his malevolence on making him a brute: he was never taught to read or write; never rebuked for any bad habit which did not annoy his keeper; never led a single step towards virtue, or guarded by a single precept against

204   EMILY BRONTË

vice. And from what I heard, Joseph contributed much to his deterioration by a narrow minded partiality which prompted him to flatter, and pet him, as a boy, because he was the head of the old family. And as he had been in the habit of accusing Catherine Earnshaw, and Heathcliff, when children, of putting the master past his patience, and compelling him to seek solace in drink, by what he termed, their "offalld ways," so at present, he laid the whole burden of Hareton's faults on the shoulders of the usurper of his property.

If the lad swore he wouldn't correct him; nor however culpably he behaved. It gave Joseph satisfaction, apparently, to watch him go the worst lengths. He allowed that he was ruined; that his soul was abandoned to perdition; but then, he reflected that Heathcliff must answer for it. Hareton's blood would be required at his hands; and there lay immense consolation in that thought.

Joseph had instilled into him a pride of name, and of his lineage; he would had he dared, have fostered hate between him and the present owner of the Heights, but his dread of that owner amounted to superstition; and he confined his feelings, regarding him, to muttered inuendo's and private comminations.

I don't pretend to be intimately acquainted with the mode of living customary in those days, at Wuthering Heights. I only speak from hearsay; for I saw little. The villagers affirmed Mr. Heathcliff was *near*, and a cruel hard landlord to his tenants; but the house, inside had regained its ancient aspect of comfort under female management; and the scenes of riot common in Hindley's time, were not now enacted within its walls. The master was too gloomy to seek companionship with any people, good or bad, and he is yet—

This, however, is not making progress with my story. Miss Cathy rejected the peace-offering of the terrier, and demanded her own dogs, Charlie and Phenix. They came limping, and hanging their heads; and we set out for home, sadly out of sorts, every one of us.

I could not wring from my little lady how she had spent the day; except that, as I supposed, the goal of her pilgrimage was Penistone Crags; and she arrived without adventure to the gate of the farmhouse, when Hareton happened to issue forth, attended by some canine followers who attacked her train.

They had a smart battle, before their owners could separate them: that formed an introduction. Catherine told Hareton who she was, and where she was going; and asked him to show her the way; finally, beguilnig [*sic*] him to accompany her.

He opened the mysteries of the Fairy cave, and twenty other queer places; but being in disgrace, I was not favoured with a description of the interesting objects she saw.

I could gather however, that her guide had been a favourite till she hurt his feelings by addressing him as a servant, and Heathcliff's housekeeper hurt hers, by calling him her cousin.

WUTHERING HEIGHTS 205

Then the language he had held to her rankled in her heart; she who was always "love," and "darling," and "queen," and "angel," with everybody at the Grange; to be insulted so shockingly by a stranger! She did not comprehend it; and hard work I had, to obtain a promise that she would not lay the grievance before her father.

I explained how he objected to the whole household at the Heights, and how sorry he would be to find she had been there; but, I insisted most on the fact, that if she revealed my negligence of his orders, he would perhaps, be so angry that I should have to leave; and Cathy couldn't bear that prospect: she pledged her word, and kept it, for my sake—after all, she was a sweet little girl.

CHAPTER V.

A LETTER, edged with black, announced the day of my master's return. Isabella was dead; and he wrote to bid me get mourning for his daughter, and arrange a room, and other accommodations, for his youthful nephew.

Catherine ran wild with joy at the idea of welcoming her father back: and indulged most sanguine anticipations of the innumerable excellencies of her "real" cousin.

The evening of their expected arrival came. Since early morning, she had been busy, ordering her own small affairs; and now, attired in her new black frock—poor thing! her aunt's death impressed her with no definite sorrow—she obliged me, by constant worrying, to walk with her, down through the grounds, to meet them.

"Linton is just six months younger than I am," she chattered as we strolled leisurely over the swells and hollows of mossy turf, under shadow of the trees. "How delightful it will be to have him for a playfellow! Aunt Isabella sent papa a beautiful lock of his hair; it was lighter than mine—more flaxen, and quite as fine. I have it carefully preserved in a little glass box; and I've often thought what pleasure it would be to see its owner—Oh! I am happy—and papa, dear, dear papa! come, Ellen, let us run! come run!"

She ran, and returned and ran again, many times before my sober footsteps reached the gate, and then she seated herself on the grassy bank beside the path, and tried to wait patiently; but that was impossible; she couldn't be still a minute.

"How long they are!" she exclaimed. "Ah, I see some dust on the road— they are coming! No! When will they be here? May we not go a little way— half a mile, Ellen, only just half a mile? Do say yes, to that clump of birches at the turn!"

I refused staunchily: and, at length, her suspense was ended: the travelling carriage rolled in sight.

Miss Cathy shrieked, and stretched out her arms, as soon as she caught her father's face, looking from the window. He descended, nearly as eager as herself; and a considerable interval elapsed, ere they had a thought to spare for any but themselves.

While they exchanged caresses, I took a peep in to see after Linton. He was asleep, in a corner, wrapped in a warm, fur-lined cloak, as if it had been winter, A pale, delicate, effeminate boy, who might have been taken for my master's younger brother, so strong was the resemblance, but there was a sickly peevishness in his aspect, that Edgar Linton never had.

WUTHERING HEIGHTS 207

The latter saw me looking; and having shaken hands, advised me to close the door, and leave him undisturbed; for the journey had fatigued him.

Cathy would fain have taken one glance; but her father told her to come on, and they walked together up the park, while I hastened before, to prepare the servants.

"Now, darling," said Mr. Linton, addressing his daughter,, as they halted at the bottom of the front steps. "Your cousin is not so strong, or so merry as you are, and he has lost his mother, remember, a very short time since, therefore, don't expect him to play, and run about with you directly. And don't harass him much by talking—let him be quiet this evening, at least, will you?"

"Yes, yes, papa," answered Catherine; "but I do want to see him; and he hasn't once looked out."

The carriage stopped; and the sleeper, being roused, was lifted to the ground by his uncle.

"This is your cousin Cathy, Linton," he said, putting their little hands together. "She's fond of you already; and mind you don't grieve her by crying to-night. Try to be cheerful now; the travelling is at an end, and you have nothing to do but rest and amuse yourself as you please."

"Let me go to bed then," answered the boy, shrinking from Catherine's salute; and he put his fingers to his eyes to remove incipient tears.

"Come, come, there's a good child," I whispered, leading him in. "You'll make her weep too—see how sorry she is for you!"

I do not know whether it were sorrow for him, but his cousin put on as sad a countenance as himself, and returned to her father. All three entered, and mounted to the library where tea was laid ready.

I proceeded to remove Linton's cap, and mantle, and placed him on a chair by the table; but he was no sooner seated than he began to cry afresh. My master inquired what was the matter.

"I can't sit on a chair," sobbed the boy.

"Go to the sofa then; and Ellen shall bring you some tea," answered his uncle, patiently.

He had been greatly tried during the journey, I felt convinced, by his fretful, ailing charge.

Linton slowly trailed himself off, and lay down. Cathy carried a foot-stool and her cup to his side.

At first she sat silent; but that could not last; she had resolved to make a pet of her little cousin, as she would have him to be; and she commenced stroking his curls, and kissing his cheek, and offering him tea in her saucer, like a baby. This pleased him, for he was not much better; he dried his eyes, and lightened into a faint smile.

"Oh, he'll do very well," said the master to me, after watching them a minute. "Very well, if we can keep him, Ellen. The company of a child of his own age will instil new spirit into him soon: and by wishing for strength he'll gain it."

208 EMILY BRONTË

Aye, if we can keep him! I mused to myself; and sore misgivings came over me that there was slight hope of that. And then, I thought, however will that weakling live at Wuthering Heights, between his father and Hareton? what playmates and instructors they'll be.

Our doubts were presently decided; even earlier than I expected. I had just taken the children up stairs, after tea was finished; and seen Linton asleep—he would not suffer me to leave him, till that was the case—I had come down, and was standing by the table in the hall, lighting a bed-room candle for Mr. Edgar, when a maid stepped out of the kitchen, and informed me that Mr. Heathcliff's servant, Joseph, was at the door, and wished to speak with the master.

"I shall ask him what he wants first," I said, in considerable trepidation. "A very unlikely hour to be troubling people, and the instant they have returned from a long journey. I don't think the master can see him."

Joseph had advanced through the kitchen, as I uttered these words, and now presented himself in the hall. He was donned in his Sunday garments, with his most sanctimonious and sourest face; and holding his hat in one hand, and his stick in the other, he proceeded to clean his shoes on the mat.

"Good evening, Joseph," I said, coldly. "What business brings you here to-night?"

"It's Maister Linton Aw mun spake tull," he answered, waving me disdainfully aside.

"Mr. Linton is going to bed; unless you have something particular to say, I'm sure he wont hear it now," I continued. "You had better sit down in there, and entrust your message to me."

"Which is his rahm?" pursued the fellow, surveying the range of closed doors.

I perceived he was bent on refusing my mediation; so very reluctantly, I went up to the library, and announced the unseasonable visiter; advising that he should be dismissed till next day.

Mr. Linton had no time to empower me to do so, for he mounted close at my heels, and pushing into the apartment, planted himself at the far side of the table, with his two fists clapped on the head of his stick, and began in an elevated tone, as if anticipating opposition.

"Hathecliff has send me for his lad, un Aw 'munn't goa back 'baht him."

Edgar Linton was silent a minute; an expression of exceeding sorrow overcast his features; he would have pitied the child on his own account; but, recalling Isabella's hopes and fears, and anxious wishes for her son, and her commendations of him to his care, he grieved bitterly at the prospect of yielding him up, and searched in his heart how it might be avoided. No plan offered itself: the very exhibition of any desire to keep him would have rendered the claimant more peremptory: there was nothing left but to resign him. However, he was not going to rouse him from his sleep.

"Tell Mr. Heathcliff," he answered, calmly, "that his son shall come to Wuthering Heights to-morrow. He is in bed, and too tired to go the distance now. You may also tell him that the mother of Linton desired him to remain under my guardianship; and, at present, his health is very precarious."

"Noa!" said Joseph, giving a thud with his prop on the floor, and assuming an authoritative air. "Noa! that manes nowt—Hathecliff maks noa 'cahnt uh t' mother, nur yah norther—bud he'll hev his lad; und Aw mun tak him—soa nah yah knaw!"

"You shall not to-night!" answered Linton, decisively. "Walk down stairs at once, and repeat to your master what I have said. Ellen, show him down. Go—"

And, aiding the indignant elder with a lift by the arm, he rid the room of him, and closed the door.

"Varrah weel!" shouted Joseph, as he slowly drew off. "Tuh morn, he's come hisseln, un' thrust *him* aht, if yah darr!"

Chapter VI.

To obviate the danger of this threat being fulfilled, Mr. Linton commissioned me to take the boy home early, on Catherine's pony, and, said he—

"As we shall now have no influence over his destiny, good or bad, you must say nothing of where he is gone to my daughter; she cannot associate with him hereafter; and it is better for her to remain in ignorance of his proximity, lest she should be restless, and anxious to visit the Heights—merely tell her, his father sent for him suddenly, and he has been obliged to leave us."

Linton was very reluctant to be roused from his bed, at five o'clock, and astonished to be informed that he must prepare for further travelling: but I softened off the matter by stating that he was going to spend some time with his father, Mr. Heathcliff, who wished to see him so much, he did not like to defer the pleasure till he should recover from his late journey.

"My father?" he cried, in strange perplexity. "Mamma never told me I had a father. Where does he live? I'd rather stay with uncle."

"He lives a little distance from the Grange," I replied, "just beyond those hills—not so far, but you may walk over here, when you get hearty. And you should be glad to go home, and to see him. You must try to love him, as you did your mother, and then he will love you."

"But why have I not heard of him before?" asked Linton; "why didn't mamma, and he live together as other people do?"

"He had business to keep him in the north," I answered; "and your mother's health required her to reside in the south."

"And why didn't mamma speak to me about him?" persevered the child. "She often talked of uncle, and I learnt to love him long ago. How am I to love papa? I don't know him."

"Oh, all children love their parents," I said. "Your mother, perhaps, thought you would want to be with him, if she mentioned him often to you. Let us make haste. An early ride on such a beautiful morning is much preferable to an hour's more sleep."

"Is *she* to go with us," he demanded. "The little girl I saw yesterday?"

"Not now," replied I.

"Is uncle?" he continued.

"No, I shall be your companion there," I said.

Linton sank back on his pillow, and fell into a brown study.

"I won't go without uncle;" he cried at length; "I can't tell where you mean to take me."

WUTHERING HEIGHTS

211

I attempted to persuade him of the naughtiness of showing reluctance to meet his father: still he obstinately resisted any progress towards dressing; and I had to call for my master's assistance, in coaxing him out of bed.

The poor thing was finally got off with several delusive assurances that his absence should be short; that Mr. Edgar and Cathy would visit him; and other promises, equally ill-founded, which I invented and reiterated, at intervals, throughout the way.

The pure heather-scented air, and the bright sunshine, and the gentle canter of Minny relieved his despondency, after a while. He began to put questions concerning his new home, and its inhabitants, with greater interest, and liveliness.

"Is Wuthering Heights as pleasant a place as Thrushcross Grange?" he inquired, turning to take a last glance into the valley, whence a light mist mounted, and formed fleecy cloud, on the skirts of the blue.

"It is not so buried in trees," I replied, "and it is not quite so large, but you can see the country beautifully, all round; and the air is healthier for you— fresher, and dryer. You will, perhaps, think the building old and dark, at first—though it is a respectable house, the next best in the neighbourhood. And you will have such nice rambles on the moors! Hareton Earnshaw—that is Miss Cathy's other cousin; and so yours in a manner—will show you all the sweetest spots; and you can bring a book in fine weather, and make a green hollow your study; and, now and then, your uncle may join you in a walk; he does, frequently, walk out on the hills."

"And what is my father like?" he asked. "Is he as young and handsome as uncle?"

"He's as young," said I "but he has black hair, and eyes; and looks sterner, and he is taller and bigger altogether. He'll not seem to you so gentle and kind at first, perhaps, because, it is not his way—still, mind you be frank and cordial with him; and naturally, he'll be fonder of you than any uncle, for you are his own."

"Black hair and eyes!" mused Linton. "I can't fancy him. Then I am not like him, am I?"

"Not much," I answered . . . Not a morsel, I thought: surveying with regret the white complexion, and slim frame of my companion, and his large languid eyes . . . his mother's eyes save that, unless a morbid touchiness kindled them, a moment, they had not a vestige of her sparkling spirit.

"How strange that he should never come to see mama, and me" he murmured. "Has he ever seen me? If he have, I must have been a baby—I remember not a single thing about him!"

"Why, Master Linton," said I, "three hundred miles is a great distance: and ten years seem very different in length, to a grown up person, compared with what they do to you. It is probable Mr. Heathcliff proposed going, from summer to summer, but never found a convenient opportunity: and now it is

212 EMILY BRONTË

too late—Don't trouble him with questions on the subject: it will disturb him for no good."

The boy was fully occupied with his own cogitations for the remainder of the ride, till we halted before the farm-house garden gate. I watched to catch his impressions in his countenanance. He surveyed the carved front, and low-browed lattices; the straggling gooseberry bushes, and crooked firs, with solemn intentness, and then shook his head: his private feelings entirely disapproved of the exterior of his new abode; but he had sense to postpone complaining—there might be compensation within.

Before he dismounted, I went and opened the door. It was half-past six; the family had just finished breakfast; the servant was clearing and wiping down the table: Joseph stood by his master's chair telling some tale concerning a lame horse; and Hareton was preparing for the hay-field.

"Hallo, Nelly!" cried Mr. Heathcliff, when he saw me. "I feared I should have to come down and fetch my property, myself—You've brought it have you? Let us see what we can make of it."

He got up and strode to the door: Hareton and Joseph followed in gaping curiosity. Poor Linton ran a frightened eye over the faces of the three.

"Sure-ly," said Joseph after a grave inspection, 'he's swopped wi' ye, maister, an' yon's his lass!"

Heathcliff having stared his son into an ague of confusion, uttered a scornful laugh.

"God! what a beauty! what a lovely, charming thing!" he exclaimed. "Haven't they reared it on snails, and sour milk, Nelly? Oh, damn my soul! but that's worse than I expected—and the devil knows I was not sanguine!"

I bid the trembling and bewildered child get down, and enter. He did not thoroughly comprehend the meaning of his father's speech, or whether it were intended for him: indeed, he was not yet certain that the grim, sneering stranger was his father; but he clung to me with growing trepidation; and on Mr. Heathcliff's taking a seat, and bidding him "come hither," he hid his face on my shoulder, and wept.

"Tut, tut!" said Heathcliff, stretching out a hand and dragging him roughly between his knees, and then holding up his head by the chin. "None of that nonsense! we're not going to hurt thee, Linton—isn't that thy name? Thou art thy mother's child, entirely! Where is *my* share in thee, puling chicken?"

He took off the boy's cap and pushed back his thick flaxen curls, felt his slender arms, and his small fingers; during which examination, Linton ceased crying, and lifted his great blue eyes to inspect the inspector.

"Do you know me?" asked Heathcliff, having satisfied himself that the limbs were all equally frail and feeble.

"No!" said Linton, with a gaze of vacant fear.

"You've heard of me, I dare say?"

"No," he replied again.

WUTHERING HEIGHTS 213

"No? What a shame of your mother, never to waken your filial regard for me! You are my son, then, I'll tell you; and your mother was a wicked slut to leave you in ignorance of the sort of father you possessed—Now, don't wince, and colour up! Though it *is* something to see you have not white blood—Be a good lad; and I'll do for you—Nelly, if you be tired you may sit down, if not get home again—I guess you'll report what you hear, and see, to the cipher at the Grange; and this thing won't be settled while you linger about it."

"Well," replied I, "I hope you'll be kind to the boy, Mr. Heathcliff, or you'll not keep him long, and he's all you have akin, in the wide world that you will ever know—remember.

"I'll be *very* kind to him you needn't fear!" he said laughing. "Only nobody else must be kind to him—I'm jealous of monopolizing his affection—And, to begin my kindness, Joseph! bring the lad some breakfast—Hareton, you infernal calf, begone to your work. Yes, Nell," he added when they were departed, "my son is prospective owner of your place, and I should not wish him to die till I was certain of being his successor. Besides, he's *mine*, and I want the triumph of seeing *my* descendent fairly lord of their estates; my child hiring their children, to till their fathers' lands for wages—That is the sole consideration which can make me endure the whelp—I despise him for himself, and hate him for the memories he revives! But, that consideration is sufficient; he's as safe with me, and shall be tended as carefully, as your master tends his own—I have a room up stairs, furnished for him, in handsome style—I've engaged a tutor, also, to come three times a week, from twenty miles distance, to teach him what he pleases to learn. I've ordered Hareton to obey him: and in fact, I've arranged every thing with a view to preserve the superior, and the gentleman in him, above his associates—I do regret however, that he so little deserves the trouble—if I wished any blessing in the world, it was to find him a worthy object of pride, and I'm bitterly disappointed with the whey-faced whining wretch!"

While he was speaking, Joseph returned, bearing a basin of milk-porridge, and placed it before Linton. He stirred round the homely mess with a look of aversion, and affirmed he could not eat it.

I saw the old man servant shared largely in his master's scorn of the child, though he was compelled to retain the sentiment in his heart, because Heathcliff plainly meant his underlings to hold him in honour.

"Cannot ate it?" repeated he, peering in Linton's face, and subduing his voice to a whisper, for fear of being overheard. "But Maister Hareton nivir ate nowt else, when he wer a little un: und what wer gooid eneugh fur him's gooid eneugh fur yah, Aw's rayther think!"

"I *shan't* eat it!" answered Linton, snappishly. "Take it away."

Joseph snatched up the food indignantly, and brought it to us.

"Is there owt ails th' victuals?" he asked, thrusting the tray under Heathcliff's nose.

EMILY BRONTË

"What should ail them?" he said.

"Wah!" answered Joseph, "yon dainty chap says he cannut ate 'em. Bud Aw guess it's raight! His mother wer just soa—we wer a'most too mucky tuh sow t' corn fur makking her breead."

"Don't mention his mother to me," said the master, angrily. "Get him something that he can eat, that's all. What is his usual food, Nelly?"

I suggested boiled milk or tea; and the housekeeper received instructions to prepare some.

Come, I reflected, his father's selfishness may contribute to his comfort. He perceives his delicate constitution, and the necessity of treating him tolerably. I'll console Mr. Edgar by acquainting him with the turn Heathcliff's humour has taken.

Having no excuse for lingering longer, I slipped out, while Linton was engaged in timidly rebuffing the advances of a friendly sheep-dog. But he was too much on the alert to be cheated—as I closed the door, I heard a cry, and a frantic repetition of the words—

"Don't leave me! I'll not stay here! I'll not stay here!"

Then the latch was raised and fell—they did not suffer him to come forth. I mounted Minny, and urged her to a trot; and so my brief guardianship ended.

Chapter VII.

We had sad work with little Cathy that day: she rose in high glee, eager to join her cousin; and such passionate tears and lamentations followed the news of his departure, that Edgar, himself, was obliged to sooth her, by affirming he should come back soon; he added, however, "if I can get him;" and there were no hopes of that.

This promise poorly pacified her; but time was more potent; and though still, at intervals, she inquired of her father, when Linton would return; before she did see him again, his features had waxed so dim in her memory that she did not recognise him.

When I chanced to encounter the housekeeper of Wuthering Heights, in paying business-visits to Gimmerton, I used to ask how the young master got on; for he lived almost as secluded as Catherine herself, and was never to be seen. I could gather from her that he continued in weak health, and was a tiresome inmate. She said Mr. Heathcliff seemed to dislike him ever longer and worse, though he took some trouble to conceal it. He had an antipathy to the sound of his voice, and could not do at all with his sitting in the same room with him many minutes together.

There seldom passed much talk between them; Linton learnt his lessons, and spent his evenings in a small apartment, they called the parlour; or else lay in bed all day; for he was constantly getting coughs, and colds, and aches, and pains of some sort.

"And I never knew such a faint-hearted creature," added the woman; "nor one so careful of hisseln. He *will* go on, if I leave the window open, a bit late in the evening. Oh! it's killing a breath of night air! And he must have a fire in the middle of summer; and Joseph's 'bacca pipe is poison; and he must always have sweets and dainties, and always milk, milk for ever—heeding naught how the rest of us are pinched in winter—and there he'll sit, wrapped in his furred cloak in his chair by the fire, and some toast and water, or other slop on the hob to sip at; and if Hareton, for pity, comes to amuse him—Hareton is not bad-natured, though he's rough—they're sure to part, one swearing, and the other crying. I believe the master would relish Earnshaw's thrashing him to a mummy, if he were not his son: and, I'm certain, he would be fit to turn him out of doors, if he knew half the nursing he gives hisseln. But then, he wont go into danger of temptation; he never enters the parlour, and should Linton show those ways in the house where he is, he sends him up stairs directly."

I divined, from this account, that utter lack of sympathy had rendered young Heathcliff selfish and disagreeable, if he were not so originally; and my

216   EMILY BRONTË

interest in him, consequently, decayed: though still I was moved with a sense of grief at his lot, and a wish that he had been left with us.

Mr. Edgar encouraged me to gain information; he thought a great deal about him, I fancy, and would have run some risk to see him; and he told me once to ask the housekeeper whether he ever came into the village?

She said he had only been twice, on horseback, accompanying his father: and both times he pretended to be quite knocked up for three or four days afterwards.

That housekeeper left, if I recollect rightly, two years after he came; and another, whom I did not know, was her successor: she lives there still.

Time wore on at the Grange in its former pleasant way, till Miss Cathy reached sixteen. On the anniversary of her birth we never manifested any signs of rejoicing, because it was, also, the anniversary of my late mistress's death. Her father invariably spent that day alone in the library; and walked, at dusk, as far as Gimmerton kirkyard, where he would frequently prolong his stay beyond midnight. Therefore Catherine was thrown on her own resources for amusement.

This twentieth of March was a beautiful spring day, and when her father had retired, my young lady came down dressed for going out, and said she had asked to have a ramble on the edge of the moors with me; and Mr. Linton had given her leave, if we went only a short distance, and were back within the hour.

"So make haste, Ellen!" she cried. "I know where I wish to go; where a colony of moor game are settled; I want to see whether they have made their nests yet."

"That must be a good distance up," I answered; "they don't breed on the edge of the moor."

"No, it's not," she said. "I've gone very near with papa."

I put on my bonnet, and sallied out; thinking nothing more of the matter. She bounded before me, and returned to my side, and was off again like a young greyhound; and, at first, I found plenty of entertainment in listening to the larks singing far and near; and enjoying the sweet, warm sunshine; and watching her, my pet, and my delight, with her golden ringlets flying loose behind, and her bright cheek, as soft and pure in its bloom, as a wild rose, and her eyes radiant with cloudless pleasure. She was a happy creature, and an angel, in those days. It's a pity she could not be content.

"Well," said I, "where are your moor-game, Miss Cathy? We should be at them—the Grange park-fence is a great way off now."

"Oh, a little further—only a little further, Ellen," was her answer, continually. "Climb to that hillock, pass that bank, and by the time you reach the other side, I shall have raised the birds."

But there were so many hillocks and banks to climb and pass, that, at length, I began to be weary, and told her we must halt, and retrace our steps.

WUTHERING HEIGHTS 217

I shouted to her, as she had outstripped me, a long way; she either did not hear, or did not regard, for she still sprang on, and I was compelled to follow. Finally, she dived into a hollow; and before I came in sight of her again, she was two miles nearer Wuthering Heights than her own home; and I beheld a couple of persons arrest her, one of whom I felt convinced was Mr. Heathcliff himself.

Cathy had been caught in the fact of plundering, or, at least, hunting out the nests of the grouse.

The Heights were Heathcliff's land, and he was reproving the poacher.

"I've neither taken any nor found any," she said, as I toiled to them, expanding her hands in corroboration of the statement. "I didn't mean to take them; but papa told me there were quantities up here, and I wished to see the eggs."

Heathcliff glanced at me with an ill-meaning smile, expressing his acquaintance with the party, and, consequently, his malevolence towards it, and demanded who "papa" was?

"Mr. Linton of Thrushcross Grange," she replied. "I thought you did not know me, or you wouldn't have spoken in that way."

"You suppose papa is highly esteemed and respected then?" he said, sarcastically.

"And what are you?" inquired Catherine, gazing curiously on the speaker. "That man I've seen before. Is he your son?"

She pointed to Hareton, the other individual; who had gained nothing but increased bulk and strength by the addition two years to his age: he seemed as awkward and rough as ever.

"Miss Cathy," I interrupted, "it will be three hours instead of one, that we are out, presently. We really must go back."

"No, that man is not my son," answered Heathcliff, pushing me aside. "But I have one, and you have seen him before too; and, though your nurse is in a hurry, I think both you and she would be the better for a little rest. Will you just turn this nab of heath, and walk into my house? You'll get home earlier for the ease; and you shall receive a kind welcome."

I whispered Catherine, that she mustn't, on any account, accede to the proposal; it was entirely out of the question.

"Why?" she asked, aloud. "I'm tired of running, and the ground is dewy—I can't sit here. Let us go, Ellen! Besides, he says I have seen his son. He's mistaken, I think; but I guess where he lives, at the farm-house I visited in coming from Penistone Craggs. Don't you?"

"I do. Come, Nelly, hold your tongue—it will be a treat for her to look in on us. Hareton get forwards with the lass. You shall walk with me, Nelly."

"No, she's not going to any such place," I cried, struggling to release my arm which he had seized; but she was almost at the door-stones already, scampering round the brow at full speed. Her appointed companion did not pretend to escort her; he shyed off by the road side, and vanished.

218 EMILY BRONTË

"Mr. Heathcliff, it's very wrong," I continued, "you know you mean no good; and there she'll see Linton, and all will be told, as soon as ever we return; and I shall have the blame."

"I want her to see Linton," he answered: he's looking better these few days; it's not not often he's fit to be seen. And we'll soon persuade her to keep the visit secret—where is the harm of it?"

"The harm of it is, that her father would hate me, if he found I suffered her to enter your house; and I am convinced you have a bad design in encouraging her to do so," I replied.

"My design is as honest as possible. I'll inform you of its whole scope," he said. "That the two cousins may fall in love, and get married. I'm acting generously to your master; his young chit has no expectations, and should she second my wishes, she'll be provided for, at once, as joint successor with Linton."

"If Linton died," I answered, "and his life is quite uncertain, Catherine would be the heir."

"No, she would not," he said. "There is no clause in the will to secure it so; his property would go to me; but, to prevent disputes, I desire their union, and am resolved to bring it about."

"And I'm resolved she shall never approach your house with me again," I returned, as we reached the gate, where Miss Cathy waited our coming.

Heathcliff bid me be quiet; and preceding us up the path, hastened to open the door. My young lady gave him several looks, as if she could not exactly make up her mind what to think of him; but now he smiled when he met her eye, and softened his voice in addressing her, and I was foolish enough to imagine the memory of her mother might disarm him from desiring her injury.

Linton stood on the hearth. He had been out, walking in the fields; for his cap was on, and he was calling to Joseph to bring him dry shoes.

He had grown tall of his age, still wanting some months of sixteen. His features were pretty yet, and his eye and complexion brighter than I remembered them, though with merely temporary lustre borrowed from the salubrious air and genial sun.

"Now, who is that?" asked Mr. Heathcliff, turning to Cathy. "Can you tell?"

"Your son?" she said, having doubtfully surveyed, first one, and then the other.

"Yes, yes," answered he; "but is this the only time you have beheld him? Think! Ah! you have a short memory. Linton, don't you recall your cousin, that you used to tease us so, with wishing to see?"

"What, Linton!" cried Cathy, kindling into joyful surprise at the name. "Is that little Linton? He's taller than I am! Are you, Linton?"

The youth stepped forward, and acknowledged himself: she kissed him fervently, and they gazed with wonder at the change time had wrought in the appearance of each.

Catherine had reached her full height; her figure was both plump and slender, elastic as steel, and her whole aspect sparkling with health and spirits. Linton's looks and movements were very languid, and his form extremely slight; but there was a grace in his manner that mitigated these defects, and rendered him not unpleasing.

After exchanging numerous marks of fondness with him, his cousin went to Mr. Heathcliff, who lingered by the door, dividing his attention between the objects inside, and those that lay without, pretending, that is, to observe the latter, and really noting the former alone.

"And you are my uncle, then!" she cried, reaching up to salute him. "I thought I liked you, though you were cross, at first. "Why don't you visit at the Grange with Linton? To live all these years such close neighbours, and never see us, is odd; what have you done so for?"

"I visited it once or twice too often before you were born," he answered. "There—damn it! If you have any kisses to spare, give them to Linton—they are thrown away on me."

"Naughty Ellen!" exclaimed Catherine, flying to attack me next with her lavish caresses. "Wicked Ellen! to try to hinder me from entering. But, I'll take this walk every morning in future—may I, uncle—and sometimes bring papa? Wont you be glad to see us?"

"Of course!" replied the uncle, with a hardly surpressed grimace, resulting from his deep aversion to both the proposed visiters. "But stay," he continued, turning towards the young lady. "Now I think of it, I'd better tell you. Mr. Linton has a prejudice against me; we quarrelled at one time of our lives, with unchristian ferocity; and, if you mention coming here to him, he'll put a veto on your visits altogether. Therefore, you must not mention it, unless you be careless of seeing your cousin hereafter—you may come, if you will, but you must not mention it."

"Why did you quarrel?" asked Catherine, considerably crest-fallen.

"He thought me too poor to wed his sister," answered Heathcliff, "and was grieved that I got her—his pride was hurt, and he'll never forgive it."

"That's wrong!" said the young lady: "sometime, I'll tell him so; but Linton and I have no share in your quarrel. I'll not come here, then, he shall come to the Grange."

"It will be too far for me," murmured her cousin, "to walk four miles would kill me. No, come here, Miss Catherine, now and then, not every morning, but once or twice a week."

The father launched towards his son a glance of bitter contempt.

"I am afraid, Nelly, I shall lose my labour," he muttered to me. "Miss Catherine, as the ninny calls her, will discover his value, and send him to the devil. Now, if it had been Hareton—do you know that, twenty times a day, I covet Hareton, with all his degradation? I'd have loved the lad had he been some one else. But I think he's safe from *her* love. I'll pit him against that

220 EMILY BRONTË

paltry creature, unless it bestir, itself briskly. We calculate it will scarcely last till it is eighteen. Oh, confound the vapid thing. He's absorbed in drying his feet, and never looks at her—Linton!"

"Yes, father," answered the boy.

"Have you nothing to show your cousin, anywhere about; not even a rabbit, or a weasel's nest? Take her into the garden, before you change your shoes; and into the stable to see your horse."

"Wouldn't you rather sit here?" asked Linton, addressing Cathy in a tone which expressed reluctance to move again.

"I don't know," she replied, casting a longing look to the door, and evidently eager to be active.

He kept his seat, and shrank closer to the fire.

Heathcliff rose, and went into the kitchen, and from thence to the yard, calling out for Hareton.

Hareton responded, and presently the two re-entered. The young man had been washing himself, as was visible by the glow on his cheeks, and his wetted hair.

"Oh, I'll ask *you*, uncle;" cried Miss Cathy, recollecting the housekeeper's assertion. "That's not my cousin, is he?"

"Yes," he replied, "your mother's nephew. Don't you like him?"

Catherine looked queer.

"Is he not a handsome lad?" he continued.

The uncivil little thing stood on tiptoe, and whispered a sentence in Heathcliff's ear.

He laughed; Hareton darkened; I perceived he was very sensitive to suspected slights, and had obviously a dim notion of his inferiority. But his master or guardian chased the frown by exclaiming—

"You'll be the favourite among us, Hareton! She says you are a—What was it? Well, something very flattering—Here! you go with her round the farm. And behave like a gentleman, mind! Don't use any bad words; and don't stare, when the young lady is not looking at you, and be ready to hide your face when she is; and, when you speak, say your words slowly, and keep your hands out of your pockets. Be off, and entertain her as nicely as you can."

He watched the couple walking past the window. Earnshaw had his countenance completely averted from his companion. He seemed studying the familiar landscape with a stranger's, and an artist's interest,

Catherine took a sly look at him, expressing small admiration. She then turned her attention to seeking out objects of amusement for herself, and tripped merrily on, lilting a tune to supply the lack of conversation.

"I've tied his tongue," observed Heathcliff. "He'll not venture a single syllable, all the time! Nelly, you recollect me at his age—nay, some years younger—Did I ever look so stupid, so 'gaumless,' as Joseph calls it."

"Worse," I replied, "because more sullen with it."

WUTHERING HEIGHTS

"I've a pleasure in him!" he continued reflecting aloud. "He has satisfied my expectations—If he were a born fool I should not enjoy it half so much—But he's no fool; and I can sympathise with all his feelings, having felt them myself—I know what he suffers now, for instance, exactly—it is merely a beginning of what he shall suffer, though. And he'll never be able to emerge from his bathos of coarseness, and ignorance. I've got him faster than his scoundrel of a father secured me, and lower; for he takes a pride in his brutishness, I've taught him to scorn everything, extra-animal, as silly and weak—Don't you think Hindley would be proud of his son, if he could see him? almost as proud as I am of mine—But there's this difference, one is gold put to the use of paving stones; and the other is tin polished to ape a service of silver—*Mine* has nothing valuable about it; yet I shall have the merit, of making it go as far as such poor stuff can go. *His* had first-rate qualities, and they are lost—rendered worse than unavailing—I have nothing to regret; he would have more than any, but I, are aware of—And the best of it is, Hareton is damnably fond of me! You'll own that I've out-matched Hindley there—If the dead villain could rise from his grave to abuse me for his offspring's wrongs, I should have the fun of seeing the said offspring fight him back again, indignant that he should dare to rail at the one friend he has in the world!"

Heathcliff chuckled a fiendish laugh at the idea; I made no reply, because I saw that he expected none.

Meantime, our young companion, who sat too removed from us to hear what was said, began to evince symptoms of uneasiness: probably repenting that he had denied himself the treat of Catherine's society, for fear of a little fatigue.

His father remarked the restless glances wandering to the window, and the hand irresolutely extended towards his cap.

"Get up, you idle boy!" he exclaimed with assumed heartiness. "Away after them . . . they are just at the corner, by the stand of hives."

Linton gathered his energies, and left the hearth. The lattice was open and, as he stepped out, I heard Cathy inquiring of her unsociable attendant, what was that inscription over the door?

Hareton stared up, and scratched his head like a true clown.

"It's some damnable writing;" he answered, "I cannot read it."

"Can't read it?" cried Catherine, "I can read it . . . It's English . . . but I want to know, why it is there."

Linton giggled—the first appearance of mirth he had exhibited.

"He does not know his letters," he said to his cousin. "Could you believe in the existence of such a colossal dunce?"

"Is he all as he should be?" asked Miss Cathy seriously, "or is he simple . . . not right? I've questioned him twice now, and each time he looked so stupid, I think he does not understand me; I can hardly understand *him* I'm sure!"

Linton repeated his laugh, and glanced at Hareton tauntingly, who certainly, did not seem quite clear of comprehension at that moment.

"There's nothing the matter, but laziness, is there, Earnshaw?" he said. "My cousin fancies you are an idiot . . . There you experience the consequence of scorning "book-larning," as you would say . . . Have you noticed, Catherine, his frightful Yorkshire pronunciation?"

"Why, where the devil is the use on't?" growled Hareton, more ready in answering his daily companion. He was about to enlarge further, but the two youngsters broke into a noisy fit of merriment; my giddy Miss being delighted to discover that she might turn his strange talk to matter of amusement.

"Where is the use of the devil in that sentence?" tittered Linton. "Papa told you not to say any bad words, and you can't open your mouth without one . . . Do try to behave like a gentleman, now do!"

"If thou wern't more a lass than a lad, I'd fell thee this minute, I would; pitiful lath of a crater!" retorted the angry boor retreating, while his face burnt with mingled rage, and mortification; for he was conscious of being insulted, and embarrassed how to resent it.

Mr. Heathcliff having overheard the conversation, as well as I, smiled when he saw him go, but immediately afterwards, cast a look of singular aversion on the flippant pair, who remained chattering in the door-way. The boy finding animation enough while discussing Hareton's faults, and deficiencies, and relating anecdotes of his goings on; and the girl relishing his pert and spiteful sayings, without considering the ill-nature they evinced: but I began to dislike, more than to compassionate, Linton, and to excuse his father, in some measure, for holding him cheap.

We staid till afternoon: I could not tear Miss Cathy away, before: but happily my master had not quitted his apartment, and remained ignorant of our prolonged absence.

As we walked home, I would fain have enlightened my charge on the characters of the people we had quitted; but she got it into her head that I was prejudiced against them.

"Aha!" she cried, "you take papa's side, Ellen—you are partial . . . I know, or else you wouldn't have cheated me so many years, into the notion that Linton lived a long way from here. I'm really extremely angry, only, I'm so pleased, I can't show it! But you must hold your tongue about my uncle . . . he's *my* uncle remember, and I'll scold papa for quarrelling with him."

And so she ran on, till I dropped endeavouring to convince her of her mistake.

She did not mention the visit that night, because she did not see Mr. Linton. Next day it all came out, sadly to my chagrin; and still I was not altogether sorry: I thought the burden of directing and warning would be more efficiently borne by him than me, but he was too timid in giving satisfactory reasons for his wish that she would shun connection with the household of the Heights, and Catherine liked good reasons for every restraint that harassed her petted will.

"Papa!" she exclaimed after the morning's salutations, "guess whom I saw yesterday, in my walk on the moors . . . Ah, papa, you started! you've not done right, have you, now? I saw—But listen, and you shall hear how I found you out, and Ellen, who is in league with you, and yet pretended to pity me so, when I kept hoping, and was always disappointed about Linton's coming back!"

She gave a faithful account of her excursion and its consequences; and my master, though he cast more than one reproachful look at me, said nothing, till she had concluded. Then he drew her to him, and asked if she knew why he had concealed Linton's near neighbourhood from her? Could she think it was to deny her a pleasure that she might harmlessly enjoy?

"It was because you disliked Mr. Heathcliff," she answered.

"Then you believe I care more for my own feelings than yours, Cathy?" he said. "No, it was not because I disliked Mr. Heathcliff; but because Mr. Heathcliff dislikes me; and is a most diabolical man, delighting to wrong and ruin those he hates, if they give him the slightest opportunity. I knew that you could not keep up an acquaintance with your cousin, without being brought into contact with him; and I knew he would detest you, on my account; so, for your own good, and nothing else, I took precautions that you should not see Linton again—I meant to explain this sometime as you grew older, and I'm sorry I delayed it!"

"But Mr. Heathcliff was quite cordial, papa," observed Catherine, not at all convinced; "and *he* didn't object to our seeing each other: he said I might come to his house, when I pleased, only I must not tell you, because you had quarrelled with him, and would not forgive him for marrying aunt Isabella. And you won't—*you* are the one to be blamed—he is willing to let *us* be friends, at least; Linton and I—and you are not."

My master, perceiving that she would not take his word for her uncle-in-law's evil disposition, gave a hasty sketch of his conduct to Isabella, and the manner in which Wuthering Heights became his property. He could not bear to discourse long upon the topic, for though he spoke little of it, he still felt the same horror, and detestation of his ancient enemy that had occupied his heart ever since Mrs. Linton's death. "She might have been living yet, if it had not been for him!" was his constant bitter reflection; and, in his eyes, Heathcliff seemed a murderer.

Miss Cathy, conversant with no bad deeds except her own slight acts of disobedience, injustice and passion, rising from hot temper, and thoughtlessness, and repented of on the day they were committed, was amazed at the blackness of spirit that could brood on, and cover revenge for years; and deliberately prosecute its plans, without a visitation of remorse. She appeared so deeply impressed and shocked at this new view of human nature—excluded from all her studies and all her ideas till now—that Mr. Edgar deemed it unnecessary to pursue the subject. He merely added,

224 EMILY BRONTË

"You will know hereafter, darling, why I wish you to avoid his house and family—now, return to your old employments and amusements, and think no more about them!"

Catherine kissed her father, and sat down quietly to her lessons for a couple of hours, according to custom: then she accompanied him into the grounds, and the whole day passed as usual: but in the evening, when she had retired to her room, and I went to help her to undress, I found her crying, on her knees by the bedside.

Oh, fie, silly child!" I exclaimed. "If you had any real griefs, you'd be ashamed to waste a tear on this little contrariety. You never had one shadow of substantial sorrow, Miss Catherine. Suppose, for a minute, that master and I were dead, and you were by yourself in the world—how would you feel, then? Compare the present occasion with such an affliction as that, and be thankful for the friends you have, instead of coveting more."

"I'm not crying for myself, Ellen," she answered, "it's for him—He expected to see me again, to-morrow, and there, he'll be so disappointed—and he'll wait for me, and I shan't come!"

"Nonsense!" said I, "do you imagine he has thought as much of you, as you have of him? Hasn't he Hareton, for a companion? Not one in a hundred would weep at losing a relation they had just seen twice, for two afternoons—Linton will conjecture how it is, and trouble himself no further about you."

"But may I not write a note to tell him why I cannot come?" she asked rising to her feet. "And just send those books, I promised to lend him—his books are not as nice as mine, and he wanted to have them extremely, when I told him how interesting they were—May I not, Ellen?"

"No, indeed, no indeed!" replied I with decision. "Then he would write to you, and there'd never be on end of it—No, Miss Catherine, the acquaintance must be dropped entirely—so papa expects, and I shall see that it is done."

"But how can one little note—" she recommenced, putting on an imploring countenance.

"Silence!" I interrupted. "We'll not begin with your little notes—Get into bed!"

She threw at me a very naughty look, so naughty that I would not kiss her good-night at first: I covered her up, and shut her door, in great displeasure—but, repenting half-way, I returned softly, and lo! there was Miss, standing at the table with a bit of blank paper before her, and a pencil in her hand, which she guiltily slipped out of sight, on my re-entrance.

"You'll get nobody to take that, Catherine," I said, "if you write it; and at present I shall put out your candle."

I set the extinguisher on the flame, receiving as I did so, a slap on my hand, and a petulant "cross thing!" I then quitted her again, and she drew the bolt in one of her worst, most peevish humours.

The letter was finished and forwarded to its destination by a milk-fetcher who came from the village, but that I didn't learn till some time afterwards. Weeks passed on, and Cathy recovered her temper, though she grew wondrous fond of stealing off to corners by herself, and often, if I came near her suddenly while reading she would start, and bend over the book, evidently desirous to hide it; and I detected edges of loose paper sticking out beyond the leaves.

She also got a trick of coming down early in the morning, and lingering about the kitchen, as if she were expecting the arrival of something; and she had a small drawer in a cabinet in the library which she would trifle over for hours, and whose key she took special care to remove when she left it.

One day, as she inspected this drawer, I observed that the play-things, and trinkets which recently formed its contents, were transmuted into bits of folded paper.

My curiosity and suspicions were roused; I determined to take a peep at her mysterious treasures; so, at night, as soon as she and my master were safe up stairs, I searched and readily found among my house keys, one that would fit the lock. Having opened, I emptied the whole contents into my apron, and took them with me to examine at leisure in my own chamber.

Though I could not but suspect, I was still surprised to discover that they were a mass of correspondence, daily almost, it must have been, from Linton Heathcliff, answers to documents forwarded by her. The earlier dated were embarrassed and short; gradually however they expanded into copious love letters, foolish as the age of the writer rendered natural, yet with touches, here and there, which I thought, were borrowed from a more experienced source.

Some of them struck me as singularly odd compounds of ardour, and flatness; commencing in strong feeling, and concluding in the affected, wordy way that a school-boy might use to a fancied, incorporeal sweetheart.

Whether they satisfied Cathy, I don't know, but they appeared very worthless trash to me.

After turning over as many as I thought proper, I tied them in a handkerchief, and set them aside, re-locking the vacant drawer.

Following her habit, my young lady descended early, and visited the kitchen: I watched her go to the door, on the arrival of a certain little boy; and, while the dairy maid filled his can, she tucked something into his jacket pocket, and plucked something out.

I went round by the garden, and laid wait for the messenger; who fought valorously to defend his trust, and we spilt the milk between us; but I succeeded in abstracting the epistle; and threatening serious consequences if he did not look sharp home, I remained under the wall, and perused Miss Cathy's affectionate composition. It was more simple and more eloquent than her cousin's, very pretty and very silly. I shook my head, and went meditating into the house.

226 EMILY BRONTË

The day being wet, she could not divert herself with rambling about the park; so, at the conclusion of her morning studies, she resorted to the solace of the drawer. Her father sat reading at the table; and I, on purpose, had sought a bit of work in some unripped fringes of the window curtain, keeping my eye steadily fixed on her proceedings.

Never did any bird flying back to a plundered nest which it had left brimful of chirping young ones, express more complete despair in its anguished cries, and flutterings, than she by her single "Oh!" And the change that transfigured her late happy countenance. Mr. Linton looked up.

"What is the matter, love? Have you hurt yourself?" he said.

His tone and look, assured her *he* had not been the discoverer of the hoard.

"No papa—" she gasped. "Ellen! Ellen! come up-stairs—I'm sick!"

I obeyed her summons, and accompanied her out.

"Oh, Ellen! you have got them," she commenced immediately, dropping on her knees, when we were enclosed alone. "O, give them to me, and I'll never never do so again! Don't tell papa—You have not told papa, Ellen, say you have not! I've been exceedingly naughty, but I won't do it any more!"

With a grave severity in my manner, I bid her stand up.

"So, I exclaimed, Miss Catherine, you are tolerably far on, it seems—you may well be ashamed of them! A fine bundle of trash you study in your leisure hours, to be sure—Why it's good enough to be printed! And what do you suppose the master will think, when I display it before him? I haven't shown it yet, but you needn't imagine I shall keep your ridiculous secrets—For shame! And you must have led the way in writing such absurdities, he would not have thought of beginning, I'm certain."

"I didn't! I didn't!" sobbed Cathy, fit to break her heart. "I didn't once think of loving him till—"

"*Loving!*" cried I, as scornfully as I could utter the word. "*Loving!* Did anybody ever hear the like! I might just as well talk of loving the miller who comes once a year to buy our corn. Pretty loving, indeed, and both times together you have seen Linton hardly four hours, in your life! Now here is the babyish trash. I'm going with it to the library; and we'll see what your father says to such *loving*."

She sprang at her precious epistles, but I held them above my head; and then she poured out further frantic entreaties that I would burn them—do anything rather than show them. And being really fully as inclined to laugh as scold, for I esteemed it all girlish vanity, I at length, relented in a measure, and asked,

"If I consent to burn them, will you promise faithfully, neither to send, nor receive a letter again, nor a book, for I perceive you have sent him books, nor locks of hair, nor rings, nor playthings?"

"We don't send playthings!" cried Catherine, her pride overcoming her shame.

WUTHERING HEIGHTS

"Nor anything at all, then, my lady!" I said. "Unless you will, here I go."

"I promise, Ellen!" she cried catching my dress. "Oh put them in the fire, do, do!"

But when I proceeded to open a place with the poker, the sacrifice was too painful to be borne—She earnestly supplicated that I would spare her one or two.

"One or two, Ellen, to keep for Linton's sake!"

I unknotted the handkerchief, and commenced dropping them in from an angle, and the flame curled up the chimney.

"I will have one, you cruel wretch!" she screamed, darting her hand into the fire, and drawing forth some half consumed fragments, at the expense of her fingers.

"Very well—and I will have some to exhibit to papa!" I answered shaking back the rest into the bundle, and turning anew to the door.

"She emptied her blackened pieces into the flames, and motioned me to finish the immolation. It was done; I stirred up the ashes, and interred them under a shovel full of coals; and she mutely, and with a sense of intense injury, retired to her private apartment. I descended to tell my master that the young lady's qualm of sickness was almost gone, but I judged it best for her to lie down a while.

She wouldn't dine; but she re-appeared at tea, pale and red about the eyes, and marvellously subdued in outward aspect.

Next morning I answered the letter by a slip of paper inscribed, "Master Heathcliff is requested to send no more notes to Miss Linton as she will not receive them." And, thenceforth the little boy came with vacant pockets.

Chapter VIII.

Summer drew to an end, and early Autumn—it was past Michaelmas, but the harvest was late that year, and a few of our fields were still uncleared.

Mr. Linton and his daughter would frequently walk out among the reapers: at the carrying of the last sheaves, they stayed till dusk, and the evening happening to be chill damp, my master caught a bad cold, that settling obstinately on his lungs, confined him indoors throughout the whole of the winter, nearly without intermission.

Poor Cathy, frightened from her little romance, had been considerably sadder and duller since its abandonment: and her father insisted on her reading less, and taking more exercise. She had his companionship no longer; I esteemed it a duty to supply its lack, as much as possible, with mine; an inefficient substitute, for I could only spare two or three hours, from my numerous diurnal occupations, to follow her footsteps, and then, my society was obviously less desirable than his.

On an afternoon in October, or the beginning of November, a fresh watery afternoon, when the turf and paths were rustling with moist, withered leaves, and the cold, blue sky was half hidden by clouds, dark grey streamers, rapidly mounting from the west, and boding abundant rain; I requested my young lady to forego her ramble because I was certain of showers. She refused; and I unwillingly donned a cloak, and took my umbrella to accompany her on a stroll to the bottom of the park; a formal walk which she generally affected if low-spirited; and that she invariably was when Mr. Edgar had been worse than ordinary; a thing never known from his confession, but guessed both by her and me from his increased silence, and the melancholy of his countenance.

She went sadly on; there was no running or bounding now; though the chill wind might well have tempted her to a race. And often, from the side of my eye, I could detect her raising a hand, and brushing something off her cheek.

I gazed round for a means of diverting her thoughts. On one side of the road rose a high, rough bank, where hazels and stunted oaks, with their roots half exposed, held uncertain tenour: the soil was too loose for the latter; and strong winds had blown some nearly horizontal. In summer, Miss Catherine delighted to climb along these trunks, and sit in the branches, swinging twenty feet above the ground; and I pleased with her agility, and her light, childish heart, still considered it proper to scold every time I caught her at such an elevation; but so that she knew there was no necessity for descending. From dinner to tea she would lie in her breeze-rocked cradle, doing nothing except singing old songs—my nursery lore—to herself, or watching the birds,

WUTHERING HEIGHTS 229

joint tenants, feed and entice their young ones to fly, or nestling with closed lids, half thinking, half dreaming, happier than words can express.

"Look, Miss!" I exclaimed, pointing to a nook under the roots of one twisted tree. "Winter is not here yet. There's a little flower, up yonder, the last bud from the multitude of blue-bells that clouded those turf steps in July with a lilac mist. Will you clamber up, and pluck it to show to papa?"

Cathy stared a long time at the lonely blossom trembling in its earthy shelter, and replied, at length—

"No, I'll not touch it—but it looks melancholy, does it not, Ellen?"

"Yes," I observed, "about as starved and sackless as you—your cheeks are bloodless; let us take hold of hands and run. You're so low, I dare say I shall keep up with you."

"No," she repeated, and continued sauntering on, pausing, at intervals, to muse over a bit of moss, or a tuft of blanched grass, or a fungus spreading its bright orange among the heaps of brown foliage; and, ever and anon, her hand was lifted to her averted face.

"Catherine, why are you crying, love?" I asked, approaching and putting my arm over her shoulder. "You mustn't cry, because papa has a cold; be thankful it is nothing worse."

She now put no further restraint on her tears; her breath was stifled by sobs.

"Oh, it *will* be something worse," she said. "And what shall I do when papa and you leave me, and I am by myself? I can't forget your words, Ellen, they are always in my ear. How life will be changed, how dreary the world will be, when papa and you are dead."

"None can tell, whether you wont die before us," I replied. "It's wrong to anticipate evil—we'll hope there are years and years to come before any of us go—master is young, and I am strong, and hardly forty-five. My mother lived till eighty, a canty dame to the last. And suppose Mr. Linton were spared till he saw sixty, that would be more years than you have counted, Miss. And would it not be foolish to mourn a calamity above twenty years beforehand?"

"But Aunt Isabella was younger than papa," she remarked, gazing up with timid hope to seek further consolation.

"Aunt Isabella had not you and me to nurse her," I replied. "She wasn't as happy as master; she hadn't as much to live for. All you need do, is to wait well on your father, and cheer him by letting him see you cheerful; and avoid giving him anxiety on any subject—mind that, Cathy! I'll not disguise, but you might kill him, if you were wild and reckless, and cherished a foolish, fanciful affection for the son of a person who would be glad to have him in his grave—and allowed him to discover that you fretted over the separation, he has judged it expedient to make."

"I fret about nothing on earth except papa's illness," answered my companion. "I care for nothing in comparison with papa. And I'll never—never—oh, never, while I have my senses, do an act, or say a word to vex him.

230 EMILY BRONTË

I love him better than myself, Ellen; and I know it by this—I pray every night that I may live after him; because I would rather be miserable than that he should be—that proves I love him better than myself."

"Good words," I replied. "But deeds must prove it also; and after he is well, remember you don't forget resolutions formed in the hour of fear."

As we talked, we neared a door that opened on the road: and my young lady, lightening into sunshine again, climbed up, and seated herself on the top of the wall, reaching over to gather some hips that bloomed scarlet on the summit branches of the wild rose trees, shadowing the highway side, the lower fruit had disappeared, but only birds could touch the upper, except from Cathy's present station.

In stretching to pull them, her hat fell off; and as the door was locked, she proposed scrambling down to recover it. I bid her be cautious lest she got a fall, and she nimbly disappeared.

But the return was no such easy matter; the stones were smooth and neatly cemented, and the rosebushes, and blackberry stragglers could yield no assistance in re-ascending. I, like a fool, didn't recollect that till I heard her laughing, and exclaiming—

"Ellen! you'll have to fetch the key, or else I must run round to the porter's lodge. I can't scale the ramparts on this side!"

"Stay where you are," I answered, "I have my bundle of keys in my pocket; perhaps I may manage to open it, if not, I'll go."

Catherine amused herself with dancing to and fro before the door, while I tried all the large keys in succession. I had applied the last, and found that none would do; so, repeating my desire that she would remain there, I was about to hurry home as fast as I could, when an approaching sound arrested me. It was the trot of a horse; Cathy's dance stopped; and in a minute the horse stopped also.

"Who is that?" I whispered.

"Ellen, I wish you could open the door," whispered back my companion, anxiously.

"Ho, Miss Linton!" cried a deep voice, (the rider's.) "I'm glad to meet you. Don't be in haste to enter, for I have an explanation to ask and obtain."

"I shant speak to you, Mr. Heathcliff!" answered Catherine. "Papa says you are a wicked man, and you hate both him and me; and Ellen says the same."

"That is nothing to the purpose," said Heathcliff. (He it was.) "I don't hate my son, I suppose, and it is concerning him, that I demand your attention. Yes! you have cause to blush. Two or three months since, were you not in the habit of writing to Linton? making love in play, eh? You deserved, both of you, flogging for that! You especially, the elder, and less sensitive, as it turns out. I've got your letters, and if you give me any pertness, I'll send them to your father. I presume you grew weary of the amusement, and dropped it, didn't you? Well, you dropped Linton with it, into a Slough of Despond. He was in earnest—in love—really. As true as I live, he's dying for you—breaking his heart at your fickleness, not figuratively, but actually. Though Hareton has made him a standing jest for six weeks, and I have used more serious measures, and attempted to frighten him out of his idiocy, he gets worse daily, and he'll be under the sod before summer, unless you restore him!"

"How can you lie so glaringly to the poor child!" I called from the inside. "Pray ride on! How can you deliberately get up such paltry falsehoods? Miss Cathy, I'll knock the lock off with a stone, you wont believe that vile nonsense. You can feel in yourself, it is impossible that a person should die for love of a stranger."

"I was not aware there were eaves-droppers," muttered the detected villain. "Worthy Mrs. Dean, I like you, but I don't like your double dealing," he added, aloud. "How could *you* lie so glaringly, as to affirm I hated the 'poor child?' And invent bugbear stories to terrify her from my door-stones? Catherine Linton, (the very name warms me), my bonny lass, I shall be from home all this week, go and see if I have not spoken truth; do, there's a darling! Just imagine your father in my place, and Linton in yours; then think how you would value your careless lover, if he refused to stir a step to comfort you, when your father, himself, entreated him; and don't, from pure stupidity, fall into the same error. I swear, on my salvation, he's going to his grave, and none but you can save him!"

The lock gave way, and I issued out.

"I swear Linton is dying," repeated Heathcliff, looking hard at me. "And grief and disappointment are hastening his death. Nelly, if you wont let her go, you can walk over yourself. But I shall not return till this time next week; and I think your master himself would scarcely object to her visiting her cousin!"

"Come in," said I, taking Cathy by the arm and half forcing her to re-enter, for she lingered, viewing, with troubled eyes, the features of the speaker, too stern to express his inward deceit.

He pushed his horse close, and, bending down, observed—

"Miss Catherine, I'll own to you that I have little patience with Linton—and Hareton and Joseph have less. I'll own that he's with a harsh set. He pines for kindness, as well as love; and a kind word from you would be his best medicine. Don't mind Mrs. Dean's cruel cautions, but be generous, and contrive to see him. He dreams of you day and night, and cannot be persuaded that you don't hate him, since you neither write nor call."

I closed the door, and rolled a stone to assist the loosened lock in holding it; and spreading my umbrella, I drew my charge underneath, for the rain began to drive through the moaning branches of the tress, and warned us to avoid delay.

Our hurry prevented any comment on the encounter with Heathcliff, as we stretched towards home; but I divined instinctively that Catherine's heart was

232 EMILY BRONTË

clouded now in double darkness. Her features were so sad, they did not seem hers: she evidently regarded what she had heard as every syllable true.

The master had retired to rest before we came in. Cathy stole to his room to inquire how he was; he had fallen asleep. She returned, and asked me to sit with her in the library. We took our tea together; and afterwards she lay down on the rug, and told me not to talk for she was weary.

I got a book, and pretended to read. As soon as she supposed me absorbed in my occupation, she recommenced her silent weeping: it appeared, at present, her favourite diversion. I suffered her to enjoy it a while; then, I expostulated; deriding and ridiculing all Mr. Heathcliff's assertions about his son; as if I were certain she would coincide. Alas! I hadn't skill to counteract the effect his account had produced; it was just what he intended.

"You may be right, Ellen," she answered; "but I shall never feel at ease till I know— and I must tell Linton it is not my fault that I don't write; and convince him that I shall not change."

What use were anger and protestations against her silly credulity? We parted that night hostile—but next day beheld me on the road to Wuthering Heights, by the side of my wilful young mistress's pony. I couldn't bear to witness her sorrow, to see her pale, dejected countenance, and heavy eyes; and I yielded in the faint hope that Linton himself might prove by his reception of us, how little of the tale was founded on fact.

Chapter IX.

The rainy night had ushered in a misty morning—half frost, half drizzle—and temporary brooks crossed our path, gurgling from the uplands. My feet were thoroughly wetted; I was cross and low, exactly the humour suited for making the most of these disagreeable things.

We entered the farm-house by the kitchen way to ascertain whether Mr. Heathcliff were really absent; because I put slight faith in his own affirmation.

Joseph seemed sitting in a sort of elysium alone, beside a roaring fire; a quart of ale on the table near him, bristling with large pieces of toasted oat cake; and his black, short pipe in his mouth.

Catherine ran to the hearth to warm herself. I asked if the master were in?

My question remained so long unanswered, that I thought the old man had grown deaf, and repeated it louder.

"Na—ay!" he snarled, or rather screamed through his nose. "Na—ay! yah muh goa back whear yah coom frough."

"Joseph," cried a peevish voice, simultaneously with me, from the inner room. "How often am I to call you? There are only a few red ashes now. Joseph! come this moment."

Vigorous puffs, and a resolute stare into the grate declared he had no ear for this appeal. The housekeeper and Hareton were invisible; one gone on an errand, and the other at his work, probably. We knew Linton's tones and entered.

"Oh, I hope you'll die in a garret! starved to death," said the boy, mistaking our approach for that of his negligent attendant.

He stopped, on observing his error; his cousin flew to him.

"Is that you, Miss Linton?" he said, raising his head from the arm of the great chair, in which he reclined. "No—don't kiss me. It takes my breath—dear me! Papa said you would call," continued he, after recovering a little from Catherine's embrace; while she stood by looking very contrite. "Will you shut the door, if you please? you left it open—and those—those *detestable* creatures wont bring coals to the fire. It's so cold!"

I stirred up the cinders, and fetched a scuttle full myself. The invalid complained of being covered with ashes; but he had a tiresome cough, and looked feverish and ill, so I did not rebuke his temper.

"Well, Linton," murmured Catherine, when his corrugated brow relaxed. "Are you glad to see me? Can I do you any good?"

"Why didn't you come before?" he said. "You should have come, instead of writing. It tired me dreadfully, writing those long letters. I'd far rather have

234 EMILY BRONTË

talked to you. Now, I can neither bear to talk, nor anything else. I wonder where Zillah is! will you, (looking at me,) step into the kitchen and see?"

I had received no thanks for my other service; and being unwilling to run to and fro at his behest, I replied—

"Nobody is out there but Joseph."

"I want to drink," he exclaimed, fretfully, turning away. "Zillah is constantly gadding off to Gimmerton since papa went. It's miserable! And I'm obliged to come down here—they resolved never to hear me up stairs."

"Is your father attentive to you. Master Heathcliff?" I asked, perceiving Catherine to be checked in her friendly advances.

"Attentive? He makes *them* a little more attentive, at least," he cried. "The wretches! Do you know. Miss Linton, that brute Hareton laughs at me—I hate him—indeed, I hate them all—they are odious beings."

Cathy began searching for some water; she lighted on a pitcher in the dresser; filled a tumbler, and brought it. He bid her add a spoonful of wine from a bottle on the table; and having swallowed a small portion, appeared more tranquil, and said she was very kind.

"And are you glad to see me?" asked she, reiterating her former question, and pleased to detect the faint dawn of a smile.

"Yes, I am—It's something new to hear a voice like yours!" he replied, "but I *have* been vexed, because you wouldn't come—And papa swore it was owing to me; he called me a pitiful, shuffling, worthless thing; and said you despised me; and if he had been in my place, he would be more the master of the Grange than your father, by this time. But you don't despise me, do you Miss—"

"I wish you would say Catherine, or Cathy!" interrupted my young lady. "Despise you? No! Next to papa, and Ellen, I love you better than anybody living. I don't love Mr. Heathcliff, though; and I dare not come when he returns; will he stay away many days?"

"Not many:" answered Linton, but he goes onto the moors frequently, since the shooting season commenced, and you might spend an hour or two with me, in his absence—Do! say you will! I think I should not be peevish with you; you'd not provoke me, and you'd always be ready to help me, wouldn't you?"

"Yes," said Catherine stroking his long soft hair, "if I could only get papa's consent, I'd spend half my time with you—Pretty Linton! I wish you were my brother!"

"And then you would like me as well as your father?" observed he more cheerfully. "But papa says you would love me better than him, and all the world, if you were my wife—so I'd rather you were that!"

"No! I should never love anybody better than papa," she returned gravely. "And people hate their wives, sometimes; but not their sisters and brothers, and if you were the latter, you would live with us, and papa would be as fond of you, as he is of me."

WUTHERING HEIGHTS   235

Linton denied that people ever hated their wives; but Cathy affirmed they did, and in her wisdom, instanced his own father's aversion to her aunt.

I endeavoured to stop her thoughtless tongue—I couldn't succeed, till everything she knew was out. Master Heathcliff, much irritated, asserted her relation was false.

"Papa told me; and papa does not tell falsehoods!" she answered pertly.

"*My* papa scorns yours!" cried Linton. "He calls him a sneaking fool!"

"Yours is a wicked man," retorted Catherine, and you are very naughty to dare to repeat what he says—He must be wicked, to have made aunt Isabella leave him as she did!"

"She didn't leave him," said the boy. "you shan't contradict me!"

"She did!" cried my young lady.

"Well I'll tell *you* something!" said Linton "Your mother hated your father, now then."

"Oh!" exclaimed Catherine, too enraged to continue.

"And she loved mine!" added he.

"You little liar! I hate you now," she panted, and her face grew red with passion.

"She did! she did!" sang Linton sinking into the recess of his chair, and leaning back his head to enjoy the agitation of the other disputant who stood behind.

"Hush, Master Heathcliff!" I said, "that's your father's tale too, I suppose."

"It isn't—you hold your tongue!" he answered, "she did, she did, Catherine, she did, she did!"

"Cathy, beside herself, gave the chair a violent push, and caused him to fall against one arm. He was immediately seized by a suffocating cough that soon ended his triumph.

It lasted so long, that it frightened even me. As to his cousin, she wept with all her might, aghast at the mischief she had done, though she said nothing.

I held him, till the fit exhausted itself. Then he thrust me away; and leant his head down, silently—Catherine quelled her lamentations also, took a seat opposite, and looked solemnly into the fire.

"How do you feel now, Master Heathcliff," I inquired after waiting ten minutes.

"I wish *she* felt as I do," he replied, "spiteful, cruel thing! Hareton never touches me, he never struck me in his life—And I was better to-day—and there—" his voice died in a whimper.

"*I* didn't strike you!" muttered Cathy chewing her lip to prevent another burst of emotion.

He sighed and moaned like one under great suffering; and kept it up for a quarter of an hour, on purpose to distress his cousin, apparently, for whenever he caught a stifled sob from her, he put renewed pain and pathos into the inflexions of his voice.

"I'm sorry I hurt you, Linton!" she said at length, racked beyond endurance. "But *I* couldn't have been hurt by that little push; and I had no idea that you could, either—you're not much, are you, Linton? Don't let me go home, thinking I've done you harm! answer, speak to me."

"I can't speak to you," he murmured, "you've hurt me so, that I shall lie awake all night, choking with this cough! If you had it you'd know what it was—but *you'll* be comfortably asleep, while I'm in agony—and nobody near me! I wonder how you would like to pass those fearful nights!" And he began to wail aloud for very pity of himself.

"Since you are in the habit of passing dreadful nights," I said, "it wont be Miss who spoils your ease; you'd be the same, had she never come—However, she shall not disturb you, again—and perhaps, you'll get quieter when we leave you."

"Must I go?" asked Catherine dolefully, bending over him. "Do you want me to go, Linton?"

"You can't alter what you've done?" he replied pettishly, shrinking from her, "unless you alter it for the worse, by teasing me into a fever!"

"Well, then I must go?" she repeated.

"Let me alone, at least," said he "I can't bear your talking!"

She lingered, and resisted my persuasions to departure, a tiresome while, but as he neither looked up, nor spoke, she finally made a movement to the door and I followed.

We were recalled by a scream—Linton had slid from his seat on to the hearthstone, and lay writhing in the mere perverseness of an indulged plague of a child, determined to be as grievous and harassing as it can.

I thoroughly guaged his disposition from his behaviour, and saw at once it would be folly to attempt humouring him. Not so my companion, she ran back in terror, knelt down, and cried, and soothed, and entreated, till he grew quiet from lack of breath, by no means from compunction at distressing her.

"I shall lift him on to the settle," I said, "and he may roll about as he pleases; we can't stop to watch him—I hope you are satisfied, Miss Cathy that *you* are not the person to benefit him, and that his condition of health is not occasioned by attachment to you. Now then, there he is! Come away, as soon as he knows there is nobody by to care for his nonsense, he'll be glad to lie still!"

She placed a cushion under his head, and offered him some water, he rejected the latter, and tossed uneasily on the former, as if it were a stone, or a block of wood.

She tried to put it more comfortably.

"I can't do with that," he said, "it's not high enough!"

Catherine brought another to lay above it.

"That's *too* high!" murmured the provoking thing.

"How must I arrange it, then?" she asked despairingly.

He twined himself up to her, as she half knelt by the settle, and converted her shoulder into a support.

WUTHERING HEIGHTS   237

"No, that won't do!" I said. "You'll be content with the cushion, Master Heathcliff! Miss has wasted too much time on you, already; we cannot remain five minutes longer."

"Yes, yes, we can!" replied Cathy. "He's good and patient, now—He's beginning to think I shall have far greater misery than he will, to-night, if I believe he is the worse for my visit; and then, I dare not come again—Tell the truth about it, Linton—for I mutsn't come, if I have hurt you."

"You must come, to cure me," he answered. "You ought to come because you have hurt me—You know you have, extremely! I was not as ill, when you entered, as I am at present—was I?"

"But you've made yourself ill by crying, and being in a passion."

"I didn't do it all," said his cousin. "However, we'll be friends now. And you want me—you would wish to see me sometimes, really?"

"I told you, I did!" he replied impatiently. "Sit on the settle and let me lean on your knee—That's as mama used to do, whole afternoons together—Sit quite still, and don't talk, but you may sing a song if you can sing, or you may say a nice, long interesting ballad—one of those you promised to teach me, or a story—I'd rather have a ballad though, begin."

Catherine repeated the longest she could remember. The employment pleased both mightily. Linton would have another, and after that another; notwithstanding my strenuous objections; and so, they went on, until the clock struck twelve, and we heard Hareton in the court, returning for his dinner.

"And to-morrow, Catherine, will you be here to-morrow?" asked young Heathcliff, holding her frock, as she rose reluctantly.

"No!" I answered, "nor next day neither," She however, gave a different response, evidently, for his forehead cleared, as she stooped, and whispered in his ear.

"You won't go to-morrow, recollect, Miss!" I commenced when we were out of the house. "You are not dreaming of it, are you?"

She smiled.

"Oh, I'll take good care!" I continued, "I'll have that lock mended, and you can escape by no way else."

"I can get over the wall," she said laughing. "The Grange is not a prison, Ellen, and you are not my jailer. And besides I'm almost seventeen. I'm a woman—and I'm certain Linton would recover quickly if he had me to look after him—I'm older than he is, you know, and wiser, less childish, am I not? And he'll soon do as I direct him with some slight coaxing—He's a pretty little darling when he's good. I'd make such a pet of him, if he were mine—We should never quarrel, should we, after we were used to each other? Don't you like him, Ellen?"

"Like him?" I exclaimed. "The worst tempered bit of a sickly slip that ever struggled into its teens! Happily, as Mr. Heathcliff conjectured, he'll not win twenty! I doubt whether he'll see spring indeed—and small loss to his family,

238 EMILY BRONTË

whenever he drops off; and lucky it is for us that his father took him—The kinder he was treated, the more tedious and selfish he'd be! I'm glad you have no chance of having him for a husband, Miss Catherine!"

My companion waxed serious at hearing this speech—To speak of his death so regardlessly wounded her feelings.

"He's younger than I," she answered, after a protracted pause of meditation, "and he ought to live the longest, he will—he must live as long as I do. He's as strong now as when he first came into the North, I'm positive of that! It's only a cold that ails him, the same as papa has—You say papa will get better, and why shouldn't he?"

"Well, well," I cried, "after all, we needn't trouble ourselves; for listen, Miss, and mind, I'll keep my word—If you attempt going to Wuthering Heights again, with, or without me, I shall inform Mr. Linton, and unless he allow it, the intimacy with your cousin must not be revived."

"It has been revived!" muttered Cathy sulkily.

"Must not be continued, then!" I said.

"We'll see!" was her reply, and she set off at a gallop, leaving me to toil in the rear.

We both reached home before our dinner-time: my master supposed we had been wandering through the park, and therefore, he demanded no explanation of our absence. As soon as I entered, I hastened to change my soaked shoes, and stockings; but sitting such a while at the Heights, had done the mischief. On the succeeding morning, I was laid up; and during three weeks I remained incapacitated for attending to my duties—a calamity never experienced prior to that period, and, never I am thankful to say since.

My little mistress behaved like an angel in coming to wait on me, and cheer my solitude: the confinement brought me exceedingly low—It is wearisome, to a stirring active body—but few have slighter reasons for complaint than I had. The moment Catherine left Mr. Linton's room, she appeared at my bed-side. Her day was divided between us; no amusement usurped a minute: she neglected her meals, her studies, and her play; and she was the fondest nurse that ever watched: she must have had a warm heart, when she loved her father so, to give so much to me!

I said her days were divided between us; but the master retired early, and I generally needed nothing after six o'clock, thus the evening was her own.

"Poor thing, I never considered what she did with herself after tea. And though frequently, when she looked in to bid me good night I remarked a fresh colour in her cheeks, and a pinkness over her slender fingers; instead of fancying the hue borrowed from a cold ride across the moors, I laid it to the charge of a hot fire in the library.

Chapter X.

At the close of three weeks, I was able to quit my chamber, and move about the house. And on the first occasion of my sitting up in the evening, I asked Catherine to read to me, because my eyes were weak. We were in the library, the master having gone to bed: she consented, rather unwillingly, I fancied; and imagining my sort of books did not suit her, I bid her please herself in the choice of what she perused.

She selected one of her own favourites, and got forward steadily about an hour; then came frequent questions.

"Ellen, are not you tired? Hadn't you better lie down now? You'll be sick, keeping up so long, Ellen."

"No, no, dear, I'm not tired," I returned, continually.

Perceiving me immovable, she essayed another method of showing her disrelish for her occupation. It changed to yawning, and stretching, and—

"Ellen, I'm tired."

"Give over then and talk," I answered.

That was worse; she fretted and sighed, and looked at her watch till eight; and finally went to her room, completely overdone with sleep, judging by her peevish, heavy look, and the constant rubbing she inflicted on her eyes.

The following night she seemed more impatient still; and on the third from recovering my company, she complained of a head-ache, and left me.

I thought her conduct odd; and having remained alone a long while, I resolved on going, and inquiring whether she were better, and asking her to come and lie on the sofa, instead of up stairs, in the dark.

No Catherine could I discover up stairs, and none below. The servants affirmed they had not seen her. I listened at Mr. Edgar's door—all was silence. I returned to her apartment, extinguished my candle, and seated myself in the window.

The moon shone bright; a sprinkling of snow covered the ground, and I reflected that she might, possibly, have taken it into her head to walk about the garden, for refreshment. I did detect a figure creeping along the inner fence of the park; but it was not my young mistress; on its emerging into the light, I recognised one of the grooms.

He stood a considerable period, viewing the carriage road through the grounds; then started off at a brisk pace, as if he had detected something, and reappeared, presently, leading Miss's pony; and there she was, just dismounted, and walking by its side.

240 EMILY BRONTË

The man took his charge stealthily across the grass towards the stable. Cathy entered by the casement-window of the drawing-room, and glided noiselessly up to where I awaited her.

She put the door gently to, slipped off her snowy shoes, untied her hat, and was proceeding, unconscious of my espionage, to lay aside her mantle, when I suddenly rose, and revealed myself. The surprise petrified her an instant: she uttered an inarticulate exclamation, and stood fixed.

"My dear Miss Catherine," I began, too vividly impressed by her recent kindness to break into a scold, "where have you been riding out at this hour? And why should you try to deceive me, by telling a tale. Where have you been? Speak!"

"To the bottom of the park," she stammered. "I didn't tell a tale."

"And no where else?" I demanded.

"No," was the muttered reply.

"Oh, Catherine," I cried, sorrowfully. "You know you have been doing wrong, or you wouldn't be driven to uttering an untruth to me. That does grieve me. I'd rather be three months ill, than hear you frame a deliberate lie."

She sprang forward, and bursting into tears, threw her arms round my neck.

"Well Ellen, I'm so afraid of you being angry," she said. "Promise not to be angry, and you shall know the very truth. I hate to hide it."

We sat down in the window-seat; I assured her I would not scold, whatever her secret might be, and I guessed it, of course, so she commenced—

"I've been to Wuthering Heights, Ellen, and I've never missed going a day since you fell ill; except thrice before, and twice after you left your room. I gave Michael books and pictures to prepare Minny every evening, and to put her back in the stable; you mustn't scold *him* either, mind. I was at the Heights by half-past six, and generally stayed till half-past eight, and then gallopped home. It was not to amuse myself that I went; I was often wretched all the time. Now and then, I was happy, once in a week perhaps. At first, I expected there would be sad work persuading you to let me keep my word to Linton, for I had engaged to call again next day, when we quitted him; but, as you stayed up stairs on the morrow, I escaped that trouble; and while Michael was refastening the lock of the park door in the afternoon, I got possession of the key, and told him how my cousin wished me to visit him, because he was sick, and couldn't come to the Grange: and how papa would object to my going. And then I negotiated with him about the pony. He is fond of reading, and he thinks of leaving soon to get married, so he offered, if I would lend him books out of the library, to do what I wished; but I preferred giving him my own, and that satisfied him better.

"On my second visit, Linton seemed in lively spirits; and Zillah, that is their housekeeper, made us a clean room, and a good fire, and told us that as Joseph was out at a prayer-meeting, and Hareton Earnshaw was off with his

WUTHERING HEIGHTS 241

dogs, robbing our woods of pheasants, as I heard afterwards, we might do what we liked.

"She brought me some warm wine and gingerbread; and appeared exceedingly good-natured; and Linton sat in the arm-chair, and I in the little rocking chair, on the hearthstone, and we laughed and talked so merrily, and found so much to say; we planned where we would go, and what we would do in summer. I needn't repeat that, because you would call it silly.

"One time, however, we were near quarrelling. He said the pleasantest manner of spending a hot July day was lying from morning till evening on a bank of heath in the middle of the moors, with the bees humming dreamily about among the bloom, and the larks singing high up over head, and the blue sky, and bright sun shining steadily and cloudlessly. That was his most perfect idea of heaven's happiness—mine was rocking in a rustling green tree, with a west wind blowing, and bright, white clouds flitting rapidly above; and not only larks, but throstles, and blackbirds, and linnets, and cuckoos pouring out music on every side, and the moors seen at a distance, broken into cool dusky dells; but close by great swells of long grass undulating in waves to the breeze; and woods and sounding water, and the whole world awake and wild with joy. He wanted all to lie in an ecstacy of peace; I wanted all to sparkle, and dance in a glorious jubilee.

"I said his heaven would be only half alive, and he said mine would be drunk; I said I should fall asleep in his, and he said he could not breathe in mine, and began to grow very snappish. At last, we agreed to try both as soon as the right weather came; and then we kissed each other and were friends. After sitting still an hour, I looked at the great room with its smooth, uncarpeted floor; and thought how nice it would be to play in, if we removed the table; and I asked Linton to call Zillah in to help us—and we'd have a game at blind-man's buff— she should try to catch us—you used to, you know, Ellen. He wouldn't; there was no pleasure in it, he said; but he consented to play at ball with me. We found two, in a cupboard, among a heap of old toys; tops, and hoops, and battledoors, and shuttlecocks. One was marked C., and the other H; I wished to have the C., because that stood for Catherine, and the H. might be for Heathcliff, his name; but the bran came out of H., and Linton didn't like it.

"I beat him constantly; and he got cross again, and coughed, and returned to his chair; that night, though, he easily recovered his good humour; he was charmed with two or three pretty songs—*your* songs, Ellen; and when I was obliged to go, he begged and entreated me to come the following evening, and I promised.

"Minny and I went flying home as light as air: and I dreamt of Wuthering Heights, and my sweet, darling cousin, till morning.

"On the morrow, I was sad; partly because you were poorly, and partly that I wished my father knew, and approved of my excursions: but it was beautiful moonlight after tea; and, as I rode on, the gloom cleared.

EMILY BRONTË

"I shall have another happy evening, I thought to myself, and what delights me more, my pretty Linton will.

"I trotted up their garden, and was turning round to the back, when that fellow Earnshaw met me, took my bridle, and bid me go in by the front entrance. He patted Minny's neck, and said she was a bonny beast, and appeared as if he wanted me to speak to him. I only told him to leave my horse alone, or else it would kick him.

"He answered in his vulgar accent.

"'It wouldn't do mitch hurt if it did;' and surveyed its legs with a smile.

"I was half inclined to make it try; however, he moved off to open the door, and, as he raised the latch, he looked up to the inscription above, and said, with a stupid mixture of awkwardness, and elation:

"'Miss Catherine! I can read yon, nah.'

"'Wonderful,' I exclaimed. 'Pray let us hear you—you *are* grown clever!'

"He spelt, and drawled over by syllables, the name—

"'Hareton Earnshaw.'

"'And the figures?' I cried, encouragingly, perceiving that he came to a dead halt.

"'I cannot tell them yet,' he answered.

"'Oh, you dunce!' I said, laughing heartily at his failure.

The fool stared, with a grin hovering about his lips, and a scowl gathering over his eyes, as if uncertain whether he might not join in my mirth; whether it were not pleasant familiarity, or what it really was, contempt.

I settled his doubts by suddenly retrieving my gravity, and desiring him to walk away, for I came to see Linton not him.

He reddened—I saw that by the moonlight—dropped his hand from the latch, and skulked off, a picture of mortified vanity. He imagined himself to be as accomplished as Linton, I suppose, because he could spell his own name; and was marvellously discomfited that I didn't think the same.

"Stop Miss Catherine, dear!" I interrupted. "I shall not scold, but I don't like your conduct there. If you had remembered that Hareton was your cousin, as much as Master Heathcliff, you would have felt how improper it was to behave in that way. At least, it was praiseworthy ambition, for him to desire to be as accomplished as Linton: and probably he did not learn merely to show off; you had made him ashamed of his ignorance, before: I have no doubt; and he wished to remedy it and please you. To sneer at his imperfect attempt was very bad breeding—had *you* been brought up in his circumstances, would you be less rude? he was as quick and as intelligent a child as ever you were, and I'm hurt that he should be despised now, because that base Heathcliff has treated him so unjustly."

"Well, Ellen, you won't cry about it, will you?" she exclaimed, surprised at my earnestness. "But wait, and you shall hear if he conned his a b c, to please me; and if it were worth while being civil to the brute." I entered, Linton was lying on the settle and half got up to welcome me.

WUTHERING HEIGHTS   243

"I'm ill to-night Catherine, love;" he said, "and you must have all the talk, and let me listen. Come, and sit by me—I was sure you wouldn't break your word, and I'll make you promise again, before you go."

"I knew now that I mustn't tease him, as he was ill; and I spoke softly and put no questions, and avoided irritating him in any way. I had brought some of my nicest books for him; he asked me to read a little of one, and I was about to comply, when Earnshaw burst the door open, having gathered venom with reflection. He advanced direct to us; seized Linton by the arm, and swung him off the seat.

"Get to thy own room!" he said in a voice almost inarticulate with passion, and his face looked swelled and furious. "Take her there if she comes to see thee—thou shalln't keep me out of this. Begone, wi' ye both!"

He swore at us, and left Linton no time to answer, nearly throwing him into the kitchen; and he clenched his fist, as I followed, seemingly longing to knock me down. I was afraid, for a moment, and I let one volume fall; he kicked it after me, and shut us out.

I heard a malignant, crackly laugh by the fire, and turning beheld that odious Joseph, standing rubbing his bony hands, and quivering.

"Aw wer sure he'd sarve ye eht! He's a grand lad! He's getten t'raight sperrit in him! *He* knaws—Aye, he knaws, as weel as Aw do, who sud be t'maister yonder—Ech, ech, ech! He mad ye skift properly! Ech, ech, ech!"

"Where must we go?" I said to my cousin, disregarding the old wretch's mockery.

"Linton was white and trembling. He was not pretty then—Ellen, Oh! no, he looked frightful! for his thin face, and large eyes were wrought into an expression of frantic, powerless fury. He grasped the handle of the door, and shook it—it was fastened inside.

"If you don't let me in I'll kill you; If you don't let me in I'll kill you!" he rather shrieked than said. "Devil! devil! I'll kill you, I'll kill you!"

"Joseph uttered his croaking laugh again.

"'Thear that's t'father!" he cried. 'That's father! We've allas summut uh orther side in us—Niver heed Hareton, lad—dunnut be 'feard—he cannot get at thee!'

"I took hold of Linton's hands, and tried to pull him away; but he shrieked so shockingly that I dared not proceed. At last, his cries were choked by a dreadful fit of coughing; blood gushed from his mouth, and he fell on the ground.

"I ran into the yard, sick with terror; and called for Zillah, as loud as I could. She soon heard me; she was milking the cows in a shed behind the barn; and hurrying from her work, she inquired what there was to do?

"I hadn't breath to explain; dragging her in, I looked about for Linton, Earnshaw had come out to examine the mischief he had caused, and he was then conveying the poor thing up-stairs. Zillah and I ascended after him; but, he stopped me, at the top of the steps, and said, I shouldn't go in, I must go home.

EMILY BRONTË

"I exclaimed that he had killed Linton and I *would* enter.

"Joseph locked the door, and declared I should do 'no sich stuff,' and asked me whether I were 'bahn to be as mad as him.'

"I stood crying, till the housekeeper re-appeared; she affirmed he would be better in a bit; but he couldn't do with that shrieking, and din, and she took me, and nearly carried me into the house.

"Ellen, I was ready to tear my hair off my head! I sobbed and wept so that my eyes were almost blind: and the ruffian you have such sympathy with, stood opposite; presuming every now and then, to bid me "wisht," and denying that it was his fault; and finally, frightened by my assertions that I would tell papa, and that he should be put in prison, and hanged, he commenced blubbering himself, and hurried out to hide his cowardly agitation.

"Still, I was not rid of him: when at length they compelled me to depart, and I had got some hundred yards off the premises, he suddenly issued from the shadow of the road-side, and checked Minny and took hold of me.

"'Miss Catherine, I'm ill grieved,' he began, 'but it's rayther too bad—'

"I gave him a cut with my whip, thinking, perhaps he would murder me— He let go, thundering one of his horrid curses, and I gallopped home more than half out of my senses.

"I didn't bid you good-night, that evening; and I didn't go to Wuthering Heights, the next—I wished to, exceedingly; but I was strangely excited, and dreaded to hear that Linton was dead, sometimes; and sometimes shuddered at the thought of encountering Hareton.

"On the third day I took courage; at least, I couldn't bear longer suspense and stole off, once more. I went at five o'clock, and walked, fancying I might manage to creep into the house, and up to Linton's room, unobserved. However, the dogs gave notice of my approach: Zillah received me, and saying "the lad was mending nicely," showed me into a small, tidy, carpeted apartment, where, to my inexpressible joy, I beheld Linton laid on a little sofa, reading one of my books. But he would neither speak to me, nor look at me, through a whole hour, Ellen—He has such an unhappy temper—and what quite confounded me, when he did open his mouth it was to utter the falsehood, that I had occasioned the uproar, and Hareton was not to blame!"

"Unable to reply, except passionately, I got up, and walked from the room. He sent after me a faint "Catherine!" he did not reckon on being answered so—but I wouldn't turn back; and the morrow was the second day on which I stayed at home, nearly determined to visit him no more.

"But it was so miserable going to bed, and getting up, and never hearing anything about him, that my resolution melted into air, before it was properly formed. It *had* appeared wrong to take the journey once; now it seemed wrong to refrain. Michael came to ask if he must saddle Minny; I said "Yes," and considered myself doing a duty as she bore me over the hills.

WUTHERING HEIGHTS

245

"I was forced to pass the front windows to get to the court; it was no use trying to conceal my presence.

"'Young master is in the house,' said Zillah as she saw me making for the parlour.

"I went in, Earnshaw was there also, but he quitted the room directly. Linton sat in the great arm chair half asleep; walking up to the fire, I began in a serious tone, partly meaning it to be true.

"As you don't like me Linton, and as you think I come on purpose to hurt you, and pretend that I do so every time, this is our last meeting—let us say good bye; and tell Mr. Heathcliff that you have no wish to see me, and that he mustn't invent any more falsehoods on the subject.

"'Sit down and take your hat off, Catherine,' he answered. 'You are so much happier than I am, you ought to be better. Papa talks enough of my defects, and shows enough scorn of me, to make it natural I should doubt myself—I doubt whether I am not altogether as worthless as he calls me, frequently; and then I feel so cross and bitter, I hate everybody! I *am* worthless, and bad in temper, and bad in spirit, almost always—and if you choose, you *may* say good-bye—you'll get rid of an annoyance—Only, Catherine, do me this justice; believe that if I might be as sweet, and as kind, and as good as you are, I would be, as willingly, and more so, than as happy and as healthy. And, believe that your kindness has made me love you deeper than if I deserved your love, and though I couldn't, and cannot help showing my nature to you, I regret it, and repent it, and shall regret, and repent it, till I die!'

"I felt he spoke the truth; and I felt I must forgive him; and, though he should quarrel the next moment, I must forgive him again. We were reconciled, but we cried, both of us, the whole time I stayed. Not entirely for sorrow, yet I *was* sorry Linton had that distorted nature. He'll never let his friends be at ease, and he'll never be at ease himself!

"I have always gone to his little parlour, since that night; because his father returned the day after. About three times, I think, we have been merry, and hopeful, as we were the first evening; the rest of my visits were dreary and troubled—now, with his selfishness and spite; and now with his sufferings: but I've learnt to endure the former with nearly as little resentment as the latter.

"Mr. Heathcliff purposely avoids me. I have hardly seen him at all. Last Sunday, indeed, coming earlier than usual, I heard him abusing poor Linton, cruelly, for his conduct of the night before. I can't tell how he knew of it, unless he listened. Linton had certainly behaved provokingly; however, it was the business of nobody but me; and I interrupted Mr. Heathcliff's lecture, by entering, and telling him so. He burst into a laugh, and went away, saying he was glad I took that view of the matter. Since then, I've told Linton he must whisper his bitter things.

"Now, Ellen, you have heard all; and I can't be prevented from going to Wuthering Heights, except by inflicting misery on two people—whereas, if

246 EMILY BRONTË

you'll only not tell papa, my going need disturb the tranquillity of none. You'll not tell, will you? It will be very heartless if you do."

"I'll make up my mind on that point by to-morrow. Miss Catherine," I replied. "It requires some study: and so I'll leave you to your rest, and go think it over."

I thought it over aloud, in my master's presence; walking straight from her room to his, and relating the whole story, with the exception of her conversations with her cousin, and any mention of Hareton.

Mr. Linton was alarmed and distressed more than he would acknowledge to me. In the morning, Catherine learnt my betrayal of her confidence, and she learnt also that her secret visits were to end.

In vain she wept and writhed against the interdict; and implored her father to have pity on Linton; all she got to comfort her was a promise that he would write, and give him leave to come to the Grange when he he pleased; but explaining that he must no longer expect to see Catherine at Wuthering Heights. Perhaps, had he been aware of his nephew's disposition and state of health, he would have seen fit to withhold even that slight consolation.

Chapter XI.

"These things happened last winter, sir," said Mrs. Dean; "hardly more than a year ago. Last winter, I did not think, at another twelve months' end, I should be amusing a stranger to the family with relating them! Yet, who knows how long you'll be a stranger? You're too young to rest always contented, living by yourself; and I some way fancy, no one could see Catherine Linton, and not love her. You smile; but why do you look so lively and interested, when I talk about her—and why have you asked me to hang her picture over your fireplace? and why—"

"Stop, my good friend!" I cried. "It may be very possible that *I* should love her; but would she love me? I doubt it too much to venture my tranquillity, by running into temptation; and then my home is not here. I'm of the busy world, and to its arms I must return. Go on. Was Catherine obedient to her father's commands?"

"She was," continued the housekeeper. "Her affection for him was still the chief sentiment in her heart; and he spoke without anger; he spoke in the deep tenderness of one about to leave his treasure amid perils and foes, where his remembered words would be the only aid that he could bequeath to guide her.

He said to me, a few days afterwards,

"I wish my nephew would write, Ellen, or call. Tell me, sincerely, what you think of him—is he changed for the better, or is there a prospect of improvement, as he grows a man?"

"He's very delicate, sir," I replied; "and scarcely likely to reach manhood; but this I can say, he does not resemble his father; and if Miss Catherine had the misfortune to marry him, he would not be beyond her control, unless she were extremely and foolishly indulgent. However, master, you'll have plenty of time to get acquainted with him, and see whether he would suit her—it wants four years and more to his being of age."

Edgar sighed; and, walking to the window, looked out towards Gimmerton Kirk. It was a misty afternoon, but the February sun shone dimly, and we could just distinguish the two fir trees in the yard, and the sparely scattered gravestones.

"I've prayed often," he half soliloquized, "for the approach of what is coming; and now I begin to shrink, and fear it. I thought the memory of the hour I came down that glen a bridegroom, would be less sweet than the anticipation that I was soon, in a few months, or, possibly, weeks, to be carried up, and laid in its lonely hollow! Ellen, I've been very happy with my little Cathy. Through winter nights and summer days she was a living hope at my

248 EMILY BRONTË

side—but I've been as happy musing by myself among those stones, under that old church—lying, through the long June evenings, on the green mound of her mother's grave, and wishing, yearning for the time when I might lie beneath it. What can I do for Cathy? How must I quit her? I'd not care one moment for Linton being Heathcliff's son; nor for his taking her from me, if he could console her for my loss. I'd not care that Heathcliff gained his ends, and triumphed in robbing me of my last blessing! But should Linton be unworthy—only a feeble tool to his father—I cannot abandon her to him! And, hard though it be to crush her buoyant spirit, I must persevere in making her sad while I live, and leaving her solitary when I die. Darling! I'd rather resign her to God, and lay her in the earth before me."

"Resign her to God, as it is, sir," I answered, "and if we should lose you—which may He forbid—under His providence, I'll stand her friend and counsellor to the last. Miss Catherine is a good girl; I don't fear that she will go wilfully wrong; and people who do their duty are always finally rewarded."

Spring advanced; yet my master gathered no real strength, though he resumed his walks in the grounds, with his daughter. To her inexperienced notions, this itself was a sign of convalescence; and then his cheek was often flushed, and his eyes were bright, she felt sure of his recovering.

On her seventeenth birthday, he did not visit the churchyard, it was raining, and I observed—

"You'll surely not go out to-night, sir?"

He answered—

"No, I'll defer it, this year, a little longer."

He wrote again to Linton, expressing his great desire to see him; and, had the invalid been presentable, I've no doubt his father would have permitted him to come. As it was, being instructed, he returned an answer, intimating that Mr. Heathcliff objected to his calling at the Grange; but his uncle's kind remembrance delighted him, and he hoped to meet him, sometimes, in his rambles, and personally to petition that his cousin and he might not remain long so utterly divided.

That part of his letter was simple, and, probably his own. Heathcliff knew he could plead eloquently enough for Catherine's company, then—

"I do not ask," he said, "that she may visit here; but, am I never to see her, because my father forbids me to go to her home, and you forbid her to come to mine? Do, now and then, ride with her towards the Heights; and let us exchange a few words, in your presence! we have done nothing to deserve this separation; and you are not angry with me—you have no reason to dislike me—you allow yourself. Dear uncle! send me a kind note to-morrow; and leave to join you anywhere you please, except at Thrushcross Grange. I believe an interview would convince you that my father's character is not mine; he affirms I am more your nephew than his son; and though I have faults which render me unworthy of Catherine, she has excused them, and, for her sake,

WUTHERING HEIGHTS 249

you should also. You inquire after my health—it is better; but while I remain cut off from all hope, and doomed to solitude, or the society of those who never did, and never will like me, how can I be cheerful and well?"

Edgar, though he felt for the boy, could not consent to grant his request; because he could not accompany Catherine.

He said, in summer, perhaps, they might meet: meantime, he wished him to continue writing at intervals, and engaged to give him what advice and comfort he was able by letter; being well aware of his hard position in his family.

Linton complied; and had he been unrestrained, would probably have spoiled all by filling his epistles with complaints and lamentations; but his father kept a sharp watch over him; and, of course, insisted on every line that my master sent being shown; so, instead of penning his peculiar personal sufferings, and distresses, the themes constantly uppermost in his thoughts, he harped on the cruel obligation of being held asunder from his friend and love; and gently intimated that Mr. Linton must allow an interview soon, or he should fear he was purposely deceiving him with empty promises.

Cathy was a powerful ally at home: and, between them, they, at length, persuaded my master to acquiesce in their having a ride or a walk together, about once a week, under my guardianship, and on the moors nearest the Grange; for June found him still declining; and, though he had set aside, yearly, a portion of his income for my young lady's fortune, he had a natural desire that she might retain, or, at least, return, in a short time, to the house of her ancestors; and he considered her only prospect of doing that was by a union with his heir; he had no idea that the latter was failing almost as fast as himself; nor had any one, I believe; no doctor visited the Heights, and no one saw Master Heathcliff to make report of his condition, among us.

I, for my part, began to fancy my forebodings were false, and that he must be actually rallying, when he mentioned riding and walking on the moors, and seemed so earnest in pursuing his object.

I could not picture a father treating a dying child as tyrannically and wickedly as I afterwards learnt Heathcliff had treated him, to compel this apparent eagerness; his efforts redoubling the more imminently his avaricious and unfeeling plans were threatened with defeat by death.

Chapter XII.

Summer was already past its prime, when Edgar reluctantly yielded his assent to their entreaties, and Catherine and I set out on our first ride to join her cousin.

"It was a close, sultry day; devoid of sunshine, but with a sky too dappled and hazy to threaten rain; and our place of meeting had been fixed at the guide-stone, by the cross-roads. On arriving there, however, a little herd-boy, despatched as a messenger, told us that—

"Maister Linton wer just ut this side th' Heights: and he'd be mitch obleeged to us to gang on a bit further."

"Then Master Linton has forgot the first injunction of his uncle," I observed: "he bid us keep on the Grange land, and here we are, off at once."

"Well, we'll turn our horses' heads round, when we reach him," answered my companion, "our excursion shall lie towards home."

But when we reached him, and that was scarcely a quarter of a mile from his own door, we found he had no horse, and we were forced to dismount, and leave ours to graze.

He lay on the heath, awaiting our approach, and did not rise till we came within a few yards. Then, he walked so feebly, and looked so pale, that I immediately exclaimed—

"Why, Master Heathcliff, you are not fit for enjoying a ramble, this morning. How ill you do look!"

Catherine surveyed him with grief and astonishment; and changed the ejaculation of joy on her lips, to one of alarm; and the congratulation on their long postponed meeting, to an anxious inquiry, whether he were worse than usual?

"No—better—better!" he panted, trembling, and retaining her hand as if he needed its support, while his large blue eyes wandered timidly over her; the hollowness round them, transforming to haggard wildness, the languid expression they once possessed.

"But you have been worse," persisted his cousin, "worse than when I saw you last—you are thinner, and—"

"I'm tired," he interrupted, hurriedly. "It is too hot for walking, let us rest here. And, in the morning, I often feel sick—papa says I grow so fast."

Badly satisfied, Cathy sat down, and he reclined beside her.

"This is something like your paradise," said she, making an effort at cheerfulness. "You recollect the two days we agreed to spend, in the place and way, each thought pleasantest? This is nearly yours, only there are clouds; but

WUTHERING HEIGHTS

then, they are so soft and mellow, it is nicer than sunshine. Next week, if you can, we'll ride down to the Grange Park, and try mine."

Linton did not appear to remember what she talked of; and he had evidently great difficulty in sustaining any kind of conversation. His lack of interest in the subjects she started, and his equal incapacity to contribute to her entertainment were so obvious, that she could not conceal her disappointment. An indefinite alteration had come over his whole person and manner. The pettishness that might be caressed into fondness, had yielded to a listless apathy; there was less of the peevish temper of a child which frets and teases on purpose to be soothed, and more of the self-absorbed moroseness of a confirmed invalid, repelling consolation, and ready to regard the good-humoured mirth of others, as an insult.

Catherine perceived, as well as I did, that he held it rather a punishment, than a gratification, to endure our company; and she made no scruple of proposing, presently, to depart.

That proposal, unexpectedly, roused Linton from his lethargy, and threw him into a strange state of agitation. He glanced fearfully towards the Heights, begging she would remain another half-hour, at least.

"But, I think," said Cathy, "you'd be more comfortable at home than sitting here; and I cannot amuse you to-day, I see, by my tales, and songs, and chatter; you have grown wiser than I, in these six months; you have little taste for my diversions now; or else, if I could amuse you, I'd willingly stay."

"Stay to rest yourself," he replied. "And, Catherine, don't think, or say that I'm *very* unwell—it is the heavy weather, and heat that make me dull; and I walked about, before you came, a great deal, for me. Tell uncle, I'm in tolerable health, will you?"

"I'll tell him that *you* say so, Linton. I couldn't affirm that you are," observed my young lady, wondering at his pertinacious assertion of what was evidently an untruth.

"And be here again next Thursday," continued he, shunning her puzzled gaze. "And give him my thanks for permitting you to come—my best thanks, Catherine. And—and, if you *did* meet my father, and he asked you about me, don't lead him to suppose that I've been extremely silent and stupid—don't look sad and downcast, as you *are* doing—he'll be angry."

"I care nothing for his anger," exclaimed Cathy, imagining she would be its object.

"But I do," said her cousin, shuddering.

"*Don't* provoke him against me, Catherine, for he is very hard."

"Is he severe to you, Master Heathcliff?" I inquired. "Has he grown weary of indulgence, and passed from passive, to active hatred?"

Linton looked at me, but did not answer; and, after keeping her seat by his side, another ten minutes, during which his head fell drowsily on his breast, and he uttered nothing except suppressed moans of exhaustion, or pain,

252 EMILY BRONTË

Cathy began to seek solace in looking for bilberries, and sharing the produce of her researches with me: she did not offer them to him, for she saw further notice would only weary and annoy.

"Is it half an hour now, Ellen!" she whispered in my ear, at last. "I can't tell why we should stay. He's asleep, and papa will be wanting us back."

"Well, we must not leave him asleep," I answered; "wait till he wakes and be patient. You were mighty eager to set off, but your longing to see poor Linton has soon evaporated!"

"Why did *he* wish to see me?" returned Catherine. "In his crossest humours, formerly, I liked him better than I do in his present curious mood. It's just as if it were a task he was compelled to perform—this interview—for fear his father should scold him. But, I'm hardly going to come to give Mr. Heathcliff pleasure; whatever reason he may have for ordering Linton to undergo this penance. And, though I'm glad he's better in health, I'm sorry he's so much less pleasant, and so much less affectionate to me."

"You think *he* is better in health, then?" I said.

"Yes," she answered; "because he always made such a great deal of his sufferings, you know. He is not tolerably well, as he told me to tell papa, but he's better, very likely."

"There you differ with me, Miss Cathy," I remarked; "I should conjecture him to be far worse."

Linton here started from his slumber in bewildered terror, and asked if any one had called his name.

"No," said Catherine; "unless in dreams. I cannot conceive how you manage to dose, out of doors, in the morning."

"I thought I heard my father," he gasped, glancing up to the frowning nab above us. "You are sure nobody spoke?"

"Quite sure," replied his cousin. "Only Ellen and I were disputing concerning your health. Are you truly stronger, Linton, than when we separated in winter? If you be, I'm certain one thing is not stronger—your regard for me—speak, are you?"

The tears gushed from Linton's eyes as he answered—

"Yes, yes, I am!"

And, still under the spell of the imaginary voice, his gaze wandered up and down to detect its owner.

Cathy rose.

"For to-day we must part," she said. "And I won't conceal that I have been sadly disappointed with our meeting, though I'll mention it to nobody but you—not that I stand in awe of Mr. Heathcliff!"

"Hush," murmured Linton; "for God's sake, hush! He's coming." And he clung to Catherine's arm, striving to detain her; but, at that announcement, she hastily disengaged herself, and whistled to Minny, who obeyed her like a dog.

WUTHERING HEIGHTS 253

"I'll be here next Thursday," she cried, springing to the saddle. "Good bye. Quick, Ellen!"

And so we left him, scarcely conscious of our departure, so absorbed was he in anticipating his father's approach.

"Before we reached home, Catherine's displeasure softened into a perplexed sensation of pity and regret largely blended with vague, uneasy doubts about Linton's actual circumstances, physical and social; in which I partook, though I counselled her not to say much, for a second journey would make us better judges.

My master requested an account of our on-goings: his nephew's offering of thanks was duly delivered, Miss Cathy gently touching on the rest: I also, threw little light on his inquiries, for I hardly knew what to hide, and what to reveal.

Chapter XIII.

Seven days glided away, every one marking its course by the henceforth rapid alteration of Edgar Linton's state. The havoc that months had previously wrought, was now emulated by the inroads of hours.

Catherine, we would fain have deluded, yet, but her own quick spirit refused to delude her. It divined, in secret, and brooded on the dreadful probability, gradually ripening into certainty.

She had not the heart to mention her ride, when Thursday came round; I mentioned it for her; and obtained permission to order her out of doors; for the library, where her father stopped a short time daily—the brief period he could bear to sit up, and his chamber had become her whole world. She grudged each moment that did not find her bending over his pillow, or seated by his side. Her countenance grew wan with watching and sorrow, and my master gladly dismissed her to what he flattered himself would be a happy change of scene and society, drawing comfort from the hope that she would not now be left entirely alone after his death.

He had a fixed idea, I guessed by several observations he let fall, that as his nephew resembled him in person, he would resemble him in mind; for Linton's letters bore few, or no indications of his defective character. And I through pardonable weakness refrained from correcting the error; asking myself what good there would be in disturbing his last moments with information that he had neither power nor opportunity to turn to account.

We deferred our excursion till the afternoon; a golden afternoon of August—every breath from the hills so full of life, that it seemed whoever respired it, though dying, might revive.

Catherine's face was just like the landscape—shadows and sunshine flitting over it, in rapid succession; but the shadows rested longer and the sunshine was more transient, and her poor little heart reproached itself for even that passing forgetfulness of its cares.

We discerned Linton watching at the same spot he had selected before. My young mistress alighted, and told me that as she was resolved to stay a very little while, I had better hold the pony and remain on horseback; but I dissented, I wouldn't risk losing sight of the charge committed to me a minute; so we climbed the slope of heath, together.

Master Heathcliff received us with greater animation on this occasion; not the animation of high spirits though, nor yet of joy; it looked more like fear.

"It is late!" he said, speaking short, and with difficulty. "Is not your father very ill? I thought you wouldn't come."

WUTHERING HEIGHTS   255

"*Why* won't you be candid?" cried Catherine, swallowing her greeting. "Why cannot you say at once, you don't want me? It is strange Linton, that for the second time, you have brought me here on purpose, apparently, to distress us both, and for no reason besides!"

Linton shivered, and glanced at her, half supplicating, half ashamed, but his cousin's patience was not sufficient to endure this enigmatical behaviour.

"My father *is* very ill," she said, "and why am I called from his bedside— why didn't you send to absolve me from my promise, when you wished I wouldn't keep it? Come! I desire an explanation—playing and trifling are completely banished out of my mind: and I can't dance attendance on your affectations now!'

"My affections!" he murmured, "what are they? For Heaven's sake Catherine, don't look so angry! Despise me as much as you please; I am a worthless, cowardly wretch—I can't be scorned enough! but I'm too mean for your anger—hate my father, and spare me, for contempt!"

"Nonsense!" cried Catherine in a passion. "Foolish, silly boy! And there! he trembles, as if I were really going to touch him! You needn't bespeak contempt, Linton; anybody will have it spontaneously, at your service. Get off! I shall return home—it is folly dragging you from the hearth-stone, and pretending—what do we pretend? Let go my frock—if I pitied you for crying, and looking so very frightened, you should spurn such pity. Ellen, tell him how disgraceful this conduct is. Rise, and don't degrade yourself into an abject reptile—*don't*."

With streaming face and an expression of agony, Linton had thrown his nerveless frame along the ground; he seemed convulsed with exquisite terror.

"Oh!" he sobbed, "I cannot bear it! Catherine, Catherine, I'm a traitor too, and I dare not tell you! But leave me and I shall be killed! *Dear* Catherine, my life is in your hands; and you have said you loved me—and if you did, it wouldn't harm you. You'll not go, then? kind, sweet, good Catherine! And perhaps you *will* consent—and he'll let me die with you!"

My young lady, on witnessing his intense anguish, stooped to raise him. The old feeling of indulgent tenderness overcame her vexation, and she grew thoroughly moved and alarmed.

"Consent to what?" she asked. "To stay? Tell me the meaning of this strange talk, and I will. You contradict your own words, and distract me! Be calm and frank, and confess at once, all that weighs on your heart. You wouldn't injure me, Linton, would you? You wouldn't let any enemy hurt me, if you could prevent it? I'll believe you are a coward, for yourself, but not a cowardly betrayer of your best friend."

"But my father threatened me," gasped the boy, clasping his attenuated fingers, "and I dread him—I dread him! I *dare* not tell!"

"Oh well!" said Catherine, with scornful compassion, "keep your secret, *I'm* no coward—save yourself, I'm not afraid!"

256 EMILY BRONTË

Her magnanimity provoked his tears; he wept wildly, kissing her supporting hands, and yet could not summon courage to speak out.

I was cogitating what the mystery might be, and determined Catherine should never suffer to benefit him or any one else, by my good will. When hearing a rustle among the ling, I looked up, and saw Mr. Heathcliff almost close upon us, descending the Heights. He didn't cast a glance towards my companions, though they were sufficiently near for Linton's sobs to be audible; but hailing me in the almost hearty tone he assumed to none besides, and the sincerity of which, I couldn't avoid doubting, he said.

"It is something to see you so near to my house, Nelly! How are you at the Grange? Let us hear! The rumour goes," he added in a lower tone, "that Edgar Linton is on his death-bed—perhaps they exaggerate his illness?"

"No; my master is dying," I replied, "it is true enough. A sad thing it will be for us all, but a blessing for him!"

"How long will he last, do you think?" he asked.

"I don't know," I said.

"Because," he continued, looking at the two young people, who were fixed under his eye—Linton appeared as if he could not venture to stir, or raise his head, and Catherine could not move, on his account—"Because that lad yonder, seems determined to beat me—and I'd thank his uncle to be quick, and go before him—Hallo! Has the whelp been playing that game long? I *did* give him some lessons about snivelling. Is he pretty lively with Miss Linton generally?"

"Lively? no—he has shown the greatest distress;" I answered. "To see him, I should say, that instead of rambling with his sweetheart on the hills, he ought to be in bed, under the hands of a doctor."

"He shall be, in a day or two," muttered Heathcliff. "But first—get up, Linton! Get up!" he shouted. "Don't grovel on the ground, there—up this moment!"

Linton had sunk prostrate again in another paroxysm of helpless fear, caused by his father's glance towards him, I suppose, there was nothing else to produce such humiliation. He made several efforts to obey, but his little strength was annihilated, for the time, and be fell back again with a moan.

Mr. Heathcliff advanced, and lifted him to lean against a ridge of turf.

"Now," said he with curbed ferocity, "I'm getting angry—and if you don't command that paltry spirit of yours—*Damn* you! Get up, directly!"

"I will, father!" he panted. "Only, let me alone, or I shall faint! I've done as you wished—I'm sure. Catherine will tell you that I—that I—have been cheerful. Ah! keep by me Catherine; give me your hand."

"Take mine," said his father, "stand on your feet! There now—she'll lend you her arm . . . that's right, look at *her*. You would imagine I was the devil himself, Miss Linton, to excite such horror. Be so kind as to walk home with him, will you? He shudders, if I touch him."

"Linton, dear!" whispered Catherine, "I can't go to Wuthering Heights . . . papa has forbidden me . . . He'll not harm you, why are you so afraid?"

"I can never re-enter that house," he answered. "I am *not* to re-enter it without you!"

"Stop . . ." cried his father. "We'll respect Catherine's filial scruples. Nelly, take him in, and I'll follow your advice concerning the doctor, without delay."

"You'll do well," replied I, "but I must remain with my mistress. To mind your son is not my business."

"You are very stiff!" said Heathcliff, "I know that—but you'll force me to pinch the baby, and make it scream, before it moves your charity. Come then, my hero. Are you willing to return, escorted by me?"

He approached once more, and made as if he would seize the fragile being; but shrinking back, Linton clung to his cousin, and implored her to accompany him with a frantic importunity that admitted no denial.

However I disapproved, I couldn't hinder her; indeed how could she have refused him herself? What was filling him with dread, we had no means of discerning, but there he was, powerless under its gripe, and any addition seemed capable of shocking him into idiocy.

We reached the threshold; Catherine walked in; and I stood waiting till she had conducted the invalid to a chair, expecting her out, immediately; when Mr. Heathcliff pushing me forward, exclaimed—

"My house is not stricken with the plague, Nelly; and I have a mind to be hospitable today; sit down, and allow me to shut the door."

He shut and locked it also, I started.

"You shall have tea, before you go home," he added. "I am by myself. Hareton is gone with some cattle to the Lees—and Zillah and Joseph are off on a journey of pleasure. And, though I'm used to being alone, I'd rather have some interesting company, if I can get it. Miss Linton, take your seat by *him*. I give you what I have; the present is hardly worth accepting; but, I have nothing else to offer. It is Linton, I mean. How she does stare! It's odd what a savage feeling I have to anything that seems afraid of me! Had I been born where laws are less strict, and tastes less dainty, I should treat myself to a slow vivifisection of those two, as an evening's amusement."

He drew in his breath, struck the table, and swore to himself.

"By hell! I hate them."

"I'm not afraid of you!" exclaimed Catherine, who could not hear the latter part of his speech.

She stepped close up; her black eyes flashing with passion and resolution.

"Give me that key—I will have it!" she said "I would'nt eat or drink here, if I were starving."

Heathcliff had the key in his hand that remained on the table. He looked up, seized with a sort of surprise at her boldness, or, possibly, reminded by her voice and glance, of the person from whom she inherited it.

258 EMILY BRONTË

She snatched at the instrument, and half succeeded in getting it out of his loosened lingers; but her action recalled him to the present; he recovered it speedily.

"Now, Catherine Linton," he said, "stand off, or I shall knock you down; and that will make Mrs. Dean mad."

Regardless of this warning, she captured his closed hand, and its contents again.

"We *will* go!" she repeated, exerting her utmost efforts to cause the iron muscles to relax; and finding that her nails made no impression, she applied her teeth pretty sharply.

Heathcliff glanced at me a glance that kept me from interfering a moment. Catherine was too intent on his fingers to notice his face. He opened them, suddenly, and resigned the object of dispute; but, ere she had well secured it, he seized her with the liberated hand, and, pulling her on his knee, administered, with the other, a shower of terrific slaps on both sides of the head, each sufficient to have fulfilled his threat, had she been able to fall.

At this diabolical violence, I rushed on him furiously.

"You villain!" I began to cry, "you villain!"

A touch on the chest silenced me; I am stout, and soon put out of breath; and, what with that and the rage, I staggered dizzily back, and felt ready to suffocate, or to burst a blood-vessel.

The scene was over in two minutes; Catherine, released, put her two hands to her temples, and looked just as if she were not sure whether her ears were off or on. She trembled like a reed, poor thing, and leant against the table perfectly bewildered.

"I know how to chastise children, you see," said the scoundrel, grimly, as he stooped to repossess himself of the key, which had dropped to the floor. "Go to Linton now, as I told you; and cry at your ease! I shall be your father to-morrow—all the father you'll have in a few days—and you shall have plenty of that—you can bear plenty—you're no weakling—you shall have a daily taste, if I catch such a devil of a temper in your eyes again!"

Cathy ran to me instead of Linton, and knelt down, and put her burning cheek on my lap, weeping aloud. Her cousin had shrunk into a corner of the settle, as quiet as a mouse, congratulating himself, I dare say, that the correction had lighted on another than him.

Mr. Heathcliff, perceiving us all confounded, rose, and expeditiously made the tea himself. The cups and saucers were laid ready. He poured it out, and handed me a cup.

"Wash away your spleen," he said. "And help your own naughty pet and mine. It is not poisoned, though I prepared it. I'm going out to seek your horses."

Our first thought, on his departure, was to force an exit somewhere. We tried the kitchen door, but that was fastened outside; we looked at the windows—they were too narrow for even Cathy's little figure.

WUTHERING HEIGHTS   259

"Master Linton," I cried, seeing we were regularly imprisoned. "You know what your diabolical father is after, and you shall tell us, or I'll box your ears, as he has done your cousin's."

"Yes, Linton; you must tell," said Catherine. "It was for your sake I came; and it will be wickedly ungrateful if you refuse."

"Give me some tea, I'm thirsty, and then I'll tell you," he answered. "Mrs. Dean, go away. I don't like you standing over me. Now, Catherine, you are letting your tears fall into my cup! I wont drink that. Give me another."

Catherine pushed another to him, and wiped her face. I felt disgusted at the little wretch's composure, since he was no longer in terror for himself. The anguish he had exhibited on the moor subsided as soon as ever he entered Wuthering Heights; so, I guessed he had been menaced with an awful visitation of wrath, if he failed in decoying us there; and, that accomplished, he had no further immediate fears.

"Papa wants us to be married," he continued, after sipping some of the liquid. "And he knows your papa wouldn't let us marry now; and he's afraid of my dying, if we wait; so we are to be married in the morning, and you are to stay here all night; and, if you do as he wishes, you shall return home next day, and take me with you."

"Take you with her, pitiful changeling?" I exclaimed. "*You* marry? Why, the man is mad, or he thinks us fools, every one. And, do you imagine that beautiful young lady, that healthy, hearty girl, will tie herself to a little perishing monkey like you? Are you cherishing the notion that *anybody*, let alone Miss Catherine Linton, would have you for a husband? You want whipping for bringing us in here at all, with your dastardly, puling tricks; and—don't look so silly now! I've a very good mind to shake you severely, for your contemptible treachery, and your imbecile conceit."

I did give him a slight shaking, but it brought on the cough, and he took to his ordinary resource of moaning and weeping, and Catherine rebuked me.

"Stay all night? No!" she said, looking slowly round. "Ellen, I'll burn that door down, but I'll get out."

And she would have commenced the execution of her threat directly, but Linton was up in alarm, for his dear self, again. He clasped her in his two feeble arms, sobbing—

"Won't you have me, and save me—not let me come to the Grange? Oh! darling Catherine! you mustn't go, and leave me, after all. You *must* obey my father, you *must*!"

"I must obey my own," she replied, "and relieve him from this cruel suspense. The whole night! What would he think? he'll be distressed already. I'll either break or burn a way out of the house. Be quiet! You're in no danger—but, if you hinder me—Linton, I love papa better than you!"

The mortal terror he felt of Mr. Heathcliff's anger, restored to the boy his coward's eloquence. Catherine was near distraught—still, she persisted that

260 EMILY BRONTË

she must go home, and tried entreaty, in her turn, persuading him to subdue his selfish agony.

While they were thus occupied, our jailer re-entered.

"Your beasts have trotted off;" he said, "and—Now, Linton! snivelling again? What has she been doing to you? Come, come—have done, and get to bed. In a month or two, my lad, you'll be able to pay her back her present tyrannies, with a vigorous hand—you're pining for pure love, are you not? nothing else in the world—and she shall have you! There, to bed! Zillah wont be here to-night; you must undress yourself. Hush! hold your noise! Once in your own room, I'll not come near you, you needn't fear. By chance, you've managed tolerably. I'll look to the rest,"

He spoke these words, holding the door open for his son to pass; and the latter achieved his exit exactly as a spaniel might which suspected the person who attended on it of designing a spiteful squeeze.

The lock was re-secured. Heathcliff approached the fire, where my mistress and I stood silent. Catherine looked up, and instinctively raised her hand to her cheek—his neighbourhood revived a painful sensation. Anybody else would have been incapable of regarding the childish act with sternness, but he scowled on her, and muttered—

"Oh, you are not afraid of me? Your courage is well disguised—you *seem* damnably afraid!"

"I *am* afraid *now*," she replied; "because if I stay, papa will be miserable; and how can I endure making him miserable—when he—when he—Mr. Heathcliff, *let* me go home! I promise to marry Linton—papa would like me to, and I love him—and why should you wish to force me to do what I'll willingly do of myself?"

"Let him dare to force you!" I cried. "There's law in the land, thank God, there is! though we *be* in an out-of-the-way place. I'd inform, if he were my own son, and it's felony without benefit of clergy!"

"Silence!" said the ruffian. "To the devil with your clamour! I don't want *you* to speak. Miss Linton, I shall enjoy myself remarkably in thinking your father will be miserable; I shall not sleep for satisfaction. You could have hit on no surer way of fixing your residence under my roof, for the next twenty-four hours, than informing me that such an event would follow. As to your promise to marry Linton; I'll take care you shall keep it, for you shall not quit the place till it is fulfilled."

"Send Ellen then, to let papa know I'm safe!" exclaimed Catherine, weeping bitterly. "Or marry me now. Poor papa! Ellen, he'll think we're lost. What shall we do?"

"Not he! He'll think you are tired of waiting on him, and run off, for a little amusement," answered Heathcliff. "You cannot deny that you entered my house of your own accord, in contempt of his injunctions to the contrary. And it is quite natural that you should desire amusement at your age; and that you

WUTHERING HEIGHTS 261

should weary of nursing a sick man, and that man, *only* your father. Catherine, his happiest days were over when your days began. He cursed you, I dare say, for coming into the world, (I did, at least). And it would just do if he cursed you as *he* went out of it. I'd join him. I don't love you! How should I? Weep away. As far as I can see, it will be your chief diversion hereafter: unless Linton make amends for other losses; and your provident parent appears to fancy he may. His letters of advice and consolation entertained me vastly. In his last, he recommended my jewel to be careful of his; and kind to her when he got her. Careful and kind—that's paternal! But Linton requires his whole stock of care and kindness for himself. Linton can play the little tyrant well. He'll undertake to torture any number of cats if their teeth be drawn, and their claws pared. You'll be able to tell his uncle fine tales of his *kindness*, when you get home again, I assure you."

"You're right there!" I said, "explain your son's character. Show his resemblance to yourself; and then, I hope, Miss Cathy will think twice, before she takes the cockatrice!"

"I don't much mind speaking of his amiable qualities now," he answered, "because she must either accept him, or remain a prisoner, and you along with her, till your master dies. I can detain you both, quite concealed, here, If you doubt, encourage her to retract her word, and you'll have an opportunity of judging!"

"I'll not retract my word," said Catherine. "I'll marry him, within this hour, if I may go to Thrushcross Grange afterwards. Mr. Heathcliff, you're a cruel man, but you're not a fiend; and you wont, from *mere* malice, destroy, irrevocably, all my happiness. If papa thought I had left him, on purpose; and if he died before I returned, could I bear to live? I've given over crying; but I'm going to kneel here, at your knee; and I'll not get up, and I'll not take my eyes from your face, till you look back at me! No, don't turn away! *do* look! You'll see nothing to provoke you. I don't hate you. I'm not angry that you struck me. Have you never loved *anybody*, in all your life, uncle? *never*? Ah! you must look once—I'm so wretched—you can't help being sorry and pitying me."

"Keep your eft's fingers off; and move, or I'll kick you!" cried Heathcliff, brutally repulsing her. "I'd rather be hugged by a snake. How the devil can you dream of fawning on me? I *detest* you!"

He shrugged his shoulders—shook himself, indeed, as if his flesh crept with aversion; and thrust back his chair: while I got up, and opened my mouth, to commence a downright torrent of abuse; but I was rendered dumb in the middle of the first sentence, by a threat that I should be shown into a room by myself, the very next syllable I uttered.

It was growing dark—we heard a sound of voices at the garden gate. Our host hurried out, instantly; *he* had his wits about him; *we* had not. There was a talk of two or three minutes, and he returned alone.

262   EMILY BRONTË

"I thought it had been your cousin Hareton," I observed to Catherine. "I wish he would arrive! Who knows but he might take our part?"

"It was three servants sent to seek you from the Grange," said Heathcliff, overhearing me. "You should have opened a lattice, and called out; but I could swear that chit is glad you didn't. She's glad to be obliged to stay, I'm certain."

At learning the chance we had missed, we both gave vent to our grief without control; and he allowed us to wail on till nine o'clock; then he bid us go up stairs, through the kitchen, to Zillah's chamber; and I whispered my companion to obey; perhaps, we might contrive to get through the window there, or into a garret, and out by its skylight.

The window, however, was narrow like those below, and the garret trap was safe from our attempts; for we were fastened in as before.

We neither of us lay down: Catherine took her station by the lattice, and watched anxiously for morning—a deep sigh being the only answer I could obtain to my frequent entreaties that she would try to rest.

I seated myself in a chair, and rocked, to and fro, passing harsh judgment on my many derelictions of duty; from which, it struck me then, all the misfortunes of all my employers sprang. It was not the case, in reality, I am aware; but it was, in my imagination, that dismal night, and I thought Heathcliff himself less guilty than I.

At seven o'clock he came, and inquired if Miss Linton had risen.

She ran to the door immediately, and answered—

"Yes."

"Here then," he said, opening it, and pulling her out.

I rose to follow, but he turned the lock again. I demanded my release.

"Be patient," he replied; "I'll send up your breakfast in a while."

I thumped on the panels, and rattled the latch angrily; and Catherine asked why I was still shut up? He answered, I must try to endure it another hour, and they went away. I endured it two or three hours; at length, I heard a footstep, not Heathcliff's.

"I've brought you something to eat," said a voice; "oppen t' door!"

Complying eagerly, I beheld Hareton, laden with food enough to last me all day.

"Tak it!" he added, thrusting the tray into my hand.

"Stay one minute," I began.

"Nay!" cried he, and retired, regardless of any prayers I could pour forth to detain him.

"And there I remained enclosed, the whole day, and the whole of the next night; and another, and another. Five nights and four days I remained, altogether, seeing nobody but Hareton, once every morning, and he was a model of a jailer—surly, and dumb, and deaf to every attempt at moving his sense of justice or compassion.

Chapter XIV.

On the fifth morning, or rather afternoon, a different step approached—lighter and shorter—and, this time, the person entered the room. It was Zillah; donned in her scarlet shawl, with a black silk bonnet on her head, and a willow basket swung to her arm.

"Eh, dear! Mrs. Dean," she exclaimed. "Well! there is a talk about you at Gimmerton. I never thought, but you were sunk in the Blackhorse marsh, and Missy with you, till master told me you'd been found, and he'd lodged you here! What, and you must have got on an island, sure? And how long were you in the hole? Did master save you, Mrs. Dean? But you're not so thin—you've not been so poorly, have you?"

"Your master is a true scoundrel!" I replied. "But he shall answer for it. He needn't have raised that tale—it shall all be laid bare!"

"What do you mean?" asked Zillah. "It's not his tale—they tell that in the village—about your being lost in the marsh; and I calls to Earnshaw, when I come in—"

"Eh, they's queer things, Mr. Hareton, happened since I went off. It's a sad pity of that likely young lass, and cant Nelly Dean."

"He stared. I thought he had not heard aught, so I told him the rumour.

"The master listened, and he just smiled to himself, and said—

"'If they have been in the marsh, they are out now, Zillah. Nelly Dean is lodged, at this minute, in your room. You can tell her to flit, when you go up; here is the key. The bog-water got into her head, and she would have run home, quite flighty, but I fixed her, till she came round to her senses. You can bid her go to the Grange, at once, if she be able, and carry a message from me, that her young lady will follow in time to attend the Squire's funeral.'"

"Mr. Edgar is not dead?" I gasped. "Oh! Zillah, Zillah!"

"No, no—sit you down, my good mistress," she replied, "you're right sickly yet. He's not dead: Doctor Kenneth thinks he may last another day—I met him on the road and asked."

Instead of sitting down, I snatched my outdoor things, and hastened below, for the way was free.

On entering the house, I looked about for some one to give information of Catherine.

The place was filled with sunshine, and the door stood wide open, but nobody seemed at hand.

As I hesitated whether to go off at once, or return and seek my mistress, a slight cough drew my attention to the hearth.

EMILY BRONTË

Linton lay on the settle, sole tenant, sucking a stick of sugar-candy, and pursuing my movements with apathetic eyes.

"Where is Miss Catherine?" I demanded, sternly, supposing I could frighten him into giving intelligence, by catching him thus, alone.

He sucked on like an innocent.

"Is she gone?" I said.

"No," he replied; "she's up stairs—she's not to go; we wont let her."

"You wont let her, little idiot!" I exclaimed. "Direct me to her room immediately, or I'll make you sing out sharply."

"Papa would make you sing out, if you attempted to get there," he answered. "He says I'm not to be soft with Catherine—she's my wife, and it's shameful that she should wish to leave me! He says, she hates me, and wants me to die, that she may have my money, but she shan't have it; and she shan't go home! she never shall! she may cry, and be sick as much as she pleases!"

He resumed his former occupation, closing his lids, as if he meant to drop asleep.

"Master Heathcliff," I resumed, "have you forgotten all Catherine's kindness to you, last winter, when you affirmed you loved her, and when she brought you books, and sung you songs, and came many a time through wind and snow to see you? She wept to miss one evening, because you would be disappointed; and you felt then, that she was a hundred times too good to you; and now you believe the lies your father tells, though you know he detests you both! And you join him against her. That's fine gratitude, is it not?"

The corner, of Linton's mouth fell, and he took the sugar-candy from his his lips.

"Did she come to Wuthering Heights, because she hated you?" I continued. "Think for yourself! As to your money, she does not even know that you will have any. And you say she's sick; and yet, you leave her alone, up there in a strange house! *You*, who have felt what it is to be so neglected! You could pity your own sufferings, and she pitied them, too, but you won't pity hers! I shed tears Master Heathcliff, you see—an elderly woman, and a servant merely—and you, after pretending such affection, and having reason to worship her, almost, store every tear you have for yourself, and lie there quite at ease. Ah! you're a heartless, selfish boy!"

"I can't stay with her," he answered crossly. "I'll not stay, by myself. She cries so I can't bear it. And she wont give over, though I say I'll call my father—I did call him once; and he threatened to strangle her, if she was not quiet, but she began again, the instant he left the room; moaning and grieving, all night long, though I screamed for vexation that I couldn't sleep."

"Is Mr. Heathcliff out," I inquired, perceiving that the wretched creature had no power to sympathise with his cousin's mental tortures.

"He's in the court," he replied, "talking to Doctor Kenneth who says uncle is dying, truly, at last—I'm glad for I shall be master of the Grange

WUTHERING HEIGHTS 265

after him—and Catherine always spoke of it, as *her* house. It isn't hers! It's mine—papa says everything she has is mine. All her nice books are mine—she offered to give me them, and her pretty birds, and her pony Minny, if I would get the key of our room, and let her out: but I told her she had nothing to give, they were all, all mine. And then she cried, and took a little picture from her neck, and said I should have that—two pictures in a gold case—on one side her mother, and on the other, uncle, when they were young. That was yesterday—I said *they* were mine, too; and tried to get them from her. The spiteful thing wouldn't let me; she pushed me off, and hurt me. I shrieked out—that frightens her—she heard papa coming, and she broke the hinges, and divided the case and gave me her mother's portrait; the other she attempted to hide; but papa asked what was the matter and I explained it. He took the one I had away; and ordered her to resign hers to me; she refused, and he—he struck her down, and wrenched it off the chain, and crushed it with his foot."

"And were you pleased to see her struck?" I asked: having my designs in encouraging his talk.

"I winked," he answered. "I wink to see my father strike a dog, or a horse, he does it so hard—yet I was glad at first—she deserved punishing for pushing me: but when papa was gone, she made me come to the window and showed me her cheek cut on the inside, against her teeth, and her mouth filling with blood: and then she gathered up the bits of the picture, and went and sat down with her face to the wall, and she has never spoken to me since; and I sometimes think she can't speak for pain. I don't like to think so! but she's a naughty thing for crying continually; and she looks so pale and wild, I'm afraid of her!"

"And you can get the key if you choose?" I said.

"Yes, when I am up-stairs," he answered "but I can't walk up-stairs now."

"In what apartment is it?" I asked.

"Oh, he cried, I shant tell *you* where it is! It is our secret. Nobody, neither Hareton, nor Zillah are to know. There! you've tired me—go away, go away!" And he turned his face onto his arm, and shut his eyes, again.

I considered it best to depart without seeing Mr. Heathcliff; and bring a rescue for my young lady, from the Grange.

On reaching it the astonishment of my fellow servants to see me, and their joy also, was intense; and when they heard that their little mistress was safe, two or three were about to hurry up, and shout the news at Mr. Edgar's door: but I bespoke the announcement of it, myself.

How changed I found him, even in those few days! He lay an image of sadness, and resignation, waiting his death. Very young he looked: though his actual age was thirty-nine; one would have called him ten years younger, at least. He thought of Catherine for he murmured her name. I touched his hand, and spoke.

266 EMILY BRONTË

"Catherine is coming, dear master!" I whispered, "she is alive, and well; and will be here I hope to-night."

I trembled at the first effects of this intelligence: he half rose up, looked eagerly round the apartment, and then sunk back in a swoon.

As soon as he recovered, I related our compulsory visit, and detention at the Heights: I said Heathcliff forced me to go in, which was not quite true; I uttered as little as possible against Linton; nor did I describe all his father's brutal conduct—my intentions being to add no bitterness, if I could help it, to his already overflowing cup.

He divined that one of his enemy's purposes was to secure the personal property, as well as the estate to his son, or rather himself; yet why he did not wait till his decease, was a puzzle to my master; because ignorant how nearly he, and his nephew would quit the world together.

However he felt his will had better be altered—instead of leaving Catherine's fortune at her own disposal, he determined to put it in the hands of trustees, for her use during life; and for her children, if she had any, after her. By that means, it could not fall to Mr. Heathcliff should Linton die.

Having received his orders, I despatched a man to fetch the attorney, and four more, provided with serviceable weapons, to demand my young lady of her jailer. Both parties were delayed very late. The single servant returned first.

He said Mr, Green, the lawyer, was out when he arrived at his house, and he had to wait two hours for his re-entrance: and then Mr. Green told him he had a little business in the village, that must be done, but he would be at Thrushcross Grange before morning.

The four men came back unaccompanied, also. They brought word that Catherine was ill, too ill to quit her room, and Heathcliff would not suffer them to see her.

I scolded the stupid fellows well, for listening to that tale, which I would not carry to my master; resolving to take a whole bevy up to the Heights, at daylight, and storm it, literally, unless the prisoner were quietly surrendered to us.

Her father *shall* see her, I vowed, and vowed again, if that devil be killed on his own doorstones, in trying to prevent it!

Happily, I was spared the journey, and the trouble.

I had gone down stairs at three o'clock to fetch a jug of water; and was passing through the hall, with it in my hand, when a sharp knock, at the front door, made me jump.

"Oh! it is Green—I said recollecting myself—only Green," and I went on, intending to send somebody else to open it; but the knock was repeated, not loud, and still importunately.

I put the jug on the bannister, and hastened to admit him, myself.

The harvest moon shone clear outside. It was not the attorney. My own sweet little mistress sprung on my neck sobbing,

WUTHERING HEIGHTS

267

"Ellen! Ellen! Is papa alive?"

"Yes!" I cried, "yes my angel he is! God be thanked, you are safe with us again!"

She wanted to run, breathless as she was, up-stairs to Mr. Linton's room; but I compelled her to sit down on a chair, and made her drink, and washed her pale face, chafing it into a faint colour with my apron. Then I said I must go first, and tell of her arrival; imploring her to say, she should be happy, with young Heathcliff. She stared, but soon comprehending why I counselled her to utter the falsehood, she assured me she would not complain.

I couldn't abide to be present at their meeting. I stood outside the chamber-door, a quarter of an hour, and hardly ventured near the bed, then.

All was composed, however; Catherine's despair was as silent as her father's joy. She supported him calmly, in appearance; and he fixed on her features his raised eyes that seemed dilating with ecstasy.

He died blissfully, Mr. Lockwood; he died so, kissing her cheek, he murmured,

"I am going to her, and you darling child shall come to us;" and never stirred or spoke again, but continued that rapt, radiant gaze, till his pulse imperceptibly stopped, and his soul departed. None could have noticed the exact minute of his death, it was so entirely without a struggle.

Whether Catherine had spent her tears, or whether the grief were too weighty to let them flow, she sat there dry-eyed till the sun rose—she sat till noon, and would still have remained, brooding over that death-bed, but I insisted on her coming away, and taking some repose.

It was well I succeeded in removing her, for at dinner-time appeared the lawyer, having called at Wuthering Heights to get his instructions how to behave. He had sold himself to Mr. Heathcliff, and that was the cause of his delay in obeying my master's summons. Fortunately, no thought of worldly affairs crossed the latter's mind, to disturb him, after his daughter's arrival.

Mr. Green took upon himself to order everything and everybody about the place. He gave all the servants but me, notice to quit. He would have carried his delegated authority to the point of insisting that Edgar Linton should not be buried beside his wife, but in the chapel, with his family. There was the will however, to hinder that, and my loud protestations against any infringement of its directions.

The funeral was hurried over; Catherine, Mrs. Linton Heathcliff now, was suffered to stay at the Grange, till her father's corpse had quitted it.

She told me that her anguish had at last spurred Linton to incur the risk of liberating her. She heard the men I sent, disputing at the door, and she gathered the sense of Heathcliff's answer. It drove her desperate—Linton, who had been conveyed up to the little parlour soon after I left, was terrified into fetching the key before his father re-ascended.

He had the cunning to unlock, and re-lock the door, without shutting it; and when he should have gone to bed, he begged to sleep with Hareton, and his petition was granted, for once.

Catherine stole out before break of day. She dare not try the doors, lest the dogs should raise an alarm; she visited the empty chambers, and examined their windows; and, luckily, lighting on her mother's, she got easily out of its lattice, and onto the ground, by means of the fir tree, close by. Her accomplice suffered for his share in the escape, notwithstanding his timid contrivances.

Chapter XV.

THE evening after the funeral, my young lady and I were seated in the library; now musing mournfully, one of us despairingly, on our loss; now venturing conjectures as to the gloomy future.

We had just agreed the best destiny which could await Catherine, would be a permission to continue resident at the Grange, at least, during Linton's life: he being allowed to join her there, and I to remain as housekeeper. That seemed rather too favourable an arrangement to be hoped for, and yet I did hope, and began to cheer up under the prospect of retaining my home, and my employment, and, above all, my beloved young mistress, when a servant—one of the discarded ones, not yet departed—rushed hastily in, and said, "that devil Heathcliff" was coming through the court, should he fasten the door in his face?

If we had been mad enough to order that proceeding, we had not time. He made no ceremony of knocking, or announcing his name; he was master, and availed himself of the master's privilege to walk straight in, without saying a word.

The sound of our informant's voice directed him to the library: he entered; and motioning him out, shut the door.

It was the same room into which he had been ushered, as a guest, eighteen years before: the same moon shone through the window; and the same autumn landscape lay outside. We had not yet lighted a candle, but all the apartment was visible, even to the portraits on the wall—the splendid head of Mrs. Linton, and the graceful one of her husband.

Heathcliff advanced to the hearth. Time had little altered his person either. There was the same man; his dark face rather sallower, and more composed, his frame a stone or two heavier, perhaps, and no other difference.

Catherine had risen with an impulse to dash out, when she saw him.

"Stop!" he said, arresting her by the arm. "No more runnings away! Where would you go? I'm come to fetch you home; and I hope you'll be a dutiful daughter, and not encourage my son to further disobedience. I was embarrassed how to punish him, when I discovered his part in the business—he's such a cobweb, a pinch would annihilate him—but, you'll see by his look that he has received his due! I brought him down one evening, the day before yesterday, and just set him in a chair, and never touched him afterwards. I sent Hareton out, and we had the room to ourselves. In two hours, I called Joseph to carry him up again; and, since then, my presence is as potent on his nerves, as a ghost; and I fancy he sees me often, though I am not near, Hareton

EMILY BRONTË

says he wakes and shrieks in the night by the hour together; and calls you to protect him from me; and, whether you like your precious mate or not, you must come—he's your concern now; I yield all my interest in him to you."

"Why not let Catherine continue here?" I pleaded, "and send Master Linton to her. As you hate them both, you'd not miss them—they *can* only be a daily plague to your un-natural heart."

"I'm seeking a tenant for the Grange," he answered; "and I want my children about me, to be sure—besides that lass owes me her services for her bread; I'm not going to nurture her in luxury and idleness after Linton is gone. Make haste and get ready now. And don't oblige me to compel you."

"I shall," said Catherine. "Linton is all I have to love in the world, and, though you have done what you could to make him hateful to me, and me to him, you *cannot* make us hate each other! and I defy you to hurt him when I am by, and I defy you to frighten me."

"You are a boastful champion!" replied Heathcliff; "but I don't like you well enough to hurt him—you shall get the full benefit of the torment, as long as it lasts. It is not I who will make him hateful to you—it is his own sweet spirit. He's as bitter as gall at your desertion, and its consequences—don't expect thanks for this noble devotion. I heard him draw a pleasant picture to Zillah of what he would do, if he were as strong as I—the inclination is there, and his very weakness will sharpen his wits to find a substitute for strength."

"I know he has a bad nature," said Catherine; "he's your son. But I'm glad I've a better, to forgive it; and I know he loves me and for that reason I love him. Mr. Heathcliff, *you* have *nobody* to love you; and, however miserable you make us, we shall still have the revenge of thinking that your cruelty rises from your greater misery! You *are* miserable, are you not? Lonely, like the devil, and envious like him? *Nobody* loves you—*nobody* will cry for you, when you die! I wouldn't be you!"

Catherine spoke with a kind of dreary triumph: she seemed to have made up her mind to enter into the spirit of her future family, and draw pleasure from the griefs of her enemies.

"You shall be sorry to be yourself presently," said her father-in-law. "If you stand there another minute. Begone, witch, and get your things."

She scornfully withdrew.

In her absence, I began to beg for Zillah's place at the Heights, offering to resign her mine; but he would suffer it on no account. He bid me be silent, and then, for the first time, allowed himself a glance round the room, and a look at the pictures. Having studied Mrs. Linton, he said—

"I shall have that at home. Not because I need it, but—"

He turned abruptly to the fire, and continued, with what, for lack of a better word, I must call a smile—

"I'll tell you what I did yesterday! I got the sexton, who was digging Linton's grave, to remove the earth off her coffin lid, and I opened it.

WUTHERING HEIGHTS 271

I thought, once, I would have stayed there, when I saw her face again—it is hers yet—he had hard work to stir me; but he said it would change, if the air blew on it, and so I struck one side of the coffin loose—and covered it up— not Linton's side, damn him! I wish he'd been soldered in lead—and I bribed the sexton to pull it away, when I'm laid there, and slide mine out too, I'll have it made so, and then, by the time Linton gets to us, he'll not know which is which!"

"You were very wicked, Mr. Heathcliff!" I exclaimed; "were you not ashamed to disturb the dead?"

"I disturbed nobody, Nelly," he replied; "and I gave some ease to myself. I shall be a great deal more comfortable now; and you'll have a better chance of keeping me underground, when I get there. Disturbed her? No! she has disturbed me, night and day, through eighteen years—incessantly— remorselessly—till yesternight—and yesternight, I was tranquil. I dreamt I was sleeping the last sleep, by that sleeper, with my heart stopped, and my cheek frozen against hers."

"And if she had been dissolved into earth, or worse, what would you have dreamt of then?" I said.

"Of dissolving with her, and being more happy still!" he answered. "Do you suppose I dread any change of that sort? I expected such a transformation on raising the lid, but I'm better pleased that it should not commence till I share it. Besides, unless I had received a distinct impression of her passion-less features, that strange feeling would hardly have been removed. It began oddly. You know, I was wild after she died, and eternally, from dawn to dawn, praying her to return to me—her spirit—I have a strong faith in ghosts; I have a conviction that they can, and do exist, among us!

"The day she was buried there came a fall of snow. In the evening I went to the churchyard. It blew bleak as winter—all round was solitary: I didn't fear that her fool of a husband would wander up the den so late—and no one else had business to bring them there.

"Being alone, and conscious two yards of loose earth was the sole barrier between us, I said to myself—

"'I'll have her in my arms again! If she be cold, I'll think it is this north wind that chills *me*, and if she be motionless, it is sleep.'

"I got a spade from the toolhouse, and began to delve with all my might—it scraped the coffin; I fell to work with my hands; the wood commenced crack-ing about the screws, I was on the point of attaining my object, when it seemed that I heard a sigh from some one above, close at the edge of the grave, and bending down.—'If I can only get this off,' muttered, 'I wish they may shovel in the earth over us both!' and I wrenched at it more desperately still. There was another sigh, close at my ear. I appeared to feel the warm breath of it displacing the sleet-laden wind. I knew no living thing in flesh and blood was by—but as certainly as you perceive the approach to some substantial body in

EMILY BRONTË

the dark, though it cannot be discerned, so certainly I felt that Cathy was there, not under me, but on the earth.

"A sudden sense of relief flowed, from my heart, through every limb. I relinquished my labour of agony, and turned consoled at once, unspeakably consoled. Her presence was with me; it remained while I re-filled the grave, and led me home. You may laugh, if you will, but I was sure I should see her there. I was sure she was with me, and I could not help talking to her.

"Having reached the Heights, I rushed eagerly to the door. It was fastened; and, I remember, that accursed Earnshaw and my wife opposed my entrance. I remember stopping to kick the breath out of him, and then hurrying up stairs, to my room, and hers—I looked round impatiently—I felt her by me—I could *almost* see her, and yet I *could not*! I ought to have sweat blood then, from the anguish of my yearning, from the fervour of my supplications to have but one glimpse! I had not one. She showed herself, as she often was in life, a devil to me! And, since then, sometimes more, and sometimes less, I've been the sport of that intolerable torture! Infernal—keeping my nerves at such a stretch, that, if they had not resembled catgut, they would, long ago, have relaxed to the feebleness of Linton's.

"When I sat in the house with Hareton, it seemed that on going out, I should meet her; when I walked on the moors I should meet her coming in. When I went from home, I hastened to return, she *must* be somewhere at the Heights, I was certain! And when I slept in her chamber—I was beaten out of that—I couldn't lie there; for the moment I closed my eyes, she was either outside the window, or sliding back the panels, or entering the room, or even resting her darling head on the same pillow as she did when a child. And I must open my lids to see. And so I opened and closed them a hundred times a-night—to be always disappointed! It racked me! I've often groaned aloud, till that old rascal Joseph, no doubt believed that my conscience was playing the fiend inside of me.

"Now since I've seen her, I'm pacified—a little. It was a strange way of killing, not by inches, but by fractions of hair-breadths, to beguile me with the spectre of a hope, through eighteen years!"

Mr. Heathcliff paused and wiped his forehead—his hair clung to it, wet with perspiration; his eyes were fixed on the red embers of the fire; the brows not contracted, but raised next the temples, diminishing the grim aspect of his countenance, but imparting a peculiar look of trouble, and a painful appearance of mental tension towards one absorbing subject. He only half addressed me, and I maintained silence—I didn't like to hear him talk!

After a short period, he resumed his meditation on the picture, took it down, and leant it against the sofa to contemplate it at better advantage; and while so occupied Catherine entered, announcing that she was ready, when her pony should be saddled.

"Send that over to-morrow," said Heathcliff to me, then turning to her he added, "You may do without your pony—it is a fine evening, and you'll need no ponies at Wuthering Heights, for what journies you take, your own feet will serve you—Come along."

"Good-bye, Ellen!" whispered my dear little mistress. As she kissed me, her lips felt like ice. "Come and see me Ellen, don't forget."

"Take care you do no such thing, Mrs. Dean!" said her new father. "When I wish to speak to you I'll come here. I want none of your prying at my house!"

He signed her to precede him; and casting back a look that cut my heart, she obeyed.

I watched them from the window, walk down the garden. Heathcliff fixed Catherine's arm under his, though she disputed the act, at first, evidently, and with rapid strides, he hurried her into the alley, whose trees concealed them.

Chapter XVI.

I HAVE paid a visit to the Heights, but I have not seen her since she left; Joseph held the door in his hand, when I called to ask after her, and wouldn't let me pass. He said Mrs. Linton was "thrang," and the master was not in. Zillah has told me something of the way they go on, otherwise I should hardly know who was dead, and who living.

She thinks Catherine, haughty, and does not like her, I can guess by her talk. My young lady asked some aid of her, when she first came, but Mr. Heathcliff told her to follow her own business, and let his daughter-in-law look after herself, and Zillah willingly acquiesced, being a narrow-minded selfish woman. Catherine evinced a child's annoyance at this neglect; repaid it with contempt, and thus enlisted my informant among her enemies, as securely as if she had done her some great wrong.

I had a long talk with Zillah, about six weeks ago, a little before you came, one day, when we foregathered on the moor; and this is what she told me.

"The first thing Mrs. Linton did," she said, "on her arrival at the Heights, was to run up-stairs without even wishing good-evening to me and Joseph; she shut herself into Linton's room, and remained till morning—then, while the master and Earnshaw were at breakfast, she entered the house and asked all in a quiver if the doctor might be sent for? her cousin was very ill."

"We know that!" answered Heathcliff, "but his life is not worth a farthing, and I won't spend a farthing on him."

"But I cannot tell how to do," she said, "and if nobody will help me, he'll die!"

"Walk out of the room!" cried the master, "and let me never hear a word more about him! None here care what becomes of him; if you do, act the nurse; if you do not, lock him up and leave him."

Then she began to bother me, and I said I'd had enough plague with the tiresome thing; we each had our tasks, and hers was to wait on Linton, Mr. Heathcliff bid me leave that labour to her.

How they managed together, I can't tell. I fancy he fretted a great deal, and moaned hisseln, night and day; and she had precious little rest, one could guess by her white face, and heavy eyes—she sometimes came into the kitchen all wildered like, and looked as if she would fain beg assistance: but I was not going to disobey the master—I never dare disobey him, Mrs. Dean, and though I thought it wrong that Kenneth should not be sent for, it was no concern of mine, either to advise or complain; and I always refused to meddle.

WUTHERING HEIGHTS 275

Once or twice, after we had gone to bed, I've happened to open my door again, and seen her sitting crying, on the stairs' top; and then I've shut myself in, quick, for fear of being moved to interfere. I did pity her then, I'm sure; still I didn't wish to lose my place, you know!

At last, one night she came boldly into my chamber, and frightened me out of my wits, by saying

"Tell Mr. Heathcliff that his son is dying—I'm sure he is, this time.—Get up, instantly, and tell him!"

Having uttered this speech, she vanished again. I lay a quarter of an hour listening and trembling—Nothing stirred—the house was quiet.

"She's mistaken, I said to myself. He's got over it. I needn't disturb them." And I began to dose. But my sleep was marred a second time, by a sharp ringing of the bell—the only bell we have, put up on purpose for Linton, and the master called to me, to see what was the matter, and inform them that he wouldn't have that noise repeated.

"I delivered Catherine's message. He cursed to himself, and in a few minutes, came out with a lighted candle, and proceeded to their room. I followed—Mrs. Heathcliff was seated by the bedside, with her hands folded on her knees. Her father-in-law went up, held the light to Linton's face, looked at him, and touched him, afterwards he turned to her.

"'Now—Catherine,' he said, 'how do you feel?'

"She was dumb.

"'How do you feel, Catherine?' he repeated.

"'He's safe, and I'm free,' she answered, 'I should feel well—but,' she continued with a bitterness she couldn't conceal, 'You have left me so long to struggle against death, alone, that I feel and see only death! I feel like death!'

"And she looked like it, too! I gave her a little wine. Hareton and Joseph who had been wakened by the ringing, and the sound of feet, and heard our talk from outside, now entered. Joseph was fain, I believe, of the lad's removal: Hareton seemed a thought bothered, though he was more taken up with staring at Catherine than thinking of Linton. But the master bid him get off to bed again—we didn't want his help. He afterwards made Joseph remove the body to his chamber, and told me to return to mine, and Mrs. Heathcliff remained by herself.

"In the morning, he sent me to tell her she must come down to breakfast—she had undressed, and appeared going to sleep; and said she was ill; at which I hardly wondered. I informed Mr. Heathcliff, and he replied,

"'Well, let her be till after the funeral; and go up now and then to get her what is needful; and as soon as she seems better, tell me.'

Cathy stayed up-stairs a fortnight, according to Zillah, who visited her twice a-day, and would have been rather more friendly, but her attempts at increasing kindness were proudly and promptly repelled.

276 EMILY BRONTË

Heathcliff went up once, to show her Linton's will. He had bequeathed the whole of his, and what had been her moveable property to his father. The poor creature was threatened, or coaxed into that act, during her week's absence, when his uncle died. The lands, being a minor he could not meddle with. However, Mr. Heathcliff has claimed, and kept them in his wife's right, and his also—I suppose legally, at any rate Catherine, destitute of cash and friends, cannot disturb his possession.

"Nobody," said Zillah, "ever approached her door, except that once, but I . . . and nobody asked anything about her. The first occasion of her coming down into the house, was on a Sunday afternoon.

"She had cried out, when I carried up her dinner that she couldn't bear any longer being in the cold; and I told her the master was going to Thrushcross Grange; and Earnshaw and I needn't hinder her from descending; so, as soon as she heard Heathcliff's horse trot off, she made her appearance, donned in black, and her yellow curls combed back behind her ears, as plain as a quaker, she couldn't comb them out.

"Joseph, and I generally go to chapel on Sundays, (the Kirk, you know, has no minister, now, explained Mrs. Dean, and they call the Methodists' or Baptists' place, I can't say which it is, at Gimmerton, a chapel.) "Joseph had gone," she continued, "but I thought proper to bide at home. Young folks are always the better for an elder's over-looking, and Hareton with all his bashfulness, isn't a model of nice behaviour. I let him know that his cousin would very likely sit with us, and she had been always used to see the Sabbath respected, so he had as good leave his guns, and bits of in-door work alone, while she stayed.

"He coloured up at the news; and cast his eyes over his hands and clothes. The train-oil, and gunpowder were shoved out of sight in a minute. I saw he meant to give her his company; and I guessed, by his way, he wanted to be presentable; so, laughing, as I durst not laugh when the master is by, I offered to help him, if he would, and joked at his confusion. He grew sullen, and began to swear.

"Now, Mrs. Dean," she went on, seeing me not pleased by her manner, "you happen think your young lady too fine for Mr. Hareton, and happen you're right—but, I own, I should love well to bring her pride a peg lower. And what will all her learning and her daintiness do for her, now? She's as poor as you, or I—poorer—I'll be bound, you're saving—and I'm doing my little all, that road."

Hareton allowed Zillah to give him her aid; and she flattered him into a good humour; so, when Catherine came, half forgetting her former insults, he tried to make himself agreeable, by the house-keeper's account.

"Missis walked in," she said, "as chill as an icicle, and as high as a princess. got up and offered her my seat in the arm-chair. No, she turned up her nose at my civility. Earnshaw rose too, and bid her come to the settle, and sit close by the fire; he was sure she was starved.

WUTHERING HEIGHTS

"'I've been starved a month and more,' she answered, resting on the word, as scornful as she could.

"And she got a chair for herself, and placed it at a distance from both of us.

"Having sat till she was warm, she began to look round, and discovered a number of books in the dresser; she was instantly upon her feet again, stretching to reach them, but they were too high up.

"Her cousin, after watching her endeavours a while, at last summoned courage to help her; she held her frock, and he filled it with the first that came to hand.

"That was a great advance for the lad—she didn't thank him; still, he felt gratified that she had accepted his assistance, and ventured to stand behind as she examined them, and even to stoop and point out what struck his fancy in certain old pictures which they contained—nor was he daunted by the saucy style in which she jerked the page from his finger; he contented himself with going a bit farther back, and looking at her, instead of the book.

"She continued reading, or seeking for something to read. His attention became, by degrees, quite centred in the study of her thick, silky curls—her face he couldn't see, and she couldn't see him. And, perhaps, not quite awake to what he did, but attracted like a child to a candle, at last, he proceeded from staring to touching; he put out his hand and stroked one curl, as gently as if it were a bird. He might have stuck a knife into her neck, she started round in such a taking.

"'Get away, this moment! How dare you touch me? Why are you stopping there?' she cried, in a tone of disgust. 'I can't endure you! I'll go up stairs again, if you come near me.'

"Mr. Hareton recoiled, looking as foolish as he could do; he sat down in the settle, very quiet, and she continued turning over her volumes, another half hour—finally, Earnshaw crossed over, and whispered to me.

"'Will you ask her to read to us, Zillah? I'm stalled of doing naught—and I do like—I could like to hear her! dunnot say I wanted it, but ask of yourseln.'

"'Mr. Hareton wishes you would read to us, ma'am,' I said, immediately. 'He'd take it very kind—he'd be much obliged.'

"She frowned; and, looking up, answered,

"'Mr. Hareton, and the whole set of you will be good enough to understand that I reject any pretence at kindness you have the hypocrisy to offer! I despise you, and will have nothing to say to any of you! When I would have given my life for one kind word, even to see one of your faces, you all kept off. But I won't complain to you! I'm driven down here by the cold, not either to amuse you, or enjoy your society.'

"'What could I ha' done?' began Earnshaw. 'How was I to blame?'

"'Oh! you are an exception,' answered Mrs. Heathcliff. 'I never missed such a concern as you.'

"'But, I offered more than once, and asked,' he said, kindling up at her pertness, 'I asked Mr. Heathcliff to let me wake for you—'

278 EMILY BRONTË

"'Be silent! I'll go out of doors, or anywhere, rather than have your disagreeable voice in my ear!' said my lady.

"Hareton muttered, she might go to hell, for him! and unslinging his gun, restrained himself from his Sunday occupations, no longer.

"He talked now, freely enough; and she presently saw fit to retreat to her solitude; but the frost had set in, and, in spite of her pride, she was forced to condescend to our company, more and more. However, I took care there should be no further scorning at my good nature—ever since, I've been as stiff as herself—and she has no lover, or liker among us—and she does not deserve one—for, let them say the least word to her, and she'll curl back without respect of any one! She'll snap at the master himself; and, as good as dares him to thrash her; and the more hurt she gets, the more venomous she grows."

At first, on hearing this account from Zillah, I determined to leave my situation, take a cottage, and get Catherine to come and live with me; but Mr. Heathcliff would as soon permit that, as he would set up Hareton in an independent house; and I can see no remedy, at present, unless she could marry again; and that scheme, it does not come within my province to arrange."

Thus ended Mrs. Dean's story. Notwithstanding the doctor's prophecy, I am rapidly recovering strength, and, though it be only the second week in January, I propose getting out on horseback, in a day or two, and riding over to Wuthering Heights, to inform my landlord that I shall spend the next six months in London; and, if he likes, he may look out for another tenant to take the place, after October—I would not pass another winter here, for much.

Chapter XVII.

Yesterday was bright, calm, and frosty. I went to the Heights as I proposed; my house-keeper entreated me to bear a little note from her to her young lady, and I did not refuse, for the worthy woman was not conscious of anything odd in her request.

The front door stood open, but the jealous gate was fastened, as at my last visit; I knocked and invoked Earnshaw from among the garden beds; he unchained it, and I entered. The fellow is as handsome a rustic as need be seen. I took particular notice of him this time; but then, he does his best, apparently, to make the least of his advantages.

I asked if Mr. Heathcliff were at home? He answered, no; but he would be in at dinner-time. It was eleven o'clock, and I announced my intention of going in, and waiting for him, at which he immediately flung down his tools and accompanied me, in the office of watchdog, not as a substitute for the host.

We entered together; Catherine was there, making herself useful in preparing some vegetables for the approaching meal; she looked more sulky, and less spirited than when I had seen her first. She hardly raised her eyes to notice me, and continued her employment with the same disregard to common forms of politeness, as before; never returning my bow and good morning, by the slightest acknowledgment.

"She does not seem so amiable," I thought, "as Mrs. Dean would persuade me to believe. She's a beauty, it is true; but not an angel."

Earnshaw surlily bid her remove her things to the kitchen.

"Remove them yourself," she said; pushing them from her, as soon as she had done; and retiring to a stool by the window, where she began to carve figures of birds and beasts, out of the turnip parings in her lap.

I approached her, pretending to desire a view of the garden; and, as I fancied, adroitly dropped Mrs. Dean's note onto her knee, unnoticed by Hareton—but she asked aloud—

"What is that?" And chucked it off.

"A letter from your old acquaintance, the housekeeper at the Grange," I answered, annoyed at her exposing my kind deed, and fearful lest it should be imagined a missive of my own.

She would gladly have gathered it up, at this information, but Hareton beat her; he seized, and put it in his waistcoat, saying Mr. Heathcliff should look at it first.

Thereat, Catherine silently turned her face from us, and, very stealthily, drew out her pocket-handkerchief and applied it to her eyes; and her cousin,

EMILY BRONTË

after struggling a while to keep down his softer feelings, pulled out the letter and flung it on the floor beside her as ungraciously as he could.

Catherine caught, and perused it eagerly; then she put a few questions to me concerning the inmates, rational and irrational, of her former home; and gazing towards the hills, murmured in soliloquy.

"I should like to be riding Minny down there! I should like to be climbing up there—Oh! I'm tired—I'm *stalled*, Hareton!"

And she leant her pretty head back against the sill, with half a yawn and half a sigh, and lapsed into an aspect of abstracted sadness, neither caring, nor knowing whether we remarked her.

"Mrs. Heathcliff," I said, after sitting some time mute, "you are not aware that I am an acquaintance of yours? so intimate, that I think it strange you won't come and speak to me. My housekeeper never wearies of talking about and praising you; and she'll be greatly disappointed if I return with no news of, or from you, except that you received her letter, and said nothing!"

She appeared to wonder at this speech and asked,

"Does Ellen like you?"

"Yes, very well," I replied unhesitatingly.

"You must tell her," she continued, "that I would answer her letter, but I have no materials for writing, not even a book from which I might tear a leaf."

"No books!" I exclaimed. "How do you contrive to live here without them? If I may take the liberty to inquire—Though provided with a large library, I'm frequently very dull at the Grange—take my books away, and I should be desperate!"

"I was always reading, when I had them;" said Catherine, "and Mr. Heathcliff never reads; so he took it into his head to destroy my books. I have not had a glimpse of one, for weeks. Only once, I searched through Joseph's store of theology; to his great irritation: and once, Hareton, I came upon a secret stock in your room . . . some Latin and Greek, and some tales and poetry; all old friends—I brought the last here—and you gathered them, as a magpie gathers silver spoons, for the mere love of stealing! They are of no use to you—or else you concealed them in the bad spirit, that as you cannot enjoy them, nobody else shall. Perhaps *your* envy counselled Mr. Heathcliff to rob me of my treasures? But, I've most of them written on my brain and printed in my heart, and you cannot deprive me of those!"

Earnshaw blushed crimson, when his cousin made this revelation of his private literary accumulations, and stammered an indignant denial of her accusations.

"Mr. Hareton is desirous of increasing his amount of knowledge," I said, coming to his rescue. "He is not *envious* but *emulous* o[f] your attainments— He'll be a clever scholar in a few years!"

"And he wants *me* to sink into a dunce, meantime," answered Catherine. "Yes, I hear him trying to spell and read to himself, and pretty blunders he

WUTHERING HEIGHTS 281

makes! I wish you would repeat Chevy Chase, as you did yesterday—It was extremely funny! I heard you . . . and I heard you turning over the dictionary, to seek out the hard words, and then cursing, because you couldn't read their explanations!"

The young man evidently thought it too bad that he should be laughed at for his ignorance, and then laughed at for trying to remove it. I had a similar notion, and, remembering Mrs. Dean's anecdote of his first attempt at enlightening the darkness in which he had been reared, I observed,

"But, Mrs. Heathcliff, we have each had a commencement, and each stumbled and tottered on the threshold, and had our teachers scorned, instead of aiding us, we should stumble and totter yet."

"Oh!" she replied, "I don't wish to limit his acquirements . . . still, he has no right to appropriate what is mine, and make it ridiculous to me with his vile mistakes and mis-pronunciations! Those books, both prose and verse, were consecrated to me by other associations, and I hate to have them debased and profaned in his mouth! Besides, of all, he has selected my favourite pieces that I love the most to repeat, as if out of deliberate malice!"

Hareton's chest heaved in silence a minute; be laboured under a severe sense of mortification and wrath, which it was no easy task to suppress.

I rose, and from a gentlemanly idea of relieving his embarrassment, took up my station in the door-way surveying the external prospect, as I stood.

He followed my example, and left the room, but presently re-appeared, bearing half-a-dozen volumes in his hands, which he threw into Catherine's lap, exclaiming,

"Take them! I never want to hear, or read, or think of them again!"

"I wont have them, now!" she answered. "I shall connect them with you, and hate them."

She opened one that had obviously been often turned over, and read a portion in the drawling tone of a beginner; then laughed, and threw it from her.

"And listen!" she continued provokingly, commencing a verse of an old ballad in the same fashion.

But his self-love would endure no further torment—I heard, and not altogether disapprovingly, a manual check given to her saucy tongue—The little wretch had done her utmost to hurt her cousin's sensitive though uncultivated feelings, and a physical argument was the only mode he had of balancing the account and repaying its effects on the inflicter.

He afterwards gathered the books and hurled them on the fire. I read in his countenance what anguish it was to offer that sacrifice to spleen—I fancied that as they consumed, he recalled the pleasure they had already imparted; and the triumph, and ever increasing pleasure he had anticipated from them—and I fancied, I guessed the incitement to his secret studies, also. He had been content with daily labour and rough animal enjyoments, till Catherine crossed his path—Shame at her scorn, and hope of her approval were his first prompters to higher pursuits; and instead of guarding him from one, and winning him the other, his endeavours to raise himself had produced just the contrary result.

"Yes, that's all the good that such a brute as you can get from them!" cried Catherine, sucking her damaged lip, and watching the conflagration with indignant eyes.

"You'd *better* hold your tongue, now!" he answered fiercely.

And his agitation precluding further speech, he advanced hastily to the entrance, where I made way for him to pass. But, ere he had crossed the door-stones, Mr. Heathcliff, coming up the causeway, encountered him and laying hold of his shoulder, asked.

"What's to do now, my lad?"

"Naught, naught!" he said, and broke away, to enjoy his grief and anger in solitude.

Heathcliff gazed after him, and sighed.

"It will be odd, if I thwart myself!" he muttered, unconscious that I was behind him. "But, when I look for his father in his face, I find *her* every day more! How the devil is he so like? I can hardly bear to see him."

He bent his eyes to the ground, and walked moodily in. There was a rest-less, anxious expression in his countenance, I had never remarked there before, and he looked sparer in person.

His daughter-in-law on perceiving him through the window, immediately escaped to the kitchen, so that I remained alone.

"I'm glad to see you out of doors again, Mr. Lockwood," he said in reply to my greeting, "from selfish motives partly, I don't think I could readily supply your loss in this desolation. I've wondered, more than once, what brought you here."

"An idle whim, I fear sir," was my answer, "or else an idle whim is going to spirit me away—I shall set out for London, next week, and I must give you warning, that I feel no disposition to retain Thrushcross Grange, beyond the twelvemonths I agreed to rent it. I believe I shall not live there any more.

"Oh, indeed! you're tired of being banished from the world, are you?" he said. "But, if you be coming to plead off paying for a place, you won't occupy, your journey is useless—I never relent in exacting my due, from any one."

"I'm coming to plead off nothing about it!" I exclaimed, considerably irri-tated. "Should you wish it, I'll settle with you now," and I drew my notebook from my pocket.

"No, no," he replied coolly, "you'll leave sufficient behind, to cover your debts, if you fail to return . . . I'm not in such a hurry—sit down and take your dinner with us—a guest that is safe from repeating his visit, can generally be made welcome—Catherine! bring the things in—where are you?"

Catherine re-appeared, bearing a tray of knives and forks.

"You may get your dinner with Joseph," muttered Heathcliff aside, "and remain in the kitchen till he is gone."

WUTHERING HEIGHTS   283

She obeyed his directions very punctually—perhaps she had no temptation to transgress. Living among clowns and misanthropists, she probably cannot appreciate a better class of people, when she meets them.

With Mr. Heathcliff, grim and saturnine, on one hand, and Hareton absolutely dumb, on the other, I made a somewhat cheerless meal, and bid adieu early—I would have departed by the back way to get a last glimpse of Catherine, and annoy old Joseph; but Hareton received orders to lead up my horse, and my host himself escorted me to the door, so I could not fulfil my wish.

"How dreary life gets over in that house!" I reflected, while riding down the road. "What a realization of something more romantic than a fairy tale it would have been for Mrs. Linton Heathcliff, had she and I struck up an attachment, as her good nurse desired, and migrated together, into the stirring atmosphere of the town!"

Chapter XVIII.

1802.—This September, I was invited to devastate the moors of a friend, in the North; and, on my journey to his abode, I unexpectedly came within fifteen miles of Gimmerton. The hostler, at a roadside public-house, was holding a pail of water to refresh my horses, when a cart of very green oats, newly reaped, passed by, and he remarked—

"Yon's frough Gimmerton, nah! They're allas three wick' after other folk wi' ther harvest."

"Gimmerton?" I repeated, my residence in that locality had already grown dim and dreamy. "Ah! I know! How far is it from this?"

"Happen fourteen mile' o'er th' hills, and a rough road," he answered.

A sudden impulse seized me to visit Thrushcross Grange. It was scarcely noon, and I conceived that I might as well pass the night under my own roof, as in an inn. Besides, I could spare a day easily, to arrange matters with my landlord, and thus save myself the trouble of invading the neighbourhood again.

Having rested a while, I directed my servant to inquire the way to the village; and, with great fatigue to our beasts, we managed the distance in some three hours.

I left him there, and proceeded down the valley alone. The grey church looked greyer, and the lonely churchyard lonelier. I distinguished a moor sheep cropping the short turf on the graves. It was sweet, warm weather—too warm for travelling; but the heat did not hinder me from enjoying the delightful scenery above and below; had I seen it nearer August, I'm sure it would have tempted me to waste a month among its solitudes. In winter, nothing more dreary, in summer, nothing more divine, than those glens shut in by hills, and those bluff, bold swells of heath.

I reached the Grange before sunset, and knocked for admittance; but the family had retreated into the back premises, I judged by one thin, blue wreath curling from the kitchen chimney, and they did not hear.

I rode into the court. Under the porch, a girl of nine or ten, sat knitting, and an old woman reclined on the horse-steps, smoking a meditative pipe.

"Is Mrs. Dean within?" I demanded of the dame.

"Mistress Dean? Nay!" she answered, "shoo doesn't bide here; shoe's up at th' Heights."

"Are you the housekeeper, then?" I continued.

"Eea, Aw keep th' hause," she replied.

"Well, I'm Mr. Lockwood, the master—Are there any rooms to lodge me in, I wonder? I wish to stay here all night."

WUTHERING HEIGHTS

285

"T' maister!" she cried in astonishment, "Whet, whoiver knew yah wur coming? Yah sud ha' send word! They's nowt norther dry—nor mensful abaht t' place—nowt there is n't!'

She threw down her pipe and bustled in, the girl followed, and I entered too; soon perceiving that her report was true, and, moreover, that I had almost upset her wits by my unwelcome apparition.

I bid her be composed—I would go out for a walk; and, meantime, she must try to prepare a corner of a sitting-room for me to sup in, and a bedroom to sleep in—No sweeping and dusting, only good fires and dry sheets were necessary.

She seemed willing to do her best; though she thrust the hearth-brush into the grates in mistake for the poker; and mal-appropriated several other articles of her craft; but I retired, confiding in her energy for a resting-place against my return.

Wuthering Heights was the goal of my proposed excursion. An afterthought brought me back, when I had quitted the court.

"All well at the Heights?" I enquired of the woman.

"Eea, f'r owt Ee knaw!" she answered, skurrying away with a pan of hot cinders.

I would have asked why Mrs. Dean had deserted the Grange; but it was impossible to delay her at such a crisis, so, I turned away and made my exit, rambling leisurely along with the glow of a sinking sun behind, and the mild glory of a rising moon in front; one fading, and the other brightening, as I quitted the park, and climbed the stony by-road branching off to Mr. Heathcliff's dwelling.

Before I arrived in sight of it, all that remained of day was a beamless, amber light along the west; but I could see every pebble on the path, and every blade of grass by that splendid moon.

I had neither to climb the gate, nor to knock—it yielded to my hand.

That is an improvement! I thought. And I noticed another, by the aid of my nostrils; a fragrance of stocks and wall flowers, wafted on the air, from amongst the homely fruit trees.

Both doors and lattices were open; and, yet, as is usually the case in a coal district, a fine, red fire illumined the chimney; the comfort which the eye derives from it, renders the extra heat endurable. But the house of Wuthering Heights is so large, that the inmates have plenty of space for withdrawing out of its influence; and, accordingly, what inmates there were had stationed themselves not far from one of the windows. I could both see them and hear them talk before I entered; and, looked and listened in consequence, being moved thereto by a mingled sense of curiosity, and envy that grew as I lingered.

"Con-*trary*!" said a voice, as sweet as a silver bell—"That for the third time, you dunce! I'm not going to tell you, again—Recollect, or I pull your hair!"

286   EMILY BRONTË

"Contrary, then," answered another, in deep, but softened tones. And now, kiss me, for minding so well."

"No, read it over first correctly, without a single mistake."

The male speaker began to read—he was a young man, respectably dressed, and seated at a table, having a book before him. His handsome features glowed with pleasure, and his eyes kept impatiently wandering from the page to a small white hand over his shoulder, which recalled him by a smart slap on the cheek, whenever its owner detected such signs of inattention.

Its owner stood behind; her light shining ringlets blending, at intervals, with his brown locks, as she bent to superintend his studies; and her face—it was lucky he could not see her face, or he would never have been so steady—I could, and I bit my lip, in spite, at having thrown away the chance I might have had, of doing something besides staring at its smiting beauty.

The task was done, not free from further blunders, but the pupil claimed a reward and received, at least five kisses, which, however, he generously returned. Then, they came to the door, and from their conversation, I judged they were about to issue out and have a walk on the moors. I supposed I should be condemned in Hareton Earnshaw's heart, if not by his mouth, to the lowest pit in the infernal regions if I showed my unfortunate person in his neighbourhood then, and feeling very mean and malignant, I skulked round to seek refuge in the kitchen.

There was unobstructed admittance on that side also; and, at the door, sat my old friend, Nelly Dean, sewing and singing a song, which was often interrupted from within, by harsh words of scorn and intolerance, uttered in far from musical accents.

"Aw'd rayther, by th' haulf, hev 'em swearing i' my lugs frough morn tuh neeght, nur hearken yah, hahsiver!" said the tenant of the kitchen, in answer to an unheard speech of Nelly's. "It's a blazing shaime, ut Aw cannut oppen t' Blessed Book, bud yah set up them glories tuh sattan, un' all t' flaysome wickednesses ut iver wer born intuh t' warld! Oh! yah're a raight nowt; un' shoo's another; un' that poor lad 'ull be lost, atween ye. Poor lad!" he added, with a groan; "he's witched, Aw'm sartin on't! O, Lord, judge 'em, fur they's norther law nur justice amang wer rullers!"

"No! or we should be sitting in flaming fagots, I suppose," retorted the singer. "But wisht, old man, and read your Bible, like a christian, and never mind me. This is 'Fairy Annie's Wedding'—a bonny tune—it goes to a dance."

Mrs. Dean was about to recommence, when I advanced, and recognising me directly, she jumped to her feet, crying—

"Why, bless you, Mr. Lockwood! How could you think of returning in this way? All's shut up at Thrushcross Grange. You should have given us notice!"

"I've arranged to be accommodated there, for as long as I shall stay," I answered. "I depart again to-morrow. And how are you transplanted here, Mrs. Dean? tell me that."

WUTHERING HEIGHTS

"Zillah left, and Mr. Heathcliff wished me to come, soon after you went to London, and stay till you returned. But, step in, pray! Have you walked from Gimmerton this evening?"

"From the Grange," I replied; "and, while they make me lodging room there, I want to finish my business with your master, because I don't think of having another opportunity in a hurry."

"What business, sir?" said Nelly, conducting me into the house. "He's gone out, at present, and wont return soon."

"About the rent," I answered.

"Oh! then it is with Mrs. Heathcliff you must settle," she observed, "or rather with me. She has not learnt to manage her affairs yet, and I act for her; there's nobody else."

I looked surprised.

"Ah! you have not heard of Heathcliff's death, I see!" she continued.

"Heathcliff dead?" I exclaimed, astonished. "How long ago?"

"Three months since—but, sit down, and let me take your hat, and I'll tell you all about it. Stop, you have had nothing to eat, have you?"

"I want nothing. I have ordered supper at home. You sit down too. I never dreamt of his dying! Let me hear how it came to pass. You say you don't expect them back for some time—the young people?"

"No—I have to scold them every evening, for their late rambles—but they don't care for me. At least, have a drink of our old ale—it will do you good—you seem weary."

She hastened to fetch it, before I could refuse, and I heard Joseph asking, whether "it warn't a crying scandal that she should have fellies at her time of life? And then, to get them jocks out uh t' Maister's cellar! He fair shaamed to 'bide still and see it."

She did not stay to retaliate, but re-entered, in a minute, bearing a reaming, silver pint, whose contents I lauded with becoming earnestness. And afterwards she furnished me with the sequel of Heathcliff's history. He had a "queer" end, as she expressed it.

"I was summoned to Wuthering Heights, within a fortnight of your leaving us," she said; "and I obeyed joyfully, for Catherine's sake.

"My first interview with her grieved and shocked me! she had altered so much since our separation. Mr. Heathcliff did not explain his reasons for taking a new mind about my coming here; he only told me he wanted me, and he was tired of seeing Catherine, I must make the little parlour my sitting room, and keep her with me. It was enough if he were obliged to see her once or twice a day.

"She seemed pleased at this arrangement; and, by degrees, I smuggled over a great number of books, and other articles, that had formed her amusement at the Grange; and flattered myself we should get on in tolerable comfort.

288 EMILY BRONTË

"The delusion did not last long. Catherine, contented at first, in a brief space grew irritable and restless. For one thing, she was forbidden to move out of the garden, and it fretted her sadly to be confined to its narrow bounds, as Spring drew on—for another, in following the house, I was forced to quit her frequently, and she complained of loneliness; she preferred quarrelling with Joseph in the kitchen, to sitting at peace in her solitude.

"I did not mind their skirmishes; but Hareton was often obliged to seek the kitchen also, when the master wanted to have the house to himself; and, though, in the beginning, she either left it at his approach, or quietly joined in my occupations, and shunned remarking, or addressing him—and though he was always as sullen and silent, as possible—after a while, she changed her behaviour, and became incapable of letting him alone. Talking at him; commenting on his stupidity and idleness; expressing her wonder how he could endure the life he lived—how he could sit a whole evening staring into the fire, and dozing.

"'He's just like a dog, is he not, Ellen?' she once observed, "or a carthorse? He does his work, eats his food, and sleeps, eternally! What a blank, dreary mind he must have! Do you ever dream, Hareton? And, if you do, what is it about? But, you can't speak to me!'

"Then she looked at him; but he would neither open his mouth, nor look again.

"'He's perhaps, dreaming now,' she continued. 'He twitched his shoulder as Juno twitches hers. Ask him, Ellen."

"'Mr. Hareton will ask the master to send you up stairs, if you don't behave!' I said. He had not only twitched his shoulder, but clenched his fist, as if tempted to use it.

"'I know why Hareton never speaks, when I am in the kitchen,' she exclaimed, on another occasion. 'He is afraid I shall laugh at him. Ellen, what do you think? He began to teach himself to read once; and, because I laughed, he burned his books, and dropped it—was he not a fool?'

"'Were not you naughty?' I said; 'answer me that.'

"'Perhaps I was,' she went on, 'but I did not expect him to be so silly. Hareton, if I gave you a book, would you take it now? I'll try!'

"She placed one she had been perusing on his hand; he flung it off, and muttered, if she did not give over, he would break her neck.

"'Well I shall put it here,' she said, 'in the table drawer, and I'm going to bed.'

"Then she whispered me to watch whether he touched it, and departed. But he would not come near it, and so I informed her in the morning, to her great disappointment. I saw she was sorry for his persevering sulkiness and indolence—her conscience reproved her for frightening him off improving himself—she had done it effectually.

But her ingenuity was at work to remedy the injury; while I ironed, or pursued other stationary employments I could not well do in in the parlour—she would bring some pleasant volume, and read it aloud to me. When Hareton

WUTHERING HEIGHTS 289

was there, she generally paused in an interesting part, and left the book lying about—that she did repeatedly; but he was as obstinate as a mule, and, instead of snatching at her bait, in wet weather he took to smoking with Joseph, and they sat like automatons, one on each side of the fire, the elder happily too deaf to understand her wicked nonsense, as he would have called it, the younger doing his best to seem to disregard it. On fine evenings the latter followed his shooting expeditions, and Catherine yawned and sighed, and teased me to talk to her, and ran off into the court or garden, the moment I began; and, as a last resource, cried and said, she was tired of living, her life was useless.

"Mr. Heathcliff, who grew more and more disinclined to society, had almost banished Earnshaw out of his apartment. Owing to an accident, at the commencement of March, he became for some days a fixture in the kitchen. His gun burst, while out on the hills, by himself; a splinter cut his arm, and he lost a good deal of blood before he could reach home. The consequence was, that, perforce, he was condemned to the fire-side and tranquillity, till he made it up again.

"It suited Catherine to have him there: at any rate, it made her hate her room up stairs, more than ever; and she would compel me to find out business below, that she might accompany me.

"On Easter Monday, Joseph went to Gimmerton fair with some cattle; and, in the afternoon, I was busy getting up linen in the kitchen—Earnshaw sat, morose as usual, at the chimney corner, and my little mistress was beguiling an idle hour with drawing pictures on the window panes, varying her amusement by smothered bursts of songs, and whispered ejaculations, and quick glances of annoyance and impatience in the direction of her cousin, who steadfastly smoked, and looked into the grate.

"At a notice that I could do with her no longer, intercepting my light, she removed to the hearthstone. I bestowed little attention on her proceedings, but, presently, I heard her begin—

"'I've found out, Hareton, that I want—that I'm glad—that I should like you to be my cousin, now, if you had not grown so cross to me, and so rough.'

"Hareton returned no answer.

"'Hareton, Hareton, Hareton! do you hear?' she continued.

"'Get off wi' ye!' he growled, with uncompromising gruffness.

"'Let me take that pipe,' she said, cautiously advancing her hand, and abstracting it from his mouth.

"Before he could attempt to recover it, it was broken, and behind the fire. He swore at her and seized another.

"'Stop,' she cried, 'you must listen to me, first; and I can't speak while those clouds are floating in my face.'

"'Will you go to the devil!' he exclaimed, ferociously, 'and let me be!'

"'No,' she persisted, 'I wont—I can't tell what to do to make you talk to me, and you are determined not to understand. When I call you stupid,

I don't mean anything—I don't mean that I despise you. Come you shall take notice of me, Hareton—you are my cousin, and you shall own me.'

"'I shall have naught to do wi' you, and your mucky pride, and your damned, mocking tricks!' he answered. 'I'll go to hell, body and soul, before I look sideways after you again! side out of t' gait, now; this minute!'

"Catherine frowned, and retreated to the window-seat, chewing her lip, and endeavouring, by humming an eccentric tune, to conceal a growing tendency to sob.

"'You should be friends with your cousin, Mr. Hareton,' I interrupted, 'since she repents of her sauciness! it would do you a great deal of good—it would make you another man, to have her for a companion.'

"'A companion?' he cried; 'when she hates me, and does not think me fit to wipe her shoon! Nay, if it made me a king, I'd not be scorned for seeking her good will any more.'

"'It is not I who hate you, it is you who hate me!' wept Cathy, no longer disguising her trouble. 'You hate me as much as Mr. Heathcliff does, and more.'

"'You're a damned liar,' began Earnshaw; 'why have I made him angry, by taking your part then, a hundred times? and that, when you sneered at, and despised me, and—Go on plaguing me, and I'll step in yonder, and say you worried me out of the kitchen!'

"'I didn't know you took my part,' she answered, drying her eyes; 'and I was miserable and bitter at every body; but, now I thank you, and beg you to forgive me, what can I do besides?'

"She returned to the hearth, and frankly extended her hand.

"He blackened, and scowled like a thunder cloud, and kept his fists resolutely clenched, and his gaze fixed on the ground.

"Catherine, by instinct, must have divined it was obdurate perversity, and not dislike, that prompted this dogged conduct; for, after remaining an instant, undecided, she stooped, and impressed on his cheek a gentle kiss.

"The little rogue thought I had not seen her, and, drawing back, she took her former station by the window, quite demurely.

"I shook my head reprovingly; and then she blushed, and whispered—

"'Well! what should I have done, Ellen? He wouldn't shake hands, and he wouldn't look—I must show him some way that I like him, that I want to be friends.'

"Whether the kiss convinced Hareton, I cannot tell; he was very careful, for some minutes, that his face should not be seen; and when he did raise it, he was sadly puzzled where to turn his eyes.

"Catherine employed herself in wrapping a handsome book neatly in white paper; and having tied it with a bit of ribband, and addressed it to 'Mr. Hareton Earnshaw,' she desired me to be her ambassadress, and convey the present to its destined recipient.

"'And tell him, if he'll take it, I'll come and teach him to read it right,' she said, 'and, if he refuse it, I'll go up stairs, and never tease him again,'

"I carried it, and repeated the message, anxiously watched by my employer. Hareton would not open his fingers, so I laid it on his knee. He did not strike it off either. I returned to my work: Catherine leaned her head and arms on the table, till she heard the slight rustle of the covering being removed, then she stole away, and quietly seated herself beside her cousin. He trembled, and his face glowed—all his rudeness, and all his surly harshness had deserted him—he could not summon courage, at first, to utter a syllable, in reply to her questioning look, and her murmured petition.

"'Say you forgive me, Hareton, do! You can make me so happy, by speaking that little word.'

"He muttered something inaudible.

"'And you'll be my friend?' added Catherine, interrogatively.

"'Nay! you'll be ashamed of me every day of your life,' he answered. 'And the more, the more you know me, and I cannot bide it.'

"'So, you wont be my friend?' she said, smiling as sweet as honey, and creeping close up.

"I overheard no further distinguishable talk; but on looking round again, I perceived two such radiant countenances bent over the page of the accepted book, that I did not doubt the treaty had been ratified, on both sides, and the enemies were, thenceforth, sworn allies.

"The work they studied was full of costly pictures; and those, and their position had charm enough to keep them unmoved, till Joseph came home. He, poor man, was perfectly aghast at the spectacle of Catherine seated on the same bench with Hareton Earnshaw, leaning her hand on his shoulder; and confounded at his favourite's endurance of her proximity. It affected him too deeply to allow an observation on the subject that night. His emotion was only revealed by the immense sighs he drew, as he solemnly spread his large bible on the table, and overlaid it with dirty bank-notes from his pocket-book, the produce of the day's transactions. At length, he summoned Hareton from his seat.

"'Tak' these in tuh t' maister, lad,' he said, 'un' bide theare; Aw's gang up tuh my awn rahm. This hoile's norther mensful, nor seemly fur us—we mun side aht, and seearch another!'

"'Come, Catherine, I said, we must 'side out,' too—I've done my ironing, are you ready to go?'

"'It is not eight o'clock!' she answered, rising unwillingly, 'Hareton, I'll leave this book upon the chimney-piece, and I'll bring some more to-morrow.'

"'Ony books ut yah leave, Aw suall tak' intuh th' hahse,' said Joseph, 'un' it 'ull be mitch if yah find 'em agean; soa, yah muh plase yourseln!'

"Cathy threatened that his library should pay for hers; and, smiling as she passed Hareton, went singing up stairs, lighter of heart, I venture to say, than

EMILY BRONTË

ever she had been under that roof before; except, perhaps, during her earliest visits to Linton.

"The intimacy, thus commenced, grew rapidly; though it encountered temporary interruptions, Earnshaw was not to be civilized with a wish; and my young lady was no philosopher, and no paragon of patience; but both their minds tending to the same point—one loving and desiring to esteem; and the other loving and desiring to be esteemed—they contrived in the end, to reach it.

"You see, Mr. Lockwood, it was easy enough to win Mrs. Heathcliff's heart; but now, I'm glad you did not try—the crown of all my wishes will be the union of those two; I shall envy no one on their wedding-day—there won't be a happier woman than myself in England!"

Chapter XIX.

"On the morrow of that Monday, Earnshaw being still unable to follow his ordinary employments, and, therefore, remaining about the house, I speedily found it would be impracticable to retain my charge beside me, as heretofore.

She got down stairs before me, and out into the garden; where she had seen her cousin performing some easy work; and when I went to bid them come to breakfast, I saw she had persuaded him to clear a large space of ground from currant and gooseberry bushes, and they were busy planning together an importation of plants from the Grange.

"I was terrified at the devastation which had been accomplished in a brief half hour; the black currant trees were the apple of Joseph's eye, and she had just fixed her choice of a flower bed in the midst of them!

"'There! That will be all shewn to the master,' I exclaimed, 'the minute it is discovered. And what excuse have you to offer for taking such liberties with the garden? We shall have a fine explosion on the head of it: see if we don't! Mr. Hareton, I wonder you should have no more wit, than to go and make that mess at her bidding!'

"'I'd forgotten they were Joseph's,' answered Earnshaw, rather puzzled, 'but I'll tell him I did it.'

"We always ate our meals with Mr. Heathcliff. I held the mistress's post in making tea and carving; so I was indispensable at table. Catherine usually sat by me; but to-day, she stole nearer to Hareton, and I presently saw she would have no more discretion in her friendship, than she had in her hostility.

"'Now, mind you don't talk with and notice your cousin too much,' were my whispered instructions as we entered the room; 'It will certainly annoy Mr. Heathcliff, and he'll be mad at you both.'

"'I'm not going to,' she answered.

"The minute after, she had sidled to him, and was sticking primroses in his plate of porridge.

"He dared not speak to her, there; he dared hardly look; and yet she went on teasing, till he was twice on the point of being provoked to laugh; and I frowned, and then, she glanced towards the master, whose mind was occupied on other subjects than his company, as his countenance evinced, and she grew serious for an instant, scrutinizing him with deep gravity. Afterwards she turned, and re-commenced her nonsense; at last, Hareton uttered a smothered laugh.

"Mr. Heathcliff started; his eye rapidly surveyed our faces. Catherine met it with her accustomed look of nervousness, and yet defiance, which he abhorred.

EMILY BRONTË

"It is well you are out of my reach;" he exclaimed. "What fiend possesses you to stare back at me, continually, with those infernal eyes? Down with them! and don't remind me of your existence again. I thought I had cured you of laughing!"

"It was me," muttered Hareton.

"What do you say?" demanded the master.

Hareton looked at his plate, and did not repeat the confession.

Mr. Heathcliff looked at him a bit, and then silently resumed his breakfast, and his interrupted musing.

We had nearly finished, and the two young people prudently shifted wider asunder, so I anticipated no further disturbance during that sitting; when Joseph appeared at the door, revealing by his quivering lip, and furious eyes, that the outrage committed on his precious shrubs was detected.

He must have seen Cathy, and her cousin about the spot, before he examined it, for while his jaws worked like those of a cow chewing its cud, and rendered his speech difficult to understand, he began:

"Aw mun hev my wage, and Aw mun goa! Aw *hed* aimed tuh dee, wheare Aw'd sarved fur sixty year; un' Aw thowt Aw'd lug my books up intuh t' garret, un' all my bits uh stuff, un' they sud hev t' kitchen tuh theirseln; fur t' sake uh quietness. It wur hard tuh gie up my awn hearthstun, bud Aw thowt Aw *could* do that! Bud, nab, shoo's taan my garden frough me, un' by th' heart! Maister, Aw cannot stand it! Yah muh bend tuh th' yoak, an ye will—*Aw*' noan used to't and an ow'd man doesn't sooin get used tuh new barthens—Aw'd rayther arn my bite, an' my sup, wi' a hammer in th' road!"

"Now, now, idiot!" interrupted Heathcliff, "cut it short! What's your grievance? I'll interfere in no quarrels between you, and Nelly—She may thrust you into the coal-hole for anything I care"

"It's noan Nelly!" answered Joseph. "Aw sudn't shift fur Nelly—Nasty, ill nowt as shoo is, Thank God! *shoo* cannot stale t'sowl uh nob'dy! Shoo wer niver soa handsome, bud whet a body mud look at her 'baht winking. It's yon flaysome, graceless quean, ut's witched ahr lad, wi' her bold een, un' her forrard ways—till—Nay! It fair brusts my heart! He's forgetten all E done fur him, un made on him, un' goan un' riven up a whole row ut t' grandest currant trees, i' t' garden!" and here he lamented outright, unmanned by a sense of his bitter injuries, and Earnshaw's ingratitude and dangerous condition.

"Is the fool drunk?" asked Mr. Heathcliff. "Hareton is it you he's finding fault with?"

"Iv'e pulled up two or three bushes," replied the young man, "but I'm going to set 'em again.

"And why have you pulled them up?" said the master.

Catherine wisely put in her tongue.

WUTHERING HEIGHTS

"We wanted to plant some flowers there," she cried. "I'm the only person to blame, for I wished him to do it."

"And who the devil gave *you* leave to touch a stick about the place?" demanded her father-in-law, much surprised, "And who ordered *you* to obey her?" he added turning to Hareton.

The latter was speechless; his cousin replied—

"You shouldn't grudge a few yards of earth, for me to ornament, when you have taken all my land!"

"Your land, insolent slut? you never had any!" said Heathcliff.

"And my money," she continued, returning his angry glare, and meantime, biting a piece of crust, the remnant of her breakfast.

"Silence!" he exclaimed. "Get done, and begone!"

"And Hareton's land, and his money," pursued the reckless thing. "Hareton, and I are friends now; and I shall tell him all about you!"

The master seemed confounded a moment, he grew pale, and rose up, eyeing her all the while, with an expression of mortal hate.

"If you strike me, Hareton will strike you!' she said, "so you may as well sit down."

"If Hareton does not turn you out of the room, I'll strike him to Hell," thundered Heathcliff. "Damnable witch! dare you pretend to rouse him against me? Off with her! Do you hear? Fling her into the kitchen! I'll kill her, Ellen Dean, if you let her come into my sight again!"

Hareton tried under his breath to persuade her to go.

"Drag her away!" he cried savagely. "Are you staying to talk?" And he approached to execute his own command.

"He'll not obey you, wicked man, any more!" said Catherine, and he'll soon detest you, as much as I do!"

"Wisht! wisht!" muttered the young man reproachfully. "I will not hear you speak so to him—Have done!"

"But you won't let him strike me?" she cried.

"Come then!" he whispered earnestly.

It was too late—Heathcliff had caught hold of her.

"Now *you* go!" he said to Earnshaw. "Accursed witch! this time she has provoked me, when I could not bear it; and I'll make her repent it for ever!"

He had his hand in her hair; Hareton attempted to release the locks, entreating him not to hurt her that once. His black eyes flashed, he seemed ready to tear Catherine in pieces, and I was just worked up to risk coming to the rescue, when of a sudden, his fingers relaxed, he shifted his grasp from her head, to her arm, and gazed intently in her face—Then, he drew his hand over his eyes, stood a moment to collect himself apparently, and turning anew to Catherine, said with assumed calmness,

"You must learn to avoid putting me in a passion, or I shall really murder you, sometime! go with Mrs. Dean, and keep with her, and confine your

296 EMILY BRONTË

insolence to her ears. As to Hareton Earnshaw if I see him listen to you, I'll send him seeking his bread where he can get it! your love will make him an outcast, and a beggar—Nelly, take her, and leave me, all of you! Leave me!"

I led my young lady out; she was too glad of her escape, to resist; the other followed, and Mr. Heathcliff had the room to himself, till dinner.

I had counselled Catherine to get hers upstairs; but, as soon as he perceived her vacant seat, he sent me to call her. He spoke to none of us, eat very little, and went out directly afterwards, intimating that he should not return before evening.

The two new friends established themselves in the house, during his absence, where I heard Hareton sternly check his cousin, on her offering a revelation of her father-in-law's conduct to his father.

He said he wouldn't suffer a word to be uttered to him, in his disparagement; if he were the devil, it didn't signify; he would stand by him; and he'd rather she would abuse himself, as she used to, than begin on Mr. Heathcliff.

Catherine was waxing cross at this; but he found means to make her hold her tongue, by asking, how she would like *him* to speak ill of her father? and then she comprehended that Earnshaw took the master's reputation home to himself: and was attached by ties stronger than reason could break—chains, forged by habit, which it would be cruel to attempt to loosen.

She showed a good heart, thenceforth, in avoiding both complaints and expressions of antipathy concerning Heathcliff; and confessed to me her sorrow that she had endeavoured to raise a bad spirit between him and Hareton—indeed, I don't believe she has ever breathed a syllable, in the latter's hearing, against her oppressor, since.

When this slight disagreement was over, they were thick again, and as busy as possible, in their several occupations, of pupil, and teacher, I came in to sit with them, after I had done my work, and I felt so soothed, and comforted to watch them, that I did not notice how time got on. You know, they both appeared in a measure, my children: I had long been proud of one, and now, I was sure, the other would be a source of equal satisfaction. His honest, warm, and intelligent nature shook off rapidly the clouds of ignorance, and degradation in which it had been bred; and Catherine's sincere commendations acted as a spur to his industry. His brightening mind brightened his features, and added spirit and nobility to their aspect—I could hardly fancy it the same individual I had beheld on the day I discovered my little lady at Wuthering Heights, after her expedition to the Crags.

While I admired, and they laboured, dusk drew on, and with it returned the master. He came upon us quite unexpectedly, entering by the front way, and had a full view of the whole three, ere we could raise our heads to glance at him.

Well, I reflected, there was never a pleasanter, or more harmless sight; and it will be a burning shame to scold them. The red fire-light glowed on their

WUTHERING HEIGHTS   297

two bonny heads, and revealed their faces, animated with the eager interest of children; for, though he was twenty-three, and she eighteen, each had so much of novelty to feel, and learn, that neither experienced, nor evinced the sentiments of sober disenchanted maturity.

They lifted their eyes together, to encounter Mr. Heathcliff—perhaps, you have never remarked that their eyes are precisely similar, and they are those of Catherine Earnshaw. The present Catherine has no other likeness to her, except a breadth of forehead, and a certain arch of the nostril that makes her appear rather haughty, whether she will, or not. With Hareton the resemblance is carried farther, it is singular, at all times—then it was particularly striking: because his senses were alert, and his mental faculties wakened to unwonted activity.

I suppose this resemblance disarmed Mr. Heathcliff: he walked to the hearth in evident agitation, but it quickly subsided, as he looked at the young man; or, I should say, altered its character, for it was there yet.

He took the book from his hand, and glanced at the open page, then returned it without any observation; merely signing Catherine away—her companion lingered very little behind her, and I was about to depart also, but he bid me sit still.

"It is a poor conclusion, is it not," he observed, having brooded a while on the scene he had just witnessed. "An absurd termination to my violent exertions? I get levers, and mattocks to demolish the two houses, and train myself to be capable of working like Hercules, and when everything is ready, and in my power, I find the will to lift a slate off either roof has vanished! My old enemies have not beaten me—now would be the precise time to revenge myself on their representatives—I could do it; and none could hinder me— But where is the use? I don't care for striking, I can't take the trouble to raise my hand! That sounds as if I had been labouring the whole time, only to exhibit a fine trait of magnanimity. It is far from being the case—I have lost the faculty of enjoying their destruction, and I am too idle to destroy for nothing.

"Nelly, there is a strange change approaching—I'm in its shadow at present—I take so little interest in my daily life, that I hardly remember to eat, and drink—Those two, who have left the room are the only objects which retain a distinct material appearance to me; and, that appearance causes me pain, amounting to agony. About *her* I won't speak; and I don't desire to think; but I earnestly wish she were invisible—her presence invokes only maddening sensations. *He* moves me differently; and yet if I could do it without seeming insane, I'd never see him again! You'll perhaps think me rather inclined to become so," he added, making an effort to smile, "if I try to describe the thousand forms of past associations, and ideas he awakens, or embodies—But you'll not talk of what I tell you, and my mind is so eternally secluded in itself, it is tempting, at last, to turn it out to another.

298   EMILY BRONTË

"Five minutes ago, Hareton seemed a personification of my youth, not a human being—I felt to him in such a variety of ways, that it would have been impossible to have accosted him rationally.

"In the first place, his startling likeness to Catherine connected him fearfully with her—That however which you may suppose the most potent to arrest my imagination, is actually the least—for what is not connected with her to me? and what does not recall her? I cannot look down to this floor, but her features are shaped on the flags! In every cloud, in every tree—filling the air at night, and caught by glimpses in every object, by day I am surrounded with her image! The most ordinary faces of men, and women—my own features mock me with a resemblance. The entire world is a dreadful collection of memoranda that she did exist, and that I have lost her!

"Well, Hareton's aspect was the ghost of my immortal love, of my wild endeavours to hold my right, my degradation, my pride, my happiness, and my anguish—

"But it is frenzy to repeat these thoughts to you; only it will let you know, why, with a reluctance to be always alone, his society is no benefit, rather an aggravation of the constant torment I suffer—and it partly contributes to render me regardless how he and his cousin go on together. I can give them no attention, any more.

"But what do you mean by a *change*, Mr. Heathcliff?" I said, alarmed at his manner, though he was neither in danger of losing his senses, nor dying, according to my judgment he was quite strong and healthy; and, as to his reason, from childhood, he had a delight in dwelling on dark things, and entertaining odd fancies—he might have had a monomania on the subject of his departed idol; but on every other point his wits were as sound as mine.

"I shall not know that, till it comes," he said, "I'm only half conscious of it now."

"You have no feeling of illness, have you?" I asked.

"No, Nelly, I have not," he answered.

"Then, you are not afraid of death?" I pursued.

"Afraid?" No!" he replied. "I have neither a fear, nor a presentiment, nor a hope of death—Why should I? With my hard constitution, and temperate mode of living, and unperilous occupations, I ought to, and probably *shall* remain above ground, till there is scarcely a black hair on my head—And yet I cannot continue in this condition!—I have to remind myself to breathe— almost to remind my heart to beat! And it is like bending back a stiff spring . . . it is by compulsion, that I do the slightest act, not prompted by one thought, and by compulsion, that I notice anything alive, or dead, which is not associated with one universal idea . . . I have a single wish, and my whole being, and faculties are yearning to attain it. They have yearned towards it so long, and so unwaveringly, that I'm convinced it *will* be reached—and *soon*—because it has devoured my existence—I am swallowed in the anticipation of its fulfilment.

"My confessions have not relieved me—but, they may account for some, otherwise unaccountable phases of humour, which I show. O, God! It is a long fight, I wish it were over!"

He began to pace the room, muttering terrible things to himself; till I was inclined to believe, as he said Joseph did, that conscience had turned his heart to an earthly hell—I wondered greatly how it would end.

Though he seldom before had revealed this state of mind, even by looks, it was his habitual mood, I had no doubt: he asserted it himself—but, not a soul, from his general bearing would have conjectured the fact. You did not, when you saw him, Mr. Lockwood—and at the period of which I speak, he was just the same as then, only fonder of continued solitude, and perhaps still more laconic in company.

Chapter XX.

For some days after that evening, Mr. Heathcliff shunned meeting us at meals; yet he would not consent, formally, to exclude Hareton and Cathy. He had an aversion to yielding so completely to his feelings, chosing, rather, to absent himself—And eating once in twenty-four hours seemed sufficient sustenance for him.

One night, after the family were in bed, I heard him go down stairs, and out at the front door: I did not hear him re-enter and, in the morning, I found he was still away.

We were in April then, the weather was sweet and warm, the grass as green as showers and sun could make it, and the two dwarf apple trees, near the southern wall, in full bloom.

"After breakfast, Catherine insisted on my bringing a chair, and sitting, with my work, under the fir trees, at the end of the house; and she beguiled Hareton, who had perfectly recovered from his accident, to dig and arrange her little garden, which was shifted to that corner by the influence of Joseph's complaints.

"I was comfortably revelling in the spring fragrance around, and the beautiful soft blue overhead, when my young lady, who had run down near the gate, to procure some primrose roots for a border, returned only half laden, and informed us that Mr. Heathcliff was coming in.

"'And he spoke to me,' she added with a perplexed countenance.

"'What did he say?' asked Hareton.

"'He told me to begone as fast as I could,' she answered. "But he looked so different from his usual look that I stopped a moment to stare at him.

"'How?' he enquired.

"'Why, almost bright and cheerful—No, almost nothing—*very much* excited, and wild and glad!' she replied.

"Night-walking amuses him, then,' "I remarked, affecting a careless manner. In reality, as surprised as she was; and, anxious to ascertain the truth of her statement, for to see the master looking glad would not be an every day spectacle, I framed an excuse to go in.

"Heathcliff stood at the open door; he was pale, and he trembled; yet, certainly, he had a strange joyful glitter in his eyes, that altered the aspect of his whole face.

"'Will you have some breakfast?' I said, 'You must be hungry rambling about all night!'

"I wanted to discover where he had been; but I did not like to ask directly.

WUTHERING HEIGHTS 301

"'No, I'm not hungry,' he answered, averting his head, and speaking rather contemptuously, as if he guessed I was trying to divine the occasion of his good humour.

"I felt perplexed—I didn't know whether it were not a proper opportunity to offer a bit of admonition.

"'I don't think it right to wander out of doors,' I observed, 'instead of being in bed: it is not wise, at any rate, this moist season. I dare say you'll catch a bad cold, or a fever—you have something the matter with you now!'

"'Nothing but what I can bear,' he replied, 'and with the greatest pleasure, provided you'll leave me alone—get in, and don't annoy me.'

"I obeyed; and, in passing, I noticed he breathed as fast as a cat.

"'Yes!' I reflected to myself, "we shall have a fit of illness. I cannot conceive what he has been doing!'

"That noon, he sat down to dinner with us, and received a heaped up plate from my hands, as if he intended to make amends for previous fasting.

"'I've neither cold, nor fever, Nelly,' he remarked, in allusion to my morning's speech. 'And I'm ready to do justice to the food you give me.'

"He took his knife and fork, and was going to commence eating, when the inclination appeared to become suddenly extinct. He laid them on the table, looked eagerly towards the window, then rose and went out.

"We saw him walking, to and fro, in the garden, while we concluded our meal; and Earnshaw said he'd go, and ask why he would not dine; he thought we had grieved him some way.

"'Well, is he coming?' cried Catherine, when her cousin returned.

"'Nay,' he answered, 'but he's not angry; he seemed rare and pleased indeed; only, I made him impatient by speaking to him twice; and then he bid me be off to you; he wondered how I could want the company of any body else.'

"I set his plate, to keep warm, on the fender: and after an hour or two, he re-entered, when the room was clear, in no degree calmer—the same unnatural—it was unnatural—appearance of joy under his black brows; the same bloodless hue: and his teeth visible, now and then, in a kind of smile; his frame shivering, not as one shivers with chill or weakness, but as a tight-stretched cord vibrates—a strong thrilling, rather than trembling.

"I will ask what is the matter, I thought, or who should? And I exclaimed—

"'Have you heard any good news, Mr. Heathcliff? You look uncommonly animated.'

"'Where should good news come from, to me?' he said. 'I'm animated with hunger; and, seemingly, I must not eat.'

"'Your dinner is here,' I returned; 'why wont you get it?'

"'I don't want it now,' he muttered, hastily. 'I'll wait till supper. And, Nelly, once for all, let me beg you to warn Hareton and the other away from me. I wish to be troubled by nobody—I wish to have this place to myself.'

EMILY BRONTË

"'Is there some new reason for this banishment?' I inquired. 'Tell me why you are so queer, Mr. Heathcliff? Where were you last night?' I'm not putting the question through idle curiosity, but—'

"'You are putting the question through very idle curiosity,' he interrupted, with a laugh. 'Yet, I'll answer it. Last night, I was on the threshold of hell. To-day, I am within sight of my heaven—I have my eyes on it—hardly three feet to sever me! And now you'd better go—You'll neither see nor hear anything to frighten you, if you refrain from prying.'

"Having swept the hearth, and wiped the table, I departed more perplexed than ever.

"He did not quit the house again that afternoon, and no one intruded on his solitude, till, at eight o'clock, I deemed it proper, though unsummoned, to carry a candle, and his supper to him.

"He was leaning against the ledge of an open lattice, but not looking out; his face was turned to the interior gloom. The fire had smouldered to ashes; the room was filled with the damp, mild air of the cloudy evening, and so still, that not only the murmur of the beck down Gimmerton was distinguishable, but its ripples and its gurgling over the pebbles, or through the large stones which it could not cover.

"I uttered an ejaculation of discontent at seeing the dismal grate, and commenced shutting the casements, one after another, till I came to his.

"'Must I close this?' I asked, in order to rouse him, for he would not stir.

"The light flashed on his features, as I spoke. Oh, Mr. Lockwood, I cannot express what a terrible start I got, by the momentary view! Those deep black eyes! That smile, and ghastly paleness! It appeared to me, not Mr. Heathcliff, but a goblin; and, in my terror, I let the candle bend towards the wall, and it left me in darkness.

"'Yes, close it,' he replied, in his familiar voice. 'There, that is pure awkwardness! Why did you hold the candle horizontally? Be quick, and bring another.'

"I hurried out in a foolish state of dread, and said to Joseph—

"'The master wishes you to take him a light, and rekindle the fire.' For I dare not go in myself again just then.

"Joseph rattled some fire into the shovel, and went; but he brought it back, immediately, with the supper tray in his other hand, explaining that Mr. Heathcliff was going to bed, and he wanted nothing to eat till morning.

"We heard him mount the stairs directly; he did not proceed to his ordinary chamber, but turned into that with the panelled bed—its window, as I mentioned before, is wide enough for anybody to get through, and it struck me, that he plotted another midnight excursion, which he had rather we had no suspicion of.

"'Is he a ghoul, or a vampire?' I mused. I had read of such hideous, incarnate demons. And then, I set myself to reflect, how I had tended him in infancy; and

WUTHERING HEIGHTS 303

watched him grow to youth; and followed him almost through his whole course; and what absurd nonsense it was to yield to that sense of horror.

"'But, where did he come from, the little dark thing, harboured by a good man to his bane?' muttered superstition, as I dozed into unconsciousness. And I began, half dreaming, to weary myself with imaging some fit parentage for him; and repeating my waking meditations, I tracked his existence over again, with grim variations; at last, picturing his death and funeral; of which, all I can remember is, being exceedingly vexed at having the task of dictating an inscription for his monument, and consulting the sexton about it; and, as he had no surname, and we could not tell his age, we were obliged to content ourselves with the single word, 'Heathcliff.' That came true; we were. If you enter the kirkyard, you'll read on his headstone, only that, and the date of his death.

"Dawn restored me to common sense. I rose, and went into the garden, as soon as I could see, to ascertain if there were any footmarks under his window. There were none.

"'He has stayed at home,' I thought, 'and he'll be all right, to-day!'

"I prepared breakfast for the household; as was my usual custom, but told Hareton, and Catherine to get theirs, ere the master came down, for he lay late. They preferred taking it out of doors, under the trees, and I set a little table to accommodate them.

"On my re-entrance, I found Mr. Heathcliff below. He and Joseph were conversing about some farming business; he gave clear, minute directions concerning the matter discussed, but he spoke rapidly, and turned his head continually aside, and had the same excited expression, even more exaggerated.

"When Joseph quitted the room, he took his seat in the place he generally chose, and I put a basin of coffee before him. He drew it nearer, and then rested his arms on the table, and looked at the opposite wall, as I supposed, surveying one particular portion, up and down, with glittering, restless eyes, and with such eager interest, that he stopped breathing, during half a minute together.

"'Come now,' I exclaimed, pushing some bread against his hand. 'Eat and drink that, while it is hot. It has been waiting near an hour.'

"He didn't notice me, and yet he smiled. I'd rather have seen him gnash his teeth than smile so.

"'Mr. Heathcliff! master!' I cried. 'Don't for God's sake, stare as if you saw an unearthly vision.'

"'Dont, for God's sake, shout so loud,' he replied. 'Turn round, and tell me, are we by ourselves?'

"'Of course,' was my answer, 'of course, we are!'

"Still, I involuntarily obeyed him, as if I were not quite sure.

"With a sweep of his hand, he cleared a vacant space in front among the breakfast things, and leant forward to gaze more at his ease.

EMILY BRONTË

"Now, I perceived he was not looking at the wall, for when I regarded him alone, it seemed, exactly, that he gazed at something within two yards distance. And, whatever it was, it communicated, apparently, both pleasure and pain, in exquisite extremes, at least, the anguished, yet raptured expression of his countenance suggested that idea.

"The fancied object was not fixed, either; his eyes pursued it with unwearied vigilance; and, even in speaking to me, were never weaned away.

"I vainly reminded him of his protracted abstinence from food; if he stirred to touch anything in compliance with my entreaties, if he stretched his hand out to get a piece of bread, his fingers clenched, before they reached it, and remained on the table, forgetful of their aim.

"I sat a model of patience, trying to attract his absorbed attention from its engrossing speculation; till he grew irritable, and got up, asking, why I would not allow him to have his own time in taking his meals? and saying that, on the next occasion, I needn't wait, I might set the things down, and go.

"Having uttered these words, he left the house; slowly sauntered down the garden path, and disappeared through the gate.

"The hours crept anxiously by: another evening came. I did not retire to rest till late, and when I did, I could not sleep. He returned after midnight, and, instead of going to bed, shut himself into the room beneath. I listened, and tossed about; and, finally, dressed, and descended. It was too irksome to lie up there, harassing my brain with a hundred idle misgivings.

"I distinguished Mr. Heathcliff's step, restlessly measuring the floor; and he frequently broke the silence, by a deep inspiration, resembling a groan. He muttered detached words, also; the only one, I could catch, was the name of Catherine, coupled with some wild term of endearment, or suffering; and spoken as one would speak to a person present —low and earnest, and wrung from the depth of his soul.

"I had not courage to walk straight into the apartment; but I desired to divert him from his reverie, and, therefore, fell foul of the kitchen fire; stirred it, and began to scrape the cinders. It drew him forth sooner than I expected. He opened the door immediately, and said—

"'Nelly, come here—is it morning? Come in with your light.'

"'It is striking four,' I answered; 'you want a candle to take up stairs—you might have lit one at this fire.'

"'No, I don't wish to go up stairs,' he said. 'Come in, and kindle *me* a fire, and do anything there is to do about the room.'

"I must blow the coals red first, before I can carry any,' I replied, getting a chair and the bellows.

"He roamed to and fro, meantime, in a state approaching distraction: his heavy sighs succeeding each other so thick as to leave no space for common breathing between.

WUTHERING HEIGHTS

"'When day breaks, I'll send for Green,' he said; 'I wish to make some legal inquiries of him, while I can bestow a thought on those matters, and while I can act calmly. I have not written my will yet, and how to leave my property, I cannot determine! I wish I could annihiliate it from the face of the earth.'

"'I would not talk so, Mr. Heathcliff,' I interposed. "Let your will be, a while—you'll be spared to repent of your many injustices, yet! I never expected that your nerves would be disordered—they are, at present, marvellously so, however; and, almost entirely, through your own fault. The way you've passed these three last days might knock up a Titan. Do take some food, and some repose. You need only look at yourself, in a glass, to see how you require both. Your cheeks are hollow, and your eyes blood-shot, like a person starving with hunger, and going blind with loss of sleep.'

"'It is not my fault, that I cannot eat or rest,' he replied. 'I assure you it is through no settled designs. I'll do both, as soon as I possibly can. But you might as well bid a man struggling in the water, rest within arms-length of the shore! I must reach it first, and then I'll rest. Well, never mind, Mr. Green; as to repenting of my injustices, I've done no injustice, and I repent of nothing— I'm too happy, and yet I'm not happy enough. My soul's bliss kills my body, but does not satisfy itself.'

"'Happy, master?' I cried. 'Strange happiness! If you would hear me without being angry, I might offer some advice that would make you happier.'

"'What is that?' he asked. 'Give it.'

"'You are aware, Mr. Heathcliff,' I said, 'that from the time you were thirteen years old, you have lived a selfish, unchristian life; and probably hardly had a Bible in your hands, during all that period. You must have forgotten the contents of the book, and you may not have space to search it now. Could it be hurtful to send for some one—some minister of any denomination, it does not matter which, to explain it, and show you how very far you have erred from its precepts, and how unfit you will be for its heaven, unless a change takes place before you die?'

"I'm rather obliged than angry, Nelly," he said, for you remind me of the manner that I desire to be buried in—It is to be carried to the churchyard, in the evening. You, and Hareton may, if you please accompany me—and mind, particularly, to notice that the sexton obeys my directions concerning the two coffins! No minister need come; nor need anything be said over me—I tell you, I have nearly attained *my* heaven; and that of others is altogether unvalued, and uncoveted by me!"

"And supposing you persevered in your obstinate fast, and died by that means, and they refused to bury you in the precincts of the Kirk?" I said shocked at his godless indifference. "How would you like it?"

"They wont do that," he replied, "if they did, you must have me removed secretly; and if you neglect it, you shall prove, practically, that the dead are not annihilated!"

EMILY BRONTË

As soon as he heard the other members of the family stirring he retired to his den, and I breathed freer—But in the afternoon, while Joseph and Hareton were at their work, he came into the kitchen again, and with a wild look, bid me come, and sit in the house—he wanted somebody with him.

I declined, telling him plainly, that his strange talk and manner, frightened me, and I had neither the nerve, nor the will to be his companion, alone.

"I believe you think me a fiend!" he said, with his dismal laugh, "something too horrible to live under a decent roof!"

Then turning to Catherine, who was there, and who drew behind me at his approach, he added, half sneeringly.

"Will *you* come, chuck?" I'll not hurt you. No! to you, I've made myself worse than the devil. Well, there is *one* who wont shrink from my company! By God! she's relentless. Oh, damn it! It's unutterably too much for flesh and blood to bear, even mine."

He solicited the society of no one more. At dusk, he went into his chamber—through the whole night, and far into the morning, we heard him groaning, and murmuring to himself. Hareton was anxious to enter, but I bid him fetch Mr. Kenneth, and he should go in, and see him.

When he came, and I requested admittance and tried to open the door, I found it locked; and Heathcliff bid us be damned. He was better, and would be left alone; so the doctor went away.

The following evening was very wet, indeed it poured down, till day-dawn; and, as I took my morning walk round the house, I observed the master's window swinging open, and the rain driving straight in.

He cannot be in bed, I thought, those showers would drench him through! He must either be up, or out. But, I'll make no more ado, I'll go boldly, and look!"

Having succeeded in obtaining entrance with another key, I ran to unclose the panels, for the chamber was vacant—quickly pushing them aside, I peeped in. Mr. Heathcliff was there—laid on his back. His eyes met mine so keen, and fierce, I started; and then, he seemed to smile.

I could not think him dead—but his face, and throat were washed with rain; the bed-clothes dripped, and he was perfectly still. The lattice, flapping to and fro, had grazed one hand that rested on the sill—no blood trickled from the broken skin, and when I put my fingers to it, I could doubt no more—he was dead and stark!

I hasped the window; I combed his black long hair from his forehead; I tried to close his eyes—to extinguish, if possible, that frightful, life-like gaze of exultation, before any one else beheld it. They would not shut—they seemed to sneer at my attempts, and his parted lips, and sharp, white teeth sneered too! Taken with another fit of cowardice, I cried out for Joseph. Joseph shuffled up, and made a noise, but resolutely refused to meddle with him.

WUTHERING HEIGHTS 307

"Th' divil's harried off his soul" he cried, "and he muh hev his carcass intuh t' bargin, for ow't Aw care! Ech! what a wicked un he looks girnning at death!" and the old sinner grinned in mockery.

I thought he intended to cut a caper round the bed; but suddenly composing himself, he fell on his knees, and raised his hands, and returned thanks that the lawful master and the ancient stock were restored to their rights.

I felt stunned by the awful event; and my memory unavoidably recurred to former times with a sort of oppressive sadness. But poor Hareton the most wronged, was the only one that really suffered much. He sat by the corpse all night, weeping in bitter earnest. He pressed its hand, and kissed the sarcastic, savage face that every one else shrank from contemplating; and bemoaned him with that strong grief which springs naturally from a generous heart, though it be tough as tempered steel.

Kenneth was perplexed to pronounce of what disorder the master died. I concealed the fact of his having swallowed nothing for four days, fearing it might lead to trouble, and then, I am persuaded he did not abstain on purpose; it was the consequence of his strange illness, not the cause.

We buried him, to the scandal of the whole neighbourhood, as he had wished. Earnshaw, and I, the sexton and six men to carry the coffin, comprehended the whole attendance.

The six men departed when they had let it down into the grave: we stayed to see it covered. Hareton, with a streaming face, dug green sods, and laid them over the brown mould himself, at present it is as smooth and verdant as its companion mounds—and I hope its tenant sleeps as soundly. But the country folks, if you asked them, would swear on their bible that he *walks*. There are those who speak to having met him near the church, and on the moor, and even within this house—Idle tales, you'll say, and so say I. Yet that old man by the kitchen fire affirms he has seen two on 'em looking out of his chamber window, on every rainy night, since his death—and an odd thing happened to me about a month ago.

I was going to the Grange one evening—a dark evening threatening thunder—and, just at the turn of the Heights, I encountered a little boy with a sheep, and two lambs before him, he was crying terribly, and I supposed the lambs were skittish, and would not be guided.

"'What is the matter, my little man?' I asked.

"'They's Heathcliff, and a woman, yonder, under t' Nab,' he blubbered, 'un' Aw darnut pass 'em.'

"I saw nothing; but neither the sheep nor he would go on, so I bid him take the road lower down.

"He probably raised the phantoms from thinking, as he traversed the moors alone, on the nonsense he had heard his parents and companions repeat—yet still, I don't like being out in the dark, now—and I don't like

308 EMILY BRONTË

being left by myself in this grim house—I cannot help it, I shall be glad when they leave it, and shift to the Grange!"

"They are going to the Grange then?" I said.

"Yes," answered Mrs. Dean, "as soon as they are married; and that will be on New Year's day."

"And who will live here then?"

"Why, Joseph will take care of the house, and, perhaps, a lad to keep him company. They will live in the kitchen, and the rest will be shut up."

"For the use of such ghosts as choose to inhabit it," I observed.

"No, Mr. Lockwood," said Nelly, shaking her head. "I believe the dead are at peace, but it is not right to speak of them with levity."

At that moment the garden gate swung to; the ramblers were returning.

"*They* are afraid of nothing," I grumbled, watching their approach through the window.

"Together they would brave satan and all his legions."

As they stepped onto the door-stones, and halted to take a last look at the moon, or, more correctly, at each other, by her light, I felt irresistibly impelled to escape them again; and, pressing a remembrance into the hand of Mrs. Dean, and disregarding her expostulations at my rudeness, I vanished through the kitchen, as they opened the house-door, and so, should have confirmed Joseph in his opinion of his fellow-servant's gay indiscretions, had he not, fortunately, recognised me for a respectable character, by the sweet ring of a sovereign at his feet.

My walk home was lengthened by a diversion in the direction of the kirk. When beneath its walls, I perceived decay had made progress, even in seven months—many a window showed black gaps deprived of glass; and slates jutted off, here and there, beyond the right line of the roof, to be gradually worked off in coming autumn storms.

I sought, and soon discovered, the three head-stones on the slope next the moor—the middle one, grey, and half buried in heath—Edgar Linton's only harmonized by the turf, and moss creeping up its foot—Heathcliff's still bare.

I lingered round them, under that benign sky; watched the moths fluttering among the heath, and hare-bells; listened to the soft wind breathing through the grass; and wondered how any one could ever imagine unquiet slumbers, for the sleepers in that quiet earth.

APPENDICES

CHARLOTTE BRONTË'S ACCOUNTS IN *1850*

i. Currer Bell [Charlotte Brontë]'s accounts in *'Wuthering Heights' and 'Agnes Grey'. By Ellis and Acton Bell. A New Edition Revised, with a Biographical Notice of the Authors, a Selection from their Literary Remains, and a Preface, by Currer Bell* (1850)

Currer Bell [Charlotte Brontë], 'Biographical Notice of Ellis and Acton Bell' (1850)

It has been thought that all the works published under the names of Currer, Ellis, and Acton Bell were, in reality, the production of one person. This mistake I endeavoured to rectify by a few words of disclaimer prefixed to the third edition of "Jane Eyre." These, too, it appears, failed to gain general credence, and now, on the occasion of a reprint of "Wuthering Heights" and "Agnes Grey," I am advised distinctly to state how the case really stands.

Indeed, I feel myself that it is time the obscurity attending those two names—Ellis and Acton—was done away. The little mystery, which formerly yielded some harmless pleasure, has lost its interest; circumstances are changed. It becomes, then, my duty to explain briefly the origin and authorship of the books written by Currer, Ellis, and Acton Bell.

About five years ago, my two sisters and myself, after a somewhat prolonged period of separation, found ourselves reunited, and at home. Resident in a remote district, where education had made little progress, and where, consequently, there was no inducement to seek social intercourse beyond our own domestic circle, we were wholly dependent on ourselves and each other, on books and study, for the enjoyments and occupations of life. The highest stimulus, as well as the liveliest pleasure we had known from childhood upwards, lay in attempts at literary composition; formerly we used to show each other what we wrote, but of late years this habit of communication and consultation had been discontinued; hence it ensued, that we were mutually ignorant of the progress we might respectively have made.

One day, in the autumn of 1845, I accidentally lighted on a MS. volume of verse in my sister Emily's handwriting. Of course, I was not surprised, knowing that she could and did write verse: I looked it over, and something more than surprise seized me—a deep conviction that these were not common effusions, nor at all like the poetry women generally write. I thought them condensed and terse, vigorous and genuine. To my ear they had also a peculiar music—wild, melancholy, and elevating.

My sister Emily was not a person of demonstrative character, nor one on the recesses of whose mind and feelings even those nearest and dearest to her

312   EMILY BRONTË

could, with impunity, intrude unlicensed; it took hours to reconcile her to the discovery I had made, and days to persuade her that such poems merited publication. I knew, however, that a mind like hers could not be without some latent spark of honourable ambition, and refused to be discouraged in my attempts to fan that spark to flame.

Meantime, my younger sister quietly produced some of her own compositions, intimating that, since Emily's had given me pleasure, I might like to look at hers. I could not but be a partial judge, yet I thought that these verses, too, had a sweet, sincere pathos of their own.

We had very early cherished the dream of one day becoming authors. This dream, never relinquished even when distance divided and absorbing tasks occupied us, now suddenly acquired strength and consistency: it took the character of a resolve. We agreed to arrange a small selection of our poems, and, if possible, to get them printed. Averse to personal publicity, we veiled our own names under those of Currer, Ellis, and Acton Bell; the ambiguous choice being dictated by a sort of conscientious scruple at assuming Christian names positively masculine, while we did not like to declare ourselves women, because—without at that time suspecting that our mode of writing and thinking was not what is called "feminine"—we had a vague impression that authoresses are liable to be looked on with prejudice; we had noticed how critics sometimes use for their chastisement the weapon of personality, and for their reward, a flattery, which is not true praise.

The bringing out of our little book was hard work. As was to be expected, neither we nor our poems were at all wanted; but for this we had been prepared at the outset; though inexperienced ourselves, we had read the experience of others. The great puzzle lay in the difficulty of getting answers of any kind from the publishers to whom we applied. Being greatly harassed by this obstacle, I ventured to apply to the Messrs. Chambers, of Edinburgh, for a word of advice; *they* may have forgotten the circumstance, but *I* have not, for from them I received a brief and business-like, but civil and sensible reply, on which we acted, and at last made a way.

The book was printed: it is scarcely known, and all of it that merits to be known are the poems of Ellis Bell. The fixed conviction I held, and hold, of the worth of these poems has not indeed received the confirmation of much favourable criticism; but I must retain it notwithstanding.

Ill-success failed to crush us: the mere effort to succeed had given a wonderful zest to existence; it must be pursued. We each set to work on a prose tale: Ellis Bell produced "Wuthering Heights," Acton Bell "Agnes Grey," and Currer Bell also wrote a narrative in one volume. These MSS. were perseveringly obtruded upon various publishers for the space of a year and a half; usually, their fate was an ignominious and abrupt dismissal.

At last "Wuthering Heights" and "Agnes Grey" were accepted on terms somewhat impoverishing to the two authors; Currer Bell's book found

CHARLOTTE BRONTË'S ACCOUNTS IN *1850*

acceptance nowhere, nor any acknowledgment of merit, so that something like the chill of despair began to invade her heart. As a forlorn hope, she tried one publishing house more—Messrs. Smith, Elder and Co. Ere long, in a much shorter space than that on which experience had taught her to calculate—there came a letter, which she opened in the dreary expectation of finding two hard, hopeless lines, intimating that Messrs. Smith, Elder and Co. "were not disposed to publish the MS.," and, instead, she took out of the envelope a letter of two pages. She read it trembling. It declined, indeed, to publish that tale, for business reasons, but it discussed its merits and demerits so courteously, so considerately, in a spirit so rational, with a discrimination so enlightened, that this very refusal cheered the author better than a vulgarly expressed acceptance would have done. It was added, that a work in three volumes would meet with careful attention.

I was then just completing "Jane Eyre," at which I had been working while the one-volume tale was plodding its weary round in London: in three weeks I sent it off; friendly and skilful hands took it in. This was in the commencement of September, 1847; it came out before the close of October following, while "Wuthering Heights" and "Agnes Grey," my sisters" works, which had already been in the press for months, still lingered under a different management.

They appeared at last. Critics failed to do them justice. The immature but very real powers revealed in "Wuthering Heights" were scarcely recognised; its import and nature were misunderstood; the identity of its author was misrepresented; it was said that this was an earlier and ruder attempt of the same pen which had produced "Jane Eyre." Unjust and grievous error! We laughed at it at first, but I deeply lament it now. Hence, I fear, arose a prejudice against the book. That writer who could attempt to palm off an inferior and immature production under cover of one successful effort, must indeed be unduly eager after the secondary and sordid result of authorship, and pitiably indifferent to its true and honourable meed. If reviewers and the public truly believed this, no wonder that they looked darkly on the cheat.

Yet I must not be understood to make these things subject for reproach or complaint; I dare not do so; respect for my sister's memory forbids me. By her any such querulous manifestation would have been regarded as an unworthy and offensive weakness.

It is my duty, as well as my pleasure, to acknowledge one exception to the general rule of criticism. One writer, endowed with the keen vision and fine sympathies of genius, has discerned the real nature of "Wuthering Heights," and has, with equal accuracy, noted its beauties and touched on its faults. Too often do reviewers remind us of the mob of Astrologers, Chaldeans, and Soothsayers gathered before the "writing on the wall," and unable to read the characters or make known the interpretation. We have a right to rejoice when a true seer comes at last, some man in whom is an excellent spirit, to whom

314 EMILY BRONTË

have been given light, wisdom, and understanding; who can accurately read the "Mene, Mene, Tekel, Upharsin" of an original mind (however unripe, however inefficiently cultured and partially expanded that mind may be); and who can say with confidence, "This is the interpretation thereof."

Yet even the writer to whom I allude shares the mistake about the authorship, and does me the injustice to suppose that there was equivoque in my former rejection of this honour (as an honour I regard it). May I assure him that I would scorn in this and in every other case to deal in equivoque; I believe language to have been given us to make our meaning clear, and not to wrap it in dishonest doubt?

"The Tenant of Wildfell Hall," by Acton Bell, had likewise an unfavourable reception. At this I cannot wonder. The choice of subject was an entire mistake. Nothing less congruous with the writer's nature could be conceived. The motives which dictated this choice were pure, but, I think, slightly morbid. She had, in the course of her life, been called on to contemplate, near at hand, and for a long time, the terrible effects of talents misused and faculties abused: hers was naturally a sensitive, reserved, and dejected nature; what she saw sank very deeply into her mind; it did her harm. She brooded over it till she believed it to be a duty to reproduce every detail (of course with fictitious characters, incidents, and situations), as a warning to others. She hated her work, but would pursue it. When reasoned with on the subject, she regarded such reasonings as a temptation to self-indulgence. She must be honest; she must not varnish, soften, nor conceal. This well-meant resolution brought on her misconstruction, and some abuse, which she bore, as it was her custom to bear whatever was unpleasant, with mild, steady patience. She was a very sincere, and practical Christian, but the tinge of religious melancholy communicated a sad shade to her brief, blameless life.

Neither Ellis nor Acton allowed herself for one moment to sink under want of encouragement; energy nerved the one, and endurance upheld the other. They were both prepared to try again; I would fain think that hope and the sense of power were yet strong within them. But a great change approached; affliction came in that shape which to anticipate is dread; to look back on, grief. In the very heat and burden of the day, the labourers failed over their work.

My sister Emily first declined. The details of her illness are deep-branded in my memory, but to dwell on them, either in thought or narrative, is not in my power. Never in all her life had she lingered over any task that lay before her, and she did not linger now. She sank rapidly. She made haste to leave us. Yet, while physically she perished, mentally she grew stronger than we had yet known her. Day by day, when I saw with what a front she met suffering, I looked on her with an anguish of wonder and love. I have seen nothing like it; but, indeed, I have never seen her parallel in anything. Stronger than a man, simpler than a child, her nature stood alone. The awful point was, that

CHARLOTTE BRONTË'S ACCOUNTS IN *1850*   315

while full of ruth for others, on herself she had no pity; the spirit was inexorable to the flesh; from the trembling hand, the unnerved limbs, the faded eyes, the same service was exacted as they had rendered in health. To stand by and witness this, and not dare to remonstrate, was a pain no words can render.

Two cruel months of hope and fear passed painfully by, and the day came at last when the terrors and pains of death were to be undergone by this treasure, which had grown dearer and dearer to our hearts as it wasted before our eyes. Towards the decline of that day, we had nothing of Emily but her mortal remains as consumption left them. She died December 19, 1848.

We thought this enough: but we were utterly and presumptuously wrong. She was not buried ere Anne fell ill. She had not been committed to the grave a fortnight, before we received distinct intimation that it was necessary to prepare our minds to see the younger sister go after the elder. Accordingly, she followed in the same path with slower step, and with a patience that equalled the other's fortitude. I have said that she was religious, and it was by leaning on those Christian doctrines in which she firmly believed, that she found support through her most painful journey. I witnessed their efficacy in her latest hour and greatest trial, and must bear my testimony to the calm triumph with which they brought her through. She died May 28, 1849.

What more shall I say about them? I cannot and need not say much more. In externals, they were two unobtrusive women; a perfectly secluded life gave them retiring manners and habits. In Emily's nature the extremes of vigour and simplicity seemed to meet. Under an unsophisticated culture, inartificial tastes, and an unpretending outside, lay a secret power and fire that might have informed the brain and kindled the veins of a hero; but she had no worldly wisdom; her powers were unadapted to the practical business of life; she would fail to defend her most manifest rights, to consult her most legitimate advantage. An interpreter ought always to have stood between her and the world. Her will was not very flexible, and it generally opposed her interest. Her temper was magnanimous, but warm and sudden; her spirit altogether unbending.

Anne's character was milder and more subdued; she wanted the power, the fire, the originality of her sister, but was well endowed with quiet virtues of her own. Long-suffering, self-denying, reflective, and intelligent, a constitutional reserve and taciturnity placed and kept her in the shade, and covered her mind, and especially her feelings, with a sort of nun-like veil, which was rarely lifted. Neither Emily nor Anne was learned; they had no thought of filling their pitchers at the well-spring of other minds; they always wrote from the impulse of nature, the dictates of intuition, and from such stores of observation as their limited experience had enabled them to amass. I may sum up all by saying, that for strangers they were nothing, for superficial observers

316   EMILY BRONTË

less than nothing; but for those who had known them all their lives in the intimacy of close relationship, they were genuinely good and truly great.

This notice has been written because I felt it a sacred duty to wipe the dust off their gravestones, and leave their dear names free from soil.

CURRER BELL

September 19, 1850

Currer Bell [Charlotte Brontë], 'Selections from the Literary Remains of Ellis and Acton Bell' (1850)

It would not have been difficult to compile a volume out of the papers left by my sisters, had I, in making the selection, dismissed from my consideration the scruples and the wishes of those whose thoughts these papers held. But this was impossible: an influence, stronger than could be exercised by any motive of expediency, necessarily regulated the selection. I have, then, culled from the mass only a little poem here and there. The whole makes but a tiny nosegay, and the colour and the perfume of the flowers are not such as fit them for festal uses.

It has been already said that my sisters wrote much in childhood and girlhood. Usually it seems a sort of injustice to expose in print the crude thoughts of the unripe mind, the rude efforts of the unpractised hand: yet I venture to give three little poems of my sister Emily's, written in her sixteenth year, because they illustrate a point in her character.

At that period she was sent to school. Her previous life, with the exception of a single half-year, had been passed in the absolute retirement of a village parsonage, amongst the hills bordering Yorkshire and Lancashire. The scenery of these hills is not grand—it is not romantic; it is scarcely striking. Long low moors, with heath, shut in little valleys, where a stream waters, here and there, a fringe of stunted copse. Mills and scattered cottages chase romance from these valleys; it is only higher up, deep in amongst the ridges of the moors, that Imagination can find rest for the sole of her foot; and even if she finds it there, she must be a solitude-loving raven, no gentle dove. If she demand beauty to inspire her, she must bring it inborn: these moors are too stern to yield to any product so delicate. The eye of the gazer must itself brim with a 'purple light,' intense enough to perpetuate the brief flower-flush of August on the heather, or the sunset smile of June; out of his heart must well the freshness, that in latter spring and early summer brightens the bracken, nurtures the moss, and cherishes the starry flowers that spangle for a few weeks the pasture of the moor-sheep. Unless that light and freshness are innate and self-sustained, the drear prospect of a Yorkshire moor will be found as barren of poetic as of agricultural interest: where the love of wild nature is strong, the locality will perhaps be

CHARLOTTE BRONTË'S ACCOUNTS IN *1850*   317

clung to with the more passionate constancy, because from the hill-lover's self comes half its charm.

My sister loved the moors. Flowers brighter than the rose bloomed in the blackest of the heath for her; out of a sullen hollow in a livid hill-side her mind could make an Eden. She found in the bleak solitude many and dear delights; and not the least and best loved was—liberty. Liberty was the breath of Emily's nostrils; without it, she perished. The change from her own home to a school, and from her own very noiseless, very secluded, but un-restricted and inartificial mode of life, to one of disciplined routine (though under the kindliest auspices) was what she failed in enduring. Her nature proved here too strong for her fortitude. Every morning when she woke, the vision of home and the moors rushed on her, and darkened and saddened the day that lay before her. Nobody knew what ailed her but me—I knew only too well. In this struggle her health was quickly broken: her white face, attenuated form, and failing strength, threatened rapid decline. I felt in my heart she would die, if she did not go home, and with this conviction obtained her recall. She had only been three months at school: and it was some years before the experiment of sending her from home was again ventured on. After the age of twenty, having meantime studied alone with diligence and perseverance, she went with me to an establishment on the continent; the same suffering and conflict ensued, heightened by the strong recoil of her upright, heretic and English spirit from the gentle Jesuitry of the foreign and Roman system. Once more she seemed sinking, but this time she rallied through the mere force of resolution: with inward remorse and shame she looked back on her former failure, and resolved to conquer in this second ordeal. She did conquer: but it cost her dear. She was never happy till she carried her hard-won knowledge back to the remote English village, the old parsonage house, and desolate Yorkshire hills. A very few years more, and she looked her last on those hills, and breathed her last in that house, and under the aisle of that obscure village church found her last resting-place. Merciful was the decree that spared her when she was a stranger in a strange land, and guarded her dying bed with kindred love and congenial constancy.

The following pieces were composed at twilight, in the schoolroom, when the leisure of the evening play-hour brought back in full tide the thought of home.

Currer Bell [Charlotte Brontë], 'Editor's Preface to the new edition of *Wuthering Heights*' (1850)

I HAVE just read over "Wuthering Heights," and, for the first time, have obtained a clear glimpse of what are termed (and, perhaps, really are) its faults; have gained a definite notion of how it appears to other people—to strangers who knew nothing of the author; who are unacquainted with the

318 EMILY BRONTË

locality where the scenes of the story are laid; to whom the inhabitants, the customs, the natural characteristics of the outlying hills and hamlets in the West-Riding of Yorkshire are things alien and unfamiliar.

To all such "Wuthering Heights" must appear a rude and strange production. The wild moors of the north of England can for them have no interest; the language, [t]he manners, the very dwellings and household customs of the scattered inhabitants of those districts, must be to such readers in a great measure unintelligible, and—where intelligible—repulsive. Men and women who, perhaps naturally very calm, and with feelings moderate in degree, and little marked in kind, have been trained from their cradle to observe the utmost evenness of manner and guardedness of language, will hardly know what to make of the rough, strong utterance, the harshly manifested passions, the unbridled aversions, and headlong partialities of unlettered moorland hinds and rugged moorland squires, who have grown up untaught and unchecked, except by mentors as harsh as themselves. A large class of readers, likewise, will suffer greatly from the introduction into the pages of this work of words—printed with, all their letters, which it has become the custom to represent by the initial and final letter only—a blank line filling the interval. I may as well say at once that, for this circumstance, it is out of my power to apologise; deeming it, myself, a rational plan to write words at full length. The practice of hinting by single letters those expletives with which profane and violent persons are wont to garnish their discourse, strikes me as a proceeding which, however well meant, is weak and futile. I cannot tell what good it does—what feeling it spares—what horror it conceals.

With regard to the rusticity of "Wuthering Heights," I admit the charge, for I feel the quality. It is rustic all through. It is moorish, and wild, and knotty as a root of heath. Nor was it natural that it should be otherwise; the author being herself a native and nursling of the moors. Doubtless, had her lot been cast in a town, her writings, if she had written at all, would have possessed another character. Even had chance or taste led her to choose a similar subject, she would have treated it otherwise. Had Ellis Bell been a lady or a gentleman accustomed to what is called "the world," her view of a remote and unreclaimed region, as well as of the dwellers therein, would have differed greatly from that actually taken by the homebred country girl. Doubtless it would have been wider—more comprehensive: whether it would have been more original or more truthful is not so certain—As far as the scenery and locality are concerned, it could scarcely have been so sympathetic: Ellis Bell did not describe as one whose eye and taste alone found pleasure in the prospect; her native hills were far more to her than a spectacle; they were what she lived in, and by, as much as the wild birds, their tenants, or as the heather, their produce. Her descriptions, then, of natural scenery, are what they should be, and all they should be.

CHARLOTTE BRONTË'S ACCOUNTS IN *1850* 319

Where delineation of human character is concerned, the case is different. I am bound to avow that she had scarcely more practical knowledge of the peasantry amongst whom she lived, than a nun has of the country people who sometimes pass her convent gates. My sister's disposition was not naturally gregarious; circumstances favoured and fostered her tendency to seclusion; except to go to church or take a walk on the hills, she rarely crossed the threshold of home. Though her feeling for the people round was benevolent, intercourse with them she never sought; nor, with very few exceptions, ever experienced. And yet she knew them: knew their ways, their language, their family histories; she could hear of them with interest, and talk of them with detail, minute, graphic, and accurate; but with them, she rarely exchanged a word. Hence it ensued that what her mind had gathered of the real concerning them, was too exclusively confined to those tragic and terrible traits of which, in listening to the secret annals of every rude vicinage, the memory is sometimes compelled to receive the impress. Her imagination, which was a spirit more sombre than sunny, more powerful than sportive, found in such traits material whence it wrought creations like Heathcliff, like Earnshaw, like Catherine.

Having formed these beings, she did not know what she had done. If the auditor of her work when read in manuscript, shuddered under the grinding influence of natures so relentless and implacable, of spirits so lost and fallen; if it was complained that the mere hearing of certain vivid and fearful scenes banished sleep by night, and disturbed mental peace by day, Ellis Bell would wonder what was meant, and suspect the complainant of affectation. Had she but lived, her mind would of itself have grown like a strong tree, loftier, straighter, wider-spreading, and its matured fruits would have attained a mellower ripeness and sunnier bloom; but on that mind time and experience alone could work: to the influence of other intellects, it was not amenable.

Having avowed that over much of "Wuthering Heights" there broods "a horror of great darkness;" that, in its storm-heated and electrical atmosphere, we seem at times to breathe lightning, let me point to those spots where clouded daylight and the eclipsed sun still attest their existence. For a specimen of true benevolence and homely fidelity, look at the character of Nelly Dean; for an example of constancy and tenderness, remark that of Edgar Linton. (Some people will think these qualities do not shine so well incarnate in a man as they would do in a woman, but Ellis Bell could never be brought to comprehend this notion: nothing moved her more than any insinuation that the faithfulness and clemency, the long-suffering and loving-kindness which are esteemed virtues in the daughters of Eve, become foibles in the sons of Adam. She held that mercy and forgiveness are the divinest attributes of the Great Being who made both man and woman, and that what clothes the Godhead in glory, can disgrace no form of feeble humanity.) There is a dry saturnine humour in the delineation of old Joseph, and some glimpses of

320   EMILY BRONTË

grace and gaiety animate the younger Catherine. Nor is even the first heroine
of the name destitute of a certain strange beauty in her fierceness, or of hon-
esty in the midst of perverted passion and passionate perversity.

Heathcliff, indeed, stands unredeemed; never once swerving in his arrow-
straight course to perdition, from the time when "the little black-haired
swarthy thing, as dark as if it came from the Devil," was first unrolled out of
the bundle and set on its feet in the farm-house kitchen, to the hour when
Nelly Dean found the grim, stalwart corpse laid on its back in the panel-
enclosed bed, with wide-gazing eyes that seemed "to sneer at her attempt to
close them, and parted lips and sharp white teeth that sneered too."

Heathcliff betrays one solitary human feeling, and that is *not* his love for
Catherine; which is a sentiment fierce and inhuman; a passion such as might
boil and glow in the bad essence of some evil genius; a fire that might form the
tormented centre—the ever-suffering soul of a magnate of the infernal world:
and by its quenchless and ceaseless ravage effect the execution of the decree
which dooms him to carry Hell with him wherever he wanders. No; the single
link that connects Heathcliff with humanity is his rudely-confessed regard
for Hareton Earnshaw—the young man whom he has ruined; and then his
half-implied esteem for Nelly Dean. These solitary traits omitted, we should
say he was child neither of Lascar nor gipsy, but a man's shape animated by
demon life—a Ghoul—an Afreet.

Whether it is right or advisable to create beings like Heathcliff, I do not
know: I scarcely think it is. But this I know: the writer who possesses the creative gift owns something of which he is not always master—something that,
at times, strangely wills and works for itself. He may lay down rules and devise
principles, and to rules and principles it will perhaps for years lie in subjec-
tion; and then, haply without any warning of revolt, there comes a time when
it will no longer consent to "harrow the valleys, or be bound with a band in
the furrow"—when it "laughs at the multitude of the city, and regards not the
crying of the driver"—when, refusing absolutely to make ropes out of sea-
sand any longer, it sets to work on statue-hewing, and you have a Pluto or a
Jove, a Tisiphone or a Psyche, a Mermaid or a Madonna, as Fate or Inspiration
direct. Be the work grim or glorious, dread or divine, you have little choice
left but quiescent adoption. As for you—the nominal artist—your share in it
has been to work passively under dictates you neither delivered nor could
question—that would not be uttered at your prayer, nor suppressed nor
changed at your caprice. If the result be attractive, the World will praise you,
who little deserve praise; if it be repulsive, the same World will blame you,
who almost as little deserve blame.

"Wuthering Heights" was hewn in a wild workshop, with simple tools,
out of homely materials. The statuary found a granite block on a solitary
moor; gazing thereon, he saw how from the crag might be elicited a head,
savage, swart, sinister; a form moulded with at least one element of

CHARLOTTE BRONTË'S ACCOUNTS IN *1850*

grandeur—power. He wrought with a rude chisel, and from no model but the vision of his meditations. With time and labour, the crag took human shape; and there it stands colossal, dark, and frowning, half statue, half rock: in the former sense, terrible and goblin-like; in the latter, almost beautiful, for its colouring is of mellow grey, and moorland moss clothes it; and heath, with its blooming bells and balmy fragrance, grows faithfully close to the giant's foot.

CURRER BELL.

ii. Early Poems about Emily Brontë

[Charlotte Brontë], 'On the Death of Emily Jane Brontë' (1848)

My darling, thou wilt never know
  The grinding agony of woe
    That we have borne for thee.
Thus may we consolation tear
E'en from the depth of our despair   5
    And wasting misery.

The nightly anguish thou art spared
When all the crushing truth is bared
    To the awakening mind,
When the galled heart is pierced with grief,   10
Till wildly it implores relief,
    But small relief can find.

Nor know'st thou what it is to lie
Looking forth with streaming eye
    On life's lone wilderness.   15
'Weary, weary, dark and drear,
How shall I the journey bear,
    The burden and distress?'

Then since thou art spared such pain
We will not wish thee here again;   20
    He that lives must mourn.
God help us through our misery
And give us rest and joy with thee
    When we reach our bourne!

December *24, 1848.*

'A' [Matthew Arnold], 'Haworth Churchyard, April 1855'

WHERE, under Loughrigg, the stream
Of Rotha sparkles, the fields
Are green, in the house of one
Friendly and gentle, now dead,
Wordsworth's son-in-law, friend—   5
Four years since, on a mark'd
Evening, a meeting I saw.

EARLY POEMS ABOUT EMILY BRONTË

Two friends met there, two fam'd
Gift'd women. The one,
Brilliant with recent renown,   10
Young, unpractis'd, had told
With a Master's accent her feign'd
History of passionate life:
The other, maturer in fame,
Earning, she too, her praise   15
First in Fiction, had since
Widen'd her sweep, and survey'd
History, Politics, Mind.

They met, held converse: they wrote
In a book which of glorious souls   20
Held memorial: Bard,
Warrior, Statesman, had left
Their names:—chief treasure of all,
Scott had consign'd there his last
Breathings of song, with a pen   25
Tottering, a death-stricken hand.

I beheld; the obscure
Saw the famous. Alas!
Years in number, it seem'd,
Lay before both, and a fame   30
Heighten'd, and multiplied power.
Behold! The elder, to-day,
Lies expecting from Death,
In mortal weakness, a last
Summons: the younger is dead.   35

First to the living we pay
Mournful homage: the Muse
Gains not an earth-deafen'd ear.

Hail to the steadfast soul,
Which, unflinching and keen,   40
Wrought to erase from its depth
Mist, and illusion, and fear!
Hail to the spirit which dar'd
Trust its own thoughts, before yet
Echoed her back by the crowd!   45
Hail to the courage which gave
Voice to its creed, ere the creed
Won consecration from Time!

EMILY BRONTË

Turn, O Death, on the vile,
Turn on the foolish the stroke 50
Hanging now o'er a head
Active, beneficent, pure!
But, if the prayer be in vain—
But, if the stroke *must* fall—
Her, whom we cannot save, 55
What might we say to console?

She will not see her country lose
Its greatness, nor the reign of fools prolong'd.
She will behold no more
This ignominious spectacle, 60
Power dropping from the hand
Of paralytic factions, and no soul
To snatch and wield it: will not see
Her fellow-people sit
Helplessly gazing on their own decline. 65

Myrtle and rose fit the young,
Laurel and oak the mature.
Private affections, for these,
Have run their circle, and left
Space for things far from themselves, 70
Thoughts of the general weal,
Country, and public cares:
Public cares, which move
Seldom and faintly the depth
Of younger passionate souls 75
Plung'd in themselves, who demand
Only to live by the heart,
Only to love and be lov'd.

How shall we honour the young,
The ardent, the gifted? How mourn? 80
Console we cannot; her ear
Is deaf. Far northward from here,
In a churchyard high mid the moors
Of Yorkshire, a little earth
Stops it for ever to praise. 85

Where, behind Keighley, the road
Up to the heart of the moors
Between heath-clad showery hills
Runs, and colliers' carts

EARLY POEMS ABOUT EMILY BRONTË

Poach the deep ways coming down, 90
And a rough, grim'd race have their homes—
There, on its slope, is built
The moorland town. But the church
Stands on the crest of the hill,
Lonely and bleak; at its side 95
The parsonage-house and the graves.

See! In the desolate house
The childless father! Alas,
Age, whom the most of us chide,
Chide, and put back, and delay— 100
Come, unupbraided for once!
Lay thy benumbing hand,
Gratefully cold, on this brow!
Shut out the grief, the despair!
Weaken the sense of his loss! 105
Deaden the infinite pain!

Another grief I see,
Younger: but this the Muse,
In pity and silent awe
Revering what she cannot soothe, 110
With veil'd face and bow'd head,
Salutes, and passes by.

Strew with roses the grave
Of the early-dying. Alas!
Early she goes on the path 115
To the Silent Country, and leaves
Half her laurels unwon,
Dying too soon: yet green
Laurels she had, and a course
Short, yet redoubled by Fame. 120

For him who must live many years
That life is best which slips away
Out of the light, and mutely; which avoids
Fame, and her less-fair followers, Envy, Strife,
Stupid Detraction, Jealousy, Cabal, 125
Insincere Praises:—which descends
The mossy quiet track to Age.

But, when immature Death
Beckons too early the guest

EMILY BRONTË

From the half-tried Banquet of Life,   130
Young, in the bloom of his days;
Leaves no leisure to press,
Slow and surely, the sweet
Of a tranquil life in the shade—
Fuller for him be the hours!   135
Give him emotion, though pain!
Let him live, let him feel, *I have liv'd.*
Heap up his moments with life!
Quicken his pulses with Fame!

And not friendless, nor yet   140
Only with strangers to meet,
Faces ungreeting and cold,
Thou, O Mourn'd One, to-day
Enterest the House of the Grave.
Those of thy blood, whom thou lov'dst,   145
Have preceded thee; young,
Loving, a sisterly band:
Some in gift, some in art
Inferior; all in fame.
They, like friends, shall receive   150
This comer, greet her with joy;
Welcome the Sister, the Friend;
Hear with delight of thy fame.

Round thee they lie; the grass
Blows from their graves toward thine.   155
She, whose genius, though not
Puissant like thine, was yet
Sweet and graceful: and She—
(How shall I sing her?), whose soul
Knew no fellow for might,   160
Passion, vehemence, grief,
Daring, since Byron died,
That world-fam'd Son of Fire; She, who sank
Baffled, unknown, self-consum'd;
Whose too-bold dying song   165
Shook, like a clarion-blast, my soul.

Of one too I have heard,
A Brother, sleeps he here?—

EARLY POEMS ABOUT EMILY BRONTË

Of all his gifted race
Not the least-gifted; young,   170
Unhappy, beautiful; the cause
Of many hopes, of many tears.
O Boy, if here thou sleep'st, sleep well!
On thee too did the Muse
Bright in thy cradle smile: 175
But some dark Shadow came
(I know not what) and interpos'd.

   Sleep, O cluster of friends,
Sleep! Or only, when May,
Brought by the West Wind, returns   180
Back to your native heaths,
And the plover is heard on the moors,
Yearly awake, to behold
The opening summer, the sky,
The shining moorland; to hear   185
The drowsy bee, as of old,
Hum o'er the thyme, the grouse
Call from the heather in bloom:

   Sleep; or only for this
Break your united repose.   190

Francis William Lauderdale Adams, 'To Emily Brontë' (1887)

'*Since* first my soul was quickened into being,
thy spirit hath been with me: In the short days
of life's laughter and love, in the long nights
of death's darker dreams, thy spirit hath been with me.

'O mine archangel, O my perpetual love   5
of strength with sweetness, stay, stay with me still!
And let me, if my steps are lending fleet
to that great Peace which I have learned to long for,

'even as thou didst—let not my Song's note fail,
but, hymning of Man's Faith and Hope with Love   10
and Knowledge, let me onward, upward go,
till I am too a spirit of that Peace.'

EMILY BRONTË

Lionel Johnson, 'Brontë' (1890)

To Hubert Crackanthorpe.

UPON the moorland winds blown forth,
Your mighty music storms our heart:
Immortal sisters of the North!
Daughters of nature: Queens of art.

Becomingly you bore that name,   5
Your Celtic name, that sounds of Greece:
Children of thunder and of flame;
Passion, that clears the air for peace.

Stoic, thy chosen title: thou,
Whose soul conversed with vehement nights,   10
Till love, with lightnings on his brow,
Met anguish, upon *Wuthering Heights.*

Thou, Stoic! Though the heart in thee
Never knew fear, yet always pain:
Not Stoic, thou! whose eyes could see   15
Passion's immeasurable gain:

Not standing from the war apart,
Not cancelling the lust of life;
But loving with triumphant heart
The impassioned glory of the strife.   20

Oh, welcome death! But first, to know
The trials and the agonies:
Oh, perfect rest! But ere life go,
To leave eternal memories.

Then down the lone moors let each wind   25
Cry round the silent house of sleep:
And there let breaths of heather find
Entrance, and there the fresh rains weep.

Rest! rest! The storm hath surged away:
The calm, the hush, the dews descend.   30
Rest now, ah, rest thee! night and day:
The circling moorlands guard their friend.

Thou too, before whose steadfast eyes
Thy conquering sister greatly died:

EARLY POEMS ABOUT EMILY BRONTË

By grace of art, that never dies,   35
She lives: thou also dost abide.

For men and women, safe from death,
Creatures of thine, our perfect friends:
Filled with imperishable breath,
Give thee back life, that never ends.   40

Oh! hearts may break, and hearts forget,
Life grow a gloomy tale to tell:
Still through the streets of bright *Villette*,
Still flashes *Paul Emanuel*!

Still, when your *Shirley* laughs and sings,   45
Suns break the clouds to welcome her:
Still winds, with music on their wings,
Drive the wild soul of *Rochester*.

Children of fire! The Muses filled
Hellas, with shrines of gleaming stone: 50
Your wasted hands had strength to build
Gray sanctuaries, hard-hewn, wind-blown.

Over their heights, all blaunched in storm,
What purple fields of tempest hang!
In splendour stands their mountain form,   55
That from the sombre quarry sprang.

Now the high gates lift up their head:
Now stormier music, than the blast,
Swells over the immortal dead:
Silent and sleeping, free at last.   60

But from the tempest, and the gloom,
The stars, the fires of God, steal forth:
Dews fall upon your heather bloom,
O royal sisters of the North!

        1890

Stephen Phillips, 'Emily Brontë' (1913)

Daughter of thunder and the northern moor,
Singer of heath and grim and cruel souls.
Yet of thy Love remembered deep in snow.
Who taught thee in that bleakness to believe,
Who told thee in that dimness so to trust   5

330 EMILY BRONTË

Holding so fast a God for all the creeds?
Loneliness only could such lightning make,
So stern, so tender! only barren hills
Could wring the woman riches out of thee.
They live not long of thy pure fire composed,   10
Earth asks but mud of those who will endure.
Some star was too impatient for thy soul,
In silence summoning through English dew.
Did Shelley linger downward to grey hairs,
Was Keats permitted that rich brain to glean,   15
Or all his glowing morning to fulfil?
Or Byron like thee in his later fire,
When the true lightning of his soul was bared
Long smouldering till the Missolonghi torch?
Soul-solitary! taught by lonely flame;   20
No need for thee to mix in civic crowds,
Knowledge was thrilled to thee upon the heath,
And wisdom came to thee from northern stars.
Yet loving thy stern verse, I most am held
By Heathcliffe following dreamily the dead.   25

Robert Bridges, 'Emily Brontë' (1923)

'Du hast Diamanten'

Thou hadst all Passion's splendour,
   Thou hadst abounding store
Of heaven's eternal jewels,
   Belovèd; what wouldst thou more?

Thine was the frolic freedom   5
   Of creatures coy and wild,
The melancholy of wisdom,
   The innocence of a child,

The mail'd will of the warrior,
   That buckled in thy breast   10
Humility as of Francis,
   The self-surrender of Christ;

And of God's cup thou drankest
   The unmingled wine of Love,
Which makes poor mortals giddy   15
   When they but sip thereof.

EARLY POEMS ABOUT EMILY BRONTË

What was't to thee thy pathway
    So rugged mean and hard,
Whereon when Death surprised thee
    Thou gav'st him no regard?   20

What was't to thee, enamour'd
    As a red rose of the sun,
If of thy myriad lovers
    Thou never sawest one?

Nor if of all thy lovers   25
    That are and were to be
None ever had their vision,
    O belovèd, of thee,

Until thy silent glory
    Went forth from earth alone,   30
Where like a star thou gleamest
    From thine immortal throne.

332 EMILY BRONTË

iii. The First Criticism

George Barnett Smith, from 'The Brontës' (1873/5)

[...] Precocity distinguished the whole trio, though that is not an unfailing sign of future celebrity. When children, their answers to questions were clever and characteristic. Emily, whose intellect was always singularly clear, firm, and logical, when asked what should be done with her brother Branwell, if he should be naughty, instantly replied, "Reason with him, and when he won't listen to reason, whip him." And as another indication of the quick ripening of faculties in this remarkable family, it may be mentioned that Mr. Brontë said he could converse with his daughter Maria on all the leading questions of the day when she was only eleven years of age. Charlotte Brontë was at an early age familiar with all the forms of suffering and death, and her life, from its commencement to its close, may be said to have been one prolonged endurance of agony. Yet the grandeur of her courage must always strike us as one of the sublimest spectacles. When a child she lost those who were dear to her, and there were none who could understand the vast yearnings of her nature. Then came the stirrings of her genius, and she longed to take flight, but her wings were weighted, and she was kept enchained to the dull earth. A few more years, and another trouble, almost worse than death, cast its horrible shadow over her path. The melancholy story of her brother Branwell, whom she loved deeply, in spite of his numberless errors and terrible slavery to one master-passion, is matter of general knowledge. To his death succeeded that of Emily Brontë, the sister whom Charlotte especially loved. To see her drift out into the great Unknown Sea was trouble inexpressible to that loving soul which had watched her with fostering care, and hoped to have witnessed the universal acknowledgment of her splendid genius.

[. . .]

Emily Brontë—for it is now time that we should say something of the two other persons in this remarkable trio—was, in certain respects, the most extraordinary of the three sisters. She has this distinction at any rate, that she has written a book which stands as completely alone in the language as does the *Paradise Lost* or the *Pilgrim's Progress*. This of itself, setting aside subject and construction, is no mean eminence. Emily Jane Brontë, as is well known, was the youngest but one of the Rev. Mr. Brontë's children, and died before she was thirty years of age. Early in life she displayed a singularly masculine bent of intellect, and astonished those with whom she came in contact by her penetration, and that settlement of character which generally only comes with age. She went from home twice, once to school and once to Brussels, but it was like the caging of a lioness, and her soul yearned for the liberty of home. When in Brussels she attracted and impressed deeply all

THE FIRST CRITICISM

those who came across her, and M. Heger declared she should have been a man, for "her powerful reason would have deduced new spheres of discovery from the knowledge of the old, and her strong, imperious will would never have been daunted by opposition or difficulty: never have given way but with life." On her return to Haworth she began to lose in beauty but to gain in impressiveness of feature, and she divided her time between homely domestic duties, studies, and rambles. Shrinking entirely from contact with the life which surrounded her, she gave herself up to nature, the result being apparent in her works, which reveal a most intimate acquaintance with the great Mother in all her moods. Her mind was absolutely free to all the lessons which she should teach, and she embraced them with the most passionate longing. "Her native hills were far more to her than a spectacle; they were what she lived in, and by, as much as the wild birds, their tenants, or as the heather, their produce." Her descriptions, then, of natural scenery, are what they should be, and all they should be. Any reader of her works must perforce acknowledge the accuracy of these observations. Her life, however, seemed to be an unprized one, except by that sister who loved her profoundly, and who keenly appreciated her genius as it essayed to unfold its wings in the sun. But whilst she lived the world made no sign of recognition of her strangely weird powers. When illness came her indomitable will still enabled her to present an unflinching front to sympathising friends. She refused to see the doctor, and would not have it that she was ill. To the last she retained an independent spirit, and on the day of her death she arose and dressed herself as usual. Her end reminds us of that of her brother Branwell whose will was so strong that he insisted on standing up to die and did actually so die. Emily did everything for herself on that last day, but as the hours drew on got manifestly worse, and could only whisper in gasps. The end came when it was too late to profit by human skill. *Wuthering Heights*, the principal work she has left behind her, shows a massive strength which is of the rarest description. Its power is absolutely Titanic: from the first page to the last it reads like the intellectual throes of a giant. It is fearful, it is true, and perhaps one of the most unpleasant books ever written: but we stand in amaze at the almost incredible fact that it was written by a slim country girl who would have passed in a crowd as an insignificant person, and who had had little or no experience of the ways of the world. In Heathcliff, Emily Brontë has drawn the greatest villain extant, after Iago. He has no match out of Shakspeare. The Mephistopheles of Goethe's *Faust* is a person of gentlemanly proclivities compared with Heathcliff. There is not a redeeming quality in him; his coarseness is very repellent; he is a unique specimen of the human tiger. Charlotte Brontë in her digest of this character finds one ameliorating circumstance in his favour, one link which connects him with humanity viz., his regard for one of his victims, Hareton Earnshaw. But we cannot agree with her: his feeling towards Earnshaw is excessively like that feline affection which sometimes destroys its

334 EMILY BRONTË

own offspring. As to his alleged esteem for Nelly Dean, perhaps also the less said about that the better. But *Wuthering Heights* is a marvellous curiosity in letters. We challenge the world to produce another work in which the whole atmosphere seems so surcharged with suppressed electricity, and bound in with the blackness of tempest and desolation. From the time when young Heathcliff is introduced to us, "as dark almost as if he came from the devil," to the last page of the story, there is nothing but savagery and ferocity, except when we are taken away from the persons to the scenes of the narratives, and treated to those pictures in which the author excels. The Heights itself, the old north-country manor-house, is made intensely real to us, but not more so than the central figure of the story, who, believing himself alone one night, throws open the lattice, and cries with terrible anguish—"Cathy ! oh, my heart's darling. Hear me this once. Catherine, at last!" Then his history is recapitulated, by one who witnessed his life in all its stages; and in the passage where Catherine informs her nurse that she has promised to marry Edgar Linton, but ought not to have done so, we get the following example of concentrated force:

"I have no more business to marry Edgar Linton than I have to be in Heaven. But it would degrade me to marry Heathcliff now; so he shall never know how I love him, and that not because he's handsome, Nelly, but because he's more myself than I am. Whatever our souls are made of, his and mine are the same; and Linton's is as different as moonbeams from lightning, or frost from fire . . . Who is to separate us? they'll meet the fate of Milo. I cannot express it; but surely you and everybody have a notion that there is, or should be, an existence of yours beyond you. What were the use of my creation if I were entirely contained here? My great miseries in this world have been Heathcliff's miseries, and I watched and felt each from the beginning; my great thought in living is himself. If all else perished and he remained, I should continue to be; and if all else remained and he were annihilated, the universe would turn to a mighty stranger; I should not seem a part of it. My love for Linton is like the foliage in the woods: time will change it, I'm well aware, as winter changes the trees. My love for Heathcliff resembles the eternal rocks beneath: a source of little visible delight, but necessary. Nelly, I *am* Heathcliff! He's always, always in my mind; not as a pleasure any more than I am always a pleasure to myself, but as my own being."

Then comes Catherine's death—when she asks forgiveness for having wronged him, and Heathcliff answers, "Kiss me again; and don't let me see your eyes! I forgive what you have done to me. I love *my* murderer but *yours*! How can I?" The tale of woe proceeds; the despairing man longing for the dead, until at last he faces death, and being asked if he will have the minister, Replies—"I tell you I have nearly attained my Heaven; and that of others is altogether unvalued and uncoveted by me." He then sleeps beside her: the tragedy of eighteen years is complete. A great deal has been said on the question whether such a book as *Wuthering Heights* ought to be written, and Charlotte Brontë herself felt impelled to utter some words of defence for it.

THE FIRST CRITICISM

Where the mind is healthy it can do no harm; but there are, possibly, organisations upon whom it might exercise a baleful influence. With regard to the drawing of Heathcliff, Currer Bell scarcely thought the creation of such beings justifiable, but she goes on to say that 'the writer who possesses the creative gift owns something of which he is not always master something that, at times, strangely wills and works for itself.' We are afraid that if this opinion were pushed to its logical issues it would be found incapable of being supported. A multiplication of such books as *Wuthering Heights* without corresponding genius would be a lamentable thing, no doubt; yet, while we cannot defend it altogether possibly as it stands, we should regret never having seen it, as one of the most extraordinary and powerful productions in the whole range of English literature. [. . .]

A. Mary F. Robinson, ' "Wuthering Heights": Its Origins' (1883)

A GREY old Parsonage standing among graves, remote from the world on its wind-beaten hill-top, all round the neighbouring summits wild with moors; a lonely place among half-dead ash-trees and stunted thorns, the world cut off on one side by the still ranks of the serried dead, and distanced on the other by mile-long stretches of heath: such, we know, was Emily Brontë's home.

An old, blind, disillusioned father, once prone to an extraordinary violence of temper, but now grown quiet with age, showing his disappointment with life by a melancholy cynicism that was quite sincere; two sisters, both beloved, one, fired with genius and quick to sentiment, hiding her enthusiasm under the cold demeanour of the ex-governess, unsuccessful, and unrecognised; the other gentler, dearer, fairer, slowly dying, inch by inch, of the blighting neighbourhood of vice. One brother, scarce less dear, of set purpose drinking himself to death out of furious thwarted passion for a mistress that he might not marry: these were the members of Emily Brontë's household.

Herself we know: inexperienced, courageous, passionate, and full of pity. Was it wonderful that she summed up life in one bitter line?—

> "Conquered good and conquering ill."

Her own circumstances proved the axiom true, and of other lives she had but little knowledge. Whom should she ask? The gentle Ellen who seemed of another world, and yet had plentiful troubles of her own? The curates she despised for their narrow priggishness? The people in the village of whom she knew nothing save when sickness, wrong, or death summoned her to their homes to give help and protection? Her life had given only one view of the world, and she could not realise that there were others which she had not seen.

"I am bound to avow," says Charlotte, "that she had scarcely more practical knowledge of the peasantry among whom she lived than a nun has of the

336 EMILY BRONTË

country people that pass her convent gates. My sister's disposition was not naturally gregarious; circumstances favoured and fostered her tendency to seclusion; except to go to church, or to take a walk on the hills, she rarely crossed the threshold of home. Though her feeling for the people round her was benevolent, intercourse with them she never sought, nor, with very few exceptions, ever experienced; and yet she knew them, knew their ways, their language, their family histories; she could hear of them with interest and talk of them with detail, minute, graphic, and accurate; but with them she rarely exchanged a word. Hence it ensued that what her mind had gathered of the real concerning them was too exclusively confined to those tragic and terrible traits of which, in listening to the secret annals of every rude vicinage, the memory is sometimes compelled to receive the impress. Her imagination, which was a spirit more sombre than sunny, more powerful than sportive, found in such traits materials whence it wrought creations like Heathcliff, like Earnshaw, like [Catherine]. Having formed these beings she did not know what she had done. If the auditors of her work, when read in manuscript, shuddered under the grinding influence of natures so relentless and implacable—of spirits so lost and fallen; if it was complained that the mere hearing of certain vivid and fearful scenes banished sleep by night and disturbed mental peace by day, Ellis Bell would wonder what was meant and suspect the complainant of affectation. Had she but lived, her mind would of itself have grown like a strong tree—loftier and straighter, wider spreading—and its matured fruits would have attained a mellower ripening and sunnier bloom; but on that mind time and experience alone could work, to the influence of other intellects it was not amenable."

Yet no human being is wholly free, none wholly independent, of surroundings. And Emily Brontë least of all could claim such immunity. We can with difficulty just imagine her a prosperous heiress, loving and loved, high-spirited and even hoydenish; but with her cavalier fantasy informed by a gracious splendour all her own, we can just imagine Emily Brontë as Shirley Keeldar, but scarcely Shirley Keeldar writing 'Wuthering Heights.' Emily Brontë away from her moors, her loneliness, her poverty, her discipline, her companionship with genius, violence and degradation, would have taken another colour, as hydrangeas grow now red, now blue, according to the nature of the soil. It was not her lack of knowledge of the world that made the novel she wrote become 'Wuthering Heights,' not her inexperience, but rather her experience, limited and perverse, indeed, and specialised by a most singular temperament, yet close and very real. Her imagination was as much inspired by the circumstances of her life, as was Anne's when she wrote the 'Tenant of Wildfell Hall,' or Charlotte's in her masterpiece 'Villette;' but, as in each case the imagination was of a different quality, experience, acting upon it, produced a distinct and dissimilar result; a result obtained no less by the contrariety than by the harmony of circumstance. For our surroundings

THE FIRST CRITICISM

affect us in two ways; subtly and permanently, tinging us through and through as wine tinges water, or, by some violent neighbourhood of antipathetic force, sending us off at a tangent as far as possible from the antagonistic presence that so detestably environs us. The fact that Charlotte Brontë knew chiefly clergymen is largely responsible for 'Shirley,' that satirical eulogy of the Church and apotheosis of Sunday-school teachers. But Emily, living in this same clerical evangelistic atmosphere, is revolted, forced to the other extreme; and, while sheltering her true opinions from herself under the all-embracing term "Broad Church," we find in her writings no belief so strong as the belief in the present use and glory of life; no love so great as her love for earth—earth the mother and grave; no assertion of immortality, but a deep certainty of rest. There is no note so often struck in all her work, and struck with such variety of emphasis, as this: that good for goodness' sake is desirable, evil for evil's sake detestable, and that for the just and the unjust alike there is rest in the grave.

This quiet clergyman's daughter, always hearing evil of Dissenters, has therefore from pure courage and revolted justice become a dissenter herself. A dissenter in more ways than one. Never was a nature more sensitive to the stupidities and narrowness of conventional opinion, a nature more likely to be found in the ranks of the opposition; and with such a nature indignation is the force that most often looses the gate of speech. The impulse to reveal wrongs and sufferings as they really are, is overwhelmingly strong; although the revelation itself be imperfect. What, then, would this inexperienced Yorkshire parson's daughter reveal? The unlikeness of life to the authorised pictures of life; the force of evil, only conquerable by the slow-revolving process of nature which admits not the eternal duration of the perverse; the grim and fearful lessons of heredity; the sufficiency of the finite to the finite, of life to life, with no other reward than the conduct of life fulfils to him that lives; the all-penetrating kinship of living things, heather-sprig, singing lark, confident child, relentless tyrant; and, not least, not least to her already in its shadow, the sure and universal peace of death.

A strange evangel from such a preacher; but a faith evermore emphasised and deeper rooted in Emily's mind by her incapacity to acquiesce in the stiff, pragmatic teaching, the narrow prejudice, of the Calvinists of Haworth. Yet this very Calvinism influenced her ideas, this doctrine she so passionately rejected, calling herself a disciple of the tolerant and thoughtful Frederick Maurice, and writing, in defiance of its flames and shriekings, the most soothing consolations to mortality that I remember in our tongue.

Nevertheless, so dual-natured is the force of environment, this antagonistic faith, repelling her to the extreme rebound of belief, did not send her out from it before she had assimilated some of its sternest tenets. From this doctrine of reward and punishment she learned that for every unchecked evil tendency there is a fearful expiation; though she placed it not indeed in the

338   EMILY BRONTË

flames of hell, but in the perverted instincts of our own children. Terrible theories of doomed incurable sin and predestined loss warned her that an evil stock will only beget contamination: the children of the mad must be liable to madness; the children of the depraved, bent towards depravity; the seed of the poison-plant springs up to blast and ruin, only to be overcome by uprooting and sterilisation, or by the judicious grafting, the patient training of many years.

Thus prejudiced and evangelical Haworth had prepared the woman who rejected its Hebraic dogma, to find out for herself the underlying truths. She accepted them in their full significance. It has been laid as a blame to her that she nowhere shows any proper abhorrence of the fiendish and vindictive Heathcliff. She who reveals him remembers the dubious parentage of that forsaken seaport baby, "Lascar or Gipsy;" she remembers the Ishmaelitish childhood, too much loved and hated, of the little interloper whose hand was against every man's hand. Remembering this, she submits as patiently to his swarthy soul and savage instincts as to his swarthy skin and "gibberish that nobody could understand." From thistles you gather no grapes.

No use, she seems to be saying, in waiting for the children of evil parents to grow, of their own will and unassisted, straight and noble. The very quality of their will is as inherited as their eyes and hair. Heathcliff is no fiend or goblin; the untrained doomed child of some half-savage sailor's holiday, violent and treacherous. And how far shall we hold the sinner responsible for a nature which is itself the punishment of some forefather's crime. Even for such there must be rest. No possibility in the just and reverent mind of Emily Brontë that the God whom she believed to be the very fount and soul of life could condemn to everlasting fire the victims of morbid tendencies not chosen by themselves. No purgatory, and no everlasting flame, is needed to purify the sins of Heathcliff; his grave on the hillside will grow as green as any other spot of grass, moor-sheep will find the grass as sweet, heath and harebells will grow of the same colour on it as over a baby's grave. For life and sin and punishment end with death to the dying man; he slips his burden then on to other shoulders, and no visions mar his rest.

"I wondered how any one could ever imagine unquiet slumbers for the sleepers in that quiet earth." So ends the last page of 'Wuthering Heights.'

So much for the theories of life and evil that the clash of circumstance and character struck out from Emily Brontë. It happened, as we know, that she had occasion to test these theories; and but for that she could never have written 'Wuthering Heights.' Not that the story, the conception, would have failed. After all there is nothing more appalling in the violent history of that upland farm than many a midland manor set thick in elms, many a wild country-house of Wales or Cornwall could unfold. Stories more socially painful than the mere brute violence of the Earnshaws; of madness and treachery, stories of girls entrapped unwillingly into a lunatic marriage that the estate

THE FIRST CRITICISM 339

might have an heir; legends of fearful violence, of outcast children, dishonoured wives, horrible and persistent evil. Who, in the secret places of his memory, stores not up such haunting gossip? And Emily, familiar with all the wild stories of Haworth for a century back, and nursed on grisly Irish horrors, tales of 1798, tales of oppression and misery, Emily, with all this eerie lore at her finger-ends, would have the less difficulty in combining and working the separate motives into a consistent whole, that she did not know the real people whose histories she knew by heart. No memory of individual manner, dominance or preference for an individual type, caught and rearranged her theories, her conception being the completer from her ignorance. This much her strong reason and her creative power enabled her to effect. But this is not all.

This is the plot; but to make a character speak, act, rave, love, live, die, through a whole lifetime of events, even as the readers feel convinced he must have acted, must have lived and died, this demands at least so much experience of a somewhat similar nature as may serve for a base to one's imagination, a reserve of certainty and reassurance on which to draw in times of perplexity and doubt. Branwell, who sat to Anne sorrily enough for the portrait of Henry Huntingdon, served his sister Emily, not indeed as a model, a thing to copy, but as a chart of proportions by which to measure, and to which to refer as for correct investiture, the inspired idea. Mr. Wemyss Reid (whose great knowledge of the Brontë history still greater kindness in admitting me to his advantages as much as might be, I cannot sufficiently acknowledge)— this capable critic perceives a *bonâ fide* resemblance between the character of Heathcliff and the character of Branwell Brontë as he appeared to his sister Emily. So much, bearing in mind the verse concerning the leveret, I own I cannot see. Branwell seems to me nearly akin to Heathcliff's miserable son than Heathcliff. But that, in depicting Heathcliff's outrageous thwarted love for [Catherine], Emily did draw upon her experience of her brother's suffering, this extract from an unpublished lecture of Mr. Reid's will sufficiently reveal:—

"It was in the enforced companionship of this lost and degraded man that Emily received, I am sure, many of the impressions which were subsequently conveyed to the pages of her book. Has it not been said over and over again by critics of every kind that 'Wuthering Heights' reads like the dream of an opium-eater? And here we find that during the whole time of the writing of the book an habitual and avowed opium-eater was at Emily's elbow. I said that perhaps the most striking part of 'Wuthering Heights' was that which deals with the relations of Heathcliff and Catharine after she had become the wife of another. Whole pages of the story are filled with the ravings and ragings of the villain against the man whose life stands between him and the woman he loves. Similar ravings are to be found in all the letters of Branwell Brontë written at this period of his career; and we may be sure that similar savings were always on his lips as, moody and more than half mad, he wandered about the rooms of the parsonage at Haworth. Nay, I have found some striking verbal coincidences between Branwell's

340 EMILY BRONTË

own language and passages in *Wuthering Heights*. In one of his letters there are these words in reference to the object of his passion: 'My own life without her will be hell. What can the so-called love of her wretched sickly husband be to her compared with mine?' Now, turn to *Wuthering Heights* and you will read these words: 'Two words would comprehend my future—death and hell. Existence after losing her would be hell. Yet I was a fool to fancy for a moment that she valued Edgar Linton's attachment more than mine. If he loved with all the powers of his puny being, he wouldn't love in eighty years as much as I could in a day.'"

So much share in 'Wuthering Heights' Branwell certainly had. He was a page of the book in which his sister studied; he served, as to an artist's temperament all things unconsciously serve, for the rough block of granite out of which the work is hewn, and, even while with difficulty enduring his vices, Emily undoubtedly learned from them those darker secrets of humanity necessary to her tragic incantation. They served her, those dreaded, passionate outbreaks of her brother's, even as the moors she loved, the fancy she courted, served her. Strange divining wand of genius, that conjures gold out of the miriest earth of common life; strange and terrible faculty laying up its stores and half-mechanically drawing its own profit out of our slightest or most miserable experiences, noting the gesture with which the mother hears of her son's ruin, catching the faint varying shadow that the white windshaken window-blind sends over the dead face by which we watch, drawing its life from a thousand deaths, humiliations, losses, with a hand in our sharpest joys and bitterest sorrows; this faculty was Emily Brontë's, and drew its profit from her brother's shame.

Here ended Branwell's share in producing 'Wuthering Heights.' But it is not well to ignore his claim to its entire authorship; for in the contemptuous silence of those who know their falsity, such slanders live and thrive like unclean insects under fallen stones. The vain boast of an unprincipled dreamer, half-mad with opium, half-drunk with gin, meaning nothing but the desire to be admired at any cost, has been given too much prominence by those lovers of sensation who prefer any startling lie to an old truth. Their ranks have been increased by the number of those who, ignorant of the true circumstances of Emily's life, found it impossible that an inexperienced girl could portray so much violence and such morbid passion. On the contrary, given these circumstances, none but a personally inexperienced girl could have treated the subject with the absolute and sexless purity which we find in 'Wuthering Heights.' How *infecte*, commonplace, and ignominious would Branwell, relying on his own recollections, have made the thwarted passion of a violent adventurer for a woman whose sickly husband both despise! That purity as of polished steel, as cold and harder than ice, that freedom in dealing with love and hate, as audacious as an infant's love for the bright flame of fire, could only belong to one whose intensity of genius was rivalled by the narrowness of her experience—an experience

THE FIRST CRITICISM

limited not only by circumstances, but by a nature impervious to any fierier sentiment than the natural love of home and her own people, beginning before remembrance and as unconscious as breathing.

The critic, having Emily's poems and the few remaining verses and letters of Branwell, cannot doubt the incapacity of that unnerved and garrulous prodigal to produce a work of art so sustained, passionate, and remote. For in no respect does the terse, fiery, imaginative style of Emily resemble the weak, disconnected, now vulgar, now pretty mannerisms of Branwell. There is, indeed, scant evidence that the writer of Emily's poems could produce 'Wuthering Heights;' but there is, at any rate, the impossibility that her work could be void of fire, concentration, and wild fancy. As great an impossibility as that vulgarity and tawdriness should not obtrude their ugly heads here and there from under Branwell's finest phrases. And since there is no single vulgar, trite, or Micawber-like effusion throughout 'Wuthering Heights;' and since Heathcliff's passion is never once treated in the despicable would-be worldly fashion in which Branwell describes his own sensations, and since at the time that 'Wuthering Heights' was written he was manifestly, and by his own confession, too physically prostrate for any literary effort, we may conclude that Branwell did not write the book.

On the other side we have not only the literary evidence of the similar qualities in 'Wuthering Heights' and in the poems of Ellis Bell, but the express and reiterated assurance of Charlotte Brontë, who never even dreamed, it would seem, that it could be supposed her brother wrote the book; the testimony of the publishers who made their treaty with Ellis Bell; of the servant Martha who saw her mistress writing it; and—most convincing of all to those who have appreciated the character of Emily Brontë—the impossibility that a spirit so upright and so careless of fame should commit a miserable fraud to obtain it.

Indeed, so baseless is this despicable rumour that to attack it seems absurd, only sometimes it is wise to risk an absurdity. Puny insects, left too long unhurt, may turn out dangerous enemies irretrievably damaging the fertile vine on which they fastened in the security of their minuteness.

To the three favouring circumstances of Emily's masterpiece, which we have already mentioned—the neighbourhood of her home, the character of her disposition, the quality of her experience—a fourth must be added, inferior in degree, and yet not absolutely unimportant. This is her acquaintance with German literature, and especially with Hoffmann's tales. In Emily Brontë's day, Romance and Germany had one significance; it is true that in London and in prose the German influence was dying out, but in distant Haworth, and in the writings of such poets as Emily would read, in Scott, in Southey, most of all in Coleridge, with whose poems her own have so distinct an affinity, it is still predominant. Of the materialistic influence of Italy, of atheist Shelley, Byron with his audacity and realism, sensuous Keats, she

EMILY BRONTË

would have little experience in her remote parsonage. And, had she known them, they would probably have made no impression on a nature only susceptible to kindred influences. Thackeray, her sister's hero, might have never lived for all the trace of him we find in Emily's writings; never is there any single allusion in her work to the most eventful period of her life, that sight of the lusher fields and taller elms of middle England; that glimpse of hurrying vast London; that night on the river, the sun slipping behind the masts, doubly large through the mist and smoke in which the houses, bridges, ships are all spectral and dim. No hint of this, nor of the sea, nor of Belgium, with its quaint foreign life; nor yet of that French style and method so carefully impressed upon her by Monsieur Héger, and which so decidedly moulded her elder sister's art. But in the midst of her business at Haworth we catch a glimpse of her reading her German book at night, as she sits on the hearthrug with her arm round Keeper's neck; glancing at it in the kitchen, where she is making bread, with the volume of her choice propped up before her; and by the style of the novel jotted down in the rough, almost simultaneously with her reading, we know that to her the study of German was not—like French and music—the mere necessary acquirement of a governess, but an influence that entered her mind and helped to shape the fashion of her thoughts.

So much preface is necessary to explain, not the genius of Emily Brontë, but the conditions of that genius—there is no use saying more. The aim of my writing has been missed if the circumstances of her career are not present in the mind of my reader. It is too late at this point to do more than enumerate them, and briefly point to their significance. Such criticism, in face of the living work, is all too much like glancing in a green and beautiful country at a map, from which one may, indeed, ascertain the roads that lead to it and away, and the size of the place in relation to surrounding districts, but which can give no recognisable likeness of the scene which lies all round us, with its fresh life forgotten and its beauty disregarded. Therefore let us make an end of theory and turn to the book on which our heroine's fame is stationed, fronting eternity. It may be that in unravelling its story and noticing the manner in which its facts of character and circumstance impressed her mind, we may, for a moment, be admitted to a more thorough and clearer insight into its working than we could earn by the completest study of external evidence, the most earnest and sympathising criticism.

Algernon Charles Swinburne, 'Emily Brontë' (1883)

To the England of our own time, it has often enough been remarked, the novel is what the drama was to the England of Shakespeare's. The same general interest produces the same incessant demand for the same inexhaustible supply of imaginative produce, in a shape more suited to the genius of a later day and the conditions of a changed society. Assuming this simple explanation to

THE FIRST CRITICISM

be sufficient for the obvious fact that in the modern world of English letters the novel is everywhere and the drama is nowhere, we may remark one radical point of difference between the taste of play-goers in the age of Shakespeare and the taste of novel-readers in our own. Tragedy was then at least as popular as either romantic or realistic comedy; whereas nothing would seem to be more unpopular with the run of modern readers than the threatening shadow of tragedy projected across the whole length of a story, inevitable and unmistakable from the lurid harshness of its dawn to the fiery softness of its sunset. The objection to a novel in which the tragic element has an air of incongruity and caprice—in which a tragic surprise is, as it were, sprung upon the reader, with a jarring shock such as might be given by the actual news of some unforeseen and grievous accident—this objection seems to me thoroughly reasonable, grounded on a true critical sense of fitness and unfitness; but the distaste for high and pure tragedy, where the close is in perfect and simple harmony with the opening, seems not less thoroughly pitiable and irrational.

A later work of indisputable power, in which the freshness of humour is as real and vital as the fervour of passion, was at once on its appearance compared with Emily Brontë's now famous story. And certainly not without good cause; for in point of local colour *Mehalah* is, as far as I know, the one other book which can bear and may challenge the comparison. Its pages, for one thing, reflect the sterile glitter and desolate fascination of the salt marshes, their minute splendours and barren beauties and multitudinous monotony of measureless expanse, with the same instinctive and unlaborious accuracy which brings all the moorland before us in a breath when we open any chapter of *Wuthering Heights*. But the accumulated horrors of the close, however possible in fact, are wanting in the one quality which justifies and ennobles all admissible horror in fiction: they hardly seem inevitable; they lack the impression of logical and moral certitude. All the realism in the world will not suffice to convey this impression: and a work of art which wants it wants the one final and irreplaceable requisite of inner harmony. Now in *Wuthering Heights* this one thing needful is as perfectly and triumphantly attained as in *King Lear* or *The Duchess of Malfy*, in *The Bride of Lammermoor* or *Notre-Dame de Paris*. From the first we breathe the fresh dark air of tragic passion and presage; and to the last the changing wind and flying sunlight are in keeping with the stormy promise of the dawn. There is no monotony, there is no repetition, but there is no discord. This is the first and last necessity, the foundation of all labour and the crown of all success, for a poem worthy of the name; and this it is that distinguishes the hand of Emily from the hand of Charlotte Brontë. All the works of the elder sister are rich in poetic spirit, poetic feeling, and poetic detail; but the younger sister's work is essentially and definitely a poem in the fullest and most positive sense of the term. It was therefore all the more proper that the honour of raising a biographical and critical monument to the author of *Wuthering Heights* should have been reserved for a poetess of

344 EMILY BRONTË

the next generation to her own. And those who had already in their mind's eye the clearest and most definite conception of Emily Brontë will be the readiest to acknowledge their obligation and express their gratitude to Miss Robinson for the additional light which she has been enabled to throw upon a great and singular character. It is true that when all has been said the main features of that character stand out before us unchanged. The sweet and noble genius of Mrs Gaskell did not enable her to see far into so strange and sublime a problem; but, after all, the main difference between the biographer of Emily and the biographer of Charlotte is that Miss Robinson has been interested and attracted where Mrs Gaskell was scared and perplexed. On one point, however, the new light afforded us is of the very utmost value and interest. We all knew how great was Emily Brontë's tenderness for the lower animals; we find, with surprise as well as admiration, that the range of this charity was so vast as to include even her own miserable brother. Of that lamentable and contemptible caitiff—contemptible not so much for his commonplace debauchery as for his abject selfishness, his lying pretention, and his nerveless cowardice—there is far too much in this memoir: it is inconceivable how any one can have put into a lady's hand such a letter as one which defaces two pages of the volume, and it may be permissible to regret that a lady should have made it public; but this error is almost atoned for by the revelation that of all the three sisters in that silent home "it was the silent Emily who had ever a cheering word for Branwell; it was Emily who still remembered that he was her brother, without that remembrance freezing her heart to numbness." That she saved his life from fire, and hid from their father the knowledge of her heroism, no one who knows anything of Emily Brontë will learn with any mixture of surprise in his sense of admiration; but it gives a new tone and colour to our sympathetic and reverent regard for her noble memory when we find in the depth of that self-reliant and stoic nature a fountain so inexhaustible of such Christlike longsuffering and compassion.

I cannot however but think that Miss Robinson makes a little too much of the influence exercised on Emily Brontë's work by the bitter, narrow, and ignoble misery of the life which she had watched burn down into such pitiful ruin that its memory is hardly redeemed by the last strange and inconsistent flash of expiring manhood which forbids us to regard with unmixed contempt the sufferer who had resolution enough to die standing if he had lived prostrate, and so make at the very last a manful end of an abject history. The impression of this miserable experience is visible only in Anne Brontë's second work, *The Tenant of Wildfell Hall*; which deserves perhaps a little more notice and recognition than it has ever received. It is ludicrously weak, palpably unreal, and apparently imitative, whenever it reminds the reader that it was written by a sister of Charlotte and Emily Brontë; but as a study of utterly flaccid and invertebrate immorality it bears signs of more faithful transcription from life than anything in *Jane Eyre* or *Wuthering Heights*. On the other

THE FIRST CRITICISM

hand, the intelligent reader of *Wuthering Heights* cannot fail to recognize that what he is reading is a tragedy simply because it is the work of a writer whose genius is essentially tragic. Those who believe that Heathcliff was called into existence by the accident that his creator had witnessed the agonies of a violent weakling in love and in disgrace might believe that Shakespeare wrote *King Lear* because he had witnessed the bad effects of parental indulgence, and that Æschylus wrote the *Eumenides* because he had witnessed the uncomfortable results of matricide. The book is what it is because the author was what she was; this is the main and central fact to be remembered. Circumstances have modified the details; they have not implanted the conception. If there were any need for explanation there would be no room for apology. As it is, the few faults of design or execution leap to sight at a first glance, and vanish in the final effect and unimpaired impression of the whole; while those who object to the violent illegalities of conduct with regard to real or personal property on which the progress of the story does undeniably depend— "a senseless piece of glaring folly," it was once called by some critic learned in the law—might as well complain, in Carlylesque phrase, that the manners are quite other than Belgravian.

It is a fine and accurate instinct that has inevitably led Miss Robinson to cite in chosen illustration of the book's quality at its highest those two incomparable pictures of dreamland and delirium which no poet that ever lived has ever surpassed for passionate and lifelike beauty of imaginative truth. But it is even somewhat less than exact to say that the latter scene "is given with a masterly pathos that Webster need not have made more strong, nor Fletcher more lovely and appealing." Fletcher could not have made it as lovely and appealing as it is; he would have made it exquisitely pretty and effectively theatrical; but the depths, the force, the sincerity, recalling here so vividly the "several forms of distraction" through which Webster's Cornelia passes after the murder of her son by his brother, excel everything else of the kind in imaginative art; not excepting, if truth may be spoken on such a subject, the madness of Ophelia or even of Madge Wildfire. It is hardly ever safe to say dogmatically what can or cannot be done by the rarest and highest genius; yet it must surely be borne in upon us all that these two crowning passages could never have been written by any one to whom the motherhood of earth was less than the brotherhood of man—to whom the anguish, the intolerable and mortal yearning, of insatiate and insuppressible homesickness, was less than the bitterest of all other sufferings endurable or conceivable in youth. But in Emily Brontë this passion was twin-born with the passion for truth and rectitude. The stale and futile epithet of Titaness has in this instance a deeper meaning than appears; her goddess mother was in both senses the same who gave birth to the divine martyr of Æschylean legend: Earth under one aspect and one name, but under the other Righteousness. And therefore was the first and last word uttered out of the depth of her nature a cry for that one thing

346   EMILY BRONTË

needful without which all virtue is as worthless as all pleasure is vile, all hope as shameful as all faith is abject—a cry for liberty.

And therefore too, perhaps we may say, it is that any seeming confusion or incoherence in her work is merely external and accidental, not inward and spiritual. Belief in the personal or positive immortality of the individual and indivisible spirit was not apparently, in her case, swallowed up or nullified or made nebulous by any doctrine or dream of simple reabsorption into some indefinite infinity of eternal life. So at least it seems to me that her last ardent confession of dauntless and triumphant faith should properly be read, however capable certain phrases in it may seem of the vaguer and more impersonal interpretation. For surely no scornfuller or stronger comment on the "unutterable" vanity of creeds could pass more naturally into a chant expressive of more profound and potent faith; a song of spiritual trust more grave and deep and passionate in the solemn ardour of its appeal than the Hymn to God of Cleanthes. Her infrangible self-reliance and lonely sublimity of spirit she had in common with him and his fellows of the Porch; it was much more than "some shy ostrich prompting" which bade her assign to an old Stoic the most personal and characteristic utterance in all her previous poems; but the double current of imaginative passion and practical compassion which made her a tragic poet and proved her a perfect woman gives as it were a living warmth and sweetness to her memory, such as might well have seemed incompatible with that sterner and colder veneration so long reserved for her spiritual kinsmen of the past. As a woman we never knew her so well as now that we have to welcome this worthy record of her life, with deeper thanks and warmer congratulations to the writer than can often be due even to the best of biographers and critics. As an author she has not perhaps even yet received her full due or taken her final place. Again and again has the same obvious objection been taken to that awkwardness of construction or presentation which no reader of *Wuthering Heights* can undertake to deny. But, to judge by the vigour with which this objection is urged, it might be supposed that the rules of narrative observed by all great novelists were of an almost legal or logical strictness and exactitude with regard to probability of detail. Now most assuredly the indirect method of relation through which the story of Heathcliff is conveyed, however unlikely or clumsy it may seem from the realistic point of view, does not make this narrative more liable to the charge of actual impossibility than others of the kind. Defoe still remains the one writer of narrative in the first person who has always kept the stringent law of possibilities before the eye of his invention. Even the admirable ingenuity and the singular painstaking which distinguish the method of Mr Wilkie Collins can only give external and transient plausibility to the record of long conversations overheard or shared in by the narrator only a few hours before the supposed date of the report drawn up from memory. The very greatest masters in their kind, Walter Scott and Charles Dickens, are of all narrators the

THE FIRST CRITICISM   347

most superbly regardless of this objection. From *Rob Roy* and *Redgauntlet*, from *David Copperfield* and *Bleak House*, we might select at almost any stage of the autobiographic record some instance of detail in which the violation of plausibility, probability, or even possibility, is at least as daring and as glaring as any to be found in the narrative of Nelly Dean. Even when that narrative is removed, so to speak, yet one degree further back—even when we are supposed to be reading a minute detail of incident and dialogue transcribed by the hand of the lay figure Mr Lockwood from Nelly Dean's report of the account conveyed to her years ago by Heathcliff's fugitive wife or gadding servant, each invested for the nonce with the peculiar force and distinctive style of the author—even then we are not asked to put such an overwhelming strain on our faculty of imaginative belief as is exacted by the great writer who invites us to accept the report drawn up by Mr Pendennis of everything that takes place—down even to the minutest points of dialogue, accent, and gesture—in the household of the Newcomes or the Firmins during the absence no less than in the presence of their friend the reporter. Yet all this we gladly and gratefully admit, without demur or cavil, to be thoroughly authentic and credible, because the whole matter of the report, however we get at it, is found when we do get at it to be vivid and lifelike as an actual experience of living fact. Here, if ever anywhere, the attainment of the end justifies the employment of the means. If we are to enjoy imaginative work at all, we must "assume the virtue" of imagination, even if we have it not; we must, as children say, "pretend" or make believe a little as a very condition of the game.

A graver and perhaps a somewhat more plausible charge is brought against the author of *Wuthering Heights* by those who find here and there in her book the savage note or the sickly symptom of a morbid ferocity. Twice or thrice especially the details of deliberate or passionate brutality in Heathcliff's treatment of his victims make the reader feel for a moment as though he were reading a police report or even a novel by some French "naturalist" of the latest and brutallest order. But the pervading atmosphere of the book is so high and healthy that the effect even of those "vivid and fearful scenes" which impaired the rest for Charlotte Brontë is almost at once neutralized—we may hardly say softened, but sweetened, dispersed, and transfigured—by the general impression of noble purity and passionate straightforwardness, which removes it at once and for ever from any such ugly possibility of association or comparison. The whole work is not more incomparable in the effect of its atmosphere or landscape than in the peculiar note of its wild and bitter pathos; but most of all is it unique in the special and distinctive character of its passion. The love which devours life itself, which devastates the present and desolates the future with unquenchable and raging fire, has nothing less pure in it than flame or sunlight. And this passionate and ardent chastity is utterly and unmistakably spontaneous and unconscious. Not till the story is ended, not till the effect of it has been thoroughly absorbed and digested,

348 EMILY BRONTË

does the reader even perceive the simple and natural absence of any grosser element, any hint or suggestion of a baser alloy in the ingredients of its human emotion than in the splendour of lightning or the roll of a gathered wave. Then, as on issuing sometimes from the tumult of charging waters, he finds with something of wonder how absolutely pure and sweet was the element of living storm with which his own nature has been for awhile made one; not a grain in it of soiling sand, not a waif of clogging weed. As was the author's life, so is her book in all things: troubled and taintless, with little of rest in it, and nothing of reproach. It may be true that not many will ever take it to their hearts; it is certain that those who do like it will like nothing very much better in the whole world of poetry or prose.

EXPLANATORY NOTES

All references to Shakespeare are to *The Oxford Shakespeare: The Complete Works*, 2nd edn, ed. Stanley Wells and Gary Taylor (Oxford: Oxford University Press, 2005); those to the Bible are to The King James Version in the 1769 Oxford 'Authorized' edition. Modern values in sterling are given using a simple multiplication of nineteenth-century sums by the Retail Price Index (RPI) of the intervening period from http://www.measuringworth.com. The modern figures are those of 2019. Methodologically, there are problems with this not least because consideration of labour value or of income value (if the capital were invested optimally) will give different and usually larger conversion figures. The RPI methodology is, nevertheless, straightforward and based on the cost of easily recognizable commodities. The results remain, all the same, indicative not definitive.

TEXTS

EMILY AND ANNE BRONTË'S DIARY PAPER, 24 NOVEMBER 1834

p. 3 *alias*: it is not clear what this means. Though a joint composition, the paper is written in EJB's hand.

Sir Robert Peel . . . Leeds: Sir Robert Peel (1788–1850), later to be British Prime Minister (1841–6), was at this point, as he remained, MP for Tamworth, Staffordshire. Peel led a minority government from 15 December 1834 to 8 April 1835, when he was obliged to resign. Early in April, Patrick Brontë was most likely the leading force behind an address sent to Sir Robert in support of his minority government. It was published in the conservative, and often anti-Catholic, *Leeds Intelligencer* (11 April 1835), p. 3. This newspaper became the still-published *Yorkshire Post* in 1866.

peeling: did EJB notice this connection with 'Peel'?

Gaaldine: see Introduction, pp. xxii–xxiii.

Sally Mosley: an occasional servant in the Parsonage, presumably. Occasional because EJB gives her whole name, which one assumes she would not have done if Sally had been a permanent or frequent presence.

EMILY AND ANNE BRONTË'S DIARY PAPER, 26 JUNE 1837

p. 4 *Eugene Aram*: was this Edward Bulwer-Lytton's novel *Eugene Aram: A Tale*, 3 vols (London: Colburn and Bentley, 1832)? *Companion* is in no doubt (p. 110). The novel narrates the story of the businessman and philologist, Eugene Aram (1704–59), who was executed in York for murdering Daniel Clark, a friend and trades associate. Thomas Hood's 'The Dream of Eugene Aram' was published in 1831, and it is possible Branwell was reading this instead.

NOTES TO PAGES 4–5

p. 4 *"Fair was the evening...the sun"*: the opening line of AB's 'Alexander and Zenobia'. See Christine Alexander, ed., *Tales of Glass Town, Angria, and Gondal: Selected Writings* (Oxford: Oxford University Press, 2010), p. 444.

birthday: Branwell was born on 26 June 1817.

POEMS IN MSS FROM 1838 TO 1846 LATER INCLUDED IN
'POEMS BY ELLIS BELL', IN *POEMS BY CURRER, ELLIS, AND ACTON
BELL*, ED. CURRER BELL, 2ND EDN (LONDON: SMITH & ELDER, 1850),
WITH OTHER PERSONAL DOCUMENTS INSERTED
AS CHRONOLOGICALLY APPROPRIATES

Order of Poems, by First Lines, in *1850**

'A little while, a little while'
'The Bluebell is the sweetest flower'
'Loud without the wind was roaring'
'Shall earth no more inspire thee'
'In summer's mellow midnight'
'Aye there it is!'
'Love is like the wild rose briar'
'Listen! when your hair, like mine'
'How few, of all the hearts that loved'
'In the earth—the earth—thou shalt be laid'
'I knew not 'twas so dire a crime'
'For him who struck thy foreign string'
'Heavy hangs the raindrop'
'Silent is the house: all are laid asleep'
'I do not weep; I would not weep'
'Often rebuked, yet always back returning'
'No coward soul is mine'

30 AUGUST 1838

p. 5 *30 August 1838 ('For him who struck thy foreign string')*: GP. The earliest EJB poem in CB's selection, which was not arranged chronologically. The title 'The Lady to her Guitar' is added in pencil in the MS. The Gondal context is lost. *1850** reads:

> FOR him who struck thy foreign string,
>   I ween this heart has ceased to care;
> Then why dost thou such feelings bring
>   To my sad spirit—old Guitar?
>
> It is as if the warm sunlight   5
>   In some deep glen should lingering stay,
> When clouds of storm, or shades of night
>   Have wrapt the parent orb away.
>
> It is as if the glassy brook
>   Should image still its willows fair,   10

NOTES TO PAGE 5

> Though years ago the woodman's stroke
> Laid low in dust their Dryad-hair.

> Even so, Guitar, thy magic tone
> Hath moved the tear and waked the sigh;
> Hath bid the ancient torrent moan,   15
> Although its very source is dry.

l. 2 *I ween this heart*: 'ween' as '*Obsolete* exc. *archaic*. 1. *transitive*. In regard to what is present or past: To think, surmise, suppose, conceive, believe, consider', *OED*. Cf. Scott's *The Lay of Last Minstrel* (1805), Canto III, st. xxxi, P. 89 [ll. 413–15]: 'Some said that there were thousands ten; | And others weened that it was nought, | But Leven clans, or Tynedale men', given in *OED*. *OED*'s last example is 1848, in Edward Bulwer-Lytton's archaicizing historical romance, *Harold: The Last of the Saxon Kings*.

17 OCTOBER 1838, 'SONG BY J. BRENZAIDA TO G.S.'

p. 5 *17 October 1838, 'Song by J. Brenzaida to G.S.'*: *GP*. CB titled it 'Love's Farewell' in the MS but 'Last Words' in *1850**. The Gondal context is lost.

The poem is 8-6-8-6 (in hymn-tune terms, 'common metre'), with a notable number of masculine rhymes. *1850** reads:

> I KNEW not 'twas so dire a crime
> To say the word, Adieu;
> But this shall be the only time
> My lips or heart shall sue.

> The wild hill-side, the winter morn,   5
> The gnarled and ancient tree,
> If in your breast they waken scorn,
> Shall wake the same in me.

> I can forget black eyes and brows,
> And lips of falsest charm,   10
> If you forget the sacred vows
> Those faithless lips could form.

> If hard commands can tame your love,
> Or strongest walls can hold,
> I would not wish to grieve above   15
> A thing so false and cold.

> And there are bosoms bound to mine
> With links both tried and strong;
> And there are eyes whose lightning shine
> Has warmed and blest me long: 20

> Those eyes shall make my only day,
> Shall set my spirit free,
> And chase the foolish thoughts away
> That mourn your memory.

352 NOTES TO PAGE 6

11 NOVEMBER 1838

p. 6 *11 November 1838 ('Loud without the wind was roaring')*: HM. *1850** reads:

LOUD without the wind was roaring
  Through th' autumnal sky;
Drenching wet, the cold rain pouring,
  Spoke of winter nigh.
    All too like that dreary eve,   5
    Did my exiled spirit grieve.
Grieved at first, but grieved not long,
  Sweet—how softly sweet!—it came;
Wild words of an ancient song,
  Undefined, without a name.   10

"It was spring, and the skylark was singing:"
  Those words they awakened a spell;
They unlocked a deep fountain, whose springing,
  Nor absence, nor distance can quell.

In the gloom of a cloudy November,   15
  They uttered the music of May;
They kindled the perishing ember
  Into fervour that could not decay.

Awaken, o'er all my dear moorland,
  West-wind, in thy glory and pride!
O! call me from valley and lowland,   20
  To walk by the hill-torrent's side!

It is swelled with the first snowy weather;
  The rocks they are icy and hoar,
And sullenly waves the long heather,   25
  And the fern leaves are sunny no more.

There are no yellow stars on the mountain;
  The bluebells have long died away,
From the brink of the moss-bedded fountain;
  From the side of the wintry brae.   30

But lovelier than corn-fields all waving
  In emerald, and vermeil, and gold,
Are the heights where the north-wind is raving,
  And the crags where I wandered of old.

It was morning: the bright sun was beaming;   35
  How sweetly it brought back to me,
The time when nor labour nor dreaming
  Broke the sleep of the happy and free.

But blithely we rose as the dawn-heaven
  Was melting to amber and blue,   40

NOTES TO PAGES 6–8

And swift were the wings to our feet given,
    As we traversed the meadows of dew.

For the moors! For the moors, where the short grass
    Like velvet beneath us should lie!
For the moors! For the moors, where each high pass   45
    Rose sunny against the clear sky!

For the moors, where the linnet was trilling
    Its song on the old granite stone;
Where the lark, the wild sky-lark, was filling
    Every breast with delight like its own!   50

What language can utter the feeling
    Which rose, when in exile afar,
On the brow of a lonely hill kneeling,
    I saw the brown heath growing there?

It was scattered and stunted, and told me   55
    That soon even that would be gone:
It whispered, "The grim walls enfold me,
    I have bloomed in my last summer's sun."

But not the loved music, whose waking
    Makes the soul of the Swiss die away,   60
Has a spell more adored and heartbreaking
    Than, for me, in that blighted heath lay.

The spirit which bent 'neath its power,
    How it longed—how it burned to be free!
If I could have wept in that hour,   65
    Those tears had been heaven to me.

Well—well; the sad minutes are moving,
    Though loaded with trouble and pain;
And some time the loved and the loving
    Shall meet on the mountains again!   70

l. 14 *Nor Absence nor Distance can quell*: given the date, this poem was written while EJB was teaching at Law Hill. See note to p. 316, '*At that period . . .*'. The distance from Haworth Parsonage to Law Hill, Southowram, on modern roads, is 12.6 miles.

l. 52 *in exile afar*: perhaps confirmation that this poem has a Gondal context as 12.6 miles (see previous note) is hardly 'exile afar'. Note that the heath references in the poem imply a Haworth context but the 'mountains' of the last line imply, probably, a Gondal one.

ll. 59–60 *But not the loved music . . . away*: a puzzle. It is not clear what the 'loved music' is (the singing linnet and skylark?), nor why it should so affect the Swiss. Gezari glosses this as follows:

[T]he Swiss, who were invaded and occupied by the French in 1798, symbolized liberty for Wordsworth. He writes of the voices of the sea and the mountains as

354   NOTES TO PAGE 8

their 'chosen Music, Liberty!' in 'Thought of a Briton on the subjugation of Switzerland' (1807). [EJB] might also be recalling 'The Swiss Emigrant's Return', a poem by CB [*The Complete Poems of Charlotte Brontë*, pp. 137–8], which appears in one of the Glass Town tales, *The Foundling* (31 May–27 June 1833):

> Yet to my spirit more sweet is the sound
> Than the music which floats over-vine-covered France (ll. 17–18).

Gezari, p. 254.

But these seem too loose as associations to give EJB's lines sharp sense. If music were in any way to be associated with liberty, apart from anything else, it is not clear why it, music, should make the 'soul' of the once-occupied Swiss 'die away' (or does this merely imply 'swoon away'?). The French occupation of Switzerland, 17 January–28 May 1798, was, in fact, welcomed by liberal sectors of the Swiss population as an act of liberation by French revolutionary forces from the *ancien régime* cantonal government of Switzerland. And, anyway, that was thirty-five years before.

Switzerland in 1838, when the poem is dated, was bitterly divided between liberals and conservatives, so there was no unified 'Swiss' opinion on 'liberty' anyway. This conflicted situation would eventually result, in 1847, in the *Sonderbundskrieg*, a short civil war, where the conservative Catholic league of seven cantons, the *Sonderbund*, was defeated by liberal forces, leading the following year to the federal constitution of 12 September 1848.

4 DECEMBER 1838

p. 8 *4 December 1838 ('A little while, a little while')*: HM. *1850** gave a very different version (which CB wrote onto the MS, deleting EJB's original):

> A LITTLE while, a little while,
>   The weary task is put away,
> And I can sing and I can smile,
>   Alike, while I have holiday.
>
> Where wilt thou go, my harassed heart—   5
>   What thought, what scene invites thee now?
> What spot, or near or far apart,
>   Has rest for thee, my weary brow?
>
> There is a spot, 'mid barren hills,
>   Where winter howls, and driving rain;   10
> But, if the dreary tempest chills,
>   There is a light that warms again.
>
> The house is old, the trees are bare,
>   Moonless above bends twilight's dome;
> But what on earth is half so dear—   15
>   So longed for—as the hearth of home?
>
> The mute bird sitting on the stone,
>   The dank moss dripping from the wall,

NOTES TO PAGE 8

The thorn-trees gaunt, the walks o'ergrown,
  I love them—how I love them all!   20

Still—as I mused—the naked room,
  The alien firelight died away;
And from the midst of cheerless gloom,
  I passed to bright, unclouded day.

A little and a lone green lane   25
  That opened on a common wide;
A distant, dreamy, dim, blue chain
  Of mountains, circling every side.

A heaven so clear, an earth so calm,
  So sweet, so soft, so hushed an air;   30
And—deepening still the dream-like charm—
  Wild moor-sheep feeding everywhere.

That was the scene, I knew it well;
  I knew the turfy pathway's sweep,
That, winding o'er each billowy swell,   35
  Marked out the tracks of wandering sheep.

Could I have lingered but an hour,
  It well had paid a week of toil;
But Truth has banished Fancy's power:
  Restraint and heavy task recoil.   40

Even as I stood with raptured eye,
  Absorbed in bliss so deep and dear,
My hour of rest had fleeted by,
  And back came labour, bondage, care.

Critics have been severe on CB's version. See, for instance: 'Charlotte has deliberately falsified the setting of the poems [see note to pp. 61–2 and 316, '*At that period...*']; she has even altered one of the poems to read as if the writer were a pupil, not a teacher: in the opening lines of [this] poem, the original [...] reads, "A little while, a little while, / *The noisy crowd are barred away*"; while in Charlotte's edited version, those lines read "A little while, a little while / *The weary task is put away*". In Charlotte's version the poem reads as if written by an unwilling student, while Emily's original is clearly from the point of view of an overworked teacher finally having some time to herself', Sarah Fermi, 'What Do We Know about Emily Jane? Some Well-known "Facts" Reconsidered', *Brontë Studies*, 44 (2019), pp. 152–61 (pp. 154–5).

This rewriting contributes to the ongoing interest in CB's erasure of EJB's time at Law Hill School and to the mystery of why she left. There has been much speculation. Chitham offers a recent possible explanation—chiefly, a difficult friendship with Jane Aspden (1813–75), a fellow teacher—in 'Law Hill and Emily Brontë: Behind Charlotte's Evasion', *Brontë Studies*, 43 (2018), pp. 176–87. Whatever happened to EJB at Law Hill, CB must have had some good reason to remove from the record, almost completely, this part of EJB's life. *LCB* speaks only of EJB 'once going as teacher to a school in Halifax for six months' (i.150), which, presumably, is all that CB

356 NOTES TO PAGES 8–10

told Mrs Gaskell. (And it is perhaps worth adding that the school wasn't in Halifax anyway, but in Southowram, to the east.)

It is also worth observing that the poem is, at one level, obviously about a schoolroom and a tired teacher while other elements—particularly in the original—imply, perhaps, a Gondal context.

18 DECEMBER 1838

p. 10 *18 December 1838 ('The blue bell is the sweetest flower')*: HM. The title is in the MS. Cf. AB's 'The Bluebell', 22 August 1840 in *The Complete Poems of Anne Brontë*, ed. Clement Shorter (London: Hodder and Stoughton, n.d. [1920]), pp. 17–19 and EJB's 'To the Blue Bell | by A.G.A.' in Gezari, p. 99. The poem is notably different in *1850**:

> THE Bluebell is the sweetest flower
> That waves in summer air:
> Its blossoms have the mightiest power
> To soothe my spirit's care.
>
> There is a spell in purple heath   5
> Too wildly, sadly dear;
> The violet has a fragrant breath,
> But fragrance will not cheer.
>
> The trees are bare, the sun is cold,
> And seldom, seldom seen;   10
> The heavens have lost their zone of gold,
> And earth her robe of green.
>
> And ice upon the glancing stream
> Has cast its sombre shade;
> And distant hills and valleys seem   15
> In frozen mist arrayed.
>
> The Bluebell cannot charm me now,
> The heath has lost its bloom;
> The violets in the glen below,
> They yield no sweet perfume.   20
>
> But, though I mourn the sweet Bluebell,
> 'Tis better far away;
> I know how fast my tears would swell
> To see it smile to-day.
>
> For, oh! when chill the sunbeams fall   25
> Adown that dreary sky,
> And gild yon dank and darkened wall
> With transient brilliancy;
>
> How do I weep, how do I pine
> For the time of flowers to come,   30
> And turn me from that fading shine,
> To mourn the fields of home!

NOTES TO PAGES 10–11   357

l. 19 *The violets in the glen below*: in the changing time-schemes of the poem, this is confusing, as violets do not flower in December. EJB perhaps means the violets that grow in the glen, which currently are not in flower. The sweet violet, *Viola odorata*, is no doubt intended, as the common dog-violet, *Viola riviniana*, is unscented.

11 SEPTEMBER 1840

p. 11 *11 September 1840 ('In summer's mellow midnight')*: HM. The title, 'The Night-Wind', added in MS. *1850** reads:

Here again is the same mind in converse with a like abstraction. The Night-Wind, breathing through an open window, has visited an ear which discerned language in its whispers.

<blockquote>

In summer's mellow midnight,
A cloudless moon shone through
Our open parlour window,
And rose-trees wet with dew.

I sat in silent musing;   5
The soft wind waved my hair;
It told me heaven was glorious,
And sleeping earth was fair.

I needed not its breathing
To bring such thoughts to me;   10
But still it whispered lowly,
"How dark the woods will be!

"The thick leaves in my murmur
"Are rustling like a dream,
"And all their myriad voices   15
"Instinct with spirit seem."

I said, "Go, gentle singer,
"Thy wooing voice is kind:
"But do not think its music
"Has power to reach my mind.   20

"Play with the scented flower,
"The young tree's supple bough,
"And leave my human feelings
"In their own course to flow."

"The wanderer would not heed me;   25
"Its kiss grew warmer still.
"O come!" it sighed so sweetly;
"I'll win thee 'gainst thy will."

"Were we not friends from childhood?
"Have I not loved thee long?   30
"As long as thou, the solemn night,
"Whose silence wakes my song?

</blockquote>

358 NOTES TO PAGES 11–12

"And when thy heart is resting
"Beneath the church-aisle stone,
"*I* shall have time for mourning, 35
"And *thou* for being alone."

Cf. AB's 'The North Wind', in *The Complete Poems of Anne Brontë*, ed. Clement Shorter (London: Hodder and Stoughton, n.d. [1920]), pp. 3–4 (in the voice of Alexandrina Zenobia).

l. 16 *Instinct with spirit seem*: 'instinct' as 'Imbued or charged with something, as a moving or animating force or principle', *OED*, which gives two examples from Shelley, who might, possibly, be on EJB's mind in this poem.

l. 26 *Its kiss grew warmer still*: the night-wind is not given a sex.

l. 34 *church-yard*: in *1850**, it might be that CB made the change to 'church-aisle' because she was thinking of where EJB was buried?

16 MAY 1841

p. 12 *16 May 1841 ('Shall earth no more inspire thee')*: HM. *1850** reads:

The following little piece has no title; but in it the Genius of a solitary region seems to address his wandering and wayward votary, and to recall within his influence the proud mind which rebelled at times against what it most loved.

SHALL earth no more inspire thee,
Thou lonely dreamer, now?
Since passion may not fire thee,
Shall nature cease to bow?

Thy mind is ever moving, 5
In regions dark to thee;
Recall its useless roving,
Come back, and dwell with me.

I know my mountain breezes
Enchant and soothe thee still, 10
I know my sunshine pleases,
Despite thy wayward will.

When day with evening blending,
Sinks from the summer sky,
I've seen thy spirit bending 15
In fond idolatry.

I've watched thee every hour;
I know my mighty sway:
I know my magic power
To drive thy griefs away. 20

Few hearts to mortals given,
On earth so wildly pine;

NOTES TO PAGES 12–13 359

> Yet few would ask a heaven
> More like this earth than thine.

> Then let my winds caress thee;   25
> Thy comrade let me be:
> Since nought beside can bless thee,
> Return—and dwell with me.

l. 4 *Shall Nature cease to bow?*: 'bow' presumably in *OED*'s sense, 10a: 'To cause to turn in a given direction; to incline, turn, direct; figurative to incline or influence (the mind). Obsolete.' *OED*'s last source is from 1705.

ll. 23–4 *Yet few would ask a Heaven…thine*: cf. p. 26 and note to p. 117, '*I broke my heart…*'.

6 JULY 1841

p. 13 *6 July 1841 ('Aye there it is!')*: HM. *1850**, significantly modifying the text, reads as follows:

> In these stanzas a louder gale has roused the sleeper on her pillow: the wakened soul struggles to blend with the story by which it is swayed:—

> AY—there it is! It wakes to-night
> Deep feelings I thought dead;
> Strong in the blast—quick gathering light—
> The heart's flame kindles red.

> "Now I can tell by thine altered cheek,   5
>   "And by thine eyes' full gaze,
> "And by the words thou scarce dost speak,
>   "How wildly fancy plays.

> "Yes—I could swear that glorious wind
>   "Has swept the world aside,   10
> "Has dashed its memory from thy mind
>   "Like foam-bells from the tide:

> "And thou art now a spirit pouring
>   "Thy presence into all:
> "The thunder of the tempest's roaring,   15
>   "The whisper of its fall:

> "An universal influence,
>   "From thine own influence free;
> "A principle of life—intense—
>   "Lost to mortality.   20

> "Thus truly, when that breast is cold,
>   "Thy prisoned soul shall rise;
> "The dungeon mingle with the mould—
>   "The captive with the skies.
> "Nature's deep being, thine shall hold,   25
>   "Her spirit all thy spirit fold,

360 NOTES TO PAGES 13–15

"Her breath absorb thy sighs.
"Mortal! though soon life's tale is told;
"Who once lives, never dies!"

EMILY BRONTË'S DIARY PAPER, 30 JULY 1841

p. 14 *Victoria and Adelaide*: the geese. Victoria for the Queen; Adelaide for the Queen of William IV (she died in 1849). Hero is a hawk (sometimes given as 'Nero').

peat-house: see note to p. 61.

are all stout and hearty: cf. note to p. 23.

John White . . . Rawden: see note to p. 75.

Luddenden foot: Branwell was made clerk-in-charge of Luddenden Foot Railway Station, in the Upper Calder Valley, on 1 April 1841 until he was dismissed in March 1842. The station finally closed in 1962.

Scarborough: between *c*.8 May 1840 and June 1845, AB was employed by the Robinsons at Thorp Green Hall.

19 DECEMBER 1841, 'A.S. TO G.S.'

p. 15 *19 December 1841, 'A.S. to G.S.'*: *GP. 1850**, titling the poem 'Encouragement', reads:

> I DO not weep; I would not weep;
>   Our mother needs no tears:
> Dry thine eyes, too; 'tis vain to keep
>   This causeless grief for years.
>
> What though her brow be changed and cold,   5
>   Her sweet eyes closed for ever?
> What though the stone—the darksome mould
>   Our mortal bodies sever?
>
> What though her hand smooth ne'er again
>   Those silken locks of thine?   10
> Nor, through long hours of future pain,
>   Her kind face o'er thee shine?
>
> Remember still, she is not dead;
>   She sees us, sister, now;
> Laid, where her angel spirit fled,   15
>   'Mid heath and frozen snow.
>
> And, from that world of heavenly light
>   Will she not always bend
> To guide us in our lifetime's night,
>   And guard us to the end?   20
>
> Thou knowest she will; and thou mayst mourn
>   That *we* are left below:
> But not that she can ne'er return
>   To share our earthly woe.

NOTES TO PAGES 16–17

LETTER TO ELLEN NUSSEY, 22? MAY 1843

p. 16 *"postage-free"*: Ellen has already pre-paid for a reply.

Charlotte has never mentioned...home: CB had returned to Brussels on 27 January 1843.

Methusaleh: the oldest-living of the Hebrew Patriarchs, dying at the age of 969.

6 SEPTEMBER 1843

p. 17 *6 September 1843 ('In the earth, the earth thou shalt be laid')*: *GP. 1850** titles this 'Warning and Reply' and presents it as follows:

> IN the earth—the earth—thou shalt be laid,
> A grey stone standing over thee;
> Black mould beneath thee spread,
> And black mould to cover thee.
>
> "Well—there is rest there,   5
> "So fast come thy prophecy;
> "The time when my sunny hair
> "Shall with grass roots entwined be."
>
> But cold—cold is that resting-place,
> Shut out from joy and liberty,   10
> And all who loved thy living face
> Will shrink from it shudderingly.
>
> "Not so. *Here* the world is chill,
> "And sworn friends fall from me:
> "But *there*—they will own me still,   15
> And prize my memory."
>
> "Farewell, then, all that love,
> All that deep sympathy:
> Sleep on: Heaven laughs above,
> Earth never misses thee.   20
>
> Turf-sod and tombstone drear
> Part human company;
> One heart breaks only—here,
> But that heart was worthy thee!

Gezari, p. 272, wonders if the speaker of the second and fourth stanzas might be Lord Alfred S., in the Gondal narratives, who haunts Aspin Castle, his ancestral home.

Note the characteristically ambiguous time scheme.

11 MARCH 1844, 'E.W. TO A.G.A.'

p. 17 *11 March 1844, 'E.W. to A.G.A.'*: *GP. 1850** calls this 'The Wanderer from the Fold', though the MS has the pencilled title 'On a life perverted'. There is an ongoing

362 NOTES TO PAGE 17

debate as to whether the poem refers to Branwell or could have subsequently been thought apt for him. *1850** reads:

How few, of all the hearts that loved,
    Are grieving for thee now;
And why should mine to-night be moved
    With such a sense of woe?

Too often thus, when left alone,   5
    Where none my thoughts can see,
Comes back a word, a passing tone
    From thy strange history.

Sometimes I seem to see thee rise,
    A glorious child, again;   10
All virtues beaming from thine eyes
    That ever honoured men:

Courage and truth, a generous breast
    Where sinless sunshine lay:
A being whose very presence blest   15
    Like gladsome summer-day.

O, fairly spread thy early sail,
    And fresh, and pure, and free,
Was the first impulse of the gale
    That urged life's wave for thee!   20

Why did the pilot, too confiding,
    Dream o'er that ocean's foam,
And trust in Pleasure's careless guiding
    To bring his vessel home?

For well he knew what dangers frowned,   25
    What mists would gather, dim;
What rocks, and shelves, and sands, lay round
    Between his port and him.

The very brightness of the sun,
    The splendour of the main,   30
The wind which bore him wildly on
    Should not have warned in vain.

An anxious gazer from the shore—
    I marked the whitening wave,
And wept above thy fate the more   35
    Because—I could not save.

It recks not now, when all is over:
    But yet my heart will be
A mourner still, though friend and lover
    Have both forgotten thee!   40

NOTES TO PAGES 17–19   363

The poem seems to echo William Cowper's 'The Castaway' (1799). Cf. AB's 'To Cowper', in *The Complete Poems of Anne Brontë*, ed. Clement Shorter (London: Hodder and Stoughton, n.d. [1920]), pp. 28–30. Mary Taylor observed that 'The Castaway' 'was known to them all, and they all at times appreciated or almost appropriated it. Charlotte told me once that Branwell had done so', quoted in *Companion*, p. 131.

The opening sentence, it has sometimes been thought, uses a formulation that imitates l. 429 of Oliver Goldsmith's *The Traveller; Or, a Prospect of Society* (1764) in a sentiment about tyranny and restraint that might have interested EJB:

> In every government, though terrors reign,
> Though tyrant kinds, or tyrant laws restrain,
> How small, of all that human hearts endure,
> That part which laws or kings can cause or cure.
>
> (ll. 427–30).

ll. 21–4 *Why did the pilot … home?*: it is faintly possible that CB published this poem in part because, by the time of *1850**, these lines reminded her of Branwell. If that were the case, then it is interesting to wonder about the last two lines of the poem as a whole and their possible awkwardness. Lydia Robinson (1799–1859) was still alive in 1850, having declined to have anything to do with Branwell after his dismissal from Thorp Green (the refusal of contact was justified on the basis of the Revd Mr Robinson's will which was alleged to contain a clause cutting Mrs Robinson from any inheritance if she saw Branwell again: in fact, the will had no such clause [Barker]). On the death of the Revd Edmund Robinson, Lydia married Sir Francis Edward Dolman Scott in 1848. We do not know what CB understood of the Thorp Green scandal as, equally, we have no certain knowledge of exactly what that scandal was. It is *possible*, for instance, that Branwell's version of a relationship with Mrs Robinson was a cover story for something else. Barker makes, however, a strong case that it was indeed an affair with Lydia Robinson that was the problem. AB's house at Thorp Green is now incorporated into the school, Queen Ethelburga's Collegiate.

l. 37 *recks*: a rare example of an EJB pun ('wrecks').

11 NOVEMBER 1844, 'FROM A DUNGEON WALL IN THE SOUTHERN COLLEGE'—JB SEPT. 1825

p. 19 *11 November 1844*: GP. The first twenty-eight lines are addressed, it is usually assumed, to 'J.B.', Julius Brenzaida; the second half, by Brenzaida to Rosina. The final six lines of the poem as printed in *1850**, where it was titled 'The Elder's Rebuke' (the MS has 'Old Man's Lecture' in pencil), are by CB:

> "LISTEN! When your hair, like mine,
> "Takes a tint of silver gray;
> "When your eyes, with dimmer shine,
> "Watch life's bubbles float away:
> "When you, young man, have borne like me   5
>
> "The weary weight of sixty-three,
> "Then shall penance sore be paid

364   NOTES TO PAGES 19–20

"For those hours so wildly squandered;
"And the words that now fall dead
    "On your ear, be deeply pondered—   10
"Pondered and approved at last:
"But their virtue will be past!

"Glorious is the prize of Duty,
    "Though she be 'a serious power';
"Treacherous all the lures of Beauty,   15
    "Thorny bud and poisonous flower!

"Mirth is but a mad beguiling
    "Of the golden-gifted time;
"Love—a demon-meteor, wiling
    "Heedless feet to gulfs of crime.   20

"Those who follow earthly pleasure,
    "Heavenly knowledge will not lead;
"Wisdom hides from them her treasure,
    "Virtue bids them evil-speed!

"Vainly may their hearts, repenting,   25
    "Seek for aid in future years;
"Wisdom, scorned, knows no relenting;
    "Virtue is not won by fears."

Thus spake the ice-blooded elder gray;
The young man scoffed as he turned away,   30
Turned to the call of a sweet lute's measure,
Waked by the lightsome touch of pleasure:
Had he ne'er met a gentler teacher,
Woe had been wrought by that pitiless preacher.

28 MAY 1845, 'A.E. AND R.C.'

p. 20 *28 May 1845, 'A.E. and R.C.'*: *GP. 1850** calls this 'The Two Children' (added
in pencil in the MS) and reads:

HEAVY hangs the rain-drop
    From the burdened spray;
Heavy broods the damp mist
    On uplands far away.

Heavy looms the dull sky,   5
    Heavy rolls the sea;
And heavy throbs the young heart
    Beneath that lonely tree.

Never has a blue streak
    Cleft the clouds since morn;   10

NOTES TO PAGE 20

Never has his grim fate
    Smiled since he was born.

Frowning on the infant,
    Shadowing childhood's joy,
Guardian-angel knows not   15
    That melancholy boy.

Day is passing swiftly
    Its sad and sombre prime;
Boyhood sad is merging
    In sadder manhood's time: 20

All the flowers are praying
    For sun, before they close,
And he prays too—unconscious—
    That sunless human rose.

Blossom—that the west-wind   25
    Has never wooed to blow,
Scentless are thy petals,
    Thy dew is cold as snow!

Soul—where kindred kindness,
    No early promise woke,   30
Barren is thy beauty,
    As weed upon a rock.

Wither—soul and blossom!
    You both were vainly given:
Earth reserves no blessing   35
    For the unblest of heaven!

————

Child of delight, with sun-bright hair,
    And sea-blue, sea-deep eyes!
Spirit of bliss! What brings thee here,
    Beneath these sullen skies?   40

Thou shouldst live in eternal spring,
    Where endless day is never dim;
Why, Seraph, has thine erring wing
    Wafted thee down to weep with him?

"Ah! Not from heaven am I descended,   45
    "Nor do I come to mingle tears;
"But sweet is day, though with shadows blended;
    "And, though clouded, sweet are youthful years.

"I—the image of light and gladness—
    "Saw and pitied that mournful boy,   50

366 NOTES TO PAGES 20-4

"And I vowed—if need were—to share his sadness,
  "And give to him my sunny joy.

"Heavy and dark the night is closing;
  "Heavy and dark may its biding be:
"Better for all from grief reposing,   55
  "And better for all who watch like me—

"Watch in love by a fevered pillow,
  "Cooling the fever with pity's balm;
"Safe as the petrel on tossing billow,
  "Safe in mine own soul's golden calm!   60

"Guardian-angel he lacks no longer;
  "Evil fortune he need not fear:
"Fate is strong, but love is stronger;
  "And *my* love is truer than angel-care."

The poem might be thought EJB's reply to Wordsworth's Immortality Ode (1807) though the matter of what exactly, and how, EJB read is, of course, complicated (see Introduction, pp. xl–xli). The Blakean feel in language—and the use of different approaches to the same topic—is most probably coincidental, as it seems unlikely, even impossible, that EJB could have known much, or anything, about the poet-engraver whose critical fortunes, as she wrote, were at their lowest point. The first complete facsimile of any work by Blake was of *The Marriage of Heaven and Hell*, by the London publisher, John Camden Hotten, in 1868. Hotten also published that year Swinburne's *William Blake: A Critical Essay*, the first major milestone in criticism in the establishment of Blake's work among a wide readership. It is a pleasing coincidence that Swinburne also did something related for the fortunes of EJB (see pp. 342–8). William Gilchrist's *Life of William Blake, 'Pictor Ignotus', With Selections from his Poems and Other Writings* was published in two volumes (London: Bell) in 1863. Swinburne's book was in effect a long review of it.

CB's stanza—the penultimate above—makes one wonder if she took the petrel image from Thomas Bewick: see note to p. 31.

LETTER TO ELLEN NUSSEY, 16? JULY 1845

p. 23 *stout*: this is the closest EJB comes in any surviving document to making a joke—and perhaps it was a family one. CB was remarkably small and slim as her surviving clothes and accessories at BPM confirm.

EMILY BRONTË'S DIARY PAPER, THURSDAY, 30 [31] JULY 1845

p. 24 *Luddenden Foot C*: see note to p. 14.
papa...eyes: Patrick would be successfully operated on for cataracts in Manchester on 26 August 1846.
30th: EJB was born on 30 July 1818.

NOTES TO PAGE 25

367

p. 25 *Branwell... week*: see note to p. 84.
black currants: cf. note to p. 293.
I conclude: cf. AB's addition:

Thursday July the 31st 1845. Yesterday was Emily's birthday, and the time when we should have opened our 1845 paper, but by mistake we opened it to day instead. How many things have happened since it was written—some pleasant, some far otherwise—Yet I was then at Thorp Green and now I am only just escaped from it. I was wishing to leave it then and if I had known that I had four years longer to stay how wretched I should have been then too. I was writing the fourth volume of Sophalal but during my stay I have had some very unpleasant and undreamt of experience of human nature—Others have seen more changes Charlotte has left Mr. White's and been twice to Brussels, where she stayed each time nearly a year. Emily has been there too, and stayed nearly a year—Branwell has left Luddenden foot, and been a tutor at Thorp Green and had much tribulation and ill health he was very ill on Tuesday but he went with John Brown to Liverpool where he now is I suppose and we hope he will be better and do better in future—This is a dismal cloudy wet evening we have had so far a very cold wet summer Charlotte has lately been to Hathersage in Derbyshire on a visit of three weeks to Ellen Nuss[e]y—she is now sitting sewing in the dining-room. Emily is ironing upstairs. I am sitting in the dining-room in the rocking-chair before the fire with my feet on the fender. Papa is in the parlour. Tabby and Martha are, I think, in the kitchen Keeper and Flossy are I do not know where. Little Dick is hopping in his cage. When the last paper was written we were thinking of setting up a school—the scheme has been dropt, and long after taken up again and dropt again because we could not get pupils—Charlotte is thinking about getting another situation—she wishes to go to Paris—Will she go? She has let Flossy in by the bye, and he is now lying on the sopha—Emily is engaged in writing the Emperor Julius's life she has read some of it, and I want very much to hear the rest—she is writing some poetry too I wonder what it is about?—I have begun the third volume of passages in the life of an individual. I wish I had finished it. This afternoon I began to set about making my grey figured silk frock that was dyed at Keighley—What sort of a hand shall I make of it? E. and I have a great deal of work to do—when shall we sensibly diminish it? I want to get a habit of early rising shall I succeed? We have not yet finished our Gondal Chronicles that we began three years and a half ago when will they be done? The Gondals are at present in a sad state the Republicans are uppermost but the Royalists are not quite overcome—the young sovereigns, with their brothers and sisters, are still at the Palace of Instruction—the Unique Society, above half a year ago, were wrecked on a desert island as they were returning from Gaaldin— they are still there but we have not played at them much yet—The Gondals in general are not in first-rate playing condition—will they improve? I wonder how we shall all be and where and how situated on the ontrolh of July 1848, when, if we are all alive, Emily will be just 30 I shall be in my 29th year, Charlotte in her 33rd, and Branwell in his 32nd; and what changes shall we have seen and known and shall we be much changed ourselves? I hope not—for the worse at least—I for my part

368　NOTES TO PAGES 25–6

cannot well be *flatter* or older in mind than I am now—Hoping for the best, I conclude.

Anne Brontë.

On the piece overall, see Introduction, pp. xxiv–xxv. Note that there are peculiar difficulties in deciding the transcription of this text and no version, to my knowledge, agrees with another.

2 JANUARY 1846

p. 26 *2 January 1846 ('No coward soul is mine')*: HM. *1850** reads:

The following are the last lines my sister Emily ever wrote.

> No coward soul is mine,
> No trembler in the world's storm-troubled sphere:
> I see Heaven's glories shine,
> And faith shines equal, arming me from fear.
>
> O God within my breast,   5
> Almighty, ever-present Deity!
> Life—that in me has rest,
> As I—undying Life—have power in thee!
>
> Vain are the thousand creeds
> That move men's hearts: unutterably vain;   10
> Worthless as withered weeds,
> Or idle froth amid the boundless main,
>
> To waken doubt in one
> Holding so fast by thine infinity;
> So surely anchored on   15
> The steadfast rock of immortality.
>
> With wide-embracing love
> Thy spirit animates eternal years,
> Pervades and broods above,
> Changes, sustains, dissolves, creates, and rears.   20
>
> Though earth and man were gone,
> And suns and universes ceased to be,
> And Thou were left alone,
> Every existence would exist in Thee.
>
> There is not room for Death,   25
> Nor atom that his might could render void:
> Thou—THOU art Being and Breath,
> And what THOU art may never be destroyed.

CB was wrong in claiming—or at least appearing to claim—that this was the last poem. The last dated poem in *GP* is 13 May 1848. Gezari adds: 'It is probably the first poem [EJB] wrote after [CB] discovered her poems' (p. 278), but it is hard to

NOTES TO PAGE 26   369

know what the evidence for this is. 'No coward soul' is, in fact, the last poem in HM, and it is possible CB simply means 'this is the last poem my sister ever wrote *in this MS*'.

Note that there has been much analysis of this poem as well as efforts to locate the source of phrases, 'coward soul' especially (for which, in fact, there are many examples in English poetry prior to 1846). But these require, for the most part, a reconstruction of EJB's putative reading, for which it is mostly impossible, unfortunately, to find much more than circumstantial evidence.

Margaret Maison observed in 'Emily Brontë and Epictetus', *Notes & Queries*, 25 (1978), pp. 230–1, a possible parallel in phrasing with the eighth strophe of 'An Irregular Ode' written by 'H.M.' and addressed to Elizabeth Carter. 'H.M.' was Hester Mulso, later Chapone: see p. xlvii n.74 in the Introduction. Carter published the 'Ode' with permission at the beginning of her edition of *All the Works of Epictetus* (1758):

> No more repine, my Coward Soul!
> The Sorrows of Mankind to share,
> Which He, who could the world controul
> Did not disdain to bear!
> Check not the Flow of sweet fraternal Love,
> By Heav'n's high King in Bounty given,
> Thy stubborn Heart to soften and improve,
> Thy earth-clad Spirit to refine,
> And gradual raise to Love divine
> And wing its soaring Flight to Heaven!

> *All the Works of Epictetus, Which are now Extant: consisting of his discourses, preserved by Arrian, in four books, the 'Enchiridion', and fragments translated from the original Greek, by Elizabeth Carter with an introduction, and notes, by the translator* (London: Richardson, 1758), unpaginated front endpapers).

ll. 19–20 *Pervades and broods…rears*: it is not hard to think here of Coleridge's statement in *Biographia Literaria* (1817): 'The IMAGINATION then, I consider either as primary, or secondary. The primary IMAGINATION I hold to be the living Power and prime Agent of all human Perception, and as a repetition in the finite mind of the eternal act of creation in the infinite I AM. The secondary Imagination I consider as an echo of the former, co-existing with the conscious will, yet still as identical with the primary in the *kind* of its agency, and differing only in *degree*, and in the *mode* of its operation. It dissolves, diffuses, dissipates, in order to recreate; or where this process is rendered impossible, yet still at all events it struggles to idealize and to unify. It is essentially *vital*, even as all objects (*as* objects) are essentially fixed and dead', *Biographia Literaria*, ed. J.T. Shawcross, 2 vols (Oxford: Clarendon, 1907), i.202. Whether this is an accidental or actual connection or otherwise, we do not, of course, know.

ll. 21–8 *Though Earth and moon…destroyed*: cf. Catherine's words about Heathcliff, p. 118.

370 NOTES TO PAGE 27

UNDATED

p. 27 *Undated ('Love is like the wild rose briar')*: HM. The title in *1850**, 'Love and Friendship', is CB's. CB's version reads:

> LOVE is like the wild rose-briar;
>   Friendship like the holly-tree.
> The holly is dark when the rose-briar blooms,
>   But which will bloom most constantly?
>
> The wild rose-briar is sweet in spring,   5
>   Its summer blossoms scent the air;
> Yet wait till winter comes again,
>   And who will call the wild-briar fair?
>
> Then, scorn the silly rose-wreath now,
>   And deck thee with the holly's sheen,   10
> That, when December blights thy brow,
>   He still may leave thy garland green.

Note that *1850** also included a poem entitled 'Stanzas'. No MS version has been found and there have long been suspicions that this is by CB (or even AB). See Introduction, p. xxxii. 'Stanzas' reads:

OFTEN REBUKED, YET ALWAYS BACK RETURNING

> OFTEN rebuked, yet always back returning
>   To those first feelings that were born with me,
> And leaving busy chase of wealth and learning
>   For idle dreams of things which cannot be:
>
> To-day, I will seek not the shadowy region;   5
>   Its unsustaining vastness waxes drear;
> And visions rising, legion after legion,
>   Bring the unreal world too strangely near.
>
> I'll walk, but not in old heroic traces,
>   And not in paths of high morality,   10
> And not among the half-distinguished faces,
>   The clouded forms of long-past history.
>
> I'll walk where my own nature would be leading:
>   It vexes me to choose another guide:
> Where the grey flocks in ferny glens are feeding;   15
>   Where the wild wind blows on the mountain side.
>
> What have those lonely mountains worth revealing?
>   More glory and more grief than I can tell:
> The earth that wakes *one* human heart to feeling
>   Can centre both the worlds of Heaven and Hell.   20

1850* also included 'The Visionary', which reads as follows:

NOTES TO PAGES 27–9 371

SILENT IS THE HOUSE: ALL ARE LAID ASLEEP

SILENT is the house: all are laid asleep:
One alone looks out o'er the snow-wreaths deep,
Watching every cloud, dreading every breeze
That whirls the wildering drift, and bends the groaning trees.

Cheerful is the hearth, soft the matted floor;   5
Not one shivering gust creeps through pane or door;
The little lamp burns straight, its rays shoot strong and far:
I trim it well, to be the wanderer's guiding-star.

Frown, my haughty sire! Chide, my angry dame!
Set your slaves to spy; threaten me with shame: 10
But neither sire nor dame, nor prying serf shall know,
What angel nightly tracks that waste of frozen snow.

What I love shall come like visitant of air,
Safe in secret power from lurking human snare;
What loves me, no word of mine shall e'er betray,   15
Though for faith unstained my life must forfeit pay.

Burn, then, little lamp; glimmer straight and clear—
Hush! A rustling wing stirs, methinks, the air:
He for whom I wait, thus ever comes to me;
Strange Power! I trust thy might; trust thou my constancy.   20

On the context of this, see Note on the Text, p. l.

ELLIS BELL [EMILY BRONTË]'S CONTRIBUTION TO *POEMS BY CURRER, ELLIS, AND ACTON BELL* (LONDON: AYLOTT AND JONES, 1846)

The name 'Aylott and Jones' first appears, to my knowledge, in a printed catalogue in 1822 (as one of the publishers of *The Works of William Robertson, D.D.*) though this must be either an error or another company. EJB's Aylott and Jones more obviously began business in the mid-1840s with a list primarily including Evangelical and theological works (some of them lectures and pamphlets). The company also, early on, published hymns; a collection of Richard Brinsley Sheridan's parliamentary oratory; and statements on philanthropy. Large-scale books were not, as fiction was not, their medium in the 1840s (I can find no evidence to support the assertion in *Companion* that they published 'Dr G. B. Cheever's life of Bunyan', p. 27 [*Lectures on the Pilgrim's Progress, and on the Life and Times of Bunyan* (London: Nelson/Fullarton, 1846)]).

The Bells' volume appeared with only two other catalogued volumes of poetry in 1846: A Young Englander, *Thirty-Six Non-Conformist Sonnets* [violently anti-Catholic] and Thomas Chamberlain, *Windsor: A Poem: Historical and Imaginative*. The catalogue for that year situated this tiny number of poetry collections within a much larger list of Evangelical and socially aware writing (including, for instance, *A Verbatim Report of the Fourth Annual Meeting of the Metropolitan Drapers' Association, formed*

372   NOTES TO PAGE 29

for the purpose of abridging the hours of business in all trades: held in Covent Garden Theatre, on Friday evening, February 27th, 1846, the Right Hon. Lord Ashley in the chair, and containing the speeches of the noble chairman; the Right Hon. Fox Maule, M.P.; Col. Fox, M.P.). Readers looking for new poetry in 1846, in other words, would hardly have turned to Aylott and Jones' catalogue first. The company later published the four (unsuccessful) instalments of the Pre-Raphaelite journal, *The Germ: Thoughts Towards Nature, in Poetry, Literature, and Art* in 1850 before abandoning the project because of poor sales. The business seems to have ceased trading under the name 'Aylott and Jones' from the beginning of the 1860s.

LCB notes:

> The publishers to whom she finally made a successful application for the production of 'Currer, Ellis, and Acton Bell's poems,' were Messrs Aylott and Jones, Paternoster Row. Mr Aylott has kindly placed the letters which she wrote to them on the subject at my disposal. The first is dated January 28th, 1846, and in it she inquires if they will publish one volume octavo of poems; if not at their own risk, on the author's account. It is signed 'C. Brontë.' They must have replied pretty speedily, for on January 31st she writes again:—
>
> 'GENTLEMEN,
>
> 'Since you agree to undertake the publication of the work respecting which I applied to you, I should wish now to know, as soon as possible, the cost of paper and printing. I will then send the necessary remittance, together with the manuscript. I should like it to be printed in one octavo volume, of the same quality of paper and size of type as Moxon's last edition of Wordsworth. The poems will occupy, I should think, from 200 to 250 pages. They are not the production of a clergyman, nor are they exclusively of a religious character; but I presume these circumstances will be immaterial. It will, perhaps, be necessary that you should see the manuscript, in order to calculate accurately the expense of publication; in that case I will send it immediately. I should like, however, previously, to have some idea of the probable cost; and if, from what I have said, you can make a rough calculation on the subject, I should be greatly obliged to you.'

In her next letter, February 6th, she says:—

> 'You will perceive that the poems are the work of three persons, relatives—their separate pieces are distinguished by their respective signatures.'

She writes again on February 15th; and on the 16th she says:—

> 'The MS. will certainly form a thinner volume than I had anticipated. I cannot name another model which I should like it precisely to resemble, yet, I think, a duodecimo form, and a somewhat reduced, though still clear type, would be preferable. I only stipulate for clear type, not too small, and good paper.'

On February 21st she selects the 'long primer type' for the poems, and will remit 31l. 10s. in a few days.

Minute as the details conveyed in these notes are, they are not trivial, because they afford such strong indications of character. If the volume was to be published at their own risk, it was necessary that the sister conducting the

NOTES TO PAGES 29–31

negotiation should make herself acquainted with the different kinds of type, and the various sizes of books. Accordingly she bought a small volume, from which to learn all she could on the subject of preparation for the press. No half-knowledge—no trusting to other people for decisions which she could make for herself; and yet a generous and full confidence, not misplaced, in the thorough probity of Messrs Aylott and Jones. The caution in ascertaining the risk before embarking in the enterprise, and the prompt payment of the money required, even before it could be said to have assumed the shape of a debt, were both parts of a self-reliant and independent character. Self-contained also was she. During the whole time that the volume of poems was in the course of preparation and publication, no word was written telling anyone, out of the household circle, what was in progress.

LCB, i. 337–9.

Aylott and Jones had their offices in 1846 at 8 Paternoster Row, next to St Paul's Cathedral. As for almost the whole of the publishing business in the area, the buildings were destroyed by aerial bombardment in the Second World War. See Margaret Willes, *In The Shadow of St. Paul's Cathedral: The Churchyard that Shaped London* (New Haven: Yale University Press, 2022).

The best review of *1846* was an unsigned piece in *The Critic* (4 July 1846), pp. 6–8, which included the lines:

Indeed it is long since we have enjoyed a volume of such genuine poetry as this. Amid the heaps of trash and trumpery in the shape of verses, which lumber the table of the literary journalist, this small book of some 170 pages only has come like a ray of sunshine, gladdening the eye with present glory, and the heart with promise of bright hours in store. Here we have good, wholesome, refreshing, vigorous poetry—no sickly affectations, no namby-pamby, no tedious imitations of familiar strains, but original thoughts, expressed in the true language of poetry—not in its cant, as is the custom with mocking-bird poets.

CH, pp. 59–60.

FAITH AND DESPONDENCY

p. 29 *Faith and Despondency*: *GP*, 6 November 1844. 'I.M. to I.G.'
l. 6 *Iernë*: minor figure from the Gondal narratives (cf. MS title).

STARS

p. 31 *Stars*: HM, untitled. 14 April 1845.
l. 12 *petrel*: a generic name for a large number of different pelagic seabirds that return to land only to breed. Thomas Bewick's *History of British Birds*, 2 vols (Newcastle: Beilby and Bewick/Walker, 1797–1804), had a section 'Of the petrel', ii.241–51, in which he noted: 'These birds are the constant, roving, adventurous inhabitants of the ocean; one species or another of them is met with by navigators in every climate, and at the greatest distances from the land. They seem to sport with the tempest, and run on foot, swim, or fly at pleasure over the foaming billows, with

374   NOTES TO PAGES 31–3

amazing velocity', ii.241. EJB had certainly looked at this book; she had copied the ring ouzel (see note to p. 182, '*ousels*') while Charlotte the 'mountain sparrow', and Branwell the goshawk. For an account of the matter overall, see Barbara T. Gates, 'Natural History', in Marianne Thormählen, ed., *The Brontës in Context* (Cambridge: Cambridge University Press, 2012), pp. 250–60.

The absence of an article, definite or indefinite, is awkward (Hewish sensibly notes of this word: 'The poem is strong enough to absorb minor flaws', p. 82; cf. l. 59 of 'The Two Children' from *1850**, note to p. 20). Bewick's book, of course, plays a memorable role in Chapter I of *JE*. For a consideration of the Bewick-related birds in *JE*, see Francis O'Gorman, '*Jane Eyre*'s Rooks and Crows', *Brontë Studies*, 46 (2021), pp. 82–7. Cf. CB's 'Lines on Bewick', in *The Complete Poems of Charlotte Brontë*, pp. 131–4.

ll. 27–8 *steep in gold... hill*: an echo of Wordsworth's 'I wandered lonely as a cloud' (1807), perhaps?

THE PHILOSOPHER

p. 32 *The Philosopher*: HM, 3 February 1845, untitled. *The Athenæum*, 1133 (4 July 1849), p. 682, quoted stanzas 3 to 5 of this poem after the comment: '[The instinct of song rises, in the poetry] of Ellis, into an inspiration, which may yet find an audience in the outer world. A fine quaint spirit has the latter, which may have things to speak that men will be glad to hear,—and an evident power of wing that may reach heights not here attempted', *CH*, p. 61. Reviewing the *1846* volume in December 1848, another journal added of Ellis: 'With very few exceptions, the poems of ELLIS deal with abstract ideas rather than actual events. He is the most metaphysical of the three', 'Poems by Currer, Ellis, and Acton Bell', *The Critic of Books, Society, Pictures, Music and Decorative Art*, 7 (15 December 1848), pp. 486–7 (p. 486).

l. 17 *Three gods*: unidentified.

l. 46 *wilder*: bewilder.

REMEMBRANCE

p. 33 *Remembrance*: GP, 3 March 1845 ('R. Alcona to J. Brenzaida'). The Gondal context is, of course, lost.

C. Day Lewis (1904–72), who had just completed his term of office as the University of Oxford's Professor of Poetry, famously observed:

> The line here is basically a pentameter: but it is pulled out of the ordinary iambic pentameter rhythm and given a different shape by three devices—by putting a stress on the first syllable of each line, by a marked cæsura after the second foot, and by the use of feminine rhymes in lines one and three of each stanza. The effect of this rhythm I find extremely powerful, extremely appropriate. It is a dragging effect, as of feet moving in a funeral march; an andante maestoso: it is the *slowest* rhythm I know in English poetry, and the most sombre.
>
> 'The Poetry of Emily Brontë', *Brontë Society Transactions*,
> 13 (1957), pp. 83–99 (p. 91).

NOTES TO PAGES 33–7

See also Introduction, p. xlii n.63. Cf. CB's 'The Grave of Percy', in *The Complete Poems of Charlotte Brontë*, pp. 184–9 and 'He saw my heart's woe', ibid., pp. 220–2.

l. 6 *northern shore*: one part of Gondal was imagined to be in the north Pacific, with landscapes like that of the Yorkshire moors and Sir Walter Scott's Scottish Borders. See Introduction, pp. xxii–xxiii.

l. 28 *mine*: possibly 'thine' in the MS.

A DEATH-SCENE

p. 34 *A Death-Scene*: GP, 2 December 1844 ('From A D— W— in the N.C.') ['From a Dungeon Wall in the Northern College']. Cf. Introduction, pp. xxiii–xxiv.

l. 9 *Edward*: from the largely lost Gondal context. In the MS, this is given as 'Elbë', Alexander, Lord of Elbë. He was a lover of A.G.A. (see note to p. 36) and his lonely grave is at Lake Elnor.

l. 11 *Arden's lake*: presumably Lake Elnor (see the previous note).

SONG

p. 36 *Song*: GP, 1 May 1844. The MS indicates that the speaker is Lord Eldred W., friend of A.G.A. (Augusta G[eraldine?] Almeda), who was the leading powerful and destructive female figure of the Gondal narratives (see p. xxii n.24). It is not difficult to see that what we know of her irascible and sexually active character finally re-appeared as the first Catherine in *WH* after EJB had killed A.G.A. off in 'A.G.A., the Death of' (begun in January 1841): Hewish notes the 'curiously logistical' title (p. 73).

l. 2 *moor-lark*: presumably the skylark, *Alauda arvensis*.

l. 3 *heather bells*: this might be a generic reference to heather in general with its bell-like flowers or to specific heather-bell, *Erica cinerea*. Cf. pp. 9–10 (esp. l. 21) and Lockwood's recollection of the graves at the end of *WH*.

ANTICIPATION

p. 37 *Anticipation*: HM, 2 June 1845.

l. 1 *How*: only the initial letter capitalized in *1846*.

l. 11 *thy own compeers*: a good example of where EJB readers can be tempted, rightly or wrongly, to be biographical. Is this Branwell, perhaps? In the month after EJB wrote, or at least dated, this poem, he would be dismissed in disgrace from Thorp Green (because, it might be, of an affair with Mrs Lydia Robinson, though the details are uncertain and contested: see note to p. 18, ll. 21–4). EJB might well have known of the scandalous behaviour, whatever it was. We do not, in addition, know what EJB understood of CB's love for Constantin Héger, though, of course, she had been with her sister on her first visit to Brussels. CB might dimly, it is possible, be included in this description of those who 'went wandering wrong'. Alternatively, the context might be a lost Gondal one. Or something completely different.

376   NOTES TO PAGES 37–45

l. 15 *died untried and young*: Maria (1814–25) and Elizabeth Brontë (1815–25)?

l. 16 *wandering wrong*: Branwell and Mrs Robinson? CB and M. Héger? See note to l. 11 above.

l. 33 *anchor of desire*: a formulation that recalls the opening of 'A Passionate Man's Pilgrimage' (1604), once ascribed to Sir Walter Raleigh (*c*.1552–1618):

> Give me my scallop shell of quiet,
> My staff of faith to walk upon,
> My scrip of joy, immortal diet,
> My bottle of salvation,
> My gown of glory, hope's true gage,
> And thus I'll take my pilgrimage. [...]

THE PRISONER (A FRAGMENT)

p. 38 *The Prisoner (A Fragment)*: from *GP*; see note below. Cf. AB's 'The Dungeon', in *The Complete Poems of Anne Brontë*, ed. Clement Shorter (London: Hodder and Stoughton, n.d. [1920]), pp. 57–8 (16 December 1844).

'JULIAN M. AND A.G. ROCHELLE'

p. 40 *'Julian M. and A.G. Rochelle'*: I reproduce the complete text of this poem from *GP* (with its inconsistences and occasional puzzles). It is dated 9 October 1845, and was first published as a whole in the Shakespeare Head *Gondal Poems: Now First Published from the MS. in the British Museum*, ed. Helen Brown and Joan Mott (Oxford: Blackwell for Shakespeare Head, 1938). See my account in 'Note on the Text', pp. xlix–li. In *1846*, an adapted extract was published as 'The Prisoner (A Fragment)'; see previous poem. CB also published another extract, from the opening, as 'The Visionary' in *1850**: see p. l and note to p. 26. In *GP*, the poem has the pencilled title 'The Signal Light'.

18 DECEMBER 1843

p. 44 *Hope*: HM, 18 December 1843. Title added in pencil.

A DAY DREAM

p. 45 *A Day Dream*: HM, 5 March 1844.

l. 1 *brae*: 'The steep bank bounding a river valley. Frequent in the collocation "banks and braes"', *OED*. Scottish and northern English. The opening word 'On' has only an initial capital letter in *1846*.

ll. 11–12 *wedding guests...there*: the single troubled wedding guest is a memory, it might be, of the auditor of Coleridge's 'The Rime of the Ancient Mariner' (first published 1798). Gezari compares: 'Oh, evil day! if I were sullen | While Earth herself is

NOTES TO PAGES 45–50

377

adorning, | This sweet May-morning', William Wordsworth, 'Ode: Intimations of Immortality from Recollections of Early Childhood' (1807), ll. 43–5 (Gezari, p. 234).

l. 28 *unreal mockery*: cf. *Macbeth*, 3.iv.106.

ll. 37–8 *Now...sure*: Gezari, p. 234, compares Wordsworth's 'Resolution and Independence' (1807), 'Now, whether it were by peculiar grace, | A leading from above, a something given [...]', ll. 50–1.

ll. 41–4 *A thousand...near*: seemingly echoing a stanza from 'The Rime of the Ancient Mariner' in the 1834 version:

> The many men, so beautiful!
> And they all dead did lie:
> And a thousand thousand slimy things
> Lived on; and so did I.

(ll. 236–9).

l. 52 *O seemed to sing, to me*: HM clearly has 'Or seemed to sing to me'.

TO IMAGINATION

p. 47 *To Imagination*: HM, 3 September 1844. In the MS, this poem is followed, as in *1846*, by 'How clear she shines'. Title added in pencil.

HOW CLEAR SHE SHINES

p. 48 *How clear she shines*: HM, 13 April 1843, the night of a full moon. There is no title in the MS.

SYMPATHY

p. 49 *Sympathy*: HM, undated and untitled.

PLEAD FOR ME

p. 49 *Plead for me*: HM, 14 October 1844, untitled.

SELF-INTERROGATION

p. 50 *Self-interrogation*: HM, 23 October 1842–6 February 1843. A poem, untitled in the MS, that was, it must be assumed, broken off in Brussels with news of Aunt Branwell's death and completed back in Haworth. The Revd William Weightman (b. 1814), who had charmed the sisters (AB had been, it might be, particularly fond of him: her poem 'I will not mourn thee, lovely one', could be about him), had died on 6 September 1842; the sisters' friend, Martha Taylor, had died of unknown causes on 12 October 1842 in Koekelberg, near Brussels. (There is a convincing argument that Martha did not, as is often asserted, die of cholera [and possibly died of appendicitis instead] in Eric Ruijssenaars, 'The True Cause of Death of Martha Taylor', Brussels Brontë Blog (18 May 2018), http://brussels-bronte.blogspot.com/2018/05/the-true-cause-of-death-of-martha-taylor.html.)

378 NOTES TO PAGES 50–7

The placing of speech marks in the poem has not yet been settled and my text, of course, follows *1846*. Editorial intervention, for clarity, in square brackets.

l. 3 *What thoughts has*: sic.

DEATH

p. 52 *Death*: HM, 10 April 1845. Untitled. Some have wondered if this is EJB thinking about the deaths of Maria and Elizabeth: cf. note to p. 37, l. 15.

STANZAS TO—

p. 53 *Stanzas to—*: HM, 14 November 1839. Untitled.

l. 4 *ruined hopes*: possibly Branwell is on EJB's mind, though is clearly not being addressed. His career as a portrait painter in Bradford, begun in July 1838, had failed a few months before EJB wrote this poem.

l. 8 *altered eye*: Gezari, p. 237, suggests a comparison with Scott's 'Lay of the Last Minstrel' (1805), 'Nor in her mother's altered eye | Dared she to look for sympathy', i.10–11. But, in fact, the phrase is a shared one. Cf. 'the altered eye of friends' in J.G. Lockhart's *Life of Sir Walter Scott*, 3 vols (Paris: Baudry, 1837), i.328; Caroline Bowles Southey, *Ellen Fitzarthur* (London: Longman, Hurst, Rees, Orme, and Brown, 1820), 'And love may gaze with altered eye', Canto I, l. 387; or Isaac d'Israeli, 'Cominge', in *Narrative Poems by I. d'Israeli* (London: Murray, 1803), 'My ruined feelings in thine altered eye', l. 74.

l. 25 *lie lightly on that breast*: Gazari, p. 237, suggests this an echo of Pope's 'Elegy to the Memory of an Unfortunate Lady': 'And the green turf lie lightly on thy breast', l. 64. But the line has, perhaps, the feel of a commonplace expression. Cf. 'Oliver Oldschool', *The Port Folio*, new series, 1 (Philadelphia: Watts, 1806), 'They bid the earth lie lightly on their former companion', p. 344.

HONOUR'S MARTYR

p. 53 *Honour's Martyr*: GP, 21 November 1844. The MS title is 'M. Douglas to E.R. Gleneden'. The Gondal context is lost.

STANZAS

p. 55 *Stanzas*: HM, 4 May 1840. Untitled.

MY COMFORTER

p. 56 *My Comforter*: HM, 10 February 1844.

THE OLD STOIC

p. 57 *The Old Stoic*: HM, 1 March 1841. Cf. 'No coward soul', p. 26. See Introduction, pp. xlvi–xlvii.

NOTES TO PAGES 57–9 379

l. 1 *Riches… esteem*: a secular response, perhaps, to Matthew 6:19–21: 'Lay not up for yourselves treasures upon earth, where moth and rust doth corrupt, and where thieves break through and steal: But lay up for yourselves treasures in heaven, where neither moth nor rust doth corrupt, and where thieves do not break through nor steal: For where your treasure is, there will your heart be also.'

l. 8 *And give me liberty*: is there any chance this could be a recollection of the only semi-recalled but still celebrated words of the lawyer Patrick Henry (1736–99), keen to make military preparations against the British Army, at the Second Virginia Convention on 23 March 1775?

> It is in vain, sir, to extenuate the matter. Gentlemen may cry, peace, peace—but there is no peace. The war is actually begun! The next gale that sweeps from the north, will bring to our ears the clash of resounding arms! Our brethren are already in the field! Why stand we here idle? What is it that gentlemen wish? What would they have? Is life so dear, or peace so sweet, as to be purchased at the price of chains and slavery? Forbid it, Almighty God!—I know not what course others may take; but as for me, [. . .] give me liberty, or give me death!
>
> William Wirt, *Sketches of the Life and Character of Patrick Henrys* (Philadelphia: Webster, 1817), p. 123.

It is worth noting how readily EJB's turn in poetry to hopes for liberty has been taken as evidence of her alleged dislike of her seemingly confined life at Haworth. In a gossipy opinion-piece in *Tait's Edinburgh Magazine* of May 1857, for instance, the writer reflected on the notion that a fly could supply EJB with poetic material and turned this into a particularly provocative image of an idea of EJB under restraint. 'The buzzing of an imprisoned blue-bottle', the writer went on, 'will always suggest Emily Brontë', 'Tangled Talk', *Tait's Edinburgh Magazine*, 24 (May 1857), pp. 292–6 (p. 293). As described in the Introduction, however, the evidence points to her active preference for privacy and for Parsonage life over anything beyond it (excepting her own imagination).

l. 11 *chainless soul*: cf. Byron's 'Eternal spirit of the chainless Mind!', 'Sonnet on Chillon' (1816), l. 1 and Emmeline Stuart-Wortley, 'Love and Freedom', *Hours at Naples, and Other Poems* (London: Saunders and Otley, 1837), 'When it [Love] burns in a Soul that is chainless and free!', l. 28.

ELLIS BELL [EMILY BRONTË], *WUTHERING HEIGHTS: A NOVEL*

Thomas Cautley Newby (1797/8?–1882), London publisher. At the time of publishing *WH*, his offices were at 72 Mortimer Street, Cavendish Square. The area at this point was dominated by the Middlesex Hospital and was not, unlike the area around St Paul's, home to many similar businesses. In 1847, Newby's new fiction, which was the majority of what he published, included: Mrs C.D. Burdett, *Walter Hamilton: A Novel*; Robert Mackenzie Daniel, *The Cardinal's Daughter*; [Mrs?] Robert Mackenzie Daniel, *Jeremiah Parkes: A Novel*; Elizabeth Caroline Grey, *Daughters: A Novel*; C.F. Henningsen, *Sixty Years Hence: A Novel*; Eliza Lynn Linton, *Azeth, the Egyptian: A Novel*; and Anthony Trollope's first novel, *The Macdermots of Ballycloran*. Non-fiction was only a small part of Newby's relatively modest publishing output and

380 NOTES TO PAGES 59–61

in 1847 included Cesare Cantù's *The Reformation in Europe*, trans. Fortunato Prandi and the first of two volumes of Count Callistus Augustus de Godde de Liancourt and James A. Manning's *Pius the Ninth: Or, The First Year of his Pontificate*.

Newby was not the most admirable of publishers. He did not, for a start, attend very carefully to the task of issuing accurately EJB and AB's texts, and did not even let them know their novels had been released, other than by sending them six copies; he later tried to claim to Harper Brothers in New York that they should take *The Tenant of Wildfell Hall* because it was by CB. Elizabeth Gaskell called him 'the mean publisher to be gibbetted' (*ODNB*). On the publication of George Eliot's *Adam Bede* (Edinburgh: Blackwood, 1859), Newby advertised *Adam Bede, Junior: A Sequel* to be published that same year, much to Eliot's irritation. Of Newby, CB wrote to W.S. Williams on 7 December 1848:

> [...] I am indeed surprised that Mr. Newby should say he is to publish another work by Ellis and Acton Bell. Acton has had quite enough of him. I think I have before intimated that the author never more intends to have Mr. Newby for a publisher. Not only does he seem to forget that engagements should be fulfilled—but by a system of petty and contemptible manœuvring he throws an air of charlatanry over the works of which he has the management: this does not suit the 'Bells'; they have their own rude north-country ideas of what is delicate, honourable and gentleman like[.]
>
> *Letters*, ii.148.

p. 61 *1801*: 1 January 1801 marked the commencement of the 1800 Acts of Union, creating the political union of Great Britain and Ireland. Patrick Brontë turned twenty-four on 17 March 1801 and the year following he would move from Ireland to St John's College, Cambridge, as an undergraduate. Maria Branwell, EJB's mother, turned eighteen in 1801, eleven years before she met her future husband, when he was serving as an external examiner in Classics at Woodhouse Grove School, Rawdon. There is an inscription above the main door of Ponden House, now Ponden Hall, a farm house (recently a bed and breakfast), approx. 2½ miles west of Haworth at Stanbury, which might have influenced EJB's imagining of the properties in *WH* (see Figures 1 and 2 and note to p. 61, '*Thrushcross Grange*'). The inscription reads: 'The Old House now standing was built by Robert Heaton for his son Michael, Anno Domini 1634. The Old Porch and Peat House were built by his grandson Robert Heaton, Anno Domini 1680. The present building was rebuilt by his descendant R.H., 1801.'

Note that the narrative of the novel proper starts with the arrival of Heathcliff in 1771. Edward Chitham pointed out in *The Birth of 'Wuthering Heights'* (Basingstoke: Macmillan, 1998), p. 104, that the name 'Hareton' is an anagram of 'R. Heaton'.

Throughout these notes, I broadly follow the chronology described by 'C.P.S.' [C.P. Sanger], *The Chronology of 'Wuthering Heights'* (London: Leonard and Virginia Woolf at the Hogarth Press, 1926).

Cf. 'By fixing, then, the date of my story Sixty Years before this present 1st November, 1805, I would have my readers understand, that they will meet in the following pages neither a romance of chivalry, nor a tale of modern manners', Sir Walter

Figure 1 Ponden Hall (photograph by the editor, 7 July 2021). EJB might have read in the library here.

Scott, *Waverley, Or, 'Tis Sixty Years Since*, ed. P.D. Garside, The Edinburgh Edition of the Waverley Novels (Edinburgh: Edinburgh University Press, 2007), p. 4.
    p. 61 *Heathcliff*: see Introduction, pp. xxix, xxxv–xxxvii. Cf. this early review:

> This is a strange book. It is not without evidences of considerable power: but, as a whole, it is wild, confused, disjointed, and improbable; and the people who make

FIGURE 2 The inscription at Ponden Hall (photograph by the editor, 7 July 2021), possibly a model—possibly not—for properties in *WH*. Like the inscription in *Wuthering Heights*, the instruction above the door at Ponden Hall is dated 1801.

up the drama, which is tragic enough in its consequences, are savages ruder than those who lived before the days of Homer. With the exception of Heathcliff, the story is confined to the family of Earnshaw, who intermarry with the Lintons; and the scene of their exploits is a rude old-fashioned house, at the top of one of the high moors or fells in the north of England. Whoever has traversed the bleak heights of Hartside or Cross Fell, on his road from Westmoreland to the dales of Yorkshire, and has been welcomed there by the winds and rain on a 'gusty day', will know how to estimate the comforts of Wuthering Heights in wintry weather. But it may be as well to give the author's own sketch of the spot, taken, it should be observed, at a more genial season: [quotation omitted, see pp. 61–3].

This Heathcliff may be considered as the hero of the book, if a hero there be. He is [an incarnation] of evil qualities; implacable hate; ingratitude, cruelty, falsehood, selfishness and revenge. He exhibits, moreover, a certain stoical endurance in early life, which enables him to 'bide his time,' and nurse up his wrath till it becomes mature and terrible; and there is only one portion of his nature, one only, wherein he appears to approximate to humanity. Like the Corsair, and other such melodramatic heroes, he is

'Linked to one virtue and a thousand crimes;'

NOTES TO PAGE 61

and it is with difficulty that we can prevail upon ourselves to believe in the appearance of such a phenomenon, so near our own dwellings as the summit of a Lancashire or Yorkshire moor.

[...] If this book be, as we apprehend it is, the first work of the author, we hope that he will produce a second,—giving himself more time in its composition than in the present case, developing his incidents more carefully, eschewing exaggeration and obscurity, and looking steadily at human life, under all its moods, for those pictures of the passions that he may desire to sketch for our public benefit. It may be well also to be sparing of certain oaths and phrases, which do not materially contribute to any character, and are by no means to be reckoned among the evidences of a writer's genius. We detest the affectation and effeminate frippery which is but too frequent in the modern novel, and willingly trust ourselves with an author who goes at once fearlessly into the moors and desolate places, for his heroes; but we must at the same time stipulate with him that he shall not drag into light all that he discovers, of coarse and loathsome, in his wanderings, but simply so much good and ill as he may find necessary to elucidate his history—so much only as may be interwoven inextricably with the persons whom he professes to paint. It is the province of an artist to modify and in some cases refine what he beholds in the ordinary world. There never was a man whose daily life (that is to say, *all* his deeds and sayings, entire and without exception) constituted fit materials for a book of fiction. Even the figures of the Greeks (which are

'In old marbles ever beautiful)'

were without doubt selected from the victors in the ancient games, and others, by Phidias and his scholars, and their forms and countenances made perfect before they were thought worthy to adorn the temple of the wise Athena.

The only book which occurs to us as resembling *Wuthering Heights* is a novel of the late Mr Hooton's,—a work of very great talent; in which the hero is a tramper or beggar, and the *dramatis personae* all derived from humble and middle life; but which, notwithstanding its defects, we remember thinking better in its peculiar kind than anything that had been produced since the days of Fielding[.]

'Wuthering Heights', *Examiner*, 2084 (8 January 1848), pp. 21–2 (pp. 21–2).

The last novel of the writer, journalist, and farmer Charles Hooton (1810?–1847) was *Launcelot Wedge* (1847), but the *Examiner* refers to *Colin Clink* (1837/1841), a 'down-in-the-world' story first issued in *Bentley's Miscellany*.

p. 61 *Lockwood*: a village/township, as EJB was writing, south west of Huddersfield. The name might just have been associated, too, with Henry Francis Lockwood (1811–78), a well-known architect based at this point in Hull. With Adolphus H. Cates, he was the author of *The History and Antiquities of the Fortifications to the City of York* (London: Weale, 1834). Thinking about the possible meaning of names in *WH*, John Sutherland observes of 'Lockwood': 'life for him is full of doors he will never go through', *Brontësaurus*, p. 49.

Thrushcross Grange: EJB's equivalent of Thornfield in *JE* and Wildfell Hall (another 'W.H.', like Wuthering Heights) for AB (see Introduction, p. xxxv). It is possible that

384   NOTES TO PAGES 61–2

EJB might have had the Heatons' Ponden Hall in mind (see note to p. 61, '*1801*'). The Brontës were certainly familiar with the Heatons who had lived at Ponden Hall for generations and the important library in the house might have been known to them (there is no certainty EJB was acquainted with this). Ponden Hall, however, is relatively modest and not set in the enormous park that surrounds Linton's house (p. 81 reveals the distance from the Grange to the gates to be two miles). In fact, Ponden Hall suggests features, more clearly, of Wuthering Heights, though not its location. See note to p. 61, '*1801*'. Shibden Hall, Halifax, might also have contributed to EJB's imagining of the Grange. But this is an uncertain topic.

It is only on subsequent readings that the significance of Heathcliff's pronouncement—and in turn its indication of EJB's sense that she knew where the novel was going from the beginning—is clear.

p. 61 *reserved*: a word associated with EJB herself. Cf. *LCB:* 'The first impression made on the visitor by the sisters of her school-friend was, that Emily was a tall, long-armed girl, more fully grown than her elder sister; extremely reserved in manner. I distinguish reserve from shyness, because I imagine shyness would please, if it knew how; whereas, reserve is indifferent whether it pleases or not. Anne, like her eldest sister, was shy; Emily was reserved', i.133. Francis A. Leyland in *The Brontë Family, with Special Reference to Patrick Branwell Brontë*, 2 vols (London: Hurst and Blackett, 1886), adds a recollection of EJB's 'extreme reserve with strangers', which, he said, 'is remembered by one who knew her there, but she was not at all of an unkindly nature; on the contrary, her disposition was generous and considerate to those with whom she was on familiar terms', i.153. It is not known who Leyland's source was.

The German mistress in *Villette*, Anna Braun, experiences, Lucy says, 'a sensation of cruel constraint from what she called our English reserve', ii.282. (It is an interesting question to wonder about the extent to which the Brontë sisters thought themselves simply English.)

There is a fresh view of EJB's 'reserve' from a contemporary perspective in Christine Blowfield, 'Emily Brontë and the Strategic Art of Social Distancing', *Brontë Studies*, 46 (2021), pp. 132–45.

pp. 61–2 *'Wuthering'* ... *weather*: *OED* does not allow for this definition directly, giving 'whithering' or 'wuthering' to mean 'rushing, whizzing, etc.; also, very large or vigorous'. *OED* cites only these words from Lockwood as the source for EJB's definition (or at least *Lockwood*'s definition). No comparison, *OED* implies, has been found in any other text. Though cf. Lucy Snowe's 'I felt sure now that I was in the pensionnat—sure by the beating rain on the casement; sure by the "wuther" of wind amongst trees', *Villette*, ii.8 (not in *OED*). The assumption must be that EJB or another sister invented the term (from 'withering'?) and no-one else took it up.

Wright only gives 'wuthering' as follows:

> WHITHERING, *ppl. adj.* Lakel. Yks. Lan. Chs. Der. Also written *withering* s.Lan.1 Chs.123 nw.Der.1; and in forms *whidderen* Lakel.2; *wuthering* m.Yks.1 Lan.1 s.Lan.1 [wi·ðərin.] Big; strong; overbearing; awkward; astonishing in any way.

Cf. 'Wuthering Heights, by Ellis Bell, is a terrific story, associated with an equally fearful and repulsive spot. It should have been called Withering Heights, for any thing

NOTES TO PAGE 62   385

from which the mind and body would more instinctively shrink, than the mansion and its tenants, cannot be imagined', 'Wuthering Heights', *New Monthly Magazine and Humorist*, 82 (January 1848), pp. 138–40 (p. 140).

Wuthering Heights is, obviously, like Thrushcross Grange, a building of the imagination. But Ponden Hall (see notes to p. 61); Shibden Hall, Halifax; the now-demolished High Sunderland Hall, Halifax; and the ruined Top Withens on the moors above Haworth are often thought to have contributed elements of it in EJB's mind. See note to p. 61, *'Thrushcross Grange'*. Chitham, pp. 111–31, argues convincingly that it was the landscape and buildings around Law Hill (see note to p. 8) that most contributed to EJB's imagination in *WH*. Halifax and its surroundings are, in this respect, EJB's imaginative equivalent for CB's Brussels in *Villette*. Intriguingly, neither Brussels nor M. Héger seems to have left any discernible trace on EJB's writing style or imagination.

p. 62 *grotesque carving*: a memory of the principal entrance to Ponden Hall, perhaps: see note to p. 61, *'1801'*; or of the two grotesques mounted on Corinthian columns at the principal entrance to High Sunderland Hall. Note that this latter doorway is depicted in one of the engravings in John Horner's *Views of the Buildings in the Town and Parish of Halifax Drawn from Nature and on Stone* (Halifax: Leyland, 1835), and the title page to Horner's book is also illustrated with a doorway with grotesque figures. One of the subscribers to this book was Miss Elizabeth Pratchett, who employed EJB briefly at Law Hill School in 1838 where she, EJB, could have seen it (the book). That does not exclude the possibility that EJB visited the façade of the house in reality (or even inside). It also does not mean that she could not have imaginatively invented such a door without any obvious models at all.

penetralium: inner-most room.

preeminently ... parlor: *1850* has 'pre-eminently' and 'parlour'.

under-drawn: to underdraw is 'To cover (the inside of a roof or the under-side of a floor) with boards or with lath and plaster', *OED. OED* gives only two examples: one from 1843 and another from 1865.

villanous: *1850* corrects to 'villainous'.

horse-pistols: large pistols 'carried at the pommel of the saddle when on horseback', *OED*.

pointer: English pointer, a sleek gun dog (usually of good nature). One of *The Athenæum*'s objections to *WH* was: 'let us hope that they [the Bells, who, the journal allows, might be one person or separate individuals] will spare us further interiors so gloomy as the one here elaborated here with such dismal minuteness', 'Our Library Table', *The Athenæum*, 1052 (25 December 1847), pp. 1324–5 (p. 1325).

He is a dark skinned gypsy: an intriguing description that constitutes one of the many puzzles EJB sets up concerning Heathcliff's origins (cf. Introduction, p. xxix).

Note that there was a black character, Quashia Quamina, in the Glass Town/Angria narratives (see, for instance, CB's 'The Green Dwarf' and 'The African Queen's Lament'). In an article about what ideas about race and slavery the sisters might have come across in Cowan Bridge, the late Sarah Fermi sums up the relationship of Quamina's narrative to that of Heathcliff and poses some questions about the school:

386　　　NOTES TO PAGES 62–4

The fictitious Quashia is adopted by the Duke [Arthur Wellesley, Duke of Wellington] and raised as a member of his family; he quarrels with the eldest son, Arthur, Marquis of Douro, and finally he rebels, inciting the Ashantees [native black inhabitants] to rise in revenge and attack the British colony. In *Wuthering Heights*, the narrative structure is [similar]: Heathcliff is adopted by Mr Earnshaw and raised as a family member; he quarrels with his foster brother, Hindley, runs away, but then returns to carry out revenge attacks on Hindley and the Lintons. Was the plot of *Wuthering Heights* based on this story of the black child, adopted by a good man to his bane? Had the outline of her novel been at the back of Emily's mind for nearly twenty years? Did she experience, perhaps, a direct contact with a black or mulatto child while at Cowan Bridge?

> Sarah Fermi, 'A Question of Colour', *Brontë Studies*,
> 40 (2015), pp. 334–42 (p. 340).

This story, incidentally, might well be based on the Duke of Wellington's actual life, assuming EJB had detailed knowledge of it. Note that, in an editorial in *The Times* on 20 October 1836—while the Angria stories were being composed—Wellington's guardianship of a young Indian had been revealed to a wide public. The editorial was a review of the second volume of Colonel John Gurwood's *The Dispatches of Field Marshal the Duke of Wellington*, 13 vols (London: Murray, 1834–9). 'You know', the Duke had written in a letter *The Times* quoted from Gurwood, 'that for some years I have had under my protection Salabut Khan, the supposed or adopted son of Dhoondiah Waugh. I have given him a sum of money, and placed him under the guardianship of the Court of Seringapatam, and I request you take him into the Rajah's service hereafter, if you should find him to be worthy of your favour', p. 4. Dhondia Wagh (d. 1800) was an Indian soldier whose rising power eventually alarmed British forces to the extent that he was defeated and killed by an army division commanded by Wellesley.

p. 63 *peeuliar*: corrected in *1850*.

"never told my love": cf. Viola's 'A blank, my lord. She never told her love', *Twelfth Night*, 2.iv.110.

mamma: more usually 'mama'. *OED* does not list this word, in its *WH* spelling, as meaning 'Mother'/'Mama'. Presumably EJB—if she actually intended this spelling—meant the word still to be pronounced /ˈmamə/. *1850* did not alter. The same spelling is also used in the *1847* edition of *Agnes Grey*.

gnarl: *OED* says 'rare' and that it means 'snarl'. Only this use in *WH* is cited.

p. 64 *phlegm*: an archaism befitting a house built in 1500: 'In ancient and medieval physiology and medicine: one of the four cardinal humours [...] described as cold and moist, and supposed when predominant to cause constitutional indolence or apathy', *OED*.

possessed swine: Jesus in the country of the Gergesenes, as KJV has it, meets two men possessed by devils, which ask to be sent into pigs nearby. 'And [Jesus] said unto them, Go. And when they were come out, they went into the herd of swine: and, behold, the whole herd of swine ran violently down a steep place into the sea, and perished in the waters', Matthew 8:32.

signet: in the sense of 'stamping with my seal of ownership': hitting to leave a mark.

NOTES TO PAGES 65-8

p. 65 *I dine...five*: on p. 212, we learn that breakfast at the Heights is almost over by 6:30 am and on p. 237 we hear that Hareton returns to the Heights at noon for 'dinner'. Ellen/Nelly, when ill, does not take anything after 'tea', which has concluded by 6pm (p. 238). Cf. the regime at Cowan Bridge School as recorded in *LCB*: 'Oatmeal porridge for breakfast; a piece of oat-cake for those who required luncheon; baked and boiled beef, and mutton, potato-pie, and plain homely puddings of different kinds for dinner. At five o'clock, bread and milk for the younger ones; and one piece of bread (this was the only time at which the food was limited) for the elder pupils, who sat up till a later meal of the same description', i.69–70. Heathcliff in 1801 always wakes the household at 4am having gone to bed at 9pm (see p. 78). Originally published in 1952, and then updated, Arnold Palmer with an Introduction by David Pocock, *Movable Feasts: Changes in English Eating Habits* (Oxford: Oxford University Press, 1984), is a detailed account of the whole general subject.

Cf. also Clement Shorter's comment: 'The children's dinner-table [at Haworth Parsonage] has been described to me by a visitor to the house. At one end sat Miss Branwell, at the other, Charlotte, with Emily and Anne on either side. Branwell was then absent. The living was of the simplest. A single joint, followed invariably by one kind or another of milk-pudding. Pastry was unknown in the Brontë household. Milk-puddings, or food composed of milk and rice, would seem to have made the principal diet of Emily and Anne Brontë, and to this they added a breakfast of Scotch porridge, which they shared with their dogs', *Charlotte Brontë and Her Circle* (London: Hodder and Stoughton, 1896), p. 60.

laith: lane.

flaysome: 'Frightful, dreadful', *OED*. The first use *OED* gives is 1790.

p. 66 *flaxen ringlets, or rather golden...neck*: in the celebrated 'Pillar' portrait of the sisters by Branwell, now in the National Portrait Gallery, London (NPG 1725), the only sister who approaches this colouring is Anne. Barker notes: 'a little plait, cut off [from Anne's hair] and carefully preserved by Patrick on 22 May 1833, suggests that [her hair] had deepened to a rich brown with a hint of auburn, though it remained fairer than her sisters'. There is an image of the lock in *ST*, no. 47.

pet: 'Offence at being or feeling slighted; a fit of peevishness or ill humour from this cause, (now) esp. a childish sulk. Frequently in *in a pet*. Also to take (the) pet: to take offence, to become bad-tempered or sulky (now rare, perhaps obsolete)', *OED*. Cf. Fergus's comment to Waverley in ch. 57 of Scott's novel: ' "You have taken pet at some of Flora's prudery["]', *Waverley, Or, 'Tis Sixty Years Since*, p. 283.

p. 67 *discussed*: in the sense of 'to examine, to investigate', *OED*. The use derives from the judiciary and is another example of Lockwood's elevated—and, often enough, out-of-place—language.

p. 68 *home and heart*: it is possible that 'home and hearth' was intended though *1850* does not change *1847* here.

man and wife: Lockwood uses the terms of the marriage service in *The Book of Common Prayer* (1662 version) where the minister, after the vows, says: 'I pronounce that they be man and wife together'. EJB's copy of *The Book of Common Prayer*, in the edition published by Parker of Cambridge, 1837, was a present from CB: *Books*.

388

NOTES TO PAGES 69–71

p. 69 *Aw woonder... afore ye!*: 'I wonder how you can manage to stand there idly and worse, when everyone has gone out. But you're a worthless person, and it's no use talking—you'll never improve from your bad ways; but, go right to the devil, like your mother before you!'

castaway: cf. Mr Brocklehurst's speech to the pupils at Lowood: ' "My dear children," pursued the black marble clergyman, with pathos, "this is a sad, a melancholy occasion; for it becomes my duty to warn you, that this girl, who might be one of God's own lambs, is a little castaway: not a member of the true flock, but evidently an interloper and an alien', *JE*, i.118.

modlled: corrected to 'modelled' in *1850*.

I fix: presumably, put pins and needles in a wax or clay model of a person as a curse. Or alternatively, as Michael Henchard fears in Chapter XXVII of Thomas Hardy's *The Mayor of Casterbridge* (1886), the roasting of a waxen image of the person to be punished. Belief in this form of folk magic was (is) of long tradition in Europe.

p. 70 *I'll not say... you!*: cf. *King Lear* (Folio), 2.ii.454–5. Cf. note to p. 71, '*King Lear*', and Introduction, p. xix.

long book: presumably EJB means a book like a ledger or butcher's book (long in the sense of page size) rather than merely a book with many pages.

Zillah: in Genesis 4, the wife of Lamech, a descendant of Cain. See note to p. 216.

visiters: corrected to 'visitors' in *1850*. This word is spelt incorrectly throughout *1847*, including in *Agnes Grey*. It is always corrected in *1850*. This must be evidence of the poor spelling of the compositor(s).

p. 71 *King Lear*: the connections are obvious: a man harshly served retreats petulantly in a state of high feeling into a storm, with denunciations of his previous hosts. But in the play, of course, the problems come from daughters not dogs. And it is hard not to forget that the imagined dogs of *King Lear*, in one of the mad scenes, are called Tray, Blanch, and Sweetheart (though they bark at Lear), and not given the powerful/fierce names of Juno, Gnasher, and Wolf. The dog, Grasper (owned by Emily or Charlotte?), was drawn by EJB in January 1834. The Ponden Hall library, famously, had a 1623 first folio, which vanished in the sale of the library in 1898. See note to p. 104, '*I have read more...*'. *Books* includes nothing by Shakespeare.

agait: 'On the way, on the road. Hence: going, in motion, in a busy state. Now Scottish and English regional (chiefly northern)', *OED*. Cf. 1. *JE*, iii.72, where Hannah says to Jane, as she seeks shelter having fled Thornfield, ' "I'm fear'd you have some ill plans agate, that bring you about folk's houses at this time o' night." ' And 2. *Shirley*, ch. XVIII, where Shirley is in a disagreement with Joe about women's roles:

'Because there is nought agate that fits women to be consarned in.'
'Indeed! There is prayer and preaching agate in that church. Are we not concerned in that?'

ii.174.

wisht: although not in *OED*, this term is still in use in Yorkshire and Scotland as a way of saying 'shush'; that is, not impolitely, 'be quiet'. *1850* gives 'wisht!'.

NOTES TO PAGES 71–4 389

p. 71 *condoled*: of 17thc origin, 'to condole' means, here, 'To grieve with; to express sympathy with another in his affliction', *OED*.

p. 72 *clothes-press... large oak case*: *OED* gives for 'clothes-press' a 'receptacle for clothes; properly a shelved recess or movable chest or case in which clothes are kept folded; but also sometimes applied to a wardrobe in which they are hung up unfolded'. *OED*'s last source is 1822. Various forms of enclosed space that included a bed, from this case to an alcove, were a shared imaginative feature for the sisters. Lucy Snowe, for instance, 'retired to my crib in a closet within [Miss Marchmont's] room' in *Villette*, i.76. And, once Lucy is in the pensionnat, 'My bed stood in a little alcove', ii.11. On p. 149 of *WH*, Catherine, in a state of madness, remembers being enclosed in 'the oak-panelled bed at home'. Joseph, we learn on p. 162, has a 'large, low, curtainless bed, with an indigo-coloured quilt' in the garret.

Catherines: an etymology of the name from the Greek Αἰκατερίνα or Αἰκατερίνη (*Aikaterína, Aikateríne*) is not certain. But the name came to be associated among early Christians with καθαρός (katharos: pure, uncontaminated).

lean type: narrow (cheap).

quarter of a century back: Catherine Earnshaw was born in 1765.

p. 73 *decypher*: *1850* has 'decipher'.

T' maister nobbut just buried... sowls!: 'The master only just buried and the Sabbath not over, and the sound of the gospel still in your ears, and dare to be larking around! Shame on you! Sit down, wicked children. There are enough good books if you will read them; sit down, and think of your souls!' 'Lugs' is from the 16thc, a colloquialism for 'ears', still in use in Yorkshire and parts of Scotland.

scroop: *OED* gives only this example, adding 'Perhaps a mistake for SCRUFF?' *1850* does not amend it. Wright gives only this example and defines it as 'the back of the cover of a book'.

p. 74 *Th' Helmet... Destruction*: 'The Helmet of Salvation' is from Ephesians 6:17. EJB might be thinking of its use as a title for several chapters in William Gurnall's much-regarded *The Christian in Complete Armour*, 3 vols (1655–62), which is, as a whole, an extended discussion of Ephesians 6:10–20. Gurnall (1616–79) was Rector of Lavenham in Suffolk. The title of *The Broad Way to Destruction* is derived from Matthew 7:13. Various pamphlets and published sermons prior to the late 18thc included the relevant words but none, so far as I know, took the simple title EJB uses.

Patrick Brontë had written polemical pamphlets/tracts himself, though by no means on such fearsome themes. See 'The Signs of the Times: or, a Familiar Treatise on Some Political Indications in the Year 1835' (Keighley: Aked, 1835) and 'A Brief Treatise on the Best Time and Mode of Baptism: chiefly in answer to a tract ["Baptism without Controversy"] of Peter Pontifex, alias the Rev. [Moses Saunders] Baptist Minister' (Keighley: Aked, 1836).

Robert Aked (1806–85), 'printer and sub-distributor of stamps', of Low Street, Keighley, also published Haworth Church's hymn-sheets and, from 1853, a temperance magazine called *The Keighley Visitor*. He also appears to have had a circulating library. Aked was, as it happens, the father-in-law of Timothy Taylor, whose brewing company began in 1858 and still continues.

gait: in its figurative sense of 'to go one's own way', *OED*. Cf. note to p. 290.

390 NOTES TO PAGE 74

p. 74 *"owd Nick"*: the devil.

scamper: including the sense here of *OED* v.1's definition: '*intransitive*. To run away, decamp, "bolt"', now obsolete. *OED* gives sources from 1687 to 1833.

"Seventy Times Seven... Gimmerden Sough": this is a gloomily comic name and title, derived from Matthew 18:21–2: 'Then came Peter to him, and said, Lord, how oft shall my brother sin against me, and I forgive him? till seven times? Jesus saith unto him, I say not unto thee, Until seven times: but, Until seventy times seven.'

Some effort has been made to identify a model for Jabes Branderham. Jabez Bunting (1779–1858), prominent preacher and Wesleyan minister, perhaps; or Jabez Burns (1805–76), a notable non-conformist preacher initially based in Yorkshire (whose Dissenting mother had named him after Bunting)? Burns briefly had a book-selling trade in Keighley. John Sutherland thinks William Grimshaw, incumbent of Haworth, 1742–63 (see below) was 'undoubtedly' the model: *Brontësaurus*, p. 20. Branderham is, more obviously, a somewhat brutal comic satire, ironically preaching about forgiveness. Cf. Mr Jabesh Rentowel, the Covenanter, for whom a crowd waits in ch. 35 of *Waverley, Or, 'Tis Sixty Years Since* 'for the out-pouring of the afternoon exhortation' (p. 184).

Jabes/z is an apt name for EJB's mischievous wit here: 'And Jabez was more honourable than his brethren: and his mother called his name Jabez, saying, Because I bare him with sorrow', 1 Chronicles 4:9. Jabez, יַעְבֵּץ, in Hebrew means 'distress/pain'. The surname contains 'brand', not inappropriate for a 'hell-fire' sermon (the term is proleptic: *OED*'s first source in relation to preaching is from 1894).

EJB might certainly, though perhaps without the definiteness John Sutherland asserts, have had in mind episodes from the history of St Michael and All Angels' Church, Haworth, including tales about its preachers. *LCB* notes:

> Mr. [George] Whitfield [1714–70, Anglican clergyman and one of the founders of Methodism] was once preaching in Haworth, and made use of some such expression, as that he hoped there was no need to say much to this congregation, as they had sat under so pious and godly a minister for so many years; 'whereupon Mr. [William] Grimshaw stood up in his place, and said with a loud voice, "Oh, sir! for God's sake do not speak so. I pray you do not flatter them. I fear the greater part of them are going to hell with their eyes open." ' But if they were so bound, it was not for want of exertion on Mr. Grimshaw's part to prevent them. He used to preach twenty or thirty times a week in private houses. If he perceived any one inattentive to his prayers, he would stop and rebuke the offender, and not go on till he saw every one on their knees. He was very earnest in enforcing the strict observance of Sunday; and would not even allow his parishioners to walk in the fields between services. He sometimes gave out a very long Psalm (tradition says the 119th), and while it was being sung, he left the reading-desk, and taking a horsewhip went into the public-houses, and flogged the loiterers into church.

i.25–6.

It is hard to be certain of the veracity of such narratives, of course. Grimshaw's teapot is *ST*, no. 5.

Gimmerton (*sic*), as we shortly find out (p. 90), is the village closest to the Heights and Thrushcross Grange. A 'gimmer' (hard 'g') is northern English and Scottish

NOTES TO PAGES 74–5 391

dialect for a ewe between first and second shearing (*OED*); 'sough', pronounced either /saʊ/ or /sʌf/, has the primary meanings of a 'rushing or murmuring sound as of wind, water, or the like': a kind of counterpart to 'wuthering'; or 'a swampy, boggy place', *OED*. Gimmerden Sough—see note to p. 230, '*Slough of Despond*'— turns out to be near a bog. But EJB might also have the Scottish sense of 'sough' in mind: 'A canting or whining manner of speaking, especially in preaching or praying', *OED*.

1998 observes:

[A]s was first pointed out by Thomas Keyworth in *The Bookman* for March 1893 ('A new identification of "Wuthering Heights"' [iii.183–5]), Emily Brontë may well have had in mind Chapel-le-Breer, also known as St Ann's Chapel or the Chapel-in-the Grove, which stood two miles from Southowram village, on the Brighouse road. A 'sough', or water channel, runs into Shibden Beck just above the site of the chapel. The fields close by were known as Sough Pastures and the farm as Sough Holme. There is no evidence that Chapel-le-Breer was ever consecrated: burials from Southowram took place at Halifax parish church. Emily Brontë attended St Anne's-in-the-Grove, a mile nearer Southowram, which had been built partly from the stones of the older chapel.

pp. 342–3.

p. 74 *Joseph for a guide*: an ironic reference to the Flight to Egypt. See, for instance, Matthew 2:14 where Joseph, having been warned in a dream, leads Mary and Jesus to safety in Egypt. Lockwood's dream and Joseph-led journey are thoroughly different. Note that it seems likely that Tabby (Tabitha Ackroyd), the Haworth Parsonage servant from about the autumn of 1825, provided a starting point for Joseph's speech (though not, so far as we know, for his religious views).

pilgrim's staff: another covertly ironic reference, this time to the difficult journey narrated in John Bunyan's *Pilgrim's Progress from This World, to That Which Is to Come* (1678). The Brontës' copy of this book—with its title page missing—is *Books*, bb13. When Patrick was in his second curacy—at Wellington, Shropshire (1809)—he made friends with the Revd Joshua Gilpin, vicar of Wrockwardine, who published a 'A new and corrected edition' of *Pilgrim's Progress*, 'in which', as the title page noted, 'the phraseology of the author is somewhat improved' (Wellington [Shropshire]: F. Houlston and Son, 1811).

p. 75 *peaty moisture … corpses deposited there*: peat and mosses assist in the preservation of corpses. An early amply documented case of such preservation was from Ireland—EJB was, of course, half-Irish—where peat bogs were, and to an extent still are, an essential source of fuel in rural areas. See Elizabeth Rawdon, Countess of Moira [north west County Down], 'Particulars relative to a Human Skeleton, and the Garments that were found thereon, when dug out of a Bog at the Foot of Drumkeragh, a Mountain in the County of Down, and Barony of Kinalearty, on Lord Moira's Estate, in the Autumn of 1780', *Archaeologia: Journal of the Society of Antiquaries, London*, 7 (1785), pp. 90–110. There is some grim foresight in this passage of Catherine's preservation after burial.

392 NOTES TO PAGES 75–6

Patrick Brontë burned peat at Haworth Parsonage (and the family kept the geese Victoria and Adelaide in the peat house at night: cf. p. 14). Ponden Hall's two-storey Peat House (see note to p. 61), where the peat upstairs was dried by the heat of the cows housed on the ground floor, was a sophisticated way of managing the fuel.

p. 75 *twenty pounds per annum*: this was nominally CB's salary as a governess, from 2 March 1841, for the family of John White at Upperwood House, Rawdon (Rawdon is now a suburb of Leeds; the house no longer exists). A subtraction was made for expenses reducing it to £16. In relative terms, £20 now = £1,786. AB was earning twice this amount at Thorp Green.

rather let him starve…own pockets: Patrick Brontë's salary at his first curacy, in Wethersfield in Essex (1806–9), had been £60 a year. The Perpetual Curacy of Haworth brought in around £200 together with a free house (the Parsonage) and while she was alive Patrick also had the support of Maria's £50 a year (in 1820, £250 was roughly the modern equivalent of £20,130). Note that it is easy to think that a 'Perpetual Curacy' was a low-status situation, not comparable, for instance, with being Vicar. But the important word is 'Perpetual': Patrick could not (easily) be removed from his post. Within the aegis of the Vicar of Bradford, the church at Haworth was properly a chapel-of-ease but, to all intents and purposes, Patrick had authority there as if, in most things, he were indeed Vicar. His principal dealings with the Vicar of Bradford seem primarily to have concerned appointments and finances, though there were occasional important difficulties. The Trustees of Haworth church had a long-standing belief, for instance, which caused some significant problems on Patrick's appointment, that they were in truth independent of the Vicar of Bradford. There were ongoing and understandable problems for the Dissenters in the parish, too, with paying church rates. And there was also, among the Anglicans as well, some enduring irritation with having to pay for both Haworth church's costs and those of Bradford. The Parish Church of Bradford (St Peter) became Bradford Cathedral in 1919.

four hundred and ninety parts: that is, of course, seventy times seven.

They were…odd trangressions: *1850* has 'character: odd transgressions'. Cf. Mark 3:28–9: 'Verily I say unto you, All sins shall be forgiven unto the sons of men, and blasphemies wherewith soever they shall blaspheme: But he that shall blaspheme against the Holy Ghost hath never forgiveness, but is in danger of eternal damnation.'

christian: 'Christian' in *1850*.

place which knows him may know him no more!: cf. Job 7:10: 'He shall return no more to his house, neither shall his place know him any more.'

Thou art the Man!: 2 Samuel 12:7. *1998*, p. 343, adds: 'The quotation was a favourite of John Wesley's: see *John Wesley's English*[: *A Study of Literary Style*], by George Lawton ([London: Allen and Unwin], 1962), 148'.

p. 76 *Brethren, execute upon him…saints!*: Psalm 149:9, 'To execute upon them the judgment written: this honour have all his saints. Praise ye the Lord.'

sconses: corrected to 'sconces' in *1850* = heads, tops of heads (*OED* n.2).

rappings and counter-rappings: it is worth confirming that EJB has no sense here of a séance association for these terms. The so-called 'Hydesville rappings', State of New York, which started the first wave of 19thc interest in séances and mediums, began in March 1848, a year after *WH*'s publication. (The term 'séance' is first listed in *OED* as from 1845.)

NOTES TO PAGE 76

p. 76 *Every man's hand was against his neighbour*: a familiar biblical expression; e.g., Zechariah 14:13: 'And it shall come to pass in that day, that a great tumult from the Lord shall be among them; and they shall lay hold every one on the hand of his neighbour, and his hand shall rise up against the hand of his neighbour.'

disagreebly: split across a line in *1847* as 'disagree-bly'; corrected to 'disagreeably' in *1850*.

firbough: *1850* has 'fir-bough'.

Catherine Linton: perhaps the most chilling words in the first half of *WH*. EJB indicates that the 'ghost' is the real person of whose circumstances—her marriage—Lockwood is, at this point, unaware. Another indicator at a local level of how exactly *WH* was planned.

LCB remembers the time after AB and EJB's deaths:

> The hours of retiring for the night had always been early in the Parsonage; now family prayers were at eight o'clock; directly after which Mr. Brontë and old Tabby went to bed, and Martha was not long in following. But Charlotte could not have slept if she had gone,—could not have rested on her desolate couch. She stopped up,—it was very tempting,—late and later, striving to beguile the lonely night with some employment, till her weak eyes failed to read or to sew, and could only weep in solitude over the dead that were not. No one on earth can even imagine what those hours were to her. All the grim superstitions of the North had been implanted in her during her childhood by the servants, who believed in them. They recurred to her now,—with no shrinking from the spirits of the Dead, but with such an intense longing once more to stand face to face with the souls of her sisters, as no one but she could have felt. It seemed as if the very strength of her yearning should have compelled them to appear. On windy nights, cries, and sobs, and wailings seemed to go round the house, as of the dearly-beloved striving to force their way to her. Some one conversing with her once objected, in my presence, to that part of 'Jane Eyre' in which she hears Rochester's voice crying out to her in a great crisis of her life, he being many, many miles distant at the time. I do not know what incident was in Miss Brontë's recollection when she replied, in a low voice, drawing in her breath, 'But it is a true thing; it really happened.'
>
> ii.147–8.

On the assertion that this part of *WH* derives from Hoffmann, see Introduction, pp. xix–xx. But clearly the idea of strange fancies/fantasies in the night while sleeping in an unfamiliar place were part of the Brontë family's imaginative repertoire. In CB's 'An Adventure in Ireland', for instance, the unnamed narrator arrives at a castle near Cahir (County Tipperary). Just before supper, the narrator learns from a young boy that the old master's ghost is sometimes seen and heard in the castle. The narrator retires to bed:

> As soon as I had laid down I began to think of what the boy had been telling me, and I confess I felt a strange kind of fear, and once or twice I even thought I could discern something white through the darkness which surrounded me. At length, by the help of reason, I succeeded in mastering these, what some would call idle fancies, and fell asleep.

394 NOTES TO PAGES 76–81

I had slept about an hour when a strange sound awoke me, and I saw looking through my curtains a skeleton wrapped in a white sheet. I was overcome with terror and tried to scream, but my tongue was paralysed and my whole frame shook with fear. In a deep hollow voice it said to me, 'Arise, that I may show thee this world's wonders,' and in an instant I found myself encompassed with clouds and darkness. But soon the roar of mighty waters fell upon my ear, and I saw some clouds of spray arising from high falls that rolled in awful majesty down tremendous precipices, and then foamed and thundered in the gulf beneath as if they had taken up their unquiet abode in some giant's cauldron [...]

> Christine Alexander, ed., *Tales of Glass Town, Angria, and Gondal: Selected Writings* (Oxford: Oxford University Press, 2010), pp. 16–17.

p. 76 *gripe*: 'The action of griping, clutching, grasping or seizing tenaciously, *esp*. with the hands, arms, claws, and the like', *OED*.

p. 77 *twenty years*: Catherine died at 2am, 20 March 1784, so it is actually seventeen years.

ideal: in *OED*'s sense 4: 'Existing only in idea; confined to thought or imagination; imaginary: opposed to real or actual. Also: not real or practical; based on an idea or fancy; fancied, visionary.'

at the—: here as elsewhere (cf. p. 80, where this habit is highlighted), Heathcliff's oath is left blank. 'At the devil's', presumably. Cf. also CB's observation on p. 318.

dose: *1850* has 'doze'.

p. 78 *changling*: *1850* has 'changeling'.

violent: in the 19thc sense of 'extreme'.

p. 79 *Grimalkin*: from Shakespeare's time onwards, a word for a cat.

ribs: 'Any one of the bars of a grate, grid, or the like; *spec.* (chiefly *Scottish* and *English regional*) a bar of a fire grate', *OED*.

p. 80 *snoozled*: an exclusively 19thc dialect/colloquial word, 'nuzzled', *OED*.

epithet . . . by a dash: 'bitch', presumably.

damnable jade: cf. CB's justification for the printing of expletives in full in *WH* on p. 318. But cf. also the note to p. 77, '*at the*—' and the note above. 'Jade' is a 'term of reprobation applied to a woman. Also used playfully, like hussy or minx', *OED*.

answered the young lady, closing her book: this seemingly habitual integration of domestic labour with reading—especially after Tabby's accident in December 1836 and Emily's effective assumption of the role of housekeeper—might mirror life at Haworth Parsonage, as recounted, not least, in *LCB*. See, for instance, note to 342, '*German book . . .*' Cf. CB's letter to Ellen Nussey on 21 December 1839, quoted in the note to p. 99, '*the scoured . . .*'.

p. 81 *quarries*: for the much-used Yorkstone/flagstone, a kind of sandstone, quarried in Yorkshire since at least the medieval period. In 1837, one William Pagitt was the only registered owner of a quarry in Keighley (*White's Directory*).

barren: as a noun, simply a tract of barren land (*OED*).

Thrushcross park: one of a number of references to the enormous estate around the Grange. A considerable property indeed (confirmed shortly by the reference to the porter's lodge). See note to p. 61, '*Thrushcross Grange*'. *1850* has 'Thrushcross Park'.

NOTES TO PAGES 81–4   395

p. 81 *to: 1850* corrects to 'two'. It was the page in EJB's own copy of *WH* that included her hand-written correction to this error, which was reproduced in 'C.K.S.' [Clement K(ing) Shorter], 'A Literary Letter: The Latest Brontë Myth', *The Sphere*, 97 (24 May 1924), p. 240. Shorter's piece is in response to Alice Law's *Patrick Branwell Brontë* (London: Philpot, 1923), which argued that Branwell was the real author of *WH* (an assertion, it might be, originally made by some of Branwell's friends). The corrections in EJB's own copy and in her own hand are part of the evidence that Shorter musters to repudiate Law's assertion. Alice Law was in turn obliged to defend herself against the novelist and suffragist May Sinclair (1863–1946) and her doubtfulness of Law's claims in 'Who Wrote "Wuthering Heights"?', *The Bookman*, 66.392 (May 1924), pp. 97–8. Law asserted there that it was likely that Branwell, having dictated portions of the book to EJB, forgot he had done so in a haze of opium. See also A. Mary F. Robinson's argument, pp. 339–41, for an earlier version of this claim about the brother.

clock chimed twelve as I entered the house: the Brontës' long-case clock, made by Barraclough of Haworth, is *ST*, no. 41. It was returned to BPM by Mrs William Heaton, a descendant of the Ponden Hall family, in 1983.

smoking coffee: steaming. This sense—'To give off or send up vapour, dust, spray, etc.; esp. to steam'—survived at least, according to *OED*, till 1869.

p. 82 *strike my colours*: to strike one's colours is a universally recognized act of a ship of war lowering its flag/battle ensign and thus declaring surrender.

mistress was married: in the spring of 1783.

indigenae: a 'native, aboriginal', *OED*. The last example *OED* gives is from 1799.

p. 83 *Very old, sir;... Miss Cathy is of us*: the idea of the 'last of the race' is well established—from Deucalion and Noah, not least. Cf. Sir Walter Scott's 'The Lay of the Last Minstrel' (1805); Mary Shelley's *The Last Man* (1826); and James Fenimore Cooper's *The Last of the Mohicans: A Narrative of 1757* (1826). The idea, momentarily echoed here, forms the topic of Fiona Stafford's *The Last of the Race: The Growth of a Myth from Milton to Darwin* (Oxford: Clarendon, 1994). By coincidence, the American painter Tompkins Harrison Matteson (1813–84) completed his *The Last of the Race*, depicting a small group of North American Indians, the only survivors of the new settlers' displacements and destruction, in 1847. The Brontës' copy of 'The Lay of the Last Minstrel' (London: Longman, 1806), inscribed by Patrick, is *Books*, bb54. Patrick bought it with some of the £4 that St John's College, following its custom, gave to him on taking his degree. Cf. the opening sentence of Ch. VIII, p. 105.

Note that *WH* is more generally interested in plots of decline and extinction: of enfeebled women (Isabella) and children (the second Catherine at her birth; Linton Heathcliff) and of childbirth itself as fatal.

whinstone: a 'name for various very hard dark-coloured rocks or stones, as greenstone, basalt, chert, or quartzose sandstone', often used figuratively for 'hard, tough', *OED*.

dunnock: a small, brown, extremely common bird, often called the hedge-sparrow, *Prunella modularis*.

p. 84 *Liverpool, to-day... long spell!*: on modern roads, the distance from Haworth to central Liverpool is 68.4 miles. *LCB* notes a letter from CB on 4 August 1839,

396   NOTES TO PAGES 84–6

describing a possible trip to Liverpool: ' "The Liverpool journey is yet a matter of talk, a sort of castle in the air; but, between you and me, I fancy it is very doubtful whether it will ever assume a more solid shape. Aunt—like many other elderly people—likes to talk of such things; but when it comes to putting them into actual execution, she rather falls off', i.197. Concerning long walks, *LCB* adds of William Grimshaw (see note to p. 74, '*Seventy Times Seven*...'): 'He had strong health and an active body, and rode far and wide over the hills, "awakening" those who had previously had no sense of religion. To save time, and be no charge to the families at whose houses he held his prayer-meetings, he carried his provisions with him; all the food he took in the day on such occasions consisting simply of a piece of bread and butter, or dry bread and a raw onion', i.26.

Branwell went to Liverpool on 28 July 1845 for a week according to EJB's diary paper: see p. 25.

p. 84 *stept*: *1850* has 'stepped'.

three kingdoms: presumably, England and Wales (regarded as one); Scotland; and Ireland. Cf. note to p. p. 32, l. 17.

flighted: '*transitive*. To put to flight, rout; hence, to frighten, scare. *Obsolete exc. Dialect*', *OED*.

gibberish...understand: on Heathcliff's origins and the narrative silences in the novel, see Introduction, p. xxix n.36.

p. 85 *its owner*: language suggestive of slavery, perhaps. Liverpool was the major European port for the transatlantic slave trade, peaking in the two decades before the abolition of the trade in 1807 (47 Geo III Sess. 1 c. 36: note that slavery itself, as distinct from the trade, was made illegal in British possessions in 1833). The Liverpool Slavery Museum estimates that nearly three-quarters of all European slave ships left from the city's docks (website). For an effort to argue that *WH* is a Wilberforcean narrative based on the experience of the plantation-owning Sill family of Dent, see Christopher Heywood, 'Yorkshire Slavery in *Wuthering Heights*', *Review of English Studies*, 38 (1987), pp. 184–98.

expences: *1850* has 'expenses'.

christian: as before, corrected to 'Christian' in *1850*.

p. 86 *measles*: Patrick Brontë owned, and annotated throughout, a first edition of Thomas John Graham's *Modern Domestic Medicine; or, A Popular Treatise Illustrating the Character, Symptoms, Causes, Distinction, and Correct Treatment of all Diseases Incident to the Human Frame* (London: Simpkin and Marshall, 1826). It is catalogued as *Books*, bb210, and, in its various editions, was extremely popular across the 19thc. Graham—whose name, 'John Graham', must surely give CB her two names for Dr John in *Villette*—observes of the effects of measles:

> When neither the habit nor mode of treatment are bad, the disease itself seldom proves fatal ; but its consequences are often troublesome. Its most frequent consequences are, the various forms of scrophula, as glandular tumours, wasting from obstruction in the mesenteric glands of the belly, obstinate sores, a weak and inflamed state of the eyes, and pulmonary consumption. A moisture on the skin at the appearance of the eruption; early and free expectoration; moderate looseness; and mild fever; are favourable symptoms.

NOTES TO PAGES 86–91

Sometimes the disease is much more violent and far less regular in its symptoms than is above described; the inquietude and restlessness being much greater, delirium supervening early, the throat being of a deep or dusky red colour, sense of great oppression about the chest, and the fever often assuming the form of typhus at an early period.

pp. 408–9.

Some of Patrick's annotations to this book can be seen at 'Modern Domestic Medicine annotated by the Brontës', British Library, https://www.bl.uk/collection-items/modern-domestic-medicine-annotated-by-the-brontes. The book is *ST*, no. 42.

p. 88 *curate*: the Earnshaw household, collectively, are, we deduce from this, members of the Church of England. (Joseph is presented more as if a (half-crazed) Dissenter, though on Mr Earnshaw's death, p. 90, his first thought is to call for a doctor and a *parson*, a term normally reserved for ministers of the Church of England.) Cf. the slightly confusing account of Mrs Dean and Joseph's religious affiliations on p. 276. Cf. also the Linton and Earnshaw Christmas church visit on p. 101.

living answer: the 'living' is a term for income from a parish though it is normally reserved for those who hold the benefice, a vicar or rector, rather than a curate (but cf. the note about a Perpetual Curate to p. 75, '*rather let him starve ...*').

pharisee: ancient Jewish group, presented in the Gospels largely as sanctimonious and over-scrupulous. In Matthew 23:27, Jesus observes: 'Woe unto you, scribes and Pharisees, hypocrites! for ye are like unto whited sepulchres, which indeed appear beautiful outward, but are within full of dead men's bones, and of all uncleanness.' The word is retained in small case in *1850*.

worrying: in the sense of harassing, or doggedly trying to wear down, rather than in the later sense of anxiety or fretfulness. This is the sense of this word throughout the novel.

p. 89 *wick*: English regional (northern): quick, *OED*.

using her hands freely: that is, as we find out, slapping people.

naughty: this word was shifting in meaning during the 19thc. EJB might mean it in the original sense of 'Morally bad, wicked', *OED*, which dated from the 15thc, or in the gradually loosening, and increasingly lighter, sense that is now the word's only meaning.

saucy: insolent, impertinent (presumably without the sexual sense, though that was available in the 19thc).

died quietly: October 1777.

done.): *1850* gives 'done.)'

p. 90 *frame*: in *OED*'s sense v. 8b: '*transitive* (reflexive). English regional (Yorkshire). To get oneself started, to organize oneself; to act or behave with evident urgency or effort. Frequently in *imperative*'.

p. 91 *gossipping*: corrected in *1850*.

symptoms portended: EJB was familiar with the symptoms of consumption/tuberculosis.

We don't in general take to foreigners here, ... first: Cf. *LCB*: 'The practical qualities of a [Yorkshire] man are held in great respect; but the want of faith in strangers and

398   NOTES TO PAGES 91–4

untried modes of action, extends itself even to the manner in which the virtues are regarded; and if they produce no immediate and tangible result, they are rather put aside as unfit for this busy, striving world; especially if they are more of a passive than an active character', i.11.

p. 91 *delf-case*: not in *OED*. Joseph Hunter's *The Hallamshire Glossary* (London: Pickering, 1829), says: 'A frame of wood, part of the furniture of a kitchen, on which are placed the articles of common porcelain which are in daily use. Probably the *case* for the *delf-ware*', p. 30. Delf-ware is more commonly Delft-ware, the well-known blue and white hand-painted pottery from the Dutch city of Delft. (Hallamshire is a historical name for a western part of South Yorkshire, most notably preserved in the contemporary Roman Catholic Diocese of Hallam, which includes Sheffield.)

p. 93 *basement*: 'The distinct lowest part of a fixed structure', *OED*: here, some sort of projection considerably beneath the window sill.

Old: it is possible that there was meant to be a new paragraph here. The word begins a new (un-indented) line in *1847* and this is an unusually long paragraph. Not changed in *1850* (but then CB's habit was to create long paragraphs anyway).

p. 94 *Linton's*: corrected in *1850*.

bull-dog: Keeper, EJB's dog, is described by the BPM as a huge bull mastiff cross (his 8″ diameter collar is still in the BPM collection). His equivalent in *Shirley*, Tartar, is described in ch. XI as between a 'mastiff and bull-dog', i.294.

She did not yell out... cow: cf. the passage from *LCB* reproduced on note to p. 61, '*reserved*'.

out-and-outer: 'A person who or thing which is in some way beyond the norm: a person of determined, adventurous, or reckless character; a person or thing of great beauty; an unqualified supporter of some cause; a thoroughgoing criminal or cheat', *OED*.

you shall... gallows: cf. the following:

The great majority of the ninety-seven offences for which the executions took place in 1785 [in London and Middlesex alone] were offences against property, there being only one case of murder, no other serious crimes against the person or sex, and none against the safety of the State or public order.

Burglary and housebreaking	43
Forgery and uttering forged instruments	4
Horse stealing	4
Larceny on a navigable river	5
Murder	1
Personating others to obtain prize money	2
Robbery on the highway and other places	31
Transportation, unlawfully returning from	4
Various (not specified)	3
Total number	97

These figures relate to one year only, but are by no means exceptional. Out of 678 offenders executed in London and Middlesex in the twenty-three years from

NOTES TO PAGES 94–104   399

1749 to 1771, seventy-two had committed murder, fifteen attempted murder, two rape, two sodomy, one high treason, and two other felonies. Thus out of 678 capital offences for which executions took place, only ninety-four were for very serious crimes against the person and the State; all the remaining 584 were for offences against property.

> Leon Radzinowicz, *A History of English Criminal Law and its Administration from 1750*, 5 vols (1948–86), i.148.

p. 94 *fortune-teller*: a figure shared with *JE* (where she, or rather he in disguise, has a significant role in the plot).

tame pheasant: there was a 'tame' pheasant at Haworth, mentioned in EJB's diary paper, 24 November 1834, called Jasper. See p. 3.

p. 95 *Lascar*: an East Indian sailor.

grey cloak: Jane Eyre has a 'grey mantle' in Chapter V (*JE*, i.83).

negus: 'a drink made from wine (usually port or sherry) mixed with hot water, sweetened with sugar and sometimes flavoured [with spices]', *OED*.

p. 97 *be be*: as in many other examples of such repetition, this occurs over a line break in *1847*.

p. 99 *the scoured and well-swept floor*: *LCB* gives a letter of CB's to Ellen Nussey from 21 December 1839, well after Tabby's accident, describing the current arrangements for management of the parsonage: 'She [Tabby] is very comfortable, and wants nothing; as she is near, we see her very often. In the meantime, Emily and I are sufficiently busy, as you may suppose: I manage the ironing, and keep the rooms clean; Emily does the baking, and attends to the kitchen. We are such odd animals, that we prefer this mode of contrivance to having a new face amongst us. Besides, we do not despair of Tabby's return, and she shall not be supplanted by a stranger in her absence. I excited aunt's wrath very much by burning the clothes, the first time I attempted to iron; but I do better now. Human feelings are queer things; I am much happier black-leading the stoves, making the beds, and sweeping the floors at home, than I should be living like a fine lady anywhere else', i.202. Cf. note to pp. 25, '*I conclude*' and 342, '*German book . . .*'.

cant lass: in its adjectival form, 'cant' is Scottish and northern English dialect for 'Bold, brisk, courageous, hearty, lusty, lively, hale', *OED*.

christmas: corrected in *1850*.

p. 100 *brow*: corrected in *1850*.

p. 102 *clarionets*: 'clarionet' is an early name for a clarinet.

p. 103 *long hours*: '*n.* now *rare* any of the late hours of the day denoted by large numbers, *esp.* midnight', *OED*. Cf. 'short hours'.

p. 104 *French cooks*: bringing all the food together to a table is the *service à la fran-çaise*, which, though the norm at the beginning of the 19thc for fine dining, was to be replaced by the *service à la russe*—where one course followed another—from about the 1870s.

I have read more than you would fancy . . . daughter: it is easy to think of EJB reading in the Ponden Hall Library here, though there is, as mentioned, no documentation proving that she did. The evidence is assessed in Bob Duckett, 'The Library at

400   NOTES TO PAGES 104–111

Ponden Hall', *Brontë Studies*, 40 (2015), pp. 104–49 (e.g., 'Emily comes closest to the Ponden library in *Wuthering Heights*. Says Nelly Dean to Lockwood, "I have read more than you would fancy, Mr Lockwood. You could not open a book in this library that I have not looked into, and got something out of also; unless it be that range of Greek and Latin, and that of French [...]" [p. 104]. The library at Thrushcross Grange is mentioned again when Lockwood exclaimed, "'No books! [...] How do you contrive to live here without them? [...] Though provided with a large library, I'm frequently very dull at the Grange—take my books away, and I should be desperate'. 'I was always reading, when I had them', said Catherine" [p. 280]. Later, Catherine reports to Hareton that '"[...] I came upon a secret stock in your room [...] some Latin and Greek, and some tales and poetry; all old friends—I brought the last here [p. 280]"'), p. 121.

p. 105 *the last of the ancient Earnshaw stock was born*: cf. note to p. 83, '*Very old...*'.
rush: in *OED*'s P1 sense for 'rush, n.': something 'slight, fragile, unreliable'. Graham observes in *Villette* that '"I am weak as a rush"', i.39.

p. 108 *lime*: the manufacturing uses of lime are multiple, from baking powder to glass, fertilizer, floor tiles, milk of magnesia, and many others.

Pennistow Crag: this becomes 'Peniston crag' and then 'Penistone crag' on p. 148. By p. 199, it is 'Penistone Craggs'. The feature is possibly inspired, if EJB needed inspiration, by Ponden Kirk, a gritstone outcrop in the moors west of Haworth. The rock feature, almost unreachable safely, has a curious hole at the base, which could be the origin of the 'fairy cave' on pp. 148, 199, and 204. Penistone /ˈpɛnɪstən/ is a Pennine market town, about 30 miles east of Manchester. *1850* changes 'Penistone' to 'Peniston' on its first appearance but makes no alteration to 'Pennistow'. See note to p. 199.

p. 111 *Earnshaw had come home rabid drunk*: Branwell is presumably on EJB's mind here (see Introduction, pp. xviii, xxxvi–xxxvii) and, if so, it is interesting to note that she elides the imagined geography of the Heights and its environment with Haworth, where the Black Bull Inn, Branwell's drinking place, is only a short walk from the Parsonage.

fowling piece: a light firearm for shooting game birds. Cf. *LCB*: '[Patrick Brontë] fearlessly took whatever side in local or national politics appeared to him right. In the days of the Luddites, he had been for the peremptory interference of the law, at a time when no magistrate could be found to act, and all the property of the West Riding was in terrible danger. He became unpopular then among the millworkers, and he esteemed his life unsafe if he took his long and lonely walks unarmed; so he began the habit, which has continued to this day, of invariably carrying a loaded pistol about with him. It lay on his dressing-table with his watch; with his watch it was put on in the morning; with his watch it was taken off at night', i.52–3. As Chitham notes, at p. 167, Patrick gave EJB shooting lessons in the Parsonage garden.

I had hit upon the plan of removing it...the gun: cf. *LCB* recollection of Branwell's last three years and the turmoil at the Parsonage: 'The sisters often listened for the report of a pistol in the dead of the night, till watchful eye and hearkening ear grew heavy and dull with the perpetual strain upon their nerves', i.333. See Introduction, pp. xviii, xxxvi–xxxvii.

NOTES TO PAGES 112–118   401

p. 112 *red herrings*: herrings turned reddish brown by being smoked.

p. 114 *"It was far in the night... heard that"*: remembering two lines from Robert Jamieson's translation of the Danish ballad 'Svend Dyring', given as 'The Ghaist's Warning' in Sir Walter Scott's note XLIX to *The Lady of the Lake* (Edinburgh: Ballantyne, 1810), pp. 376–80. The version of EJB's quotation is: "'Twas lang i' the night, and the bairnies grat: | Their mither she under the mools heard that' (grat = cried/wept; mools = mould/earth/grave): p. 377. These are not the first lines of the ballad, which tells of a mother who returns from the tomb to protect her mistreated children. Note that Nelly had just said (p. 113): 'Oh! I wonder his mother does not rise from her grave to see how you use him'. Cf. CB's 'The Fairies' Warning', in *The Complete Poems of Charlotte Brontë*, pp. 120–1.

Katherine W. Ankenbrandt, in 'Songs in *Wuthering Heights*', *Southern Folklore Quarterly*, 33 (1969), pp. 92–115, notes that 'It is very likely that, in using a stanza [*sic*] from a translated Danish ballad as a Border ballad in *Wuthering Heights*, Emily Brontë thought herself restoring part of the ancient heritage of northern Britain', (p. 101).

p. 115 *You have pledged your word, and cannot retract*: breach of promise to marry was, throughout the 19thc, a tort (civil wrong) within common law.

p. 117 *I broke my heart with weeping to come back to earth*: cf. p. 12.

He had listened till he heard... no farther: cf. Thomas Moore's *Byron's Life, Letters, and Journals in one volume* (London: Murray, 1844), pp. 27–8:

> Miss [Mary] Chaworth [of Annesley Hall, a neighbour], looked upon Byron as a mere school-boy. He was in his manners, too, at that period, rough and odd, and (as I have heard from more than one quarter) by no means popular among girls of his own age. If, at any moment, however, he had flattered himself with the hope of being loved by her, a circumstance mentioned in his 'Memoranda,' as one of the most painful of those humiliations to which the defect in his foot had exposed him, must have let the truth in, with dreadful certainty, upon his heart. He either was told of, or overheard, Miss Chaworth saying to her maid, 'Do you think I could care any thing for that lame boy?' This speech, as he himself described it, was like a shot through his heart. Though late at night when he heard it, he instantly darted out of the house, and scarcely knowing whither he ran, never stopped till he found himself at Newstead.

p. 118 *Milo*: Milo of Croton was a celebrated 6thc BC wrestler in ancient Greece. (Croton—now the Province of Crotone—is in Calabria but was an Achaean settlement. Achaea was the northernmost division of the Peloponnese.) Milo's fame is mentioned in *Troilus and Cressida* when Ulysses addresses Diomedes:

> Let Mars divide eternity in twain,
> And give him half. And for thy vigour,
> Bull-bearing Milo his addition yield
> To sinewy Ajax.

> 2.iii.240–3.

Milo's death is described in Strabo's Γεωγραφικά, *Geographica* (7 BC) in the following terms:

402   NOTES TO PAGES 118–20

And [Croton's] fame was increased by the large number of its Pythagorean philosophers, and by Milo, who was the most illustrious of athletes, and also a companion of Pythagoras, who spent a long time in the city. It is said that once, at the common mess of the philosophers, when a pillar began to give way, Milo slipped in under the burden and saved them all, and then drew himself from under it and escaped. And it is probably because he relied upon this same strength that he brought on himself the end of his life as reported by some writers; at any rate, the story is told that once, when he was travelling through a deep forest, he strayed rather far from the road, and then, on finding a large log cleft with wedges, thrust his hands and feet at the same time into the cleft and strained to split the log completely asunder; but he was only strong enough to make the wedges fall out, whereupon the two parts of the log instantly snapped together; and caught in such a trap as that, he became food for wild beasts.

6.1.12, Perseus Project.

There was a story of the sisters' nurse breaking the branch of Patrick's favourite cherry tree while pretending to be an escaping prince in a children's game. See Marion Harland, *Charlotte Brontë at Home* (New York: Putnam's, 1899), p. 32.

p. 118 *an existence of yours beyond you*: cf. 'No coward soul is mine', p. 26.

p. 119 *Und hah isn't that nowt comed...seeght*: 'And how is that nothing's [or "that nothing hasn't", i.e., the useless Heathcliff] come in from the field, by this point? What is he about? Great idle sight!'

ill eneugh for ony fahl manners: 'ill [bad] enough for only foul manners'.

pp. 119–20 *Yon lad gets war un war!...nowt!*: 'That lad gets worse and worse [...] He's left the gate swung completely open and Miss's pony has trodden down two fields or corn, and crashed through right over into the meadow. However, the master will play the devil in the morning, and he'll do well [at it]. He's patience itself with such careless, awful creatures—patience itself he is! But he'll not be always so—you see, all of you! You mustn't drive him out of his mind for nothing.'

p. 120 *Aw sud more likker look for th' horse...wi' ye!*: 'I should better look for the horse [...] It would make more sense. But, I can look for neither horse nor man in such a night as this—as black as a chimney! And Heathcliff is the chap to come at *my* whistle—no doubt he'll be less hard of hearing with *you!*'

split a tree off: on this motif, see note to p. 118, '*Milo*'.

Noah and Lot: Lot, a Patriarch in Genesis, escapes in Genesis 19 with his daughters from the destruction of Sodom by God's angels; Noah, also in Genesis, flees with his family and wild animals from the great flood (Chapters 6–9) sent by God to punish transgression.

Cf. 2 Peter 2:5–7: 'And spared not the old world, but saved Noah the eighth person, a preacher of righteousness, bringing in the flood upon the world of the ungodly; And turning the cities of Sodom and Gomorrah into ashes condemned them with an overthrow, making them an ensample unto those that after should live ungodly; And delivered just Lot, vexed with the filthy conversation of the wicked.'

Jonah: in the Book of Jonah, Jonah is required by the Lord to visit Nineveh and warn the inhabitants of the divine wrath: ' "Arise, go to Nineveh, that great city, and cry against it; for their wickedness is come up before me" ', 1:2. Jonah, however, escapes this responsibility by taking a boat to Tarshish, from which he is thrown by the

NOTES TO PAGES 120–24

angry crew who blame him for a dangerous storm (hence the connection to Mr Earnshaw). Jonah is swallowed by a great fish, inside of which he remains for three days before being vomited onto dry land. Thereafter, Jonah fulfils the Lord's original command and preaches at Nineveh.

p. 120 *should n't*: these two words are the last and first of a new line break in *1847*; 'shouldn't' in *1850*.

p. 121 *Aw's niver wonder, ...Scripture ses*—: 'I expect he is at the bottom of a bog hole. This visitation [of the storm] wasn't for nothing, and I would have you watch out. Miss,—you might be the next. Thank Heaven for everything! Everything works for good together for those that are chosen, and picked out from the dross. You know what the scripture says—'. Cf. next note. 'All warks togither for gooid' is from Romans 8:28.

And he began quoting several texts: Joseph's sense of 'the chosen' might imply Calvinist leanings/a belief in predestination. In the New Testament, the verses closest to affirming this (or rather, the verses that have been interpreted by some as affirming this) are Romans 8:28–30: 'And we know that all things work together for good to them that love God, to them who are the called according to his purpose. For whom he did foreknow, he also did predestinate to be conformed to the image of his Son, that he might be the firstborn among many brethren. Moreover whom he did predestinate, them he also called: and whom he called, them he also justified: and whom he justified, them he also glorified.'

The house door was ajar...drowsy: *1850* has: 'The house door was ajar, too; light entered from its unclosed windows; Hindley had come out, and stood on the kitchen hearth, haggard and drowsy'.

pp. 121–2 *If Aw wur yah, maister,...road*: 'If were you, master, I'd just slam the door in the faces of all of them, plain and simple! There is never a day when you are off but that cat of a Linton comes sneaking here—and Miss Nelly, she's a fine lass! She sits watching for you in the kitchen; and as you're in at one door, he's out at the other—And, then, our grand lady goes a-courting herself! It's charming behaviour, lurking among the fields, after twelve at night, with that foul, dreadful devil of a gipsy, Heathcliff. They think *I'm* blind; but I'm not, not at all. I saw young Linton both coming and going, and I saw *you* (directing his discourse to me), you good for nothing, slatternly witch! get up and bolt into the house, the minute you heard the master's horse making a clatter up the road.' Note missing terminal speech mark in *1847*.

p. 122 *yon*: one of a number of examples where the compositor appears to have inverted a letter. Corrected in *1850*.

He bled her: see note to p. 86.

p. 124 *last of the season*: another 'last of' moment (see note to p. 105, '*the last of the ancient...*'). EJB makes an unusual error in *WH*'s chronology here. The grouse season legally ends on 10 December. But that is the result of the Game Act 1831 (still in force), which was the first in the United Kingdom to limit the hunting periods for wild birds.

some other subject than pills...leeches: Thomas John Graham, see note to p. 86, widely refers to the health benefits of blistering, usually with the use of a blistering plaster. The 'therapy' is described in *Modern Domestic Medicine*, pp. 106–7. The

404   NOTES TO PAGES 124–33

theory for what was in effect a form of torture was that raising blisters drew impurities from the system. *Modern Domestic Medicine* covers the usage of the 'very serviceable' (ibid., p. 41) and widely applied leech, ibid., pp. 41–2: the theory for this was the same in terms of the drawing of impure or 'excessive' amounts of blood. Page 41 notes that drawing blood by leeches from close to any inflamed part is 'of great consequence'.

p. 124 *sizer's place*: Patrick Brontë had held a sizarship at St John's College Cambridge: that is, received financial support from the college in return for some practical contribution. Corrected to 'sizar's' in *1850*. It is worth noting that the College now was very different in some respects to that which Patrick knew: not least, the Chapel. That which Patrick would have known was demolished in the early 1860s (its ground plan remains) and replaced, 1866–9, by the present building, designed by Sir George Gilbert Scott.

p. 126 *for a soldier*: we presently learn that his 'upright carriage' suggests to Nelly that Heathcliff had had a military career.

sough: see note to p. 74, '*Seventy Times Seven...*'.

his return: i.e. Linton's.

p. 128 *fought*: a verb perhaps intended to reinforce the sense that Heathcliff has been in the army.

p. 129 *alike*: *1850* has 'alike:'.

p. 130 *christian*: corrected in *1850*.

slap me on the cheek, I'd not only turn the other: cf. Matthew 5:39: 'But I say unto you, That ye resist not evil: but whosoever shall smite thee on thy right cheek, turn to him the other also.'

p. 132 *fondling*: 'one who is fondly loved', *OED*.

dog in the manger: an expression *OED* finds first in 1573 ('A person who selfishly prevents another from having or enjoying something, even though he or she has no personal use for it'). This example is cited in *OED*. Cf. Lucy's accusation of Madame Beck: ' "Dog in the manger!" I said; for I knew she secretly wanted [M. Paul], and had always wanted him[")]', *Villette*, iii.253 (not in *OED*).

p. 133 *we's hae a Crahnr's 'quest enah...t' pikes?*: 'We'll have a coroner's inquest for sure at our place. One of them almost had his finger cut off because of holding the other from sticking himself like a calf. That's the master, you know, who is so set on going to the Grand Assizes. He is not frightened of the bench of judges, nor of Paul, nor Peter, nor John, nor Matthew, nor any of them: not he! He behaves like he longs to set his brazened face against them! And that bonny lad Heathcliff, you know, he's a rare one! He can twist his face into a laugh as well as anyone at a true devil's jest. Does he never say anything of his fine living among us when he goes to the Grange? This is the thing: up at dawn; dice, brandy, closed shutters, and candle light till next day at noon—then the fool goes swearing and raving to his room, making decent folks dig their fingers in their ears for very shame; and the knave, why, he can count his money, and eat, and sleep, and then go off to his neighbour to gossip with the wife. Of course, he tells Mistress Catherine how her father's gold runs into his pocket and her father's son gallops down the Broad road [cf. Matthew 7:13] while he runs ahead to open the gates?'

NOTES TO PAGES 134–47

p. 134 *transcient*: another misprint corrected in *1850*, though *OED* does record one example of this spelling—in 1644. Subsequent appearances of the word are standard spelling in *1847*.

p. 135 *centipede from the Indies*: almost certainly *Scolopendra gigantea*, present in the Caribbean (West Indies): a giant venomous centipede growing up to 12"/30cm in length.

wrench them: i.e. the 'talons' or nails.

silly: in the sense of 'Helpless, defenceless, powerless; frequently with the suggestion of innocence', as well as 'lacking in judgement or common sense', *OED*.

p. 137 *sand-pillar*: cf. *Agnes Grey*: 'I still preserve those relics of past sufferings and experience, like pillars of witness set up in travelling through the vale of life, to mark particular occurrences. The footsteps are obliterated now; the face of the country may be changed; but the pillar is still there, to remind me how all things were when it was reared', *1847*, iii.267. And *JE*: 'Whitcross is no town, nor even a hamlet; it is but a stone pillar set up where four roads meet: whitewashed, I suppose, to be more obvious at a distance and in darkness. Four arms spring from its summit: the nearest town to which these point is, according to the inscription, distant ten miles; the farthest, above twenty. From the well-known names of these towns I learn in what county I have lighted; a north-midland shire, dusk with moorland, ridged with mountain: this I see', iii.49–50.

p. 139 *Who is Nelly?*: *1850* corrects to 'Who is, Nelly?'.

husband: *1850* has 'husband:'.

p. 140 *prejucial*: in *1847*, this is divided across the end of one line and the beginning of another: 'preju/cial'. It is possible, again, to assume a reason for this error in that the typesetter forget how far through the word he was.

p. 142 *leveret*: a young hare (in its first year). *OED* notes the sense, 'A spiritless person', but observes that it is obsolete and can find only one source—from ?1608.

half-a-dozen: one of the odd moments that reminds us how little EJB reveals about the people at the Grange. We presently find that Linton has mustered the coachman and two gardeners.

p. 143 *this this*: divided 'this | this' between the end and the beginning of a line in *1847*.

p. 145 *time in the library*: cf. the next note.

p. 146 *among his books*: this is a detail perhaps borrowed from Patrick Brontë's life at Haworth. Note the 'of course' in this comment from Chapter III of *LCB*: 'Little Maria Brontë was delicate and small in appearance, which seemed to give greater effect to her wonderful precocity of intellect. She must have been her mother's companion and helpmate in many a household and nursery experience, for Mr. Brontë was, of course, much engaged in his study', i.45.

p. 147 *in a pet*: see note to p. 66, '*pet*'.

pigeons' feathers ... die!: Cf.

Again, the soul cannot free itself if the dying person has been laid on a bed containing pigeon feathers, or the feathers of wild birds even. Instances are on record of pigeon feathers having been placed in a small bag, and thrust under dying

406 NOTES TO PAGES 147–56

persons to hold them back, until the arrival of some loved one; but the meeting having taken place, the feathers were withdrawn, and death allowed to enter.

Richard Blakeborough, *Wit, Character, Folklore, and Customs of the North Riding of Yorkshire* (London: Frowde, 1898), p. 120.

This is, for sure, *WH*'s 'mad scene', where Catherine takes on the King Lear role of delusionary self-absorption (or indeed the Ophelia role in *Hamlet* where, mad and shortly before her death, we see her handing out flowers and herbs in 4.v). Ebenezer Cobham Brewer's *Dictionary of Phrase and Fable* (1870[–], reprinted in facsimile in Cambridge by Cambridge University Press, 2014), adds that pigeons in a number of cultures have generally been associated with misfortune. For 17thc England, Brewer observes:

He who is sprinkled with pigeon's blood will never die a natural death. A sculptor carrying home a bust of Charles I. stopped to rest on the way; at the moment a pigeon overhead was struck by a hawk, and the blood of the bird fell on the neck of the bust. The sculptor thought it ominous, and after the king was beheaded the saying became current.

p. 687.

p. 148 *moor-cock*: red grouse, *Lagopus lagopus scotica*.

fairy cave under Peniston Crag: see note to p. 108, '*Pennistow Crag*'.

elf-bolts: a term for flint arrowheads. (The word dates from a period in which prehistoric and ancient artefacts, like flint arrowheads, were not understood in relation to human history but imagined to come from fantastic realms of faerie.)

It's behind there...alone!: a scene that relates to the 'Red Room' scene in Chapter II of *JE*.

p. 149 *Who is coward now?*: cf. 'No coward soul is mine', p. 26.

firs by the lattice: cf. p. 76.

oak-panelled bed at home: cf. note to p. 72, '*clothes-press...*'.

p. 150 *it's ghosts*: corrected to 'its ghosts' in *1850*.

I'll not lie...deep: cf. 'Remembrance', pp. 33–4.

p. 152 *to tarry the event*: 'to await the outcome'.

springer: in the 19thc, springer and cocker spaniels were not as strictly delineated as to-day: both could come from the same litter. The Kennel Club recognized the English Springer Spaniel as a distinct breed in 1902. The springer was/is bred as a gun dog to 'spring' game birds (startle them into the air).

gallopping: *1850* corrects.

p. 153 *Earnshaw's*: *1850* corrected to Earnshaws'.

p. 155 *fast*: something went wrong on the right-hand end of the typography here, which I have, for once, corrected: 'fast' appears as 'fas'' and two lines lower, the 'all', which ends the line, is missing its final 'l'.

p. 156 *No mother...former self*: *1850* has: 'No mother could have nursed an only child more devotedly than Edgar tended her. Day and night he was watching, and patiently enduring all the annoyances that irritable nerves and a shaken reason could inflict; and, though Kenneth remarked that what he saved from the grave would only recompense his care by forming the source of constant future anxiety—in fact, that his health and strength were being sacrificed to preserve a mere ruin of humanity—he

NOTES TO PAGES 156–63

knew no limits in gratitude and joy when Catherine's life was declared out of danger; and hour after hour he would sit beside her, tracing the gradual return to bodily heath, and flattering his too sanguine hopes with the illusion that her mind would settle back to its right balance also, and she would soon be entirely her former self.'

p. 158 *dip candle*: 'A candle made by repeatedly dipping a wick in melted tallow, a dipped candle', *OED*.

Now…ganging: *1850* alters this to 'Now, wilt thou be ganging' [going].

mim: 'Originally and chiefly *Scottish* and *British regional*. A. *adj.* Reserved or restrained in manner or behaviour, esp. in a contrived or priggish way; affectedly modest, demure; primly silent, quiet; affectedly moderate or abstemious in diet (*rare*). Also (occasionally) of a person's appearance', *OED*.

p. 159 *Nor nuh me*: *1850* has 'None o' me'.

p. 160 *to to*: not across a line ending on this occasion; corrected in *1850*.

as as: across a line ending; corrected in *1850*.

p. 161 *If they's…hend*: 'If there's to be fresh ordering—just when I was getting used to two masters—if I'm to have a *mistress* set over my head, it's the right time to be leaving. I never *did* think to see the day when I would have to leave the old place— but I don't doubt it is near at hand!'

It racked me to recall past happiness…apparition: cf. 'Remembrance', pp. 33–4.

thible: '*Scottish* and *northern regional*. A stick for stirring porridge or anything cooked in a pot; a potstick', *OED*.

Hareton, thah willut sup thy porridge…aht: 'Hareton, you won't be tasting your porridge tonight; there'll be nothing but lumps as big as my fist. There, again! I'd fling in the bowl and all, if I were you! There, pour the scum off, and then you'll be done with it. Bang, bang. It's a mercy the bottom isn't knocked out!' *1850* leaves the unusual 'guilp' unchanged. Wright gives its meaning in West Yorkshire as the 'scum from porridge' but cites only this example.

barn: unchanged in *1850* but presumably with the Scottish sense of 'bairn', baby, young child.

p. 162 *It's weel eneugh tuh ate a few porridge in…on't*: 'It's good enough to eat some porridge in. There's a pack/sack of corn in the corner there, mightily clean; if you're afraid of dirtying your grand silk clothes, spread your handkerchief out on top of it.' 'Porridge' here is, in keeping with northern English and Scottish usage, plural.

Oh! it's Maister Hathecliff's yah're wenting?…hisseln: ' "Oh! It's Mr Heathcliff's [room] you're wanting", cried he, as if making a new discovery. "Couldn't you have said so at first? For then, I might have told you, without all this work, that it's just the one you can't see—he always keeps it locked, and nobody ever meddles [?] with it but himself.'

p. 163 *ye marred, wearisome nowt!…hahse*: 'you damaged, wearisome nobody! You have seen all but Hareton's portion of a room. There's not another hole in which to lie down in the house!'

Ech! ech!…may: ' "Ech! ech!" exclaimed Joseph. "Well done, Miss Cathy! well done, Miss Cathy! Howsoever, the master will just tumble over them [like] broken pots; and then we'll hear something; we'll hear how it is to be. Good-for-nothing mad one! you deserve to sorrow from now till Christmas, flinging the precious gifts of God underfoot in your dreadful rages. But, I'm mistaken if you will show your spirit for

408   NOTES TO PAGES 163–82

long. Will Heathcliff tolerate such bonny ways, do you think? I can't but wish he will catch in that mood. I but wish he will." '

'Plisky' is Scottish, northern English, and Irish: 'a mischievous trick, a frolic', *OED*.

p. 163 *handherchief*: *1850* corrects to 'handkerchief'.

Him as allas maks a third: the devil, presumably. A violent parody of Jesus's words in Matthew 18:20, 'For where two or three are gathered together in my name, there am I in the midst of them.'

p. 165 *As*: atypically, this first word of a chapter is set in ordinary type.

a a: again, the first is at the end of a line, the second at the beginning.

p. 167 *my future death and hell*: *1850* has 'future—death and hell'.

slut: in the sense of 'A woman of dirty, slovenly, or untidy habits or appearance', *OED*.

p. 168 *but the very morrow of our wedding... home*: cf. Catherine's dream on p. 117.

aud: more casual typesetting, with, it seems, a 'u' mistaken for an 'n'.

brach: a female hunting hound, but figuratively, at least in the 17thc, a term of abuse: bitch.

p. 169 *retain custody*: the legal rights and obligations of marriage in the first half of the 19thc, including a husband's right to confine his wife's freedoms of movement, interested the Brontë sisters. Cf. Helen Huntingdon's momentous decision in *The Tenant of Wildfell Hall* and the first Mrs Rochester in *JE*.

p. 170 *that, that*: *1850* has 'that that'.

p. 171 *dree'*: of trouble, cheerless. Used of weather, particularly in Scotland, dree/dreich means long drawn-out/tedious/monotonous. The apostrophe/speech mark is a typographical error removed in *1850*.

the daughter turned out a second edition of the mother!: this is the end of Volume I, so there is something loosely appropriate about this reference though, of course, the reader turns to the second *part* of the edition not a second edition.

p. 177 *in the earth*: cf. the opening line of 'Remembrance', p. 33.

p. 179 *satan*: 'Satan' in *1850*.

p. 180 *delivered*: in the sense of 'liberated, relieved'.

p. 182 *inhabitants*: Pauline Nestor makes the valuable observation: 'Modern editions have tended to normalize this sentence by printing "inhabitant". However both the 1847 first edition and Charlotte's 1850 amended edition use the plural of the noun, which is richly suggestive of the shared identity of Catherine and Heathcliff', *Wuthering Heights*, ed. Pauline Nestor (Harmondsworth: Penguin, 1995), p. 347.

Do you believe... Maker?: this great topic was obviously a matter discussed throughout the Parsonage. AB, notably as evidenced in *The Tenant of Wildfell Hall*, was particularly sympathetic to universalism. Cf. *Letters*, ii. 160, where AB writes to the Revd David Thom, author of *The Assurance of Faith: Or, Calvinism Identified with Universalism*, 2 vols (London: Simpkin and Marshall, 1833):

> I have seen so little of controversial Theology that I was not aware the doctrine of Universal Salvation had so able and ardent an advocate as yourself; but I cherished it from my very childhood—with a trembling hope at first, and afterwards with a firm and glad conviction of its truth.

NOTES TO PAGES 182–90 409

She added, 'in my late novel, "The Tenant of Wildfell Hall", I have given as many hints in support of the doctrine as I could venture to introduce into a work of that description', ii.160–1.

Had CB made Jane Eyre share such a view, she—Jane—would have had less of a theological basis to argue against becoming Rochester's mistress: the unintended consequence of universalism is, of course, its difficulty in policing earthly morality. *Companion* makes the intriguing point that *WH*'s 'serene ending perhaps suggests universalism', p. 516.

p. 182 *motive... motive*: the first is at the end of the last line of p. 24 in *1847* and the second at the beginning of the first line of p. 25.

ousels: EJB probably means the common European blackbird (*Turdus merula*), which is what the word first signified. It is possible that she means the ring ouzel, *Turdus torquatus*, which the term could, at this point, also signify. Her drawing from Bewick of the ring ouzel from 29 May 1829 is in BPM.

In fact, only the female blackbird and female ring ouzel build nests.

to to: again, this repetition occurs over a line break.

p. 183 *You said I killed you... take any form*: Mary Visick comments that in *1850* CB 'made the meaningless and weakening emendation: "...The murdered *do* haunt their murderers, I believe. I know that ghosts *have* wandered on earth..." ', *The Genesis of 'Wuthering Heights'* (Hong Kong: Hong Kong University Press, 1967), p. ix.

p. 184 *kirkyard*: Scottish and northern English usage.

p. 186 *back again*: unless with clear grounds against (e.g., bigamy, adultery), Heathcliff could legally oblige his wife's return.

p. 187 *pinched it to death*: pinching is the favourite chastisement of Prospero in *The Tempest*. Cf. Caliban's 'I shall be pinched to death', 5.i.279.

Pulling out the nerves with red hot pincers: it is possible EJB is thinking of the torturing to death of the would-be regicide of Louis XV, Robert-François Damiens (1715–57).

p. 188 *methodist*: *1850* corrects to 'Methodist'.

depressed: this does not have quite the modern sense of a mental health condition but rather of 'depress' in the definition of *OED* 5a: 'To lower or bring down in force, vigour, activity, intensity, or amount; to render weaker or less; to render dull or languid.'

so as by fire: 'If any man's work shall be burned, he shall suffer loss: but he himself shall be saved; yet so as by fire', 1 Corinthians 3:15.

p. 190 *girned*: in *OED*'s 1a sense of 'to girn': 'To show the teeth in rage, pain, disappointment, etc.; to snarl as a dog; to complain persistently; to be fretful or peevish'.

faithful dog: one wonders if EJB knew Edwin Landseer's 1837 painting *The Old Shepherd's Chief Mourner*, now in the V&A (FA.93[O]). Landseer might, it has been thought, have been the artist responsible for the 1834 'Brontë sisters' portrait sold by J.P. Humbert, auctioneers, in 2017. Cf. note to p. 66, '*flaxen ringlets...*'. Certainly, Branwell, while working in the railway office of Luddenden Foot, wrote a poem on 'The Old Shepherd's Chief Mourner', probably in July/early August 1841:

410   NOTES TO PAGES 190–94

The Shepherd's Cheif Mourner
vide Landseers Picture

The beams of Fame dry up Affections tears
And those who rise forget from whom they spring
Wealths golden glories pleasures glittering wind
All that man chases through his while of years
All that his hope seeks all his caution fears
Dazzle or drown those holy thoughts that cling
Round where the forms he loved lie slumbering
But not so *Thou*—Mans slave,—whose joys or cares
Mean deems so grovelling—power nor pride are thine
Nor Mans pursuits or ties—Yet oer this grave
Where lately crowds the *form* of mourning gave
I only hear *thy* low heart broken whine
I only see *Thee* left—long hours to pine
For him if love had power thy love could save[.]
The Works of Patrick Branwell Brontë, ed. Victor A.
Neufeldt, 3 vols (New York: Garland, 1997–9), iii.337.

But had Branwell seen Landseer's picture/a reproduction of it—or merely heard about it? The painting is not of a grave but of a dog resting its muzzle on a solitary coffin.

p. 191 *preter-human self denial*: *1850* has 'preterhuman self-denial'.

Whet is thur tuh do, nah?...nah?: *1850* has ' "What is ther to do, now? what is ther to do, now?', where Charlotte uses only an orthographic variant that has no effect on pronunciation. Cf. the peculiar moment in terms of word sounds in Chapter XI of *JE* when Adela first meets Jane:

'And Mademoiselle—what is your name?'
'Eyre—Jane Eyre.'
'Aire? Bah! I cannot say it.[']

i.189.

'Aire' here makes, incidentally, an interesting Yorkshire connection (the river Aire runs through Leeds) but is also a sort of homophone for Eire: Ireland.

p. 192 *guant*: corrected in *1850*.

another,,: corrected in *1850*.

an eye for an eye, a tooth for a tooth: Matthew 5:38: 'Ye have heard that it hath been said, An eye for an eye, and a tooth for a tooth.'

p. 192 *It's well people don't really rise from their grave*: cf. note to p. 114.

p. 194 *And far rather would I be condemned...again*: an extreme rewriting, perhaps, of Psalm 84:10: 'I had rather be a doorkeeper in the house of my God, than to dwell in the tents of wickedness.'

mistress,: *1850* corrects to 'mistress.'.

Linton: a related case, perhaps, to Heathcliff's name. EJB makes 'Linton' serve as both a first and a surname in the novel (although not for the same person). The doubling and compounding of individuals in *WH* is intensified by EJB's use of a tiny selection of names.

NOTES TO PAGES 195–216 411

p. 195 *because Heathcliff, had a habit of doing so*: *1850* has 'Heathcliff had a habit of doing so'.

p. 196 *No, Heathcliff's a tough...half*: missing inverted commas added in *1850*.

twenty-seven: Branwell was thirty-one when he died on 24 September 1848.

cross-roads: by long tradition, a place of burial for suicides. This was altered after the Burial of Suicide Act 1823 (4 Geo. c. 52), which allowed for churchyard burial under conditions that were further relaxed in the Interments (felo de se) Act 1882 (45 & 46 Vict. c 19).

p. 197 *Aw'd rayther...nowt uh t'soart!*: *1850* has: 'I'd rather he'd goan hisseln for t'doctor! I sud ha' taen tent o't' maister better nor him—and he warn't deead when I left, naught o't' soart!'

executed,: *1850* has 'executed.'.

a servant deprived of the advantage of wages: another slavery motif. Cf. note to p. 85, '*its owner*'.

p. 199 *Pennistone Craggs*: see note to p. 108, '*Pennistow Crag*'. *1850* changes this to 'Penistone Crags'.

p. 200 *galloway*: *1850* changes to 'Galloway'. EJB might well be using this term inexactly to indicate a large and strong pony. The true-bred Galloway—once native to northern England, especially Swaledale, and Scotland—was lost through cross-breeding at the beginning of the 19thc. Cf. the note to p. 83, '*Very old...*', on extinctions and 'last of the race'. The small case initial was an acceptable spelling. Cf. 'But poor Macwheeble [...] before he could rally his galloway, slunk to the rear amid the unrestrained laughter of the spectators', *Waverley, Or, 'Tis Sixty Years Since*, p. 289.

p. 201 *I open*: *1850* changes to 'I opened'.

p. 202 *Phenix*: *1850* gives 'Phœnix' throughout.

me me: not broken across a line. Corrected in *1850*.

p. 204 *offalld*: presumably 'awful'. *1850* leaves unchanged.

inuendo's: *1850* corrects to 'innuendoes'.

near: in the figurative sense of 'narrow, cramped' (*OED*); mean.

attacked her train: cf. the dog attack that leads to the first Catherine's consequential stay at the Grange on p. 94, which also 'formed an introduction'.

p. 206 *worrying*: see note to p. 88, '*worrying*'.

winter,: corrected to 'winter.' In *1850*.

p. 207 *daughter,,*: corrected in *1850*.

p. 208 *And then, I thought,...they'll be*: *1850* has 'And then, I thought, however will that weakling live at Wuthering Heights? Between his father and Hareton, what playmates and instructors they'll be.'

p. 209 *Noa! that manes...knaw*: 'No! That means nothing. Heathcliff takes no account of the mother, nor you neither—but he'll have his lad; and I must take him—so now you know!'

p. 210 *brown study*: in Dr Johnson's sense of 'gloomy meditations'. *OED*, citing Johnson, dates this expression to *c*.1555.

p. 212 *countenanance*: split over a line in *1847*; corrected in *1850*.

p. 216 *That housekeeper left,...there still*: an unusual error of detail here. The implication of this statement is, presumably, that Nelly does not know the present housekeeper at Wuthering Heights. Michael Grosvenor Myer rightly points out, however, that, on p. 263

412   NOTES TO PAGES 216–30

of this present edition, Zillah (the Wuthering Heights housekeeper) greets Nelly ('"Eh, dear! Mrs. Dean"') whom we are clearly intended to understand she knows perfectly well. See 'An Inconsistency in *Wuthering Heights*', *Notes & Queries*, 44 (1997), pp. 335–6.

p. 218 *not not*: again, broken across two lines in *1847*; corrected in *1850*.

p. 219 *surpressed...visiters*: both errors corrected in *1850*.

p. 220 *interest,*: *1850* has 'interest.'. Hareton has, perhaps, something of EJB's own artist's visual attentiveness.

gaumless: *OED* dates this dialect term (later 'gormless') to ?1746. Its second source is this one.

p. 221 *extra-animal*: not in *OED* but presumably 'beyond the flesh, the physical'.

p. 222 *strange talk*: Hareton's 'strange talk' can be compared to Heathcliff's on his arrival at Wuthering Heights (see p. 84 and note).

lath: *OED*, noun, 2b: 'applied to what is slender or fragile'.

compassionate: *OED*'s last example of this transitive verb is 1837, strangely given its wide use of *WH* as a source.

p. 223 *cover*: unchanged in *1850* but it is possible that 'covet' was intended.

p. 224 *Oh,*: speech marks added in *1850*.

p. 228 *Michaelmas*: 29 September.

streamers: a streamer is 'A long narrow strip of vapour, snow, etc.', *OED*. Interestingly, *OED* gives the first example as 1871.

tenour: *1850* changes this to 'tenure' unnecessarily, for 'tenour', *OED* notes, could still mean at this point: 'The action or fact of holding a tenement (esp. in *English Law*)' and 'The action or fact of holding anything material or non-material; hold upon something; maintaining a hold; occupation.'

old songs: Katherine W. Ankenbrandt, in 'Songs in *Wuthering Heights*', valuably surveys both the named texts in the novel and the 'image of the song' (though she mistakes 'Fair(y) Annie's Wedding': see note to p. 286). Ankenbrandt is particularly interested in the Danish origins of 'The Ghaist's Warning': see note to p. 114. On ballads and *WH* more generally, see Sheila Smith, '"At Once Strong and Eerie": The Supernatural in *Wuthering Heights* and its Debt to the Traditional Ballad', *Review of English Studies*, 43 (1992), pp. 498–517.

p. 229 *sackless*: '*Scottish* and *northern dialect*. Innocent of wrong intent, guileless, simple; also, of a thing, harmless. Hence, in [a] disparaging sense, feeble-minded; lacking energy, dispirited', says *OED*, giving this usage as one of its sources.

p. 229 *canty*: '*Scottish* and *northern dialect*. Cheerful, lively, gladsome; esp. in *Scottish* manifesting gladness and cheerfulness; in north of England rather = lively, brisk, active', *OED*.

p. 230 *I love him better than myself, Ellen*: a parallel statement in a very different context to the first Catherine's on p. 117.

Slough of Despond: from Bunyan's *The Pilgrim's Progress* (see note to p. 74, '*pilgrim's staff*'), the bog in which Christian sinks under the weight of his sin and sense of sinfulness: 'And he said unto me, This miry slough is such a place as cannot be mended; it is the descent whither the scum and filth that attends conviction for sin doth continually run, and therefore it is called the Slough of Despond; for still, as the sinner is awakened about his lost condition, there ariseth in his soul many fears, and doubts,

NOTES TO PAGES 230–41   413

and discouraging apprehensions, which all of them get together, and settle in this place. And this is the reason of the badness of this ground', *The Pilgrim's Progress* (London: Oxford University Press, 1903), p. 17. 'Slough' also picks up on the imagined place described in the note to p. 74, '*Seventy Times Seven . . .*'.

p. 232 *double darkness*: a good example of the problems noted in the Introduction, pp. xix–xxi, of supposed 'sources'. *2009*, p. 336, suggests an allusion to Milton's *Samson Agonistes* (*1671*): 'yield to double darkness now at hand', l. 593. But the collocation is not uncommon prior to *WH*, assuming for a moment that EJB did not independently think of the words.

silly: in *OED*'s definition II: 'Senses relating to weakness, vulnerability, or physical incapacity. [. . .] Helpless, defenceless, powerless; frequently with the suggestion of innocence or undeserved suffering.'

by the side of my wilful young mistress's pony: this is the first we have heard of Minny's bad temper. EJB seems to have displaced either Ellen's, or Ellen's view of Catherine, onto the Galloway. Cf. note to p. 200.

p. 233 *quart*: a quarter of a gallon (2 pints). *LCB* remembers the neighbourhood of CB's schooldays, saying: 'Nor was hospitality, one of the main virtues of Yorkshire, wanting. Oat-cake, cheese, and beer were freely pressed upon the visitor', i.124. Beer, naturally, was safer to drink than potentially contaminated water. Ponden Hall Library held four copies of the aptly named George Cooper's *The Modern Domestic Brewer. In two parts. Part I. Preliminary discourse, and observations on water, malt and hops; together with a dissertation on the four quarters of the year as they relate to brewing. Part II. The most approved method of brewing malt liquors, with observations on the use of the thermometer, and all other matters relating to the brewery* (London: Sherwood, Neeley and Jones, *1811*) and seven other publications on brewing. It was, indeed, an important matter.

p. 234 *shooting season*: see note to p. 24, '*last of the season*'.

p. 235 "*Cathy*: *1850* removes the speech marks.

p. 236 *guaged*: *1850* corrects to 'gauged'.

p. 237 *being in a passion*: Graham's *Modern Domestic Medicine*, see note to p. 86, '*measles*', records being in a fit of 'passion' as the cause of temporary blindness (p. 328) and even of miscarriage (p. 416).

neither," She: *1850* correctly has a full stop.

The Grange is not a prison . . . jailer: cf. 'Julian M. and A.G. Rochelle', pp. 40–4, for more of EJB's imaginative absorption with imprisonment.

p. 238 "*Poor thing, I never considered . . . library.*: an example of the irregularity of the use of speech marks in *1847*.

p. 239 *dis-relish*: *OED* gives a source of 1841 as its final example of this word ('dis-relish'), oddly, again, in the light of *OED*'s use of *WH* elsewhere.

p. 241 *gingerbread*: Gaskell remembers in *LCB* the social events after the annual 'Lecture' at Heckmondwicke: 'The rest of the day was spent in social enjoyment; great numbers of strangers flocked to the place; booths were erected for the sale of toys and gingerbread (a sort of "Holy Fair")', i.125.

throstles: song thrushes (*Turdus philomelos*).

ecstacy: *1850* gives 'ecstasy'.

414   NOTES TO PAGES 241–66

p. 241 *battledoors*: battledores (as corrected in *1850*) are small wooden and gut rackets used with shuttlecocks, the precursor of badminton rackets.

p. 242 "*'Oh, you dunce!' ...failure*: a line that inevitably makes one reflect on what kind of school EJB might have run had the plan to open one succeeded.

a b c: *1850* has 'A B C'.

p. 243 *skift*: 'To undergo shifting, change, or removal; to change one's place, etc. *Obsolete* exc. *Dialect*', *OED*, which includes this instance in its sources.

p. 244 *he did not reckon on being answered so...and*: *1850* has 'He did not reckon on being answered so: but I wouldn't turn back; and'.

p. 246 *he he*: another example of a repetition across a line ending in *1847*.

p. 248 *you have no reason to dislike me...yourself*: *1850* has 'you have no reason to dislike me, you allow, yourself'.

p. 252 *bilberries*: wild berries (usually *Vaccinium myrtillus*), like a softer blueberry, harvested principally at the end of July and in August.

p. 255 I'm *no coward*: cf. note to p. 149, '*Who is coward...*'.

p. 256 *ling*: heather, *Calluna vulgaris*.

muttered Heathcliff.: in *1847*, the full-stop is at the level of the top of the main writing line rather than the bottom.

suppose,: *1850* has 'suppose:'.

p. 257 *vivifisection*: *1850* gives 'vivisection'.

p. 260 *benefit of clergy*: provision from the Middle Ages to permit clergy charged with offences to be tried in ecclesiastical courts under canon law rather than in civil courts. It was finally abolished in the Criminal Law Act 1827 though remains a figurative expression for 'special treatment'.

p. 261 *He cursed you,...world*: cf. Job 3:1–4. 'After this opened Job his mouth, and cursed his day. And Job spake, and said, Let the day perish wherein I was born, and the night in which it was said, There is a man child conceived. Let that day be darkness; let not God regard it from above, neither let the light shine upon it.'

cockatrice: presumably in *OED*'s sense 2: ' A malicious, treacherous, or destructive person'.

eft's fingers: 'A small lizard or lizard-like animal. Now [...] chiefly applied to the Greater Water-Newt (*Triton cristatus*) and to the Smooth Newt (*Lophinus punctatus*), of the order Salamandridæ', *OED*. Presumably an indication of Catherine's slender, long (cold?) fingers.

p. 263 "*Eh, dear! Mrs. Dean,*": see note to p. 216.

cant: 'Bold, brisk, courageous, hearty, lusty, lively, hale. The Scottish sense leans to "Lively, merry, brisk"', *OED*. Cf. *Shirley*, 'Th' wife's a raight cant body', i.205.

p. 264 *his his*: not across a line end; corrected in *1850*.

p. 265 *everything she has is mine*: Mr Green, the lawyer, arrived too late (see pp. 266–7) to receive Edgar's instructions about his estate and so it has passed to young Linton.

nor Zillah are: corrected to 'nor Zillah is' in *1850*.

p. 266 *Mr,*: corrected in *1850*.

bevy: the most extended account of who staffs the Grange.

harvest moon: full moon closest to the autumnal equinox, on a night between 21 and 24 September.

NOTES TO PAGES 267–76

p. 267 *happy,*: *1850* has 'happy'.

I am going to her: cf. 'I am going to God' (and Introduction, p. xxx). The line spacing is, of course, as *1847*.

p. 268 *she got easily out of its lattice . . . close by*: cf. p. 76 and Lockwood's dream.

p. 269 *runnings*: retained in *1850*.

p. 270 *I'll tell you what I did yesterday!*: Hilda Marsden and Ian Jack make the interesting point, following Leicester Bradner, 'The Growth of *Wuthering Heights*', *Publications of the Modern Language Association of America*, 48 (1933), pp. 139–41, of comparing this narrative to the end of 'The Bride of Barna', a story issued in *Blackwood's Magazine* 48 (November 1840), pp. 680–704:

> By the side of Ellen Nugent's new-made grave sat the murderer Lawlor, enclosing in his arms the form that had once comprised all earth's love and beauty for him, and which, like a miser, with [wild] and maniac affection, he had unburied once more to clasp and contemplate. The shroud had fallen form the upper part of the body, upon which decay had as yet made slight impression. The delicate head lay reclined upon that . . . shoulder which had been its home so often, and over which now streamed the long bright hair like a flood of loosened gold.

Marsden and Jack add that the last sentence of the story is 'the strangers who dug his grave did not venture to separate in death the hapless pair who in life could never be united'. See Emily Brontë, *Wuthering Heights*, ed. Hilda Marsden and Ian Jack (Oxford: Clarendon, 1976), p. 431.

p. 271 *I dreamt I was sleeping the last sleep . . . against hers*: cf. 'Remembrance', pp. 33–4.

den: in the Scottish regional sense, 'A deep hollow between hills; a dingle', *OED*.

p. 272 *catgut*: 'The dried and twisted intestines of sheep, also of the horse and ass; used for the strings of musical instruments; also as bands in lathes, clocks, etc.', *OED*.

Joseph,: *1850* has 'Joseph'.

p. 273 *journies*: corrected to 'journeys' in *1850*.

p. 274 *"thrang"*: in the Scottish sense of 'trouble'.

farthing: the smallest denomination of currency available (a quarter of one penny).

Then she began to bother me . . . her: retained unchanged in *1850*.

p. 276 *However, Mr. Heathcliff has claimed . . . possession*: EJB shows some knowledge of the law here, at least in relation to inheritance. It is not certain from where this knowledge came. There was a notable collection of law textbooks in the library of Ponden Hall (see note to p. 104, '*I have read more . . .*'). Bob Duckett comments: 'Emily's "occult knowledge of property law in *Wuthering Heights*" [Hewish, p. 35] could have been derived from Ponden House law books written for the layman, such as Runnington's *Treatise on the Action of Ejectment* (1751) and Lovelass's *The Laws Disposing of a Person's Estate who Dies without Will or Testament* (1790). [Hewish] could also have mentioned John Paul's *Laws relating to Landlords and Tenants* (1795). Disputed inheritances apart, there were books on game laws, distress for rent, legal provision for the poor, insolvency, and laws respecting horses', 'The Library at Ponden Hall', p. 114. It is not clear to me what Hewish means by 'occult'. Again, we have no conclusive evidence EJB read in the Ponden library. Nor does the legal knowledge

416   NOTES TO PAGES 276–86

displayed in *WH* seem more than basic and could, perhaps, have been gathered from a conversation or a newspaper?

It is worth noting that EJB took charge, if that is quite the term, of the financial investments in the railways consequent on the sisters' inheritances from Aunt Branwell. The income for 1846 (£305 10/-) was more than twice that of 1845 (£116 18/4d). This material is recovered from EJB's much mutilated account booklet, begun sometime before 1845. See Hewish, p. 90. But Barker notes that EJB's 'taking charge' did not involve action: 'Emily's management seems to have consisted solely in leaving the money where it was; she made no attempt to spread the investment or put money into new ventures or different companies. By the time she and AB died, their capital was still invested exactly as it had been when Aunt Branwell first left it to them.' On 27 September 1849, CB complained to George Smith that her shares (from the inheritance from Aunt Branwell and possibly some of the £500 she received for *JE*) in the York & North Midland Railway had fallen in value: they had once yielded a dividend of 10% but now their value had fallen from the purchase price of £50 to £20 (*Letters*, ii.264).

p. 276 *quaker*: *1850* corrects to 'Quaker'.

Joseph, and I generally... a chapel: see note to p. 74, '*Seventy Times Seven...*'.

train-oil: from the boiled flesh of sea mammals, especially Right Whale blubber (this might well have been envisaged as coming from Whitby, a major whaling port at this point).

got up: *1850* restores the missing 'I' before this in *1847*.

p. 277 *hypocricy*: corrected in *1850*.

p. 281 *Chevy Chase*: a well-known Northumbrian ballad describing how the Scottish Earl Douglas disastrously mistakes a hunting party led by Percy, Earl of Northumberland, in the Cheviot Hills for an invasion of Scotland. In the ensuing fight, the Earl Douglas is killed. Cf. Landseer's *The Hunting of Chevy Chase* (1825–6), now in Birmingham Museum and Art Gallery (and cf. note to p. 190, '*faithful dog*').

enjyoments: corrected in *1850*.

p. 284 *glens*: the Scottish term rather than the Yorkshire 'dales'.

p. 285 *mensful*: menseful: '*English regional* (*northern*), *Scottish*, and *Irish English* (*northern*). Proper, seemly, decent, discreet; polite, well-mannered, hospitable; neat, tidy', *OED*.

p. 286 *Aw'd rayther, by th' haulf,...rullers!*: 'I'd rather, by the half, have them swearing in my ears from morning till night, than hear you, howsoever!' [...] 'It is a blazing shame, but I cannot open the Blessed Book, but you set up those glories to Satan, and all the dreadful wickedness that were ever born into the world. Oh, you're a right good-for-nothing; and she's another; and that poor lad will be lost between you. Poor lad!' [...] 'He's bewitched, I am certain of it. O Lord, judge them, for there's neither law nor justice among their rulers!'

christian: corrected in *1850* to 'Christian'.

Fairy Annie's Wedding: this is now recognized as a misprint (uncorrected in *1850*) for the song 'Fair Annie' (see the article cited below and its own notes). For a version of this song's text, see Helen Child Sargent and George Lyman Kittredge, eds., *English and Scottish Popular Ballads edited from the Collection of Francis James Childs* (Boston: Houghton Mifflin/Cambridge University Press, 1904), pp. 120–1. The story

NOTES TO PAGES 286–95   417

is of a woman who bears to a Lord seven children though he does not marry her, intending instead to marry another woman called Jane. But Jane, it turns out, is Annie's sister, who departs, leaving some of her marriage portion to Annie. Although the song does not make this explicit, it seems to invite the listener to believe that Annie weds her children's father (or rather the other way around) in the end.

Colin Wilcockson pointed out, in ' "Fair(y) Annie's Wedding": A Note on *Wuthering Heights*', *Essays in Criticism*, 33 (1983), pp. 259–61, that 'The ballad-story is that a lord loves a woman, makes plans to marry her sister, but finally returns to the original woman. Ellen Dean is preoccupied with a real ["real"] story about a man who passionately loves a woman, subsequently marries her sister-in-law, but is finally reunited with the ghost of his first love' (p. 260).

p. 287 *jocks*: drinks.

reaming: 'Chiefly *Scottish* and *Irish English* (*northern*). 1. *intransitive*. To froth or foam; (of a vessel) to be full of a frothy liquid', *OED*.

p. 289 *automatons*: in the earlier sense, as *OED* describes, of 'A moving device having a concealed mechanism, so it appears to operate spontaneously. Frequently (and in earliest use) in figurative and similative contexts'. *OED* gives 1616 as the first recorded source.

On Easter Monday, Joseph went to Gimmerton fair: Haworth held, as it still does, a fair on Easter Monday.

p. 290 *side out of t' gait*: 'get out of the way'. See note to p. 74, '*gait*'.

p. 293 *black currant trees*: blackcurrant bushes, *Ribes nigrum*, are meant, or 'shrubs', as they are called on p. 294. Cf. Clement Shorter's comment: 'the house [Parsonage] still retains its essentially interesting features. In the time of the Brontës, it is true, the front outlook was as desolate as to-day it is attractive. Then there was a little piece of barren ground running down to the walls of the churchyard, with here and there a currant-bush as the sole adornment', *Charlotte Brontë and Her Circle* (London: Hodder and Stoughton, 1896), p. 59. Cf. p. 25.

p. 294 *Aw mun hev my wage… in th' road!*: 'I must have my wages and I must go! I *had* aimed to die where I'd served for sixty years; and I thought I'd lug my books up into the garret, and all my bits of stuff, so they should have the kitchen to themselves, for the sake of quietness. It was hard to give up my own hearthstone, but I thought I *could* do that! But, no, she's taken my garden from me, and by the heart! Master, I cannot stand it! You must bend to the yoke, and you will—*I* am not used to it and an old man doesn't soon get used to new burdens—I'd rather earn my bit, and my supper, with a hammer in the road!'

It's noan Nelly!… i' t' garden!: 'It is not Nelly' […] 'I wouldn't leave for Nelly— Nasty, grim nothing as she is. Thank God, *she* cannot poison anyone's soul. She was never so good-looking that anyone would look at her without being surprised [at her beauty]. It that dreadful, graceless queen, who has bewitched our lad with her bold eyes and her forward ways—till—No! It nearly breaks my heart. He's forgotten all I have done for him, and taught him, and gone and pulled up a whole row of the best currant bushes in the garden!'

p. 295 *Catherine, and he'll soon detest you*: corrected in *1850* to 'Catherine; "and he'll soon detest you'.

418 NOTES TO PAGES 297–308

p. 297 *mattocks*: mattock is '[a] tool similar to a pick but with a point or chisel edge at one end of the head and an adze-like blade at the other, used for breaking up hard ground, grubbing up trees, etc.', *OED*.

strange change: cf. CB writing to Ellen Nussey on 9 October 1848:

> The past three weeks have been a dark interval in our humble home. Branwell's constitution had been failing fast all the summer—but still, neither the Doctors nor himself thought him so near his end as he was—he was entirely confined to his bed but for one single day—and was in the village two days before his death.
>
> He died, after 20 minutes' struggle, on Sunday Morning, 24th Septbr. He was perfectly conscious till the last agony came on—His mind had undergone the peculiar change which frequently precedes death, two days previously—the calm of better feelings filled it—a return of natural affection marked his last moments—he is in God's hands now—and the all-powerful—is likewise the all-merciful—a deep conviction that he rests at last—rests well after his brief, erring, suffering, feverish life fills and quiets my mind now.
>
> *Letters*, ii.125–6 (there is an adapted version in *LCB*, ii.62).

p. 298 *I have lost her*: cf. 'Remembrance', pp. 33–4.

p. 300 *chosing*: corrected in *1850*.

him, then,' "I: stray punctuation marks regularized in *1850*.

p. 302 *vampire*: *1998* observes: 'Goethe's [*Die*] *Braut von Korinth* ([" The Bride of Corinth"] 1797) was largely responsible for the vogue for vampires in European literature during the succeeding decades. Ellen Dean may be supposed to have "read of such hideous, incarnate demons" in [Byron's] *The Giaour* [1813] and elsewhere' (p. 360). John William Polidori (1795–1821), Byron's physician and uncle of D.G., C.G., and W.M. Rossetti, published 'The Vampyre: A Tale' in *The New Monthly Magazine and Universal Register* in April 1819. The story (which was first mistakenly ascribed to Byron) defined early elements of the vampire legend for English fiction. Jane in *JE* says to Rochester concerning the 'apparition' of Bertha Mason:

> 'Shall I tell you of what it reminded me?'
> 'You may.'
> 'Of the foul German spectre—the Vampyre.'
>
> ii.274.

p. 305 *annihiliate*: corrected in *1850*.

p. 306 *The lattice, flapping to and fro...broken skin*: both a recollection of the folklore tradition that the soul leaves the body through windows and of Lockwood's terrifying dream of breaking Catherine's skin on broken window glass (p. 76).

p. 308 *satan*: 'Satan' in *1850*.

I lingered round them,... quiet earth: a notable example of how *1850* subtly modified EJB's prose rhythms, here, by changing semi-colons to commas: 'I lingered round them, under that benign sky: watched the moths fluttering among the heath and harebells, listened to the soft wind breathing through the grass, and wondered how any one could ever imagine unquiet slumbers for the sleepers in that quiet earth.'

NOTES TO PAGE 311

APPENDICES

I. CURRER BELL [CHARLOTTE BRONTË]'S ACCOUNTS IN *'WUTHERING HEIGHTS' AND 'AGNES GREY'. BY ELLIS AND ACTON BELL. A NEW EDITION REVISED, WITH A BIOGRAPHICAL NOTICE OF THE AUTHORS, A SELECTION FROM THEIR LITERARY REMAINS, AND A PREFACE, BY CURRER BELL (1850)*

Currer Bell [Charlotte Brontë],
'Biographical Notice of Ellis and
Acton Bell' (1850)

Included in *1850*. CB wrote to W.S. Williams on 20 September 1850 with a rough draft of the Notice, asking him to decide whether it should be called a 'Notice' or a 'Memoir', preferring the first. *Letters*, ii.473–4.

p. 311 *It has been thought... person*: cf. 'Our Library Table', which said of *WH* and *Agnes Grey*, 'Here are two tales so nearly related to "Jane Eyre" in cast of thought, incident, and language as to excite some curiosity. All three might be the work of one hand,—but the first issued [*JE*] remains the best', *The Athenæum*, 1052 (25 December 1847), pp. 1324–5 (p. 1324). *Tait's Edinburgh Magazine*, 15 (December 1848), pp. 860–1 added that *JE* and *WH* 'appeared to be written by one hand' (p. 860).

JE was issued by the London publishers Smith, Elder on 16 October 1847; *WH* and *Agnes Grey* in December (the exact date is unknown though by 14 December copies had reached the authors). Presumably, Newby was waiting to see what the reception of *JE* was like?

Cf. CB's letter to W.S. Williams, 31 July 1848: 'Permit me to caution you not to speak of my sisters [note 's' underlined] when you write to me—I mean do not use the word in the plural. "Ellis Bell" will not endure to be alluded to under any other appellation than the "nom de plume". I committed a grave error in betraying ~~her~~ "his" identity to you and Mr. Smith—it was inadvertent—the words "we are three sisters" escaped me before I was aware—I regretted the avowal the moment I had made it; I regret it bitterly now, for I find it is against every feeling and intention of "Ellis Bell" ', *Letters*, ii.94. For a recollection of the breaking of the anonymity, see George M. Smith, 'Charlotte Brontë', *Cornhill Magazine*, 9 (December 1900), pp. 778–95. See also 'Note on the Text', p. xlix.

Note that the non-alphabetical arrangement of the names is because the order is chronological by date of birth; the poems themselves are broadly arranged in the same way. The tricky question of the selection and editing of *1846* is expertly discussed by Derek Roper, 'The Revision of Emily Brontë's Poems of 1846', *The Library*, 6 (1984), pp. 153–67.

This mistake I... 'Jane Eyre': the Preface to the third edition of *JE* reads:

> I avail myself of the opportunity which a third edition of JANE EYRE affords me, of again addressing a word to the Public, to explain that my claim to the title of novelist rests on this one work alone. If, therefore, the authorship of other works of fiction has been attributed to me, an honour is awarded where it is not merited; and consequently, denied where it is justly due.

420   NOTES TO PAGES 311–13

This explanation will serve to rectify mistakes which may already have been made, and to prevent future errors.

CURRER BELL.

April 13th, 1848.

p. 311 *About five years ago, ... home*: AB resigned her position at Thorp Green in June 1845 and returned to Haworth, where EJB already was. CB had returned from her second stay in Brussels at the end of 1844.

p. 312 *Messrs. Chambers, of Edinburgh*: W. & R. Chambers was founded by the brothers William and Robert Chambers in Edinburgh in 1832. They were best known for *Chambers's Encyclopaedia* (1859–1979). Robert, though the Brontës could not have known this, was the (anonymous) author of the widely discussed *Vestiges of the Natural History of Creation* (1844).

the worth of these poems... criticism: misleading as far as the reviews are concerned, though the sales figures of the first edition (two copies sold) are no doubt of what CB is thinking. *Tait's Edinburgh Magazine*, as cited in the note above to p. 311, was simply divided:

> The little volume of poems bears the impress of one mind. If there have been three of the family engaged on this thin book, they must be marvellously alike.
>
> The poetry is not much liked by us, but we have heard it greatly praised by others[.]

p. 860.

narrative in one volume: *The Professor: A Tale* was eventually published, posthumously, by Smith, Elder in 1857. CB scrambles the chronology here.

p. 313 *One writer, endowed...faults*: CB refers, with strange lack of detail, to the article 'Currer Bell', *Palladium* (September 1850), pp. 161–75. The reviewer—Sydney Dobell—regards all the Bell novels as by Currer Bell, starting with *WH*. The analysis of *WH* is long and includes these words:

> [...] [One] looks back at the whole story as to a world of brilliant figures in an atmosphere of mist; shapes that come out upon the eye, and burn their colours into the brain, and depart into the enveloping fog. It is the unformed writing of a giant's hand; the 'large utterance' of a baby god. In the sprawlings of the infant Hercules, however, there must have been attitudes from which the statuary might model. In the early efforts of unusual genius, there are not seldom unconscious felicities which mature years may look back upon with envy. The child's hand wanders over the strings. It cannot combine them in the chords and melodies of manhood; but its separate notes are perfect in themselves, and perhaps sound all the sweeter for the Aeolian discords from which they come.
>
> We repeat, that there are passages in this book of 'Wuthering Heights' of which any novelist, past or present, might be proud. Open the first volume at the fourteenth page, and read to the sixty-first. There are few things in modern prose to surpass these pages for native power. We cannot praise too warmly the brave simplicity, the unaffected air of intense belief, the admirable combination of extreme likelihood with the rarest originality, the nice provision of the possible even in the highest effects of the supernatural, the easy strength and instinct of keeping with

NOTES TO PAGES 313–16

which the accessory circumstances are grouped, the exquisite but unconscious art with which the chiaroscuro of the whole is managed, and the ungenial frigidity of place, time, weather, and persons, is made to heighten the unspeakable pathos of one ungovernable outburst.

The *thinking-out* of some of these pages—of pp. 52, 53, and 60 [pp. 103, 104, and 110]—is the masterpiece of a poet, rather than the hybrid creation of the novelist. The mass of readers will probably yawn over the whole; but, in the memory of those whose remembrance makes *fame*, the images in these pages will live— when every word that conveyed them is forgotten—as a recollection of *things heard and seen*. This is the highest triumph of description; and perhaps every creation of the fancy is more or less faulty, so long as, in a mind fitted to reproduce them, the images co-exist only with the words that called them up [...].

p. 166.

p. 313 *"writing on the wall"*: CB refers, strangely given the context, to the narrative of King Belshazzar, son of Nebuchadnezzar, in Daniel 5. The fingers of a man's hand write on the plaster of the palace wall the words 'MENE, MENE, TEKEL, UPHARSIN' (v. 25) and the King 'cried aloud to bring in the astrologers, the Chaldeans, and the soothsayers' (v. 7) of Babylon to interpret them. The interpretation—a fearful warning to Belshazzar—is given by Daniel:

> [26] This is the interpretation of the thing: MENE; God hath numbered thy kingdom, and finished it. [27] TEKEL; Thou art weighed in the balances, and art found wanting. [28] PERES; Thy kingdom is divided, and given to the Medes and Persians. [29] Then commanded Belshazzar, and they clothed Daniel with scarlet, and put a chain of gold about his neck, and made a proclamation concerning him, that he should be the third ruler in the kingdom. [30] In that night was Belshazzar the king of the Chaldeans slain.

p. 314 *equivoque*: *OED* B.3: 'Ambiguity of speech; double meaning in words or phrases used'. All examples/sources given in *OED* are from the 19thc.

talents misused and faculties abused: Branwell.

They were both prepared to try again: some evidence, perhaps, of the idea that EJB had a second novel in mind.

In the very heat and burden of the day: Matthew 20:12.

p. 315 *veins of a hero*: Cf. M. Héger's memory of EJB, note to p. 333, *'her powerful reason...'*.

p. 316 *gravestones*: interestingly protective/distracting/distracted, perhaps, as this suggests that both EJB and AB are buried in a churchyard. AB is indeed: in that of St Mary's Church, Scarborough. EJB, however, lies in a vault in St Michael and All Angels', Haworth. Cf. Matthew Arnold's 'Haworth Churchyard', pp. 322–7 and note to p. 322.

Currer Bell [Charlotte Brontë], 'Selections from the Literary Remains of Ellis and Acton Bell' (1850)

Included in *1850*.

p. 316 *It has been already said*: see pp. 311–12.

422   NOTES TO PAGES 316–17

p. 316 *At that period she was sent to school*: in 1824, at the age of six, EJB was sent to the Clergy Daughters' School, Cowan Bridge, with her sisters Charlotte, Maria, and Elizabeth (the latter two both shortly died). The choice of this school was largely consequent on Patrick's poverty. It was this institution, run by the Revd William Carus Wilson (1791–1859), which CB criticized in *JE*. We know little for certain about EJB's time in the school, though Chitham dates her sense of guilt to her 'complicity, even if only slightly, in the degradation and death of her eldest sister [Maria on 6 May 1825]', p. 59. Cowan Bridge is 2½ miles South East of Kirby Lonsdale and, on a direct road, 38 miles from Keighley. The building, now called Brontë School Cottage, is currently a holiday let.

But CB means EJB's brief time at Roe Head, Mirfield, when she was seventeen. CB herself had been a pupil at Roe Head from January 1831 and subsequently returned to teach: 'When Charlotte returned to Roe Head as a teacher in July 1835, Emily [...] went with her as a pupil, the first occasion she had left home since Cowan Bridge. This time, however, at seventeen, she was not the youngest but probably much the oldest pupil. With her intense reserve, social awkwardness, and lack of conventional education, it was not surprising that she stood out from the crowd and was miserable. Worst of all, the discipline of the school day and the mind-numbing boredom of rote learning left her little time or energy to indulge in the Gondal fantasy which had become an absolute necessity to her. After only three months at school, she became so ill that her father recalled her to Haworth and her place at Roe Head was taken by the more pliant Anne', *ODNB*.

Roe Head School, 22 miles South West of Leeds, was run by Margaret Wooler, and it was where CB met Ellen Nussey and Mary Taylor, important friends. It is now Holly Bank Trust's Special School.

CB completely erases EJB's time, from September 1838 to around spring 1839 as a teacher at Law Hill School. See notes to pp. 8 and 61–2, '*Wuthering...*'. As the account continues, CB asserts that EJB could not bear to be away from the moors and the Parsonage, and so had to be returned. Whatever the truth about this period, the idea of EJB fading because she was without the moors has persisted as a powerful conception. Note that CB said in a letter perhaps addressed to W.S. Williams on 22 May 1850: 'My sister Emily had a particular love for them [the moors], and there is not a knoll of heather, not a branch of fern, not a young bilberry leaf not a fluttering lark or linnet but reminds me of her', *Letters*, ii.403. Cf. Introduction, p. xviii.

Law Hill was also a working farm, and EJB must have been—like her characters at Wuthering Heights—in daily proximity with the animals. The role of the school in EJB's imagination interested early Brontë scholars from the beginning: cf. Thomas Keyworth, 'A New Identification of "Wuthering Heights"', *The Bookman*, 3 (March 1893), pp. 183–5. Law Hill School is now Law Hill House, a private residence.

single half-year: Cowan Bridge School. See note to p. 65, '*I dine...*'.

Imagination: cf. pp. xxi–xxvi.

'*purple light*': from Coleridge's 'Song of the Pixies' in its 1797 version.

p. 317 *she went with me to an establishment on the continent*: EJB was in Brussels with CB for 9 months from February 1842. Aunt Branwell (Elizabeth Branwell, b. 1776) died unexpectedly on 29 October 1842, prompting the return of CB and EJB to

NOTES TO PAGES 317-22

Haworth, though they missed the funeral (it was not usually custom, though, for ladies to attend funerals). EJB, it seems, had no desire to accompany CB on her return to Brussels on 27 January 1843.

p. 317 *Jesuitry*: CB makes Paul Emmanuel 'a sort of lay Jesuit' in *Villette*, iii.90.

The following pieces...schoolroom: the MS dates of these poems are 1838, when EJB was twenty. The school is Law Hill School. See notes to pp. 8 and 61–2, '*Wuthering...*'. Cf. CB's 'The Teacher's Monologue', in *The Complete Poems of Charlotte Brontë*, pp. 48–50.

Currer Bell [Charlotte Brontë], Editor's Preface to the new edition of *Wuthering Heights* (1850)

Part of *1850*, both titles are used.

p. 317 *I HAVE just read over "Wuthering Heights,"*: a somewhat misleading statement as it seems to imply that CB has merely reread the text and, in turn, reproduced it untouched in *1850*. Her interventions are unmentioned.

p. 318 *hinds*: a 'hind' in the sense of 'servant; esp., in later use, a farm servant, an agricultural labourer', *OED*.

p. 319 *"a horror of great darkness"*: Genesis 15:12. Reviewing *1850*, and concentrating on *WH*, *The Leader* noted: 'And yet, although there is a want of air and light in the picture we cannot deny its truth; sombre, rude, brutal, yet true. The fierce ungoverned instincts of powerful organizations, bred up amidst violence, revolt, and moral apathy, are here seen in operation; such brutes we should all be, or the most of us, were our lives as insubordinate to law; were our affections and sympathies as little cultivated, our imaginations as undirected. And herein lies the moral of the book, though most people will fail to draw the moral from very irritation at it', *The Leader* (28 December 1850), p. 953 (p. 953).

p. 320 *"the little black-haired...Devil"*: this line is not in *WH*. CB is presumably thinking somewhat hazily of the sentence on p. 84, 'though it's as dark almost as if it came from the devil'.

"to sneer at her attempt to close them...too": misquoted from p. 306.

Afreet: 'In Arabian and Muslim mythology: a powerful jinn or demon. Also in extended use', *OED*.

"harrow the valleys...furrow": cf. Job 39:10, 'Canst thou bind the unicorn with his band in the furrow? or will he harrow the valleys after thee?'

"laughs at the multitude of the city...driver": cf. Job 39:7, 'He scorneth the multitude of the city, neither regardeth he the crying of the driver.'

Tisiphone: Τισιφόνη, one of the three Erinyes, or avenging furies, of ancient Greece. She punished murderers.

II. EARLY POEMS ABOUT EMILY BRONTË

Charlotte Brontë, 'On the Death of Emily Jane Brontë' (1848)

p. 322 *Charlotte Brontë, 'On the Death of Emily Jane Brontë'*: from *The Complete Poems of Charlotte Brontë*, pp. 209–10. The poem is dated 24 December 1848 (EJB died on the 19th).

424   NOTES TO PAGES 322–3

'A' [Matthew Arnold], 'Haworth Churchyard, April 1855' (1855)

p. 322 *'A' [Matthew Arnold*], *'Haworth Churchyard, April 1855'*: first published in *Fraser's Magazine*, 51 (May 1855), pp. 527–30 and subsequently revised for *Poems by Matthew Arnold*, 2 vols (London: Macmillan, 1877), ii.239–44. This is the original version. Arnold had obviously not been told that CB—to say nothing of EJB or AB—had been interred in the family vault inside St Michael's, and believed her to be buried in the churchyard. Cf. CB's 'The Churchyard', *The Complete Poems of Charlotte Brontë*, pp. 76–7, on the death of Maria Brontë. Cf. also the note to p. 316, '*gravestones*'.

l. 1 *Loughrigg*: Loughrigg Fell, in the English Lake District, near Ambleside.

l. 2 *Rotha*: the River Rothay in the Lake District. It flows close to the churchyard of St Oswald's, Grasmere, where Wordsworth is buried. Cf. Arnold's 'Memorial Verses: April, 1850' (June 1850) on the grave of Wordsworth.

l. 5 *Wordsworth's son-in-law*: Edward Quillinan (1791–1851), Irish soldier, poet, and novelist, who married Dora Wordsworth (1804–47), the poet's daughter, on 11 May 1841. Cf. Arnold's 'Stanzas in Memory of Edward Quillinan' (publ. 1853).

ll. 8–9 *Two friends met there, two fam'd | Gift'd women*: CB and the novelist, political and social theorist, Harriet Martineau (1802–76), who had moved into The Knoll, Ambleside, in 1846 (the house has now been converted into a holiday rental).

ll. 12–13 *feign'd | History of passionate life: JE*, one assumes, though the description would also fit *Villette*.

ll. 15–16 *her praise | First in Fiction*: Martineau's first works had, in fact, been in political economy and what would now be called sociology. She published *Deerbrook: A Novel* (London: Moxon, 1839) to acclaim. *The Athenæum*, referring to one of her earlier publications, remarked: 'In the "Illustrations of Political Economy [1832–3]," Miss Martineau gave tokens, not merely of close observation of character, and a strong poetical feeling for nature, but also of such creative and dramatic power, as made us look forward with interest to a novel from her hands [...] and naturally, therefore, [we] expected, in this her more mature effort, a work of fiction whose vitality and freshness should put to shame the feverish and conventional things, which are thrust upon us by the hundred, as pictures of human life. Such a work, though not in every point equalling our expectations, is the novel before us', '"Deerbrook: A Novel" ', *The Athenæum*, 597 (1 April 1839), pp. 254–6 (p. 254).

ll. 24–6 *Scott had consign'd there ... death-stricken hand*: Sir Walter Scott had added some verses to Quillinan's album, which belonged at that point to Dora Wordsworth, at Abbotsford on 22 September 1831.

ll. 27–8 *I beheld; the obscure | Saw the famous*: replaced in the revised version of 1877 with 'Hope at that meeting smiled fair'.

ll. 32–3 *The elder, to-day, | Lies expecting from Death*: in fact, Harriet Martineau died on 27 June 1876, necessitating Arnold, in republishing the poem, to revise it. But she had suffered severely for a long time. First, in 1838, when she had collapsed at Venice. *ODNB* notes: 'The problem was a prolapsed uterus almost certainly caused by an ovarian cyst. She moved to Newcastle to be near her doctor, her brother-in-law T.M. Greenhow (1791–1881), and eventually took up residence in rented rooms in

NOTES TO PAGES 323–7

Tynemouth, where after 1842 she was largely confined to her couch. Despite the debility and frequent suffering, she led an active philanthropic and literary life and entertained a stream of visitors. The experience was turned to account in *Life in the Sickroom* ([London: Moxon,] 1844), an inspirational and instructive volume for other sufferers that evoked much admiration and almost equal hostility.'

Arnold, however, is referring to a later problem, described by *ODNB* as follows: 'In 1855 Harriet Martineau had been once more stricken with illness, caused, she believed, by heart disease—a not inaccurate, but insufficient, diagnosis. She died on 27 June 1876 at The Knoll, Ambleside. The attending physician gave as the cause of death fatty degeneration of the heart and an ovarian tumour; the tumour, which the autopsy showed to be of enormous size, had grown, severely compressing and distending the internal organs and producing the symptoms that reduced her to invalidism in the last twenty years of her life. She remained mentally alert and an excellent correspondent almost to the moment of death.'

l. 89 *colliers' carts*: on the history of coal mining in and near Keighley, see M.C. Gill, *Keighley Coal: A History of Coal Mining in the Keighley District* (Keighley: Northern Mine Research Society, 2004), available at https://www.nmrs.org.uk/assets/lookinside/bm74lookinside.pdf.

l. 90 *Poach*: in *OED*'s sense II.4 '*intransitive*. To sink into wet heavy ground in walking; to make slow progress over soft ground, or through mud or mire; to tramp heavily; to trample. Now chiefly British regional.'

l. 95 *Lonely and bleak*: in fact the church was (and its replacement still is) essentially at the top of the high street (Main Street), so not 'lonely'; and the Parsonage was, and still is, slightly above and beyond the churchyard, rather than 'at its side'. Note that the church Patrick knew was largely demolished and rebuilt between 1879 and 1881 (the original tower remains). There are current plans to open the Brontë vault to visitors.

l. 107 *Another grief I see*: CB's widower, the Revd Arthur Bell Nicholls (1819–1906).

l. 154 *Round thee they lie*: again, somewhat odd inexactness, and one wonders why Arnold did not check the details. EJB lies within the family vault and AB at Scarborough.

l. 165 *too-bold dying song*: Arnold added a note to this: 'See the last verses by Emily Brontë in *Poems by Currer, Ellis, and Acton Bell*.' This would seem to indicate that he meant 'The Old Stoic': see p. 57. But presumably he is actually thinking of *1850* and of 'No coward soul is mine' together with CB's assertion that they were the 'last lines' that EJB wrote: see p. 26 and note.

ll. 167–77 *Of one too I have heard...interpos'd*: it is possible, perhaps, that Arnold's vagueness about Branwell—who is, indeed, buried in the family vault and not in the churchyard—is deliberate to avoid addressing a difficult subject.

ll. 178–90 *Sleep, O cluster of friends...repose*: this somewhat evasive ending might have been suggested by memories of the last paragraph of *WH* (see p. 308). In 1877, Arnold added the following 'Epilogue':

> So I sang; but the Muse,
> Shaking her head, took the harp—
> Stern interrupted my strain,
> Angrily smote on the chords.

426   NOTES TO PAGES 327–9

April showers
Rush o'er the Yorkshire moors.
Stormy, through driving mist,
Loom the blurred hills; the rain
Lashes the newly-made grave.

Unquiet souls!
—In the dark fermentation of earth,
In the never idle workshop of nature,
In the eternal movement,
Ye shall find yourselves again!

Francis William Lauderdale Adams, 'To Emily Brontë' (1887)

p. 327 *Francis William Lauderdale Adams, 'To Emily Brontë'*: Adams (1862–93) was an English socialist school teacher, who published poetry, fiction, and periodical essays, and is best known for his volume *Songs of the Army of the Night* (London: Reeves, 1888). 'To Emily Brontë' was included in *The Poetical Works of Francis W.L. Adams* (London: Griffith, Farran, 1887), though I have not been able to establish if it had been previously published.

Lionel Johnson, 'Brontë' (1890)

p. 328 *Lionel Johnson, 'Brontë'*: Lionel Johnson (1867–1902), English poet and critic, most notably of Thomas Hardy, and in the circle of the Rhymers of the Cheshire Cheese, Selwyn Image, W.B. Yeats, and the *Century Guild*. This poem was included in *Poems by Lionel Johnson* (London: Elkin Mathews, 1895).

Hubert Crackanthorpe: Hubert Montague Crackanthorpe (1870–96) was an English writer most notably of short fiction in a manner suggestive of Henry James and touched by Aestheticism and Decadence. *ODNB* aptly observes: 'His work is often grouped among the coterie of other talented writers from the 1890s who died young, a roster that includes such figures as Francis Adams [see previous poem], Aubrey Beardsley, Ernest Dowson, Lionel Johnson, and H. D. Lowry.' Crackanthorpe was found drowned in the River Seine, Paris, at the age of twenty-six.

l. 6 *Celtic name*: Patrick's Irish family name (in its Anglicized version) had been Brunty/Prunty with or without an O'. βροντή (bronte) is Greek for thunder.

l. 13 *Stoic*: cf. 'The Old Stoic', p. 57.

l. 33 *Thou too*: CB.

l. 52 *hard-hewn*: Johnson is perhaps taking his cue from CB's much quoted assertion that '"Wuthering Heights" was hewn in a wild workshop': see p. 320.

l. 53 *blaunched*: 'blanched' in archaic form (*OED*'s last example comes from 1601).

l. 54 *purple fields*: cf. CB's 'The eye of the gazer must itself brim with a "purple light," intense enough to perpetuate the brief flower-flush of August on the heather, or the sunset smile of June', p. 316 and note.

l. 60 *Silent and sleeping, free at last*: cf. the end of 'The Old Stoic', p. 57.

NOTES TO PAGES 329–32 427

Stephen Phillips, 'Emily Brontë' (1913)

p. 329 *Stephen Phillips, 'Emily Brontë'*: this poem was included in Stephen Phillips (1864–1915), *Lyrics and Dramas* (London: John Lane/The Bodley Head, 1913), though I have not been able to establish if it had been previously published. Phillips was an English actor of considerable importance, poet, and novelist.

l. 6 *Holding so fast a God for all the creeds?*: cf. 'No coward soul is mine', ll. 9–10 (p. 26).

l. 13 *English dew*: cf. the fact that EJB was half Irish.

l. 15 *glean*: cf. Keats' opening two lines of the sonnet, 'When I have fears' (1818): 'When I have fears that I may cease to be | Before my pen has gleaned my teeming brain [...]'.

l. 19 *Missolonghi*: Byron died at Missolonghi, on the Gulf of Patras, Greece, on 19 April 1824.

l. 22 *thrilled*: in *OED*'s sense 3.a.: '*transitive*. To cause (a lance, dart, or the like) to pass; to dart, hurl (a piercing weapon). *Obsolete*. Perhaps sometimes including a notion of the quivering motion of the missile.' All *OED*'s examples are from the 17thc (e.g., '1609 T. Heywood *Troia Britanica* xiii. lxx He thrild a Iavelin at the Dardans brest').

Robert Bridges, 'Emily Brontë' (1923)

p. 330 *Robert Bridges, 'Emily Brontë'*: Bridges (1844–1930) was an English poet, originally a doctor, who from 1913 till his death was Poet Laureate. This poem first appeared in the *London Mercury*, 8 (June 1923), p. 120. Volume 9 of Bridges' posthumously issued *The Collected Essays, Papers, etc. of Robert Bridges*, 30 parts in 10 volumes (London: Oxford University Press, 1923–34) was *The Poems of Emily Brontë* (1932).

'*Du hast Diamanten*': the first line of LXII from Heinrich Heine, *Buch der Lieder: Die Heimkehr* ([*Book of Songs: The Homecoming*] 1823–4). In the edition of *Buch der Lieder*, edited by John Lees (London: Longmans, Green, 1920), the lyric appears on p. 110. 'You have diamonds'.

l. 11 *Francis*: St Francis of Assisi (1181/1182–3 October 1226), half-French, half-Italian saint deeply venerated across western Christendom. He relinquished the benefits of his prosperous birth to become a mendicant friar and to found religious orders. It is curious to think that Bridges has recast EJB's famous 'reserve' into 'humility', a rather different thing. But the poem more generally Christianizes EJB in a way her family would have no doubt felt well-intentioned but baffling.

III. THE FIRST CRITICISM

George Barnett Smith, from 'The Brontës' (1873/5)

First published in *The Cornhill Magazine*, 28 (July 1873), pp. 54–71 and reprinted in Smith's *Poets and Novelists: A Series of Literary Studies* (London: Smith, Elder, 1875), pp. 209–50. George Barnett Smith (1841–1909) was an English journalist, biographer, historian, and literary critic.

p. 332 '*Reason with him, and when...whip him*': from *LCB*, i.59.

he could converse with his daughter...years of age: *LCB*, i.60: 'They took a vivid interest in the public characters, and the local and the foreign as well as home

428 NOTES TO PAGES 332–5

politics discussed in the newspapers. Long before Maria Brontë died, at the age of eleven, her father used to say he could converse with her on any of the leading topics of the day with as much freedom and pleasure as with any grown-up person.'

p. 332 *Charlotte Brontë was...agony*: This sentence was changed from the original publication: "Early familiar with all the forms of suffering and death, the life of Charlotte Bronte from its commencement to its close may be said to have been one prolonged endurance of agony."

She went from home twice...Brussels: on the strange omission here, and elsewhere, of EJB's time at Law Hill, see notes to pp. 8 and 61–2, '*Wuthering...*'. Smith is following *LCB*, which is no doubt following CB.

p. 333 '*her powerful reason...life*': *LCB*, i.254. This is an extract from a much-quoted passage:

> He [M. Héger] seems to have rated Emily's genius as something even higher than Charlotte's; and her estimation of their relative powers was the same. Emily had a head for logic, and a capability of argument, unusual in a man, and rare indeed in a woman, according to M. Héger. Impairing the force of this gift, was a stubborn tenacity of will, which rendered her obtuse to all reasoning where her own wishes, or her own sense of right, was concerned. 'She should have been a man—a great navigator,' said M. Héger in speaking of her. 'Her powerful reason would have deduced new spheres of discovery from the knowledge of the old; and her strong imperious will would never have been daunted by opposition or difficulty; never have given way but with life.' And yet, moreover, her faculty of imagination was such that, if she had written a history, her view of scenes and characters would have been so vivid, and so powerfully expressed, and supported by such a show of argument, that it would have dominated over the reader, whatever might have been his previous opinions, or his cooler perceptions of its truth. But she appeared egotistical and exacting compared to Charlotte, who was always unselfish (this is M. Héger's testimony); and in the anxiety of the elder to make her younger sister contented she allowed her to exercise a kind of unconscious tyranny over her.
>
> *LCB*, i.253–4.

lose in beauty: I have been unable to trace the source of this assertion.

'*Her native hills were...produce*': see p. 318.

Branwell whose will was so strong...so die: from *LCB*, ii.78. See p. xxv n.27.

Charlotte Brontë in her digest of this character...Earnshaw: see p. 320.

p. 334 *believing himself alone...at last!*: an odd mis-remembering of one of the most powerful scenes in the novel. See p. 79.

I have no more business...being: see p. 117. Smith must be using *1850* or its successors but, whatever the case, the transcription is inaccurate.

Kiss me again...me: see p. 179.

A great deal has been said on the question...defence for it: see pp. 318–20.

p. 335 '*the writer who possesses the creative gift...itself*': see p. 320.

A. Mary F. Robinson, '"Wuthering Heights": Its Origins' (1883)

Chapter XIV from A. Mary F. Robinson's *Emily Brontë* in the 'Eminent Women Series' (London: W.H. Allen, 1883), reviewed as a whole by A.C. Swinburne in the

NOTES TO PAGES 335–40

next text (pp. 342–8). Agnes Mary Frances Robinson (1857–1944) was a prolific English writer, translator, poet, and novelist. This was the first book-length biography of EJB.

p. 335 *furious thwarted passion for a mistress ... marry*: see notes to pp. 18, ll. 21–4 and 37, l. 11.

"Conquered good and conquering ill.": see p. 33, l. 55.

"I am bound to avow ... amenable": see p. 319.

p. 337 *no assertion of ... rest*: this statement does not sit easily with the last paragraphs of *WH*.

that good for goodness' sake ... detestable: a notable effort to give *WH* a moral framework it does not have.

always hearing evil of Dissenters: Robinson, here, as elsewhere, is speculating.

Frederick Maurice: John Frederick Denison [F.D.] Maurice (1805–72), Anglican clergyman, prolific author on theological topics, and Cambridge professor. A founder of so-called Christian Socialism and of the Working Men's College. Robinson gives no source for this unlikely assertion.

p. 338 *"Lascar or Gipsy"*: see p. 320.

"gibberish that nobody could understand.": see p. 84 and note.

"I wondered how any one could ever imagine ... earth": see p. 308.

p. 339 *tales of 1798*: as well as the possible influence of Tabby's stories of Yorkshire, Patrick Brontë's narratives of Ireland and of Yorkshire life might lie somewhere at the starting point of *WH*, Gondal, etc. Cf. Ellen Nussey's recollection:

> Mr Brontë at times would relate strange stories, which had been told to him by some of the oldest inhabitants of the parish, of the extraordinary lives and doings of people who had resided in far-off, out-of-the-way places, but in contiguity with Haworth—stories which made one shiver and shrink from hearing; but they were full of grim humour and interest to Mr Brontë and his children, as revealing the characteristics of a class in the human race, and as such Emily Brontë has stereotyped them in her *Wuthering Heights*.
>
> Harold Orel, ed., *The Brontës: Interviews and Recollections*
> (London: Macmillan, 1997), p. 27.

The Irish Rebellion of 1798, *Éirí Amach 1798*, was a short-lived uprising against British rule, and the British army, by Irish nationalists assisted by French forces. It marked an influential moment in the struggle for Irish freedom (as well as having, more immediately, a role to play in prompting the Acts of Union, 1800).

Henry Huntingdon: AB's dissolute husband in *The Tenant of Wildfell Hall* is Arthur Huntingdon.

Wemyss Reid: pronounced 'Weems'. Sir Thomas Wemyss Reid (1842–1905), newspaper editor, novelist, and biographer, had a long-standing interest in the Brontës. His works include *Charlotte Brontë: A Monograph* (London: Macmillan, 1877).

leveret: see note to p. 142.

p. 340 *hewn*: cf. note to p. 52.

Here ended Branwell's ... authorship: cf. note to p. 81, '*to*'.

infecte: 'morally corrupted', *OED* (archaic).

430 NOTES TO PAGES 341-2

p. 341 *Hoffman's tales*: see Introduction, pp. xix–xx.

p. 342 *that night on the river . . . dim*: a memory of CB reaching the ship very early in the morning on 28 January 1843 that would take her to Ostend on her return to Brussels, which is, it might be, dramatized in Chapter VI of *Villette*.

German book at night: again, there is no source given for this assertion. Cf. *LCB*'s famous passage:

> This physical suffering on Emily's part when absent from Haworth, after recurring several times under similar circumstances, became at length so much an acknowledged fact, that whichever was obliged to leave home, the sisters decided that Emily must remain there, where alone she could enjoy anything like good health. She left it twice again in her life; once going as teacher to a school in Halifax for six months, and afterwards accompanying Charlotte to Brussels for ten. When at home, she took the principal part of the cooking upon herself, and did all the household ironing; and after Tabby grew old and infirm, it was Emily who made all the bread for the family; and any one passing by the kitchen-door, might have seen her studying German out of an open book, propped up before her, as she kneaded the dough; but no study, however interesting, interfered with the goodness of the bread, which was always light and excellent. Books were, indeed, a very common sight in that kitchen; the girls were taught by their father theoretically, and by their aunt, practically, that to take an active part in all household work was, in their position, woman's simple duty; but in their careful employment of time, they found many an odd five minutes for reading while watching the cakes, and managed the union of two kinds of employment better than King Alfred.

i.150–1.

There can be no certainty that this is an accurate account; obviously, Elizabeth Gaskell had never met EJB.

Algernon Charles Swinburne, 'Emily Brontë' (1883)

First published in *The Athenæum*, 2903 (16 June 1883), pp. 762–3, and reprinted in Swinburne's *Miscellanies* (London: Chatto & Windus, 1886). An early critical work from the Putney period of the poet's life (from 1879), this essay followed from Swinburne's *A Note on Charlotte Brontë* (London: Chatto & Windus, 1877). The essay is a review of A. Mary F. Robinson's *Emily Brontë* in the 'Eminent Women Series' (London: W.H. Allen, 1883): cf. previous text, pp. 335–42. Robinson herself wrote to thank Swinburne for 'your beautiful notice' on 15 June 1883 (*Uncollected Letters of Algernon Charles Swinburne*, ed. Terry L. Myers, 3 vols (London: Pickering & Chatto, 2005), ii.344).

Swinburne notes the inevitability of EJB's imagination, the convincing way in which her characters act and how her story unfolds as if there can be no alternative to it. This is a development of his praise of CB in 1877 who, he said, possessed a 'power to make us feel in every nerve, at every step forward which our imagination is compelled to take under the guidance of another's, that thus and not otherwise, but in all things altogether even as we are told and shown, it was and it must have been with the human figures set before us in their action and their suffering; that thus and not otherwise they absolutely

NOTES TO PAGES 342–5
431

must and would have felt and thought and spoken under the proposed conditions' (*A Note on Charlotte Brontë*, pp. 13–14). In the *Note*, CB is compared favourably to George Eliot whose *The Mill on the Floss* (1860), Swinburne thinks, is flawed by the improbability of the relationship between Stephen Guest and Maggie.

A review of Robinson by James Ashcroft Noble in *The Academy*, 576 (19 May 1883), p. 340 (p. 340), asserted that Swinburne 'was the first to remove Emily Brontë from out the shadow of her great sister's fame'. But there was already George Smith's 'The Brontës', *Cornhill Magazine*, 28 (July 1873), pp. 54–71. See the extract, pp. 332–5 above.

Swinburne's piece can be compared to Angus M. MacKay, 'On the Interpretation of Emily Brontë', *Westminster Review*, 150 (August 1898), pp. 203–18 as another significant periodical essay that argued for EJB's importance. This is celebratory in particular of the poetry (which, of course, was only known in part), which the essay treats in relation to what MacKay deduces was her personality. None of the essays reproduced here, naturally, knows anything of Gondal. Angus MacKay was the author of the important late-century assessment, *The Brontës: Fact and Fiction* (London: Service & Paton, 1897).

The editorial material here is a revised version of that provided in Francis O'Gorman, ed., *Algernon Charles Swinburne*, 21st-Century Oxford Authors (Oxford: Oxford University Press, 2016), pp. 628–30.

p. 343 *Mehalah*: Swinburne compares *WH* to the recent sensation of the Revd Sabine Baring-Gould's *Mehalah: A Story of the Salt Marshes* (London: Smith, Elder, 1880), a novel about a fisher-girl named Mehalah who is pursued by a Heathcliff-like villain, Elijah Rebow. The story ends with Rebow's brutal drowning of the newly married girl. *Pall Mall Gazette* said of Baring-Gould's novel: 'The fibre of the story is as rough and coarse as that of "Wuthering Heights". Even the genius of Emily Brontë was heavily handicapped by the unvarying ferocity of her savages, men and women who bit, scratched, and kicked like Liverpool corner-men' ('Mehalah', 13 November 1880, p. 12). Swinburne observed to his Balliol friend, John Nichol, on 21 June 1883, that 'I did not mean—Heaven forbid!—to set *Mehalah*, on the whole, beside or near *Wuthering Heights*: but it is the only book I know which shows anything of the same power' (*The Swinburne Letters*, ed. Cecil Y. Lang, 6 vols (New Haven: Yale University Press, 1959–62), v.27).

p. 344 *it is inconceivable how any one . . . public*: presumably the letter to Mr Grundy from Branwell disclosing his (alleged) affair with Mrs Robinson and his subsequent breakdown (Robinson, *Emily Brontë*, pp. 120–2).

"it was the silent Emily . . . numbness": Robinson, *Emily Brontë*, p. 125.

die standing: Branwell determined 'he would die as he thought no one had ever died before, standing', Robinson, *Emily Brontë*, p. 221, following *LCB*. See also p. xxv n.27. Was this true? Or village gossip? A death-bed convulsion?

p. 345 *"a senseless piece of glaring folly"*: untraced, but possibly from Swinburne's friend with whom he now shared The Pines, 11 Putney Hill, Theodore Watts-Dunton (1832–1914). Watts-Dunton had been a solicitor.

"is given with a masterly pathos . . . appealing": Robinson refers to the death of the first Catherine in *WH*: 'A fit she had had alone and untended during those three days

432   NOTES TO PAGES 345–7

of isolated starvation had unsettled Catherine's reason. The gradual coming-on of her delirium is given with a masterly pathos that Webster need not have made more strong, nor Fletcher more lovely and appealing', *Emily Brontë*, p. 190.

p. 345 *Webster's Cornelia*: in *The White Devil* (1612).

Madge Wildfire: in Scott's *The Heart of Midlothian* (1818).

divine martyr of Æschylean legend: *Prometheus Bound* ($\Pi\rho o\mu\eta\theta\epsilon\dot{v}s$ $\Delta\epsilon\sigma\mu\dot{\omega}\tau\eta s$), which Swinburne believed written by Aeschylus (a now challenged but not vanquished attribution).

p. 346 *dauntless and triumphant faith should properly be read*: Robinson asserted, following CB, that the last lines Emily wrote were the poem, 'No coward soul is mine' (*Emily Brontë*, p. 232): see p. 26 and note.

"unutterable" vanity of creeds: 'Vain are the thousand creeds | That move men's hearts: unutterably vain' ('No coward soul is mine', Robinson, *Emily Brontë*, p. 232). See p. 26.

Hymn to God of Cleanthes: Swinburne is thinking of the 'Hymn to Zeus' by the 3rdc BC Stoic philosopher-poet Cleanthes.

Porch: the Painted Porch ($\dot{\eta}$ $\pi o\iota\kappa\acute{\iota}\lambda\eta$ $\sigma\tau o\acute{a}$; 'stoa' = porch) in the Agora of Classical Athens, from where Stoicism was, it is agreed by long tradition, first taught.

"some shy ostrich prompting": 'by some shy ostrich prompting, Emily chose to call [this poem] "The Old Stoic" ', Robinson, *Emily Brontë*, p. 136. See p. 57 and note.

Wilkie Collins: Swinburne published his essay 'Wilkie Collins' in *The Fortnightly Review*, 46 (1889), pp. 589–99.

p. 347 *the report drawn up . . . Firmins*: both Thackeray's *The Newcomes: Memoirs of a Most Respectable Family*, 2 vols (1854–5) and *The Adventures of Philip on his Way Through the World: Shewing Who Robbed Him, Who Helped Him, and Who Passed Him By*, 3 vols (1862), which contains the story of the Firmins, are narrated by Arthur Pendennis, the leading character of Thackeray's *The History of Pendennis* (1848–50).

"assume the virtue": cf. *Hamlet*, 3.iv.151.

French "naturalist": Swinburne is primarily thinking of Émile Zola (1840–1902). *L'Assommoir* (1877) made a reader 'literally and actually sick', Swinburne said, 'with more pure physical horror and loathing than I could have believed it possible for any mere literary bestiality and brutality to do' (*Swinburne Letters*, iii.268). Swinburne's 'Note on a Question of the Hour', *The Athenæum*, 2590 (16 June 1877), p. 768, had been a protest about the publication of *L'Assommoir*.

"vivid and fearful scenes": CB's words, complaining that passages from *WH* kept the reader awake, from her 'Preface' (see p. 319), and often repeated. See, for instance, *LCB*, ii.38–9.

INDEX OF FIRST LINES

A little while, a little while 8
Ah! why, because the dazzling sun 31
Aye there it is! It wakes tonight 13

Cold in the earth—and the deep snow piled
  above thee 33

Death! that struck when I was most
  confiding 52

Enough of thought, philosopher! 32

For him who struck thy foreign string 5

Heavy hangs the raindrop 20
Hope was but a timid friend 44
How beautiful the earth is still 37
How clear she shines! How quietly 48
How few, of all the hearts that loved 17

I do not weep, I would not weep 15
I knew not 'twas so dire a crime 5
I'll not weep that thou art going to leave me 55
In summer's mellow midnight 11
In the dungeon-crypts, idly did I stray 38
In the earth, the earth thou shalt be laid 17

Listen! when your hair, like mine 19
Loud without the wind was roaring 6
Love is like the wild rose briar 27

No coward soul is mine 26

O day! he cannot die 34
Oh, thy bright eyes must answer now 49
On a sunny brae alone I lay 45

Riches I hold in light esteem 57

Shall earth no more inspire thee 12
Silent is the house—all are laid asleep 40

The blue bell is the sweetest flower 10
The evening passes fast away 50
The linnet in the rocky dells 36
The moon is full this winter night 53
The winter wind is loud and wild 29
There should be no despair for you 49

Well hast though spoken, and yet, not
  taught 56
Well, some may hate, and some may scorn 53
When weary with the long day's care 47

INDEX OF TITLES (WHERE GIVEN)

2 January 1846 26
4 December 1838 8
6 July 1841 13
6 September 1843 17
11 March 1844, 'E.W. to A.G.A.' 17
11 November 1838 6
11 November 1844, 'From a Dungeon Wall in
    the Southern College'—JB Sept. 1825 19
11 September 1840 11
16 May 1841 12
17 October 1838, 'Song by J. Brenzaida to
    G.S.' 5
18 December 1838 10
18 December 1843 44
19 December 1841, 'A.S. to G.S.' 15
28 May 1845, 'A.E. and R.C.' 20
30 August 1838 5

A Day Dream 45
A Death-Scene 34
Anticipation 37

Death 52

Faith and Despondency 29

Honour's Martyr 53
How clear she shines 48

Julian M. and A.G. Rochelle 40

My Comforter 56

Plead for me 49

Remembrance 33

Self-interrogation 50
Song 36
Stanzas 55
Stanzas to— 53
Stars 31
Sympathy 49

The Old Stoic 57
The Philosopher 32
The Prisoner 38
To Imagination 47

Undated ['Love is like the wild rose
    briar'] 27